THE POWER OF
CRITICAL THINKING

THE POWER OF
CRITICAL THINKING

Second Canadian Edition

Lewis Vaughn | Chris MacDonald

OXFORD
UNIVERSITY PRESS

OXFORD
UNIVERSITY PRESS

8 Sampson Mews, Suite 204, Don Mills, Ontario M3C 0H5
www.oupcanada.com

Oxford University Press is a department of the University of Oxford.
It furthers the University's objective of excellence in research, scholarship,
and education by publishing worldwide in

Oxford New York

Auckland Cape Town Dar es Salaam Hong Kong Karachi
Kuala Lumpur Madrid Melbourne Mexico City Nairobi
New Delhi Shanghai Taipei Toronto

With offices in

Argentina Austria Brazil Chile Czech Republic France Greece
Guatemala Hungary Italy Japan Poland Portugal Singapore
South Korea Switzerland Thailand Turkey Ukraine Vietnam

Oxford is a trade mark of Oxford University Press
in the UK and in certain other countries

Published in Canada
by Oxford University Press

Library and Archives Canada Cataloguing in Publication

Vaughn, Lewis
The power of critical thinking / Lewis Vaughn & Chris MacDonald. — 2nd
Canadian ed.

Includes bibliographical references and index.
ISBN 978-0-19-543122-3

1. Critical thinking—Textbooks. I. MacDonald, Chris, 1969– II. Title.

B809.2.V38 2010   160   C2009-906154-6

6 7 – 13 12

Cover image: vector works 2006–2009/Flickr/Gettyimages

This book is printed on permanent (acid-free) paper ∞.
Printed in the United States of America

Contents

Faulty Reasoning   168

PART THREE   ARGUMENTS   205

PART FOUR   EXPLANATIONS   331

9   Inference to the Best Explanation   332

10 Judging Scientific Theories   375

11 Judging Moral Arguments and Theories   425

From the Publisher

Oxford University Press is proud to present the second Canadian edition of *The Power of Critical Thinking*. This edition builds on the successful approach used in the first Canadian edition that has served instructors and students well. It gives first-time students a useful, compelling, and accurate introduction to critical thinking, reading, and learning. To that end, this edition retains qualities that will be familiar to long-time users:

1. *Comprehensive coverage of inference to the best explanation.* This textbook gives considerable attention (three chapters) to inference to the best explanation because (1) it is probably the type of inference that students use most, (2) it can be especially fertile ground for diverse cases and examples that students are likely to find intriguing, and (3) it implies a framework for thinking about claims and theories as well as a method for assessing their worth. Step-by-step instructions and plentiful examples show students how to use this kind of inference to assess theories and claims in science, pseudoscience, ethics, medicine, the media, popular culture, and many other arenas.

2. *Extensive treatment of scientific reasoning.* Users of this text have long expressed strong approval of the broad coverage of science and scientific reasoning. The text offers a chapter each on inductive reasoning and causal arguments (Chapter 8), scientific theories and inference (Chapter 9), and scientific method and theory evaluation (Chapter 10). Extended examples show how scientific reasoning can be applied to a wide range of questions in many scientific fields, everyday life, and even the realm of extraordinary phenomena.

3. *Across-the-curriculum learning.* A deliberate strategy of this book is to help students apply critical thinking principles across a broad spectrum of disciplines and subjects and, in the process, show them that such skills are broadly applicable to their lives and useful in a wide variety of interesting, real-world contexts. So the book's examples, exercises, and discussions are purposely skewed toward material drawn from politics, pop culture, philosophy, ethics, the news media, the Internet, pseudoscience, the paranormal, science, medicine, and more.

4. *Emphasis on evaluation of evidence, authority, and credibility.* Throughout this text (and especially in Chapter 4) considerable ink is expended to show students how to assess the evidence and claims proffered by experts, science, the news media, and personal experience. In each case, the relevant principles or procedures are explained and illustrated.

5. *Accessible writing style.* The intent here is to make the prose as clear and as engaging as possible without oversimplifying the material or dodging tough topics. To that end, the text is informal in tone (though sufficiently serious in content), paced to match the abilities of most students without being dull, respectful of student readers, and dabbed with humour where appropriate.

6. *Large and diverse collections of exercises.* There are hundreds of exercises, drawn from a wide range of sources and configured in a variety of forms, with selected answers given at the back of the book (Appendix B).

7. *A chapter on the 'environment' of critical thinking.* In Chapter 2 students will find a review of many of the factors that impede critical thinking—bias, habit, tradition, emotion, skewed perceptions, rationalizations, and certain philosophical outlooks. Along with explanations of how these factors affect thinking, there are suggestions on how to avoid or minimize them.

Enhanced Pedagogy

This edition of *The Power of Critical Thinking* builds on the pedagogical approach that has successfully helped students practise and refine and their critical thinking skills.

○ *'Review Notes'* appear throughout each chapter to reiterate the main points of chapter sections, improving comprehension and making later review more efficient.

Review Notes

Three Steps to Diagramming a Categorical Statement
1. Draw two overlapping circles, each one representing a term in the statement.
2. Label the circles with the terms.
3. Shade an area of a circle to show that an area is empty; insert an X to show that at least one member of a class is also a member of another class.

Food For Thought

Francis Bacon on Critical Thinking

Francis Bacon (1561–1626), the father of modern science, articulated basic principles and methods of science and advocated their use in the careful pursuit of reliable knowledge. He also warned about common mistakes in thinking that can doom the scientific enterprise and lead to biased perceptions and serious error. Bacon asserted that it is possible to prevent these mistakes through scientific, down-to-earth thinking—approximately what we would call critical thinking, a necessary and powerful tool in the search for truth. He termed the mistakes 'the idols of the mind' because he thought that people not only commit the errors but revere them as one would revere a false god.

Photo: National Portrait Gallery, London

Bacon focused on four kinds of idols that he considered especially prevalent and destructive. The first type is 'the Idols of the Tribe'—the problems in thinking that arise from human nature generally. This is the fallacy of assuming that our biased perceptions are automatically a true reflection of the objective world, and that knowledge is to be found inside us without any reference to the real world.

The second group consists of the 'Idols of the Cave'—the biases that are unique to each individual. These develop from each person's personality, education, and experiences. Bacon claimed that we each live in our own cave, 'which refracts and discolors the light of nature'.

Then there are the 'Idols of the Marketplace'—the impediments to clear thinking that develop from our imprecise and careless use of language. As Bacon said, 'the ill and unfit choice of words wonderfully obstructs the understanding.'[1]

Finally there are the 'Idols of the Theater'—the ideologies or systems of thought that are 'but so many stage-plays, representing worlds of their own creation after an unreal and scenic fashion.'[2] These barriers to good critical thinking have little or nothing to do with the real world but are nevertheless thought to be accurate and profound.

○ *'Food for Thought'* boxes provide additional, sometimes humorous, material on a topic and challenge students to apply the critical thinking skills they are learning.

Chapter 3 Making Sense of Arguments   71

Exercise 3.1

1. What is a deductive argument?
2. What is an inductive argument?
3. Are inductive arguments truth-preserving? Why or why not?
* 4. What type of arguments do the terms *valid* and *invalid* apply to?
5. What kind of guarantee does a deductive argument provide when it is valid?
6. Can an inductive argument guarantee the truth of the conclusion if the premises are true? Why or why not?
7. What is the difference between an inductively strong argument and an inductively weak one?
* 8. What is the term for valid arguments that have true premises?
9. What is the term for strong arguments that have true premises?
10. Can a valid argument have false premises and a false conclusion? Can it have false premises and a true conclusion?
11. What logical conclusion can you draw about an argument that is valid but has a false conclusion?
* 12. Is it possible for a valid argument to have true premises and a false conclusion?
13. In what way are conclusions of deductive arguments absolute?

Judging Arguments

When it comes to deductive and inductive arguments, the most important skills you can acquire are being able to identify both kinds of arguments and determining whether they are good or bad. Much of the rest of this text is devoted to helping

DILBERT: © Scott Adams/Dist. By United Feature Syndicate, Inc.

○ *Exercises* draw from a wide range of sources and are configured in a variety of forms, with selected answers given at the back of the book. Simple to complex exercises are found throughout each chapter.

Contemporary Design

An increasingly digital, quickly changing world of communication calls for a design that evolves and adapts. We have striven for a look that is contemporary yet clean, a design that reflects the vibrancy and excitement of learning how to think critically without sacrificing content or authoritativeness. The use of colour and novel design elements is a necessary acknowledgement of the changes wrought by new media and how readers expect information to be packaged and presented. At the same time we remain well aware that this is indeed a printed book, with both the limitations and the very real and enduring strengths that are a product of print's long history as the pre-eminent method of codifying and transmitting knowledge.

Aids to Student Learning

○ *Chapter Openers* preview the contents of each chapter with chapter objectives that provide a concise overview of the key concepts to be covered.

Chapter

8 Inductive Reasoning

Chapter Objectives

Enumerative Induction

You will be able to
○ define enumerative induction and explain how it's used.
○ define *target population*, *sample*, and *relevant property*.
○ understand the two ways in which an enumerative induction can fail to be strong.
○ understand the error known as hasty generalization and know how to avoid it.
○ understand the basics of opinion polls and know the definitions of *random sampling*, *self-selecting sample*, *margin of error*, and *confidence level*.

Statistical Syllogisms

You will be able to:
○ explain what a statistical syllogism is.
○ define *individual*, *group*, *characteristic*, and *proportion*.
○ understand three ways in which statistical syllogisms can fail to be strong.

Analogical Induction

You will be able to
○ formulate and evaluate an argument by analogy.
○ use the following criteria to evaluate arguments by analogy: relevant similarities, relevant dissimilarities, the number of instances compared, and diversity among cases.

Chapter 3 Making Sense of Arguments

117

Critical Thinking and Writing Exercise

From Thesis to Outline

In Module 1, we saw that the second step in writing an argumentative essay (after determining your thesis statement, or conclusion) is to create an outline. Outlines are useful because, among other things, they help avert disaster in the essay-writing phase. Imagine writing two-thirds of your essay then discovering that the second premise of your argument cannot be supported and is, in fact, false. You might have to throw out the whole argument and start over.

At the head of your outline, insert your thesis statement, expressing it as clearly and as precisely as possible. At every stage of outlining, you can then refer to the statement for guidance. The premises and conclusion of your argument (or arguments) will constitute the major points of your outline. The following, for example, is the preliminary outline for the essay discussed in Module 2:

Thesis: Allowing coal-burning power plants to emit more sulphur dioxide will most likely increase the incidence of respiratory illnesses.

I.   Excessive amounts of sulphur dioxide in the air have been linked to increases in the incidence of asthma and other respiratory illnesses.
II. Many areas of the country already have excessive amounts of sulphur dioxide in the air.
III. Most sulphur dioxide in the air comes from coal-burning power plants.
IV. Therefore, allowing coal-burning power plants to emit more sulphur dioxide will most likely increase the incidence of respiratory illnesses.

After you clearly state the premises, you need to ask yourself whether any of them need to be defended. As we discussed in Module 1, any premise likely to be questioned by your readers will need support. That is, the premise itself will need arguments to back it up, and the supporting arguments should be indicated in your outline. (Some premises, though, may not need support because they are obvious or generally accepted.) As discussed in Chapter 3, you can support a premise (claim) through deductive or inductive arguments with premises made up of examples, analogies, empirical evidence (such as scientific research or trustworthy observations), and authoritative judgments (such as those from reliable experts). Here's how the preceding outline might look with (fictional) supporting arguments clearly shown:

THESIS: Allowing coal-burning power plants to emit more sulphur dioxide will most likely increase the incidence of respiratory illnesses.

I.   Excessive amounts of sulphur dioxide in the air has been linked to increases in the incidence of asthma and other respiratory illnesses.

○ *'Writing Exercises'* introduce the rudiments of argumentative essay writing in five end-of-chapter writing lessons, or modules.

○ ***Student Activities***, included at the end of each chapter, reinforce concepts and ideas through a variety of formats, including

- *'Field Problems'* that invite students to apply newly acquired and refined critical thinking skills to 'real world' problems.
- *'Self-Assessment quizzes'* that ensure students can apply their understanding of the material.
- *'Integrative Exercises'* that help students bring information and techniques from multiple chapters together, ensuring that their understanding of critical thinking is comprehensive.
- *'Writing Assignments'* that allow students to apply their knowledge and practise working in longer formats such as essays.

374

Part IV　Explanations

Evaluate each of the following theories and indicate whether it is plausible or implausible.

15. The positions and movements of the stars and planets at the time of your birth can have a powerful effect on your life.
16. David Milgaard was sent to prison for raping and murdering a nursing assistant, Gail Miller, and he spent 21 years behind bars. Three of Milgaard's friends testified against him in court. Milgaard was released in 1997 after DNA evidence supposedly proved he didn't commit the crime. But I'll trust the word of three witnesses over some fancy scientific test any day!
17. In Area 51, the famous portion of a military base near Groom Dry Lake in Nevada, the government is concealing real alien visitors or an actual space vehicle used by the visitors to reach Earth.
18. If people are homeless, it's because they chose to be homeless. In Canada, there are a hundred ways to get out of poverty—if you want to.
19. The large network news organizations have ignored most of the anti-war protests staged since 9/11. Coverage of any anti-war sentiment seems to be against media policy. This can only mean that top network execs have decided together that such coverage is not in their best interests.
20. When the streetlights lit up the side of the building, a vague image appeared on the wall, a mixture of shadows and light. Most people say that the image shows the face of Jesus. This image is a holy sign from God.

Writing Assignments

1. In a one-page essay evaluate the theory that all major decisions made by the Canadian prime minister or the premier of your province are politically motivated and have very little to do with the merits of ideas or programs. Use the TEST formula.
2. Think of the last time you caught a cold or the flu. Write a 250-word paper evaluating at least two theories that explain how you first came into contact with the virus. Use the TEST formula.
3. Write a 500-word paper in which you use the TEST formula to assess two theories for UFO abductions. One theory is the alien theory (Hypothesis 1) as discussed in Essay 9 ('UFO Abductions') in Appendix A; the other one is the hypnosis theory, the view that no one is actually abducted but instead the idea of being abducted by aliens is inadvertently implanted in people's minds when they undergo hypnosis.

371

Chapter 9　Inference to the Best Explanation

Field Problems

1. Many companies have recently marketed products that are supposed to relieve various ills (arthritis, low back pain, migraine headaches, tennis elbow, etc.) through the use of simple magnets. This 'magnetic therapy' is said to work because magnetic fields generated by the magnets act on the body's processes or structures. Look at ads in magazines, on TV, or on the Internet to find a health claim made for one of these products. Then in a 150-word paragraph evaluate the claim in light of the criteria of simplicity and conservatism. Check for any relevant scientific research and information at www.quackwatch.com or www.sram.org/(*The Scientific Review of Alternative Medicine*).
2. Using the TEST formula, evaluate the theory that people are more likely to behave strangely or violently during a full moon than at other times. Do some research to uncover any evidence pertaining to this theory. Write a 200-word essay summarizing your findings.

Self-Assessment Quiz

1. What is the basic pattern of inference to the best explanation? How does this pattern differ from that of enumerative induction? Analogical induction?
2. What is the minimum requirement for consistency?
3. What are the criteria of adequacy?
4. According to the text, what does it mean for a theory to be testable or untestable?
5. What is the TEST formula?
6. According to the text, in theory evaluation, when is a theory properly considered the best?

Each of the following theories is offered to explain John's apparently prophetic dream that a distant cousin would die in a plane crash. Indicate which theory (a) lacks simplicity, (b) is not conservative, (c) is untestable, and (d) has the most scope. (Some theories may merit more than one of these designations.)

7. The fact that John's dream happened to be about a plane crash involving his cousin was coincidence. We have many dreams, and some are likely to match real events from time to time.
8. In his dream, John was able to see into the future and 'view' the plane crash.
9. The incident was an example of 'synchronicity', in which events are paired in unusual but predetermined ways by cosmic forces.
10. John had calculated the odds of the crash even before he dreamed about it, so the dream was not a prophecy, but a memory of his calculation.

373

Chapter 9　Inference to the Best Explanation

Integrative Exercises

These exercises refer to lessons in Chapters 3 and 6–9.

1. What is a deductive argument?
2. What is a valid argument?
3. What is an inductive argument?
4. What is the logical pattern of *modus ponens*?

For each of the following arguments, specify the conclusion and premises and say whether it is deductive or inductive. If it's deductive, use Venn diagrams or truth tables to determine its validity. If it's inductive, say whether it's an enumerative, analogical, or causal induction and whether it's strong or weak. If necessary, add implicit premises and conclusions.

5. The problem is that if people realize that they can do their own buying and selling of stocks, they won't use brokers any more. But people don't realize that yet. So people will continue to use brokers.
6. I've read a lot about relations between Canadian soldiers and the people of Afghanistan. Almost everything I've read has been positive. The Afghanis realize that our soldiers are there to help and have welcomed them with open arms. I even read about one woman whose house was damaged in a firefight between Canadian soldiers and Taliban fighters, and she said she was glad the Canadians were there.
7. Every man I know has some kind of hang-up about sex. What is it with men? They're all a bunch of sexual neurotics.
8. Either the Prime Minister visited Quebec City to shore up support for his party among Quebecers, or he went there for the poutine. He didn't go there for the poutine, so he must have gone to shore up support for his party.
9. 'Hence a young man is not a proper hearer of lectures on political science; for he is inexperienced in the actions that occur in life, but its discussions start from these and are about these; and, further, since he tends to follow his passions, his study will be vain and unprofitable, because the end aimed at is not knowledge but action.' (Aristotle, *Nichomachean Ethics*)
10. Why should Canada be sending aid to foreign countries when there are people right here in Canada who need help? Every dollar spent on foreign aid could be better spent on problems right here at home!
11. No kings are persons without power. All people without power are persons who spend their days being victims. Therefore, no kings are victims.
12. Vulgarity is rampant across the land, and Hollywood is to blame. As vulgar, sexually explicit, tasteless movies have proliferated, so has the amount of vulgarity increased.
13. He's afraid of her. He avoids her all the time, and he won't look her in the eye.
14. Most teens arrested for committing some act of violence also play a lot of violent video games. These games are causing violent behaviour among our youth.

Supplements

The Canadian Edition also includes a comprehensive online ancillary package, available at http://www.oupcanada.com/vaughn2e. An instructor's manual, a test bank, and a robust set of PowerPoint slides—animated for maximum pedagogical effectiveness—are available to adopters. (Please contact your Sales Representative for login and password information). A Student Study Guide is also available on-line, which allows the student to take advantage of a number of study notes, quizzes, and additional exercises.

COMPANION WEBSITE

Lewis Vaughn and Chris MacDonald

The Power of Critical Thinking : Second Canadian Edition
ISBN 13: 9780195431223

Inspection copy request

Ordering information

Contact & Comments

About the Book

The Power of Critical Thinking is an introductory text for courses in critical thinking. This book covers arguments, belief and doubt, faulty reasoning, deductive and inductive reasoning, and inference; it also offers an introduction to the issues specific to both scientific and moral reasoning. The authors' presentation emphasizes the application of critical thinking skills in disciplines outside of philosophy.

The text starts by examining the basic concepts required to think critically, then moves on to such compelling topics as how to assess the credibility of a website, how to judge paranormal claims, why it's important to be wary of advertising, and how psychological and social factors such as bias, habit, tradition, emotions and philosophical outlook impede clear thinking. Five writing modules walk students through the process of drafting a clear and concise analytical research paper, free of logical missteps and inaccuracies. The colloquial and friendly tone makes a potentially difficult subject very

Preface

In preparing this text for a Canadian audience I have done my best to remain true to the spirit of Lewis Vaughn's original text. Thus I have attempted to keep the text light-hearted and student-friendly, without sacrificing clarity or rigour. Though the basics have stayed the same, there have also been many changes. The changes have of course included a 'Canadianization' of spellings, and more importantly, a Canadianization of examples. The new examples are drawn from Canadian history, politics, sports and popular culture. Gone are references to the US Bill of Rights; in their place are references to the Canadian Charter of Rights and Freedoms. Gone are most references to Hillary Clinton and George W. Bush; in their place you'll find references to key figures in modern Canadian politics. Further, I have attempted to replace references to issues and debates that are salient for an American audience (such as the death penalty, the abortion debate, and separation of church and state) with ones more familiar to Canadian students (such as aboriginal land claims, environmental issues, and Quebec nationalism). These are small but crucial changes: students will be better motivated to think critically about issues that they see as relevant to them.

Acknowledgements

As the person responsible for adapting this text for a Canadian audience, I would like to take full credit for all the good bits and blame the original author, Lewis Vaughn, for any errors. Just kidding. The very high quality of the original version of the book made it very easy to produce this Canadian edition, and Lewis Vaughn deserves full credit for that. In addition, I would like to thank the many anonymous reviewers who offered a range of excellent suggestions, more of which I wish could have been integrated into the text. I also owe a debt of gratitude to a number of people at Oxford University Press Canada, including Phyllis Wilson, Peter Chambers, and Freya Godard. Finally, I would like to thank Aimee Smith and Christine Bray for their able assistance in the preparation of the text.

Reviewers

We gratefully acknowledge the contributions of the following reviewers, whose thoughtful comments and suggestions have helped to shape this new edition:

Brian van den Broek, Concordia University
Jeff Vancha, University of Regina
Leslie Burkholder, University of British Columbia
Violaine Arès, John Abbott College
Glenn Hoffmann, Ryerson University
Laura Byrne, University of Ottawa
Ken Kirkwood, University of Western Ontario
John Wilkinson, Wilfrid Laurier University

Chris MacDonald
St. Mary's University

Part One
Basics

The Power of Critical Thinking

Chapter Objectives

- To understand the meaning of *critical thinking* and the importance and meaning of the terms 'systematic', 'evaluation', 'formulation', and 'rational standards'.
- To understand how critical thinking is related to logic, the truth or falsity of statements, knowledge, and personal empowerment.

Why It Matters

You will be able to

- appreciate why critical thinking is better than the passive acceptance of beliefs.
- appreciate the relevance of the claim 'The unexamined life is not worth living' to critical thinking.
- understand why the following claims are dubious: 'Critical thinking makes people too critical or cynical', 'Critical thinking makes people cold and unemotional', and 'Critical thinking is the enemy of creativity'.
- appreciate the usefulness of critical thinking in all human endeavours.

How It Works

You will be able to

- distinguish between statements and non-statements.
- understand the basic concepts of reasons, argument, inference, premises, and conclusion.
- know how to use indicator words to help pinpoint premises and conclusions.
- distinguish between passages that do and do not contain an argument.
- identify arguments in various contexts and distinguish between arguments and superfluous material, arguments and explanations, and premises and conclusions.

Y ou came into this world without opinions or judgments or values or view-points—and now your head is overflowing with them. If you tried to write them all down, you would be busy for the rest of your life (and would probably win an award for being the world's biggest nerd). Opinions help you make your way through the world. They guide you to failure and success, ignorance and under-standing, good and bad, paralysis and empowerment. Some of your beliefs truly inform you, and some blind you. Some are true; some are not. But the question is, *which ones are which*? This kind of question—a question about the *quality* of your beliefs—is the fundamental concern of **critical thinking**.

Determining the quality or value of your beliefs is a function of thinking, and the kind of thinking that does this job best is critical thinking—a skill that higher education seeks to foster. This means that critical thinking is not about *what* you think, but *how* you think.

Notice also that the question about the quality of beliefs is not about what fac-tors *caused* you to have the beliefs that you do. A sociologist might tell you how society has influenced some of your moral choices. A psychologist might describe how your emotions cause you to cling to certain opinions. Your best friend might allege that you have unconsciously absorbed most of your beliefs directly from your parents. But none of these speculations have much to do with the central task of critical thinking.

Critical thinking focuses not on what *causes* a belief, but on *whether it is worth believing*. A belief is worth believing, or accepting, if we have *good reasons* to accept it. The better the reasons for acceptance, the more likely the belief is to be true. Critical thinking offers us a set of standards embodied in techniques, attitudes, and principles that we can use to assess beliefs and determine if they are supported by good reasons. After all, we want our beliefs to be true, to be good guides for dealing with the world—and critical thinking is the best tool we have for achieving this goal.

Here's one way to wrap up these points in a concise definition:

CRITICAL THINKING: The systematic evaluation or formulation of beliefs, or statements, by rational standards.

Critical thinking is *systematic* because it involves distinct procedures and meth-ods. It entails *evaluation* and *formulation* because it's used both to assess existing beliefs (yours or someone else's) and to devise new ones. And it operates accord-ing to *rational standards* in that beliefs are judged by how well they are supported by reasons.

The effort involved in thinking critically is well worth it, because it is one of the few tools we have to counteract the natural limitations of the human brain. Some of those limitations are pretty easy to spot, of course. All of us make mistakes of reasoning from time to time: we fail to give enough attention to key facts, we forget things, we jump to conclusions, and so on. But some errors of reasoning are more

> 'The recipe for perpetual ignorance is: be satisfied with your opinions and content with your knowledge.'
> —Elbert Hubbard

common than others. Some are so common that psychologists have studied them and given them names. These are called 'cognitive biases', and evidence suggests that some of them are nearly universal. For example, we tend to judge facts differently depending on just how they are stated, or 'framed'. We might react quite positively to an announcement that a struggling company had been able to 'save' 300 jobs (out of 1,000) but quite negatively to an announcement that the company was 'laying off' 700 people (out of 1,000)—even though the result is the exactly the same, either way. Framing the issue in terms of jobs saved—which sounds like a good thing—makes us tend to think more positively about the whole scenario. Another example: if you ask people to estimate how likely it is that 200 people will die in Canada this month in a plane crash, versus how likely it is that 200 people will die in Canada this month in car wrecks, they're likely to *over*estimate the relative likelihood of a plane crash, just because they've seen scary images on TV of planes crashing and can readily call those images to mind. In general, we tend to overestimate how common dramatic events are and underestimate how common more boring events are. (Some more of these 'cognitive biases' are touched upon again in Chapter 4.) We *know* that mistakes of reasoning like these are common, and it's easy to see how they can lead to bad conclusions and bad decisions. Our best defence is to look at the facts carefully and think critically.

Critical thinking, of course, involves **logic**. Logic is the study of good reasoning, or inference, and the rules that govern it. Critical thinking is broader than logic because it involves not only logic but also the examination of the truth or falsity of statements, the evaluation of arguments and evidence, the use of analysis and investigation, and the application of many other skills that help us decide what to believe or do.

Ultimately, what critical thinking leads you to is knowledge, understanding, and—if you put these to work—empowerment. In addition, as you're guided by your instructor through this text, you will come to appreciate some other benefits that cannot be fully explored now. Critical thinking enables problem solving, active learning, and intelligent self-improvement.

In Chapters 2 and 3 you'll get a more thorough grounding in critical thinking and logical argument as well as plenty of opportunities to practise your new skills. Consider this chapter an introduction to those important lessons.

Why It Matters

In large measure, our lives are defined by our actions and choices, and our actions and choices are guided by our thinking—so our thinking had better be good. Almost every day we are hit by a blizzard of assertions, opinions, arguments, and pronouncements from all directions. They all implore us to believe, to agree, to accept, to follow, to submit. If we care whether our choices are right and our beliefs

Food For Thought

Dumb and Dumber

Many times when we don't know something, that's bad. But when we *don't know* that we don't know something, that's worse. At least, that's the view of researchers who studied the effects of this kind of double-edged ignorance (*Journal of Personality and Social Psychology*, December 1999). In several studies, the researchers assessed the ability of study participants in areas that demanded 'knowledge, wisdom, or savvy'—logical reasoning, English grammar, and humour.

The results: People whose abilities were very weak tended to greatly overestimate them. Those who got the lowest test scores thought they had achieved much higher scores. The data suggested that the overestimations arose because the subjects couldn't distinguish accuracy from error. They didn't know what they didn't know. Ironically, when the researchers helped the participants improve their abilities and increase their knowledge, the participants could recognize their limitations.

Hmm. Increase your knowledge and recognize your limitations—isn't that what critical thinking helps you do?

Harry and Lloyd (Jim Carrey and Jeff Daniels) from the movie *Dumb & Dumber* (1994). Photo: New Line/The Kobal Collection/Fellman, Mark

true, if we want to rise above blind acceptance and arbitrary choices, we must use the tools provided by critical thinking.

Of course we always have the option of taking the easy way out. We can simply grab on to whatever beliefs or statements come blowing by in the wind, adopting viewpoints either because others favour them or because they make us feel good. But then we give up control over our lives and let the wind take us wherever it will, as if we had no more say in the outcome than a leaf in a storm.

A consequence of going with the wind is a loss of personal freedom. If you passively accept beliefs that have been handed to you by your parents, your culture, or your teachers, then those beliefs are *not really yours*. You just happened to be in a certain place and time when they were handed out. If they are not really yours and you let them guide your choices and actions, then they—not you—are in charge of

In the 1998 film *The Truman Show*, Truman is a captive in a fake world where everything he experiences is fabricated by the executives of a TV series, of which he is the unwitting star. He is a mere puppet for a hidden TV audience—until he begins to think for himself. Photo: © Photos 12/Alamy

your life. Your beliefs are yours only if you critically examine them for yourself to see if they are supported by good reasons.

To examine your beliefs in this way is to examine your life, because your beliefs in large measure define your life. To forgo such scrutiny is to abandon your chance of making your life deliberately and authentically meaningful. The great philosopher Socrates says it best: 'The unexamined life is not worth living.'

Our choice to apply critical thinking skills is not an all-or-nothing decision. Each of us uses critical thinking to some degree in our lives. We often evaluate reasons for (and against) believing that someone has committed a crime, that an earnest celebrity is deluded, that one candidate in an election is better than another, that regulation of genetically modified foods should be strengthened or weakened, that we should buy a particular kind of car, that the legendary Bigfoot does not exist, that a friend is trustworthy, that one university is superior to another, that the bill being considered in Parliament would be bad for the environment, or that Elvis is living the good life in a witness-protection program. But the more urgent consideration is not just whether we sometimes use critical thinking, but *how well* we use it.

Many people, however, will have none of this—and perhaps you are one of them. They believe that critical thinking—or what they assume to be critical thinking—makes one excessively critical or cynical, emotionally cold, and creatively constrained. For example, there are some who view anything that smacks of logic

'Are you not ashamed of caring so much for the making of money and for fame and prestige, when you neither think nor care about wisdom and truth and the improvement of your soul?'

—Socrates

and rationality as a negative enterprise designed to attack someone else's thinking and score points by putting people in their place. A few of these take the word *critical* here to mean 'faultfinding' or 'whining'.

Now, no doubt some people try to use critical thinking primarily for offensive purposes, but this approach goes against critical thinking principles. The *critical* in critical thinking is used in the sense of 'exercising or involving careful judgment or judicious evaluation'. Critical thinking is about determining what we are justified in believing, and that involves an openness to other points of view, a tolerance for opposing perspectives, a focus on the issue at hand, and fair assessments of arguments and evidence.

Some people fear that if they apply critical thinking to their lives, they will become cold and unemotional—just like a computer that works strictly according to logic and mathematical functions. But this is a confused notion. Critical thinking and feelings actually complement one another. Certainly part of thinking critically is ensuring that we don't let our emotions distort our judgments. But critical thinking can also help us clarify our feelings and deal with them more effectively. Our emotions often need the guidance of reason. Likewise, our reasoning needs our emotions. It is our feelings that motivate us to action, and without motivation our reasoning would never get off the ground.

Then there's the dubious assumption that critical thinking is the enemy of creativity. To some people, critical thinking is a sterile and rigid mode of thought that limits the imagination, hinders artistic vision, and prevents 'thinking outside the box'. But critical thinking and creative thinking are not opposed to one another. Good critical thinkers can let their imaginations run free just like anyone else. They can create and enjoy poetry, music, art, literature, and plain old fun in the same way and to the same degree as the rest of the world. Critical thinking can complement creative thinking because it is needed to assess and enhance the creation. Scientists, for example, often dream up some very fanciful theories (which are an important part of doing science). These theories pop into their heads in the same sort of ways that the ideas for a great work of art appear in the mind of its creator. But then scientists use all of their critical thinking skills to evaluate what they have produced (as artists sometimes do)—and this critical examination enables them to select the most promising theories and to weed out those that are unworkable. Critical thinking perfects the creation.

In a very important sense, critical thinking *is* thinking outside the box. When we passively absorb the ideas we encounter, when we refuse to consider any alternative explanations or theories, when we conform our ideas to the wishes of the group, and when

"Never, ever, think outside the box."

we let our thinking be controlled by bias, stereotypes, superstition, and wishful thinking, then we are deep, deep in the box. But we rise above all that when we have the courage to think critically. When we are willing to let our beliefs be tried in the court of critical reason, we open ourselves to new possibilities, the dormant seeds of creativity.

Critical thinking covers a lot of territory. It's used across the board in all disciplines, all areas of public life, all the sciences, all sectors of business, and all vocations. It has played a major role in all the great endeavours of humankind—scientific discoveries, technological innovations, philosophical insights, social and political movements, literary creation and criticism, judicial and legal reasoning, democratic nation building, and more. The *lack* of critical thinking has also left its mark. The great tragedies of history—the wars, massacres, holocausts, tyrannies, bigotries, epidemics, and witch hunts—grew out of famines of the mind where clear, careful thinking was much too scarce.

How It Works

As you can see, critical thinking has extremely broad applications. Principles and procedures used to evaluate beliefs in one discipline or issue can be used to assess beliefs in many other arenas. Good critical thinking is the same everywhere. Here are the common threads that make it universal.

Review Notes

Why Critical Thinking Matters
- Our thinking guides our actions, so it should be of high quality.
- If you have never critically examined your beliefs, they are not truly yours.
- Critical thinking is one way of defending against the 'cognitive biases' that tend to lead us to false conclusions and bad decisions.
- To examine your beliefs is to examine your life. Socrates said: 'The unexamined life is not worth living.'
- Critical thinking involves determining what we're justified in believing, being open to new perspectives, and fairly assessing the views of others and ourselves.
- Critical thinking complements both our emotions and our creativity.
- Critical thinking is thinking outside the box.

Claims and Reasons

Critical thinking is a rational, systematic process that we apply to beliefs of all kinds. Of course, we can really only evaluate beliefs that are made explicit; for obvious reasons, it's hard to evaluate beliefs that are kept hidden from us. We can only evaluate our *own* beliefs once we say (or maybe admit!) to ourselves, 'This is what I believe.' And we can only evaluate other people's beliefs by looking at the things those people actually say or write. So although we are interested in evaluating the quality of beliefs in general, we are mostly limited to evaluating beliefs that someone makes explicit by making some statement or claim. (We'll say something about the role unstated beliefs can play in arguments, and about how to bring them to light and assess them, in Chapter 3.)

A **statement** is an assertion that something is or is not the case. The following are statements:

- A triangle has three sides.
- I am cold.
- You are a liar.
- You are not a liar.
- I see blue spots before my eyes.
- $7 + 5 = 12$
- $7 + 5 = 11$
- You should never hit your mother with a shovel.
- The best explanation for his behaviour is that he was in a trance.
- The capital of Canada is Toronto.
- Rap music is better than Celtic fiddle music.
- There are black holes in space.

So statements, or claims, are the kind of things that are either true or false. (Notice that at least two of the claims above are definitely false!) They assert that some state of affairs is or is not actual. You may know that a specific statement is true, or you may know that it is false, or you may not know either way. There may be no way to find out at the time if the statement is true or false. There may be no one who believes the statement. But it would be a statement nonetheless.

Some sentences, though, do *not* express statements:

- Does a triangle have three sides?
- Is God all-powerful?
- Turn that music off.
- Stop telling lies.
- Hey, dude.
- OMG!

"What some people fail to grasp, Larry, is the difference between 'thinking outside of the box' and just being a weirdo."

© 2002 by Randy Glasbergen

The first two sentences are questions. The second two are commands or requests. The fifth sentence is a greeting. The sixth one is an exclamation that is common in email and text messaging. None asserts that something is or is not the case. They are meaningful things to say, but they're not *statements*.

When you're engaged in critical thinking, you're mostly either evaluating statements or formulating them. In both cases your primary task is to figure out how strongly to believe them. The strength of your belief should depend on the quality of the reasons in favour of the statements. Statements backed by good reasons are worthy of strong acceptance. Statements that fall short of this standard deserve weaker acceptance.

Sometimes you may not be able to assign any substantial weight at all to the reasons for or against a statement. There simply may not be enough evidence to decide rationally. Generally when that happens, good critical thinkers do not arbitrarily choose to accept or reject a statement. They suspend judgment until there is enough evidence to make an intelligent decision.

Reasons and Arguments

Reasons provide support for a statement. That is, they provide us with grounds for believing that a statement is true. Reasons are themselves expressed as statements. So a statement expressing a reason or reasons is used to show that another statement is true or likely to be true. This combination of statements—a statement (or statements) supposedly providing reasons for accepting another statement—is known as an **argument**. Arguments are the main focus of critical thinking. They are the most important tool we have for evaluating the truth of statements (our own and those of others) and for formulating statements that are worthy of acceptance. Arguments are, therefore, essential for the advancement of knowledge in all fields.

Often people use the word *argument* to indicate a debate or an angry exchange. In critical thinking, however, *argument* refers to the assertion of reasons in support of a statement.

The statements (reasons) given in support of another statement are called the **premises**. The statement that the premises are intended to support is called the **conclusion**. We can define an argument, then, like this:

ARGUMENT: A group of statements in which some of them (the premises) are intended to support another of them (the conclusion).

The following are some simple arguments:

1. Because assault rifles have no peaceful civilian use, the Canadian government should ban assault rifles.
2. *The Globe and Mail's Report on Business* says that people should invest heavily in stocks. Therefore, investing in stocks is a smart move.
3. When Judy drives her car, she's always late. Since she's driving her car now, she will be late.
4. Listen, any movie with clowns in it cannot be a good movie. Last night's movie had at least a dozen clowns in it. Consequently, it was awful.
5. The war on terrorism must include a massive military strike on nation X because without this intervention, terrorists cannot be defeated. They will always be able to find a safe haven and support in the X regime. Even if terrorists are scattered around the world, support from nation X will increase their chances of surviving and launching new attacks.
6. No one should buy a beer brewed in the US. Old Guzzler beer is brewed in the US, so no one should buy it.

Here are the same arguments where the parts are easily identified:

1. [Premise] Because assault rifles have no peaceful civilian use, [Conclusion] the Canadian government should ban assault rifles.
2. [Premise] *The Globe and Mail's Report on Business* says that people should invest heavily in stocks. [Conclusion] Therefore, investing in stocks is a smart move.
3. [Premise] When Judy drives her car, she's always late. [Premise] Since she's driving her car now, [Conclusion] she will be late.
4. [Premise] Any movie with clowns in it cannot be a good movie. [Premise] Last night's movie had at least a dozen clowns in it. [Conclusion] Consequently, it was awful.
5. [Premise] Without a military intervention in nation X, terrorists cannot be defeated. [Premise] They will always be able to find a safe haven and support in the X regime. [Premise] Even if terrorists are scattered around the world, support from nation X will increase their chances of surviving and launching new attacks. [Conclusion] The war on terrorism must include a massive military strike on nation X.
6. [Premise] No one should buy a beer brewed in the US. [Premise] Old Guzzler beer is brewed in the US. [Conclusion] So no one should buy it.

What all of these arguments have in common is that reasons (the premises) are offered to support or prove a claim (the conclusion). This logical link between premises and conclusion is what distinguishes arguments from all other kinds of discourse. This process of reasoning from a premise or premises to a conclusion based on those premises is called **inference**. Being able to identify arguments, to

'What danger can ever come from ingenious reasoning and inquiry? The worst speculative skeptic ever I knew was a much better man than the best superstitious devotee and bigot.'
—David Hume

pick them out of a block of non-argumentative prose if need be, is an important skill on which many other critical thinking skills are based.

Now consider this passage:

The cost of the new XJ fighter plane is $650 million. The cost of three AR21 fighter bombers is $1.2 billion. The Canadian government intends to fund such projects.

Is there an argument here? No. This passage consists of several claims, but no reasons are presented to support any particular claim (conclusion), including the last sentence. This passage can be turned into an argument, though, with some minor editing:

Canada's Auditor General says that any weapon that costs more than $50 million apiece will actually impair our military readiness. The cost of the new XJ fighter plane is $650 million dollars. The cost of three AR21 fighter bombers is $1.2 billion. We should never impair our readiness. Therefore, the Canadian government should cancel both these projects.

Now we have an argument because *reasons* are given for accepting a conclusion. Here's another passage:

Allisha went to the bank to get a more recent bank statement of her chequing account. The teller told her that the balance was $125. Allisha was stunned that it was so low. She called her brother to see if he had been playing one of his twisted pranks. He wasn't. Finally, she concluded that she had been a victim of bank fraud.

Where is the conclusion? Where are the reasons? There are none. This is a little story hung on some descriptive claims. But it's not an argument. It's not trying to convince you, the reader, of anything. It could be turned into an argument if, say, some of the claims were restated as reasons for the conclusion that bank fraud had been committed.

Being able to distinguish between passages that do and do not contain arguments is a very basic skill—and an extremely important one. Many people think that if they have clearly stated their beliefs on a subject, they have presented an argument. But a mere declaration of beliefs never counts as an argument. Often such assertions of opinion are just a jumble of unsupported claims. Search high and low and you will not find an argument anywhere. A writer or speaker of these claims gives the readers or listeners no grounds for believing the claims. In writing courses, the absence of supporting premises is sometimes called 'a lack of development'.

Food For Thought

Now for Something Completely Different

All your hours spent watching the TV and movie antics of Monty Python—the famous comedy sketch team—were not in vain. In at least one sketch, critical thinking has its moment in the sun. In it a man is ready and willing to pay for a good argument (in the critical-thinking sense), but, alas, the only arguments available are the quarrel type:

MAN LOOKING FOR AN ARGUMENT (M): Ah, is this the right room for an argument?

PROFESSIONAL ARGUER (A): I told you once.

M: No you haven't.

A: Yes I have.

M: When?

A: Just now.

M: No you didn't.

A: Yes I did....

M: Oh look, this isn't an argument.

A: Yes it is.

M: No it isn't. It's just contradiction.... I came here for a good argument.

A: No you didn't; no, you came here for an argument.

M: Argument isn't just contradiction.

A: It can be.

M: No it can't. An argument is a connected series of statements intended to establish a proposition.

A: No it isn't....

Photo: Columbia / The Kobal Collection

Here are three more examples of discussion without argument:

Attributing alcohol abuse by children too young to buy a drink to lack of parental discipline, intense pressure to succeed, and affluence incorrectly draws attention to proximate causes while ignoring the ultimate cause: a culture that tolerates overt and covert marketing of alcohol, tobacco and sex to these easily manipulated, voracious consumers. (Letter to the editor, *New York Times*)

Like any effective telemarketer or pushy door-to-door salesperson, Toronto city councillors angling for a pay raise won't take 'no' for an answer. After being shamed less than four months ago into abandoning an attempt to slide through a bureaucratic, under-the-radar pay increase, the councillors are making yet another pitch for more money. (Editorial, *Toronto Star*, 12 May 2006)

The Iraqi people deserve the same freedoms that I have, especially the freedom to live, which have been greatly reduced since the American invasion. (Michael White, letter to the editor, *Ottawa Citizen*, 11 May 2006)

The passage on alcohol abuse in children is not an argument but an unsupported assertion about the causes of the problems. The passage about Toronto city councillors is an expression of outrage (which may or may not be justified), but no conclusion is put forth, and no reasons supporting a conclusion are offered. Note the contentious tone in the third passage. This passage smells like an argument—it certainly expresses an opinion. But, alas, there is no argument. It's just a claim presented without support.

Sometimes people also confuse **explanations** with arguments. An argument gives us reasons for believing *that something is the case*—that a claim is true or probably true. An explanation, though, tells us *why or how something is the case*. Arguments have something to prove; explanations do not. Look carefully at this pair of statements:

1. Adam obviously stole the money, for three people saw him do it.
2. Adam stole the money because he needed it to buy food.

Statement 1 is an argument. Statement 2 is an explanation. Statement 1 tries to show that something is the case—that Adam stole the money. And the reason offered in support of this statement is that three people saw him do it. Statement 2 does not try to prove that something is the case (that Adam stole the money). Instead, it attempts to explain why something is the case (why Adam stole the money). Statement 2 takes for granted that Adam stole the money and then tries to explain *why* he did it. (Note: Explanations can be used as integral *parts* of arguments. As such they are powerful intellectual and scientific tools that help us understand the world; that is why this text has several chapters—in Part 4—devoted to explanations used in this way.)

It's not always easy to recognize an argument and to locate both premises and a conclusion, but there are a few tricks that can make the job more manageable. For one, there are **indicator words** that frequently accompany arguments and signal that a premise or conclusion is present. For example, in argument 1, presented earlier in this chapter, the indicator word *because* tips us off to the presence of the premise 'Because assault rifles have no peaceful civilian use'. In argument 2, *therefore* points to the conclusion 'Therefore, investing in stocks is a smart move.'

Here are some common **premise indicators**:

because	due to the fact that	inasmuch as
in view of the fact	being that	as indicated by
given that	since	for
seeing that	assuming that	the reason being
as	for the reason that	

And here are some common **conclusion indicators**:

therefore	it follows that	it must be that
thus	we can conclude that	as a result
which implies that	so	which means that
consequently	hence	ergo

Using indicator words to spot premises and conclusions, however, is not foolproof. They're just good clues. You will find that some of the words just listed are used when no argument is present. For example,

- I am here *because* you asked me to come.
- I haven't seen you *since* Canada Day.
- He was *so* sleepy he fell off his chair.

Note also that arguments can be put forth without the use of *any* indicator words:

> We must take steps to protect our environment. We can't rely on the government—federal and provincial regulators already have their hands full. Government can't be everywhere at once, and they usually get involved only after some environmental catastrophe has already happened.

As you may have noticed from these examples, the basic structure of arguments can have several simple variations. For one thing, arguments can have any number of premises. Arguments 1 and 2 on page 11 have one premise; arguments 3, 4, and 6, two premises; argument 5, three premises. In extended arguments that often appear in essays, editorials, reports, and other works, there can be many more premises. Also, the conclusion of an argument may not always appear after the premises. As in argument 5, the conclusion may be presented first.

Occasionally the conclusion of an argument can be disguised as a question—even though we would usually expect a question not to be a claim at all. (For purposes of examining such arguments, we may need to rewrite the conclusion as a statement; in some arguments, we may also need to do the same for the premises.)

Most of the time readers have no difficulty discerning what the implied conclusion is. See for yourself:

> Do you think for one minute that backbench Conservatives in Parliament will be happy about the Prime Minister's refusal to re-open the abortion debate? A lot of Conservative members of Parliament were elected by constituents who have very strong anti-abortion views.

Probably the best advice for anyone trying to uncover or dissect arguments is this: *Find the conclusion first*. Once you know what claim someone is trying to prove, it becomes much easier to isolate the premises. Ask yourself, 'What claim is this writer or speaker trying to persuade me to believe?' If the writer or speaker is not trying to convince you of anything, there is no argument to examine.

Arguments in the Rough

As you've probably guessed by now, in the real world, arguments almost never appear neatly labelled as they are here. As suggested earlier, they usually come imbedded in a tangle of other sentences that serve many other functions besides articulating an argument. They may be long and hard to follow. And sometimes a passage that sounds like an argument isn't one. Your main challenge is to identify the conclusion and premises without getting lost in all the 'background noise'.

Consider this passage:

> [1] A.L. Jones used flawed reasoning in his letter yesterday praising this newspaper's decision to publish announcements of same-sex unions. [2] Mr Jones asserts that same-sex unions are a fact of life and therefore should be acknowledged by the news media as a legitimate variation on social partnerships. [3] But the news media are not in the business of endorsing or

Review Notes

Claims, Reasons, and Arguments
- *Statement* (claim): An assertion that something is or is not the case.
- *Premise*: A statement given in support of another statement.
- *Conclusion*: A statement that premises are used to support.
- *Argument*: A group of statements in which some of them (the premises) are intended to support another of them (the conclusion).
- *Explanation*: A statement or statements asserting why or how something is the case.
- *Indicator words*: Words that frequently accompany arguments and signal that a premise or conclusion is present.

validating lifestyles. [4] They're supposed to report on lifestyles, not bless them. [5] In addition, by validating same-sex unions or any other lifestyle, the media abandon their objectivity and become political partisans—which would destroy whatever respect people have for news outlets. [6] All of this shows that the news media—including this newspaper—should never (explicitly or implicitly) endorse lifestyles by announcing those lifestyles to the world.

There's an argument here, but it's surrounded by extraneous material. The conclusion is sentence 6—'All of this shows that the news media—including this newspaper—should never (explicitly or implicitly) endorse lifestyles by announcing those lifestyles to the world.' Since we know what the conclusion is, we can identify the premises and separate them from other information. Sentences 1 and 2 are not premises; they're background information about the nature of the dispute. Sentence 3 presents the first premise, and sentence 4 is essentially a restatement of that premise. Sentence 5 is the second premise.

Stripped clean of non-argumentative material, the argument looks like this:

[Premise] But the news media are not in the business of endorsing or validating lifestyles. [Premise] In addition, by validating same-sex unions or any other lifestyle, the media abandon their objectivity and become political partisans—which would destroy whatever respect people have for news outlets. [Conclusion] All of this shows that the news media—including this newspaper—should never (explicitly or implicitly) endorse lifestyles by announcing those lifestyles to the world.

Now see if you can spot the conclusion and premises in this one:

[1] You have already said that you love me and that you can't imagine spending the rest of your life without me. [2] Once, you even tried to propose to me. [3] And now you claim that you need time to think about whether we should be married. [4] Well, everything that you've told me regarding our relationship has been a lie. [5] In some of your letters to a friend you admitted that you were misleading me. [6] You've been telling everyone that we are just friends, not lovers. [7] And worst of all, you've been secretly dating someone else. [8] Why are you doing this? [9] It's all been a farce, and I'm outta here.

And you thought that romantic love had nothing to do with critical thinking! In this passionate paragraph, an argument is alive and well. The conclusion is in sentence 4: 'Everything that you've told me . . . has been a lie.' Sentence 9, the concluding remark, is essentially a repetition of the conclusion. Sentences 1, 2, and 3 are background information on the current conflict. Sentences 5, 6, and 7 are the premises, the reasons that support the conclusion. And sentence 8 is an exasperated query that's not part of the argument.

'I respect faith, but doubt is what gets you an education.'
—Wilson Mizner

You will discover that in most extended argumentative passages, premises and conclusions make up only a small portion of the total number of words. A good part of the text is background information and restatements of the premises or conclusion. Most of the rest consists of explanations, digressions, examples or illustrations, and descriptive passages.

Of all these non-argumentative elements, explanations are probably most easily confused with arguments. As we've seen, arguments try to prove or demonstrate that a statement is true. They try to show *that* something is the case. Explanations, however, do not try to prove that a statement is true. They try to show *why* or *how* something is the way it is. Consider these two statements:

- People have a respect for cultural diversity because they adhere to certain ethical standards.

Food For Thought

Go Ahead, Make My Day

Occasionally you will come across an argument that makes its case by way of irony. Both the premises and conclusion may be clearly implied but nowhere stated directly. Here's an excerpt from a full-page ad in the *New York Times* featuring a big picture of Osama bin Laden, the man thought to be responsible for the terrorist attacks of 9/11. Osama is addressing America:

Photo: AFP/Getty Images

> I want you to invade Iraq. Go ahead. Send me a new generation of recruits. Your bombs will fuel their hatred of America and their desire for revenge. Americans won't be safe anywhere. Please attack Iraq. Distract yourself from fighting Al Qaeda. Divide the international community. Go ahead. Destabilize the region. Maybe Pakistan will fall—we want its nuclear weapons. Give Saddam a reason to strike first. He might draw Israel into a fight. Perfect! So please—invade Iraq. Make my day.

Here, an advocacy group is arguing for the opposite of what 'Osama' is saying:

> Don't invade Iraq. This message is the implied conclusion. The basic idea is that invading Iraq is exactly what terrorists want—so don't do it.

- People should have a respect for cultural diversity because their own ethical standards endorse it.

The first statement is an explanation. It's not trying to prove anything, and no statement is in dispute. It's trying to clarify why or how people have respect for cultural diversity. The second statement, though, is an argument. It's trying to prove, or provide support for, the idea that people should have a respect for life.

We discuss the basics of explanations in Chapter 9, and we deal with the other non-argumentative elements in Chapters 4 and 5. In the meantime, you should be able to find the conclusion and premises of an argument—even when there is a lot of non-argumentative material nearby.

Finally, as you can see, learning the principles of critical thinking or logic requires at least some prior knowledge and ability. But, you may wonder (especially if this is your first course in critical or logical reasoning), 'Where does this prior knowledge and ability come from?'—and do you have these prerequisites? Fortunately, the answer is yes. Since you are, as Aristotle says, a rational animal, you already have the necessary equipment, namely, a logical sense that helps you reason in everyday life and enables you to begin honing your critical reasoning.

Summary

Critical thinking is the systematic evaluation or formulation of beliefs, or statements, by rational standards. Critical thinking is *systematic* because it involves distinct procedures and methods. It entails *evaluation* and *formulation* because it's used both to assess existing beliefs (yours or someone else's) and to devise new ones. And it operates according to *rational standards* in that beliefs are judged according to the reasons and reasoning that support them.

Critical thinking matters because our lives are defined by our actions and choices, and our actions and choices are guided by our thinking. Critical thinking helps guide us toward beliefs that are worthy of acceptance and that can us help be successful in life, however we define success.

A consequence of not thinking critically is a loss of personal freedom. If you passively accept beliefs that have been handed to you by your family and your culture, then those beliefs are not really yours. If they are not really yours and you let them guide your choices and actions, then they—not you—are in charge of your life. Your beliefs are yours only if you examine them critically for yourself to see if they are supported by good reasons.

Some people believe that critical thinking will make them cynical, emotionally cold, and creatively constrained. But there is no good reason to believe that this is the case. Critical thinking does not necessarily lead to cynicism. It can complement our feelings by helping us sort them out. And it doesn't limit creativity—it helps perfect it.

Critical thinking is a rational, systematic process that we apply to beliefs of all kinds. As we use the term here, *belief* is just another word for statement, or claim. A *statement* is an assertion that something is or is not the case. When you're engaged in critical thinking, you are mostly either evaluating a statement or trying to formulate one. In both cases your primary task is to figure out how strongly to believe the statement (on the basis of how likely it is to be true). The strength of your belief will depend on the strength of the reasons in favour of the statement.

In critical thinking an argument is not a fight but a set of statements—statements supposedly providing reasons for accepting another statement. The statements given in support of another statement are called the *premises*. The statement that the premises are used to support is called the *conclusion*. An argument then is a group of statements in which some of them (the premises) are intended to support another of them (the conclusion).

Being able to recognize an argument is an important skill on which many other critical-thinking skills are based. The task is made easier by indicator words that often accompany arguments and signal that a premise or conclusion is present. Premise indicators include *for*, *since*, and *because*. Conclusion indicators include *so*, *therefore*, and *thus*.

Arguments almost never appear neatly labelled for identification. They usually come embedded in a lot of statements that are not part of the arguments. Arguments can be complex and long. Your main task is to identify the conclusion and premises without getting lost in the maze of words.

Key Terms

Argument: A group of statements in which some of them (the premises) are intended to support another of them (the conclusion).

Conclusion: In an argument, the statement that the premises are intended to support.

Critical thinking: The systematic evaluation or formulation of beliefs, or statements, by rational standards.

Explanation: A statement or statements intended to tell why or how something is the case.

Indicator words: Words that frequently accompany arguments and signal that a premise or conclusion is present.

Inference: The process of reasoning from a premise or premises to a conclusion based on those premises.

Logic: The study of good reasoning, or inference, and the rules that govern it.

Premise: In an argument, a statement, or reason, given in support of the conclusion.

Statement (claim): An assertion that something is or is not the case.

EXERCISES

For exercises marked with an asterisk (*), there are answers in Appendix B, 'Answers to Exercises'. Answers are not given for quizzes, integrative exercises, and writing assignments.

Exercise 1.1

Review Questions

* 1. What is critical thinking?
 2. Is critical thinking primarily concerned with *what* you think or *how* you think?
 3. Why is critical thinking systematic?
* 4. According to the text, what does it mean to say that critical thinking is done according to rational standards?
 5. According to the text, how does a lack of critical thinking cause a loss of personal freedom?
* 6. What does the term *critical* refer to in critical thinking?
 7. In what way can feelings and critical thinking complement each other?
* 8. What is a statement?
 9. Give an example of a statement. Then give an example of a sentence that is not a statement.
 10. According to the text, by what standard should we always proportion our acceptance of a statement?
* 11. What is an argument?
 12. Give an example of an argument with two premises.
 13. What is a premise?
* 14. What is a conclusion?
 15. Why can't a mere assertion or statement of beliefs constitute an argument?
 16. True or false: All disagreements contain an argument.
* 17. Does the following passage contain an argument? *Sample passage*: I couldn't disagree more with Olivia. She says that video games provoke young men to violence and other insensitive acts. But that's just not true.
 18. Does the following passage contain an argument? *Sample passage*: Alonzo asserts that the government should be able to arrest and imprison anyone if they are suspected of terrorist acts. But that's ridiculous. Doing that would be a violation of basic civil liberties guaranteed in the Canadian Charter of Rights and Freedoms.
* 19. What are indicator words?

20. List three conclusion indicator words.
21. List three premise indicator words.
22. Give an example of a short argument that uses one or more indicator words.
* 23. What is probably the best strategy for trying to find an argument in a complex passage?
24. True or false: You can almost always find an argument in narrative writing.

Exercise 1.2

Which of the following sentences are **statements**? Which are not?

* 1. Do you think that I'm guilty?
2. Do not allow your emotions to distort your thinking.
3. If someone wants to hold a protest march, they should be able to do it without interference from the police.
* 4. Now that you're mayor of the city, do you still believe that the city government is a waste of time?
5. Should our religious beliefs be guided by reason, emotion, or faith?
6. Stop driving on the left side of the road!
* 7. The Meech Lake Accord was a terrible mistake.
8. The Meech Lake Accord was not a terrible mistake.
9. I shall do my best to do my duty to God and my country.
* 10. Are you doing your best for God and country?

Exercise 1.3

Which of the following passages are arguments? For each argument specify what the conclusion is.

* 1. Rene hates Julia, and she always upsets him, so he should avoid her.
2. Rene hates Julia, and his feelings against her cause him tremendous pain.
3. God save our gracious Queen, Long live our noble Queen, God save the Queen. Send her victorious, Happy and glorious, Long to reign over us: God save the Queen.
* 4. Why do you think you have the right to park your car anywhere you please?
5. Drop your gun! You're under arrest.
6. If you smoke that cigarette in here, I will leave the room.
* 7. The *Titanic* sank, and no one came to save it.
8. I know that humans evolved from 'lower' life forms, because my biology professor taught us that in class.
9. Spiderman is a better superhero than Superman because kryptonite can't hurt him, and he doesn't have a Lois Lane around to mess things up.

10. 'Whether our argument concerns public affairs or some other subject, we must know some, if not all, of the facts about the subject on which we are to speak and argue. Otherwise, we can have no materials out of which to construct arguments.' (Aristotle, *Rhetoric*)

* 11. If guns are outlawed, then only outlaws will have guns. Don't outlaw guns.

12. If someone says something that offends me, I should have the right to stop that kind of speech. After all, words can assault people just as weapons can.

13. 'Citizens who so value their "independence" that they will not enroll in a political party are really forfeiting independence, because they abandon a share in decision-making at the primary level: the choice of the candidate.' (Bruce L. Felknor, *Dirty Politics*)

14. If someone says something that offends me, I cannot and should not try to stop them from speaking. After all, in free countries like Canada, speech—even offensive speech—is protected.

* 15. 'Piercing car alarms have disturbed my walks, café meals or my sleep at least once during every day I have lived in the city; roughly 3,650 car alarms. Once, only once, was the wail a response to theft. . . . Silent car alarms connect immediately to a security company, while the noisy ones are a problem, not a solution. They should be banned, finally.' (Letter to the editor, *New York Times*)

16. 'If history is a gauge, the US government cannot be trusted when it comes to sending our children to war. It seems that many years after Congress sends our children to war, we find out that the basic premise for the war was an intentional lie.' (Letter to the editor, *LA Daily News*)

Exercise 1.4

Which of the following passages are arguments? For each argument specify both the conclusion and the premise or premises.

* 1. Faster-than-light travel is not possible. It would violate a law of nature.

2. You have neglected your duty on several occasions, and you have been absent from work too many times. Therefore, you are not fit to serve in your current capacity.

3. Racial profiling is not an issue for white people, but it is a serious issue for visible minorities.

* 4. The flu epidemic on the East Coast is real. Government health officials say so. And I personally have read at least a dozen news stories that characterize the situation as a 'flu epidemic'.

5. Communism is crazy. Only naïve, impressionable pinheads believe that stuff.

6. People who protest Canada's military involvement in Afghanistan don't know what they're talking about. They spend all their time marching and protesting. These are the sort of people who think Canada shouldn't have a military at all.

* 7. 'I am writing about the cost of concert tickets. I am outraged at how much ticket prices are increasing every year. A few years ago, one could attend a popular concert for a decent price. Now some musicians are asking as much as $200 to $300.' (Letter to the editor, *Buffalo News*)

8. 'Comparing the culling of animals for economic reasons to the difficult decision that has to be made by thousands of women each year—whether to end a pregnancy through abortion—is reprehensible. If those who oppose abortion used their resources more wisely and became advocates of better sex education in the classroom, condom machines in all washrooms including high schools, and getting the Catholic Church to change its archaic, dangerous stance on all forms of contraceptives, I believe the rates of abortion around the world would drop significantly.' (Tony Matthews, letter to the editor, Halifax *Chronicle-Herald*, 12 May 2006)

9. Witches are real. They are mentioned in the folklore of many different cultures. There are many people today who claim to be witches. And in the US, they even put a number of witches on trial during the late seventeenth century.

* 10. Stretched upon the dark silk night, bracelets of city lights glisten brightly.

11. Vaughn's car is old. It is beat up. It is unsafe to drive. Therefore, Vaughn's car is ready for the junkyard.

Exercise 1.5

For each of the following conclusions, write at least two premises that can support it. Your proposed premises can be entirely imaginary. To concoct the premises, think of what kind of statement (if true) would persuade you to believe the conclusion.

Example

Conclusion: Pet psychics can diagnose a dog's heartburn 100 per cent of the time.
Premise 1: In the past 50 years, in hundreds of scientific tests, pet psychics were able to correctly diagnose heartburn in dogs 100 per cent of the time.
Premise 2: Scientists have confirmed the existence of energy waves that can carry information about the health of animals.

1. What this country needs is more family values.
2. All animals—rodents, dogs, apes, whatever—have moral rights, just as people do.
* 3. Aboriginal Canadians have every right to hunt and fish on their traditional lands.
4. When I looked into your eyes, time stood still.
5. All medical patients have the right to end their own lives.

* 6. When it comes to animals, MacDonald doesn't know what he's talking about.
  7. Suspicion has arisen regarding the Premier's financial dealings.
  8. The Internet is the most dangerous tool that terrorists have in their arsenal.
* 9. The Internet is the best tool that law enforcement officials have against terrorists.
  10. Pornography is good for society because it educates people about sexuality.
  11. Pornography is bad for society because it misleads people about sexuality.
* 12. *The Sopranos* is the greatest series in the history of TV.
  13. It is the duty of every student to prevent this arbitrary tuition increase.
  14. Ling cannot hold her liquor.

Exercise 1.6

For each of the following sets of premises, write a conclusion that would be supported by the premises (your conclusion should depend on both premises). Neither the conclusion nor the premises need to be statements that are true.

Example

Premise 1: The price of your shares in the stock market will continue to decline for at least a year.
Premise 2: Anyone with shares whose price will continue to decline for at least a year should sell now.
Conclusion: You should sell now.

1. Premise 1: You are afraid of heights.
    Premise 2: Anyone who is afraid of heights will fall if they climb a tree.
* 2. Premise 1: Several Canadian cities have banned smoking in bars and restaurants.
    Premise 2: Bans on smoking in bars and restaurants typically result in lower rates of smoking over all.
3. Premise 1: Several Canadian cities have banned smoking in bars and restaurants.
    Premise 2: Bans on smoking in bars and restaurants usually result in reduced profits for bars and restaurants.
* 4. Premise 1: All married people are happier than unmarried people.
    Premise 2: You are married.
5. Premise 1: If stem-cell research is banned, Edgar will be very happy.
    Premise 2: Stem-cell research is banned.
6. Premise 1: If there is no God, then there is no morality.
    Premise 2: There is no God.
7. Premise 1: There is a God.
    Premise 2: If there is a God, then life has meaning.

* 8.   Premise 1: There is a great deal of pornography of all kinds on the Internet.

Premise 2: The government has essentially established a hands-off policy toward pornography on the Internet.

Premise 3: Kids everywhere have access to pornography of all kinds on the Internet.

9.   Premise 1: People in favour of capital punishment have a complete disregard for human life.

Premise 2: Anyone who has a complete disregard for human life cannot be trusted.

Premise 3: Nancy favours capital punishment.

Exercise 1.7

For each of the following passages, determine if there is an argument present. If so, identify the premises and the conclusion.

* 1.   Advertising is not manipulative, as some people seem to think. The main thing advertising does is to provide us with information about products. And ads that don't seem to feature much information are really just trying to entertain us, not manipulate us.

2.   '[Francis Bacon] is the father of experimental philosophy. . . . In a word, there was not a man who had any idea of experimental philosophy before Chancellor Bacon; and of an infinity of experiments which have been made since his time, there is hardly a single one which has not been pointed out in his book. He had even made a good number of them himself.' (Voltaire, *On Bacon and Newton*)

* 3.   'Is there archaeological evidence for the [Biblical] Flood? If a universal Flood occurred between five and six thousand years ago, killing all humans except the eight on board the Ark, it would be abundantly clear in the archaeological record. Human history would be marked by an absolute break. We would see the devastation wrought by the catastrophe in terms of the destroyed physical remains of pre-Flood human settlements. . . . Unfortunately for the Flood enthusiasts, the destruction of all but eight of the world's people left no mark on the archaeology of human cultural evolution.' (Kenneth L. Feder, *Frauds, Myths, and Mysteries*)

4.   'Subjectivism claims that what makes an action [morally] right is that a person approves of it or believes that it's right. Although subjectivism may seem admirably egalitarian in that it takes everyone's moral judgments to be as good as everyone else's, it has some rather bizarre consequences. For one thing, it implies that each of us is morally infallible. As long as we approve of or believe in what we are doing, we can do no wrong. But this cannot be right. Suppose that Hitler believed that it was right to exterminate the Jews. Then it was right for Hitler to exterminate the Jews. . . . But what . . . Hitler did was wrong, even if [he] believed otherwise.' (Theodore Schick, Jr, *Free Inquiry Magazine*)

Field Problems

1. Obtain the 'Letters to the Editor' section of any newspaper (including student newspapers and online newspapers). Select a letter that contains at least one argument. Locate the conclusion and each premise.

2. Next go through the letters again to find one that contains no argument at all. Rewrite the letter so that it contains at least one argument. Try to preserve as much of the original letter as possible. Stay on the same topic.

Self-Assessment Quiz

1. What is an argument?

2. Name at least three premise indicators and three conclusion indicators.

3. From the following sentences, select the one that is *not* a statement:
   a. When I met you, you didn't know anything about logic.
   b. Read the story and write a complete review of it.
   c. The Canadian Charter of Rights and Freedoms guarantees the rights and freedoms set out in it subject only to such reasonable limits prescribed by law as can be demonstrably justified in a free and democratic society.
   d. The best pizza in town can be had at Luigi's.

4. From the following list, select the conclusion that is supported by the premises in the following argument:

   I spoke to a number of students on campus who see nothing wrong with downloading music from the Internet without paying for it. I tried to explain to them, but they just didn't get it. They didn't understand that taking songs without paying for them is just like shoplifting. And they didn't seem to think downloading hurts anyone, even though it means hard-working musicians aren't getting paid for their work. If some bands want to give away music for free, that's fine, but that doesn't mean that all music is then free for the taking.

   a. University students are not intelligent.
   b. Music should not be freely available on the Internet.
   c. Some university students should learn more about ethical arguments related to downloading music.
   d. University students generally don't respect the law.

5. Does the following passage contains an argument? If it does, specify the conclusion.

   We live in an incredibly over-reactionary society where the mindless forces of victim demagoguery have unfortunately joined with the child-worship industry. It is obviously tragic that a few twisted kids perpetuated such carnage there in Columbine. [Letter to the editor, Salon.com]

6. Indicate whether the following passage contains an argument. If it does, specify the conclusion.

"War doesn't solve problems; it creates them," said an Oct. 8 letter about Iraq. World War II solved problems called Nazi Germany and militaristic Japan and created alliances with the nations we crushed. . . . The Persian Gulf war solved the problem of the Iraqi invasion of Kuwait. The Civil War solved the problem of slavery. These wars created a better world. War, or the threat of it is the only way to defeat evil enemies who are a threat to us. There is no reasoning with them. There can be no peace with them . . . so it's either us or them. What creates true peace is victory." (Letter to the editor, *New York Times*)

7. Does the following passage contain an argument? If it does, specify the conclusion.

Some people seem to think that the provincial government can't do anything right. If the government raises taxes, they get upset over that. But if the government lowers taxes, those same people complain that it's going to result in the government providing fewer services. If the province introduces new programs, these folks complain that they're not as good as the old programs. But if the government doesn't do something new every year, then the complaint is that the government isn't doing enough.

Which of the following sentences and sentence fragments are likely to be conclusions, and which are likely to be premises?

8. Therefore, BC's old-growth forests will disappear within your lifetime!
9. Assuming that you will never reach Montreal.
10. This implies that you are not driving as safely as you should.
11. Given all the excitement surrounding the football team.
12. It follows that sexual harassment should be a crime.

For questions 13–15, write at least two premises for each of the numbered conclusions. You can make up the premises, but you must ensure that they support the conclusion.

13. DNA evidence should be disallowed in cases of first-degree murder.
14. Computers will never be able to converse with a human being well enough to be indistinguishable from humans.
15. The Edmonton Oilers are the greatest hockey team of all time.

Read the following argument. Then in questions 16–20, supply the information requested.

[1] Is global warming a real threat? [2] Or is it hype propagated by tree-hugging, nutty environmentalists? [3] The Prime Minister apparently thinks that the idea of global climate change is nonsense. [4] But a recent American study showed him to be wrong. [5] The US government issued a report on global warming called the *US Climate Action Report 2002*. [6] It gave no support to the idea that global warming doesn't happen and we should all go back to sleep. [7] Instead, it asserted that global warming was definitely real and that it could have catastrophic consequences if ignored. [8] For example, global climate change could cause heat waves, extreme weather, and water shortages in many parts of North America. [9] The report is also backed by many other reports, including a very influential one from the United Nations. [10] Yes, Prime Minister, global warming is real. [11] It is as real as hurricanes and ice storms.

Identify by number all the sentences in the argument that fulfill each of the following roles:

16. Conclusion.
17. Premise or premises.
18. Background information.
19. Example or illustration.
20. Repetition of conclusion or premise.

Critical Thinking and Writing Exercise

This is the first of five end-of-chapter lessons, or modules, designed to help you think about, plan, and write good argumentative essays. The modules are progressive, starting here with a few fundamentals of the writing process and then later covering basic guidelines and concepts that can help you think critically and write intelligently about arguments and issues. Though the modules are linked in some fashion to material in their corresponding chapters, they are meant to serve as a stand-alone (though cumulative) tutorial to be used as your instructor sees fit.

Arguments and Argumentative Essays

As we note in this chapter, an argument is a group of statements in which some of them (the premises) are intended to support another of them (the conclusion). This configuration of statements-supporting-another-statement is not only the basic structure of an argument—it's the general design of an argumentative essay. An argumentative essay tries to support a particular conclusion or position on an issue by offering reasons to support that conclusion. Arguments (in the critical-thinking sense) are not passionate exchanges of unsupported views or pointless contests of the is-too-is-not variety. And neither are argumentative essays. A mere sequence of statements expressing your views is not an argument, just as several pages of such statements do not constitute an argumentative essay.

So in an argumentative essay, your main task is to provide rational support for a claim. If you are successful, you will have shown that there are good reasons to accept your view of things. Readers who think critically may well be persuaded by your arguments. If you write well, you may be able to make your essay even more persuasive through rhetorical or stylistic devices that add emphasis, depth, and vividness to your prose. No one wants to read a boring essay. What you should not do, however, is rely entirely on non-argumentative elements to persuade your audience. Strong emotional appeals, for example, can indeed persuade some people, but they prove nothing. In truly effective argumentative essays, the primary persuasive device is critical reasoning.

Basic Essay Structure

Good argumentative essays generally contain the following elements, though not necessarily in the order shown here:

- Introduction (or opening)
- Statement of thesis (the claim to be supported)
- Argument supporting the thesis
- Assessment of objections
- Conclusion

In the *introduction*, you want to do at least two things: (1) grab the reader's attention and (2) provide background information for the thesis. Effective attention grabbers include startling statistics, compelling quotations, interesting anecdotes, opinions of experts, shocking or unexpected claims, and vivid imagery. Whatever attention grabbers you use, *they must be related to the topic of the essay*. There's no use telling a good story if it has nothing to do with your thesis. Providing background for your thesis often means explaining why your topic is important, telling how you became concerned, or showing that there is a problem to be solved or a question to be answered. Very often the introduction, sometimes consisting of no more than a sentence or two, is laid out in the first paragraph of the essay. In general, the shorter the introduction, the better.

The *thesis statement* also usually appears in the first paragraph. This is the statement that you hope to support or prove in your essay; it is the conclusion of the argument that you intend to present. You want to state the thesis in a single sentence and do so as early as possible in the essay. Your thesis statement is like a compass to your readers, guiding them through your essay from premise to premise, showing them a clear path. It also helps *you* stay on course by reminding you to keep every part of the essay related to your single unifying idea. Your thesis statement should be restricted to a claim that can be defended in the space allowed (often only 750 to 1,000 words). Not restricted enough: 'Tuition is too high.' Better: 'Tuition increases at Degrassi College are unacceptable.' Better still: 'The recent tuition increase at Degrassi College is unnecessary for financial reasons.' (More on how to devise a properly restricted thesis statement in a moment.)

The main body of the essay is the fully developed *argument supporting the thesis*. This means that the basic essay structure consists of the thesis statement followed by each premise or reason that supports the thesis. Each premise in turn is stated clearly, explained and illustrated sufficiently, and supported by examples, statistics, expert opinion, and other evidence. Sometimes you can develop the essay very simply by devoting a single paragraph to each premise. At other times, each premise may demand several paragraphs. In any case, you should develop just one point per paragraph, and every paragraph should be clearly related to the thesis statement.

A sketch of the argument for the Degrassi College essay, then, might look like this:

Premise: If the college has a budget surplus, then a tuition increase is unnecessary.

Premise: The college has had a budget surplus for the last five years.

Premise: If the college president says that the school is in good shape financially and therefore doesn't need a tuition increase, then it's probably true that the school doesn't need a tuition increase.

Premise: In an unguarded moment, the president admitted that the school is in good shape financially and therefore doesn't need a tuition increase.

Thesis statement: Therefore, the recent tuition increase at Degrassi College is probably unnecessary for financial reasons.

Good argumentative essays include an *assessment of objections*—an honest effort to take into account any objections that readers are likely to raise about the thesis statement or its premises. When you deal with such objections in your essay, you lend credibility to it because you're making an attempt to be fair and thorough. In addition, when you carefully examine objections, you can often see ways to make your argument or thesis statement stronger. It isn't necessary to consider every possible objection but just the strongest or the most common ones. Sometimes it's best to deal with objections when you discuss premises that are related to them. At other times it may be better to handle objections near the end of the essay after defending the premises.

Finally, your essay—unless it's very short—must have a *conclusion*. The conclusion usually appears in the last paragraph of the essay. Usually it reiterates the thesis statement (though usually not in exactly the same words). If the argument is complex or the essay is long, the conclusion may contain a summary of the argument. Good conclusions may reassert the importance of the thesis statement, challenge readers to do something about a problem, tell a story that emphasizes the relevance of the main argument, or bring out a disturbing or unexpected implication of a claim defended in the body of the essay.

Guidelines for Writing the Essay

1. *Determine your thesis statement.* Do *not* write on the first thesis idea that pops into your head. Select a topic you're interested in and narrow its scope until you have a properly restricted thesis statement. Research the topic to find out what issues are being debated. When you think you have an idea for a thesis statement, stop. Dig deeper into the idea by examining the arguments associated with that claim. Choose a thesis statement that you think you can defend. If you come to a dead end, start the process over.

2. *Create an outline.* Establish the basic framework of your outline by writing out your thesis statement and all the premises that support it. Then fill in the framework by jotting down what points you will need to make in defence of each premise. Decide what objections to your argument you will consider and how you will respond to them.

3. *Write a first draft.* As you write, don't be afraid to revise your outline or even your thesis statement. Writing will force you to think carefully about the strengths and weaknesses of your argument. If need be, write a second draft and a third. Good writers aren't afraid of revisions; they depend on them.

4. *Stay on track.* Make sure that each sentence of your essay is related somehow to your thesis statement and argument.

5. *Zero in on your audience.* Decide what audience your essay is intended for, and *write to them.* Is it readers of the local paper? Fellow students? People who are likely to disagree with you?

6. *Support your premises.* Back up the premises of your argument with examples, expert opinion, statistics, analogies, and other kinds of evidence.

7. *Let your final draft sit.* If possible, when you've finished writing your paper, set it aside and read it the next day. You may be surprised how many mistakes this fresh look can reveal. If you can't set the essay aside, ask a friend to read it and give you some constructive criticism.

Writing Assignments

1. Read Essay 7 ('Yes, Human Cloning Should Be Permitted') in Appendix A and outline the argument presented. Specify the thesis statement and each supporting premise.

2. Write a 500-word paper in which you defend a claim that *contradicts* the thesis statement in Essay 2 ('Hurray! No One's Watching'). Pretend that all the evidence cited in Essay 2 actually supports your thesis statement. You may alter the description of the evidence accordingly.

3. Study the argument presented in Essay 3 ('Marine Parks') in Appendix A. Identify the conclusion and the premises and objections considered. Then write a two-page rebuttal to the essay. That is, defend the claim that marine mammals should continue to be kept in marine parks.

4. Select an issue from the following list and write a 750-word paper defending a claim pertaining to the issue.

   • Should Canada change its constitution to recognize Quebec as a 'distinct society'?
   • When Canadian companies are operating overseas, should they follow Canadian ethical standards or the standards of their 'host' country?
   • Should the legal drinking age in your province be lowered?
   • Should the private ownership of all firearms be outlawed?

The 'Environment' of Critical Thinking

Chapter Objectives

- To appreciate that there are ways to (1) detect errors in our thinking, (2) restrain the attitudes and feelings that can distort our reasoning, and (3) achieve a level of objectivity that makes critical thinking possible
- To understand that the most common impediments to critical thinking can be sorted into two categories: (1) those hindrances that arise because of *how* we think and (2) those that occur because of *what* we think

Perils of a Haunted Mind

You will be able to

- detect and overcome self-interested thinking by (1) watching out for instances when your deliberations get personal, (2) being alert to ways that critical thinking can be undermined, and (3) ensuring that no relevant evidence or ideas have been left out.
- appreciate how group thinking can distort critical thinking.
- understand the meaning of *peer pressure*, *appeal to popularity*, *appeal to common practice*, and *stereotyping* and be able to cite examples of each.

Perils of a Haunted World View

You will be able to

- understand what a world view is and how certain crucial ideas in a world view can undermine critical thinking.
- critique the doctrine of subjective relativism.
- critique the doctrine of social relativism.
- define philosophical skepticism and how it relates to critical thinking.

Critical thinking does not happen in a vacuum but in an 'environment' that is often hostile to it. It takes place in the real world in the minds of real people who almost always have thoughts and feelings and experiences that, given half a chance, would sabotage critical reasoning at every turn. The sparkling palace of our mind is grand—except for the demons chained in the basement.

Recall our definition of critical thinking: *The systematic evaluation or formulation of beliefs, or statements, by rational standards*. This means, of course, that several factors must be present for the process of critical thinking to be fully realized. If the process fails to be systematic, or falls short of being a true evaluation or formulation, or ignores rational standards, critical thinking can't happen. Because we are fallible, there are a thousand ways that this failure of reason could come about. And there is no cure for our fallibility.

We should expect then that thinking critically will often be difficult and even unpleasant (as painful truths sometimes are), and indeed it is. But there are ways to (1) detect errors in our thinking (even subtle ones), (2) restrain the attitudes and feelings that can distort our reasoning, and (3) achieve a level of objectivity that makes critical thinking possible.

Doing all this—and doing it consistently—requires *awareness*, *practice*, and *motivation*. If we are to think critically, we must be aware, not only of what is involved in good critical thinking, but also of what can result from sloppy thinking. Then we must *practise* avoiding the pitfalls and using the skills and techniques that critical thinking requires. And we must be *motivated* to do all of this because it is unlikely that we will use critical thinking very much if we can't appreciate its value; if we can't appreciate its value, we would have little motivation to make the extra effort.

We can sort the most common impediments to critical thinking into two main categories: (1) those hindrances that arise because of *how* we think and (2) those that occur because of *what* we think. There is some overlap in these categories since how people think is often a result of what they think and vice versa. But in general, category 1 obstacles are those that come into play because of psychological factors (our fears, attitudes, motivations, and desires), and category 2 impediments are those that arise because of certain philosophical ideas we have (our beliefs about beliefs). For example, a category 1 hindrance is the tendency to conform our opinions to those of our peers. This conformism often grows out of some psychological need that is part of our personality. A common category 2 problem is the belief

"We'll probably vote for the least qualified candidate. We have no judgment skills."

Food For Thought

Francis Bacon on Critical Thinking

Francis Bacon (1561–1626), the father of modern science, articulated basic principles and methods of science and advocated their use in the careful pursuit of reliable knowledge. He also warned about common mistakes in thinking that can doom the scientific enterprise and lead to biased perceptions and serious error. Bacon asserted that it is possible to prevent these mistakes through scientific, down-to-earth thinking—approximately what we would call critical thinking, a necessary and powerful tool in the search for truth. He termed the mistakes 'the idols of the mind' because he thought that people not only commit the errors but revere them as one would revere a false god.

Photo: National Portrait Gallery, London

Bacon focused on four kinds of idols that he considered especially prevalent and destructive. The first type is 'the Idols of the Tribe'—the problems in thinking that arise from human nature generally. This is the fallacy of assuming that our biased perceptions are automatically a true reflection of the objective world, and that knowledge is to be found inside us without any reference to the real world.

The second group consists of the 'Idols of the Cave'—the biases that are unique to each individual. These develop from each person's personality, education, and experiences. Bacon claimed that we each live in our own cave, 'which refracts and discolors the light of nature'.

Then there are the 'Idols of the Marketplace'—the impediments to clear thinking that develop from our imprecise and careless use of language. As Bacon said, 'the ill and unfit choice of words wonderfully obstructs the understanding.'[1]

Finally there are the 'Idols of the Theater'—the ideologies or systems of thought that are 'but so many stage-plays, representing worlds of their own creation after an unreal and scenic fashion'.[2] These barriers to good critical thinking have little or nothing to do with the real world but are nevertheless thought to be accurate and profound.

that objectivity in thinking is impossible or that we really don't know anything or that we don't know what we think we know.

In this chapter we review the most common category 1 and 2 barriers to critical thinking and practise uncovering and neutralizing them. The motivation to learn these lessons well is up to you.

Perils of a Haunted Mind

No one is immune to category 1 obstacles. We are all heir to psychological tendencies and habits that affect our behaviour and channel our thinking. They tend to persist or recur, haunting our minds until we have the awareness and the will to break free of them.

The Almighty Self

As humans we spend a great deal of time protecting, maintaining, and comforting our own mental life, our own *selves*—a perfectly natural urge that does no harm until we push our self-serving efforts too far. How far is too far? From the standpoint of critical thinking, we have taken things too far when we accept claims for no good reason—when our thinking is no longer systematic and rational. In the service of our almighty selves, we distort our judgment and raise our risk of error, which is ironically a risk to ourselves.

Self-interested thinking takes several forms. We may decide to accept a claim *solely on the grounds that it advances, or coincides with, our interests.* You may think, 'I believe the province should lower the sales tax on anything bought at a convenience store because I own a convenience store,' or 'I am against all forms of gun control because I am a hunter,' or 'This university should not raise tuition fees because I am a student, and I don't want to pay more tuition.' There is nothing inherently wrong with accepting a claim that furthers your own interests. The problem arises when you accept a claim *solely because* it furthers your interests. Self-interest alone simply cannot establish the truth of a claim. To base your beliefs on self-interest alone is to abandon critical thinking.

Here's a classic example of self-interested thinking inspired by the film *Twelve Angry Men*:

> Twelve jurors sit in a room deliberating over whether to find the defendant guilty of murder. The accused is a Puerto Rican teenager who has grown up in the rough and impoverished streets of the inner city. At first, all but one juror (the jury foreman) vote guilty. The foreman persuades the other jurors to examine the evidence once again. Their deliberations go on for hours, and as they do, the prosecution's case slowly falls apart. Apparently damning evidence that had seemed so strong earlier was now shown to be full of holes. They take another vote, but this time 11 jurors, including the foreman, vote not guilty, while one man (juror number 10) insists that the other jurors are deluded and that the boy is undoubtedly guilty. The jurors ask him to explain his reasons. He angrily insists again that the boy is guilty, but he can't provide any evidence or reasons that suggest the boy's guilt. He just rants at the other jurors, muttering something about his dead son and

Puerto Ricans being 'no good' and 'against everything I believe in'. Finally the other jurors think they understand what's behind the seemingly irrational stance of juror number 10: He wants to convict the boy for personal reasons—perhaps because he wants to avenge his son's death, because he feels threatened by ethnic minorities, because he had been wronged by another Puerto Rican boy, or because of some other bias that has nothing to do with the guilt or innocence of the defendant.

In this example, the other members of the jury eventually realize that the judgments of juror number 10 are self-serving and linked to his own emotional needs. What gave him away? An obvious clue is his emotional protestations. But an even more telling clue is his rejection of all relevant evidence. The reasons for acquitting are perfectly clear to the other jurors, but he won't (or can't) consider them. In everyday life, these two clues often signal the presence of powerful self-interest at work.

The influence of self on your thinking can take another form. You may be tempted to accept claims *for no other reason than that they help you save face*. We all like to think of ourselves as excelling in various ways. We may believe that we are above average in intelligence, integrity, talent, compassion, physical beauty, sexual prowess, athletic ability, and much more. But we not only like to think such things about ourselves; we want others to think the same about us. The rub comes, however, when we

In *Twelve Angry Men*, one juror, for personal reasons, holds out for a guilty verdict despite overwhelming evidence that the accused is innocent. How often do you think this kind of self-interested thinking happens in real-life juries? Photo: Showtime/The Kobal Collection

DILBERT: © Scott Adams/Dist. By United Feature Syndicate, Inc.

accept or defend claims just to cover up the cracks in our image. You make a mistake, and so you blame it on someone or something else. You behave badly, and you try to justify your behaviour. You make a judgment or observation that turns out to be wrong, and you're too embarrassed or proud to admit it. (In Chapter 4 we'll learn that sometimes self-interested thinking can even alter our perceptions.)

The consequences of self-centred thinking can be self-destructive. In the realm of critical thinking, this devotion to yourself can prevent careful evaluation of claims, limit critical inquiry, blind you to the facts, provoke self-deception, engender rationalizations, lead you to suppress or ignore evidence, and beget wishful thinking. And these mistakes can decrease your chances of success (however you define success) and hamper your personal growth, maturity, and self-awareness. Such egocentrism can also leave you wide open to propaganda and manipulation by people who appeal to your personal desires and prejudices. How easy would it be for people to control your choices and thoughts if they told you exactly what you wanted to hear? (There are in-depth discussions of these lapses in critical thinking in Chapters 4 and 5.)

Other people (especially those who know you fairly well) may be amused or puzzled by your stubborn adherence to claims that obviously conflict with the evidence. Or they may think it odd that you cling to ideas or behaviour that you loudly condemn in others.

When examining a claim or making a choice, how can you overcome the excessive influence of your own needs? Sometimes you can do it only with great effort, and sometimes the task is much easier, especially if you remember these three guidelines:

- Watch out when things get very personal.
- Be alert to ways that critical thinking can be undermined.
- Ensure that nothing has been left out.

'To be conscious that you are ignorant is a great step to knowledge.'
–Benjamin Disraeli

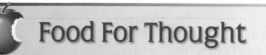

Food For Thought

When We Construct the Facts Ourselves

Psychologists have long known that a great deal of what we experience is fabricated by ourselves. That is, our own desires and expectations help form an impressive proportion of our perceptions, memories, and beliefs. Here are a few examples documented by scientific research:

Pareidolia or not: The face of Mother Teresa in a cinnamon bun? In 1996, this bun was discovered at Bongo Java, a Nashville coffee-house. Photo: www.bongojava.com

- Often what we think we see in vague stimuli turns out to be something that our minds have made up. We see bunnies, bearded men, and Elvis in formless clouds and smoke. We hear words and animal noises in garbled audio (like records played backward). This phenomenon is known as *pareidolia*. To this day tabloid newspapers run stories on the Great Stone Face of Mars, a supposed one-mile wide stone monument built by aliens. That's what some people say they see in a very fuzzy 1976 NASA photograph of the Martian surface. Scientists say it's a natural formation like a thousand others in the area. A later NASA photo was much clearer and showed that the 'face' was just an illusion of shadows and wishful thinking.

- There are probably hundreds of stories about ghosts and aliens showing up in people's bedrooms. Whatever is going on here, it certainly doesn't need to be supernatural. Researchers have shown that when people are in that drowsy state just before sleep, they often have weird hallucinations known as *hypnogogic imagery*. These images come on suddenly, are not under the sleeper's control, and can seem as real as physical objects in the room. Images range from faces in the dark to ghostly shapes and coloured geometric shapes.

- Research has shown that our memories are not exact copies of past events. The recall of eyewitnesses, for instance, is notoriously unreliable. In the act of recall, they try to reconstruct a memory—but the reconstruction is frequently inexact, resulting in distortions and missing details. Stress can exaggerate these problems. Our memories can be drastically changed if we later come across new information—even if the new information is brief and flimsy. Most amazing of all, our expectations about the way things should be can insert or delete elements of a memory. If we expect to see a gun in the hand of a bank robber, we may remember exactly that even though no gun was involved.

Part of the job of critical thinking, of course, is to counteract all these tendencies—or help you recognize them when they happen.

Watch Out When Things Get Very Personal

You are most likely to let your self-interest get in the way of clear thinking when you have a big personal stake in the conclusions you reach. You may be deeply committed to a particular view or belief, or you may desperately want a particular claim to be false or unjustified, or you may be devoted not to particular claims but to *any* claims that contradict those of someone you dislike. Such zeal can wreck any attempt at a careful, fair evaluation of a claim.

The twentieth-century philosopher Bertrand Russell asserts that the passionate holding of an opinion is a sure sign of a lack of reasons to support the opinion:

> When there are rational grounds for an opinion, people are content to set them forth and wait for them to operate. In such cases, people do not hold their opinions with passion; they hold them calmly, and set forth their reasons quietly. The opinions that are held with passion are always those for which no good ground exists; indeed the passion is the measure of the holder's lack of rational conviction.[3]

The dead giveaway that you are skewing your thinking is a surge of strong emotions (like the one that gripped juror number 10). If your evaluation or defense of a position evokes anger, passion, or fear, your thinking could be prejudiced or clouded. It is possible, of course, to be emotionally engaged in an issue and still think critically and carefully. But most of the time, getting worked up over a claim or conclusion is reason enough to suspect that your thinking is not as clear as it should be.

The rule of thumb is this: If you sense a rush of emotions when you deal with a particular issue, pause for a moment. Think about what's happening and why. Then continue at a slower pace and with greater attention to the basics of critical reasoning, double-checking to ensure that you are not ignoring or suppressing evidence or getting sloppy in your evaluations.

Be Alert to Ways That Critical Thinking Can Be Undermined

If you understand the techniques and principles of critical thinking, and you have practised applying them in a variety of situations, you are more likely than not to detect your own one-sided self-centred thinking when it occurs. An alarm should go off in your head: 'Warning—faulty reasoning!'

When your alarm sounds, double-check your thinking, look for lapses in arguments and claims, and weed them out.

Ensure That Nothing Has Been Left Out

A common flaw in reasoning is the failure to consider evidence or arguments that *do not support* your preferred claims or positions. For example, you may secretly want a particular claim to be true, so you knowingly or unknowingly look for

Food For Thought

Is It Unethical to Believe without Good Reasons?

Some philosophers have asserted that it is morally wrong to believe a proposition without justification or evidence. One of these is the famous biologist Thomas Henry Huxley. Another is the mathematician W.K. Clifford (1845–79). This is how Clifford states his view:

> It is wrong always, everywhere, and for anyone, to believe anything upon insufficient evidence. If a man, holding a belief which he was taught in childhood or persuaded of afterwards, keeps down and pushes away any doubts which arise about it in his mind ... and regards as impious those questions which cannot easily be asked without disturbing it—the life of that man is one long sin against mankind.[4]

Clifford thinks that belief without evidence is immoral because our actions are guided by our beliefs, and if our beliefs are unfounded, our actions (including morally relevant actions) are likely to be imprudent.

evidence in its favour but ignore evidence against it. The chances of making this mistake increase markedly when you are reasoning for the sake of self.

This kind of preferential treatment for some statements and not others is part of a common phenomenon called *selective attention* (see Chapters 4 and 5). In selective attention, we notice certain things and ignore others—usually without even being aware that we're doing it. We may ignore facts that contradict our beliefs and search out facts that support them. Scientific research has repeatedly confirmed this behaviour. In a typical study, researchers showed subjects both *evidence for* and *evidence against* the reality of extrasensory perception (ESP). Subjects who already doubted the existence of ESP recalled both kinds of evidence accurately. But subjects who already believed in ESP remembered both kinds of evidence as *proving* ESP. They somehow recalled even the disconfirming evidence as supporting their belief in ESP!

The remedy for this problem is to *make a conscious effort to look for opposing evidence.* Don't consider your evaluation of a statement or argument finished until you've carefully considered *all the relevant reasons.* Ask yourself, 'What is the evidence or reasons against this statement?'

This approach is at the heart of science. A basic principle of scientific work is not to accept a favoured theory until competing (alternative) theories are thoroughly examined. (More on this in Chapter 10.)

Review Notes

Avoiding Self-Interested Thinking

- Watch out when things get personal and you become emotionally invested in an issue.
- Beware of the urge to distort your thinking to save face.
- Be alert to ways that critical thinking can be undermined.
- Ensure that nothing has been left out of consideration.
- Avoid selective attention.
- Make a conscious effort to look for opposing evidence.

The Power of the Group

In the television series *Star Trek: The Next Generation*, the crew of the starship *Enterprise* encounters an unusual threat: the Borg. The Borg is a collective of individual minds that have been stripped of individuality and merged into a single group-mind with evil intentions. Much of the Borg storyline (which spans several episodes) is about the dignity and importance of individualism as opposed to the conformism of the Borg hive. The thought of losing one's self in the monolithic Borg is presented as a profound tragedy—a theme that strikes a cord with humans. Individualism, independence, and freedom of thought are what we want and what we must have.

Or so we say. Despite our apparent longings, we humans spend a great deal of our time trying to conform to groups or be part of them. We want to belong, we want the safety and comfort of numbers, and we want the approval of our beloved tribe. All that is perfectly normal. We are, after all, social creatures. Conformist tendencies are a fact of life. But trouble appears when our conformism hampers—or obliterates—critical thinking.

We all belong to multiple groups—family, employees, gender, church, club, professional society, political party, advocacy group, you name

Critical thinking helps you stay away from the Borg.
Photo: Photos 12/Alamy

... BUT WE DON'T PAY YOU LESS BECAUSE YOU'RE A WOMAN... WE PAY YOU LESS BECAUSE WE'RE MEN!

FRAN©

www.CartoonStock.com

it—and we can be susceptible to pressure from all of them. Much of the time, there is intense pressure to fit into groups and to adopt the ideas, attitudes, and goals endorsed by them. Sometimes the influence of the group is subtle but strong and can occur in the most casual, 'unofficial' gatherings. The claims and positions adopted by the group can be implicit, never spoken, but well understood. The political chat group online, the group of Christians or Muslims or Jews who happen to meet on the bus, the collection of peers who support the same political cause—all these can exert a noticeable influence on our beliefs.

Group pressure to accept a statement or act in a certain way has several different faces (some of which we cover in more detail in later chapters). When we're talking about the pressure to conform that comes from your peers, it's called—not surprisingly—**peer pressure**. When we're talking about an argument that tries to support a conclusion on the basis of the mere popularity of a belief, that's known, appropriately enough, as an **appeal to popularity** (also known as an appeal to the masses). In all cases, the lapse in critical thinking comes from the fact that the views or behaviour of the group *alone* is taken as reason to support a claim (see Chapter 5).

Group pressure can happen quickly. For example, if you're listening to a speech by a member of your own political party, you may immediately find yourself positively disposed toward the speaker—not because you agree with him but because he's a member of your group.

Group pressure can also take a while to have an effect. Consider this example:

Aimee has just become a new member of the Young Liberals club on campus. She's been considering joining ever since Frosh Week. She's away from home for the first time and hasn't made very many new friends. She likes to feel that she belongs to something, and she shares most of the group's beliefs. And the club includes some of the smartest and most active students on campus, so being part of the club makes her feel like part of the 'in' crowd. She soon finds out that she agrees with members of the club on every social and political issue—except one. Everyone else in the group is strongly in favour of decriminalizing possession of marijuana. Aimee is against that, because she's read a lot about it and the arguments against decriminalization seem to be stronger than the arguments in favour. But she doesn't want to jeopardize her membership in the club—or her new friendships—over this one issue. So, when the topic comes up, she stays quiet. The arguments she hears from her new friends seem faulty. But, as time goes on, she stops thinking about the

'Believe nothing, no matter where you read it, or who said it, no matter if I said it, unless it agrees with your own reason and your own common sense.'
—The Buddha

arguments and tries not to think about the topic at all. Over time, her views on the subject start to change, until finally she finds herself being whole-heartedly in favour of decriminalizing marijuana.

Here, the need to belong slowly usurps critical reasoning in a specific subject area (decriminalization of marijuana). On other topics, Aimee may be an astute critical thinker.

There's another kind of group influence that we have all fallen prey to: that's the pressure that comes from assuming that our own group is the best, the right one, the chosen one, and all other groups are, well, not as good. You can see this kind of ethnocentrism in religions, political parties, generations, social classes, and many other groups. The assumption that your group is better than others is at the heart of prejudice.

> 'A great many people think they are thinking when they are really rearranging their prejudices.'
> —William James

Food For Thought

Prejudice, Bias, and Racism

Group pressure often leads to prejudice, bias, and racism. (To a lesser extent, so does self-interest.) But what do these terms mean?

Prejudice in its broadest sense is a judgment or opinion—whether positive or negative—based on insufficient reasons. But usually the term is used in a more narrow way to mean a negative, or adverse, belief (most often about people) without sufficient reasons. At the heart of prejudice, then, is a failure of critical thinking. And the use of critical thinking is an important part of eradicating prejudiced views.

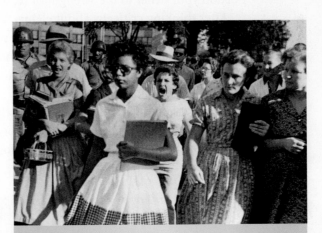

Critical thinking against racism. In 1957 during efforts to integrate schools in Little Rock, Arkansas, a black student is jeered as she attempts to attend classes at an all-white high school. Photo © Bettmann/Corbis

Bias is another word for prejudice, both in the general and the narrow sense. Sometimes the word is also used to mean an inclination of temperament or outlook—as in 'My bias is in favour of tougher laws.'

Racism is a lack of respect for the value and rights of people of different races or geographical origins. Usually this attitude is based on prejudice—specifically an unjustified belief that one group of people is somehow superior to another.

This we-are-better pressure is probably the most powerful of all. We all have certain beliefs, not because we have thought critically about them, but because our parents raised us to believe them or because the conceptual push and pull of our social group has instilled them in us. That is, we may believe what we believe—and assume that our beliefs are better than anyone else's—because we were born into a family or society that maintains such views. We may be a Catholic or a Conservative or a racist primarily because we were born into a Catholic or Conservative or racist family or society. Like the influence of the self, this endemic pressure can lead to wishful thinking, rationalization, and self-deception. Group thinking can also easily generate narrow-mindedness, resistance to change, and **stereotyping** (drawing conclusions about people without sufficient reasons). (Again, more on these problems in Chapters 4 and 5.)

As comfortable as our inherited beliefs are, when we accept them without good reason, we risk error, failure, and delusion. And as we discussed in Chapter 1, if we have certain beliefs solely because they were given to us, they are not really our beliefs. The sign of a maturing intellect is having the will and the courage to gradually eliminate those beliefs that are groundless.

For critical thinkers, the best way to deal with the power of the group is to proportion your belief to the strength of reasons.

After thinking critically about claims favoured by groups, you may find that the claims are actually on solid ground and you really do have good reason to accept them. Or you may find that there is no good reason for believing them, and so you don't accept them. Either way, critical thinking will give you a clearer view of the group and yourself.

Critical thinking then is independent thinking. And to many people, those who have most dramatically achieved independent thinking—the Aristotles, the Einsteins, the Shakespeares, the Michelangelos—are heroes.

Review Notes

Avoiding Group Pressure on Your Thinking

- Group pressure can come in the form of peer pressure, appeals to popularity, and appeals to common practice.
- Group-centred thinking can degenerate into narrow-mindedness, resistance to change, and stereotyping.
- The best way to defend yourself against group thinking is to always proportion your acceptance of a claim according to the strength of reasons.

Perils of a Haunted World View

A **world view** is a philosophy of life, a set of fundamental ideas that helps us make sense of a wide range of important issues in life. The ideas are fundamental because they help guide us in the evaluation or acceptance of many other less basic ideas. They are answers to the 'big questions' of life, such as 'What do I know?', 'Is knowledge possible?', 'What is real and what is not?', and 'How do I know which actions are morally right?'

The interesting thing about world views is that we all have one; all of us have adopted (or inherited) certain fundamental ideas about the world. You may have unknowingly absorbed the ideas from your family or society, and you may not have thought much about them, but you have a world view nonetheless. Even the rejection of all world views is a world view.

In Chapter 11 we discuss how critical thinking can help you construct a world view that is founded on good reasons. For now, we need to investigate how some elements of a world view—certain fundamental but problematic ideas—may undermine critical thinking. These notions can give rise to category 2 obstacles to critical reason, for they may affect our thinking through the content of our beliefs.

Subjective Relativism

Like science, critical thinking is based upon a number of propositions that few people would think to question. Science, for example, is based on the proposition that the world is publicly understandable—that the world has a certain structure (independent of what anyone thinks), that we can know the structure, and that this knowledge can, in principle, be acquired by anyone. Critical thinking is based on similar ideas. Among the most basic is the notion that the truth of a claim does not depend on what a person thinks. That is, your believing that something is true *does not make it true*.

The idea that truth depends on what someone believes is called **subjective relativism**, and if you accept this notion or use it to try to support a claim, you are said to be committing the **subjectivist fallacy**. This view says that truth depends, not on the way things are, but solely on what someone believes. Truth, in other words, is relative to individual persons. Truth is a matter of what a person believes—not a matter of how the world is. This means that a proposition can be true for one person but not for another. If you believe that dogs can fly, then it is true (for you) that dogs can fly. If someone else believes that dogs cannot fly, then it is true (for him) that dogs cannot fly.

You've probably encountered subjective relativism more often than you realize. You may have heard someone (maybe even yourself!) say, 'This is *my* truth, and that's *your* truth,' or, 'This statement is true *for me*.'

Many critics of subjective relativism maintain that it can undermine critical thinking in a fundamental way. In large part, critical thinking is about determining whether statements are true or false. But if we can make a statement true just by believing it to be true, then critical thinking would seem to be unnecessary. The subjectivist fallacy, they say, may be an excuse to forgo the tough job of critical inquiry.

Most philosophers see the situation this way: We use critical thinking to find out whether a statement is true or false—*objectively* true or false. Objective truth is about the world, about the way the world is regardless of what we may believe about it. To put it differently, there is a way the world is, and our beliefs do not make it. The world is the way it is, regardless of how we feel about it.

These same philosophers would probably be quick to point out that some objective truths *are* about our subjective states or processes. It might be true, for example, that you're feeling pain right now. But if so, the claim that you are feeling pain right now is an *objective* truth about your *subjective* state.

Also, they would readily admit that there are some things about ourselves that obviously *are* relative because they are one way for us and another way for someone else. You may like ice cream, but someone else may not. Your liking ice cream is then relative to you. But the truth about these states of affairs is not relative.

Subjective relativism (as well as other forms of relativism) is controversial, and we needn't spend much time on it here. But you should know at least that many philosophers have (through the use of critical thinking!) uncovered some odd implications that seem to render the view implausible. First, they point out that if we could make a statement true just by believing it to be true, we would be infallible. We

Food For Thought

Having Everything Your Own Way Is … Impossible?

If you like relativism, you'll love a notion similar to relativism that has been advocated by, among others, the actress and New Age guru Shirley MacLaine. In a nutshell the idea is that we each create our own reality—that is, each of us creates physical reality, everything from stars and galaxies to chocolate pudding. As MacLaine says, 'Life doesn't happen to us. We make it happen. Reality isn't separate from us. We are creating our reality every moment of the day.'[5] Believe it, and it will come true.

But a little critical thinking shows this theory to be flawed because it involves a logical contradiction. If we each create our own reality, what happens when people have opposing beliefs? If you believe that the Earth is round, and someone else believes that the Earth is not round, we would have a state of affairs that was both existing and not existing at the same time—which is a logical impossibility. We would have a situation like a square circle or a married bachelor, which simply can't be. Since the theory leads to such absurdities, we must conclude that we really can't create our own reality.

could not possibly be in error about anything that we sincerely believed. We could never be mistaken about where we parked the car or what we said about jelly beans or which planet is the largest or smallest. Personal infallibility is, of course, absurd, and this possibility seems to weigh heavily against subjective relativism.

Many critics think the biggest problem with subjective relativism is that it's self-defeating. It defeats itself because its truth implies its falsity. The relativist says, 'All truth is relative.' If this statement is objectively true, then it refutes itself because if it is objectively true that 'All truth is relative,' then the statement itself is an example of an objective truth. So if 'All truth is relative' is objectively true, it is objectively false.

Social Relativism

To escape the difficulties of subjective relativism, some people posit **social relativism**, the view that truth is relative to societies. The claim is that truth depends, not on an individual's beliefs, but on society's beliefs. So a claim can be true for the Chinese but false for Americans, true for college students but false for public officials, true for Protestants or Muslims but false for atheists. To many, this kind of relativism, like the subjective kind, also seems to render critical thinking superfluous.

Social relativism is attractive to many because it seems to imply an admirable egalitarianism—the notion that the beliefs of different societies are all equal. In general, respect for other cultures is a good thing. But a lot of philosophers maintain that social relativism has most of the same defects that subjective relativism has. For example, according to social relativism, individuals aren't infallible, but societies are. In other words, it implies that the beliefs of whole societies cannot be mistaken. But this notion of societal infallibility is no more plausible than the idea of individual infallibility. Is it plausible that no society has ever been wrong about anything—never been wrong about the causes of disease, the best form of government, the number of planets in our solar system, the burning of witches, the Nazi policies that resulted in the killing of six million Jews?

Critics like to point out that just as subjective relativism is self-defeating, so is social relativism. The claim that 'all truth is relative to societies' is self-defeating because if it is objectively true, it is an example of an objective truth—and that means that the claim (that all truth is relative) must be objectively false.

If you accept relativism, you may be tempted to care very little about critical thinking, and that would be your loss. Fortunately, there is no good reason why you should neglect critical thinking in the name of relativism.[6]

> 'What we need is not the will to believe, but the will to find out.'
> —Bertrand Russell

Skepticism

If knowledge were impossible, critical thinking—as a way of coming to know the truth or falsity of claims—would seem to be out of a job. Most of us, though, believe that we *can* acquire knowledge. We think that we know a great many things—that we are alive, that our shoes are a certain colour, that there is a tree on the lawn, that the Earth is not flat, that rabbits cannot fly, that 2 + 2 = 4. But not everyone would agree. There are some who believe that we know much less than we think we do or nothing at all. This view is known as **philosophical skepticism**, and thinkers who raise doubts about how much we know are known as **philosophical skeptics**.

This is no place to dive into a debate on skepticism, but we can take a quick look at the most important type of philosophical skepticism and see what, if anything, it has to do with critical thinking. This form of skepticism says that knowledge requires certainty—if we are to know anything, we must be certain of it. This means that our knowledge isn't knowledge unless it is beyond any *possibility* of doubt. If knowledge requires certainty, however, there is very little that we know because there are always considerations that can undermine our certainty.

But it seems that our knowledge *does not* require certainty. All of us can cite many situations in which we do seem to have knowledge—even though we do not have absolutely conclusive reasons. We usually would claim to know, for example, that it is raining, that our dog has spots, that we were born, and that the Moon is not made of green cheese—even though we are not absolutely certain of any of these. These situations suggest that we do know many things. We know them not because they are beyond all *possible* doubt, but because they are beyond all *reasonable* doubt. Doubt is always possible, but it is not always reasonable. Rejecting a reasonable claim to knowledge just because of the bare possibility that you may be wrong is neither reasonable nor necessary.

Critical thinking does have a job to do in our efforts to acquire knowledge. Its task, however, is not to help us find claims that we cannot possibly doubt but to help us evaluate claims that vary in degrees of reasonable doubt—that is, from weak reasons (or no reasons) to very strong reasons.

Summary

Critical thinking takes place in a mental environment consisting of our experiences, thoughts, and feelings. Some elements in this inner environment can sabotage our efforts to think critically or can at least make critical thinking more difficult. Fortunately, we can exert some control over these elements. With practice, we can detect errors in our thinking, restrain attitudes and feelings that can disrupt our reasoning, and achieve enough objectivity to make critical thinking possible.

The most common of these hindrances to critical thinking fall into two main categories: (1) those obstacles that crop up because of *how* we think and (2) those that occur because of *what* we think. The first category is composed of psychological factors such as our fears, attitudes, motivations, and desires. The second category is made up of certain philosophical beliefs.

None of us is immune to the psychological obstacles. Among them are the products of egocentric thinking. We may accept a claim solely because it advances our interests or just because it helps us save face. To overcome these pressures, we must (1) be aware of strong emotions that can warp our thinking, (2) be alert to ways that critical thinking can be undermined, and (3) ensure that we take into account *all* relevant factors when we evaluate a claim.

The first category of hindrances also includes those that arise because of group pressure. These obstacles include conformist pressures from groups that we belong to and ethnocentric urges to think that our group is superior to others. The best defense against group pressure is to proportion our beliefs according to the strength of reasons.

We may also have certain core beliefs that can undermine critical thinking (the second category of hindrances). Subjective relativism is the view that truth depends solely on what someone believes—a notion that may make critical thinking look superfluous. But subjective relativism leads to some strange consequences. For example, if the doctrine were true, each of us would be infallible. Also, subjective relativism has a logical problem—it's self-defeating. Its truth implies its falsity. There are no good reasons to accept this form of relativism.

Social relativism is the view that truth is relative to societies—a claim that would also seem to make critical thinking unnecessary. But this notion is undermined by the same kinds of problems that plague subjective relativism.

Philosophical skepticism is the doctrine that we know much less than we think we do. One form of philosophical skepticism says we cannot know anything unless the belief is beyond all possible doubt. But this is not a plausible criterion for knowledge. To be knowledge, claims need not be beyond all possible doubt but beyond all *reasonable* doubt.

Key Terms

Appeal to common practice: The fallacy of accepting or rejecting a claim solely on the basis of what groups of people generally do or how they behave (when the action or behaviour is irrelevant to the truth of the claim).

Appeal to popularity (or to the masses): The fallacy of arguing that a claim must be true merely because a substantial number of people believe it.

Peer pressure: Group pressure to accept or reject a claim solely on the basis of what one's peers think or do.

Philosophical skepticism: The view that we know much less than we think we do or that we know nothing at all.

Philosophical skeptics: Those who embrace philosophical skepticism.

Social relativism: The view that truth is relative to societies.

Stereotyping: Drawing conclusions about people without sufficient reasons.

Subjective relativism: The idea that truth depends on what someone believes.

Subjectivist fallacy: Accepting the notion of subjective relativism or using it to try to support a claim.

World view: A philosophy of life; a set of fundamental ideas that helps us make sense of a wide range of important issues in life. A world view defines for us what exists, what should be, and what we can know.

EXERCISES

The answers to exercises marked with an asterisk (*) are given in 'Answers to Exercises' (Appendix B). Answers are not given for quizzes, integrative exercises, or writing assignments.

Exercise 2.1

Review Questions

* 1. According to the text's definition of critical thinking, what factors must be present for critical thinking to be realized?
  2. What are the two main categories of common obstacles to critical thinking?
  3. What did W.K. Clifford say about the morality of believing claims?
  4. What is stereotyping?
* 5. From the standpoint of critical thinking, what event signals that we have allowed our bias in favour of ourselves go too far?
  6. According to the text, what effect can our urge to save face have on our thinking?
* 7. When are you most likely to let your self-interest get in the way of clear thinking?
  8. According to the text, what should you do if you sense a rush of emotion when you think about a particular issue?
  9. What is selective attention?
  10. According to the text, how might selective attention affect your thinking when you are examining evidence for or against a claim?
* 11. How might the influence of a group that you belong to affect your attempts to think critically?
  12. According to the text, what is the most powerful group pressure of all?
  13. What is the appeal to popularity?
* 14. What is a world view?
  15. What is subjective relativism?
  16. According to the text, how could subjective relativism make critical thinking unnecessary?
* 17. Is critical thinking concerned with the *objective* or the *subjective* truth of claims?
  18. What is social relativism?
  19. What is philosophical skepticism?

20. Does our knowledge require certainty?

* 21. What kind of doubt is involved in the acquisition of knowledge?

Exercise 2.2

Indicate whether each of the following passages most likely contains examples of self-interested thinking, face-saving, or group pressure. Some of these are really tough!

* 1. Mary: Animals have the same rights as humans.
      Jenna: What makes you think that?
      Mary: I love animals, and there are so many that are treated horribly all over the world. It's heartbreaking.

  2. Jonathan: My essay is better than Julio's.
      Betty: Why do you think yours is better than all the others? Do you agree that the content and writing of all the essays are similar?
      Jonathan: Well, yes.
      Betty: Do you agree that all the other indicators of quality are nearly identical?
      Jonathan: Yes, but mine is still better.

  3. Dear friends, as your Member of Parliament I will continue my tireless work on your behalf. I will continue to use my considerable talents to make this riding even better. I will continue to let my integrity be the guide for all my actions.

* 4. We cannot allow those people to move into this neighbourhood. They're not like us.

  5. I oppose women becoming members of this club. If I endorsed their claims, every friend I've got in the club would turn their backs on me.

  6. His statements about the West Bank are all false, of course. He's an Israeli.

* 7. Hinduism is superior to all other religions. I was raised Hindu, and all my relatives are Hindus. This is the only religion I've known, and the only one I need.

  8. I'm due to receive tenure next year, so I am in favour of continuing the tradition of tenure at this university.

  9. Canada is the greatest nation on the face of the earth. I don't know anything about other countries, and I don't want to know.

* 10. If Joan is appointed to the committee, I am guaranteed to have a job for the rest of my life. I wholeheartedly favour Joan's appointment.

  11. Free speech should not extend to pornographers. Right now they are allowed to espouse their smut on the Internet and many other places. That's just not how I was raised.

Exercise 2.3

Read each of the following claims. Then select from the list any statements that, if true, would constitute good reasons for accepting the claim. Be careful: in some questions, none of the choices is correct.

* 1. John: The newspaper account of the charges of pedophilia lodged against Father J. Miller, a Catholic priest in our town, should never have been printed.
     a. The charges are false.
     b. John is a Catholic.
     c. Important evidence that would exonerate Father Miller was not mentioned in the newspaper account.
     d. The town is predominately Catholic.

  2. Alice: The speed limit on Highway 401 should be 120 km/h.
     a. Raising the speed limit to 120 km/h would result in faster and safer traffic.
     b. The provincial ministry of transportation did a study showing that Highway 401 should have a limit of 120 km/h.
     c. Alice travels Highway 401 and needs to drive 120 km/h to get to work on time.
     d. Alice drives Highway 401 every day.

* 3. Janette: Women are less violent and less emotional than men.
     a. A study from McGill shows that women are less violent and less emotional than men.
     b. Janette is a woman.
     c. Janette is a member of a group of women who are fighting for the rights of women.
     d. Janette and all her friends are women.

  4. Brie: People should buy stocks in TELUS, an action that will push the price per share higher.
     a. Brie owns a large proportion of TELUS stocks.
     b. Brie is chair of the board at TELUS.
     c. The stock market is weak.
     d. Brie has a large family to support.

  5. Colonel Lewis: Canada's peacekeepers must stay in Afghanistan until the Taliban are destroyed, even if it means that some Canadian lives will be lost.
     a. Taliban fighters have killed three of Colonel Lewis's soldiers.
     b. Canadians are proud of their nation's reputation in peacekeeping.
     c. Colonel Lewis is loyal to his troops, all of whom want to attack the Taliban.
     d. Fighting the Taliban is unlikely to result in Canadian casualties, and it will make Afghanistan a great place to live.

* 6. Ivana: Gay marriage is always wrong.
     a. All of Ivana's friends agree that gay marriage is wrong.
     b. If Ivana favoured gay marriage, her friends would abandon her.
     c. Ivana is president of the League of Traditional Families.

  d. Ivana has already made her views known and cannot change her mind without seeming to be inconsistent.

7. Angelo: Marijuana should be legalized.

  a. All of Angelo's friends smoke marijuana.

  b. Legalizing marijuana would reduce the consumption of marijuana and save lives, money, and resources.

  c. Angelo has already said on television that marijuana should be legalized.

  d. Angelo likes to smoke marijuana.

Exercise 2.4

Read the following passages. Say whether each one contains examples of the kind of group pressure that encourages people to conform (peer pressure or appeal to popularity) or the type that urges people to think that one's own group is better than others. For each example of group pressure, specify the possible negative consequences. A couple of these are very difficult to classify.

* 1. Marie-Eve is deeply religious, attending church regularly and trying to abide by church law and the Scriptures. She has never considered any other path. She believes that laws should be passed that forbid Sunday shopping and that designate Easter as a national statutory holiday.

2. John goes to a prestigious university where many students use illegal drugs. Nearly everyone in John's frat house uses them. So far, he hasn't tried any, but his frat brothers frequently ask if he wants some. And he has noticed that he is rarely invited to any frat parties.

* 3. An Atlantic Canadian university has invited a famous writer to be a guest speaker in the campus-wide distinguished-speaker series. She is an accomplished poet and essayist. She is also a Marxist and favours more socialism in Canada. During her speech she is shouted down by a small group of conservative students and faculty.

4. Yang Lei is a conservative columnist for one of the best conservative journals in the country. But she yearns for greener pastures—namely, a regular column for a weekly news magazine. She gets her dream job, though the magazine does have liberal leanings. The first few columns she writes for the magazine are a shock to her friends. Politically, they are middle-of-the-road or even suspiciously left-leaning.

5. Alex is a grade-four teacher at a suburban elementary school in Alberta. He is liked by students and teachers alike, and he has superior teaching skills. He is also a homosexual. When a group of fundamentalist Muslims learn that Alex is gay, they pressure the school board to fire him.

6. Sylvia writes a column for the university newspaper. In her last column, she argues that in a time of national crisis, the RCMP should have the power to arrest and detain literally anyone suspected of terrorism. Her arguments are

well supported and are presented with a tone of tolerance for those who disagree with her. And most students do disagree—vehemently. Hundreds of letters to the editor arrive at the newspaper, each one denouncing Sylvia and calling her a fascist and a few names that could not be published. In Sylvia's next column, she apologizes for her statements, says that she made serious errors, and declares that her statements should be viewed as hypothetical.

* 7. Advertisement: When you make the best car in the world, everyone wants it. Audi TT. A car in demand.

Exercise 2.5

Read the following scenarios. Indicate whether each one contains examples of self-interested thinking or face-saving and, for each instance, specify the possible negative consequences.

* 1. Neera thinks she is a superior student whose writing and math are excellent. She frequently says so to her friends and sometimes ridicules other people's grades. She predicts that her final grade in her Critical Thinking class will be an A+. When she writes the final exam, she's calm, alert, and eager to do really well. After the exam, she says that she feels great. When grades are announced, she finds she's got a B. She explains that the exam was bogus and was obviously marked badly, and besides, she's not a good exam writer.

* 2. City councillor Jackson is in a position to cast the deciding vote on two proposals for the development of a new city park. Proposal 1 offers a parcel of land near Jackson's house, which affords him a beautiful view. Its drawbacks are that it costs twice as much as proposal 2 and is not easily accessible to most of the public. Proposal 2 suggests a parcel of land near the centre of town. It is convenient to the public, has a more beautiful setting, and will raise property values in the area. Councillor Jackson says that the obvious best choice is proposal 1.

3. Antonio is a university student who responds predictably to his scores on tests. If the score is high, he remarks that he hardly studied at all and that his score ranks among the highest in the class. If the score is low, he says the instructor grades unfairly, the test was flawed, and he intends to protest his grade to the grade-review committee.

4. Sheila is a bright medical scientist. For years she has been working on a series of clinical studies that could establish her favourite medical hypothesis—that high doses of vitamin E can cure skin cancer. Each study in the series has added more evidence suggesting that the hypothesis is probably true. The last study in the series is crucial. It is a much larger study than the others, and it will confirm or invalidate the usefulness of vitamin E for skin cancer. When the study is completed, she examines the data. Instead of confirming her hypothesis, the study suggests not only that her pet idea is unfounded but also that the doses of vitamin E used are toxic, causing terrible side effects in

patients. She concludes, though, that the study results do not disconfirm her hypothesis but are merely inconclusive.

5. David and Max are in a heated debate about the theory of biological evolution. David rejects the theory in favour of creationism, which says that life on earth was created or facilitated by a supreme intelligence. Max rejects creationism in favour of evolution. David marshals an abundance of facts that seem to prove his case. In addition, he alleges that evolution is false because there are huge gaps in the fossil record suggesting that there has never been a smooth, tidy progression of species from earlier forms to later forms. Max has no answer for this fossil-record gap argument and looks exasperated. David is about to declare victory when Max suddenly begins to quote the research findings of reputable biologists showing that there really are no gaps. After the debate some of Max's friends quietly congratulate him for being clever enough to quote research findings that are fictitious.

Field Problems

1. Recall a situation in your past in which your beliefs were skewed by self-interest, face-saving, or group pressure. Think about (1) how one or more of these three factors affected your beliefs, (2) what the consequences (negative or positive) of the event were, and (3) what beliefs you might have acquired if you had used critical thinking. Take notes to help you remember the facts and be prepared to present your story in class.

2. Recall a situation in which the beliefs of someone you know were skewed by self-interest, face-saving, or group pressure to conform. Identify the three factors mentioned in the preceding question.

Self-Assessment Quiz

1. According to the definition of critical thinking given in the text, what factors must be present for critical thinking to take place?

2. From the standpoint of critical thinking, what event signals that we have allowed our bias in favour of ourselves go too far?

3. According to the text, how might selective attention affect your thinking when you are examining evidence for or against a claim?

4. According to the text, what is probably the most powerful group pressure of all?

5. According to the text, what is a world view?

6. What kind of doubt is involved in the acquisition of knowledge?

7. According to the text, why is it important to look for opposing evidence when evaluating claims?

Read the following scenarios. Say whether each one contains examples of self-interested thinking, face-saving, or both.

8. Trevor predicts that Farley Windblower will win the 2011 mayoral election in his city. In fact, he bets money on it and brags that he always predicts the winners. Windblower then loses by the widest margin in the city's history. At first, Trevor refuses to pay the bet but finally gives in. He claims that the election was rigged from the very beginning.

9. Lois strongly believes in UFO abductions—people being kidnapped by space aliens. She says she has absolute proof: a small piece of metal that she says is 'not of this earth' and a cut on her shin that she says came from alien probes. However, several metallurgists in the area say the piece of metal is ordinary aluminum. And her daughter reminds her that she got the cut on her shin when she ran into a desk drawer. Lois doesn't say anything else about her 'evidence', but she asserts that the real proof is in the skies in the form of alien spacecraft.

10. One day Julie and Jill hear their instructor read a list of arguments for and against abortion. Half the arguments are pro, and half are con. Julie is on the pro side, Jill on the con side. Later when they discuss the abortion arguments, they recall the facts differently. Julie remembers that most of the arguments were for abortion rights. Jill remembers only the arguments against abortion and can't recall any pro arguments.

Specify whether the following passages are examples of face-saving, self-serving, or group-pressure thinking, or a combination of these.

11. The world would be better off if the New Democrats ran everything.
12. Everyone believes in affirmative action. That fact alone ought to persuade you to do the same.
13. Look, every student I know cheats on exams once in a while. So why not you? Why do you have to be such a Boy Scout?
14. People should do whatever makes them happy.
15. Member of Parliament Aneesah Syed: 'Anyone who doesn't believe in God shouldn't have a say in how this nation is run. I don't think that atheists should even be citizens.'
16. Yes, I smoked marijuana in college, but I didn't inhale.
17. In Canada about 90 per cent of the population has some kind of religious belief or denominational affiliation. In light of this, how can you say you're an unbeliever? If you're an unbeliever, you're un-Canadian.

Read each of the following passages and say whether it is an example of the subjectivist fallacy or social relativism.

18. This may not be your truth, but it's my truth.
19. It's true for me that killing innocent civilians is morally wrong. It may not be true for you.
20. Chinese diplomat: 'My country cannot be judged by some universal standard. It must be judged by its own unique criteria and norms.'

Integrative Exercises

These exercises pertain to material in Chapters 1 and 2.

1. What is an argument?
2. What is a statement, or claim? (Give an example of a statement and an example of a sentence that is not a statement.)
3. In what ways can a group that you belong to affect your evaluation of a claim?
4. According to the text, what critical-thinking principle should you invoke when you're trying to think clearly under group pressure?

For each of the following passages indicate whether it contains an argument. For each argument, specify what the conclusion is and whether the passage contains an appeal to popularity or peer pressure.

5. You can never escape your past because your memory will always remind you of it.
6. Cloning any biological entity (including humans) is not worth the risk involved. Scientists have already reported some unexpected, dangerous side effects in the cloning of plants, and Dolly, the famous cloned sheep, has exhibited some cellular abnormalities.
7. Cloning is perfectly safe. It's only religious nuts and conservative politicians who are making a big fuss about it.
8. It will be a great day when the Department of National Defence has to have a bake sale to raise money for bombs and guns and education gets billions of dollars.
9. Capitalism is an immoral, oppressive system. That's just the way I was raised.
10. Most Canadians believe that the prime minister is doing a great job. You can't argue with the people. Therefore, he is doing a great job.
11. All your friends think your views on abortion are ridiculous. That should be proof enough that you're wrong.

Read each of the following claims. Then select from the list any statements that, if true, would constitute good reasons for accepting the claim. Some statements may have no good reasons listed.

12. Corporation executives who 'cook the books' should be imprisoned.
    a. Everyone in the business world believes that cooking the books should be punished by imprisonment.
    b. Polls show that most Canadians are in favour of imprisoning executives who cook the books.
    c. In Russia it is common practice to imprison executives who cook the books.
    d. Imprisoning executives who cook the books is the only way to save Canadian business from disaster and the only morally correct course of action.
13. Psychic predictions in tabloid newspapers are almost always accurate.
    a. This claim is true for me, even if it isn't true for you.

b. It is impossible to know anything, so there is no way that anyone can legitimately claim that tabloid psychics are almost always right.

c. Massive amounts of research into psychic phenomena prove that tabloid psychics are usually correct in their predictions.

d. Believing that psychics cannot predict anything accurately is close-minded and petty. I refuse to be that way.

14. There is an afterlife. After you die, your essence lives on.

a. I have to believe in an afterlife. The alternative is too terrible to contemplate.

b. Over 80 per cent of Canadians believe in an afterlife.

c. This society believes that there is an afterlife.

d. On the radio I told two million people that there is an afterlife. So I have to believe in it. Otherwise, I'll look like a fool.

For each of the following passages, determine whether an argument is present and whether peer pressure or an appeal to popularity is being used. Some passages may not contain arguments, and some may not contain examples of group pressure.

15. 'Barbara Ehrenreich wrote tongue-in-cheek in her June column, "First, challenge anyone to find in the Bible . . . a single phrase or sentence forbidding the fondling or sodomizing of altar boys." . . . In fact, the Bible does have at least a single phrase or sentence forbidding just such a thing. In 1 Corinthians 6:9 (New International Version), Paul has a list of those who will not inherit the Kingdom. Although far from settled, one of the words in the list suggests that men in a mentoring relationship with young boys are "wicked" if they engage in sexual acts with the boys.' (Letter to the editor, *The Progressive*, July 2002)

16. '[A] political scientist at the Massachusetts Institute of Technology says, "I expect robust Internet voting by 2010." He may be right, but would this be a good thing? Remote voting by way of the Internet would privatize one of our few remaining civic rituals. Balloting technology is not politically neutral. The history of elections administration in this country shows that different ways of voting allocate political values differently.' (Letter to the editor, *New York Times*)

17. You must reject the proposition that rising levels of gun violence in Canada's major cities proves the need for the federal government's Firearm Registry. First, there's no documented connection between violence and the availability of guns. Second, if you accept the need for a Registry, you'll be the laughing-stock of all your fellow Westerners!

18. To teens, getting fake IDs to sneak into bars and pubs may seem like a good idea, but it's not. I think every teenager who tries it should be arrested.

19. Every thinking person in this country would disagree with you.

Critical Thinking and Writing Exercise

From Issue to Thesis

For many students, the biggest challenge in writing an argumentative essay is deciding on an appropriate thesis—the claim, or conclusion, that the essay is designed to support or prove. Very often, when an essay runs off the track and crashes, the derailment can be traced to a thesis that was bad from the beginning.

Picking a thesis out of the air and beginning to write is usually a mistake. Any thesis statement that you craft without knowing anything about the subject is likely to be ill-formed or indefensible. It's better to begin by selecting an issue—a question that's controversial or in dispute—then researching it to determine what arguments or viewpoints are involved. To research it, you can survey the views of people or organizations involved in the controversy. Read articles and books, talk to people, and do some research online. This process should not only inform you about various viewpoints but also tell you what arguments are used to support them. It should also help you narrow the issue down to one that you can easily address in the space you have.

Suppose you begin with the issue of whether Canada has serious industrial pollution problems. After investigating this issue, you would probably see that it is much too broad to be addressed in a short paper. You should then restrict the issue to something more manageable—for example, whether recent legislation to allow coal-burning power plants to emit more sulphur dioxide will harm people's health. With the scope of the issue narrowed, you can explore arguments on both sides. You cannot examine every single argument, but you should assess the strongest ones, including those that you devise yourself. You can then use what you've already learned about arguments to select one that you think provides good support for its conclusion. The premises and conclusion of this argument can then serve as the bare-bones outline of your essay. Your argument might look like this:

[Premise 1] Excessive amounts of sulphur dioxide in the air have been linked to increases in the incidence of asthma and other respiratory illnesses.
[Premise 2] Many areas of the country already have excessive amounts of sulphur dioxide in the air.
[Premise 3] Most sulphur dioxide in the air comes from coal-burning power plants.
[Conclusion] Therefore, allowing coal-burning power plants to emit more sulphur dioxide will most likely increase the incidence of respiratory illnesses.

For the sake of the example, the premises of this argument are made up. But the argument of your essay must be real, with each premise that could be called into question supported by an additional argument. After all, your readers are not likely to accept the conclusion of your argument if they doubt your premises.

In some cases, your paper may contain more than one argument supporting a single conclusion, or it may offer a critique of someone else's argument. In either case, investigating an issue and the arguments involved will follow the pattern just suggested. In a critique of an argument (or arguments), you offer reasons why the argument fails and thus support the thesis that the conclusion is false.

This process of devising a thesis statement and crafting an argument to back it up is not linear. You will probably have to experiment with several arguments before you find one that's suitable. Even after you decide on an argument, you may later discover that its premises are dubious or that they cannot be adequately supported. Then you will have to backtrack to investigate a better argument. Backtracking in this preliminary stage is relatively easy. But if you postpone this rethinking process until you are almost finished with your first draft, it will be harder—and more painful.

Argument and Emotion

As we saw earlier, the point of an argument is to provide rational support for a claim by supplying good reasons for accepting a conclusion. And argument, of course, is the main focus of a good argumentative essay. Nonetheless, experienced writers often enhance the persuasive power of their argumentative essays through the use of various emotional appeals. Inexperienced writers, though, sometimes get the argumentative and emotional elements confused or out of balance. To avoid such problems, try to stick to these rules of thumb:

- Be fair to the opposing view. Summarize or restate the opposing arguments accurately. Avoid sarcasm, ridicule, or loaded (emotive) words in describing other viewpoints. Don't say, for example, 'this so-called argument', 'that ridiculous view', or 'this idiotic proposal'.
- Be fair to your opponent. Avoid personal attacks, insults, stereotyping, and innuendo. Keep the main focus on the quality of your opponent's arguments, not his or her character.
- Avoid appeals to your own self-interest or the wishes of your preferred group.
- If you have strong feelings about an issue, try to channel those feelings into creating the best arguments possible—not into emotional displays on paper.

Writing Assignments

1. Read Essay 2 ('Hurray! No One's Watching') in Appendix A and write a summary of the essay in 75–100 words. Mention the thesis statement and each supporting premise.

2. Study the argument presented in Essay 6 ('Misleading the Patient for Fun and Profit') in Appendix A. Identify the conclusion and the premises and objections considered. Then write a two-page rebuttal to the essay. That is, defend the claim that it is morally right to promote unproven treatments.

3. Select an issue from the following list and write a three-page paper defending a statement pertaining to the issue. Follow the procedure discussed in the text for identifying a thesis and an appropriate argument to defend it.

    - Are the media biased?
    - Should a single corporation be allowed to buy up as many media outlets (newspapers, radio and TV stations, book publishers, etc.) as it wants?
    - Should the Canadian government be allowed to arrest and indefinitely imprison, without trial, any Canadian citizen who is suspected of terrorism?
    - Should racial profiling be used to do security screening of airplane passengers?

Chapter 3

Making Sense of Arguments

Chapter Objectives

Argument Basics

You will be able to

- ○ distinguish between deductive and inductive arguments.
- ○ understand the terms *valid*, *invalid*, and *sound*.
- ○ understand the terms *strong*, *weak*, and *cogent*.

Judging Arguments

You will be able to

- ○ follow the four-step procedure for determining whether an argument is deductive or inductive, good or bad.
- ○ obtain a familiarity with indicator words that suggest that an argument is deductive or inductive.

Finding Missing Parts

You will be able to

- ○ use the three-step procedure for uncovering implicit premises.

Argument Patterns

You will be able to

○ memorize and be able to recognize the argument patterns known as *modus ponens, modus tollens, hypothetical syllogism, denying the antecedent, affirming the consequent,* and *disjunctive syllogism.*

○ use the counter-example method for determining if a deductive argument is valid or invalid.

Diagramming Arguments

You will be able to

○ understand the definition of *dependent* and *independent premises.*

○ follow the three-step procedure to diagram arguments, both simple and complex ones, including those embedded in extraneous material.

Assessing Long Arguments

You will be able to

○ understand the challenges involved in assessing long arguments.

○ follow the procedure for diagramming long arguments.

In this chapter we resume our discussion of arguments begun in Chapter 1, delve deeper into the dynamics and structure of different types of argument, and get a lot more practice in identifying and critiquing simple (and not so simple) arguments in their 'natural habitat'.

Remember, in Chapter 1 we defined an argument as a group of statements in which some of them (the premises) are intended to support another of them (the conclusion). An essential skill is the ability to identify arguments in real-life contexts and to distinguish them from non-arguments. To recognize an argument you must be able to identify the premises and the conclusion. Indicator words such as *because* and *since* often signal the presence of premises, and words such as *therefore* and *thus* can point to a conclusion.

Argument Basics

The point of *devising* an argument is to try to show that a statement, or claim, is worthy of acceptance. The point of *evaluating* an argument is to see whether this task has been successful—whether the argument shows that the statement (the conclusion) really is worthy of acceptance. When the argument shows that the statement is worthy of acceptance, we say that the argument is *good*. When the argument fails to show that the statement is worthy of acceptance, we say that the argument is *bad*. There are different ways, however, that an argument can be good or bad. There are different ways because there are different types of arguments.

Arguments come in two forms—**deductive** and **inductive**. A deductive argument is intended to provide logically *conclusive* support for its conclusion. An inductive argument is intended to provide *probable*—not conclusive—support for its conclusion.

A deductive argument that succeeds in providing such decisive logical support is said to be **valid**; a deductive argument that fails to provide such support is said to be **invalid**. A deductively valid argument is such that if its premises are true, its conclusion *must* be true. That is, if the premises are true, there is no way that the conclusion can be false. In logic, *valid* is not a synonym for true. A deductively valid argument simply has the kind of logical structure that *guarantees* the truth of the conclusion *if* the premises are true. 'Logical structure' refers, not to the content of an argument, but to its construction, that is, the way the premises and conclusion

Food For Thought

Persuading or Reasoning?

There is a fundamental distinction in critical thinking between persuading and reasoning. Persuading someone to agree with you is not the same thing as presenting them with a good argument. You can influence people's opinions by using words to appeal to their ego, gullibility, bigotry, greed, anger, prejudice, and more. You just have to use emotional language, psychological ploys, semantic or syntactic tricks, and outright lies. But having done so, you would not have demonstrated that any belief is true or warranted. You would not have shown that a claim is worthy of acceptance. This latter task is a matter of logic and argument. The techniques of raw persuasion are not.

Certainly the presentation of a good argument (in the critical-thinking sense) can sometimes be psychologically compelling. And there are times when persuasion through psychological or emotional appeals is appropriate, even necessary. You just have to keep these two functions straight in your mind.

Great persuaders aren't necessarily great critical thinkers. Photo: The Art Archive

fit together. Because of the guarantee of truth in the conclusion, deductively valid arguments are said to be **truth-preserving**.

Here's a simple deductively valid argument:

All dogs have fleas.
Bowser is a dog.
So Bowser has fleas.

And here's a golden oldie:

All men are mortal.
Socrates is a man.
Therefore, Socrates is mortal.

And one in regular paragraph form:

[Premise] If abortion is the taking of a human life, then it's murder. [Premise] It is the taking of a human life. [Conclusion] So it necessarily follows that abortion is murder.

In each of these arguments, if the premises are true, the conclusion must be absolutely, positively true. It is impossible for the premises to

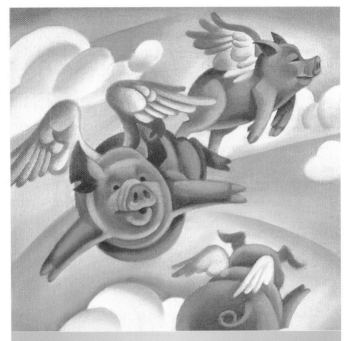

An argument containing a false premise such as 'All pigs can fly' may be logically valid—but definitely flawed (and a little strange). © LaFleur Studio/Images.com.

be true and the conclusions false. The conclusion *follows logically* from the premises. And the order of the premises makes no difference.

A deductively *invalid* version of these arguments might look like this:

All dogs are mammals.
All cows are mammals.
Therefore, all dogs are cows.

If Socrates has horns, he is mortal.
Socrates is mortal.
Therefore, Socrates has horns.

In each of these, the conclusion does *not* follow logically from the premises. Each is an attempt at a deductively valid argument, but the attempt fails. And, again, this would be the case regardless of the order of the premises. Note that even an argument with a conclusion that is obviously true can be invalid if that conclusion is not supported by the premises offered. Look at this argument, for example:

All poodles have short tails.
All poodles have fur.
Therefore all poodles are dogs.

The conclusion here is obviously true, but the argument is invalid: the conclusion doesn't *follow from* the premises offered.

An inductive argument that succeeds in providing probable—but not conclusive—logical support for its conclusion is said to be **strong**. An inductive argument that fails to provide such support is said to be **weak**. An inductively strong argument is such that if its premises are true, its conclusion is *probably* or *likely* to be true. The structure of an inductively strong argument cannot guarantee that the conclusion is true if the premises are true—but the conclusion can be rendered probable and worthy of acceptance. (Here again, the structure and content of an argument are distinct elements.) Because the truth of the conclusion cannot be guaranteed by the truth of the premises, inductive arguments are not truth-preserving.

Let's turn our first two deductively valid arguments into inductively strong arguments:

> Most dogs have fleas.
> Therefore, Bowser, my dog, probably has fleas.

> Ninety-eight per cent of humans are mortal.
> Socrates is human.
> Therefore, Socrates is likely to be mortal.

Notice that in the first argument, it's entirely possible for the premise to be true and the conclusion false. After all, if only *most* dogs have fleas, there is no guarantee that Bowser has fleas. Yet the premise, if true, makes the conclusion probably true. Likewise, in the second argument it is possible that even if 98 per cent of humans are mortal and Socrates is human, the conclusion that Socrates is mortal could be false. But the premises, if true, make it likely that the conclusion is true.

Logical validity or logical strength is an essential characteristic of good arguments. But there is more to good arguments than having the proper structure. Good arguments also have *true premises*. A good argument is one that has the proper structure—*and* true premises. Take a look at this argument:

> All pigs can fly.
> Vaughn is a pig.
> Therefore, Vaughn can fly.

The premises of this argument are false—but the conclusion follows logically from those premises. It's a deductively valid argument with all the parts in the right place—even though the premises are false. But it is not a good argument, because a good argument must have true premises, and this argument doesn't. A deductively valid argument that has true premises is said to be **sound**. A sound argument is a good argument that gives you good reasons for accepting its conclusion.

Note, however, that deductively valid arguments can have true or false premises and true or false conclusions. Specifically, deductively valid arguments can have

"In the midst of chaos, Larry is the clear voice of reason. Get him the hell out of here."

false premises and a false conclusion, false premises and a true conclusion, and true premises and a true conclusion. A valid argument, though, cannot have true premises and a false conclusion—that's impossible. See for yourself:

False Premises, False Conclusion
All dogs have flippers.
All cats are dogs.
Therefore, all cats have flippers.

False Premises, True Conclusion
Bowser is a cat.
All cats are mammals.
Therefore, Bowser is a mammal.

True Premises, True Conclusion
Bowser is a dog.
All dogs are mammals.
Therefore, Bowser is a mammal.

A good inductive argument must also have true premises. For example:

Scientific studies show that 99 per cent of dogs have three eyes.
So it's likely that the next dog I see will have three eyes.

This is an inductively strong argument, but it's not a good argument because its premise is false. When inductively strong arguments have true premises, they are said to be **cogent**. Good inductive arguments are cogent. Bad inductive arguments are not cogent.

You may have noticed another important difference between deductive and inductive arguments. The kind of support that a deductive argument can give a conclusion is *absolute*. Either the conclusion is shown to be true, or it is not. There is no sliding scale of truth or falsity. The support that an inductive argument can provide a conclusion, however, can vary from weak to extremely strong.

Both deductive and inductive arguments can be manipulated in various ways to yield new insights. For example, let's say that you have formulated a valid deductive argument and you know that the conclusion is false. From these facts you can infer that at least one of the premises is false. Using this tack, you can demonstrate that a premise is false because in a valid argument it leads to an absurd conclusion. Or let's say that you've fashioned a valid argument and you know that your premises are true. Then you can infer that the conclusion must be true—even if it's contrary to your expectations. Or maybe you put forth a strong inductive argument and you know that the premises are questionable. Then you know that the conclusion also can't be trusted.

Review Notes

Deductive and Inductive Arguments

- A deductive argument is intended to provide conclusive support for its conclusion.
- A deductive argument that succeeds in providing conclusive support for its premise is said to be valid. A valid argument is such that if its premises are true, its conclusion must be true.
- A deductively valid argument with true premises is said to be sound.
- An inductive argument is intended to provide probable support for its conclusion.
- An inductive argument that succeeds in providing probable support for its conclusion is said to be strong. A strong argument is such that if its premises are true, its conclusion is probably true.
- An inductively strong argument with true premises is said to be cogent.

Exercise 3.1

1. What is a deductive argument?
2. What is an inductive argument?
3. Are inductive arguments truth-preserving? Why or why not?
* 4. What type of arguments do the terms *valid* and *invalid* apply to?
5. What kind of guarantee does a deductive argument provide when it is valid?
6. Can an inductive argument guarantee the truth of the conclusion if the premises are true? Why or why not?
7. What is the difference between an inductively strong argument and an inductively weak one?
* 8. What is the term for valid arguments that have true premises?
9. What is the term for strong arguments that have true premises?
10. Can a valid argument have false premises and a false conclusion? Can it have false premises and a true conclusion?
11. What logical conclusion can you draw about an argument that is valid but has a false conclusion?
* 12. Is it possible for a valid argument to have true premises and a false conclusion?
13. In what way are conclusions of deductive arguments absolute?

Judging Arguments

When it comes to deductive and inductive arguments, the most important skills you can acquire are being able to identify both kinds of arguments and determining whether they are good or bad. Much of the rest of this text is devoted to helping

DILBERT: © Scott Adams/Dist. By United Feature Syndicate, Inc.

you become proficient in these skills. This chapter will serve as your first lesson and give you a chance to practise what you learn.

So the obvious questions here are the following: When you come face to face with an argument to evaluate, (1) how can you tell whether it's deductive or inductive, and (2) how can you determine whether it gives you good reasons for accepting the conclusion (whether it's sound or cogent)? The following is a suggested four-step procedure for answering these questions, one that will be elaborated on here and in later chapters.

Step 1. Find the conclusion of the argument and then its premises. Use the techniques you learned in Chapter 1. You'll have plenty of chances to hone this skill in later chapters.

Step 2. Ask: Is it the case that if the premises are true the conclusion *must* be true? If the answer is yes, treat the argument as *deductive*, for it is very likely meant to offer conclusive support for its conclusion. The argument, then, is deductively valid, and you should check to see if it's sound. If the answer is no, proceed to the next step.

Step 3. Ask: Is it the case that if the premises are true, its conclusion is *probably* true? If the answer is yes, treat the argument as *inductive*, for it is very likely meant to offer probable support for its conclusion. The argument, then, is inductively strong, and you should check to see if it's cogent. If the answer is no, proceed to the next step.

Step 4. Ask: Is the argument intended to offer conclusive or probable support for its conclusion but *fails* to do so? If you reach this step, you will have already eliminated two possibilities: a valid argument and a strong one. The remaining options are an invalid argument or a weak one. So here you must discover what type of (failed) argument is intended. These two guidelines can help you do that.

> GUIDELINE 1: Generally if an argument looks deductive or inductive because of its form, assume that it is intended to be so.

Bad arguments may sometimes look like good arguments because the arrangement of their premises and conclusion—their form—is similar to that found in reliable arguments. (You saw some of these reliable argument forms in the argument examples presented earlier in this chapter.) Such argument forms are an indication of what kind of argument is intended, and that fact gives you some guidance on determining argument type.

> GUIDELINE 2: Generally if an argument looks deductive or inductive because of indicator words (and its form yields no clues), assume that it is intended to be so.

Arguments are often accompanied by words or phrases that identify them as deductive or inductive. Terms that signal a deductive argument include 'It necessarily follows that', 'it logically follows that', 'absolutely', 'necessarily', and 'certainly'. Words signalling an inductive argument include 'likely', 'probably', 'chances are', 'odds are', and 'it is plausible that'. Such indicator words, though, are not foolproof clues to the type of argument because they are sometimes used in misleading ways. For example, someone might end an inductively strong argument with a conclusion prefaced with 'it necessarily follows that', suggesting that the argument is deductively valid. But argument-type indicators may still be useful, especially when the argument form yields no clues (when guideline 1 doesn't apply).

In step 4, once you discover which kind of argument is intended, you will know that it is either invalid or weak (because in steps 2 and 3 we eliminated the possibility of a valid or strong argument). The only remaining task is to determine whether the premises are true.[1]

Let's try out the four-step procedure on a few arguments. Consider this one:

[Premise] Unless we do something about the massive AIDS epidemic in Africa, the whole continent will be decimated within six months. [Premise] Unfortunately we won't do anything about the AIDS epidemic in Africa. [Conclusion] It necessarily follows that the population of Africa will be decimated within six months.

Step 1 is already done for us; the premises and conclusion are clearly labelled. In step 2, we must ask, 'Is it the case that if the premises are true, the conclusion must be true?' The answer is yes, if it's true that the AIDS epidemic in Africa will decimate the population in six months unless 'we do something', and it's true that 'we won't do anything', then the conclusion that the population of Africa will be decimated in six months *must* be true. So this argument is deductively valid. To determine if it's sound, we would need to check to see if the premises are true. In this case, the first premise is false because, under current conditions, it would take longer than six months for the epidemic to decimate the population of the whole continent. The other premise ('we won't do anything') is at least dubious since we can't predict the future. So what we have here is a deductively valid argument that's unsound—a bad argument.

Now let's analyze this one:

[Premise] The Quebec-based French-language group 'l'impératif français' works diligently to make sure businesses in Quebec use French in their daily operations. [Premise] The Quebec government has affirmed its commitment to preserving the French language. [Premise] And most Canadians are in favour of official bilingualism. [Conclusion] Let's face it, the French language is guaranteed to survive in Quebec!

From step 2 we can see that even if the three premises of this argument are all true, the conclusion can still be false. After all, even if everything described in the premises is true, the French language could still die out in Quebec (perhaps because new immigrants speak English or other languages, or because of the influence of American TV, movies, and magazines). So the argument can't be deductively valid. But if we go through step 3, we can see that if all the premises are true, the conclusion is likely to be true, making the argument inductively strong. If the premises *are* true, the argument would be cogent.

See what you think of this one:

[Premise] If you act like Bart Simpson, you will be respected by all your classmates. [Premise] But you don't act like Bart Simpson. [Conclusion] It follows that you will not be respected by all of your classmates.

This argument flunks the tests in steps 2 and 3: It is not deductively valid, and it is not inductively strong. But it does resemble a deductive argument in two ways. First, it displays a pattern of reasoning that can, at first glance, seem deductive. Actually, it uses an argument pattern that is always deductively *invalid* (called denying the antecedent, an argument form we will look at shortly). This alone should be evidence enough that the argument is indeed deductive but invalid. But it also contains an argument-indicator phrase ('it follows that') that suggests an attempt at a deductive form.

You'll get a lot more exposure to argument forms and indicator words in the rest of this chapter (and the rest of this text). Ultimately, practice in distinguishing different types of arguments and their relative worth is the only way to gain proficiency (and confidence!) in making these judgments.

So far we've spent most of our time assessing the logical structure of arguments—that is, whether they are valid or invalid, or strong or weak. We haven't focused as much attention on evaluating the truth of premises because that's a big issue that's best considered separately—which is what we do in Part 2 of this book.

Food For Thought

When Reasoning Crashes ... Leave the Scene of the Accident
Sometimes an argument goes off into a ditch and you don't know why. Here's an example of a wrecked argument from the great American satirical writer Ambrose Bierce (1842–1914?). What's wrong here?

Sixty men can do a piece of work sixty times as quickly as one man.
One man can dig a posthole in sixty seconds.
Therefore, sixty men can dig a posthole in one second.

Exercise 3.2

For each of the following arguments, follow the four-step procedure to determine whether it is deductive or inductive, valid or invalid, and strong or weak. State the results of applying each step.

Example 1

Colonel Mustard did not commit the murder. Someone who had committed the murder would have dirt on his shoes and blood on his hands. Colonel Mustard has neither.

Step 1: Conclusion: Colonel Mustard did not commit the murder. Premises: Someone who had committed the murder would have dirt on his shoes and blood on his hands. Colonel Mustard has neither.
Step 2: Deductively valid.
Step 3: Does not apply.
Step 4: Does not apply.

Example 2

Most people who smoke pot are irresponsible and forgetful. Looks like you smoke pot all the time. Ergo, you're irresponsible and forgetful. Can you remember that?

Step 1: Conclusion: Ergo, you're irresponsible and forgetful. Premises: Most people who smoke pot are irresponsible and forgetful. Looks like you smoke pot all the time.
Step 2: Not deductively valid.
Step 3: Inductively strong.
Step 4: Does not apply.

* 1. Ethel graduated from Queen's University. If she graduated from Queen's, she probably has a superior intellect. She has a superior intellect.
2. You *must* be under 30! You're a university student, and all university students are under 30.
3. If you go to that party you're completely nuts. You're going to the party. It necessarily follows that you're nuts.
4. 'Good sense is of all things in the world the most equally distributed, for everybody thinks himself so abundantly provided with it, that even those most difficult to please in all other matters do not commonly desire more of it than they already possess.' (René Descartes, *A Discourse on Method*)
5. All philosophers are absent-minded. All philosophers are teachers. It necessarily follows that all absent-minded people are teachers.
* 6. Every musician has had special training, and everyone with special training has a university degree. Thus, every musician has a university degree.
7. People with high IQs also have psychic abilities. People with high grades—which are comparable to high IQ scores—also probably have psychic abilities.

8. If Elvis Presley's name is spelled wrong on his tombstone, there must be some kind of conspiracy surrounding the death of the King. His name is spelled wrong. Therefore, there's a conspiracy.

* 9. Some actors sing, and some play a musical instrument. So some actors who sing also play a musical instrument.

10. Anyone who is not a bigot will agree that Chris is a good fellow. Some people in this neighbourhood think that he's anything but a good fellow. Some people in this neighbourhood are bigots.

11. 'In the actual living of life there is no logic, for life is superior to logic.' (Daisetz Teitaro Suzuki, *Essays in Zen Buddhism*)

12. A vase was found broken on the floor; some money had been taken out of the safe; and there were strange scratches on the wall. It therefore follows that someone obviously burglarized the place.

13. All the evidence in this trial suggests that Paul Bernardo is guilty of murder. Let's face it: he's probably guilty.

14. If everything were all right, there would be no blood on the floor. Of course, there is plenty of blood on the floor. Therefore, everything is not all right.

* 15. If minds are identical to brains—that is, if one's mind is nothing but a brain—androids could never have minds because they wouldn't have brains. Clearly, a mind is nothing but a brain, so it's impossible for androids to have minds.

16. 'From infancy, almost, the average girl is told that marriage is her ultimate goal; therefore her training and education must be directed towards that end.' (Emma Goldman, 'Marriage and Love')

17. If you have scratches on your body that you can't account for, and you feel that you have been visited by space aliens, then you really have been visited by space aliens. You have such scratches, and you have experienced such feelings. Doubtless space aliens have visited you.

18. If bombs are falling on London, war has started. The bombs are falling now. War has begun.

Exercise 3.3

For each of the following arguments, indicate whether it is valid or invalid, strong or weak.

1. Joe says that the food in the restaurant is first-rate. So it's first-rate.

2. Social welfare is by definition a handout to people who have not worked for it. But giving people money they have not earned through labour is not helping anyone. It follows then that social welfare does not help anyone.

* 3. If *The Globe and Mail* reports that war has started in Iraq, then war has started in Iraq. *The Globe and Mail* has reported exactly that. War must have started.

4. If $r = 12$, then $s = 8$; $r = 12$; therefore, $s = 8$.

5. Any sitcom that tries to imitate *Seinfeld* probably sucks. All of this season's sitcoms try to imitate *Seinfeld*. They've gotta suck.

6. 'Poetry is finer and more philosophical than history; for poetry expresses the universal and history only the particular.' (Aristotle, *Poetics*)

7. Either you're lying or you're not telling the whole story. You're obviously not lying, so you're just relating part of the story.

* 8. Either your thinking is logical or it is emotional. It's obviously not logical. It's emotional.

9. It is unwise to touch that electrical wire. It might be hot.

10. A recent Gallup poll says that 69 per cent of Canadians believe in the existence of heaven, but only 43 per cent say they believe in hell. People are just too willing to engage in wishful thinking.

11. Stem-cell research encourages abortions because abortions are a prime source for stem cells. Anything that encourages abortions should be banned. We ought to ban all stem-cell research.

12. 'We say that a person behaves in a given way because he possesses a philosophy, but we infer the philosophy from the behavior and therefore cannot use it in any satisfactory way as an explanation, at least until it is in turn explained.' (B.F. Skinner, *Beyond Freedom and Dignity*)

13. You failed the last three tests. You didn't show up for the last eight classes. And you haven't written any of the essays. Looks like you don't know the material.

* 14. Bachelors are unmarried. George is a bachelor. He has never taken a wife.

15. Bachelors are unmarried, and George acts as if he's not married. He's a bachelor for sure.

16. If there is a tax cut this year, the deficit will rise. There has already been a tax cut. The deficit is sure to rise.

17. If the universe had a beginning, then it was caused to begin. We know that the universe did have a beginning in the form of the Big Bang. So it was caused to come into existence. If it was caused to come into existence, that cause must have been God. God caused the universe to come into existence.

* 18. If the United States is willing to wage war in the Middle East, it can only be because it wants the oil supplies in the region. Obviously the United States is willing to go to war there. The United States wants that oil.

19. 'Someone must have been telling lies about Joseph K., for without having done anything wrong he was arrested one fine morning.' (Franz Kafka, *The Trial*)

20. Anyone willing to take the lives of innocent people for a cause is a terrorist. Many Christians, Jews, and Muslims have taken innocent lives in the name of their religious cause. Many Christians, Jews, and Muslims have been terrorists.

21. If he comes back, it's probably because he wants money. There he is. He wants money.

22. If you're 18, you're eligible to vote. But you're only seventeen. You're not eligible to vote.

* 23. I like geometry. My geometry teacher likes me. Therefore I will pass my geometry course with flying colours.

Food For Thought

How to Win Any Argument ... at a Party

The humorist Dave Barry has a lot of advice for you on how to win arguments at social gatherings—and alienate all your friends. So if you want to formulate good arguments, read the rest of this book. But if you want to win arguments and destroy your social life, follow Barry's advice precisely:

I argue very well. Ask any of my remaining friends. I can win an argument on any topic, against any opponent. People know this, and steer clear of me at parties. Often, as a sign of their great respect, they don't even invite me. You too can win arguments. Simply follow these rules:

Drink Liquor. Suppose you're at a party and some hotshot intellectual is expounding on the economy of Peru, a subject you know nothing about. If you're drinking some health-fanatic drink like grapefruit juice, you'll hang back, afraid to display your ignorance, while the hotshot enthralls your date. But if you drink several large martinis, you'll discover you have STRONG VIEWS about the Peruvian economy. You'll be a WEALTH of information. You'll argue forcefully, offering searing insights and possibly upsetting furniture. People will be impressed. Some may leave the room.

Make Things Up. Suppose, in the Peruvian economy argument, you are trying to prove Peruvians are underpaid, a position you base solely on the fact that YOU are underpaid, and you're damned if you're going to let a bunch of Peruvians be better off. DON'T say: 'I think Peruvians are underpaid.' Say: 'The average Peruvian's salary in 1981 dollars adjusted for the revised tax base is $1,452.81 per annum, which is $836.07 before the mean gross poverty level.' NOTE: Always make up exact figures. If an opponent asks you where you got your information, make THAT up too. Say: 'This information comes from Dr Hovel T. Moon's study for the Buford Commission published May 9, 1982. Didn't you read it?' Say this in the same tone of voice you would use to say 'You left your soiled underwear in my bath house.'

Use Meaningless But Weighty-Sounding Words and Phrases. Memorize this list:

Let me put it this way
In terms of
Vis-à-vis
Per se
As it were
Qua
So to speak

You should also memorize some Latin abbreviations such as 'QED', 'e.g.', and 'i.e.'. These are all short for 'I speak Latin, and you do not.'[2]

Finding Missing Parts

Sometimes arguments not only are faulty but also have a few pieces missing. Premises (and sometimes even conclusions)—material needed to make the argument work—are often left unstated. These implicit premises, or assumptions, are essential to the argument. Of course, certain assumptions are frequently left unsaid for good reason: they are obvious and understood by all parties to the argument, and boredom would set in fast if you actually tried to mention them all. If you wish to prove that 'Socrates is mortal', you normally wouldn't need to explain what *mortal* means and that the name 'Socrates' refers to an ancient philosopher, and not to a type of garden tool. But many arguments do have unstated premises that are not only necessary to the chain of reasoning but also must be made explicit to fully evaluate the arguments.

For instance:

Handguns are rare in Canada, but the availability of shotguns and rifles poses a risk of death and injury. Shotguns and rifles should be banned, too!

Notice that there is a kind of disconnect between the premise and the conclusion. The conclusion is about banning something, but the premises—the reasons given—don't say anything about banning anything. The conclusion follows from the premise *only* if we assume an additional premise, perhaps something like this: 'Anything that poses any risk of death or injury should be banned.' With this additional premise, the argument becomes:

Handguns are rare in Canada, but the availability of shotguns and rifles poses a risk to public safety. Anything that poses any risk of death or injury should be banned. Therefore, shotguns and rifles should be banned, too!

Now that all the premises are spelled out, you can evaluate the *full* argument just as you would any other. Not only that, but you can see that the unstated premise is questionable, which is the case with many implicit premises. Not everyone would agree that anything raising the risk of death or injury should be banned, for if that were the case we would have to outlaw cars, airplanes, most prescription drugs, most occupations, and who knows how many kitchen appliances! Many unstated premises are like this one—they're controversial and therefore should not be left unexamined.

Here's another argument with an unstated premise:

Anyone who craves political power cannot be trusted to serve the public interest. So I say Premier Blowhard can't be trusted to serve the public interest.

As stated, this argument seems like a rush to judgment because the first premise concerns *anyone* who craves power, and suddenly Premier Blowhard is denounced as untrustworthy. Something's missing. What we need is another premise connecting the first premise to the conclusion: 'Premier Blowhard craves political power.' Now let's plug the implicit premise into the argument:

> Anyone who craves political power cannot be trusted to serve the public interest. Premier Blowhard craves political power. He can't be trusted to serve the public interest.

So exactly when should we try to ferret out an unstated premise? The obvious answer is that we should do so when there appears to be something essential missing—an implied, logical link between premises and conclusion that is not a common-sense, generally accepted assumption. Such implicit premises should never be taken for granted because, among other things, they are often deliberately hidden or downplayed to make the argument seem stronger.

Be aware, though, that many times the problem with an argument is not unstated premises, but invalid or weak structure. Consider this:

> If Tariq works harder, he will pass his calculus course. But he will not work harder, so he will not pass calculus.

This argument is invalid; the conclusion does not follow from the premises. Like most invalid arguments, it can't be salvaged without altering it beyond what is clearly implied. It's just a bad argument. The same goes for weak arguments. They usually can't be fixed up without adding or changing premises gratuitously. Remember, the point of articulating unstated premises is to make explicit what is already implicit. Your job as a critical thinker is not to make bad arguments good; that task falls to the one who puts forth the argument in the first place.

To make sure that your investigation of implicit premises is thorough and reasonable, work through the following three-step process.[3]

Step 1. Search for a credible premise that would make the argument *valid*, one that would furnish the needed link between premise (or premises) and conclusion. Choose the supplied premise that

a.   is most plausible

and

b.   fits best with the author's intent.

The first stipulation (a) means that you should look for premises that are either true or, at least, not obviously false. The second stipulation (b) means that premises should fit—that is, at least not conflict—with what seems to be the author's point or purpose (which, of course, is often difficult to discern).

These two requirements embody what is sometimes known as 'the Principle of Charity in Interpretation' or just 'the Principle of Charity'. The Principle of Charity says that, whenever we find someone's meaning unclear, we should attempt to interpret it in a way that makes sense. That's the *fair* thing to do, and it's the thing that's most likely to aid in clear communication. And when it comes to *criticizing* someone else's argument, you want to be especially fair in stating what you think their argument is. Criticizing a version of their argument into which you've inserted a silly or irrelevant premise isn't very productive, and it isn't very fair.

If the premise you supply is plausible and fitting (with the author's intent), use it to fill out the argument. If the premise you supplied is either not plausible or not fitting, go to step 2.

Step 2. Search for a credible premise that would make the argument as *strong* as possible. Choose the supplied premise that fulfills stipulations (a) and (b). If the premise you supply is plausible and fitting, use it to fill out the argument. If it is either not plausible or not fitting, consider the argument beyond repair and reject it.

Step 3. Evaluate the reconstituted argument. If you're able to identify a credible implicit premise that makes the argument either valid or strong, assess this revised version of the argument, paying particular attention to the plausibility of the other premise or premises.

www.CartoonStock.com

Now let's apply the procedure above to a few arguments:

If the Bank of Canada lowers interest rates one more time, there will be a deep recession. I'm telling you there's going to be a deep recession.

The first step is to see if there's a credible premise that would make the argument valid. We can see right away that one premise will do the trick: 'The Bank of Canada has lowered interest rates again.' Adding it to the argument will supply the link needed between the existing premise and the conclusion. We also can see that our new premise is plausible (the Bank of Canada has lowered interest rates many times) and seems to fit with the point of the argument (to prove that there will be a recession). Our resulting argument, though, is probably not a good one because the premise about the effect of the Bank of Canada's lowering interest rates is dubious.

Now examine this one:

Security officer Jones lied on her employment application about whether she had a criminal record. Security officer Jones will do a bad job of screening passengers for weapons.

The sentence 'Security officer Jones will do a bad job of screening passengers for weapons' is the conclusion here. To try to make this argument valid, we would need a premise like 'Any security officer at Pearson International Airport who has lied on his or her employment application about having a criminal record will do a bad job of screening passengers for weapons.' This premise fits the point of the argument, but it isn't plausible. Surely it cannot be the case that *any* security officer who has lied will do a bad job of screening. A more plausible premise is 'Most security officers at Pearson International Airport who have lied on their employment applications about having a criminal record will do a bad job of screening passengers for weapons.' This premise will do, and this is now a good argument—assuming that the other premise is true.

What about this one:

> The use of marijuana should be legal because it's an act that brings pleasure to people's lives.

To make this argument valid, we would need to add this premise (or one like it): 'Any act that brings pleasure to people's lives should be legal.' But this premise is hard to accept since many heinous acts—such as murder and theft—may bring pleasure to some people, yet few of us would think those acts should be legal. To try to make the argument strong, we might add this premise instead: 'Some acts should be legal simply because they bring pleasure to people's lives.' This premise is actually controversial in some quarters, but it at least is not obviously false. It also fits with the point of the argument. If we decide that the premise is neither plausible nor fitting, we would declare the argument beyond repair.

Exercise 3.4

I. For each of the following arguments, state the implicit premises that will make the argument valid.

Example

The engine is sputtering. It must be out of gas.
Implicit premise: Whenever the engine sputters, it's out of gas.

* 1. Any Member of Parliament who is caught misusing campaign funds should resign his seat. The Honourable Member from Algoma-Manitoulin-Kapuskasing should resign.
2. Jenna is a highly motivated runner, so she is sure to finish the race.
3. In the first week at the box office, the movie grossed over $30 million. So it's sure to win at least one Oscar.
4. The RCMP doesn't have a very serious focus on stopping terrorism. A major terrorist attack *will* happen in this country.
* 5. The author of this new book on interventionist wars is either biased or incompetent as a journalist. So she's biased.

6. The conflict in Indonesia is a genuine war. So it can't possibly be morally justified.

7. The government of Saudi Arabia is bound to fall! After all, the Taliban regime in Afghanistan fell because it persecuted women.

8. The Canadian government should limit its military activities to the western hemisphere because it doesn't have the resources to cover the whole world.

* 9. If the engine starts right away, it's because of the tune-up I gave it. Must be because of the tune-up I gave it.

10. Taslima did not criticize US military action in the Gulf War or in the war in Afghanistan. She must be pro-American.

II. For each of the following arguments, change or add a premise that will make the argument strong.

1. Coach Johnson once fell asleep during a game. He's probably not a very good coach.

2. Aziz regularly eats at McDonald's, so Aziz is likely to gain a few pounds.

* 3. Six out of ten of my teenage friends love rap music. So 60 per cent of all teens love rap music.

4. Seventy-one per cent of the faculty and staff at Spadina College are New Democrats. So most of the students are probably New Democrats.

5. Miriam was in the library when the books were stolen from the librarian's desk. She was also seen hanging around the desk. So she's probably the one who stole them.

* 6. If Assad's fingerprints are on the vase, then he's probably the one who broke it. He's probably the one who broke it.

7. If the Prime Minister needs more money to balance the federal budget, he will get it by cutting defence spending. Well, he's almost certainly going to get it by cutting defence spending.

8. Ninety per cent of students at the University of Northern Saskatchewan graduate with a BA degree. Li Fong will probably graduate from the University of Northern Saskatchewan with a BA degree.

* 9. The murder rates in the Atlantic provinces are very low. The murder rates in most large cities in the western provinces are very low. So the murder rate in Toronto must be very low.

10. John has a typical Canadian diet. His fat intake is probably excessively high.

Food For Thought

Arguments on the Net

The Internet is fertile ground for all manner of arguments—good, bad, benign, and benighted. Here's one that has gone around the world a few times in cyberspace:

> Hillary Clinton supports gun-control legislation.
> All fascist regimes of the twentieth century have passed gun-control legislation.
> Therefore, Hillary Clinton is a fascist.

What's wrong with this argument? If you don't know, the following section on argument patterns will help you. An important clue that something is fishy here is that any argument of this form can be used to try to 'frame' anybody. Consider:

> Vaughn likes salads and can be trained to do tricks.
> Hamsters like salads and can be trained to do tricks.
> Therefore, Vaughn is a hamster.

Argument Patterns

Earlier we discussed the importance of being familiar with patterns, or forms, of argument, that is, the structures on which the content is laid. The point was that knowing some common argument forms makes it easier to determine whether an argument is deductive or inductive. But being familiar with argument forms is also helpful in many other aspects of argument evaluation. Let's take a closer look at some of these forms.

Since argument forms are structures distinct from the content of an argument, we can easily signify different forms by using letters to represent statements in the arguments. Each letter represents a different statement in much the same way that letters are used to represent values in a mathematical equation. Consider this argument:

> If the job is worth doing, then it's worth doing well.
> The job is worth doing.
> Therefore, it's worth doing well.

We can represent this argument like this:

> If p, then q.
> p.
> Therefore, q.

Notice that the first line in the argument is a compound statement—it's composed of at least two constituent statements, which are represented in this case by p and q. So we have two statements in this argument that are arranged into an argument form, one that is both very common and always valid. We can plug any statements we want into this form, and we will still get a valid argument. The premises may be true or false, but the form will be valid.

Some of the more common argument patterns that you encounter are like this pattern—they're deductive and **conditional**. They are conditional in that they contain at least one conditional, or if-then, premise. The first statement in a conditional premise (the *if* part), is known as the **antecedent**. The second statement (the *then* part) is known as the **consequent**.

The conditional pattern shown here is called **affirming the antecedent** or, to use the Latin term, ***modus ponens***. Any argument in the *modus ponens* form is valid—if the premises are true, the conclusion absolutely must be true. In the argument form shown here, this means that if 'If p, then q' and 'p' are both true, the conclusion has to be true also. These facts, then, provide a way to quickly size up any conditional argument. If it's in the form of *modus ponens*, it's valid, regardless of the content of the statements.

Review Notes

Valid Conditional Argument Forms

Affirming the Antecedent

(*Modus Ponens*)

If p, then q.

p

Therefore, q.

Example

If Spot barks, a burglar is in the house.

Spot is barking.

Therefore, a burglar is in the house

Denying the Consequent

(*Modus Tollens*)

If p, then q.

Not q.

Therefore, not p.

Example

If it's raining, the park is closed.

The park is not closed.

Therefore, it's not raining.

Hypothetical Syllogism

If p, then q.

If q, then r.

Therefore, if p, then r.

If Ajax steals the money, he will go to jail.

If Ajax goes to jail, his family will suffer.

Therefore, if Ajax steals the money, his family will suffer.

Another common conditional argument form is called **denying the consequent**, or *modus tollens*:

If Austin is happy, then Barb is happy.
Barb is not happy.
Therefore, Austin is not happy.

The form of *modus tollens* is:

If *p*, then *q*.
Not *q*.
Therefore, not *p*.

Like *modus ponens*, *modus tollens* is always valid. If the premises are true, the conclusion must be true. So any argument that's in the *modus tollens* pattern is valid.

A third common conditional argument form is called **hypothetical syllogism**. *Hypothetical* is just another term for conditional. A **syllogism** is an argument (usually deductive) made up of three statements—two premises and a conclusion. (*Modus ponens* and *modus tollens* are also syllogisms. We'll discuss 'categorical' syllogisms—deductive syllogisms which show the logical relationships between three categories of things—in Chapter 7, and we'll discuss inductive 'statistical' syllogisms in Chapter 8.) In a hypothetical syllogism, all three statements are conditional, and the argument is always valid:

If the ball drops, the lever turns to the right.
If the lever turns to the right, the engine will stop.
Therefore, if the ball drops, the engine will stop.

Here's the symbolized version:

If *p*, then *q*.
If *q*, then *r*.
Therefore, if p, then *r*.

People often use hypothetical syllogisms to reason about causal chains of events. They try to show that one event will lead inexorably to a sequence of events that will finally conclude in a single event that seems far removed from the first. This linkage has prompted some to label hypothetical syllogisms 'chain arguments'.

Here's another example of a hypothetical syllogism:

If the Habs lose this game, they're out of the playoffs.
If they're out of the playoffs, there will be riots in Montreal.
Therefore, if the Habs lose this game, there will be riots in Montreal.

Because the *structure* of this argument is the same as the structure of the previous argument (that is, they're both hypothetical syllogisms), the symbolized version is exactly the same:

If *p*, then *q*.
If *q*, then *r*.
Therefore, if *p*, then *r*.

There are two common conditional argument forms that are *not* valid, though they strongly resemble valid forms. One is called **denying the antecedent**. For example:

If Einstein invented the steam engine, then he's a great scientist.
Einstein did not invent the steam engine.
Therefore, he is not a great scientist.

Denying the antecedent is represented like this:

If *p*, then *q*.
Not *p*.
Therefore, not *q*.

You can see the problem with this form in the preceding argument. Even if the antecedent is false (if Einstein did not invent the steam engine), that doesn't show that he's not a great scientist, because he could be a great scientist on account of some other great achievement. Thus, denying the antecedent is clearly an invalid pattern because it's possible for the premises to be true and the conclusion false.

Here's another example of this form:

If science can prove that God is dead, then God is dead.
Science cannot prove that God is dead.
Therefore, God is not dead.

Even if science cannot prove that God is dead, that in itself does not show that God is not dead. Perhaps God is dead even though science cannot prove it. In other words, it's possible for both premises to be true while the conclusion is false.

There's another common invalid form you should know about: **affirming the consequent**. Here's an instance of this form:

If Brandon is the capital of Manitoba, then Brandon is in Manitoba.
Brandon is in Manitoba.
Therefore, Brandon is the capital of Manitoba.

We represent this form like this:

If *p*, then *q*.
q.
Therefore, *p*.

'Mistakes are made on two counts: an argument is either based on error or incorrectly developed.'
—Thomas Aquinas

Obviously, in this form it's possible for the premises to be true while the conclusion is false, as this example shows. This pattern, therefore, is invalid.

Finally, we come to a common non-conditional argument form called **disjunctive syllogism**. It's valid and extremely simple:

Either Ralph walked the dog, or he stayed home.
He didn't walk the dog.
Therefore, he stayed home.

The symbolized form:

Either *p* or *q*.
Not *p*.
Therefore, *q*.

Keep in mind that in a disjunctive syllogism, either disjunct can be denied, not just the first one. Here's an example in which the second of the two disjuncts is denied:

Either Rick Mercer was joking, or he is out of touch with current events.
But I *know* he's not out of touch with current events!
So, he must have been joking.

These six deductive argument forms (four valid ones and two invalid ones) can help you streamline the process of argument evaluation. If you want to find out quickly if a deductive argument is valid, you can use these patterns to do that. (Remember, a good deductive argument has both a valid form and true premises.) You need only to see if the argument fits one of the forms. If it fits a valid form, it's valid. If it fits an invalid form, it's invalid. If it doesn't fit any of the forms, then you need to find another way to evaluate the argument. The easiest way to use this form-comparison technique is to memorize all six forms so that you can recognize them whenever they arise.

Sometimes you can see right away that an argument has a valid or invalid form. At other times, you may need a little help figuring this out, or you may want to use a more explicit test of validity. In either case, the *counter-example method* can help. With this technique you check for validity by simply devising a parallel argument that has the same form as the argument you're evaluating (the test argument) but has obviously *true premises and a false conclusion*. Recall that any argument having true premises and a false conclusion cannot be valid. So if you can invent such an argument that also has the same pattern as the test argument, you've proved that the test argument is invalid.

Let's say that you are confronted with this argument:

If old-fashioned values are lost, then young people will abandon marriage.
Young people have abandoned marriage.
Therefore, old-fashioned values have been lost!

Review Notes

Invalid Conditional Argument Forms

Affirming the Consequent
If *p*, then *q*.
q.
Therefore, *p*.

Example
If the cat is on the mat, she is asleep.
She is asleep.
Therefore, she is on the mat.

Denying the Antecedent
If *p*, then *q*.
Not *p*.
Therefore, not *q*.

Example
If the cat is on the mat, she is asleep.
She is not on the mat.
Therefore, she is not asleep.

And to check this test argument, you come up with this parallel argument:

If George is a dog, then he is warm-blooded.
George is warm-blooded.
Therefore, he is a dog.

This argument has the same pattern as the previous one—but the premises are true and the conclusion is false. So the test argument is invalid. You may have already guessed that it is an instance of affirming the consequent. The counter-example method, though, works not just for the deductive forms we've discussed but for all deductive forms. (We will discuss other deductive forms in upcoming chapters.)

Review Notes

Disjunctive Syllogism

Symbolized Version
Either *p* or *q*.
Not *p*.
Therefore, *q*.

Example
Either we light the fire or we will freeze.
We will not light the fire.
Therefore, we will freeze.

Exercise 3.5

For each of the following arguments, determine whether it is valid or invalid and indicate the argument pattern.

* 1. If the Vikings built that wall, there would be archeological evidence of that.
   But there is no such evidence.
   So the Vikings did not build that wall.

 2. If the butler didn't kill the master, then the maid did.
   The butler didn't kill him.
   So the maid killed him.

 3. Either John drove home or he stayed late.
   He didn't drive home.
   Therefore, he stayed late.

 4. If the South Africans have nuclear weapons, the South African jungle will be radioactive.
   The South African jungle is radioactive.
   Therefore, the South Africans have nuclear weapons.

 5. If the South Africans have nuclear weapons, the South African jungle will be radioactive.
   The South Africans do not have nuclear weapons.
   Therefore, the South African jungle is not radioactive.

* 6. If CBC News omits important news stories, then it is irresponsible.
   It is not irresponsible.
   So CBC News does not omit important news stories.

 7. If ESP (extrasensory perception) were real, psychic predictions would be completely reliable.
   Psychic predictions are completely reliable.
   Therefore, ESP is real.

 8. If ESP (extrasensory perception) were real, psychic predictions would be completely reliable.
   ESP is not real.
   Therefore, psychic predictions are not completely reliable.

* 9. If ESP (extrasensory perception) were real, psychic predictions would be completely reliable.
   ESP is real.
   Therefore, psychic predictions are completely reliable.

 10. If laws could stop crime, there would be no crime.
   But there is crime.
   Therefore, laws cannot stop crime.

 11. If I perceive what appears to be a red door, then there really is a red door there.
   There really is a red door there.
   Therefore, I perceive what appears to be a red door.

12. If it rains, Alex will get wet.

If Alex gets wet, he will be upset.

Therefore, if it rains, Alex will be upset.

Exercise 3.6

For each of the following premises, fill out the rest of the argument to make it valid in two different ways—*modus ponens* and *modus tollens*.

1. If the theory of evolution were untrue, biology would make no sense.
* 2. If Lino is telling the truth, he will admit to all charges.
3. If some wars are just, then pacifism is false.
4 If the new vaccine prevents the spread of the virus, the researchers who developed the vaccine should get the Nobel Prize.
* 5. If religious conflict in Nigeria continues, thousands more will die.
6. If *p*, then *q*.
7. If the glaciers are melting, global warming has increased.
8. If there is such a thing as moral progress—that is, social changes in which we judge states of affairs to be 'better' now than before—then the Enlightenment ideal of moral perfection is possible.
* 9. If solar power can supply six megawatts of power in Vancouver (which is certainly not the sunniest place in the world), then solar power can transform the energy systems in sunnier places like Edmonton and Calgary.
10. If my honourable colleague would stop listening to only his own voice for more than 60 seconds, he would doubtless be astonished that there are other minds in the world with other ideas.

Exercise 3.7

Use the counter-example method to create a parallel argument for each of the invalid arguments in Exercise 3.5. Write out each parallel argument and represent its form with letters as discussed earlier. Answers are provided for 4, 5, 7, 8, and 11.

Example

Test Argument:

If the prime minister cuts taxes again, there will be a long-term recession.

There will be a long-term recession.

Therefore, the prime minister will cut taxes.

Parallel Argument:

If Conrad Black could fly, he would be famous.

He is famous.

Therefore, he can fly.

If *a*, then *b*.

b.

Therefore, *a*.

Diagramming Arguments

Most of the arguments we've looked at so far have been relatively simple. When arguments are more complex (in real life they usually are!), you may find it increasingly difficult to sort out premises from conclusions and parts of an argument from non-argumentative background noise. If you can visualize the structure of an argument, though, the job gets much easier. That's where argument diagramming comes in.

Let's begin by diagramming the following very simple argument, before moving on to more complicated ones:

Barack Obama has great ideas for preserving the natural environment. You bet he does! Therefore Obama being elected is good for Canada.

The first thing we do is underline any premise- or conclusion-indicator words (e.g., 'therefore', 'since', and 'because'):

Barack Obama has great ideas for preserving the natural environment. You bet he does! <u>Therefore</u> Obama being elected is good for Canada.

Next we number all the statements (and *only* the statements) in the passage in sequential order.

(1) Barack Obama has great ideas for preserving the natural environment.
(2) You bet he does! (3) Therefore Obama being elected is good for Canada.

And then we cross out all extraneous statements—those that are neither premises nor conclusions, those that are redundant, and those that are nothing more than background information or other logically irrelevant material.

(1) Barack Obama has great ideas for preserving the natural environment.
(2) ~~You bet he does!~~ (3) Therefore Obama being elected is good for Canada.

We've crossed out claim (2) because it is redundant—it just reaffirms what is said in claim (1).

Finally, we draw the diagram. Place the numbers of the premises inside squares and above the number for the conclusion, which is itself placed inside a circle. (In our diagramming method, squares will always represent premises, and circles will always represent conclusions.) Then draw arrows from the premises to the conclusion they support. Each arrow represents a logical relationship between premise and conclusion, a relationship that we normally indicate with the word 'therefore' or 'is a reason or premise for'.

This diagram is very simple, because the argument it represents is very simple. It has just one premise and one conclusion. And it has just one arrow, showing that premise (1) is being used here in support of conclusion (3).

Now we're ready to try a slightly more complicated example.

> What do I think of shopping at the Bay? I'll tell you! They've got great prices, and they've got a good selection of men's clothes. So the Bay is a great place to shop!

The first thing we do is underline any premise- or conclusion-indicator words (e.g., 'therefore', 'since', and 'because'):

> What do I think of shopping at the Bay? I'll tell you! They've got great prices, and they've got a good selection of men's clothes. <u>So</u> the Bay is a great place to shop!

Next we number all the statements (and *only* the statements) in the passage in sequential order.

> What do I think of shopping at the Bay? (1) I'll tell you! (2) They've got great prices, and (3) they've got a good selection of men's clothes. (4) <u>So</u> the Bay is a great place to shop!

We haven't numbered that first sentence, because it's a question, not a statement—it's merely there to introduce the topic.

And then we cross out all extraneous statements—those that are neither premises nor conclusions, those that are redundant, etc.

> ~~What do I think of shopping at the Bay?~~ (1) ~~I'll tell you!~~ (2) They've got great prices, and (3) they've got a good selection of men's clothes. (4) <u>So</u> the Bay is a great place to shop!

We've crossed out the first two sentences because they're not essential to the structure of this argument. The first sentence isn't a statement at all. And the second one, though it *is* a statement, doesn't really have any content: it just announces that an argument is on its way.

Finally, we draw the diagram. Place the numbers of the premises inside squares and put the number for the conclusion inside a circle. Put the premises above the conclusion on your page. Then draw arrows from the premises to the conclusion they support.

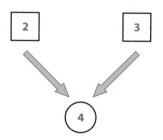

Here we see that our diagram—our argument—is one step more complicated than in our previous example. This one has two premises, each lending some support to the conclusion. The logical 'flow' from the two premises to the conclusion is represented by the two arrows.

Next, let's try something more complicated still.

> There is no question in my mind. I therefore maintain that Colonel Mustard is the murderer. Because if he did it, he would probably have bloodstains on the sleeve of his shirt. The bloodstains are tiny, but they are there. Any observant person could see them. Also the murder weapon was within the colonel's reach for quite a while before the crime was committed. And since of all the people in the house at the time he alone does not have an airtight alibi, he must be the killer.

Again, the first thing we do is underline any premise- or conclusion-indicator words (e.g., 'therefore', 'since', and 'because'):

> There is no question in my mind. I <u>therefore</u> maintain that Colonel Mustard is the murderer. <u>Because</u> if he did it, he would probably have bloodstains on the sleeve of his shirt. The bloodstains are tiny, but they are there. Any observant person could see them. Also the murder weapon was within the colonel's reach for quite a while before the crime was committed. And <u>since</u> of all the people in the house at the time he alone does not have an airtight alibi, he must be the killer.

Next we number all the statements (and *only* the statements) in the passage in sequential order. (For the purposes of diagramming, an if-then statement is considered one statement, and multiple statements in a single compound sentence are to be counted as separate statements. Such statements are usually joined by 'and', 'or', and 'but'.)

(1) There is no question in my mind. (2) I <u>therefore</u> maintain that Colonel Mustard is the murderer. (3) <u>Because</u> if he did it, he would probably have bloodstains on the sleeve of his shirt. (4) The bloodstains are tiny, but they are there. (5) Any observant person could see them. (6) Also the murder weapon was within the colonel's reach for quite a while before the crime was committed. (7) And <u>since</u> of all the people in the house at the time he alone does not have an airtight alibi, (8) he must be the killer.

And then we cross out all extraneous statements noise, redundancies, and anything else that is neither a premise nor a conclusion.

Allen is far less argumentative since Angie's introduction to falconry.

By permission of the Jerry Van Amerongen and Creators Syndicate, Inc.

(1) ~~There is no question in my mind~~. (2) I <u>therefore</u> maintain that Colonel Mustard is the murderer. (3) <u>Because</u> if he did it, he would probably have bloodstains on the sleeve of his shirt. (4) The bloodstains are tiny, but they are there. (5) ~~Any observant person could see them~~. (6) Also the murder weapon was within the colonel's reach for quite a while before the crime was committed. (7) And <u>since</u> of all the people in the house at the time he alone does not have an airtight alibi, ~~he must be the killer~~.

Finally, we draw the diagram. Again, place the numbers of the premises inside squares and above the number for the conclusion, which is itself placed inside a circle. Squares will represent premises, and circles will represent conclusions.. Draw arrows from the premises to the conclusion they support.

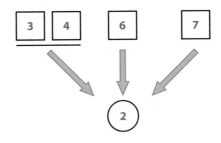

In this diagram you can see that premises 3 and 4 are handled differently from premises 6 and 7. The reason is that some premises are **independent** and some are **dependent**.

An independent premise offers support to a conclusion *without the help of any other premises*. If other premises are omitted or undermined in an argument, the support supplied by an independent premise does not change. We represent this fact in the diagram by drawing separate arrows from premises 6 and 7 to the conclusion. Premise 6 gives independent support to the conclusion, and premise 7 gives independent support to the conclusion. If we delete one of these premises, the support that the other one gives does not change.

Premises 3 and 4 are dependent premises. They do depend on each other to jointly provide support to a conclusion. If either premise 3 or 4 is removed, the support that the remaining premise supplies is undermined or completely cancelled out. By itself, premise 3 ('Because if he did it, he would probably have bloodstains on the sleeve of his shirt') offers no support whatsoever to the conclusion ('Colonel Mustard is the murderer'). And by itself, premise 4 ('The bloodstains are tiny, but they are there') doesn't lend any support to the conclusion. But together, premises 3 and 4 offer a good reason to accept the conclusion. We represent dependent premises by underlining them *together*, as in our diagram. Since dependent premises together act as a single premise, or reason, we draw a single arrow from the combined premises (3 and 4, each inside its own square) to the conclusion. With the diagram complete, we can see clearly that two independent premises and one set of dependent premises provide support for the conclusion (statement 2).

Now, consider this argument:

(1) The famous trial lawyer Clarence Darrow (1857–1938) made a name for himself by using the 'determinism defence' to get his clients acquitted of serious crimes. (2) The crux of this approach is the idea that humans are not really responsible for anything they do because they cannot choose freely—they are 'determined', predestined, if you will, by nature (or God) to be the way they are. (3) So in a sense, Darrow says, humans are like wind-up toys with no control over any action or decision. (4) They have no free will. (5) Remember that Darrow was a renowned agnostic who was skeptical of all religious claims. (6) But Darrow is wrong about human free will for two reasons. (7) First, in our moral life, our own common-sense experience suggests that sometimes people are free to make moral decisions. (8) We should not abandon what our common-sense experience tells us without good reason—and (9) Darrow has given us no good reason. (10) Second, Darrow's determinism is not confirmed by science, as he claims—but actually conflicts with science. (11) Modern science says that there are many things (at the subatomic level of matter) that are not determined at all: (12) They just happen.

Indicator words are scarce in this argument, unless you count the words 'first' and 'second' as signifying premises. After we number the statements consecutively, cross out extraneous statements, the argument looks like this:

(1) ~~The famous trial lawyer Clarence Darrow (1857–1938) made a name for himself by using the 'determinism defense' to get his clients acquitted of serious crimes.~~ (2) ~~The crux of this approach is the idea that humans are not really responsible for anything they do because they cannot choose freely—they are 'determined', predestined, if you will, by nature (or God) to be the way they are.~~ (3) ~~So in a sense, Darrow says, humans are like wind-up toys with no control over any action or decision.~~ (4) ~~They have no free will.~~ (5) ~~Remember that Darrow was a renowned agnostic who was skeptical of all religious claims.~~ (6) But Darrow is wrong about human free will for two reasons. (7) First, in our moral life, our own common-sense experience suggests that sometimes people are free to make moral decisions. (8) We should not abandon what our common-sense experience tells us without good reason—and (9) Darrow has given us no good reason. (10) Second, Darrow's determinism is not confirmed by science, as he claims—but actually conflicts with science. (11) Modern science says that there are many things (at the subatomic level of matter) that are not determined at all: (12) ~~They just happen.~~

Clarence Darrow was skilled at argumentation, which he used to good effect in his most famous case, the so-called Scopes Monkey Trial of 1925, in which he defended a man (John Scopes) charged with teaching evolution in a public school. Photo: © Bettmann / Corbis

To simplify things, we can eliminate several statements right away. Statements 1 through 4 are just background information on Darrow's views. Statement 5 is irrelevant to the argument; his agnosticism has no logical connection to the premises or conclusion. Statement 12 is a rewording of statement 11.

After this elimination process, only the following premises and conclusion (statement 6) remain:

(6) But Darrow is wrong about human free will for two reasons.

(7) First, in our moral life, our common-sense experience suggests that sometimes people are free to make moral decisions.

(8) We should not abandon what our common-sense experience tells us without good reason.

(9) Darrow has given us no good reason.

(10) Darrow's determinism is not confirmed by science, as he claims—but actually conflicts with science.

(11) Modern science says that there are many things (mostly at the subatomic level of matter) that are not determined at all.

The question is, how are these premises related to the conclusion? Well, premises 7, 8, and 9 are dependent premises supporting the conclusion. Taken separately, these premises are weak, but together they constitute a plausible reason for accepting statement 6. Premise 10 directly supports the conclusion, and it in turn is supported by premise 11. These logical relationships can be diagrammed like this:

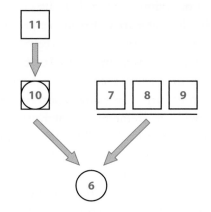

Notice how statement 10 is diagrammed. It is a premise leading to the conclusion (6), so it needs to be inside a square. But it is also a conclusion (from premise 11), so it also needs to be inside a circle. The circle-square combination indicates that the statement is a sub-conclusion, a statement that serves as both a premise *and* a conclusion.

Review Notes

Diagramming Arguments: Step by Step

1. Underline all premise or conclusion indicator words such as 'since', 'therefore', and 'because'. Then number the statements.
2. Cross out all extraneous material—redundancies, irrelevant sentences, questions, exclamations.
3. Draw the diagram, using numbered squares to represent premises and numbered circles to represent conclusions. Connect premises and conclusions with arrows showing logical connections. Include both dependent and independent premises, and draw a line under dependent premises to connect them.

Now read this passage:

As the Islamic clerics cling to power in Iran, students there are agitating for greater freedom and less suppression of views that the clerics dislike. Even though ultimate power in Iran rests with the mullahs, it is not at all certain where the nation is headed. Here's a radical suggestion: the Islamic republic in Iran will fall within the next five years. Why do I say this? Because the majority of Iranians are in favour of democratic reforms, and no regime can stand for very long when citizens are demanding access to the political process. Also, Iran today is a mirror image of the Soviet Union before it broke apart—there's widespread dissatisfaction and dissent at a time when the regime seems to be trying to hold the people's loyalty. Every nation that has taken such a path has imploded within five years. Finally, the old Iranian trick of gaining support for the government by fomenting hatred of America will not work anymore because Iran is now trying to be friends with the United States.

When we number the statements and underline the indicators, we get this:

(1) As the Islamic clerics cling to power in Iran, students there are agitating for greater freedom and less suppression of views that the clerics dislike. (2) Even though ultimate power in Iran rests with the mullahs, it is not at all certain where the nation is headed. Here's a radical suggestion: (3) The Islamic republic in Iran will fall within the next five years. Why do I say this? (4) <u>Because</u> the majority of Iranians are in favour of democratic reforms, (5) and no regime can stand for very long when citizens are demanding access to the political process. (6) Also, Iran today is a mirror image of the Soviet Union before it broke apart—there's widespread dissatisfaction and dissent at a time when the regime seems to be trying to hold the people's loyalty. (7) Every nation that has taken such a path has imploded within five years. (8) Finally, the old Iranian trick of gaining support for the government by fomenting hatred of America will not work anymore (9) <u>because</u> Iran is now trying to be friends with the United States.

And here's the passage with the premises and conclusion underlined and the extraneous material crossed out:

~~(1) As the Islamic clerics cling to power in Iran, students there are agitating for greater freedom and less suppression of views that the clerics dislike.~~ ~~(2) Even though ultimate power in Iran rests with the mullahs, it is not at all certain where the nation is headed.~~ Here's a radical suggestion: (3) The Islamic republic in Iran will fall within the next five years. ~~Why do I say this?~~ (4) <u>Because</u> the majority of Iranians are in favour of democratic reforms (5) and no regime can stand for very long when citizens are demanding access to the political process. (6) Also, Iran today is a mirror image of the Soviet Union before it broke apart—there's widespread dissatisfaction and dissent at a time when the regime seems to be trying to hold the people's loyalty. (7) Every nation that has taken such a path has imploded within five years. (8) Finally, the old Iranian trick of gaining support for the government by fomenting hatred of America will not work anymore (9) <u>because</u> Iran is now trying to be friends with the United States.

The conclusion is statement 3, and the premises are statements 4 through 9. The first two statements are extraneous. Statements 4 and 5 are dependent premises, and so are statements 6 and 7. Statements 8 and 9 constitute an argument that gives support to the conclusion of the passage. Statement 8 is the conclusion; statement 9, the premise. Notice also that the sentence 'Why do I say this?' is not diagrammed at all, or even numbered, because it's not a statement. The diagram of this argument is as follows:

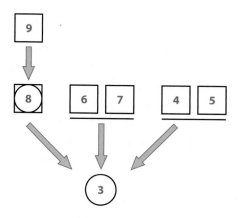

By the time you work through the diagramming exercises in this chapter, you will probably be fairly proficient in diagramming arguments of all kinds. Just as important, you will have a better appreciation of how arguments are built, how they are dissected, and how you can judge their value in a penetrating, systematic way.

Exercise 3.8

For each of the following diagrams, devise an argument whose premises and conclusion can be accurately depicted in the diagram. Write out the argument, number each statement, and insert the numbers into the diagram at the right places.

 1.

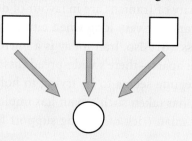

2.

3.

* 4.

5.

6.

7.

Exercise 3.9

Diagram the following arguments using the procedure discussed in the text.

1. I shouldn't take physics this semester. My course load is already too heavy. There's no room for the course in my schedule. And I don't like physics.
2. The Prime Minister is soft on the environment. He has weakened clean air regulations and lifted restrictions on logging in the West.
3. Mayor LeClerc is either dishonest or incompetent. He's not incompetent, though, because he's expert at getting self-serving by-laws passed by City Council. I guess he's just dishonest.
4. If an individual in a coma is no longer a person, then giving him a drug to kill him is not murder. Such an individual is in fact not a person. Therefore, giving him the drug is not murder.
5. I think City Council should pass a by-law prohibiting smoking in all and restaurants and bars. It won't be a popular move, but it's clearly the best thing from a public-health point of view. By passing such a by-law, City Council would be setting a good example and reminding everyone what a serious risk smoking poses.

* 6. If Marla buys the house in the suburbs, she will be happier and healthier. She is buying the house in the suburbs. So she will be happier and healthier.

7. If you gain too much weight, your blood pressure will increase. If your blood pressure increases, your risk of stroke or heart attack rises. Therefore, gaining too much weight can increase your risk of stroke and heart attack.

8. 'Grow accustomed to the belief that death is nothing to us, since every good and evil lie in sensation. However, death is the deprivation of sensation. Therefore . . . death is nothing to us.' (Epicurus)

9. 'A cause-and-effect relationship is drawn [by those opposed to pornography] between men viewing pornography and men attacking women, especially in the form of rape. But studies and experts disagree as to whether any relationship exists between pornography and violence, between images and behavior. Even the pro-censorship Meese Commission Report admitted that the data connecting pornography to violence was unreliable.' (*Free Inquiry*, Fall 1997)

* 10. The existence of planets outside our solar system is a myth. There is no reliable empirical evidence at all showing that planets exist outside our solar system.

11. If Li Yang gets a high score on her test, she will have a perfect grade point average. If she gets a low score, she will drop out of school. She will get a high score on the test, so she will have a perfect grade point average.

12. Most philosophers are nerds, and Chris is a philosopher. Therefore, Chris is probably a nerd. Therefore, Chris probably has poor social skills, because most nerds have poor social skills.

13. Bill is a student at Queen's. No student at Queen's has won the Nobel Prize. Therefore, Bill has not won the Nobel Prize.

14. 'An international agreement proscribes the use of gas and so germ warfare must be developed.' (Germaine Greer, *The Female Eunuch*)

15. The only valid reasons for dishonourably discharging someone from the Canadian Armed Forces are health problems and violations of military regulations. So if Amal says he was dishonourably discharged for simply being gay, he is lying or is mistaken. He is not lying. So he is mistaken.

16. 'It is clear that archaeologists have not yet come to terms with dowsing [the practice of searching for underground water or treasure by paranormal means]. Where it has been the subject of tests, the tests have been so poorly designed and executed that any conclusion whatsoever could have been drawn from them. The fact that such tests are usually carried out only by researchers with a prior positive view of dowsing means that the conclusions will likely also be positive. The normal processes of peer review and scholarly discussion have also failed to uncover the lack of properly controlled test conditions in such studies as those of Bailey et al. and Locock, causing a generation of students and general readers in the United Kingdom, at least, to remain under the impression that the reality of archaeological dowsing had been all but confirmed by science.' (*Skeptical Inquirer*, March/April 1999)

* 17. There are at least two main views regarding the morality of war. Pacifism is the view that no war is ever justified because it involves the taking of human life. Just-war theory is the view that *some* wars are justified for various reasons—mostly because they help prevent great evils (such as massacres, 'ethnic cleansing', or world domination by a madman like Hitler) or because they are a means of self-defence. I think our own moral sense tells us that occasionally (as in the case of the Second World War, for example) violence is morally justified. It would be hard for anyone to deny that a war to prevent something like the Holocaust is morally right.

18. Some say that those without strong religious beliefs—non-believers in one form or another—cannot be moral. But millions upon millions of people have been non-believers or non-theists and yet have produced some of the most noble and most morally principled civilizations in history. Consider the Buddhists of Asia and the Confucianists of China. Consider also the great secular philosophers from the ancient Greeks to the likes of Bertrand Russell and John Searle of the twentieth century.

19. Maggie, Pierre, or Ling broke the window and stole the vase. Pierre couldn't have done it because he was studying in his room and was observed the whole time. Maggie couldn't have done it because she was out of town at the time and has witnesses to prove it. So the thief had to be Ling.

* 20. The picnic will probably be spoiled because there is a 90 per cent probability of rain.

21. The CN Tower will probably be attacked by terrorists within the next two years. The latest intelligence reports from CSIS confirm this prediction. Plus terrorists have already stated publicly that they intend to destroy various symbolic structures or monuments in the Canada, including the CN Tower and the Parliament Buildings.

22. We shouldn't pay Edward an allowance because he never does any work around the house, and he will probably just waste the money because he has no conception of the value of anything.

Assessing Long Arguments

The general principles of diagramming can help you when you have to evaluate arguments that are much longer and more complicated than most of those in this chapter. Some arguments are embedded in extended passages, persuasive essays, long reports, and even whole books. In such cases, the kind of *detailed* argument diagramming we use to analyze short passages won't help you much. In very lengthy works, our three-step diagramming procedure would be tedious and time-consuming—if not maddening. But the *general approach* used in the procedure *is* relevant to longer arguments.

When you have to evaluate a very long passage, you are almost always faced with three obstacles:

1. Only a small part of the writing may contain statements that serve as the premises and conclusion. (The rest is background information, reiterations of ideas, descriptions, examples, illustrations, asides, irrelevancies, and more.)
2. The premises or conclusion may be implicit.
3. Many longer works purporting to be filled with arguments contain very few arguments or none at all. (It's common for many books—even best sellers—to pretend to make a case for something but to be without any genuine arguments.)

Fortunately, you can usually overcome these impediments if you're willing to put in some extra effort. The following is a four-step procedure that can help.

Step 1. Study the text until you thoroughly understand it. You can't find the conclusion or premises until you know what you're looking for—and that requires having a clear idea of what the author is driving at. Don't try to find the conclusion or premises until you 'get it'. This understanding entails having an overview of a great deal of text, a bird's-eye view of the whole work.

Step 2. Find the conclusion. When you evaluate extended arguments, your first task, as in shorter writings, is to find the conclusion. There may be several main conclusions or one primary conclusion with several sub-conclusions (as depicted in some of the previous argument diagrams). Or the conclusion may be nowhere explicitly stated but embodied in metaphorical language or implied by large amounts of prose. In any case, your job is to come up with a single conclusion statement for each conclusion—even if you have to paraphrase large sections of text to do it.

Step 3. Identify the premises. Like the hunt for a conclusion, unearthing the premises may involve condensing large sections of text into manageable form— namely, single premise statements. To do this you need to disregard extraneous material and keep your eye on the 'big picture'. Just as in shorter arguments, premises in longer pieces may be implicit. At this stage you shouldn't try to incorporate the details of evidence into the premises, though you must take them into account to fully understand the argument.

Step 4. Diagram the argument. After you identify the premises and conclusion, diagram them just as you would a much shorter argument.

Food For Thought

No Arguments, Just Fluff

Once you get really good at spotting arguments in a variety of passages, you may be shocked to see that a massive amount of persuasive writing contains no arguments at all. Apparently many people—including some very good writers—think that if they clearly express their opinions, they have given an argument. You could look at this state of affairs as evidence that people are irrational—or you could view it as a time-saver since there's no need to waste your time on a bunch of unsupported opinions.

Unsupported opinions are everywhere, but they seem to permeate political writing, letters to the editor, and anything that's labelled 'spiritual'. Sometimes opinions are so weakly supported that they're almost indistinguishable from completely unsupported ones. Here's a taste:

> My family and friends have season tickets for the Buffalo Bandits. The disrespect that is shown to America by this team is appalling, particularly in this time of war. As both the Canadian and American national anthems are sung before each game, members of the team are hopping around, tugging at their uniforms, talking and carrying on amongst themselves. The players can't even wait for the national anthem to finish before they run off to their respective field positions. Whether one is for or against the war is irrelevant. Have some respect for America and what it stands for. (Letter to the editor, *Buffalo News* website)

There's no argument there, just indignation.

> So after a decade of progress, we have our smog problem back (as if it ever left). Another problem overlooked? Couldn't be because of all the giant behemoths (SUVs) on the road, could it? Nah. Or letting all the trucks from south of the border into our country without safety and smog inspections could it? Nah. It couldn't be because the government needs to have control of all it surveys? Nah. It must be something simpler, you think? Nah. (Letter to the editor, *Daily News* [Los Angeles] website)

There's no argument there either.

> How little is said or taught of the soul-life and its complete identification with the human being! To most men the soul is something apart from themselves that is only to be talked of and trusted in on special occasions: There is no real companionship, no intimate affiliation, between men's minds and souls in their everyday existence. Now there is in every man a divine power, and when that divinity, which is real self, is acknowledged and understood by the mind, it takes a very active part in man's life—indeed, it could fill at the very least one-half of his thought-life. [http://www.theosophy-nw.org/theosnw/path/oc-kt.htm Theosophy website]

Nope.

Let's see how this procedure works on the following selection:

The Case for Discrimination

Edgardo Cureg was about to catch a Continental Airlines flight home on New Year's Eve when he ran into a former professor of his. Cureg lent the professor his cell phone and, once on board, went to the professor's seat to retrieve it. Another passenger saw the two 'brown-skinned men' (Cureg is of Filipino descent, the professor Sri Lankan) conferring and became alarmed that they, and another man, were 'behaving suspiciously'. The three men were taken off the plane and forced to get later flights. The incident is now the subject of a lawsuit by the ACLU.

Several features of Cureg's story are worth noting. First, he was treated unfairly, in that he was embarrassed and inconvenienced because he was wrongly suspected of being a terrorist. Second, he was not treated unfairly, because he was not wrongly suspected. A fellow passenger, taking account of his apparent ethnicity, his sex and age, and his behavior, could reasonably come to the conclusion that he was suspicious. Third, passengers' anxieties, and their inclination to take security matters into their own hands, increase when they have good reason to worry that the authorities are not taking all reasonable steps to look into suspicious characters themselves. . . .

Racial profiling of passengers at check-in is not a panacea. John Walker Lindh could have a ticket; a weapon could be planted on an unwitting 73-year-old nun. But profiling is a way of allocating sufficiently the resources devoted to security. A security system has to, yes, discriminate—among levels of threat. (*National Review*, 1 July 2002)

> 'Our minds anywhere, when left to themselves, are always thus busily drawing conclusions from false premises.'
> —Henry David Thoreau

In this example, the author has given us a break by alluding to the conclusion in the title: Discrimination by racial profiling is a justified security measure. Notice that this conclusion is not explicitly stated in the text but is implied by various remarks, including 'A security system has to, yes, discriminate.' Given this conclusion, we can see that the entire first paragraph is background information—specifically, an example of racial profiling. The first premise is implicit. We glean it from the comments in the second paragraph: racial profiling is a reasonable response in light of our legitimate concerns about security. The second premise is explicit: profiling is a way of allocating the resources devoted to security.

Laid out in neat order, this argument looks like this:

(1) Racial profiling is a reasonable response in light of our legitimate concerns about security.
(2) Profiling is a way of allocating sufficiently the resources devoted to security.
(3) Therefore, discrimination by racial profiling is a justified security measure.

The diagram of this argument looks like this:

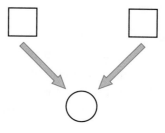

A fact that can further complicate the argument structure of a long passage is that complex arguments can sometimes be made up of simpler arguments (sub-arguments). For example, the conclusion of a simple argument can serve as a premise in another simple argument, with the resulting chain of arguments constituting a larger complex argument. Such a chain can be long. The complex argument can also be a mix of both deductive and inductive arguments. Fortunately, all you need to successfully analyze these complex arguments is mastery of the elementary skills discussed earlier. (Recall that we used both a circle *and* a square to indicate that a particular statement is acting as both a premise of one sub-argument and the conclusion of another sub-argument.)

The best way to learn how to assess long passages is to practise, which you can do in the following exercises. Be forewarned, however, that this skill depends heavily on your ability to understand the passage in question. If you do grasp the author's purpose, you can more easily paraphrase the premises and conclusion and uncover implicit statements. You will also be better at telling extraneous stuff from the real meat of the argument. In the 'Critical Thinking and Writing' section for this chapter, we continue this discussion of evaluating long arguments.

Exercise 3.10

For each of the following passages, (1) list the conclusion and premises and (2) diagram the argument.

* 1. 'There are those who maintain . . . that even if God is not required as the author of the moral law, he is nevertheless required as the enforcer of it, for without the threat of divine punishment, people will not act morally. But this position is [not plausible]. In the first place, as an empirical hypothesis about the psychology of human beings, it is questionable. There is no unambiguous evidence that theists are more moral than non-theists. Not only have psychological studies failed to find a significant correlation between frequency of religious

worship and moral conduct, but convicted criminals are much more likely to be theists than atheists. Second, the threat of divine punishment cannot impose a moral obligation, for might does not make right. Threats extort; they do not create a moral duty.' (*Free Inquiry*, Summer 1997)

2. I love your magazine but when I read your article on our new Prime Minister, I couldn't help but wonder whether the author is on drugs! He certainly has every right to speak out against the Prime Minister, but when he refers to him as 'some rich guy who has no idea what it's like to put in an honest day's work' it reminds me of the garbage rhetoric we're used to hearing from socialists, tree-huggers, and other left-wing nut-jobs. That kind of *ad hominem* attack is not only disrespectful to a man who is doing a damned good job as leader of our country (his party now enjoys a 52 per cent approval rating); garbage criticisms like that detract from the whole point of the article.

3. 'The fifth way [of proving that God exists] is taken from the governance of the world. We see that things that lack knowledge, such as natural bodies, act for an end, and this is evident from their acting always, or nearly always, in the same way, so as to obtain the best result. Hence it is plain that they achieve their end, not fortuitously, but designedly. Now whatever lacks knowledge cannot move towards an end, unless it be directed by some being endowed with knowledge and intelligence; as the arrow is directed by the archer. Therefore some intelligent being exists by whom all natural things are directed to their end; and this being we call God.' (Thomas Aquinas, *Summa Theologica*)

4. 'The first thing that must occur to anyone studying moral subjectivism [the view that the rightness or wrongness of an action depends on the beliefs of an individual or group] seriously is that the view allows the possibility that an action can be both right and not right, or wrong and not wrong, etc. This possibility exists because, as we have seen, the subjectivist claims that the moral character of an action is determined by individual subjective states; and these states can vary from person to person, even when directed toward the same action on the same occasion. Hence one and the same action can evidently be determined to have—simultaneously—radically different moral characters. . . . [If] subjectivism . . . does generate such contradictory conclusions, the position is certainly untenable.' (Phillip Montague, *Reason and Responsibility*)

5. I just heard about another lawsuit accusing the Vatican of hiding instances of sexual abuse by priests in Canada and the US. Sexual abuse is never ok, but I think such cases should be dismissed by courts in light of the community stature and function of priests and the benefits that accrue to society in the aftermath of the decision. Let's consider community stature first. The community stature of priests must always be taken into account in these abuse cases. A priest is not just anybody; he performs a special role in society—namely, to provide spiritual guidance and to remind people that there is both a moral

order and a divine order in the world. The priest's role is special because it helps to underpin and secure society itself. Anything that could undermine this role must be neutralized as soon as possible. Among those things that can weaken the priestly role are publicity, public debate, and legal actions. Abuse cases are better handled in private by those who are keenly aware of the importance of a positive public image of priests. And what of the benefits of curtailing the legal proceedings? The benefits to society of dismissing the legal case outweigh all the alleged disadvantages of continuing with public hearings. The primary benefit is the continued nurturing of the community's faith, without which the community would cease to function effectively.

Summary

Arguments come in two forms: deductive and inductive. A deductive argument is intended to provide logically conclusive support for a conclusion; an inductive one is intended to provide probable support for a conclusion. Deductive arguments can be valid or invalid whereas inductive arguments are strong or weak. A valid argument with true premises is said to be sound. A strong argument with true premises is said to be cogent.

Evaluating an argument is the most important skill of critical thinking. It involves finding the conclusion and premises, checking to see if the argument is deductive or inductive, determining its validity or strength, and discovering if the premises are true or false. Sometimes you also have to ferret out implicit, or unstated, premises.

Arguments can come in certain common patterns, or forms. Two valid forms that you will often run into are *modus ponens* (affirming the antecedent) and *modus tollens* (denying the consequent). Two common invalid forms are denying the antecedent and affirming the consequent.

Analyzing the structure of arguments is easier if you diagram them. Argument diagrams can help you visualize the function of premises and conclusions and the relationships among complex arguments with several sub-arguments.

Assessing very long arguments can be challenging because they may contain lots of verbiage but few or no arguments, and many premises can be implicit. Evaluating long arguments, though, requires the same basic steps as assessing short ones. (1) Ensure that you understand the argument, (2) find the conclusion, (3) find the premises, and (4) diagram the argument to clarify logical relationships.

Key Terms

Affirming the antecedent/*modus ponens*: A valid argument form:

> If *p*, then *q*.
> *p*.
> Therefore, *q*.

Affirming the consequent: An invalid argument form:

> If *p*, then *q*.
> *q*.
> Therefore, *p*.

Antecedent: The first part of a conditional statement (If *p*, then *q*), the component that begins with the word *if*.

Cogent argument: A strong inductive argument with all true premises.

Conditional statement: An 'if-then' statement; it consists of the antecedent (the part introduced by the word *if*) and the consequent (the part introduced by the word *then*).

Consequent: The part of a conditional statement (If *p*, then *q*) introduced by the word *then*.

Deductive argument: An argument intended to provide logically conclusive support for its conclusion.

Denying the antecedent: An invalid argument form:

> If *p*, then *q*.
> Not *p*.
> Therefore, not *q*.

Denying the consequent/*modus tollens*: A valid argument form:

> If *p*, then *q*.
> Not *q*.
> Therefore, not *p*.

Dependent premise: A premise that depends on at least one other premise to provide joint support to a conclusion. If a dependent premise is removed, the support that its linked dependent premises supply to the conclusion is undermined or completely cancelled out.

Disjunctive syllogism: A valid argument form:

> Either *p* or *q*.
> Not *p*.
> Therefore, *q*.

In the second premise of the syllogism, either disjunct can be denied.

Hypothetical syllogism: A valid argument made up of three hypothetical, or conditional, statements:

> If *p*, then *q*.
> If *q*, then *r*.
> Therefore, if *p*, then *r*.

Independent premise: A premise that does not depend on other premises to provide support to a conclusion. If an independent premise is removed, the support that other premises supply to the conclusion is not affected.

Inductive argument: An argument in which the premises are intended to provide probable, not conclusive, support for its conclusion.

Invalid argument: A deductive argument that fails to provide conclusive support for its conclusion.

Sound: Said of a deductively valid argument that has true premises.

Strong argument: An inductive argument that succeeds in providing probable—but not conclusive—support for its conclusion.

Syllogism: A deductive argument made up of three statements—two premises and a conclusion. See *modus ponens* and *modus tollens*.

Truth-preserving: A characteristic of a valid deductive argument in which the logical structure guarantees the truth of the conclusion if the premises are true.

Valid argument: A deductive argument that succeeds in providing conclusive support for its conclusion.

Weak argument: An inductive argument that fails to provide strong support for its conclusion.

Field Problems

1. Find a passage of 150–200 words claiming to present an argument for a particular view but actually being devoid of arguments. Look in magazine or newspaper letters to the editor or advocacy or political websites. Then rewrite the passage and include an argument for the original view.
2. Visit a website intended to support a particular view on a social or political issue. Using the information on the website, write a 300-word passage containing an argument for a view that the website might endorse.

Self-Assessment Quiz

1. What is a deductive argument? An inductive argument?
2. What is a valid argument? An invalid one? What is a strong inductive argument?
3. What is a sound argument?

Say whether the following arguments are deductive or inductive.

4. If you refuse to surrender, then you will be arrested. You refuse to surrender. Prepare yourself: you will be arrested.
5. There's an 80 per cent chance that the hurricane will veer northward tomorrow and hit Halifax. So Halifax will probably feel the force of the hurricane tomorrow.
6. Ethel is reckless. She is going to have an accident sooner or later.
7. Whatever Jack Layton says is true. He says that the Liberals are corrupt. So the Liberals are corrupt.

In each of the following arguments, identify the implicit premise that will make the argument either valid or strong.

8. Jones has never openly criticized substance abuse or excessive consumption of alcohol. He is a druggie.

9.   Maria failed her driving test three times. She's probably not paying attention.

10. If 60 per cent of people believe in astrology or tarot cards, the future of the country does not look bright. Grades in university science courses will probably drop dramatically.

11. For each of the following exercises, give an example of the argument pattern indicated.

   a.   *Modus ponens.*
   b.   *Modus tollens.*
   c.   Denying the antecedent.
   d.   Affirming the consequent.

Diagram the following arguments.

12. Cole is up to no good. He's been acting suspiciously for days, and he told Rachel that he was going to steal something valuable.

13. The sitcom *Corner Gas* is becoming really lame. The writing is predictable and plodding. The acting is worse than ever.

14. If dolphins have minds comparable to ours, then these creatures are self-conscious, intelligent, and creative. If they are self-conscious, then they should react appropriately when they see their reflections in a mirror. They do react appropriately. If they're intelligent, they should be able to solve complex problems. They can solve such problems. If they're creative, they should be able to create some form of art. In a rudimentary way, they do create art. They are definitely self-conscious, intelligent, and creative.

15. If the dictum to always tell the truth in all circumstances is a valid moral principle, then it should fit well with our considered moral judgments. But it does not fit well with our considered moral judgments because there are times when lying is actually the right thing to do, as when we lie to save a life. So the dictum to always tell the truth is not a valid moral principle.

16. I don't think that I should vote for any independent candidate in the next election. Independents never win, and I want the person I vote for to win. Also, independents have a tendency to be a little wacky. And we definitely don't need any more wacky politicians in power.

17. Creationism is an inadequate theory about the origins of life. It conflicts with science, and it is incapable of predicting any new facts.

Integrative Exercises

These exercises pertain to material in Chapters 1–3. For each of the following passages say whether it contains an argument. If it does, specify the conclusion and premises, any argument-indicator words, whether the argument is deductive or inductive, and whether it contains an example of face-saving or group-pressure thinking. Also identify any implicit premises and diagram the argument.

1. If Anne is in town, then she's staying at the Barbary Hotel. She's in town. Therefore, she's staying at the Barbary Hotel.

2. If the death penalty deterred anyone from crime, there would be a lower crime rate in countries that have the death penalty than in countries that do not. But crime rates are often higher in countries with the death penalty. So the death penalty is really no crime deterrent.

3. 'In the wake of the attacks of September 11th, 2001, the governments of Canada and the United States have passed sweeping anti-terrorism bills that effectively lay the groundwork for the criminalization of ideas. One consequence has been . . . the policing of freedom of expression. In Canada, a post-September 11th exhibit of contemporary Arab-Canadian art at the National Museum in Ottawa was abruptly cancelled by the organizers to allow the curators to "reconsider" the political works on display: the exhibition did go ahead as scheduled, but only after a determined public campaign challenging the museum's actions.' (*Alternative Press Review*, Spring 2002)

4. '[Is] there scientific evidence that prayer really works? . . . The problem with . . . any so-called controlled experiment regarding prayer is that *there can be no such thing as a controlled experiment concerning prayer*. You can never divide people into groups that received prayer and those that did not. The main reason is that there is no way to know that someone did not receive prayer. How would anyone know that some distant relative was not praying for a member of the group . . . identified as having received no prayer?' (*Free Inquiry*, Summer 1997)

5. The media in Canada are no longer simply reporting on the story, they have become the story. For weeks, Canadian media consumers have been spoon-fed an endless series of lamentations from some members of the Ottawa press corps over media access. (Editorial, *The National Post*, 26 April 2006)

6. '[C]urrent-day Christians use violence to spread their right-to-life message. These Christians, often referred to as the religious right, are well known for violent demonstrations against Planned Parenthood and other abortion clinics. Doctors and other personnel are threatened with death, clinics have been bombed, there have even been cases of doctors being murdered.' (Letter to the editor, *Daily Wildcat*, 17 September 2002)

7. Everyone knows how beneficial an operating casino can be to a city of this size. But since establishing a casino here is prohibitively expensive, we need to try to institute gambling on a smaller scale—by placing a few slot machines in government buildings.

8. The financial health of the banking industry will improve dramatically in the next few months. This improvement will immediately lead to more lenient loan terms for individuals. So it's better to wait a few months to ask a bank for a loan.

9. We evaluated the accuracy of recent news reports on a wide range of news topics. We focused on reports aired or published by three major media outlets. We found that 40 per cent of their news reports were highly inaccurate. So, though it's hard to believe, 40 per cent of all the news reports that people are exposed to are questionable.

10. A recent poll shows that 57 per cent of Canadians believe in life after death. In addition, there are thousands of first-person reports of either contacting dead people or seeing their spirit. Life after death is a reality.

11. These are Canadian geese. Canadian geese mate for life, so these Canadian geese are paired up forever.

12. If sex education in the schools can reduce the teen pregnancy rate or help delay the onset of teen sexual activity, I'm all for it. A recent study of several hundred teens showed that sex education in school lowered the incidence of teen pregnancy. We should have sex ed in all public schools.

13. The worst calamity that will befall the world in the next twenty years will be the use of small nuclear weapons by terrorists or rogue states. The death toll from such a state of affairs is likely to be higher than that of any other kind of human devastation. The United Nations just issued a report that comes to the same conclusion. We should act now to prevent the proliferation of nuclear weapons and nuclear-weapons-grade material from falling into the wrong hands.

14. Many surveys show that most people not only believe in 'remote viewing' (the ability to observe distant locations without using the physical senses) but also think that science has already proved its existence. This demonstrates that the majority of people are scientifically illiterate. If they understood the least bit about the methods of science and how it reaches conclusions, they would denounce silly ideas like remote viewing—or at least not accept them blindly.

15. Magazines regularly publish articles on 'the sexiest man alive' or 'the most beautiful woman in the world'. All you have to do to see that these claims of superior attractiveness are crazy is to stroll down any main thoroughfare in any nation's capital. There you will see people—male and female—who make the magazines' favourite personifications of beauty or sexiness look like dogs.

16. The biblical story of Noah and the ark is immediately shown to be a fraud or fantasy by one fact: the volume of dung produced by the ark's animals (one pair of everything!) would fill a hundred arks, and shovelling all that stuff overboard would have taken scores of labourers working round the clock for two years.

17. Peanuts are good for you. A million little monkeys can't be wrong.

18. 'There is no justice in the world. Amelia Earhart's plane went down, and despite fifty years of looking, no one has ever been able to find her. But Yasser Arafat's plane goes down, and he's rescued in fifteen minutes.' (Jay Leno, *The Tonight Show*)

19. 'So Stephen Harper has officially declared that the time for debating Canada's presence in Afghanistan is over (*Now* magazine, 16–22 March 2006). I have the utmost respect for our soldiers, but don't we owe it to them to have a legitimate debate on the issue to ensure they're there for the right reasons? Years into the mission, the government has completely lost sight of why we went in the first place and has become more concerned with saving face. Now that we're being told Canada might be in Afghanistan upwards of 10 years, there's never been a more important time for debating the issue. This idea of giving the government unquestioned support for war is dangerously close to the backwards mentality of the US.' (Letter to the editor, *Now* magazine, 23–29 March 2006)

20. Freedom is a necessary component of the good life. The good life is something that every human being has a right to. Everything that humans have a right to should be acquired by any means necessary. Therefore, any war conducted to secure freedom for any of us is justified.

Critical Thinking and Writing Exercise

From Thesis to Outline

In Module 1, we saw that the second step in writing an argumentative essay (after determining your thesis statement, or conclusion) is to create an outline. Outlines are useful because, among other things, they help avert disaster in the essay-writing phase. Imagine writing two-thirds of your essay then discovering that the second premise of your argument cannot be supported and is, in fact, false. You might have to throw out the whole argument and start over.

At the head of your outline, insert your thesis statement, expressing it as clearly and as precisely as possible. At every stage of outlining, you can then refer to the statement for guidance. The premises and conclusion of your argument (or arguments) will constitute the major points of your outline. The following, for example, is the preliminary outline for the essay discussed in Module 2:

Thesis: Allowing coal-burning power plants to emit more sulphur dioxide will most likely increase the incidence of respiratory illnesses.

I.   Excessive amounts of sulphur dioxide in the air have been linked to increases in the incidence of asthma and other respiratory illnesses.
II. Many areas of the country already have excessive amounts of sulphur dioxide in the air.
III. Most sulphur dioxide in the air comes from coal-burning power plants.
IV. Therefore, allowing coal-burning power plants to emit more sulphur dioxide will most likely increase the incidence of respiratory illnesses.

After you clearly state the premises, you need to ask yourself whether any of them need to be defended. As we discussed in Module 1, any premise likely to be questioned by your readers will need support. That is, the premise itself will need arguments to back it up, and the supporting arguments should be indicated in your outline. (Some premises, though, may not need support because they are obvious or generally accepted.) As discussed in Chapter 3, you can support a premise (claim) through deductive or inductive arguments with premises made up of examples, analogies, empirical evidence (such as scientific research or trustworthy observations), and authoritative judgments (such as those from reliable experts). Here's how the preceding outline might look with (fictional) supporting arguments clearly shown:

THESIS: Allowing coal-burning power plants to emit more sulphur dioxide will most likely increase the incidence of respiratory illnesses.

I.   Excessive amounts of sulphur dioxide in the air has been linked to increases in the incidence of asthma and other respiratory illnesses.

A. Environment Canada data show an association between high amounts sulphur dioxide and increased respiratory illnesses.

B. Cities that monitor air pollution have noted increases in hospital admissions for asthma and other respiratory illnesses when sulphur dioxide emissions are high.

II. Many areas of the country already have excessive amounts of sulphur dioxide in the air.

A. Scientists have reported high levels of sulphur dioxide in the air in fifteen major cities.

III. Most sulphur dioxide in the air comes from coal-burning power plants.

A. Many environmental scientists assert that coal-burning power plants are the source of most sulphur dioxide.

B. A few owners of coal-burning power plants admit that their plants emit most of the sulphur dioxide in their region.

IV. Therefore, allowing coal-burning power plants to emit more sulphur dioxide will most likely increase the incidence of respiratory illnesses.

You should expand your outline until you've indicated how you intend to provide support for each claim that requires it. This level of detail helps ensure that you will not encounter any nasty surprises in the writing phase.

Your essay should somehow address objections or criticisms that your readers are likely to raise and your outline should show how you intend to do this. Answering objections can make your case stronger and lend credibility to you as the writer. Sometimes it's best to address objections where they are likely to arise—in connection with specific premises or arguments. At other times, your essay may be more effective if you deal with objections at the end of it, near the conclusion.

As you work through your outline, don't be afraid to rework your thesis statement or to make changes in arguments. Satisfy yourself that the outline is complete and that it reflects a logical progression of points.

Argument and Ambiguity

Good writing is clear writing. Writing that lacks clarity is ineffective—not to mention exasperating to its readers and sometimes embarrassing to its writer. An argument with unclear premises or conclusion is likewise ineffective. The lack of clarity undermines the argument, perhaps even rendering it useless.

Ambiguity is one of the many ways that a piece of writing can be unclear. A term or statement is ambiguous if it has more than one meaning and if the context doesn't reveal which meaning is intended. Consider these claims:

1. Morgan ate the ice cream with relish.
2. Kids make nutritious snacks.
3. A quarter of a million Chinese live on water.

4. John met the girl that he married at a dance.
5. Helen saw the bird with powerful binoculars.
6. Luc hit the boy with a book.
7. The guy was all over the road; I had to swerve a number of times before I hit him.
8. Officers help dog bite victims.
9. Include your children when baking cookies.

All these claims are ambiguous, but they are ambiguous in different ways. Claims 1, 2, and 3 involve *semantic ambiguities*. Semantic ambiguities are due to possible multiple meanings of a word or phase. In claim 1 the phrase 'with relish' could mean 'accompanied by a condiment' or 'with pleasure or delight'. In claim 2 the word 'make' could mean either 'prepare' or 'constitute'—a difference between the kids' making food and *being* food. In claim 3 the phrase 'live on water' could mean 'subsist by ingesting water' or 'reside on water'—a distinction between the culinary and the sociological.

Semantic ambiguities often spark unnecessary and tedious debates. Disputants, for example, may disagree dramatically over whether a photo in a magazine is pornographic—but they disagree only because they have different ideas about what the term 'pornographic' means. They may actually be in agreement about which photos they find offensive. But to one person, 'pornographic' may describe any representation of nudity. To another person, 'pornographic' may refer only to depictions of sexual acts.

Claims 4, 5, and 6 involve *syntactic ambiguities*. Syntactic ambiguities arise because of the sloppy way that words are combined. In claim 4 did John meet his bride-to-be at a dance, or did he marry her at a dance? In claim 5 did Helen use the binoculars, or did the bird use them? In claim 6 did Luc use a book to smack the boy, or did Luc smack a boy who was carrying a book?

Claims 7, 8, and 9 are not plainly either semantically or syntactically ambiguous, but they are unclear (and silly) just the same. In claim 7 was the writer deliberately trying to hit the guy or not? In claim 8 are the officers helping people who had been bitten or are they using dogs to bite people? In claim 9 are we supposed to bake cookies alongside our children—or bake the children *into the cookies*?

As a critical reader, your job is to be on alert for possible ambiguities, to understand the contexts that can help clear up ambiguities, and to constantly ask, 'What does this mean?' If the meaning of a claim is unclear, you are under no obligation to accept it. Likewise, if an argument contains ambiguous claims, you need not accept the argument.

As a critical writer, your job is *not* to suppose that your readers will understand exactly what you mean but to strive to be perfectly clear about what you mean. Inexperienced writers too often assume that because they know what they mean, others will know too. The best corrective for unclear or ambiguous writing is the objective stance—the viewing of your writing from the standpoint of others. Good writers try hard to view their writing as others will, to step back mentally and try to imagine coming to their writing for the first time. In effect, they ask themselves, 'Will my audience understand what I mean?' Achieving an objective attitude toward your writing is not easy. One thing that helps is to put your writing aside for a day or two after you complete it and then read it cold. Often after this 'cooling down' period, passages that you thought were unambiguous turn out to be murky.

Another good tactic, of course, is to state explicitly what you intend your words to mean, by offering a definition. But of course, you can't offer definitions for *every* word you use—not without ruining the 'flow' of your essay. So definitions, while useful, must be used sparingly. (For more about definitions, see 'Defining Terms' on page 165.)

Writing Assignments

1. Create an outline for Essay 3 ('Marine Parks') in Appendix A. Specify the thesis statement, each premise, arguments supporting premises, any objections considered, and the conclusion.

2. Study the argument presented in Essay 7 ('Yes, Human Cloning Should Be Permitted') in Appendix A. Identify the conclusion and the premises and objections considered. Then write a two-page critique of the essay's argument.

3. Select an issue from the following list and write a three-page paper defending a claim pertaining to the issue. Follow the procedure discussed in the text for outlining the essay and choosing a thesis and an appropriate argument to defend it. Where necessary, clarify terms.

    - Should same-sex marriage be allowed in Canada?
    - In the fight against terrorism, should law-enforcement agencies be allowed to spy on Canadian citizens by monitoring their email, wiretapping their phones, and checking records from public libraries—all without warrants?
    - Should a city government be allowed to ban art exhibits if they are deemed anti-religious or blasphemous?
    - Does pornography lead to violence against women?

Part Two
Reasons

Chapter 4

Reasons for Belief and Doubt

Chapter Objectives

When Claims Conflict

You will be able to

- understand that when a claim conflicts with other claims we have good reason to accept, we have good grounds for doubting it.
- recognize that if a claim conflicts with our background information, we have good reason to doubt it.
- appreciate that when we are confronted with a claim that is neither completely dubious nor fully credible, we should proportion our belief to the evidence.
- realize that it is not reasonable to believe a claim when there is no good reason for doing so.

Experts and Evidence

You will be able to

- understand what makes someone an expert and what does not.
- understand that if a claim conflicts with expert opinion, we have good reason to doubt it.
- realize that when the experts disagree about a claim, we have good reason to doubt it.
- recognize fallacious appeals to authority.
- distinguish true experts from non-experts by using the four indicators of expertise.

Personal Experience

You will be able to

○ understand that it is reasonable to accept the evidence provided by personal experience only if there is no good reason to doubt it.

○ appreciate the importance of the common factors that can give us good reason to doubt the reliability of personal experience—impairment, expectation, and innumeracy.

Fooling Ourselves

You will be able to

○ appreciate why we need to resist the human tendency to resist contrary evidence.

○ become sensitive to the possibility of confirmation bias.

○ be alert to the possibility of the availability error.

Claims in the News

You will be able to

○ gain a basic understanding of how the news media work and what factors influence the claims that they generate.

○ understand the skills involved in evaluating claims in the news.

Advertising and Persuasion

You will be able to

○ understand and apply the guiding principle for thinking critically about advertising.

○ gain familiarity with common tactics of persuasion used in advertising.

Let's remind ourselves once again why we've come this way. If we care whether our beliefs are true or reliable, whether we can safely use them to guide our steps and inform our choices, then we must care about the reasons for accepting those beliefs. The better the reasons for acceptance, the more likely are the beliefs, or statements, to be true. Inadequate reasons, no reasons, or fake reasons (discussed in the next chapter) should lead us not to accept a statement, but to doubt it.

As we saw in earlier chapters, the reasons for accepting a statement are often spelled out in the form of an argument, with the statement being the conclusion. The reasons and conclusion together might compose a deductive argument or an inductive argument. In such cases, the reasons are normally there in plain sight. But in our daily lives statements, or claims, usually confront us alone without any accompanying stated reasons. An unsupported claim may be the premise of an argument (and its truth value may then determine whether the argument is sound or cogent). Or it may simply be a stand-alone assertion of fact. Either way, if we care whether the claim is acceptable, we must try to evaluate the claim as it stands.

'The whole problem with the world is that fools and fanatics are always so certain of themselves, but wiser people so full of doubts.'
—Bertrand Russell

Of course, it helps to be knowledgeable about the subject matter of a claim. But it can be even more useful to understand and apply some critical-thinking principles for assessing unsupported claims. Let's take a close look at these principles.

Food For Thought

Favourite Unsupported Claims

In the Information Age, you don't have to look far for unsupported claims. They jump out at you from all directions. Many of them are a joy to behold because they are so imaginative, unusual, or provocative. They don't offer much of a challenge for critical thinkers, but they are certainly fun. The following is a little sampling from cyberspace.

- 'The reason why they call it KFC is because they cannot use the word chicken anymore. Why? KFC does not use real chickens. They actually use genetically manipulated organisms. These so called "chickens" are kept alive by tubes inserted into their bodies to pump blood and nutrients throughout their structure. They have no beaks, no feathers, and no feet. Their bone structure is dramatically shrunk to get more meat out of them. This is great for KFC because they do not have to pay so much for their production costs. There is no more plucking of the feathers or the removal of the beaks and feet. The government has told them to change all of their menus so they do NOT say chicken anywhere. If you look closely you will notice this. Listen to their commercials, I guarantee you will not see or hear the word chicken.'
- '[Enron founder Kenneth] Lay's powerful friends helped him fake his death to escape sentencing in one of the biggest corporate frauds in US history.'
- 'Phasing out the human race by voluntarily ceasing to breed will allow Earth's biosphere to return to good health. Crowded conditions and resource shortages will improve as we become less dense.'
- 'The Reverse Speech phenomenon, discovered by Australian researcher David John Oates, demonstrates that a person's true thoughts and feelings are naturally imbedded backwards in his speech.'
- 'Most people are not aware that the cartoonish "Bigfoot" figure is a distorted product of ancient and modern stories describing a real, but unacknowledged species that is still occasionally observed today in North American forests.'
- 'The main goal of the Bodhi Foundation is to present The Truth—The Sacred Secrets about Angels and to prevent damage to Invisible Worlds because of spacecrafts or high-altitude satellites or the shooting of high-powered lasers from Earth Countries.'
- 'Clothing designer Liz Claiborne appeared on a national television talk show and said that she was a Satan worshipper and that the profits of her company were being given to the Church of Satan.'

When Claims Conflict

Suppose you come across this claim in a reputable local newspaper:

[Claim 1] The historic CHUM–CityTV Building at the corner of Queen and John was demolished yesterday to make way for a parking lot.

But say you have very good reasons to believe this claim:

[Claim 2] The historic CHUM–CityTV Building at the corner of Queen and John was NOT demolished yesterday to make way for a parking lot.

What do you make of such a conflict between claims? Well, as a good critical thinker, you can know at least that you have good reason to doubt claim 1 and therefore have no good grounds for accepting it. You have good reason to doubt it because it conflicts with another claim you have good reason to believe (claim 2). When two claims conflict, they simply cannot both be true; at least one of them has to be false. So this principle comes into play:

If a claim conflicts with other claims we have good reason to accept, we have good grounds for doubting it.

With conflicting claims, you are not justified in believing either one of them until you resolve the conflict. Sometimes this job is easy. If, for example, the competing claims are reports of personal observations, you can often decide between them by making further observations. If a friend says your dog is sleeping on top of your car, and you say your dog is not sleeping on top of your car (because you checked a short time ago), you can see who's right by simply looking at the roof of your car. (Remember, though, that even personal observations can sometimes mislead us, as we'll soon see.)

Many times, however, sorting out conflicting claims requires a deeper inquiry. You may need to do some research to see what evidence exists for each of the claims. In the best-case scenario, you may quickly discover that one of the claims is not credible because it comes from an unreliable source (a subject taken up in the next few pages).

Now suppose that you're confronted with another type of conflict—this time a conflict between a claim and your **background information**. Background information is that huge collection of very well-supported beliefs that we all rely on to inform our actions and choices. A great deal of this lore consists of basic facts about everyday things, beliefs based on very good evidence (including our own personal observations and excellent authority), and justified claims that we would regard as 'common sense' or 'common knowledge'. Suppose then that you're asked to accept this unsupported claim:

Some babies can bench-press a five-hundred-pound weight.

Food For Thought

Fact and Opinion

When we evaluate claims, we are often concerned with making a distinction between facts and opinions. But just what is the difference? We normally use the word 'fact' in two senses. First, we may use it to refer to a state of affairs—as in 'Examine the evidence and find out the facts.' Second, and more commonly, we use fact to refer to true statements—as in 'John smashed the dinnerware—that's a fact.' Thus, we say that some claims, or statements, are facts (or factual) and some are not. We use the word opinion, however, to refer to a belief—as in 'It's John's opinion that he did not smash the dinnerware.' Some opinions are true, so they are facts. Some opinions are not true, so they are not facts.

Sometimes we may hear somebody say, 'That's a matter of opinion.' What does this mean? Often it's equivalent to something like 'Opinions differ on this issue' or 'There are many different opinions on this.' But it also frequently means that the issue is not a matter of objective fact but is entirely subjective, a matter of individual taste. Statements expressing matters of opinion in this latter sense are not the kind of things that people can disagree on, just as two people cannot sensibly disagree about whether they like chocolate ice cream.

You are not likely to give much credence to this claim for the simple reason that it conflicts with an enormous number of your background beliefs concerning human physiology, gravity, weightlifting, and who knows what else.

Or how about this claim:

The Prime Minister is entirely under the control of the chief justice of the Supreme Court of Canada.

This claim is not as outlandish as the previous one, but it too conflicts with our background beliefs, specifically those having to do with the structure and workings of the Canadian government. So we would have good reason to doubt this one also.

The principle exemplified here is:

If a claim conflicts with our background information, we have good reason to doubt it.

Other things being equal, the more background information the claim conflicts with, the more reason we have to doubt it. We would normally—and rightfully—assign a low probability to any claim that conflicts with a great deal of our background information.

You would be entitled, for example, to have some doubt about the claim that Joan is late for work if it conflicts with your background information that Joan has never been late for work in the ten years you've known her. But you are entitled to have very strong doubts about, and to assign very low credibility to, the claim that André can turn a stone into gold just by touching it. You could even reasonably dismiss the claim out of hand. Such a claim conflicts with too much of what we know about the physical world.

It's always possible, of course, that a conflicting claim is true and some of our background information is unfounded. So many times it's reasonable for us to examine a conflicting claim more closely. If we find that it has no good reasons in its favour and that it is not credible, we may reject it. If, on the other hand, we discover that there are strong reasons for accepting the new claim, we may need to revise our background information. For example, we may be forced to accept the claim about André's golden touch (and to rethink some of our background information) if the claim is backed by strong supporting evidence. Our background information would be in need of some serious revision if André could produce this stone-to-gold transformation repeatedly under scientifically controlled conditions that ruled out error, fraud, and trickery.

So it is not reasonable to accept a claim if there is good reason to doubt it. And sometimes, if the claim is dubious enough, we may be justified in dismissing a claim out of hand. But what should we believe about a claim that is not quite dubious enough to discard immediately and yet not worthy of complete acceptance? We should measure out our belief according to the strength of reasons. That is,

We should proportion our belief to the evidence.

The more evidence a claim has in its favour, the stronger our belief in it should be. Weak evidence for a claim warrants weak belief; strong evidence warrants strong belief. And the strength of our beliefs should vary across this spectrum as the evidence dictates.

Implicit in all of the foregoing is a principle that deserves to be explicit because it's so often ignored:

It's not reasonable to believe a claim when there is no good reason for doing so.

The famous twentieth-century philosopher Bertrand Russell tried hard to drive this idea home. As he put it, 'It is undesirable to believe a proposition when there is no ground whatever for supposing it true.'[1] Russell claimed that if the use of this principle became widespread, social life and political systems would be transformed.

> 'A belief which leaves no place for doubt is not a belief; it is a superstition.'
> —José Bergamin

Experts and Evidence

When an unsupported claim doesn't conflict with what we already know, we are often justified in believing it because it comes from experts. An **expert** is someone who is more knowledgeable in a particular subject area or field than most other people are. Experts provide us with reasons for believing a claim because, in their specialty areas, they are more likely to be right than we are. They are more likely to be right because (1) they have access to more information on the subject than we do and (2) they are better at judging that information than we are. Experts are familiar with the established facts and existing data in their field and know how to properly evaluate that information. Essentially, this means that they have a handle on the information and know how to assess the evidence and arguments for particular claims involving that information. They are true authorities on a specified subject. Someone who knows the lore of a field but can't evaluate the reliability of a claim is no expert.

In a complex world where we can never be knowledgeable in every field, we must rely on experts—a perfectly legitimate state of affairs. But good critical thinkers are careful about expert opinion, guiding their use of experts by some common-sense principles. One such principle is this:

If a claim conflicts with expert opinion, we have good reason to doubt it.

This tenet follows from our definition of experts. If they really are more likely to be right than non-experts about claims in their field, then any claims that conflict with expert opinion are, at least initially, dubious.

Here's the companion principle to the first:

When the experts disagree about a claim, we have good reason to doubt it.

If a claim is in dispute among experts, then non-experts can have no good reason for accepting (or rejecting) it. Throwing up your hands and arbitrarily deciding to believe or disbelieve the claim is not a reasonable response. The claim must remain in doubt until the experts resolve the conflict or you resolve the conflict yourself by becoming informed enough to decide competently on the issues and evidence involved—a course that's possible but usually not feasible for non-experts.

Sometimes we may have good reason to be suspicious of unsupported claims, even when they are purportedly derived from expert opinion. Our doubt is justified when a claim comes from someone deemed to be an expert who in fact is not an expert. When we rely on such bogus expert opinion, we commit the fallacy known as the **appeal to authority**.

The fallacious appeal to authority usually happens in one of two ways. First, we may find ourselves disregarding this important rule of thumb: just because someone is an expert in one field, he or she is not necessarily an expert in another. The opinion of experts generally carries more weight than our own—but only in their

"None of my friends could diagnose the symptoms, Doctor. You're my last hope!"

Medical Economics

areas of expertise. Any opinions that they proffer outside their fields are no more authoritative than those of non-experts. Outside their fields, they are not experts.

We needn't look far for real-life examples of such skewed appeals to authority. On any day of the week we may be urged to accept claims in one field that are based on the opinion of an expert from unrelated fields. An electrical engineer or Nobel Prize–winning chemist may assert that certain herbs can cure cancer. A radio talk-show host with a degree in physiology may give advice in psychology. A professor of genetics declares that human clones would have a distorted sense of identity. A botanist may say that the evidence for the existence of ESP is conclusive. Sometimes the lack of relevant expertise is quite subtle: a scientist with expertise relevant to detecting global warming may not have the relevant expertise to tell us what we can or should *do about* global warming. The point is not that these experts can't be right, but that their expertise in a particular field doesn't give us reason to believe their pronouncements in another. There is no such thing as a general expert, only experts in specific subject areas.

Second, we may fall into a fallacious appeal to authority by regarding a non-expert as an expert. We forget that a non-expert—even one with prestige, status, or sex appeal—is still a non-expert. Movie stars, TV actors, renowned athletes, and famous politicians endorse products of all kinds in TV and print advertising. But when they speak outside their areas of talent and experience (which is almost

Food For Thought

Are Doctors Experts?

Yes and no. Physicians are certainly experts in the healing arts, in diagnosing and treating disease and injury. They know and understand the relevant facts and they have the where-withal to make good judgments regarding those facts. But are physicians experts in determining whether a particular treatment is safe and effective? Contrary to what many believe, the answer is, in general, no. Determining the safety and efficacy of treatments is a job for scientists (who may also be physicians). Medical scientists conduct controlled studies to try to ascertain whether treatment X can safely alleviate disease A—something that usually cannot be determined by a doctor interacting with her patients in a clinical setting. Medical studies are designed to control all kinds of extraneous variables that can skew the study results, the same extraneous variables that are often present in the doctor's office.

Critical thinkers should keep this distinction in mind because they will often hear people assert that Treatment Y works just because Dr Wonderful says so.

(For an example of the process used for testing medical treatments, see the section on 'Testing Scientific Theories' on page 382.)

Fallacious appeal to authority: Talk show host Larry King has done numerous commercials touting supplement products such as Ginsana brand ginseng and Garlique brand garlic pills. Photo: Allstar Picture Library/Alamy

'An expert is a man who has made all the mistakes which can be made in a very narrow field.'
—Niels Bohr

always the case), they give us no good reason for believing that the products are as advertised. Advertisers, of course, know this, but they hope that we will buy the products anyway because of the appeal or attractiveness of the celebrity endorsers.

Historically the regarding of a non-expert as an expert has probably been the most prevalent form of the appeal to authority—with disastrous results. Political, religious, tribal, and cultural leaders have often been considered to be authorities, not because they knew the facts and could judge the evidence correctly, but because culture, tradition, or whim dictated that they be regarded as authorities. When these 'authorities' spoke, people listened and believed—then went to war, persecuted unbelievers, or undertook countless other ill-conceived projects. If we are to avoid this trap, we must look beyond mere labels and titles and ask, 'Does this person provide us with any good reasons or evidence?'

This question, of course, is just another way of asking if someone is a true expert. How can we tell? To be considered an expert, someone must have shown that he or she can assess relevant evidence and arguments and arrive at well-supported conclusions in a particular field. What are the indicators that someone has this essential kind of expertise? There are several that provide clues to someone's ability, but they do not guarantee the possession of true expertise.

In most fields, the following two indicators are considered minimal prerequisites for being considered an expert:

1. Education and training from reputable institutions or programs in the relevant field (usually evidenced by degrees or certificates).
2. Experience in making reliable judgments in the field (generally the more years of experience the better).

But, unfortunately, people can have the requisite education and experience and still not know what they're talking about in the field in question. Sadly, in the real world there are well-trained, experienced auto mechanics who do terrible work—and tenured PhD's whose professional judgment is iffy. Two additional indicators, though, are more revealing:

3. Reputation among peers (as reflected in the opinions of others in the same field, relevant prestigious awards, and positions of authority).
4. Professional accomplishments.

These two indicators are more helpful because they are very likely to be correlated with the intellectual qualities expected in true experts. People with excellent reputations among their professional peers and with significant accomplishments to their credit are usually true experts.

As we've seen, we are often justified in believing an unsupported claim because it's based on expert opinion. But if we have reason to doubt the opinion of the experts, we are not justified in believing the claim on the basis of that opinion. And chief among possible reasons for doubt (aside from conflicting expert opinion) is bias. When experts are biased, they are motivated by something other than the search for the truth—perhaps financial gain, loyalty to a cause, professional ambition, emotional needs, political outlook, sectarian dogma, personal ideology, or some other judgment-distorting factor. Therefore, if we have reason to believe that an expert is biased, we are not justified in accepting the expert's opinion.

But how can we tell when experts are biased? There are no hard-and-fast rules here. In the more obvious cases, we often suspect bias when an expert is being paid

Food For Thought

Evaluating Internet Sources

Can you trust the information you find on the Internet? In most cases, no. But if you understand how to judge the reliability of websites, and you're willing to spend some time doing the judging, you can often uncover material that is trustworthy and useful. Finding credible information online takes some effort because, unlike books and magazines, most of the information on the Internet is not screened by editors, fact-checkers, or anyone else before it hits cyberspace. Anyone can say anything on the Internet. Thus the watchwords of online research should be reasonable skepticism. If you want to know more about evaluating online sources, a good place to start is a college or university library. Many of them have free websites featuring excellent guides to Internet research. Duke University, for example, has such a site (http://www.lib.duke.edu/libguide/evaluating_web.htm). Among other things, it offers a checklist of questions to ask about online sources to help you assess their credibility. Some of these questions follow, broken down by category.

Authority

- Who wrote the material? Look for the author's name near the top or the bottom of the website. If you can't find a name, look for a copyright credit (©) or link to an organization.
- What are the author's credentials? Look for biographical information or the author's affiliations (university department, organization, corporate title, etc.).
- Could the credentials be made up? Anyone who has visited a chat room knows that people don't always identify themselves accurately.
- Did the author include contact information? Look for an email link, address, or phone number for the author. A responsible author should give you the means to contact him or her.

Whose Website Is This?

- What organization is sponsoring the website? Look at the domain (.com, .edu, .org, etc.). Look for an 'about this site' link. Also look for a tilde (~) in the URL, which usually identifies a personal directory on a website. Be careful of a website that has a tilde in its URL. Internet service provider sites (AOL, Sympatico, MSN, etc.) and online community sites (MySpace, Friendster, GeoCities, etc.) feature personal pages. Be careful of online material from those sites, too.

Purpose or Intended Audience

- What is the purpose of the site? Why did the author create it? The purpose could be advertising, advocacy, news, entertainment, opinion, fandom, scholarship, satire, and so on. Some pages have more than one purpose. For example, http://www.dowjones.com provides free business information but also encourages you to subscribe to the *Wall Street Journal* or other Dow Jones products.

Current?

- Is there a date at the top or bottom of the website? But note: A recent date doesn't necessarily mean the information is current. The content might be years out of date even if the given date is recent. (The last update of the page might have consisted of someone changing an email address or fixing a typo.)
- Is the information up to date? This takes a little more time to determine. Compare the information on the website to information available through other sources. Broken links are one measure of an out-of-date page. In general, information about science, technology, and business ages quickly. Information in the humanities and social sciences ages less quickly. However, depending on your research, old information can still be perfectly valid.

Objectivity versus Bias

- Is the author being objective or biased? Biased information is not necessarily 'bad', but you must take the bias into account when interpreting or using the information given. Look at the facts the author provides, and the facts the author doesn't provide. Are the facts cited accurately and completely? Is the author fair, balanced, and moderate in his or her views, or overly emotional or extreme? Taking the author's credentials into account, try to identify any conflict of interest. Determine if the advertising is clearly separated from the objective information on the page.

Support

- Does the author support the information he or she uses? Look for links or citations to sources. Some academic websites include bibliographies.
- Is the support respectable? Does the material cite well-known sources or authorities? Does the website cite a variety of sources? Do other websites on the same topic cite some of the same sources? The website in question should have a mix of internal links (links to websites on the same site or by the same author) and external links (links to other sources or experts). If a website makes it hard for you to check the support, be suspicious.[2]

by special-interest groups or companies to render an opinion, or when the expert expresses very strong belief in a claim even though there is no evidence to support it, or when the expert stands to gain financially from the actions or policies that he or she supports.

It's true that many experts can render unbiased opinions and do high-quality research even when they have a conflict of interest. Nevertheless, in such situations we have reasonable grounds to suspect bias—unless we have good reason to believe that the suspicion is unwarranted. These good reasons might include the fact that the expert's previous opinions in similar circumstances have been reliable or that he or she has a solid reputation for always offering unbiased assessments.

Finally, keep in mind that there are certain kinds of issues that we probably don't want experts to settle for us. Indeed, in most cases the experts cannot settle them for us. These issues usually involve moral, social, or political questions. If we're intellectually conscientious, we want to provide our own final answers to such questions, though we may draw heavily on the analyses and arguments provided by experts. We may study what the experts have to say and the conclusions they draw. But we want ultimately to come to our own conclusions. We prefer this approach in large part because the questions are so important and because the

Food For Thought

Do Non-experts Know Best?

Some people have a bias against experts—all experts. Their thoughts on the subject might run something like this: 'It's the uneducated ones, the simple seekers of knowledge who are the truly wise, for their thinking has not yet been corrupted by ivory-tower learning and highbrow theorizing that's out of touch with the real world. Thus the wisdom of the non-expert is to be preferred over the expert whenever possible.' This attitude is, oddly enough, sometimes embraced by very highly educated people. There's a strong strain of it, for example, among New Agers and advocates of some alternative, or unconventional, medicine.

This non-expertism is related to the appeal to ignorance discussed in Chapter 5. (The appeal to ignorance says that since there's no evidence refuting a position, it must be true.) The problem is that both tacks, though psychologically compelling, are fallacious. A lack of good reasons—evidence or expert testimony—does not constitute proof of a claim.

The history of science shows that virtually all notable scientific discoveries have been made by true experts—men and women who were fully knowledgeable about their subject matter. There have been many more instances, however, of cocksure non-experts who proposed theories, cures, and solutions to problems that turned out to be worthless.

Review Notes

Conflicting Claims

- If a claim conflicts with other claims that we have good reason to accept, we have good grounds for doubting it.
- If a claim conflicts with our background information, we have good reason to doubt it.
- We should proportion our belief to the evidence.
- It's not reasonable to believe a claim when there is no good reason for doing so.
- If a claim conflicts with expert opinion, we have good reason to doubt it.
- When the experts disagree about a claim, we have good reason to doubt it.

answers we give help define who we are. What's more, the experts usually disagree on these issues. So even if we wanted the experts to settle one of these questions for us, they probably couldn't.

Personal Experience

We accept a great many claims because they are based on personal experience—our own or someone else's. Personal experience, broadly defined, arises from our senses, our memory, and our judgment involved in those faculties. In countless cases, personal experience is our evidence (or part of the evidence) that something is or is not the case. You believe that Jack caused the traffic accident because you, or someone else, witnessed it. You think that the herbal tea cured your headache because the pain went away after you drank it. You believe that your friend can bend spoons with her mind because you saw her do it at a party. You're sure that it was the other guy, not you, who threw the first punch, because that's how you remember the incident. Or, as a member of a jury, you vote to convict the defendant because eyewitness testimony puts him at the scene of the crime with a gun in his hand. But can you trust personal experience to reveal the truth?

The answer is a qualified 'yes'. And here's the qualification in the form of an important principle:

> *It's reasonable to accept the evidence provided by personal experience only if there's no good reason to doubt it.*

If we have no good reason to doubt what our personal experience reveals to us, then we're justified in believing it. This means that if our faculties are working properly and our use of them is unimpeded by anything in our environment, we're entitled to accept what our personal experience tells us. If we seem to see a cat on the mat under good viewing conditions—that is, we have no reason to believe that our observations are impaired by, say, poor lighting, cracked glasses, or too many beers—then we're justified in believing that there's a cat on the mat.

The problem is that personal experience, though generally reliable, is not infallible. Under certain circumstances, our senses, memory, and judgment can't be trusted. It's easy enough to identify these circumstances in an abstract way, as you'll see later. The harder job is (1) to determine when they actually occur in real-life situations and (2) to avoid them or taking them into account.

The rest of this section is a rundown of some of the more common factors that can give us good reason to doubt the reliability of personal experience.

Impairment

This should be obvious: If our perceptual powers are somehow impaired or impeded, we have reason to doubt them. The unambiguous cases are those in which our senses are debilitated because we are ill, injured, tired, stressed out, excited, drugged, drunk, distracted, or disoriented. And just as clear are the situations that interfere with sensory input—when our environment is, say, too dark, too bright, too noisy, or too hazy. If any of these factors are in play, the risk of misperception is high, which gives us reason to doubt the trustworthiness of what we experience.

Memories can be affected by many of the same factors that interfere with accurate perception. They are especially susceptible to distortion if they are formed during times of stress—which helps explain why the memories of people who witness crimes or alleged ghosts are so often unreliable. These situations are understandably stressful.

The impairment of our faculties is complicated by the peculiar way they operate. Contrary to what many believe, they are not like recording devices that make exact mental copies of objects and events in the world. Research suggests that they are more like artists who use bits of sensory data or memory fragments to concoct creative representations of things, not exact replicas. Our perception and memory are constructive, which means that what we perceive and remember is to some degree fabricated by our minds. For example, you see a man standing in the shadows by the road—then discover when you get closer that the man is a tree stump. Or you are anxiously awaiting a phone call from Aunt Mary, and when a call comes and you hear the person's voice, you're sure it's her—then realize that it's some guy asking for a charitable donation. Or while you're in the shower you hear the phone ring—but no one is calling, and the ringing is something your mind is making up.

The constructive workings of our minds help us solve problems and deal effectively with our environment. But they can also hinder us by manufacturing too much of our experiences from too little data. Unfortunately, the constructive tendency is

> 'Besides learning to see, there is another art to be learned—not to see what is not.'
> —Maria Mitchell

Food For Thought

Tinkering with Your Memory

The memories of eyewitnesses are notoriously unreliable. One reason is that your memory of an event can be altered if you later receive new information regarding the event. Research shows that your memory can be changed in this way, but you won't know it. You will be sincerely convinced that your altered memory is the original memory. Research studies have uncovered this phenomenon again and again. Here's a description of the classic case:

> Once upon a time, a man (whom we'll call Mike) stumbled upon an armed robbery in a hardware store. The robber rummaged around the cluttered store brandishing a silver weapon; finally, he stole all the money. Then, almost as an afterthought, he grabbed a hand calculator and a hammer, putting these in his satchel as he left the store. The police were summoned immediately, but before they arrived, Mike talked to another customer about the robbery. We'll call her Maria. Maria told Mike that she saw the robber grab a calculator and a screwdriver, stuffing them in his satchel as he left the store. The police arrived, and when they questioned Mike, he recounted the robbery at some length. He described in detail the silver weapon, the money, and the calculator. When the police asked him about a tool that they heard had been taken, 'Did you see if it was a hammer or a screwdriver?' he said, 'Screwdriver'.[3]

most likely to lead us astray precisely when our powers of perception and memory are impaired or impeded. Competent investigators of alleged paranormal phenomena understand this and are rightfully skeptical of paranormal claims based on observations made under dubious conditions like those mentioned here. Under the right conditions, the mind is very good at showing us UFOs and midnight ghosts that aren't there. Likewise, juries are expected to be suspicious of the testimony of eyewitnesses who swear they plainly saw the dirty deed committed but were frightened, enraged, or a little tipsy at the time.

Expectation

A tricky thing about perception is that we often perceive exactly what we expect to perceive—regardless of whether there's anything there to detect. Ever watch the second hand on an electric clock move—then suddenly realize that the clock is not running at all? Ever been walking through a crowd looking for a friend and hear her call your name—then find out later that she was ten blocks away at the time? Such experiences—the result again of the constructive tendencies of mind—are common examples of how expectation can distort your perceptions.

Food For Thought

Look! Martian Canals

How easy it is for even a trained observer to see what isn't there! This famous example, one of many, is explained by the psychologist Terrence Hines:

Lowell's drawings of Martian canals. Photo: Lowell Observatory Archives

> The constructive nature of perception accounts for a famous astronomical illusion—the canals of Mars. These were first reported in 1877 by the Italian astronomer Schiaparelli. They were popularized in the early twentieth century by the American astronomer Percival Lowell. . . . Lowell argued that the canals were constructed by an advanced Martian civilization. It turns out, however, that the canals of Mars don't exist. [Carl Sagan and P. Fox (1975)] . . . have compared the photos taken by Mariner 9, which photographed the entire Martian surface, with maps of the canals. When the actual Martian surface is examined, there are no canals and no other physical features that could account for what Schiaparelli and Lowell reported. So, where did the canals come from? Sagan and Fox state that 'the vast majority of the canals appear to be largely self-generated by the visual observers of the canal school, and stand as monuments to the imprecision of the human eye-brain-hand system under difficult observing conditions.'[4]

Scientific research shows that expectation can have a more powerful effect on our experiences than most people think. In numerous studies, subjects who expected to see a flash of light, smell a certain odour, or feel an electric shock did indeed experience these things—even though suitable stimuli were never present. The mere suggestion that the stimuli would occur was enough to cause the subjects to perceive, or apparently perceive, things that did not exist.

Our tendency to sometimes perceive things that are not really there is especially pronounced when the stimuli are vague or ambiguous. For example, we may perceive completely formless stimuli—clouds, smoke, 'white noise', garbled voices, random-patterned wallpaper, blurry photos, lights in the night sky, stains on the ceiling—yet think we observe very distinct images or sounds. In the formlessness

Food For Thought

Expecting Racism?

Many studies demonstrate the effect of expectation and belief on our perceptions, but one classic study seems to really hit home. Years ago researchers asked students to look at a picture and describe what they saw. It showed two men standing next to one another in a subway car. One man was white, the other black. The white man was holding an open straight razor. Later the students were asked to recall what they saw. Half of them said that the razor was in the black man's hand.

we may see ghosts, faces, and words and hear songs, screams, or verbal warnings. We may see or hear exactly what we expect to see or hear. Or the mere suggestion of what we should perceive helps us perceive it. This phenomenon is a kind of illusion known as *pareidolia*. It's the reason some people claim to hear Satanic messages when rock music is played backwards, or to observe a giant stone face in fuzzy pictures of the surface of Mars, or to see the perfect likeness of Jesus in the marks left on a burnt tortilla by the pan it was fried in.

Scientists are keenly aware of the possible distorting influence of expectancy, so they try to design experiments that minimize it. We too need to minimize it as much as possible. Our strong expectations are a signal that we should double-check our sensory information and be careful about the conclusions we draw from it.

Innumeracy

When we make an off-the-cuff judgment about the chances of something happening (whether an event in the past or one in the future), we should be extra careful. Why? Because, generally, we humans are terrible at calculating probabilities.

Here's a classic example. Imagine there are 23 students, including you, in your classroom. What are the chances that at least two of the students have exactly the same birthday? (Not the same date of birth, but the same birthday out of the 365 possible ones.) The answer is neither 1 chance in 365 ($1/365$), nor 1 in 52 ($1/52$). It's 1 chance in 2 ($1/2$, or fifty-fifty)—a completely counterintuitive result.

A common error is the misjudging of coincidences. Many of us often believe that an event is simply too improbable to be a mere coincidence and that something else must surely must be going on—such as paranormal or supernatural activity. But we mustn't forget that amazing coincidences occur all the time and, in fact, must occur according to elementary laws of statistics. The probability that a particular strange event will occur—say, that an ice cube tossed out of an airplane will hit the roof of a barn—may be extremely low, maybe one in a billion. But that same event given enough opportunities to occur may be highly probable over the long haul. It may be unlikely in any given instance for you to flip a coin and get tails seven times in a row. But this 'streak' is virtually certain to happen if you flip the coin enough times.

What are the odds that someone will be thinking of a person she knew, or had heard of, and then suddenly learn that the person is seriously ill or dead? Believe it or not, such a strange event is likely to occur several times a day. If we make the reasonable assumption that someone would recognize the names of a few thousand people (both famous and not so famous) and that a person would, each year, learn of the illness or death of several of those people, then the chances of our eerie coincidence happening to someone somewhere are pretty good. We could reasonably expect that each day several people would have this experience.[5]

Another error is to think that previous events can affect the probabilities in the random event at hand. This mistake is known as the **gambler's fallacy**. Let's say you toss an unbiased coin six times in a row. On the first toss, the odds are, of course, one in two, or fifty-fifty, that it will land tails. It lands tails. Astoundingly, on the other five tosses the coin also lands tails. That's six tails in a row. So what are the odds that the coin will land tails on the seventh toss? Answer: fifty–fifty. Each toss has exactly the same probability of landing tails (or heads): fifty–fifty. The coin does not remember previous tosses. To think otherwise is to commit the gambler's fallacy. You see it a lot in casinos, sporting events, and—alas—everyday decision making.

The lesson here is not that we should mistrust all judgment about probabilities, but that we shouldn't rely solely on our intuitive sense in evaluating them. Relying entirely on intuition, or 'gut feeling', in assessing probabilities is usually not a reason to trust the assessment, but to doubt it.

> 'The first principle is that you must not fool yourself—and you are the easiest person to fool.'
> —Richard P. Feynman

Review Notes

Personal Experience

- It's reasonable to accept the evidence provided by personal experience only if there's no good reason to doubt it.
- If our perceptual powers are impaired or impeded, we have reason to doubt them.
- Our perception and memory are constructive, which means that our minds are capable of manufacturing what we experience.
- We often perceive exactly what we expect to perceive, and this tendency is enhanced when stimuli are vague or ambiguous.
- The gambler's fallacy is the mistake of thinking that previous events can affect the probabilities in the random event at hand.

Fooling Ourselves

As we've seen, it is not reasonable to believe a claim unless we have good reason for doing so. If we care whether our beliefs about the world are reliable, we must base them on the relevant evidence. Beliefs backed by good evidence are more likely to be true, and true beliefs are more likely to help us get what we want out of life.

The kink in this straightforward arrangement is that we too often fail to give evidence its due. We ignore evidence, deny it, manipulate it, and distort it. Somehow there is very little comfort in knowing that everyone occasionally does this dance. What truly is encouraging is that we can learn to be alert to missteps in using and assessing evidence and that we can usually minimize, though not eliminate, the problems. This section looks at three of the most common and most serious mistakes we make when we deal with evidence.

Resisting Contrary Evidence

An all too human tendency is to try to resist evidence that flies in the face of our cherished beliefs. We may deny evidence, or ignore it, or reinterpret it so it fits better with our prejudices. Resisting evidence may be psychologically comforting (for a while, anyway), but it thwarts any search for knowledge and stunts our understanding.

As we will see in Chapter 10, the will to resist contrary evidence is especially strong—and tempting—in forays into the paranormal. Remember the study mentioned in Chapter 2 about researchers who showed subjects both evidence

A scene from *Fairy Tale: A True Story*. Hoaxed twice—once by the original (and charming) English pranksters and once by Hollywood. Photo: Icon / The Kobal Collection

for and evidence against the reality of extrasensory perception (ESP)? The subjects who already had doubts about the existence of ESP recalled both kinds of evidence accurately. But the true believers—the subjects who already believed in ESP—remembered both kinds of evidence as proving ESP. They resisted the disconfirming evidence by mentally transforming it into confirming evidence. These results are typical of studies focusing on the paranormal.

Another typical case involves believers in the paranormal who, when confronted with evidence counting against their beliefs, simply refuse to accept it. For example, belief in fairies was given a boost many years ago when two little girls presented the world with photographs they had allegedly taken of fairies playing with them in the garden. (The episode was the basis for the 1997 movie *Fairy Tale: A True Story.*) The photos looked fake, the fairies resembling cut-outs from a children's book— which is exactly what they were. But brushing that aside, many people (including the renowned writer Sir Arthur Conan Doyle, creator of the fictional Sherlock Holmes) were convinced that the photos showed real fairies. Many years later when the girls were grown up, they confessed that the whole thing had been a hoax. But some believers—even those who heard the confession first-hand—refused to accept it![6]

But we need not look to the fringes of reality to find instances of the denial of evidence. Scientific research and common-sense experience show that the practice permeates all walks of life. A political activist may refuse to consider evidence that conflicts with his party's principles. A scientist may be so committed to her theory that she refuses to accept any evidence that undermines it. An administrator of a grand program may insist that it is a huge success despite all evidence to the contrary.

Often our resistance to contrary evidence takes a subtle form. If we encounter evidence against our views, we frequently don't reject it outright. We simply apply more critical scrutiny to it than we would to evidence in favour of our views, or we seek out additional confirming information, or we find a way to interpret the data so it doesn't conflict with our expectations.

In one study, proponents and opponents of the death penalty were presented with evidence about whether capital punishment deterred crime. Both those opposed to and in favour of capital punishment were given two types of evidence—(1) some that supported the practice and (2) some that discredited it. Psychologist Thomas Gilovich describes the outcome of the study:

> The results of this experiment were striking. The participants considered the study that provided evidence consistent with their prior beliefs—regardless of what type of study that was—to be a well-conducted piece of research that provided important evidence concerning the effectiveness of capital punishment. In contrast, they uncovered numerous flaws in the research that contradicted their initial beliefs. . . . Rather than ignoring outright the evidence at variance with their expectations, the participants cognitively transformed

it into evidence that was considered relatively uninformative and could be assigned little weight.[7]

There is no cure for our tendency to resist opposing evidence. The only available remedy is our commitment to examine our favourite claims critically—which means trying our best to be even-handed in scrutinizing the evidence we like and the evidence we don't.

Looking For Confirming Evidence

We often not only resist conflicting evidence, but also seek out and use only confirming evidence—a phenomenon known as confirmation bias. When we go out of our way to find only confirming evidence, we can end up accepting a claim that's not true, seeing relationships that aren't there, and finding confirmation that isn't genuine.

In scientific research on confirmation bias, when subjects are asked to assess a claim, they often look for confirming evidence only, even though disconfirming evidence may be just as revealing. For example, in one study, a group of subjects was asked to assess whether practising before a tennis match was linked to winning the match; another group, whether practising before a match was linked to losing the match. All the subjects were asked to select the kind of evidence (regarding practice and winning or losing matches) that they thought would be the most helpful in answering the relevant question. Not surprisingly, the subjects deciding whether pre-game practising was linked to winning focused on how many times players practised and then won the match. And subjects assessing whether practising was associated with losing focused on how many times players practised and then lost the match.[8]

Sometimes we look for confirming evidence even when disconfirming evidence is more telling. For example, take this claim: all swans are white. You can easily find confirming instances; white swans are plentiful and ubiquitous. But even seeing thousands of white swans will not conclusively confirm that all swans are white, because there may be swans in places where you haven't looked. But all you have to do is find one black swan to conclusively show that the claim is false. (People used to believe that the claim was absolutely true—until black swans were discovered in Australia.) In such cases, confirmation bias can lead us way off course.

The moral to this story is that when we evaluate claims, we should look for disconfirming as well as confirming evidence. Doing so requires a conscious effort to consider, not only the information that supports what we want to believe, but also the information that conflicts with it. We have to seek out disconfirming evidence just as we keep an eye out for confirming evidence—an approach that goes against our grain. We naturally gravitate to people and policies we agree with, to the books that support our views, to the magazines and newspapers that echo our political outlook. Acquiring a broader, smarter, more critical perspective takes effort—and courage.

Food For Thought

This Is Lunacy!

When there's full moon, do people get crazy? Do they behave like lunatics? Folklore says that they do, and many people believe that there's a lunar effect on the way people act. But numerous studies have shown that there is absolutely no causal connection between the moon and human behaviour. So why do so many people believe in lunar power? Part of the reason is the availability error. Since strange behaviour is more noticeable (and so more available) than normal behaviour, we tend to think that weird behaviour is more frequent. And if we look only for confirming instances (and we do), we're likely to believe that the moon is indeed the cause of a lot of peculiar behaviour. Of course, many people behave strangely with or without a full moon.

Photo: Universal / The Kobal Collection

Preferring Available Evidence

Another common mistake in evaluating evidence is the availability error. We commit this blunder when we rely on evidence, not because it's trustworthy, but because it's memorable or striking—that is, psychologically available. In such cases, we put stock in evidence that's psychologically impressive or persuasive, not necessarily logically acceptable. You fall for the availability error if you vote to convict a murder suspect because he looks menacing, not because the evidence points to his guilt; or if you decide that a Honda Civic is an unsafe vehicle because you saw one get smashed up in a highway accident; or if, just because you watched a TV news report about a mugging in your city, you believe that the risk of being mugged is extremely high.

Being taken in by the availability error can lead to some serious misjudgments about the risks involved in various situations. Some people (are you one of them?) believe that air travel is more dangerous than many other modes of transportation, so they shun travel by airplane in favour of the car. Their conclusion is based on nothing more than a few vivid media reports of tragic plane crashes, such as the terrorist attacks of 9/11. But research shows that per mile travelled, flying is far safer than travelling by car. Researchers have calculated that driving a particular distance (say, from Toronto, Ontario, to Fredericton, New Brunswick) is about 65 times as risky as a non-stop flight of the same distance. The fact is, there are plenty of less vivid and less memorable (that is, psychologically unavailable) things that are much more dangerous than air travel: falling down stairs, drowning, choking, and accidental poisoning.[9]

Social psychologist John Ruscio gives another example:

> Aside from a close miss by what was reported to be a falling airplane part early in *The Truman Show*, I cannot personally recall ever having heard of such an accident, fictitious or real. Students over the years have told me that they recall stories of people having found fallen airplane parts, but not of an actual fatality resulting from such falling parts. Shark attacks, on the other hand, are easily imagined and widely reported. Moreover, in the first movie that comes to my mind, the shark in *Jaws* actually did cause several fatalities. It may come as some surprise, then, to learn that in an average year in the United States thirty times more people are killed by falling airplane parts than by shark attacks.[10]

The availability error is very likely at work in many controversies regarding environmental hazards. Because the alleged hazard and its effects can be easily and vividly imagined and the scientific data on the issue are not so concrete or memorable, the imagined danger can provoke a public scare even though the fear is completely unwarranted. Brain cancer from the use of cell phones and autism from childhood vaccines—both these putative hazards have provoked fear and public demands for action. But scientific studies have shown these concerns to be groundless.[11] Many environmental hazards are real, of course. But concluding that they exist solely on the basis of scary thoughts is to commit the availability error.

If we're in the habit of basing our judgments on evidence that's merely psychologically available, we will frequently commit the error known as hasty generalization, a mistake discussed in detail in Chapter 8. We're guilty of hasty generalization when we draw a conclusion about a whole group on the basis of an inadequate sample of the group. We fall into this trap when we assert something like this: 'Honda Civics are pieces of junk. I owned one for three months, and it gave me nothing but trouble.' Since our experience with a car is immediate and personal, for many of us it can be a short step from this psychologically available evidence to a very hasty conclusion. If we give in to the availability error and stick to our guns about Civics being no good in the face of evidence to the contrary (say, automobile-reliability research done by the Consumer's Union or similar organizations), we should get an F in critical thinking.

Claims in the News

In the Information Age, we are drenched with, well, information. And the news media are a major source of the information that drenches us everyday. Through newspapers, magazines, television, radio, and the Internet, information about what's happening in the world hits us like rain almost every waking hour. The claims—supported and unsupported—just keep coming at us. How can we cope with such an onslaught?

Once again, critical thinking must play a big role. Remember that information is just pieces of data, bundles of claims—not necessarily true, not always useful, and not the same thing as knowledge. Knowledge is true belief supported by good reasons; information doesn't have this lofty status. And to transform information into knowledge—our most useful commodity—we need critical thinking. Through critical thinking we can make sense of a great deal of the information coming from the news media. As you will see, most of the rest is not relevant and not worth our time.

Let's begin by looking at how the news media work, how and why they generate the claims that they do. Then we'll see how to examine critically these claims embedded in news reports, broadcasts, and multimedia presentations.

Inside the News

The news media include hundreds of newspapers (among the biggest and the best are the *Globe and Mail*, the *Washington Post*, the *New York Times*, and the *Los Angeles Times*), network news organizations (CTV, CBC, Global), cable news networks (CBC Newsworld, CTV Newsnet), local and national radio broadcasts, local television news, American public television and radio, news magazines (notably *Macleans*, and *L'Actualité*), and numerous news-containing websites. Most news can be found in newspapers, where news stories are generally longer, more comprehensive, and more in-depth than those of any other news source. Newspapers, especially the good ones, devote far more resources to gathering and reporting news than the electronic and Internet media do, usually employing many more reporters and producing many more news stories. A large daily newspaper may contain 100,000 words, while a nightly television news broadcast may contain fewer than 4,000. Other kinds of news sources (especially television stations and websites) are far more numerous than newspapers and are the primary news sources for millions of people even though they provide less news.

But not all news is created equal. Some news stories or reports are good, some are bad; some are reliable and informative, some are not. Most probably lie somewhere in between. The quality of news reporting depends on many factors, probably most of which are not under the control of the reporters.

Foremost among such factors is money. After all, news outlets—whether print, electronic, or online—are businesses with profit margins to maintain, salaries to pay, and shareholders to please. A news organization makes most of its money, not from selling its product (news) through subscriptions or direct sales, but from selling opportunities for other companies to advertise to the news outlet's audience. The organization wants a big audience because big audiences can bring in big advertising dollars.

> 'Everything is being compressed into tiny tablets. You take a little pill of news every day—23 minutes—and that's supposed to be enough.'
> —Walter Cronkite

Cartoon courtesy of Don Addis.

The pressure on the news organizations to turn an acceptable profit is immense and has been growing in the past two decades. The old ideal of journalism as primarily a public service and not a cash cow has seldom been able to withstand the corporate push for profits. The effects of this trend on the nature and quality of the news have been profound. Two veteran newsmen from the *Washington Post* explain some of the changes this way:

Most newspapers have shrunk their reporting staffs, along with the space they devote to news, to increase their owners' profits. Most owners and publishers have forced their editors to focus more on the bottom line than on good journalism. Papers have tried to attract readers and advertisers with light features and stories that please advertisers—shopping is a favorite—and by de-emphasizing serious reporting on business, government, the country and the world.

If most newspapers have done poorly, local television stations have been worse. Typically, local stations provide little real news, no matter how many hours they devote to 'news' programs. Their reporting staffs are dramatically smaller than even the staffs of shrunken newspapers in the same cities. The television stations have attracted viewers—and the advertising that rewards their owners with extraordinary profits—with the melodrama, violence and entertainment of 'action news' formulas, the frivolity of 'happy talk' among their anchors and the technological gimmicks of computer graphics and 'live' remote broadcasting.

The national television networks have trimmed their reporting staffs and closed foreign reporting bureaus to cut their owners' costs. They have tried to attract viewers by diluting their expensive newscasts with lifestyle, celebrity and entertainment features, and by filling their low-budget high-profit, prime-time 'newsmagazines' with sensational sex, crime, and court stories.

All-news cable television channels and radio stations—to which the networks have ceded much of the routine coverage of serious national and foreign news—fill many of their hours as cheaply as possible with repetitive, bare-bones news summaries and talk shows that present biased opinions and argument as though they were news.[12]

Deliberately or unconsciously, editors and reporters may skew their reporting so as not to offend their advertisers, their audience, or their shareholders. They may also moderate their reporting to keep their sources of information open. Reporters get a great deal of their news from sources such as government officials, corporate public relations people, and advocacy-group spokespersons. A reporter who irritates these sources by writing stories that they don't like could end up being shunned by the sources. There is always the temptation, then, to craft inoffensive or watered-down stories to please the source. Not all news people give in to the temptation, but many do.

Editors and reporters are the ones who decide what's newsworthy and what isn't. And these decisions can help give us a clearer picture of the world or a more distorted one. The distortion can happen in several ways. First, it can arise when reporters do what we might call passive reporting. Most reporters aren't investigative reporters, going off into the world and digging up the hard facts. Often, the news is simply handed to them by spokespersons and public relations experts hired by governments, corporations, and others who want to get their own version of the facts into the news media. In these situations, reporters may report only what they're told at press conferences or in press releases. The result is canned news that's slanted toward the views of the people who supply it.

Second, for a variety of reasons, publishers, editors, producers, and reporters may decide not to cover certain stories or specific aspects of a story. With so much going on in the world, some selectivity is necessary and inevitable. Too often, though, decisions not to cover something can lead the public to conclude that there is nothing happening when in fact something very important is happening. During the run-up to the war in Iraq, some massive anti-war protests occurred in the United States and Europe. But, at least at first, the mainstream American news media didn't cover them, leading some observers to accuse the news media of bias in favour of the war. Likewise, some observers complain that the Canadian news media don't cover many international stories that news organizations in other countries cover in depth, such as famines and human-rights violations in developing nations. The result, the complaint goes, is that Canadians may be blithely ignorant of what's really happening in the world. Also, many times the news media forgo covering a story because they deem it too complex or too unexciting for an audience hungry for titillation, scandal, and entertainment. The RCMP chasing a local bandit on Highway 102 may get a full hour of TV coverage, but a debate over the role of the monarchy in Canada may get two minutes, or less.

Third, editors, reporters, and producers can dramatically alter our perception of the news by playing certain aspects up or down. Television and radio news broadcasts can make a trivial news item seem momentous just by making it the lead story in the broadcast. Or they can make an important story seem inconsequential by devoting only 15 seconds to it near the end of the broadcast. Newspapers can play the same game by putting a story on the front page with a big headline and compelling photo—or embedding it on page 22 with a tiny headline. Parts of a story can also be arranged for the same effect, with the most telling information mentioned last.

Every piece of news is filtered through a reporter (as well as an editor or producer), most of whom try hard to get the story right. But reporters are subject to

Food For Thought

Man Shoots Neighbour with Machete

Man shoots neighbour with machete? Yes—so says a headline that actually appeared in a large-circulation newspaper. Probably every newspaper in North America has been guilty of running such ambiguously goofy headlines. Here are a few more:

- Iraqi Head Seeks Arms
- Study Finds Sex, Pregnancy Link
- Kicking Baby Considered to Be Healthy
- Typhoon Rips Through Cemetery; Hundreds Dead
- Lack of Brains Hinders Research
- Panda Mating Fails; Veterinarian Takes Over

many pressures—internal and external—to push the story this way or that, to stray far from the laudable ideal of objective reporting based on professional journalistic standards. Reporters can slant the news by using loaded language (discussed in Chapter 5), manipulating the tone of the writing, leaving out (or leaving in) certain details, putting facts in conspicuous (or inconspicuous) positions, inserting arguments and personal opinions, dramatizing parts of the story, and appealing to the reader's prejudices.

Unfortunately, there is a trend these days for reporters to deliberately make themselves part of the story—to editorialize as they report the story, to try to exhibit attitudes common in the community, to offer subtle value judgments that the audience is likely to approve of. Here's an extreme example. On the nightly news, a film clip shows the arrest of activists who have chained themselves to some logging machines in a forest in British Columbia, and the reporter on the scene tells the TV audience, 'Once again, the police are jailing those who interfere with loggers' right to feed their families.' Or maybe the reporter takes the opposite tack: 'Once again, the police are jailing citizens fighting to protect our shared natural heritage.'

All of this suggests that we should not assume without good reason that a news report is giving us an entirely accurate representation of events. And deciding whether in fact we have good reason is a job for critical thinking.

Sorting Out the News

Sometimes you won't be able to tell whether a news report is trustworthy, no matter how carefully you scrutinize it. Your only recourse then is reasonable skepticism.

But most times you can at least get a few clues to the reliability of the report by taking the following critical approach.

Consider Whether the Report Conflicts with What You Have Good Reason to Believe

A report that conflicts with other reports that you believe are reliable or with facts you already know is not trustworthy. Likewise, a report that conflicts with expert opinion should not be accepted.

Look for Reporter Slanting

Look for slanting in news accounts just as you would look for it in any set of claims. Check for loaded or biased language; arguments or unsupported opinion; emotional appeals; appeals to authority, popularity, and tradition; and biased or subjective tone.

Consider the Source

Ask what the source is of the information presented in the story. Did the reporter uncover the facts herself—or does the information come directly from the government, corporations, or interest groups? How does the reporter know that the information is accurate? Does the information seem to be a simple statement of facts—or a pack of assertions designed to put someone in the best possible light?

Check for Missing Information

Be suspicious if essential facts are not presented in the story or if it seems so heavily edited that the context of remarks is mysterious. Sound bites, for example, are easy to take out of context because they usually have no context.

Look for False Emphasis

The size of headlines, the position of stories, the order in which facts are presented—all these things can give unmerited emphasis to a story or some of its claims. To counteract this tactic, ask if the emphasis is really deserved—or, more broadly, if the story or story part is really as significant as the reporter would have you believe.

Check Alternative News Sources

How can you tell if the news you're getting is incomplete—if there's important news you're not seeing? You can't, unless you check alternative news sources for any missing stories. Reading a variety of newspapers, newsmagazines, journals of opinion, and websites is the best way to ensure that you're getting the big picture. To avoid confirmation bias, and to ensure that you're fully informed, you should read not only those sources that agree with you but also those that don't.

> 'News reports stand up as people, and people wither into editorials. Clichés walk around on two legs while men are having theirs shot off.'
> —Karl Kraus

Advertising and Persuasion

Advertising is like air. It is everywhere, so pervasive and so natural that we forget it's there, sinking into and changing us every day. Advertising messages hit us rapid-fire and nonstop from television, radio, email, websites, blogs, podcasts, movie theatres, magazines, newsletters, newspapers, book covers, junk mail, telephones, fax machines, product labels, billboards, vehicle signs, T-shirts, wall posters, flyers, and who knows what else. Ads permeate all media—print, film, video, television, radio, and cyberspace. Caught in this whirl of words and sounds and images, we can easily overlook the obvious and disconcerting facts behind them: (1) All advertising is designed to influence, persuade, or manipulate us; (2) to an impressive degree and in many ways, it *does* successfully influence, persuade, or manipulate us; and (3) we are often oblivious to—or in outright denial about—how effectively advertising influences, persuades, or manipulates us.

The purpose of advertising is to sell products and services, promote causes or candidates, or alter attitudes and opinions. How well advertising does these jobs can be measured in money. Advertising in most media can cost a great deal. A single full-page magazine ad can cost tens of thousands of dollars; a thirty-second TV ad can run into the millions (especially on Super Bowl Sunday). But companies are willing to pay the price because advertising works. The revenues garnered from advertising can outweigh its costs by wide margins; in the case of a magazine ad or a TV spot, the gain could easily be hundreds of thousands or millions of dollars. In addition, advertisers and advertising agencies invest heavily each year in scientific consumer research to determine how to configure ads precisely to elicit the desired response from people. Again, they make these investments because there is a sure payoff. Consumers usually respond just as the research says they will. How do your eyes track across a newspaper ad when you are looking at it? Would you respond

DILBERT: © Scott Adams/Dist. By United Feature Syndicate, Inc.

better to a TV commercial if the voice-over came from Peter Mansbridge or from Nelly Furtado? Would the magazine ad be more likely to sell you the cottage cheese if the headline used the word *creamy* instead of *smooth*? Would the ad copy on the junk-mail envelope increase sales if it were red instead of blue? You may not care about any of this, but advertisers do because such seemingly trivial bits of information can help them influence you in ways you barely suspect.

However averse we are (or think we are) to advertising or to its aims, we cannot deny its appeal. We like advertising, at least some of it. We can easily point to ads that annoy us or insult our intelligence, but most of us can also recall ones that are entertaining, funny, inspiring, even informative. How, then, should good critical thinkers think about advertising? Our guiding principle should be:

We generally have good reason to doubt advertising claims and to be wary of advertising's persuasive powers.

This means that usually the most reasonable response to advertising is a degree of suspicion. If we prefer truth over falsehood, if we would rather not be mistaken or bamboozled, if we want to make informed choices involving our time and money, then a general wariness toward advertising ploys is justified. This principle does not assume that all ad claims are false or that advertising cannot be genuinely informative or useful. It simply says that we should not accept uncritically an ad's message or impact on us.

There are several reasons for this cautious approach. First, recall the purpose of advertising—to *sell or promote something*, whether a product, service, person, or idea. To put the point bluntly, though advertising can be both truthful and helpful, its primary function is *not* to provide objective and accurate information to consumers. Advertisers will tell you many good things about their products but are unlikely to mention all the bad. Their main job is *not* to help consumers make fully informed, rational choices about available options. Advertising is advertising—it is not intended to be an impartial search for facts or a program of consumer protection. We are therefore justified in maintaining the same attitude toward advertising that we would toward a complete stranger who wants to sell us something. His motives are obviously financial while his commitment to honesty is unknown.

Second, advertising has a reputation for—and a history of—misleading messages. The world is filled with ads that make dubious or false claims, use fallacious arguments (stated or implied), and employ psychological tricks to manipulate consumer responses.

Some of these methods fit neatly in our rundown of fallacies in Chapters 4 and 5. Ads frequently employ fallacious appeals to authority ('As an Olympic gold medal winner, I can tell you that PowerVitamin 2000 really works!'), appeals to emotion ('Enjoy the goodness and warmth of Big-Brand Soup, just like mother used to make'), appeals to popularity ('*The Globe and Mail*: Canada's Most Trusted News Source'), hasty generalizations ('Mothers everywhere will love Softie Diapers—our test mothers sure did!'), and faulty analogies ('As a businessman, I saved General Motors. As president, I can save this country').

But advertisers also use an array of other persuasive techniques, most of which do not involve making explicit claims or providing good reasons for acting or choosing. The following are some of the more common ones.

Identification

Many ads persuade by simply inviting the consumer to identify with attractive people (real or imagined) or groups. Most ads featuring celebrity endorsements use this ploy. The idea is to get you to identify so strongly with a celebrity that you feel his or her product choices are *your* preferred choices. Without providing a single good reason or argument, endorsement ads say, in effect, that if Christina Aguilera prefers Pepsi, if Halle Berry likes Revlon, if Michael Jordan loves Nike, maybe you should, too.

Slogans

Catchy, memorable phrases are the stock-in-trade of advertising. How could we forget such gems as: 'Nike. Just do it' (Nike); 'Reach out and touch someone' (AT&T); 'Like a rock' (Chevrolet); 'Don't leave home without it' (American Express); 'Built Ford tough!' (Ford); or 'You've Always Got Time for Tim Hortons' (Tim Hortons)? Such catchphrases may not say much, but they do get our attention, engender appealing emotions or concepts, and associate them with products or companies— again and again and again. Through repetition that seems to embed themselves in our brains, slogans surreptitiously get us to feel that one product or brand is better than another.

Misleading Comparisons

In advertising, comparisons can mislead in many ways. Consider these examples:

1. BeClean Paper Towels are 30 per cent more absorbent.
2. Big sale! The SuperX CD Player for less than the suggested retail price!
3. Simply better tasting tacos. No question.
4. X phone lets you call anywhere cheaper. Just 5 cents per minute compared with Y phone, which charges 10 cents a minute.

The problem with example 1 is its vagueness, which is of course deliberate. What does '30 per cent more absorbent' mean? Thirty per cent more absorbent than they used to be? Thirty per cent more absorbent than similar products are? If the latter, what similar products are we talking about? Are BeClean Paper Towels being compared to the *least* absorbent paper towels on the market? The *30 per cent* may seem impressive—until we know what it actually refers to. (Another relevant question is how absorbency was determined. As you might imagine, there are many ways to perform such tests, some of them likely to yield more impressive numbers than others.)

The claim in example 2 may or may not be touting a true bargain. We would probably view the 'Big sale' in a different light if we knew whether the store's *regular* prices are below the suggested retail prices or if *all* stores sell the CD player below the suggested retail.

Example 3 contains the same sort of vagueness we find in example 1 plus an additional sort of emptiness. The phrase 'better-tasting tacos' is a claim about a subjective state of affairs—a claim that *anyone* could make about his or her own eating experience. You and a thousand other people might try the tacos and think they taste terrible. So the claim tells you nothing about whether you will like the tacos. The claim would be empty even if it were stretched to 'The best-tasting tacos on earth!' In the ad world, such exaggerations are known as *puffery*, which is regarded in advertising law as hype that few people take seriously.

Example 4 is misleading because it tries to compare apples and oranges. The service offered by X Phone is not like that offered by Y Phone. The former gives you bare-bones service for 5 cents a minute; the latter gives you the same plus caller ID, call waiting, and free long distance on weekends. So comparing the two according to the per-minute charge alone is deceptive.

Weasel Words

When advertisers want to *appear* to make a strong claim but avoid blatant lying or deception, they use what are known as *weasel words*. Weasel words water down a claim in subtle ways—just enough to ensure that it is technically true but superficially misleading. Consider:

1. You may have already won a new 2007 Ford pickup truck!
2. Some doctors recommend ginseng for sexual dysfunction.
3. Relieves up to 60 per cent of headaches in chronic headache sufferers.

Example 1 is typical junk-mail hype that seems to promise a valuable prize. But the weasel word 'may' weakens the claim. Technically, you *may* have actually won since your winning is at least (remotely) possible. But in the typical sweepstakes, the odds of your winning anything are millions to one. Yes, you *may* have already won—and you *may* get hit by an asteroid tomorrow. Example 2 plays on the weasel word 'some'. It is probably true that *some* (meaning at least one) doctors recommend ginseng for sexual dysfunction, but a huge majority of them do not. Using *some*, we could craft an infinite number of technically true but misleading (and ridiculous) claims about what doctors do and don't do. In Example 3 the weasel words are 'up to'. Notice that many states of affairs would be consistent with this (vague) statement. It would be true even if just 1 per cent of headaches were relieved in almost all headache sufferers.

Other weasels include *as many as, reportedly, possibly, virtually, many, seems*, and *perhaps*. Such words, of course, can have perfectly respectable uses as necessary qualifiers in many contexts. The problems arise when they are used not to qualify but to mislead.

Summary

Many times we need to be able to evaluate an unsupported claim—a claim that isn't backed by an argument. There are several critical-thinking principles that can help us do this. An important one is: If a claim conflicts with other claims we have good reason to accept, we have good grounds for doubting it. Sometimes the conflict is between a claim and your background information. Background information is the large collection of very well-supported beliefs that we rely on to inform our actions and choices. The relevant principle then is this: If a claim conflicts with our background information, we have good reason to doubt the claim.

It's not reasonable to accept a claim if there is good reason to doubt it. In the case of claims that we can neither accept nor reject outright, we should proportion our belief to the evidence.

An expert is someone who is more knowledgeable than most people in a particular subject area. The important principle here is this: If a claim conflicts with expert opinion, we have good reason to doubt it. We must couple this principle with another one: When the experts disagree about a claim, we have good reason to doubt it. When we rely on bogus expert opinion, we commit the fallacy known as the appeal to authority.

Many claims are based on nothing more than personal experience, ours or someone else's. We can trust our personal experience—to a point. The guiding principle is that it's reasonable to accept the evidence provided by personal experience only if there's no reason to doubt it. Some common factors that can raise such doubts are impairment (stress, injury, distraction, emotional upset, and the like), expectation, and our limited abilities in judging probabilities.

Some of the common mistakes we make in evaluating claims are resisting contrary evidence, looking for confirming evidence, and preferring available evidence. To counteract these tendencies, we need to take deliberate steps to examine even our most cherished claims critically, to search for disconfirming evidence as well as confirming, and to look beyond evidence that is merely the most striking or memorable.

Many of the unsupported claims we encounter are in news reports. Reporters, editors, and producers are under many pressures that can lead to biased or misleading reporting. The biggest factor is money—the drive for profits in news organizations, especially those owned by large corporations or conglomerates. Reporters themselves may introduce inaccuracies, biases, and personal opinions. And the people who produce the news may decide not to cover certain stories (or aspects of stories), thereby sometimes giving a skewed or erroneous picture of an issue or event.

The best defense against being misled by news reports is a reasonable skepticism and a critical approach that involves, among other things, looking for slanting, examining sources, checking for missing facts, and being on the lookout for false emphasis.

Advertising is another possible source of unsupported or misleading claims. We should realize that we generally have good reason to doubt advertising claims and to be wary of the persuasive powers of advertising.

Key Terms

Appeal to authority: The fallacy of relying on the opinion of someone deemed to be an expert who in fact is *not* an expert.

Background information: The large collection of very well-supported beliefs that we all rely on to inform our actions and choices. It consists of basic facts about everyday things, beliefs based on very good evidence (including our own personal observations and excellent authority), and justified claims that we would regard as 'common sense' or 'common knowledge'.

Expert: Someone who is more knowledgeable in a particular subject area or field than most others are.

Gambler's fallacy: The error of thinking that previous events can affect the probabilities in the random event at hand.

Exercises

Exercise 4.1

Review Questions

1. What is a person's background information?
2. What is the most reasonable attitude toward a claim that conflicts with other claims you have good reason to believe?
3. What degree of probability should we assign to a claim that conflicts with our background information?
* 4. What is the most reasonable attitude toward a claim that is neither worthy of acceptance nor deserving of outright rejection?
5. What is an expert?
6. What should our attitude be toward a claim that conflicts with expert opinion?
7. What should our attitude be toward a claim when experts disagree about it?
8. What is the fallacy of the appeal to authority?
9. What, in most fields, are the two minimal prerequisites for being considered an expert?
* 10. Beyond the minimal prerequisites, what are two more telling indicators that someone is an expert?

11. Under what three circumstances should we suspect that an expert might be biased?
12. When is it reasonable to accept the evidence provided by personal experience?
13. What are two factors that can give us good reason to doubt the reliability of personal experience?
14. What is the gambler's fallacy?
15. What are some ways that people resist contrary evidence?
16. What is confirmation bias?
* 17. How can critical thinkers counteract confirmation bias?
18. What is the availability error?
19. What is the connection between availability error and hasty generalization?
20. According to the text, other than reporters and editors themselves, what is the foremost factor influencing the quality of news reporting?
21. According to the text, what are three techniques for critically evaluating the reliability of news reports?

Exercise 4.2

On the basis of claims you already have good reason to believe, your background information, and your assessment of the credibility of any cited experts, indicate for each of the following claims whether you would accept it, reject it, or proportion your belief to the evidence. Give reasons for your answers. If you decide to proportion your belief to the evidence, state generally what degree of plausibility you would assign to the claim.

1. Israeli psychic Uri Geller can bend spoons with his mind.
2. In Russia, some people live to be 150 years old.
3. Every year in Canada over 300 people die of leprosy.
* 4. According to Dr Feelgood, the spokesperson for Acme Mattresses, the EasyRest 2000 from Acme is the best mattress in the world for back-pain sufferers.
5. Some bars in the suburbs of Vancouver have been entertaining their nightly patrons with pygmy hippo tossing.
* 6. Every person has innate psychic ability that, when properly cultivated, can enable him or her to read another person's mind.
7. The Prime Minister of Canada works with the government of the United States to suppress the economic power of French Canadians.
8. Molly, a 34-year-old bank manager, says that stock prices will plummet dramatically in two months and will trigger another deep year-long recession.
9. A photo exists showing a shark attacking a diver who is climbing into a helicopter.

* 10. Fifteen women have died after smelling a free sample of perfume that they received in the mail.

11. A chain letter describing the struggles of a nine-year-old girl with incurable cancer is circulating on the Internet. The more people who receive the letter, the better the little girl's chances of survival.

12. A report from the Health Canada says there is no evidence that high doses of the herb ephedra can cure cancer.

13. Giant albino alligators crawl through the underground sewers of Toronto.

* 14. Crop circles—large-scale geometric patterns pressed into fields of grain or hay—are the work of space aliens.

15. Crop circles are the work of human hoaxers.

16. The prime minister's economic plan to lower taxes and dramatically greatly increase government spending will not cause fiscal deficits.

* 17. Dr Xavier, a world-famous astrologer, says the position of the sun, planets, and stars at your birth influences your choice of careers and your marital status.

18. Eleanor Morgan, a Nobel Prize–winning economist, says that modern democratic systems (including developed nations) are not viable.

19. Eating meat rots your colon.

20. The highway speed limit in Alberta is 120 km/h.

Exercise 4.3

For each of the following claims, decide whether you agree or disagree with it. If you agree with a claim, say what evidence would persuade you to reject the statement. If you disagree with a claim, say what evidence would persuade you to accept the statement. In each case, ask yourself if you would really change your mind if presented with the evidence you suggested.

1. Canada's system of universal, free health care should be protected at all costs.

2. The current 'fiscal imbalance' should be corrected, so that Canada's provinces will have the financial resources to pay for health care and education.

* 3. An alien spacecraft crashed in Roswell, New Mexico, in 1947.

4. The Earth is only 10,000 years old.

5. There is life on Mars.

6. Some people can twist their heads around on their necks a complete 360 degrees.

7. On Tuesday, a new computer virus will shut down every network and every PC in the world.

* 8. Meditation and controlled breathing can shrink cancerous tumors.

9. All swans are white.

10. 'Corporate welfare'—tax breaks and other special considerations for businesses—should be discontinued.

Exercise 4.4

Examine the following newspaper story and answer the questions that follow.

Work Farce

26 June 2003—Brazen Department of Education construction employees ripped off the city by clocking in but doing little or no work—instead spending their days at the gym, shopping, or moonlighting, a sting operation by Schools Investigator Richard Condon's office found.

Checks of 13 workers—some chosen randomly, others on the basis of complaints—who were monitored beginning last August found eight of them doing little or no work.

The slackers will soon find themselves in handcuffs and unemployment lines, authorities said. . . . Condon charged that time cheating by phantom workers is 'common practice'.

'Time abuse is a financial drain on the city's public school system. No doubt it plays a role in the overtime that is paid to skilled trade workers,' Condon said. . . .

Condon did not release the names of the slackers because they're about to be arrested, he said. Chancellor Joel Klein said they will be fired 'immediately'.[13]

1. Is the story slanted toward or against a particular group? How?
2. Are there instances of loaded or biased language or emotional appeals in the story or headline? If so, give examples.
3. What is the main source for this story?

Field Problems

1. Find a controversial newspaper story posted on the Internet and answer the questions in Exercise 4-4 about it.
2. Write down a claim in which you strongly believe. Select one that pertains to an important social, religious, or political issue. Then say what evidence would persuade you to change your mind about the claim.

Self-Assessment Quiz

1. How should a critical thinker regard an unsupported claim that conflicts with a great deal of his or her background information?

2. State, in your own words, Bertrand Russell's principle regarding unsupported claims.
3. Name four factors to consider in deciding whether someone should be considered an expert.
4. According to the text, what are some telltale signs that an expert may be biased?
5. Name three types of perceptual impairment that can give us good reason to doubt the reliability of our personal experience.

For each of the following situations and the claim associated with it, indicate whether there may be good reasons to doubt the claim and, if so, specify the reasons.

6. Standing on a street corner in heavy fog, Eve thinks that she sees an old friend walking away from her on the other side of the street. She says to herself, 'That's Radha Kooner.'
7. While playing an old rock tune backwards, Elton thinks he hears a sentence on the tape. It's almost inaudible, but he thinks it says, 'Hello, Elton, long time no see.'
8. Constable Jones views the videotape of the robbery at the Tim Hortons, which occurred last night. He sees the robber look into the camera. 'I know that guy,' he says. 'I put him away last year on a similar charge.'

For each of the following claims, say whether it is: (a) probably true, (b) probably false, (c) almost certainly true, (d) almost certainly false, or (e) none of the above.

9. 'Most people are not aware that the cartoonish "Bigfoot" figure is a distorted product of ancient and modern stories describing a real, but unacknowledged species that is still occasionally observed today in North American forests.' (The Bigfoot Field Researchers Organization)
10. Health Canada says that about 100 children a year die as a result of their mothers smoking during pregnancy and exposure to smoke at home.
11. Nobody in the world is truly altruistic. Everyone is out for himself alone.
12. School violence is caused mainly by hypocrisy on the part of teachers and school administrators.
13. 'The world shadow government behind the US government is at it again, destroying US buildings and killing people with staged acts of terrorism [on 9/11/01], the intent of which being—among other things—to start WWIII.' (Website devoted to 9/11 theories)
14. 'What is Pre-Birth Communication? It's something that many people experience, yet very few talk about—the sense that somehow we are in contact with a being who is not yet born! It may be a vivid dream, the touch of an invisible presence, a telepathic message announcing pregnancy, or many other types of encounter. It is a mystery, one that challenges our ideas about ourselves and our children.' (Website on pre-birth communication)

15. Physicians, drug companies, the food industry, the National Cancer Institute of Canada, and the Canadian Cancer Society are all fighting to prevent 'natural' cancer cures such as vitamin supplements and herbs from being used by cancer patients.
16. Medieval history is a lie—or, rather, it doesn't exist. Monks made it up on the basis of a corrupt copy of ancient history.

Read the following news story and then answer questions 17–20.

Soldiers Sweep up Saddam's Hit Goons

1 July 2003—WASHINGTON—US troops captured 319 suspected Ba'ath Party murderers as part of a tough new crackdown on regime diehards yesterday, as Defense Secretary Donald Rumsfeld forcefully denied that the United States is getting into a 'quagmire' in Iraq.

Military officials said US forces carried out 27 raids and also seized more than $9 million in cash as well as hundreds of machine guns and grenade launchers over the past two days as part of Operation Sidewinder.

The military offensive is a get-tough display of American power aimed at defeating Saddam Hussein's loyalists and outside terrorists responsible for hit-and-run attacks on US troops and sabotage of Iraq's power and water services. But the Iraqi goon squads continued their guerrilla-style campaign yesterday, ambushing a US Avenger air-defense vehicle in the ultra-tense town of Fallujah, wounding Jeremy Little, an Australian-born sound man for NBC news.

The Pentagon says 65 soldiers have been killed and scores more wounded in a series of ambushes and attacks by Saddam loyalists since the war was declared over May 1.

But at a Pentagon briefing, Rumsfeld tried to counter growing criticism in Congress and in the media over the US policy toward Iraq and angrily denied that the US is getting into another Vietnam War quagmire. . . .

Rumsfeld admitted that fighting in Iraq 'will go on for some time', but said 'more and more Iraqis' are starting to cooperate with coalition forces in their hunt for Saddam's goon squads.[14]

17. Is the story slanted toward or against a particular group mentioned in the story? How?
18. Are there instances of loaded or biased language or emotional appeals in the story or headline? If so, give examples.
19. What is the main source for this story?
20. Is this story lacking another perspective on the events? Is there more to the story that isn't mentioned? If so, explain.

Integrative Exercises

These exercises pertain to material in Chapters 1–4.

1. What is a deductive argument? An inductive one?
2. What is a valid argument? A strong one?
3. What is an expert?
4. What is the appeal to authority?

For each of the following arguments, specify the conclusion and premises and say whether it is deductive or inductive. If it's inductive, say whether it is strong or weak; if deductive, say whether it is valid or invalid. If necessary, add implicit premises and conclusions.

5. 'In Canada, the new Canadian Strategy on HIV/AIDS contains, for the first time, a component on legal, ethical, and human-rights issues. This represents a huge step forward and a recognition that these issues must be an integral part of any strategy to fight HIV, for three reasons: because work aimed at ensuring that laws and policies facilitate rather than hinder efforts to prevent HIV/AIDS must be supported; because work aimed at ensuring that laws and policies facilitate rather than hinder efforts to provide care, treatment and support to people with HIV/AIDS must be supported; and because work aimed at ensuring that laws and policies respect and protect the rights of people with HIV/AIDS and those affected by the disease must be supported.' (Editorial, *Canadian HIV/AIDS Policy & Law Newsletter*, Volume 4, Number 2/3, Spring 1999)
6. 'We believe that affirmative action has been good for the country because it creates diverse student populations that give everyone a shot at the top—the American promise.' (Editorial, *Times Herald-Record*, Middletown, NY)
7. If Quebec separates from Canada, Quebec will suffer economically. Fortunately, Quebec won't separate from Canada. So, Quebec will not suffer economically.
8. No one is going to support the Prime Minister if he follows the United States in refusing to lower greenhouse gas emissions. But it looks as if he's going to follow the US. Thus, no one will support him.
9. For years, the grass simply would not grow, no matter how much watering or fertilizing she did. But after adding Miracle Sprout, the grass started to grow and spread throughout the property. Miracle Sprout did the trick.
10. 'Of course, Banzhaf's argument—that so-called "fast food" fare, like cigarettes, is addictive and causes illness and death—is ludicrous. Food supports life and only contributes to obesity when it is overused, that is, when we consume more calories (regardless of the source) than are expended in exercise. You will become overweight whether your excess calories come from beer, butter, beans, or burgers.' (Editorial, *New York Post*)

11. Of course Canadians should retain their link to the British Monarchy. Sure, Canada is a democracy now. But our link to the Monarchy is an important reminder of our history, and an important part of what makes us different from other North American countries.

12. Yes, the Monarchy is part of our heritage. But Canada is a modern democracy, and in a modern democracy there is simply no room for the remnants of an outdated form of authoritarian rule.

13. If you care about the environment, you drive a compact car. If you don't care about the environment, you drive an SUV. You do drive an SUV; so you don't care about the environment!

14. Vitamin X can lower blood pressure in middle-aged adults. At least four well-controlled scientific studies of nearly three thousand people prove it.

15. Franklin is either evil or crazy. He's definitely not crazy, so he must be evil.

16. If Julio doesn't pay his bills, he will be bankrupt. He will pay his bills. Therefore, he will not be bankrupt.

For each of the following unsupported claims, specify whether it seems worthy of acceptance, rejection, or a degree of belief in between.

17. I saw a ghost last night. I awoke in the middle of the night, looked up, and saw the figure of a woman at the foot of my bed. But I was too drowsy to pay much attention then. I fell back into a deep sleep.

18. My doctor says that drinking 10 glasses of water every day can prevent heart disease, diabetes, and high blood pressure.

19. Wearing an evil grin on his face when he was captured, the goon had to be the guy who committed the recent Stanley Park mugging.

20. The contractor for the giant high-rise says that constructing it makes good economic sense.

Critical Thinking and Writing Exercise

From Outline to First Draft

If you have developed a detailed outline, then you have a path to follow as you write. And while you're writing an argumentative essay, having a path is much better than searching for one. Your outline should make the writing much easier.

No outline is a finished work, however. As you write, you may discover that your arguments are not as strong as you thought, or that other arguments would be better, or that changing a point here and there would make an argument more effective. If so, you should amend your outline and then continue writing. The act of writing is often an act of discovery, and good writers are not afraid of revisions or multiple drafts.

Recall from Module 1 that good argumentative essays generally comprise these elements:

Introduction (or opening)
Statement of thesis (the claim to be supported)
Argument supporting the thesis
Assessment of objections
Conclusion

Start your draft with a solid opening that draws your readers into your essay and prepares the way for your arguments. Good openings are interesting, informative, and short. Grab the attention of your readers with a bold statement of your thesis, a provocative quotation, a compelling story, or interesting facts. Prepare the way for your arguments by explaining why the question you're addressing is important, why you're concerned about it, or why it involves a pressing problem. Don't assume that your readers will see immediately that the issue you're dealing with is worth their time.

Include a clear statement of your thesis in your opening (in the first paragraph or very close by). In many cases, you will want to tell the reader how you plan to develop your argument or how the rest of the essay will unfold (without going into lengthy detail). In any case, by the time your audience reads through your opening, they should know exactly what you intend to prove and why.

Consider this opening for our imaginary essay on air pollution from Module 3:

Respiratory experts at Health Canada say that sulphur dioxide in the air is a poison that we should avoid. Yet the provincial government wants to loosen environmental rules to allow coal-burning power plants to emit more sulphur dioxide than they already do. That's a bad idea. The latest evidence shows that letting the plants emit more of this poison will most likely increase the incidence of respiratory illnesses in hundreds of communities.

This opening gets the reader's attention by sounding the alarm about a serious health hazard. It provides enough background information to help us understand the seriousness of the problem. And the thesis statement in the last sentence announces what the essay will try to prove.

The body of your essay should fully develop the arguments for your thesis statement, or conclusion. You should devote at least one paragraph to each premise, though several paragraphs may be necessary. You may opt to deal with objections to your argument as you go along, perhaps as you put forth each premise or at the end of the essay just before the conclusion. Each paragraph should develop and explain just one idea, which is usually expressed in a topic sentence. Each sentence in each paragraph should relate to the paragraph's main idea. Any sentence that has no clear connection to the main idea should be deleted or revised. Be sure to link paragraphs together in a logical sequence using transitional words and phrases or direct references to material in preceding paragraphs.

Here are two paragraphs that might follow the air pollution opening:

Scientists used to wonder whether there is a connection between airborne sulphur dioxide and respiratory illness—but no more. Research has repeatedly shown a strong link between high levels of sulphur dioxide in the air and diseases that affect the lungs. For example, data from studies conducted by the Environmental Protection Agency (EPA) in the United States show that when levels of airborne sulphur dioxide in urban areas reach what the EPA calls the 'high normal' range, the incidence of respiratory illnesses increases dramatically. According to several EPA surveys of air quality, many major cities (not just Los Angeles, California) often have high normal levels of sulphur dioxide in the air. In addition, data from health departments in large cities show that when levels of airborne sulphur dioxide are at their highest, hospital admissions for asthma and other respiratory ills also increase.

These findings, however, tell only half the story. Many parts of the country have more than just occasional surges in levels of airborne sulphur dioxide. They must endure unsafe levels continuously. New studies from Health Canada demonstrate that in at least ten major cities, the amount of sulphur dioxide in the air is excessive all the time.

In this passage, a single paragraph is devoted to each premise. Each paragraph develops a single idea, which is stated in a topic sentence. (The topic sentence for the first paragraph is 'Research has repeatedly shown a strong link between high levels of sulphur dioxide in the air and diseases that affect the lungs.' For the second paragraph, the topic sentence is '[Many parts of the country] must endure unsafe levels continuously.') Each sentence in each paragraph relates to the topic sentence, and the relationships among the sentences are clear. Likewise the connection between the discussion in the first paragraph and that of the second is apparent.

The transitional sentence in the second paragraph ('These findings, however, tell only half the story.') helps bridge the gap between the paragraphs. Both of them help support the thesis statement.

How you end your essay is often as important as how you start it. In short or simple essays, there may be no need for a conclusion. The thesis may be clear and emphatic without a conclusion. In many cases, however, an essay is strengthened by a conclusion, and sometimes a conclusion is absolutely essential. Often without an effective conclusion, an essay may seem to end pointlessly or to be incomplete. The typical conclusion reiterates or reaffirms the thesis statement without being repetitious. Or the conclusion of the essay's argument serves as the conclusion for the whole essay. In long or complex essays, the conclusion often includes a summary of the main points discussed.

Sometimes a conclusion is a call to action, an invitation to the reader to do something about a problem. Sometimes it relates a story that underscores the importance of the essay's argument. Sometimes it highlights a provocative aspect of a claim defended earlier. In all cases it serves to increase the impact of the essay.

The conclusion, however, is not the place to launch into a completely different issue, make entirely unsubstantiated claims, malign those who disagree with you, or pretend that your argument is stronger than it really is. These tacks will not strengthen your essay but weaken it.

Defining Terms

Your essay will do its job only if it is understood, and it will be understood only if the meaning of its terms is clear. As noted in Module 3, sometimes a dispute can hang on the meaning of a single term. Clarify the meaning, and the disagreement dissolves. In an argumentative essay, clarifying terms often comes down to offering precise definitions of words that are crucial to your argument.

There are several different kinds of definitions. A lexical definition reports the meaning that a term has among those who use the language. For example, among English-speaking people, the word 'rain' is used to refer to condensed atmospheric moisture falling in drops, which is the lexical definition. A stipulative definition reports a meaning that a term is deliberately assigned, often for the sake of convenience or economy of expression. If you assign a meaning to a familiar term or to a term that you invent, you give a stipulative definition. A precising definition reports a meaning designed to decrease ambiguity or vagueness. It qualifies an existing term by giving it a more precise definition. Someone, for example, might offer a precising definition for the word 'old' (as it applies to the age of humans) by specifying that 'old' refers to anyone over eighty. A persuasive definition reports a meaning designed to influence attitudes or beliefs. It is usually not meant to be purely informative but is calculated to appeal to someone's emotions. Someone who opposes taxation, for example, might define 'taxation' as 'a form of state-run extortion'. Someone who thinks that taxation is generally a good thing might define 'taxation' as 'a way for individuals to contribute financially to important social programs'.

In general, any definition you offer should decrease vagueness or ambiguity and thereby increase the effectiveness of your writing. Your definitions should also be consistent. If you provide a definition for a term in your essay, then you should stick to that definition throughout. Altering the meaning of a term in mid-essay or using more than one term to refer to the same thing can be confusing to the reader—and might even subvert your essay's argument.

Good writers are also very much aware of another kind of meaning—the meaning that comes from a word's connotations. Connotations are the feelings, attitudes, or images associated with a word, beyond the literal meaning of the term. Consider these words: 'food', 'sustenance,' 'cuisine', and 'grub'. These terms have nearly the same literal meaning, but they differ in the emotions or attitudes they convey. Or what about these terms: 'tavern', 'saloon,' 'bar', 'watering hole', and 'dive'. They refer to the same kind of establishment, but the images or emotions conveyed are diverse, ranging from the respectable and pleasant (tavern) to the lowly and odious (dive).

Good writers make use of both the literal meaning of words and their connotations. Connotations, however, can sometimes mislead by obscuring or minimizing the facts. In debates about, for example, those who want greater independence for Quebec may characterize their position as favouring 'sovereignty and self-determination'. Those opposed to it might label it as 'seeking to break up Canada'. Both these labels are meant to provoke certain attitudes toward the subject matter—attitudes that may not be supported by any evidence or argument. Words used to convey positive or neutral attitudes or emotions in place of more negative ones are known as euphemisms. Words used to convey negative attitudes or emotions in place of neutral or positive ones are called dysphemisms. Consider the disparate impact on the reader of these pairs of terms, both of which refer to the same thing:

downsized	fired
revenue enhancements	tax increases
full-figured	fat
guerrillas	freedom fighters
resolute	pigheaded
emphatic	pushy
sweat	perspire
crippled	disabled
lie	incomplete truth
passed away	died

Keep in mind that euphemisms often perform a useful social purpose by allowing us to discuss sensitive subjects in an inoffensive way. We may spare people's feelings by saying that their loved ones 'have passed on' rather than that they 'have died', or that their dog 'was put to sleep' rather than 'killed'. Nevertheless, as critical thinkers, we should be on guard against the deceptive use of connotations. As critical writers, we should rely primarily on argument and evidence to make our case.

Writing Assignments

1. Write an alternative opening for Essay 3 ('Marine Parks') in Appendix A. If you want, you may invent quotations or stories.
2. Write an outline for Essay 4 ('The Kalam Cosmological Argument') in Appendix A. Include a thesis statement, each premise, and points supporting each premise.
3. Study Essay 8 ('The Cohabitation Epidemic') in Appendix A. Identify the rhetorical use of any euphemisms or dysphemisms.
4. Select one of the following topics and extract an issue from it that you can write about. Investigate arguments on both sides of the issue, and write a three-page paper defending your chosen thesis.

    - the morning-after pill
    - drug testing
    - vegetarianism
    - the Kyoto Accord
    - same-sex marriages
    - censorship media bias
    - commercial whaling
    - North Korea and nuclear weapons
    - endangered species
    - animal rights
    - Oscar nominations
    - Aboriginal land claims
    - date rape
    - tougher sentences for child molesters
    - oil drilling in national parks.

5. Write a two-page rebuttal to Essay 7 ('Yes, Human Cloning Should Be Permitted') in Appendix A. Use the testimony of experts to help defend your view.

Faulty Reasoning

Chapter Objectives

Irrelevant Premises

You will be able to

○ recognize fallacies of irrelevant premises (genetic fallacy, composition, division, appeal to the person, equivocation, appeal to popularity, appeal to tradition, appeal to ignorance, appeal to emotion, red herring, and straw man).

○ understand the concept of burden of proof and when it applies.

Unacceptable Premises

You will be able to

○ recognize fallacies of unacceptable premises (begging the question, false dilemma, slippery slope, hasty generalization, and faulty analogy).

An argument is meant to prove a point—to provide good reasons for accepting a claim. As you know, sometimes an argument succeeds, and sometimes it doesn't. When it doesn't, the problem will be that the premises are false, or the reasoning is faulty, or both. In any case, the argument is defective, bad, or bogus—call it what you will. There are countless ways that an argument can be defective. But there are certain types of defective arguments that recur so frequently that they have names (given to them, in many cases, by ancient philosophers or medieval scholars) and are usually gathered into critical-thinking texts so students can become aware of them. Such common, flawed arguments are known as **fallacies**, and they are therefore said to be fallacious.

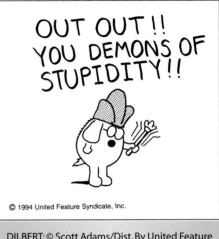

DILBERT: © Scott Adams/Dist. By United Feature Syndicate, Inc.

Fallacies are often beguiling; they can *seem* plausible. Time and again they are *psychologically* persuasive though *logically* impotent. The primary reason for studying fallacies, then, is to be able to detect them so you're not taken in by them.

We can divide fallacies into two broad categories: (1) those that have *irrelevant* premises and (2) those that have *unacceptable* premises.[1] Irrelevant premises have no bearing on the truth of the conclusion. An argument may seem to offer reasons for accepting the conclusion, but the 'reasons' have nothing to do with the conclusion. Unacceptable premises are relevant to the conclusion but are nonetheless dubious in some way. An argument may have premises that pertain to the conclusion, but they do not adequately support it. Premises can be unacceptable because they are as dubious as the claim they're intended to support, because the evidence they offer is too weak to support the conclusion adequately, or because they're otherwise so defective that they provide no support at all.

So, in good arguments, premises must be both relevant and acceptable. In fallacious arguments, at least one of these requirements is not met.

In this chapter we examine numerous fallacies of both types. We won't be able to discuss all known fallacies—there are just too many. But we will scrutinize the most common ones. By the time you have finished this chapter, you should be able to spot these fallacies a mile away.

Irrelevant Premises

Genetic Fallacy

The **genetic fallacy** consists of arguing that a claim is true or false solely because of its origin. For example:

> Selena's argument regarding Aboriginal rights can't be right because she's of European descent.

We should reject that proposal for solving the current welfare mess. It comes straight from the New Democratic Party.

Russell's idea about tax hikes came to him in a dream, so it must be junk.

These arguments fail because they reject a claim solely on the basis of where it comes from, not on its merits. In most cases, the source of an idea is irrelevant to its truth. Good ideas can come from questionable sources. Bad ideas can come from impeccable sources. Generally, judging a claim only by its source is a recipe for error.

There are times, however, when the origins of a claim can be a relevant factor. In court cases, when an eyewitness account comes from someone known to be a pathological liar, the jury is entitled to doubt the account.

Appeal to the Person

The fallacy of **appeal to the person** (or *ad hominem*, meaning 'to the man') is to reject a claim by criticizing the person who makes it rather than the claim itself. For example:

Watanabe has argued for an increase in the tax on cigarettes. But he once ran as the NDP candidate in a provincial election, so he's a raving socialist who thinks all taxes are good. Anything he has to say on this issue is sure to be loony.

We should reject Chen's argument for life on other planets. He dabbles in the paranormal.

You can't believe anything Beauchemin says about federalism. She's a known separatist.

You can't believe anything Morris says about welfare reform. He's a left-leaning softy.

Such arguments are fallacious because they attempt to discredit a claim by appealing to something that's almost always irrelevant to it, such as a person's character, motives, or personal circumstances. Claims must be judged on their own merits; they are not guilty by association. We are never justified in rejecting a claim because of a person's faults unless we can show how a person's faults translate into faults in the claim—and this is almost never the case. Even when a person's character *is* relevant to the truth of claims (as when we must consider the merits of testimonial evidence), we are not justified in believing a claim false just because the person's character is dubious. If the person's character is dubious, we are left with no reason to think the claim is either true *or* false.

The fallacy of appeal to the person is usually regarded as a special case of the genetic fallacy, discussed earlier in this chapter. What distinguishes an appeal to the person is that it not only *mentions* a person as the origin of an argument, but it also *attacks* the person (usually his or her character) and usually ignores the argument altogether.

The fallacy of appeal to the person comes in several varieties. One is the personal attack (mentioned earlier), which often simply consists of insults. The gist of these arguments is familiar enough. The arguer suggests that X's claims, ideas, or theories should be rejected because X is a radical, reactionary, extremist, right-winger, left-winger, fool, bonehead, moron, nutbar, or scum of the earth. Whatever psychological impact such terms of abuse may have, logically they carry no weight at all.

Another form of this fallacy emphasizes, not a person's character, but his or her circumstances. Here someone making a claim is accused of inconsistency—specifically, of maintaining a view that is inconsistent with his or her previous views or social or political commitments.

> Edgar asserts that global warming is real, but he's a card-carrying member of a political party that is officially skeptical about climate change. So he can't believe in global warming; he's got to deny it.

> Madison *says* she's in favour of higher levels of immigration, but you can't take her seriously. That view goes against everything her whole family believes in.

These arguments are fallacious if they're implying that a claim must be true (or false) just because it's inconsistent with some aspect of the claimant's circumstances. The circumstances are irrelevant to the truth of the claim.

When such arguments are put forth as charges of hypocrisy, we get another *ad hominem* fallacy known as **tu quoque** (or 'you're another'). The fallacious reasoning goes like this: Ellen claims that X, but Ellen doesn't practice/live by/condone X herself—so X is false. Look:

> West-coast granola crunchers tell us we shouldn't drive SUVs because they use too much gas and are bad for the environment. But they drive SUVs themselves. What hypocrites! I think we can safely reject their stupid pronouncements.

But whether someone is hypocritical about their claims can have no bearing on the truth of those claims. We may, of course, condemn someone for hypocrisy, but we logically cannot use that hypocrisy as a justification for rejecting his or her views. Their views must stand or fall on their own merits.

In another variation of circumstantial *ad hominem* reasoning, someone might deduce that a claim is false because the person making it, given his or her circumstances, would be *expected* to make it. For example:

> Wilson claims that the political system in Cuba is exemplary. But he *has* to say that. He's a card-carrying communist. So forget what he says.

But whether Wilson is a communist, and whether he would be expected or required to have certain views because of his connection to communism, is irrelevant to the truth of his claim.

Food For Thought

Fighting Fire with Fire

Political discourse is a massive breeding ground for *ad hominem* arguments. In this example, the writer uses an *ad hominem* attack while accusing her opponents of using *ad hominem* attacks!

> The Liberal Party has no real policy direction—nothing Canadian voters would be interested in, anyway. So, instead of coming up with new ideas, they just accuse the Conservatives and NDP of every flaw or failing that comes to mind. So Canadians should ignore the Liberal Party's whining criticisms of the Government's new environmental-policy initiatives.

Finally, we have the *ad hominem* tactic known as 'poisoning the well'. In this one, someone argues like this: X has no regard for the truth or has non-rational motives for espousing a claim, so nothing that X says should be believed—including the claim in question. The idea is that just as you can't get safe water out of a poisoned well, you can't get reliable claims out of a discredited claimant. This tack is fallacious because the fact that someone might have dubious reasons for making a claim does not show that the claim is false, nor does it mean that everything that comes out of the 'poisoned well' can be automatically dismissed.

Composition

The fallacy of **composition** is to argue that what is true of the parts must be true of the whole. The error here is to think that the characteristics of the parts are somehow transferred to the whole, something that is not always the case. Likewise, the error is committed whenever we assume that what's true of a member of a group is true of the group as a whole. For example,

The atoms that make up the human body are invisible. Therefore, the human body is invisible.

Each member of the club is productive and effective. So the club will be productive and effective.

Each note in the song sounds great. Therefore, the whole song will sound great.

Every part of this motorcycle is lightweight; therefore, the whole motorcycle is lightweight.

Sometimes, of course, the parts do share the same characteristics as the whole. We may safely conclude that since all the parts of the house are made of wood, the house itself is made of wood. We commit the fallacy of composition, though, when we assume that a particular case must be like this.

The fallacy of composition often shows up in statistical arguments. Consider:

> The average small investor puts $2,000 into the stock market every year. The average large investor puts $100,000 into stocks each year. Therefore, the group of large investors as a whole invests more money in the stock market than the small-investor group does.

The fact that the average small investor invests less than the average large investor does not mean that small investors as a group invest less than large investors as a group. After all, there may be many more small investors than large investors.

Division

The flip side of the fallacy of composition is the fallacy of **division**—arguing that what is true of the whole must be true of the parts. The fallacy is also committed when we assume that what is true of a group is true of individuals in the group.

> This machine is heavy. Therefore, all the parts of this machine are heavy.

> The building Dimitri lives in is huge, so his apartment must be huge.

> University students study every conceivable subject. So that university student over there also studies every conceivable subject.

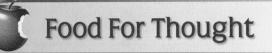

Food For Thought

The High Cost of a Fallacy

Did you know that fallacies can sell cars? Take a look at this conversation:

BRUNO: I really like this car. Looks like a babe magnet. Is it very expensive?

SALESPERSON: Oh, the price is very reasonable. You can easily afford it. The payments are only $190 a month.

BRUNO: Wow, I'll take it.

SALESPERSON: (Thinking to himself) Sucker. He just bought a $30,000 car.

The fallacy of composition strikes again.

These arguments are fallacious because they assume that characteristics of the whole are transferred to the parts or that traits of the group must be the same as traits of individuals in the group.

Like the fallacy of composition, the fallacy of division is frequently used in statistical arguments:

Of course Mike can run faster than Colleen! It's well known that men are, on average, faster runners than women.

Just because the average score for fourth-year students is higher than the average score for second-year students, it doesn't mean that anyone in fourth year must have a higher score than anyone in second year. The scores of individuals, which make up the average, may vary greatly.

Equivocation

The fallacy of **equivocation** is the use of a word in two different senses in an argument. For example:

The end of everything is its perfection.
The end of life is death.
Therefore, death is the perfection of life.

Only man is rational.
No woman is a man.
Therefore, no woman is rational.

Laws can only be created by law-givers.
There are many laws of nature.
Therefore, there must be a Law-Giver, namely, God.

Food For Thought

Bamboozling the Taxpayers

Suppose you hear these words in a speech by a national politician: 'My tax-cut plan will be a windfall for the Canadian taxpayer. Under my plan, the average tax savings will be $1,100 per person. Think of what each of you could do with that much extra income.'

Sounds like great news—except that this is an example of the fallacy of division. Just because the tax savings for Canadian taxpayers as a group is an average of $1,100, it doesn't mean that each individual taxpayer will get $1,100. It's possible that only a few taxpayers will get $1,100 or more while most won't get any tax break at all.

In the first argument, *end* is used in two different senses. In the first premise it means purpose, but in the second it means termination. Because of this flip-flop in meanings, the conclusion doesn't follow from the premises—but it looks as if it should.

In the second argument, *man* is the equivocal term. In the first premise it means humankind, but in the second, male. So the conclusion doesn't follow, making it appear that a sound argument has banished women's rationality.

In the third argument, *laws* is used in two senses—rules of human behaviour in the first premise, regularities of nature (as in 'law of gravity') in the second. Consequently, the conclusion trying to establish the existence of God doesn't follow.

The fallacy of equivocation occurs whenever a word has one meaning in one premise and another meaning in another premise or the conclusion. This switch of senses always invalidates the argument.

Equivocation often plays a central part in arguments over abortion because so much depends on the meaning of terms referring to the unborn. Consider:

Everyone agrees that a fetus is a human.
All human beings have a right to life.
Therefore, a fetus has a right to life.

In the first premise, *human* is used in the sense of something having human physical characteristics such as human DNA. In the second premise, the word is used with *beings* in the sense of a person with moral rights. Because of this shift in meaning, the argument fails.

Appeal to Popularity

The fallacy of the **appeal to popularity** (or to the masses) is to argue that a claim must be true merely because a substantial number of people believe it. The basic pattern of this fallacy is 'Everyone (or almost everyone, most people, many people) believes X, so X must be true.' For example:

Most people approve of the provincial government's decision not to pay for *in vitro* fertilization treatments. So I guess that decision must be a good one.

Of course Nova Scotia's rules for new drivers are justified. Everyone believes that they're justified.

The vast majority of Canadians believe that the monarchy is a good thing.

These arguments are fallacious because they assume that a proposition is true merely because a great number of people believe it. But as far as the truth of a claim is concerned, what many people believe is irrelevant. Many people used to believe that certain women were witches and should be burned, that slavery was perfectly acceptable, that Earth was the centre of the universe, and that bleeding and purging were cures for just about every illness. Large groups of people are no more infallible than an individual is. Their belief in a proposition, by itself, is no indication of truth.

What many other people believe, however, can be an indication of truth if they are experts or have expert knowledge in the issue at hand. If almost all farmers say that the fall harvest will be abundant, ordinarily we should believe them.

When the argument at hand is not about what many people *believe*, but rather about what many people *do*, we may have a case of **appeal to common practice**. For example:

> Of course it's OK to speed! Everybody does it.

> But Mom, why can't I get a tattoo? All the other girls in my class already have one!

> There's nothing wrong with cheating a bit on your taxes. I read somewhere that nearly half of all taxpayers lie about *something* on their tax returns.

The problem, here, is very similar to the problem with appeal to popularity. The fact that a lot of people *do* something is generally not an indication that it's ethical, polite, or wise for you to do it too.

Appeal to Tradition

The **appeal to tradition** is arguing that a claim must be true just because it's part of a tradition. For example:

> Acupuncture has been used for a thousand years in China. It must work.

> Of course publishing pornography is wrong. In this community there's a tradition of condemning it that goes back 50 years.

Such appeals are fallacious because tradition, like the masses, can be wrong. Remember that an established tradition barred women from voting, stripped Canada's Aboriginal peoples of their land, promoted the vengeful policy of 'an eye for an eye', and sanctioned the sacrifice of innocents to the gods.

Be careful, though. It is also not reasonable to automatically reject a claim because it's traditional. The point is that a tradition should be neither accepted nor rejected without good reason. Knee-jerk acceptance of tradition is as bad as knee-jerk rejection.

Appeal to Ignorance

The **appeal to ignorance** consists of arguing that a lack of evidence proves something. In one type of this fallacy, the problem arises by thinking that a claim must be true because it hasn't been shown to be false. For example:

> No one has shown that ghosts aren't real, so they must be real.

It's clear that God exists because science hasn't proved that he doesn't exist.

You can't disprove my theory that the current 'Stanley Cup' is a fake, and that the real one is hidden in Wayne Gretzky's basement. Therefore, my theory is correct.

The problem here is that a lack of evidence is supposed to prove something—but it can't. A lack of evidence alone can neither prove nor disprove a proposition. A lack of evidence simply reveals our ignorance about something.

In another variation of this fallacy, the breakdown in logic comes when you argue that a claim must be false because it hasn't been proved to be true. Look at these:

No one has shown that ghosts are real, so they must not exist.

It's clear that God doesn't exist because science hasn't proved that he does.

You can't prove your theory that the current 'Stanley Cup' is a fake, and that the real one is hidden in Wayne Gretzky's basement. Therefore, your theory is false.

Again, the moral is: Lack of evidence proves nothing. It does not give us a reason for believing a claim.

But what if our moral were wrong? If we could prove something with a lack of evidence, we could prove almost anything. You can't prove that invisible men aren't having a keg party on Mars—does this mean that it's true that invisible men are having a keg party on Mars? You can't prove that Socrates belched at his famous trial—does this prove that he didn't belch?

There are cases, however, that may seem like appeals to ignorance but actually are not. Sometimes when we carefully search for something, and such a thorough search is likely to uncover it if there is anything to uncover, the failure to find what we're looking for can show that it probably isn't there. A botanist, for example, may scan a forest looking for a rare plant but not find it even though she looks in all the likely places. In this case, her lack of evidence—her not finding the plant after a thorough search—may be good evidence that the plant doesn't exist in that environment. This conclusion would not rest on ignorance, but on the knowledge that in these circumstances any thorough search would probably reveal the sought-after object if it was there at all.

This kind of inductive reasoning is widespread in science. Drugs, for example, are tested for toxicity on rodents or other animals before they are given to humans. If after extensive testing no toxic effects are observed in the animals (which are supposed to be relevantly similar to humans), the lack of toxicity is considered evidence that the drug will probably not cause toxic effects in humans. Likewise, in the realm of extraordinary claims, some scientists regard the failure to find the

Loch Ness monster or Bigfoot after decades of searching to be evidence that these creatures do not exist.

Appeals to ignorance involve the notion of **burden of proof**. Burden of proof is the weight of evidence or argument required by one side in a debate or disagreement (in the critical thinking sense). Problems arise when the burden of proof is placed on the wrong side. For example, if Louise declares that 'no one has shown that gremlins aren't real, so they must be real,' she implicitly puts the burden of proof on those who don't agree with her. She's asserting, in effect, 'I say that gremlins are real, and it's up to you to prove I'm wrong.' Or to put it another way, 'I'm entitled to believe that gremlins are real unless you prove that they're not.' But as we saw earlier, this line is just an appeal to ignorance, and the burden of proof for showing that gremlins are real rests with *her*—not with those who don't share her belief. If her claim is unsupported, you need not accept it. If you take the bait and try to prove that gremlins don't exist, you are accepting a burden of proof that should fall on Louise's shoulders, not yours.

Usually, the burden of proof rests on the side that makes a positive claim—an assertion that something exists or is the case, rather than that something does not exist or is not the case. So in general, if a person (the claimant) makes an unsupported positive claim, he or she must provide evidence for it if the claim is to be accepted. If you doubt the claim, you are under no obligation to prove it wrong. You need not—and should not—accept it without good reasons (which the claimant should provide). Of course, you also should not reject the claim without good reasons. If the claimant does give you reasons for accepting the claim, you can either accept them or reject them. If you reject them, you are obligated to explain the reasons for your rejection.

Appeal to Emotion

The fallacy of the **appeal to emotion** is the use of emotions as premises in an argument. That is, it consists of trying to persuade someone of a conclusion solely by arousing his or her feelings rather than presenting relevant reasons. When you use this fallacy, you appeal to people's guilt, anger, pity, fear, compassion, resentment, pride—but not to good reasons that could give logical support to your case. Take a look:

> You should hire me for this network analyst position. I'm the best person for the job. If I don't get a job soon my wife will leave me, and I won't have enough money to pay for my mother's heart medication. Come on, give me a break.

> Political ad: If school music programs are cut as part of the School Board's new budget, we will save money—and lose our children to a world without music, a landscape without song. Let the children sing. Write to your member of the School Board now and let them know what you think!

As arguments, these passages are fallacious, not just because they appeal to strong emotions, but because they appeal to almost *nothing but* strong emotions. They urge us to accept a conclusion but offer no good reasons for doing so. We may feel compassion for the job hunter and his mother, but those feelings have no bearing on whether he is truly the best person for the job. We may recoil from the idea of children in a stark, tuneless world, but that overblown image and the emotions it evokes in us provide no logical support for the conclusion.

This kind of wielding of emotion in discourse is an example of *rhetoric*, the use of non-argumentative, emotive words and phrases to persuade or influence an audience. Arguments try to persuade through logic and reasons. Rhetoric tries to persuade primarily through the artful use of language. There's nothing inherently wrong with using rhetoric, but its use becomes fallacious when there's an attempt to support a conclusion by rhetoric alone.

President Richard M. Nixon's famous 'Checkers' speech of 1952 was a masterful appeal to emotion—a rhetorical tour de force that probably saved his career. Photo: Time and Life Pictures/Getty Images

But in such cases the fallacy is easily avoided. Good writers often combine arguments with appeals to emotion in the same piece of writing, and no fallacy need enter the picture. A strong argument is presented, and it's reinforced by strong feelings. Consider this piece of persuasive prose regarding the legal drinking age in various American states:

> I am a mother though my child is dead. He did not die of an incurable disease, of a virus beyond the ken of medical science. He was not taken from me by a foreign enemy while defending his country. No, he was needlessly slaughtered on the highway. A drunk driver ran broadside into his motorcycle. My son was shot fifty feet through the air by the collision and hit the blacktop at forty-five miles per hour.
>
> My son's assassin is not yet out of high school and yet that boy was able to walk into a liquor store and purchase two six-packs of beer, most of which he drank that evening. This boy does not have the mental capability to graduate from high school in the prescribed time (he was held back in his senior year), and yet the law has given him the right to purchase alcohol and decide for himself what is appropriate behaviour with regard to alcoholic consumption. I do not trust most of my adult friends to make such mature judgments. How can anyone trust the eighteen-year-old?

"Phew! Fooling some of the people all of the time is damn hard work."

www.CartoonStock.com

The law must change. Statistics have shown that states that have a minimum drinking age of twenty-one years also have significantly fewer automobile accidents caused by drunken teenagers. I lost my son, but why do any of the rest of us have to suffer as I have? Please, support legislation to increase the drinking age to twenty-one.[2]

There are appeals here to the reader's sympathy and indignation—but also an argument using statistics to support a conclusion about the need for new legislation.

Red Herring

'Discourse on virtue and they pass by in droves; whistle and dance the shimmy, and you've got an audience.'
—Diogenes

Perhaps the most blatant fallacy of irrelevance is the **red herring**, the deliberate raising of an irrelevant issue during an argument. This fallacy gets its name from the practice of dragging a smelly fish across a trail to throw a hunting dog off the scent. The basic pattern is to put forth a claim and then couple it with additional claims that may seem to support it but in fact are mere distractions. For instance:

Canada needs tougher immigration policies. I've got a neighbour who says we should let in *more* immigrants. The 60s … boy, what a great time that was for druggies and wackos! You should see the way that hippie dresses. . . . He hasn't figured out that the 60s are over!

The federal government should bring in mandatory minimum sentences for a greater range of serious crimes. I'm telling you, crime is a terrible thing when it happens to you. It causes death, pain, and fear. And I wouldn't want to wish these things on anyone.

Notice what's happening, here. In the first example, the issue is whether Canada should have tougher immigration policies. But the arguer shifts the subject to the intelligence and dress of one particular person who favours more immigration. That person's intelligence and way of dressing, of course, have nothing to do with the main issue. The argument is bogus. In the second example, the issue is whether the federal government should institute more mandatory minimum sentences. But the subject gets changed to the terrible costs of crime, which is only remotely related to the main issue. (There's also an appeal to fear, here.) We can agree that crime can have awful consequences, but this fact has little to do with the merits and demerits of instituting mandatory minimum sentences.

Straw Man

Related to red herring is the fallacy of the **straw man**—the distorting, weakening, or oversimplifying of someone's position so it can be more easily attacked or refuted. A straw-man argument distracts the listener by focusing on a distorted version of the target argument, rather than focusing on that argument itself. A straw-man argument works like this. Reinterpret claim X so that it becomes the weak or absurd claim Y. Attack claim Y. Conclude that X is unfounded. For example:

> David says he's in favour of equal marriage rights for gays. Obviously, he thinks gay relationships deserve special treatment, and that the gay lifestyle should be celebrated and promoted. Do you really want your kids being taught that the gay lifestyle is best? David does, and he's dead wrong.

> The Official Opposition is opposed to the Government's plan to increase spending on Canada's military. Why does the Opposition always want to leave Canada defenceless? Why do they want the military's budget cut? They want Canada to be stuck with a military that can't defend our borders, let alone participate in our proud tradition of peacekeeping overseas.

> The Premier says that the federal government ought to correct the 'fiscal imbalance' by transferring more money to the provinces and territories. I think if he had his way, the federal government would give up all its powers, and eventually waste away to nothing at all. Then there'd be nothing left to hold this country together. We can't let that happen! Oppose the Premier's plan!

In the first passage, David is in favour of equal marriage rights for gays. His opponent, however, distorts his view, claiming that David is actually in favour of teaching children that the gay lifestyle is *best*. David, of course, is not asserting this. This *distorted version* of David's position is easy to ridicule and reject, seemingly allowing his actual view to be summarily dismissed.

In the second passage, the Official Opposition is against increasing military spending. Their position, though, is twisted into the claim that the military's budget should actually be *reduced* to such an extent that the military becomes useless. But it is unlikely that that is what the Opposition really wants. They simply don't want the military's budget *increased*.

The third passage is typical of the kind of fallacious arguments that crop up in debates over federal–provincial relations. Here, the Premier wants the federal government to transfer more money to the provinces, in order to help correct what some people see as the 'fiscal imbalance' (i.e., the supposed mismatch between the responsibility the provinces have for major expenditures such as health care and education, and their relative lack of money compared to the federal government). But the Premier's view gets characterized as implying a wasting away of the federal government. But wanting to make *some* change in the balance of power (and financial ability) between the two levels of government is a far cry from wanting the federal government to have no role at all. Characterizing the Premier's point of view as so extreme, however, is a way to generate strong opposition to it. Note that in debates over federal–provincial relations, the straw-man tack is also taken to bolster the other side of the dispute. Those who favour *greater* powers for the federal

Review Notes

Fallacies with Irrelevant Premises

- *Genetic fallacy:* Arguing that a claim is true or false solely because of its origin.
- *Appeal to the person:* Rejecting a claim by criticizing the person who makes it rather than the claim itself.
- *Composition:* Arguing that what is true of the parts must be true of the whole.
- *Division:* Arguing that what is true of the whole must be true of the parts or that what is true of a group is true of individuals in the group.
- *Equivocation:* The use of a word in two different senses in an argument.
- *Appeal to popularity:* Arguing that a claim must be true merely because a substantial number of people believe it.
- *Appeal to common practice:* Arguing that a practice is ethical or wise merely because a substantial number of people do it.
- *Appeal to tradition:* Arguing that a claim must be true or good just because it's part of a tradition.
- *Appeal to ignorance:* Arguing that a lack of evidence proves something.
- *Appeal to emotion:* The use of emotions as premises in an argument.
- *Red herring:* An irrelevant issue raised during an argument.
- *Straw man:* A distorted, weakened, or oversimplified representation of someone's position that can be more easily attacked or refuted than the true position.

government are sometimes characterized as wanting to reduce the provinces to mere administrators of federal decisions and policies. But, of course, from the fact that someone wants to increase the powers of the federal government, it does not follow that they want to render the provinces entirely powerless.

Unacceptable Premises

Begging the Question

The fallacy of **begging the question** (or arguing in a circle) is the attempt to establish the conclusion of an argument by using that conclusion as a premise. To beg the question is to argue that a proposition is true because the very same proposition supports it:

p
Therefore, *p*.

The classic question-begging argument goes like this:

> God exists. We know that God exists because the Bible says so, and we should believe what the Bible says because God wrote it.

Or, more formally:

> The Bible says that God exists.
> The Bible is true because God wrote it.
> Therefore, God exists.

This argument assumes at the outset the very proposition ('God exists') that it is trying to prove. Any argument that does this is fallacious.

Unfortunately, most question-begging arguments are not as obviously fallacious as '*p* is true because *p* is true.' They may be hard to recognize because they are intricate or confusing. Consider this argument:

> It is in every case immoral to lie to someone, even if the lie could save a life. Even in extreme circumstances a lie is still a lie. All lies are immoral because the very act of prevarication in all circumstances is contrary to ethical principles.

At first glance, this argument may seem reasonable, but it's not. It reduces to this circular reasoning: 'Lying is always immoral because lying is always immoral.'

Among the more subtle examples of question begging is this famous one, a favourite of critical thinking texts:

> To allow every man unbounded freedom of speech must always be, on the whole, advantageous to the state; for it is highly conducive to the interests of the community that each individual should enjoy a liberty, perfectly unlimited, of expressing his sentiments.[3]

This argument, as well as the one preceding it, demonstrates the easiest way to subtly beg the question: just repeat the conclusion as a premise, but use different words.

False Dilemma

The fallacy of **false dilemma** consists either:

- of asserting that there are only two alternatives to consider when there are actually more than two, or

or

- of asserting that there are two distinct alternatives which may in fact not be mutually exclusive.

Let's start with the first kind. Here's an example:

> Look, either you're in favour of government support for the arts, or you're an uncultured thug. You're not in favour of government support for the arts. So you're an uncultured thug.

> 'Truth, like light, is blinding. Lies, on the other hand, are a beautiful dusk, which enhances the value of each object.'
> —Albert Camus

Food For Thought

Are We Begging the Question Yet?

In everyday usage, the phrase 'beg the question' often refers to the famous fallacy. But many times it does not. It is sometimes used (some would say misused) to mean something like 'prompts the question' or 'raises the question', as in, 'The rise in the crime rate begs the question of whether we have enough police officers on the job.' As a critical thinker, you need to make sure you don't get these two uses confused.

This argument contends that there are only two alternatives to choose from: either you're in favour of the government spending money to support the arts (painters, musicians, etc.) or you're an uncultured thug. But this argument works only if there really are just two alternatives. (A 'dilemma' is a situation where there are two equally undesirable possibilities.) But here there are actually other plausible possibilities. Maybe you like art, but don't want to see the government spending tax dollars on it. Maybe you spend a lot of money on art, and just don't think it's necessary for the arts to be supported by government. Because these possibilities are excluded, the argument is fallacious.

Again:

Either those lights you saw in the night sky were alien spacecraft (UFOs), or you were hallucinating. You obviously weren't hallucinating. So they had to be UFOs.

This argument says that there are only two possibilities: The lights were UFOs, or you hallucinated the whole thing. And they must have been UFOs because you weren't hallucinating. But as is the case with the majority of alleged paranormal events, there are many more possible explanations than most people realize. The lights could have been commercial aircraft, military aircraft, meteors, atmospheric conditions, or the planet Venus (which, believe it or not, is often mistaken for a UFO). Since the argument ignores these reasonable possibilities, it's fallacious.

Finally:

We must legalize drugs. We either legalize them or pay a heavy toll in lives and the taxpayers' money to continue the war on drugs. And we cannot afford to pay such a high price.

At first glance, these two alternatives may seem to exhaust the possibilities. But there is at least one other option—to launch a massive effort to prevent drug use and thereby reduce the demand for illegal drugs. The argument does not work because it fails to consider this possibility.

Note that these three arguments are expressed in disjunctive (either-or) form. But they can just as easily be expressed in a conditional (if-then) form, which says the same thing:

> Look, if you aren't in favour of government support for the arts, you're an uncultured thug. You're not in favour of government support for the arts. So you're an uncultured thug.

> If those lights you saw in the night sky were not alien spacecraft (UFOs), then you were hallucinating. You obviously weren't hallucinating. So they had to be UFOs.

> We must legalize drugs. If we don't legalize them, then we will pay a heavy toll in lives and the taxpayer's money to continue the war on drugs. And we cannot afford to pay such a high price.

Food For Thought

False Dilemmas, Evolution, and Creationism

False dilemmas seem to crop up in all kinds of controversies, including debates in science and philosophy. The following is an example of how the fallacy is thought to arise in the ongoing dispute between creationism and evolution.

> Creationists also assume that any data that counts against evolution counts in favor of creationism. But to argue in this way is to commit the fallacy of false dilemma: it presents two alternatives as mutually exclusive when, in fact, they aren't. Gish sets up the dilemma this way: 'Either the Universe arose through naturalistic, mechanistic evolutionary processes, or it was created supernaturally.' This argument is a false dilemma for a number of reasons. In the first place, there is no need to assume that the universe was created even if evolution is not supported. The universe, as many non-Western peoples believe, may be eternal, that is, without beginning or end. . . . Second, evolution is not the only natural account of creation, and Genesis is not the only supernatural account. Theories of creation are as varied as the cultures that conceived them. The Vikings believed that the universe developed naturally from the void whereas the Gnostics believed that it's the supernatural work of the devil. Thus, even if the creationists could totally discredit evolution, they would not thereby prove their own position, for there are many other alternatives.[4]

Sometimes we encounter stand-alone disjunctive phrases rather than full-blown false dilemma arguments. These are false choices often presented as one-liners or headlines in tabloid newspapers, TV news programs, and magazines. For example:

Provincial Parks: Natural Wonder or Economic Opportunity?

Microsoft: Bad Cop or Evil Giant?

Is the Government Incompetent or Just Evil?

By limiting the possibilities, these headlines can imply that almost any outlandish state of affairs is actual—without even directly asserting anything.

People are often taken in by false dilemmas because they don't think beyond the alternatives laid before them. Out of fear, the need for simple answers, or a failure of imagination, they don't ask, 'Is there another possibility?' To ask this is to think outside the box and reduce the likelihood of falling for simplistic answers.

False dilemmas also arise when the arguer asserts that there are two distinct alternatives when in fact the two options offered may not be mutually exclusive. For example:

She's either a lawyer or a doctor, but I can't figure out which!

This counts as a false dilemma because these two possibilities—being a lawyer and being a doctor—are not in fact mutually exclusive. It is possible to be both, and some people *are* both.

Here's another example:

Why are you so concerned about the rights of the *accused*? Are you interested in the rights of accused criminals, or the rights of their victims?

Again, this is a false dilemma because the two options being offered are not necessarily in opposition to each other. We can be concerned with protecting the rights of those accused of crimes (for example, presuming them 'innocent until proved guilty') while at the same time wanting to work to assist and protect the victims of crime. In the face of a false dilemma of this kind, we should reply, 'Why can't I do both?'

Slippery Slope

The fallacy of **slippery slope** is to argue, without good reasons, that taking a particular step will inevitably lead to a further, undesirable step (or steps). The idea behind the metaphor, of course, is that if you take the first step on a slippery slope, you will have to take others because, well, the slope is slippery. A familiar slippery-slope pattern is 'Doing action A will lead to action B, which will lead to action C, which will result in calamitous action D. Therefore, you should not do action A.' It's fallacious when there is no good reason to think that doing action A will actually result in undesirable action D. Take a look at this classic example:

> Americans absolutely must not lose the war in Vietnam. If South Vietnam falls to the communists, then Thailand will fall to them. If Thailand falls to them, then South Korea will fall to them. And before you know it, all of Southeast Asia will be under communist control.

This argument was a commonplace during the Cold War. It was known as the domino theory because it asserted that if one country in Southeast Asia succumbed to communism, they all would succumb, just as a whole row of dominoes will fall if the first one is pushed over. It was fallacious because there was no good evidence that the dominoes would inevitably fall as predicted. In fact, after South Vietnam was defeated, they did not fall as predicted.

Here are some more examples:

> If supporters of the federal government's Firearms Registry get their way, all recreational and hunting weapons will have to be registered with the federal government. Next thing you know, it'll be illegal to own a gun for target practice, or to go hunting for rabbits, like my Dad and I did when I was a boy. Eventually, the government will want to know if you own *any* weapon, whether it's a pocket knife or a baseball bat. So if you support the Firearms Registry, you're inviting the government to invade your privacy and interfere with your basic freedoms.

> We must ban pornography in all forms. Otherwise, rape and other sex crimes will be as common as jaywalking.

> All Canadians should oppose gay marriage. If gay marriage is allowed, before you know it anything goes—polygamy, incest, marrying animals . . . who knows!

These arguments follow the basic slippery-slope pattern. They are fallacies, not because they assert that one event or state of affairs can inevitably lead to others, but because there is no good reason to believe the assertions. Some arguments may look like slippery-slope fallacies but are not because there is good reason to think that the steps are connected as described. Observe:

> If you have Lyme disease, you definitely should get medical treatment. Without treatment, you could develop life-threatening complications. Man, you could die. You should see your doctor now.

This is not a fallacious slippery-slope argument. There are good reasons to believe that the series of events mentioned would actually happen.

Review Notes

Fallacies with Unacceptable Premises

- *Begging the question:* The attempt to establish the conclusion of an argument by using that conclusion as a premise.
- *False dilemma:* Asserting that there are only two alternatives to consider when there are actually more than two.
- *Slippery slope:* Arguing, without good reasons, that taking a particular step will inevitably lead to a further, undesirable step (or steps).
- *Hasty generalization:* The drawing of a conclusion about a target group based on an inadequate sample size.
- *Faulty analogy:* An argument in which the things being compared are not sufficiently similar in relevant ways.

Hasty Generalization

'One cool judgment is worth a thousand hasty counsels.'
—Woodrow Wilson

In Chapter 4 we pointed out the connection between the availability error and the fallacy known as **hasty generalization**. In Chapter 8 we will examine hasty generalizations at length. Here we need only recall that we are guilty of hasty generalization when we draw a conclusion about a whole group based on an inadequate sample of the group. This mistake is a genuine fallacy of unacceptable premises because the premises stating the sample size are relevant to the conclusion, but they provide inadequate evidence. For example:

You should buy a Dell computer. They're great. I bought one last year, and it has given me nothing but flawless performance.

The only male professor I've had this year was a chauvinist pig. All the male professors at this school must be chauvinist pigs.

Psychology majors are incredibly ignorant about human psychology. Believe me, I know what I'm talking about: My best friend is a psych major. What an ignoramus!

The French are snobby and rude. Remember those two high-and-mighty guys with really bad manners? They're French. I rest my case.

The food at Pappie's Restaurant is awful. I had a sandwich there once, and the bread was stale.

Faulty Analogy

We will also discuss **arguments by analogy** in Chapter 8. Like hasty generalizations, defective arguments by analogy, or **faulty analogies**, are also fallacies involving unacceptable premises. An analogy is a comparison of two or more things alike
in specific respects. An argument by analogy reasons this way. Because two or more
things are similar in several respects, they must be similar in some further respect.
For example:

> The last time we went on vacation and left you in charge of the house, you
> said you wanted to have 'a few friends' over for a party, and the house was a
> mess when we got home. Likewise, this time you say you want to have 'a few
> friends' over. So if we let you, I'm sure the house will be a disaster area when
> we get home!

> A watch is a mechanism of exquisite complexity with numerous parts pre-
> cisely arranged and accurately adjusted to achieve a purpose—a purpose
> imposed by the watch's designer. Likewise the universe has exquisite com-
> plexity with countless parts—from atoms to asteroids—that fit together pre-
> cisely and accurately to produce certain effects as though arranged by plan.
> Therefore, the universe must also have a designer.

In a faulty analogy, the things being compared are not sufficiently similar in
relevant ways. Such analogical arguments are said to be weak. For instance, you
could argue that:

> Dogs are warm-blooded, nurse their young, and give birth to puppies.
> Humans are warm-blooded and nurse their young. Therefore, humans give
> birth to puppies too.

This argument by analogy is about as weak as they come—and a little silly. Dogs
and humans are not sufficiently similar in relevant ways (in physiology, for one
thing) to justify such a strange conclusion.

Summary

Certain types of defective arguments that occur frequently are known as fallacies.
Fallacies are often psychologically persuasive but logically flawed. We can divide
fallacies into two broad categories: (1) those that have *irrelevant* premises and (2)
those that have *unacceptable* premises.

Fallacies with irrelevant premises include the genetic fallacy (arguing that a
claim is true or false solely because of its origin), composition (arguing that what
is true of the parts must be true of the whole), division (arguing that what is true
of the whole must be true of the parts or that what is true of a group is true of

individuals in the group), appeal to the person (rejecting a claim by criticizing the person who makes it rather than the claim itself), equivocation (the use of a word in two different senses in an argument), appeal to popularity (arguing that a claim must be true merely because a substantial number of people believe it), appeal to ignorance (arguing that a lack of evidence proves something), appeal to tradition (arguing that a claim must be true or good just because it's part of a tradition), appeal to emotion (the use of emotions as premises in an argument), red herring (the deliberate raising of an irrelevant issue during an argument), and straw man (the distorting, weakening, or oversimplifying of someone's position so it can be more easily attacked or refuted).

Fallacies with unacceptable premises include begging the question (the attempt to establish the conclusion of an argument by using that conclusion as a premise), slippery slope (arguing, without good reasons, that taking a particular step will inevitably lead to a further, undesirable step or steps), hasty generalization (the drawing of a conclusion about a group based on an inadequate sample of the group), and faulty analogy (an argument in which the things being compared are not sufficiently similar in relevant ways).

Key Terms

Appeal to common practice: The fallacy of arguing that a practice is ethical or wise merely because a substantial number of people do it.

Appeal to emotion: The fallacy of using emotions in place of relevant reasons as premises in an argument.

Appeal to ignorance: The fallacy of arguing that a lack of evidence proves something. In one type of this fallacy, the problem arises by thinking that a claim must be true because it hasn't been shown to be false. In another type, the breakdown in logic comes when you argue that a claim must be false because it hasn't been proved to be true.

Appeal to popularity (or to the masses): The fallacy of arguing that a claim must be true merely because a substantial number of people believe it.

Appeal to the person/*ad hominem* (appeal to the person): The fallacy of rejecting a claim by criticizing the person who makes it rather than the claim itself. *Ad hominem* means 'to the man'.

Appeal to tradition: The fallacy of arguing that a claim must be true just because it's part of a tradition.

Argument by analogy (analogical induction): An argument making use of analogy, reasoning that because two or more things are similar in several respects, they must be similar in some further respect.

Begging the question: The fallacy of attempting to establish the conclusion of an argument by using that conclusion as a premise. Also called arguing in a circle.

Burden of proof: The weight of evidence or argument required by one side in a debate or disagreement.

Composition: The fallacy of arguing that what is true of the parts must be true of the whole. The error is thinking that the characteristics of the parts are somehow transferred to the whole, something that is not always the case.

Division: The fallacy of arguing that what is true of the whole must be true of the parts. The error is thinking that characteristics of the whole must transfer to the parts or that traits of the group must be the same as traits of individuals in the group.

Equivocation: The fallacy of using a word in two different senses in an argument.

Fallacy: An argument form that is both common and defective; a recurring mistake in reasoning.

False dilemma: The fallacy of asserting that there are only two alternatives to consider when there are actually more than two.

Faulty analogy: A defective argument by analogy.

Genetic fallacy: The fallacy of arguing that a claim is true or false solely because of its origin.

Hasty generalization: The fallacy of drawing a conclusion about a target group on the basis of too small a sample.

Red herring: The fallacy of deliberately raising an irrelevant issue during an argument. The basic pattern is to put forth a claim and then couple it with additional claims that may seem to support it but, in fact, are mere distractions.

Slippery slope: The fallacy of arguing, without good reasons, that taking a particular step will inevitably lead to further, undesirable steps.

Straw man: The fallacy of distorting, weakening, or oversimplifying someone's position so it can be more easily attacked or refuted.

Tu quoque ('**you're another**'): A type of *ad hominem* fallacy that argues that a claim must be true (or false) just because the claimant is hypocritical.

Exercises

Exercise 5.1

Review Questions

1. According to the text, what are the two broad categories of fallacies?
2. What is the genetic fallacy?
3. Can the origin of a claim ever be relevant to deciding its truth or falsity?
* 4. What is the fallacy of composition?
5. What are the two forms of the fallacy of division?
6. Why are appeals to the person fallacious?
7. What type of *ad hominem* argument is put forth as a charge of hypocrisy?
8. What is the fallacy of poisoning the well?
9. What is the fallacy of equivocation?
* 10. Why are appeals to popularity fallacious?
11. What is the appeal to tradition?
12. What are the two forms of the appeal to ignorance?
13. What is the proper response to an appeal to ignorance?
14. What is rhetoric?
* 15. According to the text, is it ever legitimate to use rhetoric and argument together?

16. What is the fallacy of red herring?
17. What is the basic pattern of argument of the straw-man fallacy?
18. What is the fallacy of begging the question?
* 19. Why are people often taken in by false dilemmas?
20. What is the burden of proof?
21. What is the fallacy of slippery slope?

Exercise 5.2

In the following passages, identify any fallacies of irrelevance (genetic fallacy, composition, division, appeal to the person, equivocation, appeal to popularity, appeal to ignorance, appeal to tradition, appeal to emotion, red herring, and straw man). Some passages may contain more than one fallacy, and a few may contain no fallacies at all.

* 1. 'Seeing that the eye and hand and foot and every one of our members has some obvious function, must we not believe that in like manner a human being has a function over and above these particular functions?' (Aristotle)

2. The federal budget deficits are destroying this country. Just ask any working stiff; he'll tell you.

3. The hippies of the sixties railed against the materialistic, capitalistic system, and everyone who prospered in it. But all their bellyaching was crap because they were a bunch of hypocrites, living off their rich mothers and fathers.

4. The North American Free Trade Agreement is ruining this country. Just ask any working stiff; he'll tell you.

* 5. The *National Post* says that a proposal to force companies to embrace Corporate Social Responsibility amounts to a denial of the basic principles of the market economy. But you know that's false—the *National Post* is a notorious right-wing rag!

6. Geraldo says that students who cheat on exams should not automatically be expelled from school. But it's ridiculous to insist that students should never be punished for cheating.

7. Of course there is a God. Almost every civilization in history has believed in a deity of some kind.

8. My sweater is blue. Therefore, the atoms that make up the sweater are blue.

9. The prime minister is lying about his intelligence briefings since almost everyone surveyed in national polls thinks he's lying.

* 10. Kelly says that many women who live in predominantly Muslim countries are discriminated against. But how the heck would she know? She's not a Muslim.

11. A lot of people think that football jocks are stupid and boorish. That's a crock. Anyone who had seen the fantastic game that our team played on Saturday, with three touchdowns before halftime, would not believe such rubbish.

12. Does acupuncture work? Can it cure disease? Of course. It has been used in China by folk practitioners for at least 3,000 years.

13. The study found that 80 per cent of women who took the drug daily had no recurrence of breast cancer. But that doesn't mean anything. The study was funded in part by the company that makes the drug.

* 14. 'The only proof capable of being given that an object is visible, is that people actually see it. The only proof that a sound is audible, is that people hear it: and so of the other sources of our experience. In like manner, I apprehend, the sole evidence it is possible to produce that anything is desirable, is that people actually desire it.' (John Stuart Mill)

15. The new StratoCar is the best automobile on the road. Picture the admiring glances you'll get when you take a cruise in your StratoCar through town. Imagine the power and speed!

16. Gremlins exist, that's for sure. No scientist has ever proved that they don't exist.

17. 'The most blatant occurrence of recent years is all these knuckleheads running around protesting nuclear power—all these stupid people who do not research at all and who go out and march, pretending they care about the human race, and then go off in their automobiles and kill one another.' (Ray Bradbury)

18. Do herbal remedies work? There can be no doubt, for they have been used in traditional medicine for thousands of years!

19. Is the Bible divinely inspired? There can be no doubt that it is, for it has been a best-seller for thousands of years.

* 20. The former mayor was convicted of drug possession, and he spent time in jail. So you can safely ignore anything he has to say about legalizing drugs.

21. I believe that baby-carrying storks are real creatures. No one has ever proved that they don't exist.

22. Professor, I deserve a better grade than a D on my paper. Look, my parents just got a divorce. If they see that I got a D, they will just blame each other, and the fighting will start all over again. Give me a break.

23. Only man has morals. No woman is a man. Therefore, no woman has morals.

24. Every player on the team is the best in the league. So the team itself is the best in the league.

Exercise 5.3

In the following passages, identify any fallacies of unacceptable premises (begging the question, false dilemma, slippery slope, hasty generalization, and faulty analogy). Some passages may contain more than one fallacy, and a few may contain no fallacies at all.

1. Random drug testing in competitive sports is very effective in reducing drug use by athletes because the regular use of the testing makes drug use less likely.

2. If today we allow voluntary, physician-assisted suicide, then tomorrow we'll have non-voluntary physician-assisted suicide on unconscious or incompetent patients. Then we'll have involuntary physician-assisted 'suicide', on unwilling patients. Soon, no hospital patient will be safe from 'helpful' physicians!

3. Three thieves are dividing up the $7,000 they just stole from the local bank. Robber number one gives $2,000 to robber number two, $2,000 to robber number three, and $3,000 to himself. Robber number two says, 'How come you get $3,000?' Robber number one says, 'Because I am the leader.' 'How come you're the leader?' 'Because I have more money.'

* 4. Either God exists or he does not exist. If he exists, and you believe, you will gain heaven; if he exists and you don't believe, you will lose nothing. If he does not exist, and you believe, you won't lose much. If he does not exist, and you don't believe, you still won't lose much. The best gamble then is to believe.

5. Ivan doesn't talk about his political views. He's got to be either a Grit or a Tory. And he's certainly no Grit. So he must be a Tory!

* 6. I used to work with this engineering major, and, man, they are really socially inept.

7. I met these two guys on a plane, and they said they were from Edmonton. They were total druggies. Almost everyone in that city must be on drugs.

8. Some people are fools, and some people are married to fools.

9. Bill is an investment banker, drives a Lexus, is overweight, and votes Conservative. John is also an investment banker, drives a Lexus, and is overweight. So John probably votes Conservative too.

* 10. Either we fire this guy or we send a message to other employees that it's okay to be late for work. Clearly, we need to fire him.

Exercise 5.4

For each of the following claims, devise an argument using the fallacy shown in parentheses. Make the argument as persuasive as possible.

1. The provincial budget deficit will destroy the economy. (red herring)
2. *Shane* is the best movie Western ever made. (appeal to popularity)
* 3. Mrs Anan does not deserve the Nobel Prize. (appeal to the person)
4. Vampires—the blood-sucking phantoms of folklore—are real. (appeal to ignorance)
5. Internet pornography can destroy this country. (slippery slope)
* 6. It's great that Scouts Canada welcomes gay kids as members. (begging the question)
7. Quebec should separate from Canada. (false dilemma)
8. That economics seminar is absolutely the worst course offered at the university. (hasty generalization)

9. Pope John Paul II was a moral giant. (appeal to emotion)
10. The Nigerian court was right to sentence that woman to be stoned to death for adultery. (appeal to popularity)
* 11. Newfoundland's fisheries are a mess because the Department of Fisheries and Oceans—a federal department—has too much power over them. (red herring)
12. All efforts should be made to ban trade in exotic pets such as tigers. (genetic fallacy)

Field Problems

1. Find, in a magazine or newspaper, a letter to the editor that contains at least one fallacy. Point out the fallacious part, name the fallacy involved, and then rewrite the passage to eliminate the fallacy and strengthen the argument. (To rework the argument effectively, you may have to make up some facts.)
2. Select a page of editorials or letters from a newspaper (it should contain several opinions on various issues). Scan the entire page, circling and labelling any examples of fallacies. Find at least three examples.

Self-Assessment Quiz

Name the fallacy or fallacies in the following passages.

1. The Mayor is a racist! At a City Council meeting last night, he said that he won't support our proposal to name a street after Nelson Mandela. How can we tolerate elected officials who say that minorities shouldn't have rights?
2. You think that welfare mothers would actually prefer to have jobs? Prove it, and until you do they are all lazy moochers.
3. Legislation to officially recognize gay marriage was opposed by crazy religious groups across the country—which proves that the legislation is on the right track!
4. '[George W.] Bush lies about important things like the economy, his tax cuts, his education, our reasons for going to war and drunk driving. But I think he lies only when he feels he has to. He knows that most of the time Fox News, the *Wall Street Journal* and Rush Limbaugh are only too glad to do it for him.' (Al Franken)
5. 'Jews are part of the Soviet people. They are a fine people, intelligent, very valued in the Soviet Union. Therefore, the problem of the Jews in the Soviet Union does not exist.' (Mikhail Gorbachev)
6. You can safely ignore Helena's argument for a freeze on tuition because she's active in the Canadian Federation of Students.

7. You advocate a woman's right to abortion because you do not understand how hideous and monstrous an abortion procedure is, how it tears a living fetus away from the uterine wall, crushes it to bleeding pieces, and sucks it away into oblivion.

8. That is a lousy book. It did not sell well at all.

9. All of us cannot be loved because all of us cannot be the focus of deep affection.

10. 'If the parts of the Universe are not accidental, how can the whole Universe be considered as the result of chance? Therefore the existence of the Universe is not due to chance.' (Moses Maimonides)

11. This government is either one of the best or one of the worst. It is certainly not one of the best, so we must count it among those at the bottom of the heap.

12. Atheistic philosophers have been trying for thousands of years to prove that there is no God, and they haven't succeeded yet. This shows that there is indeed a God after all.

13. How can you, with a straight face, argue that animals have rights and expect me to believe you? You eat meat!

14. Judges should not hand down anything but maximum sentences for all convicted criminals. If you start making exceptions, prosecutors will start asking for lighter sentences. Next thing you know, every criminal will be getting off with mere warnings.

15. Either you're a Catholic, or you're a godless heathen!

16. Why on earth would you want to hire someone like Crystal? I doubt she's reliable. After all, look at how she dresses!

17. If he truly loved me, he would have written me a letter and said so. He didn't do that, so he obviously hates me.

18. When I was in elementary school, we were supposed to stand and recite 'The Lord's Prayer' every day before class. That was dead wrong. No child should have to submit to such brainwashing.

19. Ranjit was caught cheating on his final exam. But why should he be punished when a dozen other people cheated last year in the same course?

20. My Mom says I shouldn't be staying out late and partying. But Grandma says that Mom was a huge partier when she was my age. So why should I listen to what Mom says?

 ## Integrative Exercises

These exercises pertain to material in Chapters 1–5.

For each of the following passages, say whether it contains an argument. If it does, specify the conclusion and premises, whether the argument is deductive or inductive, whether it is a good argument (sound or cogent), and whether it is a fallacy. Some passages may contain no argument.

1. Amanda denies that she votes Liberal, so she must vote Liberal.

2. You say that there are no such things as ghosts, but can you prove that they don't exist?

3. 'Didn't Tom Cruise make a stock-car movie in which he destroyed thirty-five cars, burned thousands of gallons of gasoline, and wasted dozens of tires? If I were given the opportunity, I'd say to Tom Cruise, "Tom, most people don't own thirty-five cars in their *life*, and you just trashed thirty-five cars for a movie. Now you're telling other people not to pollute the planet? Shut up, sir."' (Rush Limbaugh)

4. 'The large number of female voters for Arnold Schwarzenegger in California announces one thing: the death of feminism. That so many women would ignore his sexual misconduct and vote for him bespeaks the re-emergence of the reckless phallus.' (Letter to the editor, *Newsday*)

5. Alanis Morissette and Shania Twain are vegetarians. And Nazi leader Adolf Hitler was also a vegetarian. We are forced to conclude that Morissette and Twain are Nazis!

6. If Parliament ratifies the Kyoto protocol, Canada will slide backwards economically, until we join the ranks of Third World nations and need to look to wealthier neighbours for handouts!

7. Multiculturalism makes for a better society. Everybody knows that, even if they won't admit it.

8. Thinking is like swimming. Just as in swimming it's easy to float on the top but hard to dive deep, it's easy in thinking to float along on the surface of an issue but difficult to use your intellect to delve down into the layers.

9. 'If a cell, under appropriate conditions, becomes a person in the space of a few years, there can surely be no difficulty in understanding how, under appropriate conditions, a cell may, in the course of untold millions of years, give origin to the human race.' (Herbert Spencer)

10. The chancellor is either a crook or a nut. He is a crook. Thus, he is no nut.

11. Everything must either happen by random accident or by divine intervention. Nothing happens by pure accident, so everything must happen because of divine intervention.

12. Children should never be spanked. Spanking is harmful. I've talked to three mothers about this issue, and they all agree that spanking harms a child's self-esteem and development.

13. The Eagles are the most popular rock group in history because they have sold the most records.

14. My professor says that telling a lie is never morally permissible. But that's ridiculous. The other day I heard him tell a bold-faced lie to one of his students.

15. 'Not all forms of gender discrimination are unethical. There are a number of exclusively male or female fitness clubs around the country utilized by religious individuals who shun the meat market scene. If a woman wants to spare herself the embarrassment of being ogled in her sports bra while doing thigh-thrusts, it is her right to work out with women only. Similarly, if a man wants to spare himself the temptation of working out with lingerie models, he should be allowed membership to strictly male fitness clubs. It would be unreasonable to require non-discrimination of these private clubs, or to make them build separate facilities to accommodate everyone.' (Letter to the editor, *Arizona Daily Wildcat*)

16. 'Highway checkpoints, drug testing, ubiquitous security cameras and now the government's insistence on the use of sophisticated software tools to spy on the American people all point to a single vision. This vision was shared with us years ago, in George Orwell's book *1984*. Big Brother is indeed watching.'(Letter to the editor, *Buffalo News*)

17. There are those on campus who would defend a professor's right to question the teachings of Islam. But there is no such right. Racism is wrong, and will always be wrong.

18. 'It is impossible to make people understand their ignorance; for it requires knowledge to perceive it and therefore he that can perceive it hath it not.' (Jeremy Taylor)

19. If you give that homeless guy fifty cents today, tomorrow he will want a dollar, then five dollars, then ten, and where will it stop? Before you know it, *you're* homeless.

20. What your dad told you about staying away from boys is true. If it weren't true, he wouldn't have said it!

Critical Thinking and Writing Exercise

An Annotated Sample Paper

Let's see how the lessons of the four previous modules might be applied in an actual student essay.[5] The essay on the following pages incorporates the main elements of good argumentative papers and, as even the best essays do, exhibits both strengths and weaknesses—many of which are noted in the margins. Read the paper carefully, taking in the annotations as you go and making sure you understand each point before moving on to the next.

Free Speech on Campus

In order to meet the goals and purposes of higher education, free speech must remain intact. Thus, the University of Missouri should not adopt a campus hate speech code. ①The First Amendment protects all speech outside the university setting, and what happens outside of the university setting also should be allowed inside. ②Without an open forum for thought, though it may include hate speech, the university fails in its mission to provide a realistic experience for its students. By abolishing hate speech on university campuses, that open forum for discovery and knowledge is eliminated. As a result, learning and knowledge are stunted. ③ Without the exchange of controversial ideas and opinions, there can be no real change in our society. Experiencing and debating is almost always better than suppressing, because censoring speech can never invoke real change.

Seems to be three arguments to discuss but this summary does not make that as clear as it should.

Thesis statement

Summarizes the arguments to be made.

The First Amendment protects the right for every person to express opinions about the government and about each other. It actually 'protects speech no matter how offensive the content' (Hate Speech on Campus, 1996). Just because something is offensive to one person does not mean it is offensive to another. Justice John M. Harlan wrote in Cohen v. California (1971), 'One man's vulgarity is another's lyric' (Free Speech, 1996). In other words, just because something is offensive to one person does not mean that it is offensive by definition.

Provides background for first argument.

Needs a more explicit transition to first argument.

Sources cited

Speech that is protected outside of the university setting also should be protected inside. Some would argue that hate speech hinders the abilities of minority students to learn, but part of the goal of higher education is to put students out of their comfort zone and to challenge their ways of thinking. In response to a sexual-harassment policy being implemented at the University of Massachusetts, lawyer Harvey A. Silvergate (1995) wrote a memo to university administrators opposing the proposal.

First argument for thesis

Responds to an objection to thesis.

One of the primary purposes of a college education and experience is to challenge students, to make them question their comfortable lives and assumptions in short, to discomfort them in one way or another. (Silvergate, 1995)

In the same memo, Silvergate also wrote:

If I am allowed to say something on the street corner, in a letter to the editor of a newspaper, or on a radio talk show, surely I should be allowed to say it on the campus of the University of Massachusetts.

Not clear how these quotations— which refer to sexual harassment— relate to hate speech.

First argument for thesis

This is equally true for the University of Missouri. What can possibly be gained by excluding an element of real life such as offensive speech from the campus experience? The university would only serve to deceive its students by shielding them from realistic situations while they are in school. This, in turn, only serves to place them into the real world with false expectations.

Alternatively, exploring and debating is almost always better than suppressing. The organization Justice on Campus (1995) contends that:

Introduces quotation

When we hear speech or see images that offend us, nothing is more human than our urge to suppress or to destroy them. But as deeply human is our need to think and to share our thoughts with others. Censorship is the greatest evil because the censor's goal is to imprison the human spirit.

Second argument for thesis

In addition to providing a realistic picture of nonacademic life, allowing all types of speech on campus encourages an open forum for the discussion of all types of ideas. Discussion of controversial issues and different points of view are the fuel for a useful education. That is why higher education has a responsibility to ensure that all forms of speech are protected, analyzed, and addressed. 'The right of free speech is indivisible. When one of us is denied this right, all of us are denied' (Hate Speech on Campus, 1996). By denying one point of view, we eliminate the open forum. A speech code on any university campus only hinders the ability of students and faculty to fully explore the market of ideas available to them. The University of Missouri is no exception to the idea that academic freedom is the bedrock of a free society.

*Third argument
for thesis*

If we do not allow open expression, however hateful it is, then there can be no change, no growth. Racism, sexism, ageism, etc. are not going to diminish without being addressed in higher education. As noted by the ACLU (Hate Speech on Campus, 1995),'Verbal purity is not social change.' Barring certain types of speech would be a seeming quick fix for issues such as racism, sexism, ageism, and homophobia, which often comprise hate speech. But racist statements are not the real problem between the races; racism is. If we bar all racially biased comments on campus, all we have done is fuel the racism. We have then given hatred the power to lurk and grow within us instead of communicating and debating about it in the open.

If hate speech is not allowed to occur openly, the problem of racism is never addressed. Like racism, hate speech itself is not the problem; hate is. As members of a society, we must communicate in order to solve problems and grow as individuals. This includes addressing hateful ideas and opinions. We can make no progress if we do not allow offensive kinds of speech to exist on campus. By barring them, we run the risk of being silenced ourselves.

*Conclusion
Summarizes
main
arguments.*

A hate speech code at the University of Missouri would be detrimental to everyone, from students to faculty. The First Amendment protects all kinds of speech, including the offensive. It does this in order to ensure that all voices are heard and that all issues can be addressed. To go through college with the idea that offensive speech does not happen is detrimental to students and to the society in which they live. The educational system is based on the idea that communication leads to learning and that learning leads to personal growth. Without the open forum for thought and the freedom to express controversial ideas, a higher education is worthless. Moreover, no one ever solved a controversial gender issue or a racial conflict in silence. There must be communication so that debate can tran-

*Restatement of
thesis*

spire. In order for any change in our society to transpire, offensive speech must be allowed to continue. It can only be addressed and learned from if it is equally protected by the Constitution. Mike Godwin, of the Electronic Frontier Foundation, says, 'when it comes to the Bill of Rights, what you don't use, you lose. The First Amendment is a terrible thing to waste' (Comments and quotes, 1995). If anyone has a responsibility to use the freedom granted by the First Amendment, higher education is at the top of the list.

References

American Civil Liberties Union. (1996). Hate speech on campus. [Online]. Available:
   http://www.aclu.org/library/pbp16.html

American Civil Liberties Union. (1996). Free speech. [Online]. Available:
   www.aclu.org/issues/freespeech/isfs.html

Justice on Campus. (1996). Comments and quotes on sexual harassment and free speech. [Online]. Available:
   http://joc.mit.edu/comments.html

Justice on Campus. (1995). Speech codes and disciplinary charges. [Online]. Available:
   http://joc.mit.edu/roundup.html

Silvergate, H. A. (1995, November 23). Memo from Harvey Silvergate. [Online]. Available:
   http://joc.mit.edu/amherst/silvergate.112495.txt

Writing Assignments

1. In a 300-word essay, argue that women are more nurturing and caring than men are. Avoid fallacies. Then write a one-page critique of the first paper, paying special attention to any fallacies you uncover.

2. Write a 500-word rebuttal to Essay 8 ('The Cohabitation Epidemic') in Appendix A, pointing out as many fallacies as possible.

3. Write a 300-word paper arguing that the speed limit on all highways in your province should be raised to 120 km/h. Include at least three fallacies in the paper. Exchange your paper with a classmate who has done the same assignment. Pinpoint the fallacies in each other's papers.

Part Three
Arguments

Chapter 6

Deductive Reasoning: Propositional Logic

Chapter Objectives

Connectives and Truth Values

You will be able to

- understand the purpose and uses of propositional logic.
- understand the meaning, the symbols, and the uses of the four logical connectives—conjunction, disjunction, negation, and conditional.
- define statement and explain the distinction between simple and compound statements.
- translate simple statements into symbolic form.
- construct a truth table and use it to test the validity of arguments.
- identify the situations in which conjunctions, disjunctions, negations, and conditionals are true or false.
- understand the structure of conditional statements and the various ways in which they can be expressed.

Checking for Validity

You will be able to

- determine the validity of the very simple arguments using truth tables.
- use parentheses to express statements in symbolic form.
- use the short method to evaluate complex arguments.

For centuries, philosophers, monks, scientists, linguists, and students have been enthralled by logic. Yes, *logic*. For many people—including some great thinkers such as Aristotle, Gottfried Leibniz, and Bertrand Russell—logic has been, ironically, a passion, something deemed worthy of deep study and long devotion. For hundreds of years, logic (along with philosophy) was a required course in universities and was regarded as one of the grand pillars upon which a liberal arts education was based (the others were grammar, rhetoric, arithmetic, music, astronomy, and geometry). Even today scholars continue to be drawn into the depths of logic, never seeming to tire of exploration and application.

But why do they bother? Why do they seem to think that logic is anything other than the dry and dusty preoccupation of dry and dusty philosophers? Well, maybe they bother because the study and use of logic, like the study and use of mathematics, is an exercise in exactitude, precision, clarity, and—above all—definite answers. All of which can be very satisfying. Or perhaps they bother because logic is the study of good reasoning or thinking and is therefore concerned with every decision and every judgment we make.

Logic also produces real results for us. Out of the study of logic have come discoveries now used in electronic engineering, set theory, linguistics, mathematics, and, of course, philosophy. Investigations in logic have yielded insights that made the invention of digital computers possible.

Of course, what you really want to know is what coursework in logic can do for *you*. Well, in this chapter you get a preliminary answer to that question. Here we take up an exploration of **propositional logic** (or truth-functional logic)—the branch of deductive reasoning that deals with the logical relationships among statements. In propositional logic, we use symbols to represent and clarify these relationships. If you master this material, you should reap at least two rewards right off. The first is a more thorough understanding of the power, precision, and dynamics of deductive reasoning. The second is the ability to evaluate the validity of very complex arguments.

How complex? Take a look at this deductive argument. Can you tell if it's valid?

(1) Canada will be a just society only if it improves the situation of its Aboriginal peoples.
(2) Canada will improve the situation of its Aboriginal peoples only if doing so will not significantly reduce the standard of living of middle-class Canadians.
(3) If the standard of living of middle-class Canadians is reduced, then either Canada will not be a just society or it will not improve the situation of its Aboriginal peoples.

"My lawyer says I can sue the school because they're violating my right to be stupid."

© 1996 by Randy Glasbergen.

Food For Thought

What Hath Critical Thinking Wrought?

Every year the science humour magazine *Annals of Improbable Research* awards its infamous 'Ig Nobel Prizes', which honour people whose achievements 'cannot or should not be reproduced'. We're talking here about actual research of dubious or curious value. We could argue that many Ig Nobel winners are living examples of what can happen when there are serious lapses in critical thinking. On the other hand, some of the wacky Ig Nobel accomplishments have the intended (or unintended) effect of making people laugh and then really think. You can judge the merits for yourself. Here's a partial list of the Ig Nobel Prizes for 2006:

- Physics: Basile Audoly and Sebastien Neukirch of the Université Pierre et Marie Curie, in Paris, for their insights into why, when you bend dry spaghetti, it often breaks into more than two pieces.
- Ornithology: Ivan R. Schwab, of the University of California Davis, and the late Philip R.A. May of the University of California Los Angeles, for exploring and explaining why woodpeckers don't get headaches.
- Medicine: Francis M. Fesmire of the University of Tennessee College of Medicine, for his medical case report 'Termination of Intractable Hiccups with Digital Rectal Massage'.
- Acoustics: D. Lynn Halpern (of Harvard Vanguard Medical Associates, Brandeis University, and Northwestern University), Randolph Blake (of Vanderbilt University and Northwestern University) and James Hillenbrand (of Western Michigan University and Northwestern University) for conducting experiments to learn why people dislike the sound of fingernails scraping on a blackboard.[1]

(4) Canada will not improve the situation of its Aboriginal peoples.

(5) Therefore, Canada will not be a just society.

If you don't know anything about propositional logic, the only way you can check this argument for validity is to use brute brainpower. You just have to think it through, and the thinking it through will not be easy. But with a grounding in propositional logic, you can figure this one out in straightforward fashion.

Connectives and Truth Values

As we've seen, arguments are composed of statements. In Chapter 3 we used symbols to represent the statements. Each symbol stood, not for a logical relationship between statements, but for a single statement. Propositional logic takes this symbolization to another level by using symbols to stand not just for statements but also for the *relationships between statements*—relationships that we specified previously with logical connective words, or connectives, such as 'if . . . then' and 'or'. Propositional logic gets this work done by using the symbol language of **symbolic logic**, a branch of logic in its own right.

Because these logical connectives specify the relationships between statements, they shape the *form* of the argument. Recall that the validity of an argument is a matter of the argument's form; that's why we can judge the validity of an argument apart from any consideration of the truth of its premises. So propositional logic helps us assess the validity of an argument without being distracted by non-formal elements, such as the particular words used to express content.

So the symbols used to express an argument are of two types. The first you're already familiar with; they're the letters, or **variables**, you use to represent propositions. For example, if *p*, then *q*. (There's no particular distinction in the letters *p* and *q*; any letters will do, as long as you use them consistently. That is, once you've chosen *p* to represent, say, 'Alice rode her bike,' *p* must consistently represent this same statement throughout the argument.) The second kind are the symbols for the logical connectives that indicate relationships between statements.

The following table presents the symbols for, and the meaning of, four logical connectives.

Symbol	Meaning	Example
&	Conjunction (and)	$p \& q$
		Alice rode her bike, and John walked.
$\vee$	Disjunction (or)	$p \vee q$
		Either Alice rode her bike, or John walked.
~	Negation (not)	$\sim p$
		Alice did not ride her bike.
		(or)
		It is not the case that Alice rode her bike.
$\longrightarrow$	Conditional (if–then)	$p \longrightarrow q$
		If Alice rode her bike, then John walked.

These connectives are used in compound statements such as 'The air is clean, and the sky is blue' or 'If you stay up late, you will sleep in tomorrow.' Remember that a **statement** (or claim) is an assertion that something is or is not the case. In other words, it is the kind of thing that can be either true or false. A **simple statement** is one that does not contain any other statements as constituents. And a **compound statement** is composed of at least two simple statements.

Every statement has a truth value. That is, a statement is either true or false. Or to be more precise, a true statement has a truth value of *true*, and a false statement has a truth value of *false*. In contrast, questions and exclamations don't have truth values: they are neither true nor false.

Now let's say that we have converted an argument into its symbolic form, and we list all the *possible* truth values of the argument's variables (statements). In other words, we list under what circumstances a statement is true or false because of the influence of the logical connectives. How would this information help us?

It could help us quickly uncover the validity or invalidity of the whole argument. Given the possible truth values of some statements in the argument, and given the relationships of the statements with one another as governed by the logical connectives, we could infer the possible truth values of all the other statements. Then we would have to answer just one question: *Is there a combination of truth values in the argument such that the premises could be true and the conclusion false?* If the answer is yes, then the argument is invalid. If there is no such circumstance, the argument is valid.

If you're a little fuzzy on all this, don't worry. It will become clearer as you digest the following examples and learn more about the dance between connectives and truth values. Let's look next at each of the four logical connectives introduced above.

Conjunction

Two simple statements joined by a connective to form a compound statement are known as a **conjunction**. Each of the component statements is called a **conjunct**. For example:

Julio is here, and Juan is here.

Which we symbolize like this:

p & *q*

The grammatical conjunction *and* is one of several terms that can express logical conjunction. Some others are *but*, *yet*, *nevertheless*, *while*, *also*, and *moreover*. In propositional logic, all these are logically equivalent; they are therefore properly symbolized by the ampersand (&). *Caution:* Make sure the connective really is conjoining two distinct statements and not a set of compound nouns as in 'We went to Jack's bar *and* grill' or 'Céline *and* Marie were a team.'

The truth-value of a conjunction is determined by the truth-value of its parts, that is, by the truth-value of its conjuncts. For example, look at this conjunction:

Last night I had a Coke, and I also had an order of poutine.

That conjunction is true if, and only if, it's true *both* that you had a Coke last night, and that you had poutine last night. Maybe you did have Coke last night, and maybe you didn't. Maybe you had poutine last night, and maybe you didn't.

To identify and keep track of all the possible truth values of a conjunction, we can create a **truth table**, which is just a graphic way of displaying all the possibilities. Here's the truth table for the conjunction p & q:

p	q	p & q
T	T	T
T	F	F
F	T	F
F	F	F

At the top of the table, you see a column heading for each of the component statements (in this case, one for p and one for q) and one the conjunction (p & q) itself. The Ts and Fs below the line are abbreviations for *true* and *false*. The first two columns of Ts and Fs represent the four possible sets of truth values for the variables. Either p is true and q is true, or p is true and q is false, or p is false and q is true, or p is false and q is also false. Those are the only four combinations that are possible. The table shows, in other words, that there are only four combinations of truth values for the pair of variables p and q: T T, T F, F T, and F F. These are the only combinations possible for *any* conjunction (or any other two-variable compound).

The last column of Ts and Fs (under p & q) shows the possible truth values for the conjunction as a whole, given the four possible combinations of truth values of the pair of variables. This means that if you plug into the conjunction every possible pair of truth values, the conjunction will yield only these four truth values: T, F, F, and F.

In ordinary language, this is what each of the rows is saying:

Row 1: When p is true and q is true, p & q is true.
Row 2: When p is true and q is false, p & q is false.
Row 3: When p is false and q is true, p & q is false.
Row 4: When p is false and q is false, p & q is false.

(Think this through for yourself, using the example given above. If it's true that I had Coke last night, and also true that I had poutine last night, then the statement 'I had Coke and also had poutine last night' is clearly true. But if it's true that I had Coke last night but false that I had poutine last night, then 'I had Coke and also had poutine last night' is, as a whole, false. And so on.)

Maybe you've already guessed (by studying the truth table) an important fact about the truth value of a conjunction: *If just one statement in the conjunction is false, the whole conjunction is false; only if both conjuncts are true is the whole conjunction true.* The previous truth table reflects this state of affairs. In the table, we see that p & q is true only when p is true and q is true (in the first row)—and

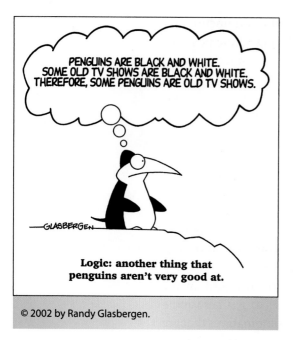

PENGUINS ARE BLACK AND WHITE.
SOME OLD TV SHOWS ARE BLACK AND WHITE.
THEREFORE, SOME PENGUINS ARE OLD TV SHOWS.

—GLASBERGEN

**Logic: another thing that
penguins aren't very good at.**

© 2002 by Randy Glasbergen.

that *p* & *q* is false whenever at least one of the component statements is false (in the other three rows). This should make perfect sense to you because in everyday speech, if one-half of a conjunction is false, we would normally regard the *whole* conjunction as false.

It's a good idea to remember the exact sequence of Ts and Fs in the first two columns of the previous truth table. That way you won't have to guess to make sure you include every possible combination of truth values. The first few columns in any truth table are usually entered automatically as guides.

Disjunction

In a conjunction we assert that *p* and *q* are both true and that if just one conjunct is false, the whole conjunction is false. But in a **disjunction**, we assert that either *p* or *q* is true (though both might be) and that even if one of the statements is false, the whole disjunction is still true. Each statement in a disjunction is called a **disjunct**. For example:

Either Joan is angry, or Ann is serene.

which we symbolize as

p ∨ *q*

or

Either Joan or Ann will row the boat.

which we also symbolize as

p ∨ *q*

The symbol for disjunction (∨) is called a wedge, which is roughly equivalent to the word *or*. The word *unless* is also sometimes used in place of *or* to form a disjunction, as in 'I will go to the movies unless I stay home.' The words *either* and *neither* usually signal the beginning of a disjunction.

The truth table for a disjunction looks like this:

p	*q*	*p* ∨ *q*
T	T	T
T	F	T
F	T	T
F	F	F

The table shows us that $p \vee q$ is true in every possible combination of Ts and Fs—except one, where both p and q are false (in the last row). This situation just reflects the fact that for a disjunction to be true, only one of the disjuncts must be true. The disjunction here, for example, is true if (1) Joan is angry or (2) Ann is serene or (3) Joan is angry and Ann is serene.

An important point to keep in mind is that in English the word 'or' has two meanings. It can mean 'one or the other, or both', which is called the *inclusive* sense.

> 'Logic is not a body of doctrine, but a mirror-image of the world. Logic is transcendental.'
> —Ludwig Wittgenstein

Food For Thought

Arguments We Have Known and Loved

Virtually every field has its share of well-worn arguments that are used to establish this theory or that proposition. But the discipline of philosophy—because it is, well, philosophy—is studded from end to end with influential arguments, including some especially famous ones.

If all that exists is matter in motion, then there are no disembodied spirits.
All that exists is matter in motion.
Therefore, there are no disembodied spirits.

Whatever begins to exist has a cause.
The universe began to exist.
Therefore, the universe had a cause, namely God.

There is unnecessary evil in the world.
If there were an all-powerful, all-knowing, all-good being, there would be no unnecessary evil in the world.
Therefore, there is no all-powerful, all-knowing, all-good being.

If it's true that all our actions are determined by an indefinitely long chain of prior events, then people cannot perform free actions.
It's true that all our actions are determined by an indefinitely long chain of prior events.
Therefore, people cannot perform free actions.

We can't be certain that we are not dreaming.
If we can't be certain that we are not dreaming, we cannot be certain that what we sense is real.
If we cannot be certain that what we sense is real, we cannot acquire knowledge through sense experience.
Therefore, we cannot acquire knowledge through sense experience.

In this sense, $p \lor q$ means 'p or q or both' ('If he's sick or tired, he won't go jogging'). But 'or' can also mean 'either but not both', which is called the *exclusive* sense. In the exclusive sense, $p \lor q$ means 'p or q but not both' ('You can have either the chicken or the fish as your in-flight meal'). Standard practice in logic is to assume the inclusive sense when dealing with disjunctions. This approach is reflected in the truth table for a disjunction, and it simplifies the evaluation of disjunctive arguments. It has no effect on our evaluation of disjunctive syllogisms (discussed in Chapter 3); they would be valid forms regardless of whether the disjunction was construed as inclusive or exclusive. Look:

> Either p or q.
> Not p.
> Therefore, q.

In the disjunctive syllogism, one of the disjuncts is denied, so the argument is valid in any case. But if one of the disjuncts is affirmed, the argument is invalid when the disjunction is inclusive:

> Either p or q.
> p.
> Therefore, not-q.

Obviously, if the disjunction means 'p or q or both', then by affirming p we cannot conclude not-q.

If we know that the disjuncts in a disjunctive premise really are exclusive options ('either a boy or a girl'), then we can safely assume the exclusive meaning of 'or' and examine the argument accordingly. Otherwise it's safest to stick to the inclusive sense.

Negation

A negation is the denial of a statement, which we indicate with the word 'not' or a term that means the same thing. For example, the negation of the statement 'The price of eggs in China is steep' is

> The price of eggs in China is not steep.

or

> It is not the case that the price of eggs in China is steep.

or

> It is false that the price of eggs in China is steep.

Assuming we use p to represent the foregoing statement, here's how we would symbolize its negation:

> $\sim p$

The symbol ~ is called a 'tilde', and when we state ~*p* aloud, we say 'not-*p*'. When it appears in front of a statement, it indicates the reversal of the statement's truth value. A true statement becomes false; a false statement becomes true. One interesting consequence of this reversal is that a *double negation* is the same thing as *no* negation. For example, take the foregoing negation ('The price of eggs in China is not steep'). If you negate this negation ('It is not the case that the price of eggs in China is not steep') you end up with the positive statement, 'The price of eggs in China is steep.' The truth table for a negation explains why such reversals can happen:

p	~*p*
T	F
F	T

Conditional

Remember conditional statements? We looked at them when we discussed valid and invalid argument forms (*modus ponens*, denying the antecedent, etc.). The basic form of a conditional is 'if . . . then . . .'. For example: 'If the cat is on the mat, then the rat will stay home.' Symbolized, a conditional looks like this: *p* ∨ *q*, where an arrow represents the connective. Recall also that in a conditional, the first part (*p*) is the antecedent, and the second part (*q*) is the consequent.

Notice that a conditional asserts only that if the antecedent is true, then the consequent must be true. It does not assert that the antecedent is actually true or that the consequent is actually true—but only that under specified conditions a certain state of affairs will be actual.

At first, you may find that the truth table for conditionals seems a little odd. But it makes good sense when you think about it:

p	*q*	*p* → *q*
T	T	T
T	F	F
F	T	T
F	F	T

The table shows that a conditional is false in only one situation—when the antecedent is true and the consequent is false. Put more precisely, a conditional statement is false if and only if its antecedent is true and its consequent is false. In all other possible combinations of truth values, a conditional is true—and this is the part that may strike you as odd.

Let's take each of the four combinations in turn and see how they work in this conditional statement: 'If George is paid a dollar, then he'll jump out the window.'

The question we can ask is this: 'Under what circumstances is the conditional statement (the whole statement, antecedent and consequent together) true?' Well, it should be clear that if George is indeed paid a dollar, and if he does jump out the window, then the whole conditional would be true. This is the situation in the first row of the truth table.

What about the last row—what if the antecedent is false and the consequent is false? If it is false that George is paid a dollar, and it's false that he jumps out the window, there is no reason to think that the conditional itself is false. George could reasonably assert that the conditional statement isn't false if he isn't paid a dollar and doesn't jump out the window.

George could also reasonably assert that the conditional isn't false even when the antecedent is false and the consequent is true (the situation in the third row). If George isn't paid a dollar, and he still jumps out the window, that doesn't prove that the conditional is false.

This path brings us back to the fact that a conditional statement is false *only* when the antecedent is true and the consequent is false.

Conditional statements can be expressed in ways other than the if–then configuration, the standard form. Here are some conditionals in various patterns with each one paired with the standard-form version:

1. You will fall off that ladder if you're not careful.
   If you're not careful, you will fall off that ladder.

2. Gregory will excel in school provided that he studies hard.
   If Gregory studies hard, then he will excel in school.

3. Jenna would not have wrecked the car if she had not tried to beat that light.
   If Jenna had not tried to beat that light, she would not have wrecked the car.

4. I'll ride the bus only if I'm late.
   If I ride the bus, then I'm late.

5. Whenever I think, I get a headache.
   If I think, I get a headache.

6. I will walk the dog unless it's raining.
   If it's not raining, I will walk the dog.

Among these patterns, pair 4 and pair 6 are likely to cause you the most trouble. In pair 4, 'only if' is the troublesome term. Just remember that 'only if' introduces the *consequent* of a conditional. So in 'I'll ride the bus only if I'm late,' 'only if' indicates that the consequent is 'I'm late.' So the antecedent is 'If I ride the bus.' You have to move 'if' to the front of the antecedent to put the statement in standard form. In pair 6, 'unless' is the sticking point. You need to understand that 'unless' introduces the antecedent and means 'if not'. So here 'unless it's raining' becomes 'if it's not raining' in the antecedent position.

Review Notes

Statements and Connectives

- A simple statement, or claim, is one that does not contain any other statements as constituents. A compound statement is one composed of at least two simple statements.
- Logical connectives

  Conjunction (and): & If just one statement in a conjunction is false, the whole conjunction is false.

  Disjunction (or): ∨ A disjunction is true even if one of the disjuncts is false.

  Negation (not): ~ A negation 'reverses' the truth value of any statement.

  Conditional (if–then): → A conditional is false if and only if its antecedent is true and its consequent is false.

- Words used in conditionals

  if—introduces the antecedent; If p, then $q = p \rightarrow q$

  only if—introduces the consequent; p only if $q = p \rightarrow q$

  provided—introduces the antecedent; p provided $q = q \rightarrow p$

  unless—introduces the antecedent; p unless $q = {\sim}q \rightarrow p$

  whenever—introduces antecedent; whenever $p, q = p \rightarrow q$

Because of such variations in conditional statements, it's important to translate conditionals into standard form before you try to assess their validity. To do that, you must identify the antecedent and consequent and put them in proper order (antecedent before consequent).

Exercise 6.1

Identify each of the following statements as a conjunction, disjunction, or conditional; identify its component statements; and indicate the symbol used to represent the connective.

* 1. The Liberals raised taxes, and the Conservatives cut programs.
  2. Either I walk home, or I drive Ralph's car.
  3. If the Maple Leafs win this game, they'll be in the playoffs.
  4. It is not the case that the Maple Leafs won.
* 5. If Taslima can read your mind, then you're in trouble.
  6. Either the newspaper ad was misleading, or it was meant as a joke.

* 7. If God is all-powerful, then he can prevent evil in the world.
  8. He supported the revolution, and he was arrested without being charged.

Exercise 6.2

Translate each of the following statements into symbolic form. Use the letters in parentheses to represent each component statement. (Assume that the letters stand for positive statements so that a negated statement is indicated by putting a tilde [~] in front of a letter.)

* 1. Either Herman does his homework, or he goofs off. (*p, q*)
  2. If Herman does his homework, then he will have time to go to the party. (*s, t*)
  3. It is not the case that Hans had access to the murder weapon. (*a*)
* 4. People die, but books live forever. (*e, f*)
  5. Touching your tongue to metal in very cold weather is not a good idea. (*d*)
  6. Provided Alex returns the money, he will not be prosecuted. (*x, y*)
  7. Human cloning will become widespread unless the government interferes. (*p, q*)
* 8. He will not benefit from instruction, and he will not learn on his own. (*g, h*)
  9. Ottawa gets a lot of snow in winter, and everybody hates it. (*j, k*)
  10. His tampering with the judicial system is not appropriate. (*b*)
  11. You will eventually discover the correct formula if you work systematically. (*x, y*)
  12. He's either a nut or a brilliant eccentric. (*p, q*)
  13. If Socrates is a man, he is mortal. (*d, e*)
* 14. It is not the case that the zoo won't accept any more mammals. (*p*)
  15. Either disembodied spirits exist, or psychic hoaxes are rampant. (*s, t*)
  16. Mickey Mouse wanted to get married, but Minnie said 'no'. (*p, q*)

Exercise 6.3

Say which of the following compound statements are true and which are false on the basis of what you know about the truth-value of their components.

  1. Dogs are mammals ∨ Snakes are marsupials
* 2. Alligators are reptiles & Dogs are reptiles
  3. ~ Dogs are reptiles & ~ Alligators are mammals
  4. Dogs can bark → Dogs can talk
  5. Dogs can talk → Dogs are reptiles
* 6. ~ Dogs are mammals ∨ Snakes are reptiles
  7. ~ Alligators are reptiles → Alligators are mammals
* 8. Alligators can bark & ~ Dogs are reptiles
  9. ~ ~ Dogs are mammals ∨ Snakes are reptiles
  10. ~ ~ Dogs are mammals → ~ ~ Snakes are reptiles

Exercise 6.4

Indicate which of the following symbolized statements are true and which are false. Assume that the statements represented by the variables *a*, *b*, and *c* are true, and that the statements represented by *p*, *q*, and *r* are false.

   1. *a* & *p*
* 2. *b* ∨ *r*
   3. *c* → *q*
   4. ~*b* ∨ *c*
* 5. ~*b* → ~*q*
   6. *a* & ~*q*
   7. *b* ∨ ~*p*
   8. *a* & *c*
   9. *b* → ~*c*
* 10. *p* → ~*r*

Exercise 6.5

Translate each of the symbolic statements in Exercise 6.4 into a logically equivalent statement in English. Assume that the letters stand for positive statements. Possible answers are provided at the back of the book for 2, 5, and 10.

Exercise 6.6

Translate each of the following statements into symbolic form. Assume that the letters you use stand for positive statements.

   1. If you visited northern Manitoba in December, then you must have seen polar bears.
* 2. Either Canada will become more European, or Canada will become more American.
   3. Either the ancient Greek temples were built by ancient Greeks, or they were built by Romans who imitated the Greeks.
   4. The Egyptian pyramids were not built by ancient alien visitors from space, and they certainly were not built by Egyptians taught by alien visitors from space.
* 5. Science will never triumph over religion unless science can offer a spiritual experience.
   6. If it was wrong for our ancestors to take land from Canada's Aboriginal peoples, then it's wrong for us to keep that land now.
   7. I will fly to Vancouver, but I will not meet you in Calgary.

8. It is not the case that philosophy is dead, and it is not true that science has replaced it.

*9. Provided I pass my logic course, I will finally be able to understand political arguments.

10. The provincial deficit is out of control, but most voters are not worried.

Checking for Validity

Now you're ready to put what you've learned about truth tables to use in determining the validity of arguments. The truth-table test of validity is based on an elementary fact about validity that you've already encountered: *It's impossible for a valid argument to have true premises and a false conclusion.* So any procedure that allows us to easily check if the premises are true and the conclusion is false will help us test an argument for validity. Truth tables can do this. Devising truth tables for arguments, then, can reveal the underlying structure—the form—of the arguments, even those that are fairly complex.

Simple Arguments

Let's start by analyzing a very simple argument involving a conjunction:

Ducks have webbed feet.
Ducks have feathers.
Therefore, ducks have webbed feet and ducks have feathers.

We symbolize the argument like this:

p
q
$\therefore p \& q$

Here we have each premise and the conclusion represented by variables, giving us a good look at the logical form of the argument. The symbol $\therefore$ indicates that a conclusion follows (it's often translated as 'therefore'). The argument is, of course, valid—a fact that you can quickly see without the aid of a truth table. But it makes for a simple illustration:

p	q	$p \& q$
T	T	T
T	F	F
F	T	F
F	F	F

Review Notes

Common Argument Forms Symbolized

Modus Ponens (Valid)	Modus Tollens (Valid)
$p \rightarrow q$	$p \rightarrow q$
p	$\sim q$
$\therefore q$	$\therefore \sim p$

Hypothetical Syllogism (Valid)	Disjunctive Syllogism (Valid)
$p \rightarrow q$	$p \vee q$
$q \rightarrow r$	$\sim p$
$\therefore p \rightarrow r$	$\therefore q$

Denying the Antecedent (Invalid)	Affirming the Consequent (Invalid)
$p \rightarrow q$	$p \rightarrow q$
$\sim p$	q
$\therefore \sim q$	$\therefore p$

This truth table is a repeat of the one we looked at in the section on conjunctions. The top line of the table shows the two premises of the argument and its conclusion with their truth values listed below. Like all truth tables, this one shows every possible combination of truth values for the premises and conclusion.

When dealing with simple arguments, the first two columns of a truth table are guide columns in which the variables, or letters, of the argument are listed, followed by a column for each premise and then a column for the conclusion. In this case, though, the guide columns happen to be identical to the premise columns, so we won't repeat them.

Now we can ask the big question: 'Does the truth table show (in any row) a state of affairs in which the premises of the argument are true and the conclusion false?' If we can find even *one* instance of this arrangement, we will have shown that the argument is invalid. Remember that we are trying to judge the *validity* of an argument, which is a matter of argument *form*. So if we can discover that it's *possible* for a particular argument form to have true premises and a false conclusion, we will know without further investigation that the argument is invalid. Not only that, but we will know that *any* argument of the same pattern is invalid. The truth table can tell us definitively whether an argument is invalid because the table includes every possible combination of truth values. If the truth table doesn't reveal a situation in which the argument has true premises and a false conclusion, then the argument is valid.

As you can see in the previous table, there is no row in which the premises are true (T T) and the conclusion false (F). Therefore, the argument is valid.

Here's a slightly more complex argument:

If the icebergs melt, the lowlands will flood.
The icebergs will not melt.
Therefore, the lowlands will not flood.

You should recognize this argument as an instance of denying the antecedent. Here it is symbolized, with negation and conditional connectives:

$p \rightarrow q$
$\sim p$
$\therefore \sim q$

And here's the truth table for the argument, with the premises and conclusion indicated for clarity:

p	q	$p \rightarrow q$ Premise	$\sim p$ Premise	$\sim q$ Conclusion
T	T	T	F	F
T	F	F	F	T
F	T	T	T	F
F	F	T	T	T

(Adding the labels 'premise' and 'conclusion' is totally optional. We won't always do that here in the text. But it may prove helpful in your own work.)

You can begin checking for validity in two different ways. You can first inspect all rows that have a false conclusion and then see if the premises in that row are true, indicating an invalid argument. Or you can zero in on rows showing all true premises and then check to see if they have false conclusions. In this case, the third row tells the tale: both premises are true and the conclusion is false. So the argument is invalid, and we need not check any other rows.

As we saw earlier, the truth value of a compound statement depends on the truth value of its components. That's why it's a good idea to start out with guide columns in a truth table. The truth value of these variables (letters) determines the truth value of statements that are comprised of the variables. The truth value of these compound units in turn determines the truth value of any larger compound units.

In the truth table just given, the truth value of $\sim p$ is the contradictory of p, and the truth value of $\sim q$ is the contradictory of q. So whatever the truth value of a statement, the tilde ($\sim$) reverses it, from true to false or false to true.

Now let's try this one:

Either we fight for freedom or we give in to tyranny.
We won't fight for freedom.
Therefore, we will give in to tyranny.

Symbolized, it looks like this:

$p \lor q$
$\sim p$
$\therefore q$

And here is its truth table:

p	q	$p \lor q$ Premise	$\sim p$ Premise	q Conclusion
T	T	T	F	T
T	F	T	F	F
F	T	T	T	T
F	F	F	T	F

(Again, we've labelled the premises and conclusion in this truth table, just to help you out, though it's not strictly part of the method.)

Is this argument valid? To find out, we need to check the table for any row that shows true premises and a false conclusion. The third row is the only one in which both premises are true—but the conclusion is also true. So this argument is valid.

Tricky Arguments

Arguments can get more complicated when variables and connectives are intricately combined into larger compounds and when the number of variables increases. In both these situations, truth tables can help you unravel the complexities. Let's examine an argument that has both these wrinkles. We'll go right to the symbolized form:

$p \rightarrow \sim(q \,\&\, r)$
p
$\therefore \sim(q \,\&\, r)$

Notice in these premises the use of parentheses to join variables. The parentheses enable us to symbolize arguments more precisely and to avoid confusion. In math, there is an obvious difference between $2 \times (3 + 4)$, which equals 14, and $(2 \times 3) + 4$, which equals 10. Likewise, there is a crucial difference between $p \rightarrow \sim(q \,\&\, r)$ and $(p \rightarrow \sim q) \,\&\, r$. The former symbolization would express a conditional such as 'If it rains tomorrow, then Alice and Eric will not go to the movies.' But the latter symbolization would represent a very different conditional, such as 'If it rains tomorrow, then Alice will not go to the movies, and Eric will go to the movies.' Such differences, of course, can affect the truth values of a statement and require a different truth table.

Food For Thought

From Here to Absurdity

One kind of powerful argument that you frequently encounter is known as *reductio ad absurdum* (reduction to absurdity). The basic idea behind it is that if the contradictory (negation) of a statement leads to a conclusion that is absurd (logically self-contradictory) or just clearly false, then the negation of the original statement is false and the original statement itself must be true. You must accept the statement because denying it forces you to accept something that is unacceptable. So if you want to demonstrate that a statement is true (or false), you assume the negation of the statement (assume it 'for the sake of argument') and show that it leads to an absurd or false statement. Here's the form of this type of argument:

p
$p \rightarrow q$
$\sim q$
$\therefore \sim p$

In plain English, this says: Let's suppose that p is true. If p is true, then q must be true. But there's no way that q can be true. (Or, q being true is absurd.) So it must not be the case that p is true. For example:

Suppose that broccoli really is poisonous.
If broccoli really were poisonous, then a broccoli fan like me would be dead by now.
But obviously I'm not dead.
Therefore, clearly broccoli is not poisonous.

Here's another, somewhat different example:

You claim that all points of view are equally good.
But *my* point of view is just that *your* claim is false.
Thus if your claim is true, then I'm *right* that it's false, which is absurd.
So, your claim must be false.

Here's a distinction involving parentheses that's worth committing to memory. Consider these two statements:

$\sim(q \,\&\, r)$
It is not the case that Leo sings the blues and Fats sings the blues.

$\sim q \,\&\, \sim r$
Leo does not sing the blues, and Fats does not sing the blues.

The first statement asserts that it is not the case that *both* Leo and Fats sing the blues. That is, it's not true that Leo and Fats are concurrently in the habit of singing the blues. Maybe Leo sings the blues, and Fats doesn't, or vice versa. On the other hand, the second statement says that Leo doesn't sing the blues and neither does Fats. If we hope that at least one of these guys sings the blues, we're out of luck.

Here's another distinction worth knowing. Look at these two statements:

$\sim(q \vee r)$
It is not the case that either Leo sings the blues or Fats sings the blues.

$\sim q \vee \sim r$
Either Leo does not sing the blues or Fats does not sing the blues.

The first statement says that neither Leo nor Fats sings the blues. The second statement says that it is not the case that Leo *and* Fats sing the blues.

Correctly symbolizing statements with parentheses is a straightforward business, but it requires close attention to what's being said. Your best clues to where to insert parentheses comes from the words *either* and *neither*, conjunction and disjunction words such as *and* and *or*, and the punctuation in the sentences. Notice how the sentence clues in the following statements inform how the statements are symbolized:

If the next Prime Minister is from Ontario, then neither the West nor Atlantic Canada will be happy.

We can symbolize the statements with the following variables:

p—The next Prime Minister is from Ontario.
q—The West will be happy.
r—Atlantic Canada will be happy.
$p \rightarrow \sim(q \vee r)$

And:

Either Jon Stewart is funny or the show is rigged, or the network has made a bad investment.

p—Jon Stewart is funny.
q—The show is rigged.
r—The network has made a bad investment.
$(p \vee q) \vee r$

Arguments like these that have three variables instead of two may look scary, but they're not. The steps you use to check the validity of a three-variable argument are the same ones you apply in two-variable arguments. You devise a truth table, calculate truth values, and check for true premises with a false conclusion. The truth table, of course, has an additional guide column for the third variable, and there are more rows to accommodate the larger number of possible true-false combinations. In a two-variable table there are four rows; in a three-variable table there are eight and thus eight combinations of truth values. Notice how the guide columns are laid out:

p	q	r
T	T	T
T	T	F
T	F	T
T	F	F
F	T	T
F	T	F
F	F	T
F	F	F

To remember the truth values in each guide column, think: The first column is four Ts, then four Fs; the second column is alternating pairs of truth values beginning with T T; and the third column is alternating Ts and Fs starting with T.

Now let's test this argument for validity:

If the Flames won game one, but didn't win game two, then they've only won one game. But it's not true that they won game one but didn't win game two. Therefore, it's not the case that they've only won one game.

p—The Flames won game one.
q—The Flames won game two.
r—The Flames have only won one game.

$(p \,\&\, {\sim}q) \rightarrow r$
${\sim}(p \,\&\, {\sim}q)$
$\therefore {\sim}r$

And here's the truth table for the argument:

	1 p	2 q	3 r	4 p & ~q	5 (p & ~q) → r	6 ~(p & ~q)	7 ~r
1	T	T	T	F	T	T	F
2	T	T	F	F	F	T	T
3	T	F	T	T	T	F	F
4	T	F	F	T	T	F	T
5	F	T	T	F	T	T	F
6	F	T	F	F	T	T	T
7	F	F	T	F	T	T	F
8	F	F	F	F	T	T	T

This truth table has seven columns, and you can guess why six of them are there. The first three are the guide columns, and the last three are for the two premises and the conclusion. Column 4 is there because it simplifies the assigning of truth values to columns 5, 6, and 7—it is a component of the two premises. If we wanted, we could add more columns for other components such as ~r if the additions would make it easier to create the truth table.

The truth values for p & $\sim q$ are, of course, determined by the truth values of its conjuncts. If just one conjunct is false, the conjunction is false (as it is in rows 1, 2, and 5 through 8). Only in rows 3 and 4 is the conjunction true. The truth value of the conditional $(p$ & $\sim q) \rightarrow r$ is based on the truth values of $(p$ & $\sim q)$ and r, with the conditional being false only when $(p$ & $\sim q)$ is true and r is false (row 4). In all other rows the conditional is true. The truth value of the premise $\sim(p$ & $\sim q)$ is the contradictory of the truth value for $(p$ & $\sim q)$. Likewise, the truth value of $\sim r$ is the contradictory of r.

Is there any row in which the premises are true and the conclusion false? Yes, that's the situation in rows 1, 5, and 7, so the argument is invalid.

Streamlined Evaluation

With truth tables, you can accurately assess the validity of any propositional argument, even some fairly complicated ones. But as the arguments get more complicated (when they have more than two or three variables, for example), you may want a more efficient technique for calculating validity. Here's a good alternative method—one that just happens to be easier to master if you already know the ins and outs of truth tables.

In this approach—which we'll call the *short method*—we don't bother to produce a whole truth table, but we do try to construct some truth-table rows (maybe only one if we're lucky). The basic strategy is based on the same fact we relied on in the truth-table test: it's impossible for a valid argument to have true premises and a false conclusion. So we try to discover if there's a way to make the conclusion false and the premises true by assigning various truth values to the argument's components. That is, we try to prove that the argument is invalid. If we can do this, then we'll have the proof we need.

Let's try the short method on this argument:

$\sim q$
$p \rightarrow (q \vee r)$
r
$\therefore p$

First we write out the argument so that the premises and conclusion are in a single row:

$\sim q$ $p \rightarrow (q \vee r)$ r p

Now we examine the conclusion. What truth value must we assign to it to ensure that it's false? Obviously the answer is *false*—because there is only one variable in the conclusion, and the conclusion must be false. So we label *p* with an F in the conclusion and everyplace else in the argument. Then our row looks like this:

$$\sim q \qquad p \rightarrow (q \vee r) \qquad r \qquad p$$
$$ F F$$

Just one caution: As you work through the short method, you must remember that the truth values you mark under the argument row *apply to the variables (letters) only, not the premises.* To avoid any confusion, if you want you can write the truth values for the premises *above* the argument row. In this way you can indicate either (1) the premise truth values that you're trying for or (2) the premise truth values that result from your truth value assignments.

Review Notes

The Short Method: Step by Step

1. Write out the symbolized argument in a single row.
2. Assign truth values to the variables in the conclusion to make the conclusion false. (Write the appropriate Ts or Fs below the row.) Assign these truth values to the same variables elsewhere.
3. Consistently assign truth values to variables in the premises. Assign truth values first to premises where specific truth values are 'locked in'.
4. Try to make assignments that yield a false conclusion and true premises. If you can, the argument is invalid. If not, the argument is valid.

In this argument we can also tell right away that *r must* be true because it is a premise in the argument, and we're trying to see if we can make all the premises true (and the conclusion false). Then we have:

$$\sim q \qquad p \rightarrow (q \vee r) \qquad r \qquad p$$
$$ F \qquad\quad T \qquad T \qquad F$$

Now we look at the first column because it will be easy to determine its truth value. Since the first premise must be true and it's a negation, *q* must be false. This fills out the whole argument with truth values:

$$\sim q \qquad p \rightarrow (q \vee r) \qquad r \qquad p$$
$$ F \qquad F \quad F \quad T \qquad T \qquad F$$

We've shown then that the first and third premises are true. And we can now see that the second premise must also be true: The disjunction $(q \lor r)$ is true because one of the disjuncts is true (r). And the conditional (made up of p and the disjunction) is true because a false antecedent (p) and a true consequent $(q \lor r)$ yields a true conditional.

We have thus shown that this argument can have a false conclusion and true premises—the sign of an invalid argument.

Now let's try the short method on this argument:

$p \rightarrow q$

$q \rightarrow r$

$\sim r$

$\therefore \sim p$

$p \rightarrow q \qquad q \rightarrow r \qquad \sim r \qquad \sim p$

Again, we start with the conclusion. Since the conclusion is a negation $(\sim p)$, we know that there is only one way that the conclusion could be false—if p is true. We then must make p true every place else in the argument:

$p \rightarrow q$	$q \rightarrow r$	$\sim r$	$\sim p$
T			T

We now turn to the first premise, a simple conditional. The antecedent (p) is true, which means that if the conditional is to be true, its consequent (q) cannot be false (a true antecedent and a false consequent yields a false conditional). So we're forced to assign these truth values:

$p \rightarrow q$	$q \rightarrow r$	$\sim r$	$\sim p$
T T	T		T

That leaves just r to deal with. Again we are forced to assign a truth value to it. Because the premise is a negation and it must be true, r has to be false. But if r is false, the second premise (another simple conditional) must be false (truth values for the premises are shown *above* the argument row):

T	F	T	F
$p \rightarrow q$	$q \rightarrow r$	$\sim r$	$\sim p$
T T	T F	F	T

So we see that since there is only one way for the conclusion to be false, we are locked into truth values that prevented us from having all true premises. We simply cannot consistently assign truth values to this argument that will give us a false conclusion and true premises. Therefore, this argument is valid.

In using the short method like this, your overall goal is to see if you can prove invalidity in the most efficient way possible. You want to get the job done without a lot of unnecessary steps. The best strategy for doing this is to look for truth value assignments *that cannot be any other way* given the truth value assignments in the conclusion. That is, focus on premises with assignments that are 'locked into' the argument by the truth values you've given the conclusion. Make assignments in those premises first, regardless of which premise you start with.

In the foregoing arguments, the conclusions could be made false in only one way, and that made the rest of the work easier. But sometimes a conclusion can be made false in more than one way. In such cases, your strategy should be to try each possibility—each way that the conclusion can be false—until you get what you're after: an argument with true premises and a false conclusion. As soon as you get it, stop. You've proven that the argument form is invalid, and there's no reason to continue making assignments. If you try all the possibilities and still can't prove invalidity, the argument is valid.

Let's take a look at one of these multiple-possibility arguments:

$$p \rightarrow q$$
$$q \lor r$$
$$\sim q$$
$$\therefore p \,\&\, r$$

$$p \rightarrow q \quad q \lor r \quad \sim q \quad p \,\&\, r$$

In this argument the conclusion is a conjunction, and that means it can be made false by any one of these combinations of truth values: F–T, T–F, and F–F. If we make separate rows for each of these possibilities, they look like this:

	$p \rightarrow q$	$q \lor r$	$\sim q$	$p \,\&\, r$	
1	F	T		F	T
2	T	F		T	F
3	F	F		F	F

So can we consistently assign truth values to make the premises true and the conclusion false in any of these rows? We can forget about row 2 because in the first premise, *q* must be true (to avoid making the conditional false). And if *q* is true, the third premise would be false. Likewise, we must throw out row 3 because *q* again must be true (to ensure that the disjunction is true). And if *q* is true, we run into the same problem we have in row 2—the third premise must be false. Row 1, though, works. To make the third premise true, we must make *q* false. And when we assign a truth value of false to *q* in the rest of the argument, we make the premises true and the conclusion false. Therefore, the argument is invalid.

Exercise 6.7

Construct a truth table for each of the statements in Exercise 6.3. Answers are given at the back of the book for 2, 6, and 8.

Exercise 6.8

Construct a truth table for each of the following arguments and show whether the argument is valid or invalid.

1. a & b
    $\therefore a$

* 2. $p \rightarrow q$
    p
    $\therefore q$

3. $p \vee q$
    p
    $\therefore \sim q$

4. $p \rightarrow q$
    $\sim p$
    $\therefore q$

5. a & b
    $\sim a$
    $\therefore b$

6. $p \rightarrow q$
    $q \rightarrow r$
    $\therefore q$

* 7. $p \rightarrow q$
    $\sim q$ & r
    $\therefore r$

8. $a \vee (b$ & $c)$
    $\sim(b$ & $c)$
    $\therefore a$

9. $x \rightarrow y$
    $y \rightarrow z$
    $\therefore x \rightarrow z$

10. $p \rightarrow q$
    $\therefore p \rightarrow (p$ & $q)$

11. $a \rightarrow b$
    $b \rightarrow c$
    $\therefore (b$ & $c) \vee (a$ & $b)$

12. $a \vee (b \rightarrow c)$
    b & $\sim c$
    $\therefore \sim a$

13. $(p \vee q) \rightarrow (p$ & $q)$
    p & q
    $\therefore p \vee q$

* 14. $p \rightarrow q$
    $\sim(q \vee r)$
    $\therefore \sim p$

15. $(d \vee e) \rightarrow (d$ & $e)$
    $\sim(d \vee e)$
    $\therefore \sim(d$ & $e)$

16. $(p \rightarrow q) \rightarrow (p \rightarrow r)$
    $\sim(p \rightarrow q)$
    $\sim r$
    $\therefore p$

17. $(d \vee e) \rightarrow f$
    $f \rightarrow (d$ & $e)$
    $\therefore (d$ & $e) \rightarrow (d \vee e)$

18. $\sim(d$ & $e)$
    $e \vee f$
    $\therefore \sim d$ & e

19. d & $(\sim e$ A $\sim d)$
    $f \rightarrow \sim e$
    $\therefore f$

20. $d \vee \sim e$
    $f \rightarrow e$
    $\therefore d \rightarrow \sim f$

Exercise 6.9

For each of the following arguments, translate it into symbols, construct a truth table, and determine its validity.

1.   If there is no rain soon, the crops will die. If the crops die, there will be no food for the coming winter. The crops will not die. Therefore, there will be rain soon.

2.   If we give kidnappers the money that they demand, then further kidnappings will be encouraged. If we do not give kidnappers the money that they demand, the kidnappers will kill the hostages. We will not give kidnappers the money that they demand. Therefore, the kidnappers will kill the hostages.

* 3.   Jake is the plumber or Jake is the carpenter. Jake is not the carpenter. Therefore, Jake is the plumber.

4.   'Men, it is assumed, act in economic matters only in response to pecuniary compensation or to force. Force in the modern society is largely, although by no means completely, obsolete. So only pecuniary compensation remains of importance.' (John Kenneth Galbraith, *The New Industrial State*)

5.   If the lake freezes, then the lake-effect snow will stop. If the lake-effect snow stops, the streets will be easier to plow. Therefore, the streets will be easier to plow.

6.   Either Emilio walks or he takes the train. And either Joanne takes the train or she does not take the train. If Emilio walks, then Joanne takes the train. Emilio takes the train. So Joanne will not take the train.

7.   UN peacekeepers will not attack the local militants, provided that the militants behave themselves. The militants will not make trouble if the UN peacekeepers don't attack. Therefore, UN peacekeepers will not attack the local militants, and the militants will not make trouble.

8.   'If then, it is agreed that things are either the result of coincidence or for an end, and these cannot be the result of coincidence or spontaneity, it follows that they must be for an end.' (Aristotle, *Physics*)

9.   Either there is evidence that women of supernatural powers (i.e., witches) exist, or there is no such evidence. If there is no such evidence, then we have no reason to believe in witches. If there is evidence, we do have reason to believe in witches. There is no such evidence. Therefore, we have no reason to believe in witches.

10.   Either the herbal remedy alleviated the symptoms, or the placebo effect alleviated the symptoms. If the placebo effect is responsible for easing the symptoms, then the herbal remedy is worthless. The herbal remedy alleviated the symptoms. So the herbal remedy is not worthless.

* 11.   Unless both Mary goes and Henry goes, the party will be a disaster. The party will be a disaster. Therefore, both Mary and Henry will not go.

Exercise 6.10

Use the short method to check the validity of the following arguments in Exercise 6.8: 1, 3, 5, 9, 10, 15, 16, and 18. Write the symbolized argument in one row and assign truth values to each variable. Then above the argument row, assign truth values to the premises and conclusion. Answers are provided for 3, 10, and 15.

Summary

In propositional logic we use symbols to stand for the relationships between state-ments—that is, to indicate the form of an argument. These relationships are made possible by logical connectives such as conjunction (and), disjunction (or), nega-tion (not), and conditional (If . . . then . . .). Connectives are used in compound statements, each of which is composed of at least two simple statements. A state-ment is a sentence that can be either true or false.

To indicate the possible truth values of statements and arguments, we can con-struct truth tables, a graphic way of displaying all the truth value possibilities. A conjunction is false if at least one of its statement components (conjuncts) is false. A disjunction is still true even if one of its component statements (disjuncts) is false. A negation is the denial of a statement. The negation of any statement chan-ges the statement's truth value to its contradictory (false to true and true to false). A conditional statement is false in only one situation—when the antecedent is true and the consequent is false.

The use of truth tables to determine the validity of an argument is based on the fact that it's impossible for a valid argument to have true premises and a false conclusion. A basic truth table consists of two or more guide columns listing all the truth value possibilities, followed by a column for each premise and the conclusion. We can add other columns to help us determine the truth values of components of the argument.

Some arguments are complex when variables and connectives are combined into larger compounds and when the number of variables increases. To prevent confusion, we can use parentheses in symbolized arguments to show how state-ment or premise components go together.

You can check the validity of arguments not only with truth tables but also with the short method. In this procedure we try to discover if there is a way to make the conclusion false and the premises true by assigning various truth values to the argument's components.

Key Terms

Compound statement: A statement composed of at least two constituent, or simple, statements.

Conjunct: One of two simple statements joined by a connective to form a compound statement.

Conjunction: Two simple statements joined by a connective to form a compound statement.

Disjunct: A simple statement that is a component of a disjunction.

Disjunction: A compound statement of the form 'Either *p* or *q*.' A disjunction is true even if only one disjunct is true, and false only if both disjuncts are false.

Propositional logic: The branch of deductive reasoning that deals with the logical relationships among statements.

Simple statement: A statement that doesn't contain any other statements as constituents.

Statement (claim): An assertion that something is or is not the case.

Symbolic logic: Modern deductive logic that uses symbolic language to do its work.

Truth table: A table that specifies the truth values for claim variables and combinations of claim variables in symbolized statements or arguments.

Variables: In modern logic, the symbols, or letters, used to express a statement.

Field Problems

1. Find three deductive arguments on the Internet or in a university newspaper. Symbolize the arguments and determine the validity of each one by making a truth table.

2. Find a deductive argument in one of your textbooks (excluding this one). Symbolize it and create a truth table to test its validity. Then devise a different argument that uses the same argument form as the one you found.

Self-Assessment Quiz

1. What are the four logical connectives used in this chapter? How is each one symbolized?

2. Construct the truth table for each logical connective.

3. Under what circumstances is a conjunction false?

4. Under what circumstances is a conditional false?

5. Which of the following symbolized statements are true and which are false? Assume that *a*, *b*, and *c* are true, and *p*, *q*, and *r* are false.

    $c \rightarrow q$

    a & $\sim q$

    $a \lor \sim c$

6. Put the following statement into symbolic form: 'You will go far if you study hard.'

7. Put the following statement into symbolic form: 'Either the Earth is flat or it is hollow.'

8. Construct a truth table for each of the following arguments and indicate whether the argument is valid or invalid.

$p \rightarrow q$ $p \vee (q \& r)$
$q \rightarrow r$ $\sim(q \& r)$
$\therefore q$ $\therefore p$

9. Translate this argument into symbols, construct its truth table, and indicate whether the argument is valid.

If the temperature rises, then the water will rise. If the water rises, the dam will break. Either the water rises, or it doesn't rise. The water will not rise. Therefore the dam will not break.

10. Translate this argument into symbols, construct its truth table, and indicate whether the argument is valid.

Either Joe goes to the movie, or Julia goes to the movie. If the movie is *The Matrix*, then Julia goes to the movie. So if Joe goes to the movie, the movie is not *The Matrix*.

Construct arguments in English for each of the following symbolized arguments.

11. $x \rightarrow y$ 14. $(p \vee q) \rightarrow (p \& q)$
    $y \rightarrow z$ $p \& q$
    $\therefore x \rightarrow z$ $\therefore p \vee q$

12. $a \rightarrow b$ 15. $p \rightarrow q$
    $\therefore a \rightarrow (a \& b)$ $\sim p$
                                     $\therefore q$

13. $a \& b$
    $\sim b$
    $\therefore a$

Use the short method to check the validity of the following arguments. Write out the argument in a single row and assign truth values to each variable.

16. $p \rightarrow q$ 19. $p \vee (q \& r)$
    $\sim q$ $\sim p$
    $\therefore \sim p$ $\sim q$

17. $p \& q$ $\therefore r$
    $q \rightarrow r$ 20. $a \rightarrow b$
    $\sim q$ $b \rightarrow c$
    $\therefore r$ $\therefore (b \& c) \vee (a \& b)$

18. $p \rightarrow q$
    $q \rightarrow r$
    $\therefore p \rightarrow r$

Integrative Exercises

These exercises pertain to material in Chapters 1–6.

1. What is critical thinking?
2. What is an argument?
3. What are the symbols for the four logical connectives, and what do they mean?
4. True or false: A mere assertion or statement of beliefs constitutes an argument.
5. Can a deductive argument guarantee the truth of its conclusion?

For each of the following arguments, specify the conclusion and premises and indicate any argument indicator words. Symbolize the argument and construct a truth table to determine the argument's validity.

6. If there are no clouds tonight, I will be able to see Venus and you will be able to see Saturn. There will be clouds tonight, so you will not be able to see Saturn.
7. If this bill is passed, the public will demand that the Minister of Health resign. The public, though, will never demand the resignation of a cabinet minister. The bill will not be passed.
8. Either the crippled economy or the sex scandals will drive the British prime minister from office. If inflation rises, then we will have a crippled economy. Inflation will not rise. Therefore, the sex scandals will drive the British prime minister from office.
9. Jones is either crazy or very shrewd. He definitely isn't very shrewd, so he's not crazy either.
10. I will go to market unless the farmer objects, and I will stay home if the cows are sick. The cows aren't sick, therefore I will go to market.

For each of the following arguments, determine whether it is deductive or inductive, valid or invalid, and strong or weak.

11. Either Ellen is shy or she is not. If her cheeks turn red, she's shy. If they don't turn red, she's not shy. Her cheeks are red. Ellen is shy.
12. Assad graduated from McGill. If he graduated from McGill, he's probably very competitive. He's probably very competitive.
13. 'And certainly if its essence and power are infinite, its goodness must be infinite, since a thing whose essence is finite has finite goodness.' (Roger Bacon, *The Opus Majus*)
14. The comet has appeared in the sky every sixty years for the past four centuries. It will appear in the sky again, right on schedule.
15. Use the short method to check the validity of this argument:

$a \rightarrow b$
$\sim b$
$\therefore \sim a$

16. Use the short method to check the validity of this argument:

$p \rightarrow q$
p
$\therefore \sim q$

For each of the following arguments, identify the implicit premise that will make the argument valid.

17. Canadians dominate the National Hockey League. So, Canada will likely win gold in Olympic Men's Hockey.
18. The movie *Harry Potter* is a huge box office success. Obviously it is a great film.
19. Tariq prays constantly. He's sure to succeed in all that he does.
20. The Prime Minister interfered in the decision making of a Crown Corporation in order to benefit a friend of his. The Prime Minister should therefore resign.

Writing Assignments

1. In a one-page essay, devise a deductive argument in which you argue for (or against) the idea that freedom of speech or press should be restricted on university campuses.
2. Select an issue from the following list and write a 500-word paper defending a claim pertaining to the issue. Use one or more deductive arguments to make your case.
   - Should there be restrictions on who can speak or what can be said at university graduation ceremonies?
   - Should private clubs be permitted to ban members of the opposite sex from membership?
   - Should Canada continue its policy of 'official bilingualism'?
   - Should there be restrictions on what university professors can say in the courses they teach?
3. Outline the argument in Essay 5 ('The Naturalist and the Supernaturalist') in Appendix A, indicating the premises and the conclusion. Determine whether the argument is deductive or inductive.

Chapter 7

Deductive Reasoning: Categorical Logic

Chapter Objectives

Statements and Classes

You will be able to

- ○ understand how categorical logic differs from propositional logic.
- ○ define *subject term*, *predicate term*, *copula*, *quantifier*, *quantity*, and *quality*.
- ○ memorize the four standard-form categorical statements.

Translations and Standard Form

You will be able to

- ○ translate ordinary statements into standard categorical form.
- ○ translate singular statements into standard form.

Diagramming Categorical Statements

You will be able to

- ○ construct a Venn diagram for any categorical statement.
- ○ memorize the Venn diagrams for the four standard-form categorical statements.
- ○ use Venn diagrams to tell if two statements are, or are not, equivalent.

Sizing Up Categorical Statements

You will be able to

- ○ understand the structure of categorical syllogisms.
- ○ check the validity of a categorical argument by drawing Venn diagrams.

As we've seen, in propositional logic the basic unit of our concern is the *statement*. Simple statements make up compound statements joined by logical connectives. And the truth value of a compound statement is a function of the truth values of the *component statements*. This important fact is the reason propositional logic is also called *truth-functional logic*. In truth-functional logic we ignore the deeper relationships among the internal parts of a statement.

Categorical logic is different. The basic unit of concern in categorical logic is the *statement component*. We study the relationships, not between statements, but between the subject and predicate of a statement.

Both types of reasoning are deductive, and in both our ultimate goal is the evaluation of arguments. In propositional logic this task is made easier with truth tables and truth-table–like calculations. In categorical logic the primary tools are diagrams and calculation rules.

In categorical reasoning the statements, or claims, of interest are **categorical statements**—those that make simple assertions about categories, or classes, of things. They say how certain classes of things are, or are not, included in other classes of things. For example: 'All cows are herbivores', 'No gardeners are plumbers', or 'Some businesspeople are cheats'. Categorical statements like these play their part without the complexities that arise from conjunctive, disjunctive, or conditional statements.

Like propositional logic, categorical logic is inescapable in daily life. Without thinking much about the process, we often use arguments composed of categorical statements. We may reason, for example, that no pocket knives are things permitted on a commercial airplane because no sharp instruments are things allowed on a commercial airplane, and all pocket knives are sharp instruments. In a real-life situation, we wouldn't state the argument so formally (and awkwardly), and we would probably make one of these premises implicit because it's too obvious to mention. Also, this whole process would likely happen in seconds, with the argument zipping through our heads at top speed.

There are several good reasons why categorical logic—first formulated by Aristotle over two thousand years ago—is still around. Chief among these are that (1) we cannot avoid it and (2) we need it. If that is so, then learning how to use it well can only help us.

"**MEMO: It has come to my attention that every time we solve one problem, we create two more. From now on, all problem solving is forbidden.**"

© 2001 by Randy Glasbergen.

Statements and Classes

The words in categorical statements that name classes, or categories, of things are called terms. Each categorical statement has both a **subject term** and a **predicate term**. For example:

All cats are carnivores.

The subject term here is *cats*, and the predicate term is *carnivores*. The statement says that the class of *cats* is included in the class of *carnivores*. We can express the form of the statement like this:

All S are P.

By convention, S stands for the subject term in a categorical statement; P, the predicate term.

This kind of statement—All S are P—is one of four **standard forms of categorical statements**. Here are all four of them together:

1. All S are P. (All cats are carnivores.)
2. No S are P. (No cats are carnivores.)
3. Some S are P. (Some cats are carnivores.)
4. Some S are not P. (Some cats are not carnivores.)

Standard-form statement 2, 'No S are P', asserts that no member of the S class is included in the P class (no members of the class of cats are part of the class of carnivores). Statement 3, 'Some S are P', asserts that some members of the S class are also members of the P class (some members of the class of cats are also members of the class of carnivores). Statement 4, 'Some S are not P', asserts that some members of the S class are not members of the P class (some members of the class of cats are not members of the class of carnivores).

For the sake of simplicity, the terms in these statements about cats are single words, just nouns naming a class. But subject and predicate terms can also consist of noun phrases and pronouns. Noun phrases are used because several words may be needed to specify a class. Sometimes a noun like *cats* won't do, but a noun phrase like 'cats that live outdoors and hunt mice' will.

In standard-form categorical statements, subject and predicate terms can't be *anything but* nouns, pronouns, and noun phrases. Only nouns, pronouns, and noun phrases can properly designate classes. So the statement 'All cats are carnivores' is in standard form, but 'All cats are carnivorous' is not.

As you might guess, many categorical statements you'll run into don't strictly fit any of these four patterns. But they should—if you want to easily evaluate the validity of arguments containing these statements. So part of the job of assessing such arguments is to translate the categorical statements found 'in the wild' into the tamer and clearer configurations of the standard forms. The challenge is to do these translations while being faithful to the meaning of the original.

Now, to translate categorical statements accurately, you need to know more about how they're put together. Categorical statements have four parts and several characteristics expressed in these parts. You already know about two of these parts, the subject term and the predicate term. They are joined together by a third part called the **copula**, a linking verb—either 'are' or 'are not'.

The fourth part is the **quantifier**, a word that expresses the **quantity**, or number, of a categorical statement. The acceptable quantifiers are 'all', 'no', or 'some'. The quantifiers 'all' and 'no' in front of a categorical statement tell us that it's *universal*—it applies to every member of a class. The quantifier 'some' at the beginning of a categorical statement says that the statement is *particular*—it applies to at least one member of a class.

Categorical statements can vary not only in quantity, but also in the characteristic of **quality**, being either *affirmative* or *negative*. A categorical statement that *affirms* that a class is entirely or partly included in another class is said to be affirmative in quality. A categorical statement that *denies* that a class is entirely or partly included in another class is said to be negative in quality.

With this technical vocabulary we can describe each of the standard forms of statements noted earlier.

1. All *S* are *P*. (All cats are carnivores.)
   This standard-form statement has a universal quantity and an affirmative quality. It *affirms* that *all* cats are included in the class of carnivores. So we characterize it as a *universal affirmative* statement, or claim.
2. No *S* are *P*. (No cats are carnivores.)
   This one *denies* that *all* cats are included in the class of carnivores. Put another way, the whole class of cats is *excluded* from the class of carnivores. It's a *universal negative* statement.
3. Some *S* are *P*. (Some cats are carnivores.)
   This one *affirms* that only *some* cats are included in the class of carnivores. It's a *particular affirmative* statement.
4. Some *S* are not *P*. (Some cats are not carnivores.)
   This one *denies* that only *some* cats are included in the class of carnivores. It doesn't refer to the whole class of cats, just as statement 3 doesn't refer to the whole class. But it denies, instead of affirms, that the partial class of cats is included in the class of carnivores. It's a *particular negative* statement.

Here are the four standard forms of categorical statements again with their quality and quantity listed:

A: All *S* are *P*. (universal affirmative)
E: No *S* are *P*. (universal negative)
I: Some *S* are *P*. (particular affirmative)
O: Some *S* are not *P*. (particular negative)

Notice that this time the statements are preceded, not by numbers, but by the letters A, E, I, and O. These letters are the traditional designations for the four logical forms of categorical statements. We can say then, for example, that this or that statement is an A-statement or an O-statement, indicating the pattern of the arguments in an easy shorthand.

Something important to remember, even if it's obvious, is that all categorical statements should fit into one of these four standard forms, and all statements that do fit into one of these have the *same* form.

Exercise 7.1

For each of the following statements, identify the subject and predicate terms and the name of the form (universal affirmative, universal negative, particular affirmative, or particular negative). Also, state the traditional letter designation for each form (A, E, I, O).

* 1. No scientists are Baptists.
2. Some plants are trees.
3. No cats that have lived over 15 years in a domestic setting are pets free of all health problems.
4. Some mammals are not whales.
* 5. All theologians who have studied arguments for the existence of God are scholars with serious misgivings about the traditional notion of omnipotence.
6. No football players are A-students.
7. All refugees from unstable countries are poor people.
* 8. Some who play the stock market are not millionaires.
9. No taxpayers from the 2003 tax year are embezzlers.
10. No Canadian banks that had dealings with Enron are institutions that deserve our business!
11. All cancer survivors in the clinical study are coffee drinkers.
* 12. Some terrorists are Saudi citizens.
13. No pro-democracy students in China are outside agitators.
14. Some congressional Republican leaders are pro-lifers.
15. Some proposals for two-tier health care are not viable options.
* 16. No 'new Canadians' are supporters of changes in the immigration rules.
17. All child-abuse caseworkers are overburdened civil servants.

Translations and Standard Form

This is worth repeating: We translate ordinary statements into standard-form categorical statements so that we can handle them more efficiently. We want to handle them efficiently so that we can more easily evaluate the validity of arguments composed of categorical statements. Translation is necessary to bring out the underlying structure of statements. It is also important because ordinary language is too imprecise and ambiguous to use in the analysis of statements and arguments. You will appreciate this fact more as you work with categorical statements.

Translating statements into standard form is a straightforward process consisting of a few simple steps and some rules of thumb. Knowing the steps and the rules is important, but getting some *practice* translating statements is vital if you want to know how to translate fast and accurately. If you don't understand a particular point, you'll have an easier time if you go over it until you do rather than skipping it and looking at it later.

Just as a reminder, here's the pattern of all standard-form categorical statements:

Quantifier . . . Subject Term . . . Copula . . . Predicate Term

Food For Thought

Categorical Inspiration

Categorical statements don't have to sound like dry logical assertions. Artists, authors, poets, and songwriters have often used categorical statements to inspire. Here are a few examples:

'Every child is an artist.' (Pablo Picasso)

'All the world's a stage, And all the men and women merely players.' (William Shakespeare, *As You Like It*)

'Every adversity, every failure and every headache carries with it the seed of an equivalent or a greater benefit.' (Napoleon Hill, *Think and Grow Rich*)

'Let every man be respected as an individual and no man idolized.' (Albert Einstein)

'No woman can call herself free who does not own and control her body. No woman can call herself free until she can choose consciously whether she will or will not be a mother.' (Margaret Sanger)

'Love is the only gold.' (Lord Alfred Tennyson)

'All you need is love.' (John Lennon)

You need to know how to handle each of these parts. Since the copula must always be either 'are' or 'are not', you don't have to spend a lot time trying to determine the correct verb. But pinning down the terms and quantifiers is a little more challenging.

Terms

In translating statements, your first order of business is usually to identify the terms and ensure that they designate classes. Once you identify the terms and distinguish the subject term from the predicate term, you'll know in what order the terms must appear in the statement because the subject term must always precede the predicate term. Identifying the terms, though, often involves rewording them so they actually name classes. Consider these translations:

[Original] All dogs are loyal.
[Translation] All dogs are loyal animals.

[Original] Some bachelors waste money.
[Translation] Some bachelors are people who waste money.

[Original] No nations can survive without secure borders.
[Translation] No nations are things that can survive without secure borders.

Sometimes it's easy to locate statement terms but not as easy to tell which is the subject term and which is the predicate term. This can happen when the order of the subject and predicate is reversed:

Beyond the mountains stood the redwood trees.

Here the subject is 'the redwood trees'. The sentence has a normal variation of subject–predicate order, common in English. If you understand the structure of such grammatical reversals, you should be able to identify the true subject and predicate terms.

Difficulty distinguishing subject and predicate terms can also arise when the word 'only' is in a statement. For example, which is the subject term and which is the predicate in these A-statements?

1. Only palm readers are wise counsellors.
2. Only if something is a music file is it an MP3.
3. Hamburgers are the only entrees.
4. The only crimes prosecuted are murders.

We can figure out statements 1 and 2 by using this formula: *The words 'only' and 'only if' precede the predicate term in an A-statement.* So the correct translations are:

1. All wise counsellors are palm readers.
2. All MP3s are music files.

Review Notes

The Four Standard-Form Categorical Statements

A: All *S* are *P*. (universal affirmative)   'All cats are felines.'

E: No *S* are *P*. (universal negative)   'No cats are felines.'

I: Some *S* are *P*. (particular affirmative)   'Some cats are felines.'

O: Some *S* are not *P*. (particular negative)   'Some cats are not felines.'

The translations of statements 3 and 4 follow this formula: *The words 'the only' precede the subject term in an A-statement.* Therefore the correct translations are:

3. All entrees are hamburgers.
4. All prosecuted crimes are murders.

Now, what are the terms in these statements?

5. Jamie Foxx is an actor.
6. Toronto is Canada's finest city.
7. Sunday is the first day of the week.
8. *The Matrix* is an amazing movie.
9. Alicia is not a good student.

> 'Men are apt to mistake the strength of their feeling for the strength of their argument. The heated mind resents the chill touch and relentless scrutiny of logic.'
> –William E. Gladstone

Food For Thought

Standard Form versus Fuzziness

We take the trouble to translate categorical statements into standard form for several reasons—one of them being that language is fuzzy, fuzzy, fuzzy. The famed logician Bertrand Russell agreed: 'Because language is misleading, as well as because it is diffuse and inexact when applied to logic (for which it was never intended), logical symbolism is absolutely necessary to any exact or thorough treatment of our subject' (*Introduction to Mathematical Philosophy*).

We can see a good example of language fuzziness in this type of categorical statement: 'All S are not P.' Take the statement 'All Bigfoot monsters are not apes.' Does this mean that (1) no Bigfoot monsters are apes or (2) that some Bigfoot monsters are not apes? Statement 1 is an E-statement; statement 2 is an O-statement. To defeat fuzziness, we have to apply some categorical logic and translate the original sentence into either an E- or O-statement.

These are known as **singular statements**. Each one asserts something about a single person or thing, including objects, places, and times. Each subject term is a noun (including names), pronoun, or noun phrase referring to an individual, particular item. In a way, the predicate terms specify classes but, alas, the subject terms don't. We can transform such statements, though, into universal statements (A-statements or E-statements). The trick is to think of each subject term as naming a class in which there's just one member. We can, for example, treat the subject term in statement 5 ('Jamie Foxx') as designating a class with Jamie Foxx as one member of that class, like this:

5. All persons identical with Jamie Foxx are actors.

We can translate our other singular statements in similar fashion:

6. All places identical with Toronto are places that are Canada's finest city.
7. All days identical with Sunday are the first days of the week.
8. All things identical with the film *The Matrix* are amazing movies.
9. No persons identical with Alicia are good students.

Now we can see more clearly that statements 5–8 are A-statements and that statement 9 is an E-statement.

Granted, translations of ordinary statements into standard-form categorical statements can sometimes sound awkward, as the preceding translations surely do. But when we translate statements, we put them into a form that makes their logical connections transparent—an agreeable state of affairs when we're trying to check the validity of complex arguments.

Quantifiers

Some quantifiers may be in non-standard form, and some may be unexpressed. Consider these statements:

1. Every hockey player is an athlete.
2. Whoever is an artist is a genius.
3. Sharks are good swimmers.
4. Nothing breakable is a warehouse item.
5. Comets are ice balls.

Each is a universal statement with a non-standard or unexpressed quantifier. Here are the translations with the proper quantifiers:

1. All hockey players are athletes.
2. All artists are geniuses.
3. All sharks are good swimmers.
4. No breakable things are warehouse items.
5. All comets are ice balls.

Statements 1, 2, and 4 have non-standard quantifiers; statements 3 and 5 have unexpressed quantifiers. Fortunately, most non-standard quantifiers are fairly

Food For Thought

Let Us Count the Ways ...

Plenty of non-standard statements are equivalents of categorical statements in standard form.

A-Statement: 'All S Are P'

Only celebrities are spoiled brats.

Mathematicians are good acrobats.

Every general is a leader.

Only if something is a plant is it a flower.

Any car is a vehicle.

Something is a breakfast only if it is a meal.

Whatever is a beaver is a rodent.

Every pediatrician is a doctor.

If something is not a vegetable, then it is not a potato.

All dictators are thugs.

E-Statement: 'No S Are P'

If anything is a feather, then it is not a flower.

All humans are non-reptiles.

Territories are not provinces.

Nothing that is a mind is a body.

Nothing red is a banana.

None of the vegetables are fruits.

It is false that some vegetables are fruits.

I-Statement: 'Some S Are P'

There are engineers who are painters.

Most criminals are morons.

Several diplomats are egomaniacs.

At least one survivor is a hero.

A few lotteries are scams.

Many Europeans are Germans.

O-Statement: 'Some S Are Not P'

Some philosophers are non-reptiles.

Some non-reptiles are philosophers.

Not all comedians are Canadian.

Many tents are not teepees.

Many maple trees are not sugar maples.

Most Quebecers are not separatists.

There are non-reptile philosophers.

Canadians are not always peacekeepers.

A few rock stars are not maniacs.

easy to decipher. 'Every professor', for example, obviously means all the professors. 'Nothing' and 'none' mean not any, which refers to all of them, whatever they are. Usually, unexpressed quantifiers are readily understood because of the nature of the terms. The statement 'Sharks are good swimmers' clearly refers to all sharks, not just some of them. In some statements, though, the unexpressed quantifier is not obvious, as, for example, in 'Trent University students are radicals.' Is it '*All* Trent students' or '*Some* Trent students'? When in doubt, assume the quantifier that you think would make the statement most likely to be true. In this case, 'All Trent students . . .' is a sweeping generalization that's unlikely to apply to every single Trent student. The claim more likely to be true is 'Some Trent students . . .'.

Now consider these statements:

6. There are government workers who are spies.
7. Most movie stars are snobs.
8. Several politicians are space aliens.

These are all particular categorical statements. Their translations are:

6. Some government workers are spies.
7. Some movie stars are snobs.
8. Some politicians are space aliens.

The quantifier 'some' is appropriate in all these statements because, in logic, it means 'at least one'. We therefore have only two options for expressing quantity in categorical statements: *all* and *fewer than all*. 'Most', 'a few', 'several', 'almost all', and similar terms are all translated as 'some'. Part of the reason for logic's restrictive definition of 'some' is that, in everyday language, 'some' is extremely vague. The word could mean 'most', 'two or three', 'ten or more', 'many', who knows? Logic, though, needs precision—more precision than is found in ordinary discourse.

Exercise 7.2

Translate each of the following statements into standard categorical form and say whether the form is A, E, I, or O.

* 1. All Habs fans are fanatical.
  2. Some government programs are wasteful.
  3. 'Brave are the hearts that beat beneath Scottish skies.' ('Scotland the Brave')
  4. 'People who whisper lie.' (Swedish proverb)
* 5. Only cell phone companies that keep up with the latest technology are good investments.

6.   Only if something has a backbeat is it a rock-and-roll song.
7.   'People with pinched faces often have poisonous hearts.' (Chinese proverb)
8.   Nothing that is a snake is a mammal.
* 9.   'All intelligent thoughts have already been thought.' (Johann Wolfgang von Goethe)
10.   'The only good human is a dead human.' (*Planet of the Apes*)
11.   Gregory is a Liberal.
12.   Players who were injured in training didn't suit up for the opening game.
* 13. Some things are meant to be forgotten.
14.   'There is no excellence without difficulty.' (Ovid)
15.   Jonathan is not a very brave pilot.
16.   'All's well that ends well.' (Shakespeare)

Exercise 7.3

Follow the instructions given for Exercise 7.2.

* 1.   Only poets are guardians of the soul.
2.   Any earthquake is a potential disaster.
3.   'People who wish to salute the free and independent side of their evolutionary character acquire cats.' (Anna Quindlen)
* 4.   All androids like Commander Data are non-human.
* 5.   Nothing that satisfies the heart is a material thing.
6.   Some young people are non-Catholics.
7.   Every political party that gets at least 20 per cent of the vote in a general election is a major player in Canadian politics.
* 8.   Most treatments said to be part of 'alternative medicine' are unproven.
9.   There are products advertised on the Internet that are unsafe devices.
10.   'People who love only once in their lives are . . . shallow people.' (Oscar Wilde)
11.   Some Acadians settled on what is called the 'French Shore' of Nova Scotia.
* 12.   Friday is the only day that gives her any joy.
13.   Many critical-thinking textbooks make good bedtime reading.
14.   'All prejudices may be traced to the intestines.' (Friedrich Nietzsche)
* 15.   The picture hanging on the wall is crooked.
16.   Whoever seeks the truth through philosophy is a free person.
17.   'He that is born to be hanged will never be drowned.' (French proverb)
18.   Only artists are visionaries.
19.   Not all writers are poets.
* 20.   'A nation without a conscience is a nation without a soul.' (Winston Churchill)

Diagramming Categorical Statements

If you want more help in understanding the relationships between subject and predicate terms, you're in luck. You can represent such relationships graphically with the use of **Venn diagrams** (named after the British logician and mathematician John Venn). The diagrams consist of overlapping circles, each one representing a class specified by a term in a categorical statement. Here's an example:

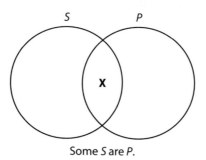

Some S are P.

This is the diagram for an I-statement: 'Some *S* are *P*.' The circle on the left represents the class of *S*; the circle on the right, the class of *P*. The area on the left contains only members of the *S* class. The area on the right contains only members of the *P* class. The area where the circles overlap means that both *S* members and *P* members are present. The X in the overlapped area, however, gives more specific information. It shows that *at least one S* member is a *P* member. That is, there is at least one *S* that also is a *P*. This diagram, of course, represents *any* statement of the form 'Some *S* are *P*'—like, for instance, 'Some cars are Fords.' The X on the diagram where the circles overlap, then, would mean that at least one car is a Ford.

Now here's the diagram for an O-statement—'Some *S* are not *P*':

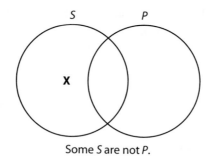

Some S are not P.

Here the X is in the *S* circle but outside the *P* circle, indicating that at least one *S* is not a *P*. In our car example (in which the *S* circle represents the class of cars and the *P* circle represents the class of Fords), this diagram would show that at least one car is not a Ford.

Here's the diagram for an A-statement—'All *S* are *P*':

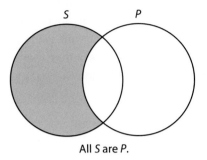

S   P

All *S* are *P*.

This diagram asserts that all members of the *S* class are also members of the *P* class. ('All cars are Fords.') Notice that the part of the diagram where the *S* circle does not overlap the *P* circle is shaded, showing that that area is 'empty', or without any members. (If you want, think of it this way: in the shaded area, the lights are out because no one is home!) And this means that there are no members of *S* that are not also members of *P*. The remaining part of the *S* circle overlaps with the *P* circle, showing that *S* members are also *P* members.

Review Notes

Three Steps to Diagramming a Categorical Statement
1. Draw two overlapping circles, each one representing a term in the statement.
2. Label the circles with the terms.
3. Shade an area of a circle to show that an area is empty; insert an X to show that at least one member of a class is also a member of another class.

Finally, the diagram for an E-statement—'No *S* are *P*':

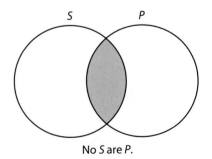

S   P

No *S* are *P*.

Here the area where the S circle and the P circle overlap is shaded (empty), meaning that there is no situation in which S overlaps with P (in which members of S are also members of P). So no members of S are also members of P ('No cars are Fords').

Venn diagrams can come in handy when you want to know whether two categorical statements are equivalent, that is, whether they say the same thing. If the diagrams for the statements are identical, then the statements are equivalent.

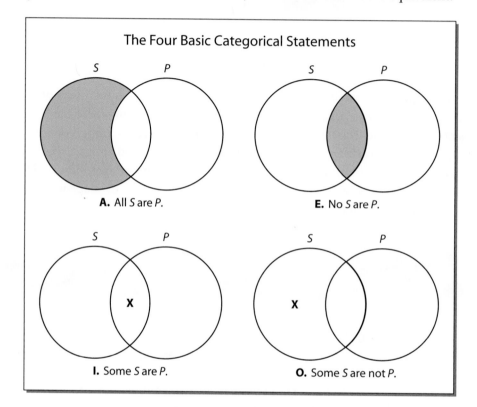

The Four Basic Categorical Statements

A. All S are P.

E. No S are P.

I. Some S are P.

O. Some S are not P.

Let's say that you want to know whether the following two statements say the same thing:

No S are P.
No P are S.

If you diagram them both, you get your answer:

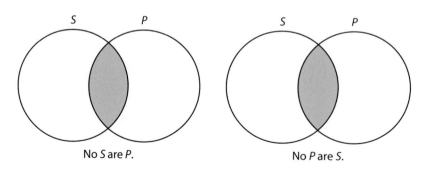

No S are P.

No P are S.

You can see that the diagrams are identical—they both show the area of over-lap between the two circles as shaded, signifying that there are no members of *S* that are also members of *P*, and vice versa. So the first statement ('No *S* are *P*,' an E-statement) says the same thing as the second statement ('No *P* are *S*').

Likewise, if we compare the diagrams for 'Some *S* are *P*' (I-statement) and 'Some *P* are *S*', we can see that these statements are also equivalent:

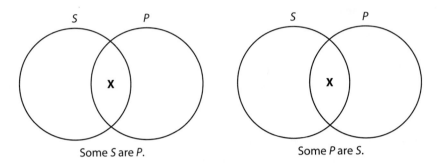

Some *S* are *P*.   Some *P* are *S*.

On the other hand, by comparing diagrams we can see that A-statements and E-statements are *not* equivalent (something you knew already, of course):

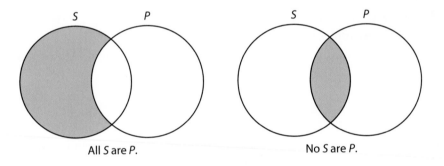

All *S* are *P*.   No *S* are *P*.

Let's examine one final pair of statements:

All *S* are *P*.
No *S* are non-*P*.

The diagrams clearly show that these are equivalent:

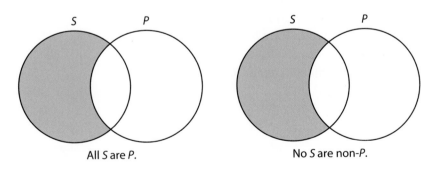

All *S* are *P*.   No *S* are non-*P*.

Exercise 7.4

Construct Venn diagrams for each of the following statements. Specify both the subject and predicate terms. If necessary, translate the statement into standard form before diagramming (A, E, I, or O).

* 1. No one is exempt from federal income tax.
  2. No creed can be inviolable.
  3. No one can drop out of school when they're thirteen.
  4. Some birds are flightless.
* 5. Nothing is more pitiable than the reasons of an unreasonable man.
  6. John Locke is one of the few philosophers whose ideas have truly shaped the modern world.
  7. Some snakes are not poisonous.
* 8. Some good talkers are good listeners.
  9. It is false that some businessmen are crooks.
  10. Some people with excellent reputations are not persons of excellent character.
  11. Black dogs didn't get fed.
* 12. Every corporation has social obligations.
  13. Rainbows are always misleading.
  14. There are bad apples in every barrel.
  15. 'Few friendships could survive the moodiness of love affairs.' (Mason Cooley)

Exercise 7.5

Construct Venn diagrams for each statement in the following pairs, and then say whether the statements are equivalent.

* 1. No P are S; No S are P.
  2. Some S are P; Some P are S.
* 3. All S are P; All P are S.
  4. No S are P; All P are non-S.
  5. All S are P; Some P are non-S.
* 6. All P are non-S; All S are non-P.
  7. No non-S are P; No non-P are S.
  8. No S are P; No P are S.
* 9. Some S are not P; Some P are not S.
  10. All S are non-P; No P are S.

Sizing Up Categorical Syllogisms

Once you understand the workings of categorical statements, you're ready to explore the dynamics of categorical arguments, or—more precisely—categorical syllogisms. As we saw in Chapter 3, a syllogism is a deductive argument made up of three statements: two premises and a conclusion. A categorical syllogism is one consisting of three categorical statements (A, E, I, or O) interlinked in a specific way. You can see the interlinking structure in this categorical syllogism:

'Logical consequences are the scarecrows of fools and the beacons of wise men.'
—Thomas Henry Huxley

(1) All elected officials are civil servants.
(2) All politicians are elected officials.
(3) Therefore, all politicians are civil servants.

If we diagram this argument as we did in Chapter 3, we come up with this structure:

But this kind of diagram, though handy in truth-functional logic, isn't much help here because it doesn't reveal the internal components and interlinking structure of the statements. Observe that each categorical statement has, as usual, two terms. But there are a total of only three terms in a categorical syllogism, each term being mentioned twice but in different statements. So in the preceding argument, *politicians* appears in statements 2 and 3; *elected officials*, in 1 and 2; and *civil servants*, in 1 and 3.

In a categorical syllogism, we refer to the predicate term in the conclusion (*civil servants*, in this case) as the *predicate term* for the whole argument. The predicate term also appears in one of the premises (premise 1, in the example above). The subject term in the conclusion is treated as the *subject term* for the whole argument. The subject term also occurs in one of the premises (premise 2, in the argument above). The other term, the one that appears once in each premise but not in the conclusion, is referred to as the *middle term*. If we map out the argument with the terms labelled in this way, here's what we get:

Premise (1) [Middle term] [Predicate term].
Premise (2) [Subject term] [Middle term].
Conclusion (3) Therefore, [Subject term] [Predicate term].

We can symbolize this argument form with letters:

(1) All *M* are *P*.
(2) All *S* are *M*.
(3) Therefore, all *S* are *P*.

Here, *M* stands for the middle term; *P* for the predicate term; and *S* for the subject term.

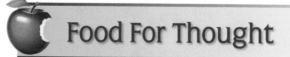

Food For Thought

Living by the Rules

Drawing Venn diagrams is a good way to both visualize what a syllogism is saying and test it for validity. But you can also check validity without diagrams. One technique is to assess the validity of a syllogism by determining if the argument follows certain rules. Some of these rules involve the fine points of syllogistic structure. But others are drawn from simple facts about syllogisms that you probably already know—or have suspected. Here are three such rules:

1. A valid categorical syllogism must possess precisely three terms.
2. A valid categorical syllogism cannot have two negative premises.
3. A valid categorical syllogism with at least one negative premise must have a negative conclusion.

Any standard-form categorical syllogism that breaks even one of these rules is invalid. (On the other hand, a categorical syllogism that does not violate any of these rules is not necessarily valid. It may be defective for other reasons.)

Here are some syllogisms that violate at least one rule:

All snakes are reptiles.
All reptiles are cold-blooded creatures.
Therefore, all lizards are cold-blooded creatures.
(Violates rule 1.)

No criminals are law-enforcement officers.
Some law-enforcement officers are not bank robbers.
Therefore, some bank robbers are not criminals.
(Violates rule 2.)

No Italians are Asians.
Some Inuit are Italians.
Therefore, some Inuit are Asians.
(Violates rule 3.)

So a categorical syllogism is one that has:

1. Three categorical statements—two premises and a conclusion.
2. Exactly three terms, with each term appearing twice in the argument.
3. One of the terms (the middle term) appearing in each premise but not the conclusion.
4. Another term (the predicate term) appearing as the predicate term in the conclusion and also in one of the premises.
5. Another term (the subject term) appearing as the subject term in the conclusion and also in one of the premises.

A valid categorical syllogism, like a valid deductive argument of any other sort, is such that if its premises are true, its conclusion *must* be true. (That is, if the premises are true, the conclusion cannot possibly be false.) This fact, of course, you already know. Of more interest now is how we can *check the validity* of categorical syllogisms. Fortunately, there are several ways, the simplest of which is the Venn diagramming method. This technique involves drawing a circle for each term (the subject, predicate, and middle term) in the argument (giving us three overlapping circles), then diagramming the premises on these circles (using shading and x's, as discussed in the previous section). If the resulting diagram reflects the assertion in the conclusion, the argument is valid.

If you know how to diagram categorical statements, you can diagram an entire categorical argument. Remember that since a categorical statement has two terms, we need two circles to diagram it—one circle for each term. And since a categorical syllogism has three terms, we need three circles, overlapping like this:

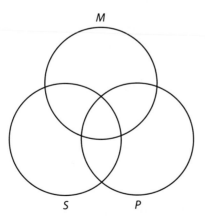

The top circle represents the class designated by the middle term (*M*); the bottom left circle, the subject term (*S*); and the bottom right circle, the predicate term (*P*). The two lower circles together represent the conclusion since they stand for the relationship between the subject and predicate terms (*S* and *P*).

Let's diagram our syllogism about politicians and civil servants, diagramming one statement, or premise, at a time. We can start by labelling the diagram like this, with three empty, overlapping circles:

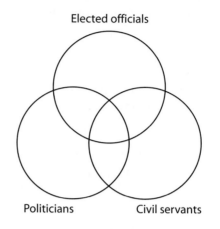

Now, we diagram the first premise ('All elected officials are civil servants'). To do this, we look *only* at the two circles involved in Premise 1—namely the 'elected officials' circle and the 'civil servants' circle. For now, *ignore the other circle entirely*. Premise 1 is an A-statement. So, to represent premise 1, we shade the part of the elected officials circle that does *not* overlap with the civil servants circle. This signifies that all the existing elected officials are also civil servants:

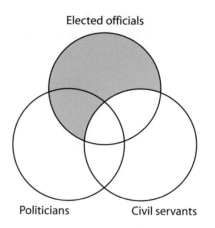

Notice that, if you just look at the two circles we're working with here, the diagram looks exactly like our original A-statement diagram on page 251. Diagrams of A-statements *always* look like that!

Next, we diagram premise 2 ('All politicians are elected officials'). Premise 2 is another A-statement, so we diagram it by shading the part of the politicians circle that does not overlap with the elected officials circle:

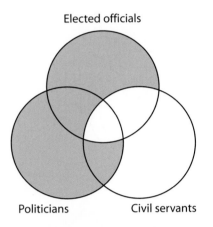

Elected officials

Politicians   Civil servants

Now, we *stop drawing*. We diagram *only* the premises. We never, ever diagram the conclusion.

Why is that? Why not diagram the conclusion too? Recall that in a valid deductive argument, the premises imply the conclusion. So, once we diagram the premises, the resulting combined diagram is already supposed to represent the information in the conclusion ('Therefore, all politicians are civil servants'). We can see that the politicians circle is shaded everywhere—except in the area that overlaps the civil servant circle. And this is how the diagram of the syllogism *should* be shaded to depict the statement 'All politicians are civil servants.' (Look at the diagram, and ask yourself: where are the politicians? Most of the politician circle is shaded—empty. The only place you can find any politicians is in an area that overlaps with the civil servant circle. Hence, all politicians are civil servants.)

So the diagram does express what's asserted in the conclusion of our argument. The argument is therefore valid. If you diagram the premises of a categorical syllogism and the resulting combined diagram says the same thing as the conclusion, the syllogism is valid. If the diagram does not 'contain' the conclusion (if information is missing), the syllogism is invalid.

This syllogism has two universal ('All') premises (both A-statements). Let's diagram one that has a particular ('Some') premise:

All robots are drudges.
Some professors are robots.
Therefore, some professors are drudges.

Here's the diagram properly labelled:

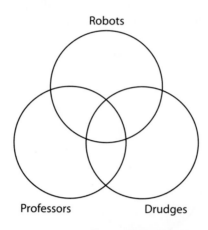

Robots

Professors   Drudges

Review Notes

Five Steps to Checking Validity with Venn Diagrams

1. Draw three overlapping circles, each circle representing a term in the syllogism, with the two circles representing the subject and predicate terms placed on the bottom.
2. Label the circles with the terms.
3. Diagram the first premise. (Diagram universal premises first. When diagramming a particular premise, if it's unclear where to place an X in a circle section, place it on the dividing line between subsections.)
4. Diagram the second premise.
5. Check to see if the diagram represents what is asserted in the conclusion. If it does, the argument is valid; if not, it's invalid.

We'll diagram the first premise first ('All robots are drudges')—but not just because it happens to be the first premise. In categorical syllogisms with both a universal and a particular premise, we should always diagram the universal premise first. The reason is that diagramming the particular premise first can lead to confusion. For example, in the argument in question, if we were to diagram the particular premise first ('Some professors are robots'), we would end up with an X in the area where the robots and professors circles overlap. That section, however, is split into two subsections by the drudges circle:

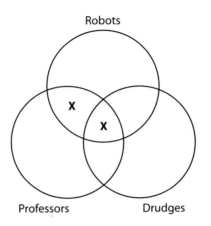

So then the question arises in which subsection we should place the X. Should we put the X in the area overlapping with the drudges circle—or in the part not overlapping with the drudges circle? Our choice *does* affect what the diagram says about the validity of the argument. But if we diagram the universal premise first, the decision of where to insert the X is made for us because there would be only one relevant subsection left (and we can't place an X in a shaded area):

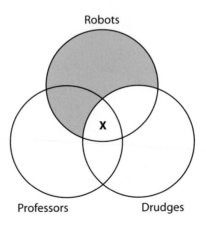

The resulting diagram represents the statement that some professors are drudges, which is what the conclusion asserts. The syllogism, then, is valid.

But sometimes, diagramming the universal premise first still leaves us with a question about where the X should go. Consider this syllogism:

All barbers are singers.
Some Italians are singers.
Therefore, some Italians are barbers.

When we diagram the universal premise first, we see that the section where the Italians and singers circles overlap is divided between a subsection including barbers and a subsection excluding barbers. So the X could go in either subsection, and we have no way of knowing which:

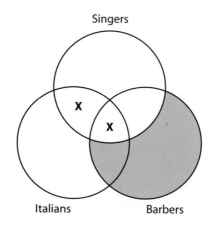

But we can't leave the diagram like that; it's too unclear! In situations like this, the best approach is to indicate our lack of information by placing the X on the border between the two subsections, like this:

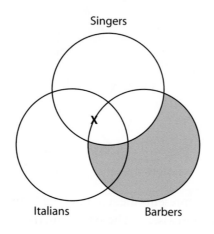

An X placed in this position means that among things that are both Italians and singers, something is either a barber or not a barber. Now, the conclusion says that some Italians are barbers. This conclusion is represented in the diagram only if there is an X *unquestionably* in the area where the barbers and Italians circles overlap. But we don't have an X unquestionably in that region; we have only an X that *may or may not be there*. That is, there's a question of just where the X is. Therefore, the diagram does not assert what the conclusion does, and the argument is invalid.

Exercise 7.6

For each of the following arguments, label the subject term, predicate term, and middle term. Then translate each syllogism into symbolic form using *S*, *P*, and *M* to represent the terms.

1. No apples are vegetables. Some plants are vegetables. So some plants are not apples.
* 2. All horses are mammals, and no mammals are lizards. Therefore, no lizards are horses.
3. All cars are self-propelled vehicles, and all motorcycles are self-propelled vehicles. Thus, all motorcycles are cars.
4. Some roses are yellow flowers. All roses are plants. Therefore, some plants are yellow flowers.
5. All roads are highways to Rome, but no mere paths are roads. So no mere paths are highways to Rome.
* 6. Some DVDs are not film classics, but all black and white movies are film classics. Therefore, some black and white movies are not DVDs.
7. All prime ministers are leaders, but some statesmen are not prime ministers. So some statesmen are not leaders.
8. All politicians are campaigners. All campaigners are money-grubbers. Therefore all politicians are money-grubbers.
* 9. No elm trees are cacti. Some tall plants are elm trees. So some tall plants are not cacti.
10. All thieves are criminals. All thieves are dangers to society. Therefore, all dangers to society are criminals.

Exercise 7.7

Draw Venn diagrams to test the validity of each of the arguments in Exercise 7.6. Answers are given for 2, 6, and 9.

Exercise 7.8

Translate each of the following arguments into categorical syllogistic form (premise, premise, conclusion), symbolize the argument (by using the conventional *S*, *P*, *M* variables), and draw a Venn diagram to test its validity.

* 1. Some architectural structures are non-traditional designs, for all houses are architectural structures and some houses are non-traditional designs.

2. All bacon burgers are heart-attack–inducing foods because all bacon burgers are high-fat foods, and some heart attack-inducing foods are not high-fat foods.

* 3. All SUVs are evil vehicles because all SUVs are gas-guzzlers and all gas-guzzlers are evil vehicles.

4. Some famous men are not racists since all racists are enemies of justice, and some famous men are not enemies of justice.

5. No persons dedicated to the public good are politicians, because all politicians are self-promoters. And no self-promoters are persons dedicated to the public good.

6. Some philosophers are musicians. Therefore, some trumpet players are philosophers since all trumpet players are musicians.

7. All civil libertarians are defenders of freedom of expression. Some defenders of freedom of expression are pornographers. Therefore, some civil libertarians are pornographers.

* 8. No wimps are social activists because no wimps are people of honest and strong convictions. And all social activists are people of honest and strong convictions.

9. Most people who drive SUVs are instant-gratification freaks who don't care about the environment or environmental issues. Instant-gratification freaks who don't care about the environment or environmental issues are the true enemies of the planet. Therefore, people who drive SUVs are the true enemies of the planet.

10. Vitamin pills are useless gimmicks promoted as sure cures for a variety of illnesses. Some useless gimmicks promoted as sure cures, though, are placebos that can make people feel good. So some vitamin pills are placebos that can make people feel good even if they don't cure anything.

Summary

Every categorical statement has a subject term and a predicate term. There are four standard forms of categorical statements: (1) universal affirmative ('All dogs are mammals'), (2) universal negative ('No dogs are mammals'), (3) particular affirmative ('Some dogs are mammals'), and (4) particular negative ('Some dogs are not mammals').

Categorical statements must be translated into standard form before you can work with them. Translating involves identifying terms, ensuring that they designate classes, and determining the quantifiers. Drawing Venn diagrams is a good way to visualize categorical statements and to tell whether one statement is equivalent to another.

A categorical syllogism is an argument consisting of three categorical statements (two premises and a conclusion) that are interlinked in a structured way.

The syllogism consists of a subject term, predicate term, and middle term. The middle term appears once in each premise. The subject term appears in one premise and the conclusion, and the predicate term appears in the other premise and the conclusion. You can use Venn diagrams to represent categorical statements, showing how the terms are related.

The easiest way to check the validity of a categorical syllogism is to draw a three-circle Venn diagram—three overlapping circles with the relationship between terms depicted graphically. If, after diagramming each premise, the diagram reflects what is asserted in the conclusion, the argument is valid. If it does not, the argument is invalid.

Key Terms

Categorical logic: A form of logic whose focus is categorical statements, which make assertions about categories, or classes, of things.

Categorical statement: A statement, or claim, that makes a simple assertion about categories, or classes, of things.

Copula: One of four components of a standard-form categorical statement; a linking verb—either 'are' or 'are not'—that joins the subject term and the predicate term.

Predicate term: The second class, or group, named in a standard-form categorical statement.

Quality: A characteristic of a categorical statement, determined by whether the statement affirms or denies that a class is entirely or partly included in another class. A categorical statement that affirms is said to be affirmative in quality; one that denies is said to be negative in quality.

Quantifier: In categorical statements, a word used to indicate the number of things with specified characteristics. The acceptable quantifiers are 'all', 'no', or 'some'. The quantifier 'all' or 'no' in front of a categorical statement tell us that it's *universal*—it applies to every member of a class.

The quantifier 'some' at the beginning of a categorical statement says that the statement is *particular*—it applies to some but not all members of a class.

Quantity: In categorical statements, the attribute of number, specified by the words 'all', 'no', or 'some'.

Singular statements: In categorical logic, statements that assert something about a single person or thing, including objects, places, and times.

Standard-form categorical statement: In categorical logic, a categorical statement that takes one of these four forms:

1. All *S* are *P*. (All cats are carnivores.)
2. No *S* are *P*. (No cats are carnivores.)
3. Some *S* are *P*. (Some cats are carnivores.)
4. Some *S* are not *P*. (Some cats are not carnivores.)

Subject term: The first class, or group, named in a standard-form categorical statement.

Venn diagrams: Diagrams consisting of overlapping circles that represent graphically the relationships between subject and predicate terms in categorical statements.

Field Problems

1. Do a search on the Internet for the term 'rant' or 'rants'. You will get an enormous list of websites featuring off-the-cuff opinions and tirades on countless topics—everything from religion and politics to celebrity fashion, cheese, bad drivers, Rice Krispies, and many subjects that can't be discussed in a textbook. From this mélange, pick out an *invalid* categorical syllogism and write a 100- to 150-word paragraph assessing the soundness of the argument (both its truth and validity) and how it might be rewritten to be made valid.

2. Check recent news reports to find one categorical statement made by the Prime Minister of Canada, a federal cabinet minister, or one of the premiers. Translate the statement into standard form. (1) Construct a *valid* categorical syllogism using the statement as the conclusion and supplying whatever premises you deem appropriate. Assume that your premises are true. (2) Then construct an *invalid* syllogism using the same statement as the conclusion and supplying premises, also assumed to be true. In both arguments, try to keep the statements as realistic as possible (for example, close to what you may actually read in a news magazine).

Self-Assessment Quiz

1. What is a quantifier? What are the two quantities that can be expressed in categorical statements?
2. What are the two qualities that can be expressed in categorical statements?
3. What are the four standard-form categorical statements? (Specify them by quality and quantity and by letter designation.)

For each of the following statements, identify the subject and predicate terms, the quality, the quantity, and the name of the form (universal affirmative, universal negative, particular affirmative, or particular negative).

4. Some tax cuts are economic mistakes.
5. No philosophers are five-year-old kids.
6. All patients treated with herbal medicine are Chinese.
7. Some ghost stories are not fabrications devised by true believers.

Translate each of the following statements into standard categorical form and indicate whether the form is A, E, I, or O.

8. Only if something is a watercraft is it a canoe.
9. 'Baseball is pastoral.' (George Carlin)
10. Sheila is the finest scholar in the department.
11. No one with any sense would drive a car without headlights on a rainy night.

12. 'Slow and steady wins the race.' (Aesop)
13. A politician is someone who firmly believes that getting elected makes one smart.
14. 'A fanatic is someone who can't change his mind and won't change the subject.' (Winston Churchill)

Construct Venn diagrams to test the validity of each of the following syllogisms.

15. All M are P. Some S are M. Therefore, some S are P.
16. No M are P. No S are M. Therefore, all S are P.
17. All P are M. No S are M. Therefore, no S are P.
18. Some P are not M. All S are M. Therefore, some S are not P.
19. All M are P. All M are S. Therefore, all S are P.
20. Some S are M. All M are P. Therefore, some S are P.

Integrative Exercises

These exercises pertain to material in Chapters 3–7.

For each of the following arguments, determine whether it is deductive or inductive, valid or invalid, strong or weak. Then diagram it using the lines-and-arrows method discussed in Chapter 3. Also state whether the argument contains any appeals to popularity or common practice.

1. 'Proposals to reduce the criminal offence of euthanasia have been advanced, especially in light of the Latimer case. Some wish to create a new category of "compassionate homicide". For three reasons, it would be unwise public policy to enact this type of provision. (a) Killing someone is not an act of compassion. Compassionate homicide is an ethically flawed concept. (b) A separate crime for euthanasia would be discriminatory by (i) depriving the lives of sick and disabled persons of equal protection from murder; (ii) signifying that the lives of sick and disabled persons have less value than others. (c) Public safety would be endangered.' (Euthanasia Prevention Coalition of BC)

2. 'Encouragement of contempt for laws is more dangerous to society than occasional use of marijuana. Severe laws against marijuana do not discourage use of marijuana, but rather breed this contempt not only for drug laws, but for laws in general. Therefore severe laws against marijuana are more dangerous to society than the activity which they are designed to prevent.' (A. Blakeslee)

3. Psychic powers (ESP, telepathy, and clairvoyance) are a myth. Hundreds of studies have failed to detect any genuine effects of such phenomena. Numerous case histories and other research over the past one hundred years reveal that most putative 'psychics' have turned out to be frauds or incapable of reliably producing the desired results. And no researchers in this field have ever devised a plausible theory that explains how psychic powers work.

4. It is ridiculous for City Council to pass a bylaw that bans smoking in all public places, including bars and private clubs. Many people enjoy smoking cigarettes and cigars, and in many cultures, smoking has cultural and religious significance. A bylaw outlawing all forms of smoking is morally and legally unjustifiable.

For each of the following arguments, name the argument pattern—*modus ponens, modus tollens*, affirming the consequent, denying the antecedent, or none of these.

5. If minds are identical to bodies, then whatever is true of minds is true of bodies, and vice versa. But minds are indivisible (they cannot be divided into parts) and bodies are divisible (we can break down a body into many parts and in many ways). Therefore, minds are not identical to bodies.
6. If Vaughn is boring, no student can stand to listen to his lectures for more than sixty seconds. Vaughn is not boring, so students can stand to listen to him for more than a minute.
7. If there were structures in nature that were so complex that they could not possibly have evolved through natural selection, the theory of evolution must be false. There are such structures, however—like the human eye. Consequently evolution cannot be the right explanation for the existence of the peculiar life forms found on Earth.

Say which of the following symbolized statements are true and which are false. Assume that the variables a, b, and c are true, and p, q, and r are false.

8. $\sim b \lor r$
9. $a \mathbin{\&} \sim p$
10. $p \rightarrow \sim a$
11. $b \rightarrow r$

For each of the following arguments, specify the conclusion and premises (including any implied premises). Symbolize the argument and construct a truth table to determine the validity of the argument.

12. If the nuclear power industry improves its safety record and solves the nuclear waste problem, it will become the number one source of energy in the world. But it will never be able to change its safety record or solve the waste problem. Consequently the industry will not become the primary source of the world's energy.
13. Either Katharine inherited money from her grandparents or she won the lottery. But she certainly did not inherit money from her grandparents. So she won the lottery.
14. The surgery will be a success if blood loss can be controlled. The surgery is a success and the patient has spoken to the press. So blood loss must have been controlled.

15. If the other nine provinces want to keep Canada strong and united, then they will continue to recognize Quebec's special place in Confederation. If they continue to recognize Quebec's special place in Confederation, then Quebec's distinct culture will survive. Quebec's distinct culture will survive, so the other nine provinces will continue to recognize Quebec's special place in Confederation.

Translate each of the following arguments into categorical syllogistic form (premise, premise, conclusion), symbolize the argument (using the conventional *S*, *P*, *M* variables), and draw a Venn diagram to test its validity.

16. Some Muslims are not Sunni Muslims, for some Muslims are Shiite Muslims and no Shiite Muslims are Sunni Muslims.
17. Some TV shows are reality shows, and no reality shows are good shows. So some TV shows are not good shows.
18. Some sociopaths are not criminals, but all serial killers are criminals. It follows that some sociopaths are not serial killers.
19. Mayor McTaggart will not support any proposal to soften the anti-smoking bylaw. He's a physician, and physicians never support proposals to soften anti-smoking by-laws.
20. Some contagious diseases are diseases caused by the influenza virus, and diseases caused by the influenza virus are always dangerous diseases. So some contagious diseases are dangerous diseases.

Writing Assignments

1. Write a two-page essay arguing either for or against recycling. Cast your argument as a categorical syllogism.
2. Write a two-page rebuttal to Essay 5 ('The Naturalist and the Supernaturalist') in Appendix A.
3. Read Essay 4 ('The Kalam Cosmological Argument') in Appendix A, noting the premises and conclusions of any arguments. Write a three-page rebuttal.

Inductive Reasoning

Chapter Objectives

Enumerative Induction

You will be able to

○ define enumerative induction and explain how it's used.

○ define *target population*, *sample*, and *relevant property*.

○ understand the two ways in which an enumerative induction can fail to be strong.

○ understand the error known as hasty generalization and know how to avoid it.

○ understand the basics of opinion polls and know the definitions of *random sampling*, *self-selecting sample*, *margin of error*, and *confidence level*.

Statistical Syllogisms

You will be able to:

○ explain what a statistical syllogism is.

○ define individual, group, characteristic, and proportion.

○ understand three ways in which statistical syllogisms can fail to be strong.

Analogical Induction

You will be able to

○ formulate and evaluate an argument by analogy.

○ use the following criteria to evaluate arguments by analogy: relevant similarities, relevant dissimilarities, the number of instances compared, and diversity among cases.

Causal Arguments

You will be able to

- define causal claims and arguments.
- apply Mill's methods to the evaluation of causal arguments.
- recognize the ways in which people can make errors in causal reasoning.
- recognize and know how to avoid the post hoc fallacy.
- define *necessary* and *sufficient conditions*.
- distinguish between necessary and sufficient conditions in everyday contexts.

We now pass from an exploration of deductive arguments to a close examination of inductive ones—a very small step since both these argument types are common features of our everyday lives. Recall that a deductive argument is intended to provide logically conclusive support for its conclusion; such an argument is either valid or invalid, sound or unsound. An inductive argument, on the other hand, is intended to supply only probable support for its conclusion, earning the label of 'strong' if it succeeds in providing such support and 'weak' if it fails. The conclusion of an inductively strong argument is simply more likely to be true than not. If the argument's premises are true, it is said to be cogent. Unlike valid deductive arguments, an inductively strong argument cannot guarantee that the conclusion is true—but it can render the conclusion probably true, even highly likely to be true. Inductive arguments, then, cannot give us certainty, but they can give us high levels of probability—high enough at least to help us acquire knowledge in everything from physics to bird-watching.

Deductive logic is the invisible framework on which much of our reasoning hangs and the solid bond that holds together the logical lattices of mathematics, computer science, and other theoretical or abstract disciplines. Inductive reasoning, though, gives us most of what we know about the empirical workings of the world, allowing us in science and in ordinary experience to soar reliably from what we know to what we don't. It allows us to reason 'beyond the evidence'—from bits of what is already known to conclusions about what those bits suggest is probably true.

Inductive arguments come in several forms. In this chapter we will examine four of them and, as in previous chapters, we will focus on how to evaluate their merits in real-life contexts.

> 'The rules of probable inference are the most difficult part of logic, but also the most useful.'
> —Bertrand Russell

Enumerative Induction

As you may have noticed in Chapter 3, sometimes an inductive argument reasons from premises about a group, or class, of things to a conclusion about a single member of the group (that is, from general to particular). For example:

"There are lies, damn lies, and statistics. We're looking for someone who can make all three of these work for us."

www.CartoonStock.com

Almost all of the students attending this university are tree huggers.
Wei-en attends this university.
Therefore, Wei-en is probably a tree hugger.

Eighty-two per cent of residents in this neighbourhood buy Girl Guide cookies.
Sam is a resident of this neighbourhood.
Therefore, Sam will probably buy Girl Guide cookies.

Far more inductive arguments, however, reason from premises about individual members of a group to conclusions about the group as a whole (from particular to general). In such cases we begin with observations about some members of the group and end with a generalization about all of them. This argument pattern is called **enumerative induction**, and it's a way of reasoning that we all find both natural and useful.

Most peace activists I know are kind-hearted. So probably all peace activists are kind-hearted.

Every Gizmo computer I've bought in the last two years has had a faulty monitor. Therefore all Gizmo computers probably have faulty monitors.

Forty per cent of the pickles that you've pulled out of the barrel are exceptionally good. So 40 per cent of all the pickles in the barrel are probably exceptionally good.

More formally, enumerative induction has this form:
X per cent of the observed members of group A have property P. Therefore, X per cent of all members of group A probably have property P.

In this formal guise, our pickle argument looks like this:
Forty per cent of the observed pickles from the barrel are exceptionally good. Therefore, 40 per cent of all the pickles in the barrel are probably exceptionally good.

Enumerative induction comes with some useful terminology. The group as a whole—the whole collection of individuals in question—is called the **target population** or **target group**. The observed members of the target group are called the **sample members** or **sample**. And the property we're interested in is called the **relevant property** or **property in question**. In the foregoing example, the target group is the pickles in the barrel. The sample is the observed pickles. And the property is the quality of being exceptionally good.

Now, using this terminology we can study arguments by enumeration a little closer. Remember that an inductive argument cannot only be strong or weak, but it can also *vary* in its strength—in the degree of support that the premises give to the conclusion. So the strength of the argument depends on the premises as well as on how much is claimed in the conclusion. Let's look at some examples.

Argument 1
All the corporate executives Jacques has worked for have been crooks.
Therefore, all corporate executives are probably crooks.

The target group is corporate executives, the sample is the corporate executives Jacques has worked for, and the relevant property is being a crook. We don't know how many corporate executives Jacques has worked for, but we must assume from what we know about career paths in corporate Canada that the number is small, probably no more than a dozen. Neither do we know exactly how many corporate executives there are, but we can safely guess that there are thousands or tens of thousands. It should be obvious then that this enumerative inductive falls short on at least one score: the sample is too small. We simply cannot draw reliable conclusions about all corporate executives on the basis of a mere handful of them. The argument is weak.

With such a small sample of the target group, we can't even conclude that *most* corporate executives are crooks. But we can make argument 1 strong by revising the conclusion to read, '*Some* corporate executives are probably crooks.' This is a much more limited generalization that requires a more limited supporting premise.

We can fault this argument on another count: the sample is not representative of the target group. With thousands of corporate executives working for thousands of corporations, we must assume that corporate executives—in temperament, morality, demographics, and many other factors—are a diverse lot. It is therefore highly unlikely that Jacques's former bosses are representative of all corporate executives in their crookedness (the relevant property). And if the sample is not representative of the whole, we cannot use it to draw accurate conclusions about the whole. Argument 1 is weak for that additional reason.

Consider this one:

Argument 2
All of the blue herons that we've examined at many different sites in the nature preserve (about 200 birds) have had birth defects.
Therefore, most of the blue herons in the nature preserve probably have birth defects.

In this argument the target group is the blue herons in the nature preserve, the sample is the 200 blue herons examined, and the relevant property is having birth defects. We would normally consider this a very strong enumerative induction. Assuming that the premise is true, we would probably be surprised to discover that only a tiny minority of the target group had birth defects. Since the sample was drawn from many parts of the preserve, we would deem it representative of the target group. And because of the general uniformity of characteristics among birds in the wild, we would assume that a sample of 200 birds would be large enough to strongly support the conclusion. As it stands, argument 2 is strong.

On the other hand, a conclusion asserting that *all* of the target group had birth defects would normally go beyond what the evidence in the premise would support. There could easily be at least some blue herons in the preserve (assuming it to be large enough) that don't have birth defects, even if most do.

So you can see that an enumerative inductive argument can fail to be strong in the two following major ways. Its sample can be (1) too small or (2) not representative. Of course, it's possible for an enumerative induction to be perfectly strong but to have false premises, in which case the argument isn't cogent. That is, the data (or evidence) stated in the premises could have been misinterpreted, fabricated, or misstated.

Sample Size

Let's say that you decide to conduct a survey of university students to determine their attitude toward federal-government deficits. So you stand around in the student centre and query the first five students that pass by. Four out of the five say that deficits don't matter. You conclude that 80 per cent (four-fifths) of the student body believe that deficits don't matter. Should you send your findings to the school newspaper—or maybe even to the CBC?

Food For Thought

Do You Really Need to Know This?
Here's a little reminder that many inductive generalizations you come across are just not worth knowing, whether they're well founded or not. Consider the following, compliments of DumbFacts.com:

- In the course of a lifetime the average person will grow two metres of nose hair.
- The starfish is the only animal that can turn its stomach inside out.
- More people use blue toothbrushes than red ones.
- The average adult male shaves off one pound of beard per year.
- Men get hiccups more often than women do.
- Banging your head against a wall uses 150 calories an hour.
- According to the World Health Organization, there are approximately 100 million acts of sexual intercourse each day.

No way. This survey is a joke—the sample is much too small to yield any reliable information about the attitudes of the students as a whole. That verdict may seem obvious, but just about everyone at one time or another probably makes this kind of mistake, which is known as **hasty generalization**. We're guilty of hasty generalization whenever we draw a conclusion about a target group on the basis of a too small sample. People regularly make this mistake when dealing with all sorts of enumerative inductive evidence—political polls, consumer opinion surveys, scientific studies (especially medical research), quality-control checks, anecdotal reports, and many others.

In our everyday experience, we may casually make, hear, or read hasty generalizations like this:

> You should buy a Dell computer. They're great. I bought one last year, and it has given me nothing but flawless performance.

> The only male professor I've had this year was a chauvinist pig. All the male professors at this school must be chauvinist pigs.

> Psychology majors are incredibly ignorant about human psychology. Believe me, I know what I'm talking about. My best friend is a psych major. What an ignoramus!

> The French are snobby and rude. Remember those two arrogant guys with really bad manners? They're French. I rest my case.

> The food at Pappie's Restaurant is awful. I had a sandwich there once, and the bread was stale.

In general, the larger the sample, the more likely it is to reliably reflect the nature of the larger group. In many cases our common sense tells us when a sample is or is not large enough to draw reliable conclusions about a particular target group. A good rule of thumb is this: *The more homogeneous a target group is in traits relevant to the property in question, the smaller the sample can be; the less homogeneous, the larger the sample should be.*

For example, if we want to determine whether cottontail rabbits have teeth, we need to survey only a tiny handful of cottontail rabbits (maybe even just one) because cottontail rabbits are fairly uniform in their physical characteristics. In this sense, if you've seen one cottontail rabbit, you've seen them all. On the other hand, if we want to know the sexual preferences of Asian Canadians who live in suburbs, surveying just a few won't do. Questioning a sample of two or 20 or even 200 suburban Asian Canadians will not give us a reliable read on the sexual preferences of the target group. In social, psychological, and cultural properties, people are too diverse to judge a large target group by just a few of its members. In biological properties, however, *homo sapiens* is relatively uniform. We need to survey only one normal member of the species to find out if humans have ears.

Representativeness

In addition to being the proper size, a sample must be a **representative sample**—it must resemble the target group in all the ways that matter. If it does not properly represent the target group, it's a **biased sample**. An enumerative inductive argument is strong only if the sample is representative of the whole.

Many arguments using unrepresentative samples are ludicrous; others are more subtle.

> University students are glad that the Conservative Party is in power in Ottawa. Surveys of the members of the Campus Conservatives club on several university campuses prove this.

> Most nurses in this hospital are burned out, stressed out, and overworked. Just ask the ones who work in the emergency department. They'll tell you they're absolutely miserable.

> No one is happy. Almost everyone is complaining about something. Just look at the letters to the editor in any big city newspaper. Complaints, complaints, complaints.

To be truly representative, the sample must be like the target group by (1) having all the same relevant characteristics and (2) having them in the same proportions that the target group does. The 'relevant characteristics' are features that could influence the property in question. For example, let's say that you want to survey adult residents of Big City to determine whether they favour distributing condoms in high schools. Features of the residents that could influence whether they favour condom distribution include political party affiliation, ethnic background, and being Catholic. So the sample of residents should have all of these features and have them in the same proportions as the target group (residents of Big City). If half the adult residents of Big City are Catholic, for example, then half the sample should consist of residents who are Catholic.

Say that we want to determine how the 10,000 eligible voters in a small town intend to vote in an upcoming federal election. We survey 1,000 of them, which should be more than enough for our purposes. But the voters we poll are almost all over 70 years old and live in nursing homes. Our sample is biased because it does not reflect the makeup of the target group, most of whom are people under 45 who live in their own homes, work in factories or offices, and have school-age children. Any enumerative argument based on this survey would be weak.

We are often guilty of biased sampling in everyday situations. One way this happens is through a phenomenon called *selective attention* (see Chapters 2 and 4), that is, the tendency to observe and remember things that reinforce our beliefs and to gloss over and dismiss things that undercut those beliefs. We may tell our friends that *The Sopranos* is a lousy TV series because we remember that three episodes were boring—but we conveniently forget the four other episodes that we thought were superb. Or we may be convinced that Dr Jones is one of

'Public opinion polls are rather like children in a garden, digging things up all the time to see how they're growing.'
—J.B. Priestley

the legendary 'absent-minded professors'. But this generalization seems plausible to us only because we're on the lookout for instances in which the professor's behaviour seems to fit the stereotype, and we don't notice instances that contradict the stereotype.

Food For Thought

How Survey Questions Go Wrong

Many opinion polls are untrustworthy because of flaws in the way the questions are asked. The sample may be large enough and representative in all the right ways, but the poll is still dubious. Here are a few of the most common problems.

Phrasing of Questions

Poll results can be dramatically skewed simply by the way the questions are worded. A poll might ask, for example, 'Are you in favour of Quebec tearing Canada in half by separating?' The question is apparently about Quebec's sovereignty. But the wording of the question practically guarantees that a very large percentage of respondents will answer 'no'. The politically and emotionally charged characterization of separation as 'tearing Canada in half' would likely persuade many respondents to avoid answering 'yes'. More neutral wording of the question would probably elicit a very different set of responses.

Here's another example. Imagine a poll of people in your town that discovers that 95 per cent of the sample group approved of efforts by the municipal government to eliminate smoking in public places. Next, imagine that to get this huge approval rating, the survey question was worded like this: 'Do you think that the government should work diligently to protect children, including by taking certain measures that would put some restrictions on when and where people can smoke?' Who would say 'no' to protecting children? We shouldn't be surprised if such a question elicited an overwhelming number of 'shoulds'.

Such biased wording is often the result of sloppiness on the part of pollsters. Many other times it's a deliberate attempt to manipulate the poll results. The crucial test of polling questions is whether they're likely to bias responses in one direction or another. Fair questions aren't skewed this way—or are skewed as little as possible.

Order of Questions

The order in which questions are asked in a poll can also affect the poll results. Pollsters know that if the economy is in bad shape and they ask people about the economic mess first and then ask them how they like the prime minister, the respondents are likely to give the prime minister lower marks than if the order of the questions were reversed. Likewise, if you're asked specific questions about crimes that have been committed in your hometown, then you're asked if you feel safe from crime, you're more likely to say no than if you're asked the questions in reverse order.

Restricted Choices

Opinion polls frequently condense broad spectrums of opinions on issues into a few conve-nient choices. Some of this condensation is necessary to make the polling process manage-able. But some of it is both unnecessary and manipulative and therefore seriously distorts the opinions of those polled. Daniel Goleman of the *New York Times* offers this example: 'In one survey . . . people were asked if they felt "the courts deal too harshly or not harshly enough with criminals". When offered just the two options, 6 per cent said "too harshly" and 78 per cent answered "not harshly enough". But when a third alternative was added—"don't have enough information about the courts to say"—29 per cent took that option, and 60 per cent answered "not harshly enough".'

Opinion Polls

Enumerative inductions reach a high level of sophistication in the form of opinion polls conducted by professional polling organizations. Opinion polls are used to arrive at generalizations about everything from the outcome of federal elections to public sentiments about cloning babies to the consumer's appetite for tacos. But as complex as they are, opinion polls are still essentially inductive arguments (or the basis of inductive arguments) and must be judged accordingly.

So as inductive arguments, opinion polls should (1) be strong and (2) have true premises. More precisely, any opinion poll worth believing must (1) use a sample that is large enough to represent the target population accurately in all the relevant population features and (2) generate accurate data (that is, the results must correctly reflect what they purport to be about). A poll can fail to meet this latter requirement through data-processing errors, botched polling interviews, poorly phrased questions, and the like. (See the box 'How Survey Questions Go Wrong.')

In national polling, samples need not be enormous to be accurate reflections of the larger target population. Modern sampling procedures used in national polls can produce representative samples that are surprisingly small. Polling organizations such as Environics and Ipsos-Reid regularly conduct polls in which the target group is Canadian adults (more than 25 million), and the representative sample consists of only one thousand to fifteen hundred individuals.

"I don't have any political opinions - would you like to hear about my symptoms?"

www.CartoonStock.com

How can a sample of 1,000 be representative of more than 25 million people? By using **random sampling**. To ensure that a sample is truly representative of the target group, the sample must be selected *randomly* from the target group. In a simple random selection, every member of the target group has an equal chance of being selected for the sample. Imagine that you want to select a representative sample from, say, 1,000 people at a football game, and you know very little about the characteristics of this target population. Your best bet for getting a representative sample of this group is to choose the sample members at random. Any non-random selection based on preconceived notions about what characteristics are representative will likely result in a biased sample.

Selecting a sample in truly random fashion is easier said than done (humans have a difficult time selecting anything in a genuinely random way). Even a simple process such as trying to pick names arbitrarily off a list of registered voters is not likely to be truly random. Your choices may be skewed, for example, by unconscious

Food For Thought

Mean, Median, and Mode

If you read enough opinion polls, you will surely encounter one of these terms: mean, median, or mode. These concepts are invaluable in expressing statistical facts, but they can be confusing. Mean is simply an average. The mean of these four numbers—6, 7, 4, and 3—is 5 (6 + 7 + 4 + 3 = 20 divided by 4 = 5). The median is the middle point of a series of values, meaning that half the values are above the point, and half the values are below the point. The median of these eleven values—3, 5, 7, 13, 14, 17, 21, 23, 24, 27, 30—is 17 (the number in the middle). The mode is the most common value. The mode in this series of values—7, 13, 13, 13, 14, 17, 21, 21, 27, 30, 30—is 13 (the most frequently appearing value).

The notions of mean, median, and mode are often manipulated to mislead people. For example, let's say that the dictator of Little Island Nation (population 1,000) proposes a big tax cut for everyone, declaring that the mean tax savings will be $5,000 (the total tax cut divided by 1,000 taxpayers). The Islanders begin to gleefully envision how they will spend their $5,000. But then they learn that the mean figure has been skewed higher because of a few millionaires whose tax savings will be $100,000 or more. The tax savings for the vast majority of taxpayers is actually less than $500. The $5,000 figure that the dictator tossed out is the true mean, but it is painfully misleading. To the Islanders, what is much more revealing is the median tax savings, which is is $400. The mode, the most common figure, is $300. When they get all the facts, the Islanders stage a revolt—the first one in history caused by a better understanding of statistics.

preferences for certain names or by boredom and fatigue. Researchers and pollsters use various techniques to help them get close to true randomization. They may, for instance, assign a number to each member of a population then use a random-number generator to make the selections.

   One approach that definitely does *not* yield a random sample is allowing survey subjects to choose themselves. The result of this process is called a *self-selecting sample*—a type of sample that usually tells you very little about the target population. We would get a self-selecting sample if we published a questionnaire in a magazine and asked readers to fill it out and mail it in or if during a TV or radio news broadcast, we asked people to cast their vote on a particular issue by clicking options on a website or emailing their responses. In such cases, the sample is likely to be biased in favour of subjects who, for example, just happen to be especially opinionated or passionate; who may have strong views about the topic of the survey and are eager to spout off; or who may simply like to fill out questionnaires. Magazines, newspapers, talk shows, and news programs sometimes acknowledge the use of self-selecting samples by labelling the survey in question as 'unscientific'. But whether or not that term is used, the media frequently tout the results of such distorted surveys as though the numbers actually proved something.

   So a well-conducted poll using a random sample of 1,000–1,500 people can reliably reflect the opinions of the whole adult population. Even so, if a second well-conducted poll is done in exactly the same way, the results will not be identical to that of the first poll. The reason is that every instance of sampling is only an approximation of the results that you would get if you polled every single individual in a target group. And, by chance, each attempt at sampling will yield slightly different results. If you dipped a bucket into a pond to get a one gallon sample of water, each bucketful would be slightly different in its biological and chemical content—even if the pond's content was very uniform.

   Such differences are referred to as the **margin of error** for a particular sampling or poll. Competently executed opinion polls will state their results along with a margin of error. A poll, for example, might say that Candidate X will receive 62 per cent of the popular vote, plus or minus 3 percentage points (a common margin of error for polls). The usual way of expressing this number is 62 per cent ±3. This means that the percentage of people in the target population who will likely vote for Candidate X is between 59 and 65 per cent.

   Connected to the concept of margin of error is the notion of **confidence level**. In statistical theory, the confidence level is the probability that the sample will accurately represent the target group within the margin of error. A confidence level of 95 per cent (the usual value) means that there is a 95 per cent chance that the results from polling the sample (taking into account the margin of error) will accurately reflect the results that we would get if we polled the entire target population. So if our aforementioned poll has a 95 per cent confidence level, we know that there's a

'It is the mark of a truly intelligent person to be moved by statistics.'
–George Bernard Shaw

Food For Thought

Polling the Clueless

Sometimes polls end up surveying, not the views of people with genuine opinions, but what has been called 'non-attitudes'. This happens when respondents answer polling questions even though they have no real opinion on the subject or no idea what the questions are really about. Presumably, people—being people—would rather give a bogus answer than admit that they are clueless.

In one landmark poll conducted in the US many years ago, respondents were asked, 'Some people say that the 1975 Public Affairs Act should be repealed. Do you agree or disagree with this idea?' One-third of those polled offered their opinion on the issue. Trouble was, the Public Affairs Act did not exist. The pollsters made it up.

95 per cent chance that the sampling results of 62 per cent ±3 points will accurately reflect the situation in the whole target group. Of course, this confidence level also means that there's a 5 per cent chance that the poll results will *not* be accurate.

Note that 'confidence level' refers only to sampling error, that is, the probability that the sample does not accurately reflecting the true values in the target population. It doesn't tell you anything about any other kinds of polling errors, such as bias, that can occur because of poorly worded questions or researchers who may consciously or unconsciously influence the kind of answers received.

Sample size, margin of error, and confidence level are all related in interesting ways.

Thank you for taking part in this poll, sir. Here's the first question: What the heck makes you so arrogant to think your opinion could have any kind of importance, sir?

www.CartoonStock.com

- Up to a point, the larger the sample, the smaller the margin of error because the larger the sample, the more representative it is likely to be. Generally, for national polls, a sample size of 600 yields a margin of error of 4 per cent; a sample of 1,000, 3 per cent; and a sample of 1,500, 2.5 per cent. But enlarging the sample substantially, to well beyond 1,000, does not substantially decrease the margin of error. Enlarging the sample from 1,500 to 10,000, for example, pushes the margin of error down to only 1 per cent.

- The lower the confidence level, the smaller the sample size can be. If you're willing to have less confidence in your polling results, a smaller sample will do. If you can accept a confidence level of only 90 per cent (meaning there is a 10 per cent chance of getting inaccurate results), you don't need a sample size of 1,500 to poll the adult population.
- The larger the margin of error, the higher the confidence level can be. With a large margin of error (20 per cent, for example), you will naturally have more confidence that your survey results will fall within this wide range. This idea is the statistical equivalent of a point made earlier: you can have more confidence in your enumerative inductive argument if you qualify, or decrease the precision of, the conclusion.
- Here's a table showing roughly the relationship between sample size and margin of error for large populations (assuming a 95 per cent confidence level):

Survey Sample Size	Margin of Error
10,000	1%
2,000	2%
1,500	2.5%
1,000	3%
500	4.5%
100	10%

Review Notes

Enumerative Induction

- *Target group:* The class of individuals about which an inductive generalization is made.
- *Sample:* The observed members of a target group.
- *Relevant property:* The property under study in a target group.
- *Hasty generalization:* The drawing of a conclusion about a target group on the basis of a sample that's too small.
- *Biased sample:* A sample that is not representative of its target group.
- *Simple random sampling:* The selecting of a sample to ensure that each member of the target group has an equal chance of being chosen.
- *Margin of error:* The variation between the values derived from a sample and the true values of the whole target group.
- *Confidence level:* The probability that the sample will accurately represent the target group within the margin of error.

To sum up: An enumerative induction, like any other inductive argument, must be strong and have true premises for us to be justified in accepting the conclusion. A strong enumerative induction must be based on a sample that is both large enough and representative. An opinion poll, as a sophisticated enumerative induction, must use a sufficiently large and representative sample and ensure that the data gathered reflect accurately what's being measured.

Exercise 8.1

For each of the following enumerative inductions, (1) identify the target group, sample, and relevant property; (2) indicate whether the argument is strong or weak; and (3) if it's weak, say whether the problem is a sample that's too small, not representative, or both. Assume that the information provided in the premises of each argument is true.

* 1. Two-thirds of the adults in Toronto say they are in favour of permitting gay marriage. And almost 70 per cent of Montrealers do, too. This makes it perfectly clear that a large majority of people in this country are in favour of gay marriage.

2. Most people are fed up with celebrities who get on their soapbox and air their political opinions. When people on the street have been asked by TV reporters how they feel about this issue, they almost always say that they wish celebrities would keep their opinions to themselves.

3. Doctors used to think that anti-arrhythmic drugs were the cure for irregular heartbeats. They over-prescribed these drugs and 50,000 patients died. Doctors used to believe that the cure for ulcers was a bland diet, but that turned out to be wrong too. Every new treatment we see these days sounds great. But history tells us that they will all turn out to be worthless.

* 4. I've asked at least a dozen first-year students at this university whether Canada should offer support to the American war effort in Iraq, and they all have said no. So most of the students at this university are against such support.

5. A random, nationwide poll of several thousand dog owners shows that 80 per cent of them are against banning vicious breeds of dogs. Thus, most adults oppose laws designed to outlaw specific breeds of dogs.

6. In every winter for the past 20 years Montreal has received several feet of snow. Therefore, Montreal is likely to get several feet of snow in the next 50 winters.

7. Most newspaper reports of deaths involve either homicide or car crashes. Therefore, homicide and car crashes must be the leading causes of death.

* 8. Eighty-five per cent of dentists who suggest that their patients chew gum recommend Brand X gum. Therefore, 85 per cent of dentists recommend Brand X gum.

9. Two hundred samples of water taken from many sites all along Lake Ontario show unsafe concentrations of toxic chemicals. Obviously the water in Lake Ontario is unsafe.

10. Clearly there is an epidemic of child abductions in this country. In the past year, major network news organizations have reported five cases of children who were abducted by strangers.

11. University fraternities are magnets for all sorts of illegal activity. Last year several frat brothers were arrested at a frat-house party. And this year a fraternity was actually kicked off campus for violating under-age drinking laws.

* 12. Most Canadians are happy with their jobs and derive a great deal of satisfaction from them. A survey of 1,500 adults with an annual income of $48,000 to $60,000, employed in various occupations, supports this assertion. When these subjects were asked if they were happy and satisfied with their jobs, 82 per cent said yes.

Exercise 8.2

For each of the enumerative inductions in Exercise 8.1, indicate whether the argument is strong or weak. If it's strong, explain how the sample could be modified to make the argument weak. If it's weak, explain how the sample could be modified to make the argument strong. Keep the modifications as realistic as possible. Answers are supplied for 1, 4, 8, and 12.

Exercise 8.3

For each of the following opinion polls, (1) determine whether the poll results offer strong support for the pollster's conclusion, and if they don't, (2) specify the source of the problem (sample too small, unrepresentative sample, or non-random sampling). Assume that the conducting of each survey is free of technical errors, such as mistakes in data processing or improper polling interviews.

* 1. The website of the *Toronto Star* invites visitors to 'speak out' by participating in 'Today's Poll'. One day, the question is: 'Should Canada hold talks with Hezbollah, as one Liberal MP has suggested?' That day, 3,241 people visit the website and give their answers. Of those, 2,206 answer 'no'. I therefore conclude that 68 per cent of Torontonians oppose the idea of Canada holding talks with Hezbollah.

2. Anita conducts a survey to determine if Canadians are willing to support the arts by contributing money directly to local theatre groups. One night she and her assistants interview 500 people who are attending a performance of a musical at the city's biggest theatre. To help ensure random selection, they

purposely select every other patron they encounter for interviewing. There is only one interview question: 'Are you willing to support the arts by giving money to local theatre groups?' Ninety-four per cent of the interviewees answer yes. Anita later reports that a large majority of Canadians are willing to support the arts by giving money to local theatre groups.

3. A prominent sociologist wants to determine the sexual attitudes of women aged 25 to 45. The main question to be asked is whether heterosexual women in this age group feel satisfied with their partners' sexual performance. The sociologist interviews 200 of her Facebook friends who belong to the target group. She also asks 200 of her female colleagues at her university to complete and return a survey asking the key question. She gets 78 completed surveys back from women in the target group. She finds that 75 per cent of all the interviewees say that they are not satisfied with their partners' performance. She concludes that most heterosexual women aged 25 to 45 aren't happy with the sexual performance of their partners.

4. A national polling organization surveys 1,500 obstetrician-gynecologists chosen randomly from a national registry of this medical specialty. The survey question is whether obstetrician-gynecologists provide quality care for pregnant women. Ninety-eight per cent of those surveyed say yes. The pollsters conclude that almost all physicians think that obstetrician-gynecologists provide quality care for pregnant women.

5. A national women's magazine publishes a questionnaire on sexual harassment in the workplace. Respondents are asked to complete the questionnaire and mail it in to the magazine. The magazine receives over 20,000 completed questionnaires in the mail. Sixty-two per cent of the respondents say that they've been sexually harassed at work. The magazine reports that most women have been sexually harassed at work.

Exercise 8.4

For each of the following arguments, say which conclusions from the accompanying list would be strongly supported by the premise given. Assume that all statements are true.

* 1. Seventy-two per cent of the 300 university students who responded to a questionnaire published in the campus newspaper are opposed to the federal government's economic policies.
    a. Some readers of the campus newspaper are opposed to the federal government's economic policies.
    b. Seventy-two per cent of the students attending this school are opposed to the federal government's economic policies.
    c. Some students attending this school are opposed to the federal government's economic policies.

d. Most readers of the campus newspaper are opposed to the federal government's economic policies.

e. Seventy-two per cent of the readers of the campus newspaper are opposed to the federal government's economic policies.

2. By listening to music, 43 per cent of arthritis patients at the Drexell Clinic experience a decrease in pain in their knee and finger joints.

a. By listening to music, 43 per cent of arthritis patients can experience a decrease in pain in their knee and finger joints.

b. By listening to music, some arthritis patients can experience a decrease in pain in their knee and finger joints.

c. By listening to music, some arthritis patients at the Drexell Clinic can experience a decrease in pain in their knee and finger joints.

d. By listening to music, many arthritis patients can experience a decrease in pain in their knee and finger joints.

3. Four out of five of the university's English majors hate anything written by William Faulkner.

a. Eighty per cent of the university's English majors hate anything written by William Faulkner.

b. Most students at this university hate anything written by William Faulkner.

c. Most university students hate anything written by William Faulkner.

d. English majors at this university hate anything written by William Faulkner.

4. Alonzo has been driving his Ford Fiesta for seven years without any problems. His friend has the same kind of car and has been driving it for five years trouble-free.

a. Ford Fiestas are trouble-free cars.

b. Most Ford Fiestas are trouble-free cars.

c. Some Ford Fiestas are trouble-free cars.

d. Many Ford Fiestas are trouble-free cars.

5. Seventy-seven per cent of adults interviewed in three Edmonton shopping malls (650 people) say they will vote Conservative in the next federal election.

a. Most people will vote Conservative in the next federal election.

b. Seventy-seven per cent of adult residents of Edmonton will vote Conservative in the next federal election.

c. Many people in Edmonton will vote Conservative in the next federal election.

d. A substantial percentage of people who shop at malls in Edmonton will vote Conservative in the next federal election.

Exercise 8.5

The following statements suggest modifications to each of the opinion polls in Exercise 8.3. In each case, determine whether the modification (and any associated change in poll results) would make the pollster's conclusion more likely to be true or not more likely to be true.

* 1. Six thousand people visit the website on the day that the poll is taken (instead of 3,241), and of those, 4,000 answer 'no' to the question (instead of 2,206).

  2. Anita supplements her research by conducting phone interviews of a random sample of 800 adult residents of her city (population one million), asking a slightly modified question: 'Are you willing to support the arts by giving money to local theatre groups?' She conducts a similar poll in another large city. In both polls, at least 60 per cent of respondents say yes.

  3. The sociologist interviews 300 of her Facebook friends (instead of 200) who belong to the target group, and she asks 400 (instead of 200) of her female colleagues at her university to complete and return a survey asking the key question. Again, 75 per cent of respondents say that they are not satisfied with their partners' performance.

  4. The national polling organization surveys 1,500 physicians of various specialties chosen randomly from a national registry. Ninety-five per cent of the respondents say that obstetrician-gynecologists provide quality care for pregnant women.

  5. The magazine receives over 30,000 completed questionnaires in the mail (instead of 20,000). Fifty-five per cent of the respondents say that they've been sexually harassed at work.

Statistical Syllogisms

Very often we have incomplete, but reasonably reliable, information about a group or category of things, and on the basis of that knowledge we can reach conclusions about particular members of that group or category. Will it be cold in Winnipeg on 12 January of next year? We don't know for sure, but we know that *most* January days in Winnipeg are cold, so we can reason inductively to a pretty firm conclusion. Will my flight from Halifax to Vancouver get there safely? Well, *virtually all* commercial air flights in Canada—hundreds every day—land perfectly safely. So we can assert pretty confidently that, yes, your flight will get to Vancouver just fine. Is that conclusion a *deductive certainty*? No, but it's still very, very reliable.

In Chapter 7 we dealt with categorical syllogisms, which were deductive arguments consisting of three elements: two categorical premises and a categorical conclusion. But there are also *statistical syllogisms*, which are *inductive* arguments that apply a statistical generalization—a claim about what is true of *most* members of a group or category—to a specific member of that group or category. Here are a few examples:

Argument 1
Premise 1: Over 80 per cent of Canadians live in cities.
Premise 2: You're a Canadian.
Conclusion: So you live in a city.

Argument 2
Premise 1: Most pro basketball players are well over six feet tall.
Premise 2: Paul plays for the Raptors.
Conclusion: Paul is over six feet tall.

Argument 3
Premise 1: Almost all countries in Africa are very poor.
Premise 2: Zimbabwe is in Africa
Conclusion: Thus, Zimbabwe is very poor!

Here is the pattern that all statistical syllogisms follow, when spelled out fully:

Premise 1: A proportion X of the group M have characteristic P.
Premise 2: Individual S is member of group M.
Conclusion: Individual S has characteristic P.

It is important, in analyzing a statistical syllogism, to be able to identify:

- The *individual* being examined.
- The *group* to which that individual is said to belong.
- The *characteristic* being attributed.
- The *proportion* of the group said to have that characteristic.

Sometimes, the proportion will take the form of an actual statistic. That's where the term *statistical* syllogism comes from. It might be stated as a percentage (as in argument 1, above) or it could also be a fraction (such as 9/10). Sometimes specific numbers aren't available and an arguer will use a word like 'most' or 'almost all' or 'most of the time'. The point is that the first premise is a *generalization*—a statement (usually rooted in some evidence) about the members of a group or class. (In fact, very often the first premise of a statistical syllogism will be arrived at by—that is, it will be the *conclusion* of—an argument using enumerative induction. We'll return to this point shortly.)

Because they are a type of inductive argument, statistical syllogisms—even good ones, with acceptable premises—cannot guarantee their conclusions. So, sometimes they can lead us astray. For example, imagine you're in southern Ontario, and a friend points out a scary-looking spider in a woodpile. 'It's okay,' you say. 'Spiders in Canada are generally harmless. So I'm sure it can't hurt you.' That's a statistical syllogism. But is the conclusion true?

Here's that same argument, with its premises and conclusion spelled out:

Premise 1: In general, the spiders that live in Canada are harmless.
Premise 2 (unstated): That spider there is in Canada.
Conclusion: That spider is harmless.

If the spider in question is a black widow spider (a spider whose natural habitat includes parts of southern Ontario), your conclusion would be false—reasonable, but false!

Evaluating Statistical Syllogisms

Since statistical syllogisms, though very useful, are never airtight, we need a method for evaluating them.

Acceptable Premises

The first thing to consider, of course, is whether we have good reason to believe the premises. How is it that the generalization expressed in the first premise was arrived at? Is it common knowledge (such as 'Most birds can fly' or 'Most water on earth is salt water')? Is it based on a careful survey, one with a large enough, randomly selected sample? Here we can apply all the tools learned in the previous section on enumerative induction. If the grounding of the generalization is weak, then the argument is weak.

Statistical Strength

Second, and perhaps most obviously, we should ask ourselves: just how strong is the generalization being offered? Clearly if our argument (about some member of the class M) is based on claim that, say, '65 per cent of M are P', that's not nearly as strong as if that same argument were based on claim that '99 per cent of M are P.' We should clearly ask questions, then, when vague words such as 'most' or 'lots of' are used in statistical syllogisms. 'Most' might just mean '51 per cent of.' And that's a pretty weak basis for a conclusion about any particular member of that group.

Typical or Randomly Selected

Statistical syllogisms take a generalization about a group or class and apply that generalization to a specific, individual member of that group or class. This will make most sense for members that we have reason to believe are typical of that group or class. It is most reasonable to assume that the individual is typical when he, she, or it is selected randomly from the population. If you know, for example, that '85 per cent of Canadians don't know CPR', then it's reasonable to suspect, of any randomly selected Canadian, that he or she doesn't know CPR. But if you're talking to someone wearing a white coat at a hospital or working at a fire station, it's much less reasonable to assume that *that* person is part of the 85 per cent of Canadians who don't know CPR. That person, in fact, is highly likely to be part of the other 15 per cent. Or how about this: if I ask you, 'How much do you think this stamp is worth?', you might well respond, 'Well, most stamps are worth the value printed on them, and that one says '42 cents,' so it's worth 42 cents!' In most circumstances, that might be a strong argument. But what if you have reason to believe that this particular stamp isn't a typical stamp. What if you happen to know that I'm a collector of rare and valuable stamps? In that situation, it's much more likely that the stamp I'm showing you is *not* a random or typical stamp, and so it would be unwise to jump too quickly to the conclusion that it's not worth much. Thus we should always consider whether the individual person or item under consideration is likely to be a typical member of the group, or whether you have reason to believe that he, she, or it is an exception to the rule.

Exercise 8.6

For each of the following statistical syllogisms, identify (1) the individual being examined; (2) the group to which that individual is said to belong; (3) the characteristic being attributed to that group and individual; and (4) the proportion of the group that is said to have that characteristic. You may need to supply missing parts.

* 1.   'Sixty-seven per cent of all geeks play computer games. June is a geek. So, June plays computer games.'

  2.   'Most happily married couples vacation together. Ben and Jessica are happily married. So, they must vacation together.'

  3.   'Gary drives too fast. He drives a Porsche, and almost all Porsche drivers drive too fast.'

* 4.   'Almost every meal I've eaten at the Poolhouse Café has been wonderful. I'm sure the next one will be, too.'

* 5.   'That car of yours will never make it to Saskatoon. Most Fords are pieces of junk!'

Exercise 8.7

Determine the most likely source of weakness for the following statistical syllogisms. (State whether the most likely problem is unacceptable premise, statistical weakness, or non-typical individual. Give a few words of explanation for why you think the argument is weak in that particular way.)

* 1. 'Ninety per cent of women are left-handed. You're a woman. So, you're left-handed.'
* 2. 'Professor Norman grew up in a small mining town. Most people who grow up in small mining towns have never read Plato. So Professor Norman has never read Plato.'
  3. 'I'm sure that if you adopt that abused beagle, it will make a great pet for your kids. Beagles are generally very gentle, lovable dogs.'
* 4. 'Most people in this town who voted—53 per cent of voters—voted for Mayor Doran. You voted. So you supported Mayor Doran.'
  5. 'I've met plenty of lawyers, and they're all crooks. You're a lawyer, eh? Well, then you must be a crook!'

Analogical Induction

An **analogy** is a comparison of two or more things alike in specific respects. In literature, science, and everyday life, analogies are used to explain or describe something. Analogies (often in the form of similes) can be powerful literary devices, both unforgettable and moving:

> . . . the evening is spread out against the sky
> Like a patient etherized upon a table . . .
>> (T. S. Eliot)

> As cold waters to a thirsty soul,
> so is good news from a far country.
>> (Proverbs 25:25)

> . . . Out, out brief candle!
> Life's but a walking shadow, a poor player
> That struts and frets his hour upon the stage
> And then is heard no more. It is a tale
> Told by an idiot, full of sound and fury,
> Signifying nothing.
>> (*Macbeth*, Act V]

But an analogy can also be used to *argue inductively for a conclusion*. Such an argument is known as an **analogical induction**, or simply an **argument by analogy**. An analogical induction reasons this way: because two or more things are similar in several respects, they must be similar in some further respect. For example:

> Humans can move about, solve mathematical equations, win chess games, and feel pain.
> Robots are like humans in that they can move about, solve mathematical equations, and win chess games.
> Therefore, it's probable that robots can also feel pain.

This argument says that because robots are like humans in several ways (ways that are already known or agreed on), they must be like humans in yet another way (a way that the argument is meant to establish).

So analogical induction has this pattern:

> Thing A has properties P_1, P_2, and P_3 plus the property P_4.
> Thing B has properties P_1, P_2, and P_3.
> Therefore, thing B probably has property P_4.

Argument by analogy, like all inductive reasoning, can establish conclusions only with a degree of probability. The greater the degree of similarity between the two things being compared, the more probable the conclusion is.

Recall that enumerative inductive has this form:

> X per cent of the observed members of group A have property P.
> Therefore, X per cent of all members of group A probably have property P.

Thus, the most blatant difference between these two forms of induction is that enumerative induction argues from some members of a group to the group as a whole, but analogical induction reasons from some (one or more) individuals to one further individual. Looked at another way, enumerative induction argues from the properties of a sample to the properties of the whole group; analogical induction reasons from the properties of one or more individuals to the properties of another individual.

Arguments by analogy are probably used (and misused) in every area of human endeavour—but especially in law, science, medicine, ethics, archaeology, and forensics. Here are a few examples.

Argument 4: Medical Science

Mice are mammals, have a mammalian circulatory system, have typical mammalian biochemical reactions, respond readily to high-blood-pressure drugs, and experience a reduction in blood cholesterol when given the new Drug Z. Humans are mammals, have a mammalian circulatory system, have typical mammalian biochemical reactions, and respond readily to high-blood-pressure drugs. Therefore, humans will also experience a reduction in blood cholesterol when given the new Drug Z.

Argument 5: Religion

A watch is a mechanism of exquisite complexity with numerous parts precisely arranged and accurately adjusted to achieve a purpose—a purpose imposed by the watch's designer. Likewise the universe has exquisite complexity with countless parts—from atoms to asteroids—that fit together precisely and accurately to produce certain effects as though arranged by plan. Therefore, the universe must also have a designer.

Argument 6: Law

The case before the court involves a search by the city police of a homeless man's cardboard shelter. At issue is whether it was improper for the police to enter the man's shelter without either permission or a warrant in order to search for evidence of a crime. A similar case—a relevant precedent—involved a search by the RCMP of an equipment trailer in which a man was living. In that case, the court ruled that the RCMP had violated section 8 of the Canadian Charter of Rights and Freedoms (the section that says, 'Everyone has the right to be secure against unreasonable search or seizure.') Therefore, the court should also rule that the search by the city police of the homeless man's shelter violated section 8 of the Charter.

Argument 7: Forensics

Whenever we have observed this pattern in the spatter of blood, we have subsequently learned that the gunshot victim was about four feet from the gun when it was fired and was facing away from the assailant. In this crime scene, we have exactly the same pattern of blood spatter. Therefore, the victim was about four feet from the gun when it was fired and was facing away from the assailant.

Arguments by analogy are easy to formulate—perhaps too easy. To use an analogy to support a particular conclusion, all you have to do is find two things with some similarities and then reason that the two things are similar in yet another way. You could easily reach some very silly conclusions. You could argue this, for instance: Birds have two legs, two eyes, breathe air, and fly; and humans have two legs, two eyes, and breathe air; therefore, humans can also fly. So the question is, how do we sort out the good analogical inductions from the bad (or really wacky)? How do we judge which ones have conclusions worth accepting and which ones don't?

Fortunately, there are some criteria we can use to judge the strength of arguments by analogy:

1. Relevant similarities
2. Relevant dissimilarities
3. The number of instances compared
4. Diversity among cases

If you find yourself thinking that they make perfect sense, that's probably because you already use these criteria in your own arguments by analogy.

Food For Thought

Analogical Induction in Moral Reasoning

In Chapter 11 you will study in detail the uses of argument and critical thinking in moral reasoning. For now, it's sufficient to know this: When we try to show that a particular action is right or wrong, we often rely on argument by analogy. We argue that since an action is relevantly similar to another action, and the former action is clearly right (or wrong), then we should regard the latter action in the same way. For example, we might propose an argument like this:

Premise 1: Caring more for the members of one's own family than outsiders is morally permissible.

Premise 2: Canada's policy of giving more aid to its own citizens than to those of other countries is relevantly similar to caring more for the members of one's own family than outsiders.

Conclusion: Therefore, Canada's policy of giving more aid to its own citizens than those of other countries is probably morally permissible.

Here, as in any argument by analogy, the conclusion can be established only with a degree of probability. And we would evaluate its strength in the same way we would any other analogical argument.

Relevant Similarities

The more relevant similarities there are between the things being compared, the more probable the conclusion. Consider this argument:

> In the Vietnam War, the United States had not articulated a clear rationale for fighting there, and the United States lost. Likewise, in the present war the United States has not articulated a clear rationale for fighting. Therefore, the United States will lose this war too.

There is just one relevant similarity noted here (the lack of rationale). As it stands, this argument is weak; the two wars are only dimly analogous. A single similarity between two wars in different eras is not enough to strongly support the conclusion. But watch what happens if we add more similarities:

> In the Vietnam War, the United States had not articulated a clear rationale for fighting, there was no plan for ending the involvement of US forces (no

exit strategy), US military tactics were inconsistent, and the military's view of enemy strength was unrealistic. The United States lost the Vietnam War. Likewise, in the present war, the United States has not articulated a clear rationale for fighting, there is no exit strategy, US tactics are inconsistent, and the military's view of enemy strength is naive. Therefore, the United States will also lose this war.

With these additional similarities between the Vietnam War and the current conflict, the argument is considerably stronger. (The premises, of course, may be false, rendering the argument not cogent, even if the inference were strong.) Arguments 4–7 (medical science, religion, law, and forensics) can also be strengthened by citing additional relevant similarities between the things compared.

Notice that this first criterion involves *relevant* similarities. The similarities cited in an analogical induction can't strengthen the argument at all if they have nothing to do with the conclusion. A similarity (or dissimilarity) is relevant to an argument by analogy if it has an effect on whether the conclusion is probably true. The argument on war that was just given mentions five different similarities between the Vietnam War and the present war, and each similarity is relevant because it has some bearing on the probability of the conclusion. But what if we added these similarities?

1. In both wars, some combatants have green eyes.
2. In both wars, some soldiers are taller than others.
3. In both wars, ticket sales to movies in the United States increase.

These factors would make no difference to the probability of the conclusion. They're irrelevant and can neither strengthen nor weaken the argument.

Of course, it's not always obvious what counts as a *relevant* similarity. In order to be relevant, a similarity cited as part of an analogical argument clearly has to be connected in some significant way to the conclusion being argued for. There's no plausible connection, for example, between the colour of soldiers' eyes and their success in war. So that factor isn't relevant. In some cases, an explanation may be required to show *why* a particular similarity is actually relevant. In this regard, the burden of proof (as discussed in Chapter 5) is on the person putting forward the argument.

Relevant Dissimilarities

Generally, the more relevant dissimilarities—or disanalogies—there are between the things being compared, the less probable the conclusion. Dissimilarities weaken arguments by analogy. Consider argument 4 (regarding Drug Z). What if we discover that cholesterol-lowering drugs that work in mice almost never work in humans? This one dissimilarity would severely weaken the argument and make the conclusion much less probable.

Pointing out dissimilarities in an analogical induction is a common way to undermine the argument. Sometimes finding one relevant dissimilarity is enough to show that the argument should be rejected. A familiar response to argument 5 (the watch argument) is to point out a crucial dissimilarity between a watch and the universe: The universe may resemble a watch (or mechanism) in some ways, but it also resembles a living thing, which a watch does not.

The Number of Instances Compared

The greater the number of instances, or cases, that show the relevant similarities, the stronger the argument. In the war argument, for example, there is only one instance that has all the relevant similarities: the Vietnam War. But what if there were five additional instances—five different wars that have the relevant similarities to the present war? The argument would be strengthened. The Vietnam War, though it is relevantly similar to the present war, may be an anomaly, a war with a unique set of properties. But citing other cases that are relevantly similar to the present war shows that the relevant set of similarities is no fluke.

Argument 7 (the forensics induction) is an especially strong argument in part because it cites numerous cases. It implies the existence of such instances when it says 'Whenever we have observed this pattern . . .'.

Diversity among Cases

As we've seen, dissimilarities between the things being compared weaken an argument by analogy. Such dissimilarities suggest that the things being compared are not strongly analogous. And we've noted that several cases (instead of just one) that exhibit the similarities can strengthen the argument. In applying this criterion, however, we focus on a very different point: The greater the diversity among the cases that exhibit the relevant similarities, the stronger the argument.

Take a look at the following argument:

(1) In my first year of university, one of my courses was taught by a young philosophy professor who handed out a very clear syllabus, explained his expectations, and demonstrated early on that he was always willing to answer any question, and the course ended up being a very good course.

(2) In my second year of university, one of my courses was taught by a middle-aged sociology professor who handed out a very clear syllabus, explained his expectations, and demonstrated early on that he was always willing to answer any question, and the course ended up being a very good course.

(3) In my third year of university, one of my courses was taught by a very old English professor who handed out a very clear syllabus, explained his expectations, and demonstrated early on that he was always willing to answer any question, and the course ended up being a very good course.

(4) Now I'm in my fourth year, and I've got a middle-aged philosophy professor who has handed out a very clear syllabus, has explained his expectations, and has demonstrated early on that he is willing to answer any question.
(5) Therefore, this new course will be a good course, too.

Here we have several similarities in question, and they exist between the new professor situation (described in premise 4) and three other professors (detailed in premises 1–3). But what makes this argument especially strong is that the cases are diverse despite the handful of similarities—one case involves a young philosophy professor; another, a middle-aged sociology professor; and finally a very old English professor. This state of affairs suggests that the similarities are not accidental or contrived but are strongly linked even in a variety of situations.

As you know, an inductive argument cannot guarantee the truth of the conclusion, and analogical inductions are no exception. But by carefully applying the foregoing criteria, we can increase our chances of arriving at well-supported conclusions (or of identifying those conclusions that are not). This is happily the case—even though there is no magic formula for using the criteria in real-life situations.

Review Notes

Analogical Induction

Analogical Argument Pattern

> Thing A has properties P_1, P_2, and P_3, plus the property P_4.
> Thing B has properties P_1, P_2, and P_3.
> Therefore, thing B probably has property P_4.

Criteria for Judging Arguments by Analogy

1. The number of relevant similarities.
2. The number of relevant dissimilarities.
3. The number of instances compared.
4. The diversity among cases.

Exercise 8.8

Evaluate each of the following passages and indicate whether it contains (a) an argument by analogy, (b) a literary analogy, or (c) an enumerative induction. If the passage contains an argument by analogy, indicate the total number of things (instances) being compared, the relevant similarities mentioned or implied, the conclusion, and whether the argument is strong or weak.

1. Thinking is like a game of chess, in which every piece is related to every other and every move is part of the realization of a hundred possible strategies.

* 2. 'Duct tape is like the force. It has a light side, a dark side, and it holds the universe together.' (Carl Zwanzig)

3. Girls are smarter than boys. Girls in the debating club always argue better than boys. And the mean grade point average of the girls in the glee club is higher than that of the boys in the club.

4. 'Howard Hughes was able to afford the luxury of madness, like a man who not only thinks he is Napoleon but hires an army to prove it.' (Ted Morgan)

5. 'Look around the world: contemplate the whole and every part of it: you will find it to be nothing but one great machine, subdivided into an infinite number of lesser machines, which again admit of subdivisions, to a degree beyond what human senses and faculties can trace and explain. All these various machines, and even their most minute parts, are adjusted to each other with an accuracy, which ravishes into admiration all men, who have ever contemplated them. The curious adapting of means to ends, throughout all nature, resembles exactly, though it much exceeds, the production of human contrivance; of human design, thought, wisdom, and intelligence. Since therefore the effects resemble each other, we are led to infer, by all the rules of analogy, that the causes also resemble; and that the Author of Nature is somewhat similar to the mind of men; though possessed of much larger faculties, proportioned to the grandeur of the work, which he has executed. By this argument *a posteriori*, and by this argument alone, do we prove at once the existence of a Deity, and his similarity to human mind and intelligence.' (David Hume)

* 6. My brother was always good at arithmetic, so he'll be a whiz at algebra.

7. Tolerating a vicious dictator is like tolerating a bully on the block. If you let the bully push you around, sooner or later he will beat you up and take everything you have. If you let a dictator have his way, he will abuse his people and rob them of life and liberty. If you stand up to the bully just once or—better yet—knock him senseless with a stick, he will never bother you again. Likewise, if you refuse to be coerced by a dictator or if you attack him, his reign will be over. Therefore, the best course of action for people oppressed by a dictator is to resist and attack.

* 8. I like hamburger, and I like steak, and I like roast beef. So I will like tripe.

9. 'The brain secretes thought as the stomach secretes gastric juice, the liver bile, and the kidneys urine.' (Karl Vogt)

10. George has loved every Chevrolet he has owned in the past 25 years. So he will probably love the Chevrolet he bought yesterday.

11. How does one know that there exists in the world other minds—that is, others having feelings and other subjective experiences? One can observe that one's own experiences are connected to publicly observable phenomena, that other people exhibit publicly observable phenomena, and therefore other people also must have subjective experiences. For example, one may observe that when one stubs a toe, one feels pain and cries 'ouch'. Then if other people—who are physically similar to oneself—also stub their toes and cry 'ouch', one can conclude that they also experience pain.

* 12. 'Character is the foundation stone upon which one must build to win respect. Just as no worthy building can be erected on a weak foundation, so no lasting reputation worthy of respect can be built on a weak character.' (R.C. Samsel)

Exercise 8.9

Evaluate each of the following arguments by analogy, indicating (1) the things (instances) being compared, (2) the relevant similarities mentioned or implied, (3) whether diversity among multiple cases is a significant factor, (4) the conclusion, and (5) whether the argument is strong or weak.

* 1. Like former Prime Minister Pierre Elliott Trudeau, Liberal leader Michael Ignatieff is both a fearsome intellectual and a charismatic speaker. Also like Trudeau, Ignatieff is a passionate defender of social justice. Ignatieff, too, will likely eventually be one of Canada's great prime ministers.

2. The United Nations failed to intervene in Bosnia to prevent massive human-rights violations and ethnic cleansing. It also failed to act to stop the murders of close to a million innocent people in Rwanda. The UN will not intervene to stop any widespread slaughter of innocents in Nigeria.

3. 'If a single cell, under appropriate conditions, becomes a person in the space of a few years, there can surely be no difficulty in understanding how, under appropriate conditions, a cell may, in the course of untold millions of years, give origin to the human race.' (Herbert Spencer)

4. Several new, modern manufacturing plants in the Toronto area have brought jobs to that area as well as improving the city's tax base, without causing significant amounts of pollution or noise or disrupting traffic. The same can be said for two new plants that have opened up on the outskirts of Montreal, as well

as plants in Edmonton and Calgary. A plant built in Halifax will provide all the same benefits, also without disadvantages.

* 5. A well-established moral principle is that one is morally justified in using deadly force in self-defence when one is threatened with death or great pain from an assailant. A disease such as terminal cancer can also threaten one with death or great pain. So suicide—a use of deadly force—must sometimes be morally justified when it is an act of self-defence against an assailant (terminal disease) that threatens death or great pain.

6. 'If we survey the universe, so far as it falls under our knowledge, it bears a great resemblance to an animal or organized body, and seems actuated with a like principle of life and motion. A continual circulation of matter in it produces no disorder: a continual waste in every part is incessantly repaired: The closest sympathy is perceived throughout the whole system. And each part or member, in performing its proper offices, operates both to its own preservation and to that of the whole. The world, therefore, I infer, is an animal, and the Deity is the soul of the world, activating it and activated by it.' (Philo, in Hume's *Dialogues Concerning Natural Religion*)

7. 'The mass of men serve the State thus, not as men mainly, but as machines, with their bodies. They are the standing army, and the militia, jailers, constables, *posse comitatus*, &c. In most cases there is no free exercise whatever of the judgment or of the moral sense; but they put themselves on a level with wood and earth and stones, and wooden men can perhaps be manufactured that will serve the purpose as well. Such command no more respect than men of straw, or a lump of dirt.' (Henry David Thoreau)

Causal Arguments

Our world is a shifting, multifarious, complicated web of causes and effects—and that's an oversimplification. Incredibly, the normal human response to the apparent causal chaos is to jump in and ask what causes what. What causes breast cancer? What made Malcolm steal the car? What produced that rash on Norah's arm? What brought the universe into existence? Why have the New Democrats never won a federal election? When we answer such questions (or try to), we make a **causal claim**—a statement about the causes of things. And when we try to prove or support a causal claim, we make a **causal argument**—an inductive argument whose conclusion contains a causal claim.

Causal arguments, being inductive, can give us only probable conclusions. If the premises of a strong causal argument are true, then the conclusion is only probably

'I would rather discover a single causal connection than win the throne of Persia.'

—Democritus

true, with the probability varying from merely likely to highly probable. The probabilistic nature of causal arguments, however, is not a failing or weakness. Causal reasoning is simply different from deductive reasoning, and it is our primary method of acquiring knowledge about the workings of the world. The great human enterprise known as science is concerned mainly with causal processes and causal arguments, and few people would consider this work inferior or unreliable because it was not deductively unshakeable. We now have very strong inductive arguments, for example, in favour of the claim that cigarettes cause cancer, that the HIV virus causes AIDS, and that chlorofluorocarbons cause depletion of Earth's ozone layer. Each of those causal conclusions is very reliable and constitutes a firm basis for guiding individual and collective behaviour.

"This is a little embarrassing to admit, but everything that happens happens for no real reason."

Causal arguments can come in several inductive forms, some of which you already know about. For example, we sometimes reason about cause and effect by using enumerative induction:

> One time, when I made the aluminum rod come in contact with the rotating circular-saw blade, sparks flew.
>
> Another time, when I made the aluminum rod come in contact with the rotating circular-saw blade, sparks flew.
>
> Many other times, when I made the aluminum rod come in contact with the rotating circular-saw blade, sparks flew.
>
> Therefore, making the aluminum rod come in contact with the rotating circular-saw blade always causes sparks to fly.

Occasionally, we may argue to a causal conclusion by using analogical induction:

> Ten years ago a massive surge in worldwide oil prices caused a recession.
>
> Five years ago a massive surge in worldwide oil prices caused a recession.
>
> Therefore, the current massive surge in worldwide oil prices will cause a recession.

Most often, though, we use another type of induction in which we reason to a causal conclusion by pinpointing the best explanation for a particular effect. Let's say that after a hail storm you discover that the roof of your car, which you had left

Food For Thought

Semmelweis, Clean Hands, and Childbed Fever

One of the most famous cases of successful causal reasoning in the history of science is the case of nineteenth-century Hungarian physician, Ignaz Semmelweis. Semmelweis worked in the maternity section of the Vienna General Hospital, in Austria. During that time period, childbirth was quite dangerous; in fact, many women died in the process. Semmelweis noticed, however, a pattern. He noticed that women in one of the hospital's two maternity wards were several times more likely to die of a disease now known as 'puerperal fever' (also known as 'childbed fever') than were women in the other. He also noticed that women in the safer ward were cared for by midwives; women in the more dangerous ward were cared for by physicians, who often examined their patients directly after performing autopsies. Could there be a connection?

Ignaz Semmelweis (1818–65)

Could the physicians be transferring something from the cadavers to their pregnant patients? Semmelweis believed so (even though scientists had not yet discovered the role of germs in producing disease). He instituted a policy under which all medical personnel were required to wash their hands with a chlorine solution after performing autopsies. In the months that followed, the death rate among women in the previously more dangerous ward dropped from 10 per cent to about 3 per cent. Semmelweis's careful causal reasoning saved lives.

parked outside in the driveway, has a hundred tiny dents in it. You might reason like this: The dents could have been caused by the mischievous kids next door, by a flock of lunatic woodpeckers, or by the hail storm. After considering these options (and a few others), you decide that the best explanation (or hypothesis) for the dents is the hail storm. So you conclude that the hail storm caused the dents in your car's roof.

This is a very powerful and versatile form of inductive reasoning called **inference to the best explanation**. It's the essence of scientific thinking and a mainstay of our everyday problem solving and knowledge acquisition (whether causal or non-causal). Because of the importance and usefulness of such reasoning, this book devotes three chapters to it in Part 4. So we won't try to cover the same ground here. Instead, we'll concentrate on some other inductive patterns of reasoning that have traditionally been used to assess causal connections.

Testing for Causes

The English philosopher John Stuart Mill (1806–73) noted several ways of evaluating causal arguments and formulated them into what are now known as 'Mill's methods' of inductive inference. Despite their fancy name, however, the methods are basically common sense and are used by just about everyone. They also happen to be the basis of a great deal of scientific testing. Let's look at a few of the more important ones.

Agreement or Difference

A modified version of Mill's *Method of Agreement* says that if two or more occurrences of a phenomenon have only one relevant factor in common, that factor must be the cause.

Imagine that dozens of people stop into Elmo's corner bar after work as they usually do and that ten of them come down with an intestinal illness one hour after leaving the premises. What caused them to become ill? There are a lot of possibilities. Maybe a waiter who had a flu-like illness sneezed into their drinks, or the free tacos had gone bad, or another patron had a viral infection and passed it along via a handshake. But let's say that there is only one relevant factor that's common to all ten people who got sick: They all had a drink from the same bottle of wine. We could then plausibly conclude that something in the wine probably caused the illness.

Public health officials often use the Method of Agreement, especially when they're trying to determine the cause of an unusual illness in a population of several thousand people. They might be puzzled, say, by an unusually large number of cases of rare liver disease in a city. If they discover that all the people affected have the same poison in their bloodstreams—and this is the only common relevant factor—they have reason to believe that the poison is the cause of the liver disease. In such situations, the poison may turn out to have an industrial or agricultural source.

Here's a schematic of an argument based on the Method of Agreement:

Instance 1: Factors a, b, and c are followed by E.
Instance 2: Factors a, c, and d are followed by E.
Instance 3: Factors b and c are followed by E.
Instance 4: Factors c and d are followed by E.
Therefore, factor c is probably the cause of E.

There's only one factor—factor c—that consistently accompanies effect E. The other factors are sometimes present and sometimes not. We conclude then that factor c brings about E.

Mill's (modified) *Method of Difference* says that the relevant factor that is present when a phenomenon occurs and that is absent when the phenomenon does not occur must be the cause. Here we look, not for factors that the instances of the phenomenon have in common, but for factors that are points of difference among the instances.

Suppose that the performance of football players on a CFL team has been consistently excellent except for six players who have recently been playing the worst games of their careers. The only relevant difference between the high- and low-performing players is that the latter have been taking daily doses of Brand X herbal supplements. If the supplement dosing is really the *only* relevant difference, we could plausibly conclude that the supplements are causing the lousy performance. (Finding out if the supplements are indeed the only relevant difference, of course, is easier said than done.)

So arguments based on the Method of Difference have this form:

Instance 1: Factors *a*, *b*, and *c* are followed by *E*.
Instance 2: Factors *a* and *b* are not followed by *E*.
Therefore, factor *c* is probably the cause of *E*.

Both Agreement and Difference

If we combine these two reasoning patterns, we get a modified version of what Mill called the *Joint Method of Agreement and Difference*. Using this joint method is, obviously, just a matter of applying both methods simultaneously—a procedure that generally increases the probability that the conclusion is true. This combined method, then, says that the likely cause is the one isolated when you (1) identify the relevant factors common to occurrences of the phenomenon (the Method of Agreement) and (2) discard any of these that are present even when there are no occurrences (the Method of Difference).

Let's apply this combined method to the mystery illness at Elmo's bar. Say that among the ten patrons who become ill, the common factors are that they all drank from the same bottle of wine and they all had the free tacos. So we reason that the likely cause is either the wine or the tacos. After further investigation, though, we find that other patrons who ate the tacos did not become ill. We conclude that the wine is the culprit.

The schematic for arguments based on the Joint Method of Agreement and Difference is:

Instance 1: Factors *a*, *b*, and *c* are followed by *E*.
Instance 2: Factors *a*, *b*, and *d* are followed by *E*.
Instance 3: Factors *b* and *c* are not followed by *E*.
Instance 4: Factors *b* and *d* are not followed by *E*.
Therefore, factor *a* is probably the cause of *E*.

Factors *a* and *b* are the only relevant factors that are accompanied by *E*. But we can eliminate *b* as a possibility because when it's present, *E* doesn't occur. So *b* can't be the cause of *E*; *a* is most likely the cause.

You can see the Joint Method of Agreement and Difference at work in modern 'controlled trials' used to test the effectiveness of medical treatments. In these experiments, there are two groups of subjects—one known as the experimental group; the other, the control group. The experimental group receives the treatment being tested, usually a new drug. The control group receives a bogus, or inactive, treatment (referred to as a placebo). This setup helps ensure that the two groups are as similar as possible and that they differ in only one respect—the use of the genuine treatment. A controlled trial, then, reveals the relevant factor *common* to the occurrence of the effect, which is the subjects' response to the treatment (Method of Agreement). And it shows the only important difference between the occurrence and nonoccurrence of the effect: the use of the treatment being tested.

Correlation

In many cases, relevant factors aren't merely present or absent during occurrences of the phenomenon—they are closely *correlated* with the occurrences. The cause of an occurrence varies as the occurrence (effect) does. For such situations Mill formulated the *Method of Concomitant Variation*. This method says that when two events are correlated—when one varies in close connection with the other—they are probably causally related.

If you observe that the longer you boil eggs, the harder they get (and no other relevant factors complicate this relationship), you can safely conclude that this correlation between boiling and hardening is a causal connection. You have good evidence that the boiling causes the hardening.

In medical science, such correlations are highly prized because direct evidence of cause and effect is so hard to come by. Correlations are often indirect evidence of one thing causing another. In exploring the link between cigarette smoking and lung cancer, for example, researchers discovered first that people who smoke cigarettes are more likely to get lung cancer than those who don't smoke. But later research also showed that the more cigarettes people smoke, the higher their risk of lung cancer. Medical scientists call such a correlation a *dose-response relationship*. The higher the dose of the element in question (smoking), the higher the response (the more cases of lung cancer). This dose-response relationship between cigarette smoking and lung cancer is, when combined with other data, strong evidence that smoking causes lung cancer.

Food For Thought

Is It Causal Confusion or ESP?

For over two decades, scientist-writer Susan Blackmore (with degrees in psychology, physiology, and parapsychology) has been investigating the psychology of 'psychic', or paranormal, experience. Her central hypothesis has been that people's supposed experience of extrasensory perception, or ESP (telepathy, clairvoyance, and precognition), is the result of errors in causal thinking. Specifically, people tend to mistake coincidence for causal connection. She writes:

> My hypothesis is that psychic experiences are comparable to visual illusions. The experience is real enough, but its origin lies in internal processes, not peculiarities in the observable world. Like visual illusions they arise from cognitive processes that are usually appropriate but under certain circumstances give rise to the wrong answer. In other words, they are a price we pay for using efficient heuristics.

> In the case of vision, illusions arise when, for example, depth is seen in two-dimensional figures and constancy mechanisms give the answer that would be correct for real depth. The equivalent in the case of psychic experiences may be the illusion that a cause is operating and an explanation is required when in fact none is. In other words, psychic experiences are illusions of causality. . . .

> Experiences of telepathy, clairvoyance, and precognition imply a coincidence that is 'too good to be just chance'. This is so whether the experience involves dreaming about a person's death and that person dies within a few hours, feeling the urge to pick up one's partner from the station and in fact he was stranded and needed help, or betting on a horse that later wins a race.

> Some people's response to such events is to say, 'That was just a chance coincidence'; while others' is to say, 'That cannot be chance.' In the latter case the person will then look for a causal explanation for the coincidence. If none can be found, a 'cause', such as ESP, may be invoked. Alternatively, some kind of noncausal but meaningful connection may be sought, such as Jung's 'acausal connecting principle'.

> There are two possible types of error that may be made here. First, people may treat connected events as chance coincidences, thereby missing real connections between events and failing to look for explanations. Second, they may treat chance events as connected and seek for explanations where none is required. In the real world of inadequate information and complex interactions one would expect errors of both types to occur. It is the latter type that, I suggest, gives rise to experiences of ESP. . . .

> One prediction of this approach is that those people who more frequently look for explanations of chance coincidences are more likely to have psychic experiences.

Therefore, sheep [believers in ESP] should be those who underestimate the probability of chance coincidences.

It has long been known that probability judgments can be extremely inaccurate. Kahneman and Tversky (1973) have explored some of the heuristics, such as 'representativeness' and 'availability', that people [are subject to]. [Other researchers (Fall 1982; Falk and MacGregor 1983) found that adding] specific but superfluous detail can make coincidences seem more surprising, and things that happen to subjects themselves seem more surprising to them than the same things happening to other people.…

There is, however, little research relating these misjudgments to belief in the paranormal or to having psychic experiences. Blackmore and Troscianko (1985) found that sheep performed worse than goats [skeptics about ESP] on a variety of probability tasks. For example, in questions testing for responsiveness to sample size, sheep did significantly worse than goats. The well-known birthday question was asked: How many people would you need to have at a party to have a 50:50 chance that two have the same birthday? … As predicted, goats got the answer right significantly more often than sheep.

Subjects also played a coin-tossing computer game and were asked to guess how many hits they would be likely to get by chance. The correct answer, 10 hits in 20 trials, seems to be rather obvious. However, the sheep gave a significantly lower mean estimate of only 7.9, while goats gave a more accurate estimate of 9.6.[1]

We can represent arguments based on the Method of Concomitant Variation like this:

Instance 1: Factors a, b, and c are correlated with E.
Instance 2: Factors a, b, and increased-c are correlated with increased E.
Instance 3: Factors a, b, and decreased-c are correlated with decreased E.
Therefore, factor c is causally connected with E.

A very important cautionary note must accompany this discussion of correlation: Correlation, of course, does not always mean that a causal relationship is present. A correlation could just be a coincidence (see later). An increase in home PC sales is correlated with a rise in the incidence of AIDS in Africa, but this doesn't mean that one is in any way causally linked with the other.

Causal Confusions

Mill's methods and other forms of causal reasoning may be common sense, but they're not foolproof. No inductive procedure can guarantee the truth of the conclusion. More to the point, it's easy to commit errors in cause-and-effect reasoning—regardless of the method used—by failing to take into account pertinent aspects of the situation. This section describes some of the more common causal blunders to which we're all prey.

Misidentifying Relevant Factors

A key issue in any type of causal reasoning is whether the factors preceding an effect are truly relevant to that effect. In the Method of Agreement, for example, it's easy to find a preceding factor common to all occurrences of a phenomenon. But that factor may be irrelevant. In the case of Elmo's bar, what if all those who became ill had black hair? So what? We know that hair colour is very unlikely to be related to intestinal illness. *Relevant* factors include only those things that could possibly be causally connected to the occurrence of the phenomenon being studied. We could reasonably judge that factors relevant to the intestinal illness would include all the conditions that might help transmit bacteria or viruses.

Your ability to identify relevant factors depends mostly on your background knowledge—what you know about the kinds of conditions that could produce the occurrences in which you're interested. Lack of background knowledge might lead you to dismiss or ignore relevant factors or to assume that irrelevant factors must play a role. The only cure for this inadequacy is deeper study of the causal possibilities in question.

Mishandling Multiple Factors

Most of the time, the biggest difficulty in evaluating causal connections is not that there are so few relevant factors to consider—but that there are so many. Too often the Method of Agreement and the Method of Difference are rendered useless because they cannot, by themselves, narrow the possibilities to just one. At the same time, ordinary causal reasoning is often flawed because of the failure to consider *all* the relevant antecedent factors. (Later chapters will refer to this problem as the failure to consider alternative explanations.)

Sometimes this kind of oversight happens because we simply don't look hard enough for possible causes. At other times, we miss relevant factors because we don't know enough about the causal processes involved. This again is a function of skimpy background knowledge. Either way, there is no countermeasure better than your own determination to dig out the whole truth.

Being Misled by Coincidence

Sometimes ordinary events are paired in unusual or interesting ways. You think of Quebec, then suddenly a TV ad announces low-cost fares to Montreal; you receive some email just as your doorbell and the phone both ring or you stand in the lobby of a hotel thinking of an old friend and then see her walk by. Plenty of interesting pairings can also show up in scientific research. Scientists might find, for example, that men with the highest rates of heart disease may also have a higher daily intake

Food For Thought

Coincidence, Birth Dates, and American Presidents

When we're tempted to say that the conjunction of two events 'couldn't be just coincidence', we should think twice. People are often very bad at determining the true likelihood of events. Recall the birth-date problem mentioned in Chapter 4. It's the classic example of misjudged probabilities: In a random selection of 23 people, what is the probability that at least two of them will have the same birth date? The answer: 50 per cent, or fifty-fifty People are usually shocked when they hear the answer. Part of the reason is that they usually underestimate how often oddball coincidences occur and fail to see that such strange conjunctions must occur from time to time. Here's a succinct explanation of the problem from social psychologist David G. Myers:

Photo: Courtesy of the Library of Congress (LC-USZ62-12950)

> We've all marveled at such coincidences in our own lives. Checking out a photocopy counter from the Hope University library desk, I confused the clerk when giving my six-digit department charge number—which just happened at that moment to be identical to the counter's six-digit number on which the last user had finished. Shortly after my daughter, Laura Myers, bought two pairs of shoes, we were astounded to discover that the two brand names on the boxes were 'Laura' and 'Myers'. And then there are those remarkable coincidences that, with added digging, have been embellished into really fun stories, such as the familiar Lincoln-Kennedy coincidences (both with seven letters in their last names, elected 100 years apart, assassinated on a Friday while beside their wives, one in Ford's theater, the other in a Ford Motor Co. car, and so forth). We also have enjoyed newspaper accounts of astonishing happenings, such as when twins Lorraine and Levinia Christmas, driving to deliver Christmas presents to each other near Flitcham, England, collided.

Photo: © Arthur Rothstein/Corbis

My favorite is this little known fact: In Psalm 46 of the King James Bible, published in the year that Shakespeare turned 46, the 46th word is 'shake' and the 46th word from the end is 'spear'. (More remarkable than this coincidence is that someone should have noted this!) ...

'In reality,' says mathematician John Allen Paulos, 'the most astonishingly incredible coincidence imaginable would be the complete absence of all coincidences.' When Evelyn Marie Adams won the New Jersey lottery twice, newspapers reported the odds of her feat as 1 in 17 trillion—the odds that a given person buying a single ticket for two New Jersey lotteries would win both. But statisticians Stephen Samuels and George McCabe report that, given the millions of people who buy US state lottery tickets, it was 'practically a sure thing' that someday, somewhere, someone would hit a state jackpot twice. Consider: An event that happens to but one in a billion people in a day happens 2000 times a year. A day when nothing weird happened would actually be the weirdest day of all.[2]

of water. Or women with the lowest risk of breast cancer may own Toyotas. Such pairings are very probably just coincidence, merely interesting correlations of events. A problem arises, though, when we think that there nevertheless *must be* a causal connection involved.

For several reasons, we may very much want a coincidence to be a cause-and-effect relationship, so we come to believe that the pairing *is* causal. Just as often we may mistake causes for coincidences because we're impressed or excited about the conjunction of events. Since the pairing of events may seem 'too much of a coincidence' to be coincidence, we conclude that one event must have caused the other. You may be thinking about how nice it would be for your sister to call you from her home in the Yukon—then the phone rings, and it's her! You're tempted to conclude that your wishing caused her to call. But such an event, though intriguing and seemingly improbable, is not really so extraordinary. Given the ordinary laws of statistics, incredible coincidences are common and must occur. Any event, even one that seems shockingly improbable, is actually very probable over the long haul. Given enough opportunities to occur, events like this surprising phone call are virtually certain to happen to *someone*.

People are especially prone to think 'it can't be just coincidence' because, for several psychological reasons, they misjudge the probabilities involved. They may think, for example, that a phone call from someone at the moment they're thinking of that person is incredible—but only because they've forgotten about all the times they've thought of that person and the phone *didn't* ring. Such probability misjudgments are a major source of beliefs about the paranormal or supernatural, topics that we address in Chapter 10. (See also the box 'Is It Causal Confusion or ESP?' in this chapter.)

Unfortunately, there is no foolproof way to distinguish coincidence from cause and effect. But this rule of thumb can help:

Don't assume that a causal connection exists unless you have good reason for doing so.

Generally, you have a good reason if the connection passes one or more standard causal tests (such as the ones we've been discussing)—and if you can rule out any relevant factors that might undermine the verdict of those tests. Usually, when a cause-effect connection is uncertain, only further evaluation or research can clear things up.

Confusing Cause with Temporal Order

A particularly common type of misjudgment about coincidences is the logical fallacy known as ***post hoc, ergo propter hoc*** ('after that, therefore because of that'). It is true that a cause must precede its effect. But just because one event precedes another, that doesn't mean that the earlier one *caused* the later. To think so is to be taken in by this fallacy. Outrageous examples of post hoc arguments include 'The rooster crowed, then the sun came up, so the rooster's crowing caused the sunrise!' and 'Jasmine left her umbrella at home on Monday, and that caused it to rain.' You can clearly see the error in such cases, but consider these arguments:

Argument 8
After the training for police officers was enhanced, violent crime in the city decreased by 10 per cent. So enhanced training caused the decline in violent crime.

Argument 9
An hour after Julio drank the cola, his headache went away. The cola cured his headache.

Argument 10
As soon as Smith took office and implemented policies that reflected his conservative theory of economics, the economy went into a downward slide characterized by slow growth and high unemployment. Therefore, the Smith policies caused the current economic doldrums.

Argument 11
I wore my black shirt on Tuesday and got an F on a math quiz. I wore the same shirt the next day and flunked my psych exam. That shirt's bad luck.

The conclusion of argument 8 is based on nothing more than the fact that the enhanced training preceded the reduction in violent crime. But crime rates can decrease for many reasons, and the enhanced training may have had nothing to do with the decline in crime. For the argument to be strong, other considerations besides temporal order would have to apply—for example, that other possible causes or antecedent factors had been ruled out; that there was a close correlation between amount of training and decline in crime rates; or that in previous years (or in comparable cities) enhanced training was always followed by a decline in violent crime (or no change in training was always followed by steady crime rates).

Argument 9 is also purely post hoc. Such reasoning is extremely common and underlies almost all folk remedies and a great deal of quackery and bogus self-cures. You take a vitamin E capsule, and eight hours later your headache is gone. But was it really the vitamin E that did the trick? Or was it some other overlooked factor, such as something you ate, the medication you took (or didn't take), the nap you had, the change in environment (from, say, indoors to outdoors), or the stress reduction you felt when you had pleasant thoughts? Would your headache have gone away on its own anyway? Was it the *placebo effect*—the tendency for people to feel better when treated even when the treatment is fake or inactive? A chief function of controlled medical testing is to evaluate cause-and-effect relationships by systematically ruling out post hoc thinking and irrelevant factors.

Argument 10 is typical post hoc reasoning from the political sphere. Unless there are other good reasons for thinking that the economic policy is causally connected to specific economic events, the argument is weak and the conclusion unreliable.

Argument 11 is 100 per cent post hoc and undiluted superstition. There is no difference in kind between this argument and much of the notorious post hoc reasoning of centuries ago: 'That girl gave me the evil eye. The next day I broke my leg. That proves she's a witch, and the Elders of Salem should have her put to death!'

Ignoring Common-Causal Factor

Sometimes A and B are correlated with each other, and genuinely causally connected, but A doesn't cause B and B doesn't cause A. Rather, both A and B are caused by some third factor, C. One often-cited example is this: there is a correlation between sales in ice cream and deaths due to drowning. Does ice cream cause people to drown? No. Does drowning somehow cause a rise in ice cream sales? Highly unlikely! The truth is that both of those things are more common during a particular season, namely summer. In the heat of summer, more people go swimming and therefore the rate of drownings goes up. And sales of ice cream likewise go up in summer. So, summertime is the common causal factor shared by those two variables. (Note: 'common' here means 'shared,' not 'frequent.') Another example: imagine reading about a survey that suggests that people with access to high-speed Internet tend to go out to see bands play live more than people with poor Internet access. Is there a causal connection between the two? Well, there might be: maybe people use the Internet to find out when good bands are playing, and people without good Internet access are left out. But maybe more likely is that there's common causal factor connecting the two: people who live in the city are much more likely to have high-speed Internet than people who live in rural areas. People who live in the city also tend to live near lots of clubs and bars where they can see live music. More evidence would be needed before we could be certain what the real causal story is.

Confusing Cause and Effect

Sometimes we may realize that there's a causal relationship between two factors but we may not know which factor is the cause and which is the effect. We may be confused, in other words, about the answers to questions like these:

> Does your coffee drinking cause you to feel stressed out—or do your feelings of being stressed out cause you to drink coffee?

> Does participation in high-school sports produce desirable virtues such as courage and self-reliance—or do the virtues of courage and self-reliance lead students to participate in high-school sports?

> Does regular exercise make people healthy—or are healthy people naturally prone to regular exercise?

As you can see, it's not always a simple matter to discern what the nature of a causal link is. Again, we must rely on our rule of thumb: *don't assume that a causal connection exists unless you have good reason for doing so.* This tenet applies not only to our ordinary experience, but also to all states of affairs involving cause and effect, including scientific investigations.

How many women did the post hoc fallacy doom in Salem? Photo: The Art Archive/Culver Pictures

In everyday life, sorting cause from effect is often easy because the situations we confront are frequently simple and familiar—as when we're trying to discover what caused the kettle to boil over. Here, we naturally rely on Mill's methods or other types of causal reasoning. But as we've seen, in many other common circumstances, things aren't so simple. We often cannot be sure that we've identified all the relevant factors or ruled out the influence of coincidence or correctly distinguished cause and effect. Our rule of thumb, then, should be our guide in all the doubtful cases.

Science faces all the same kinds of challenges in its pursuit of causal explanations. And despite its sophisticated methods and investigative tools, it must expend a great deal of effort to pin down causal connections. Identifying the cause of a disease, for example, usually requires, not one study or experiment, but many. The main reason is that it's always tough to uncover relevant factors and exclude

'Shallow men believe in luck. Strong men believe in cause and effect.'
—Ralph Waldo Emerson

Review Notes

Causal Confusions
- Misidentifying relevant factors
- Overlooking relevant factors
- Confusing coincidence with cause
- Confusing cause with temporal order (post hoc fallacy)
- Confusing cause and effect

irrelevant or misleading factors. That's why we should apply our rule of thumb even to scientific research that purports to identify a causal link. In Chapters 9 and 10, we'll explore procedures for evaluating scientific research and for applying our rule of thumb with more precision.

Necessary and Sufficient Conditions

To fully appreciate the dynamics of cause and effect and to be able to skilfully assess causal arguments, you must understand two other important concepts: **necessary condition** and **sufficient condition**. Causal processes always occur under specific conditions. So we often speak of cause and effect in terms of *the conditions for the occurrence of an event*. Scientists, philosophers, and others go a step further and emphasize a distinction between necessary and sufficient conditions for the occurrence of an event:

> *A necessary condition for the occurrence of an event is one without which the event cannot occur.*

> *A sufficient condition for the occurrence of an event is one that guarantees that the event occurs.*

Suppose you drop a water-filled balloon from the top of a building (aiming it at your least favourite professor, of course), and it breaks on the pavement. What are the *necessary* conditions for the breaking of the balloon (the effect)? There are several, including (1) your releasing the balloon, (2) the force of gravity acting on the water, (3) the weakness of the material that the balloon is made of (its breakability), and (4) the hardness of the pavement. If any one of these conditions is not present, the water balloon will not break. To state the obvious, if you don't release the balloon, it won't drop. If gravity is not in force, the balloon won't fall. If the balloon material isn't breakable, it won't break. If the pavement isn't hard enough, even a breakable balloon won't rupture. (For the sake of illustration, this list of necessary conditions is incomplete. Many, if not most, events in nature have large numbers of necessary conditions.)

What are the *sufficient* conditions for the balloon's breaking? Not one of the four conditions by itself is sufficient to cause the balloon to break. None *guarantees* the occurrence of the effect; none suffices to produce the event. But all the necessary conditions combined (these four and others) are sufficient to guarantee the balloon's breaking.

Failing to feed a healthy goldfish for a few weeks is a sure way to kill it. So this deprivation is a sufficient condition for its death, as is removing the water from its fishbowl. But neither taking away the fish's food nor draining its bowl is a necessary condition for a goldfish's death because its death can be caused without resorting to either of these methods. On the other hand, necessary conditions for *sustaining* the fish's life include feeding it, providing it with water to live in, ensuring that the water is properly oxygenated, and so on. Again, in this instance, the whole set of the necessary conditions would constitute a sufficient condition for sustaining the fish's life.

In cases in which a complete set of necessary conditions constitutes a sufficient condition for an event, we say that the conditions are *individually necessary and jointly sufficient* for an event to occur. As the previous examples suggest, however, it's possible to have a set of conditions that are individually necessary but *not* jointly sufficient. Say some of the conditions necessary for sustaining the goldfish's life are present, but not all of them are. Because some necessary conditions are missing, the sufficient condition for keeping the fish alive would not exist. On the other hand, it is also possible to have a set of conditions that are jointly sufficient but not individually necessary. By not feeding a goldfish for weeks we would create a set of conditions sufficient for the death of the fish. But these conditions are not necessary for the death of a goldfish because we could ensure its death in other ways.

So there are conditions that are necessary but not sufficient for the occurrence of an event, and conditions that are sufficient but not necessary. There are also conditions that are *both* necessary and sufficient for an event. The Earth's being more massive than the moon is both a necessary and sufficient condition for the moon's being less massive than the Earth. A piece of paper's being heated to a sufficiently high temperature in the presence of oxygen is both a necessary and sufficient condition for the combustion of the paper.

In some situations, depending on our interests or practical concerns, we may focus on necessary causal conditions, and in other situations, on sufficient causal conditions. When we're interested in preventing or eliminating a state of affairs, we often zero in on necessary causal conditions. If you were a scientist trying to discover how to prevent mosquito infestations, you would try to determine the necessary conditions for the occurrence of mosquito infestations. Uncovering and understanding just one necessary condition could give you everything you need to control the problem. If you found out, for example, that a necessary condition for mosquito breeding is standing water, you would need to look no further for an answer. Eliminating the standing water would prevent infestations.

When we're interested in *bringing about* a state of affairs, we're likely to focus on sufficient causal conditions. If you were a doctor devoted to treating clogged arteries in your patients, you would seek out treatments scientifically proven to be sufficient for alleviating the condition. The treatments might include surgery to remove the blockage or a procedure called balloon angioplasty to widen artery passageways.

Your success in appraising causal arguments often depends heavily on your ability to distinguish between statements expressing causes as necessary conditions and statements expressing causes as sufficient conditions. Consider:

> In the current situation, the Prime Minister will call an election if Parliament doesn't vote in favour of his proposal to cut taxes.

This statement says that the condition required for the Prime Minister to call an election is Parliament not supporting his proposal to cut taxes. But is this a necessary or sufficient condition? The use of the word 'if' by itself signals a sufficient condition. If sufficient condition is what's meant, then the statement says that Parliament's refusal to support the tax cuts will automatically trigger an election call. This outcome is assured if Parliament doesn't co-operate.

But if the statement is meant to express the idea that Parliament's refusal to support the tax cut is a necessary condition, then we're talking about a very different situation. If Parliament's refusal is a necessary condition, then it *will not* unavoidably trigger an election call because the refusal may not be the *only* necessary condition. The idea of necessary condition is expressed by the phrase 'only if' before the stipulated condition. To express necessary condition, the statement should read:

> In the current situation, the Prime Minister will call an election only if Parliament doesn't vote in favour of his proposal to cut taxes.

So depending on the kind of causal condition meant, the statement could describe an election that's sure to happen if the condition obtains—or an election that may not occur even if the condition obtains.

As you might expect, conditions that are *both* necessary and sufficient are indicated by the phrase 'if and only if'. For example:

> The paper will combust if and only if it's heated to a sufficiently high temperature in the presence of oxygen.

None of this discussion, however, should lead you to think that a causal condition must be *either* necessary or sufficient. It could be neither:

> Late delivery of the package caused John to miss his deadline.

> Ricardo's stubbornness caused the negotiations to break down.

Exercise 8.10

Analyze each of the following causal arguments. Identify the conclusion and say whether the argument appeals to the method of agreement, the method of difference, the joint method of agreement and difference, or correlation. In some cases the conclusion may be implied but not stated. Say whether the argument is strong or weak.

1. Forty-five patients were admitted to Children's Hospital for pneumonia in December. They were all given standard treatment for pneumonia. After five days, 30 of them were well enough to go home. The other 15, however, somehow acquired other infections and were not well enough to be released for two weeks. The only relevant factor common to these 15 is that they all stayed in the same ward (different from the ward that the other group stayed in). Something about staying in that ward is the cause of the prolonged illness.

* 2. Research suggests that eating lots of fruits and vegetables may provide some protection against several types of cancer. Studies have revealed that the risk of getting cancer associated with the lowest intakes of fruits and vegetables is twice as high as that associated with the highest intakes. This association holds for several types of cancer, including cancers of the breast, colon, pancreas, and bladder.

3. 'An experimental vaccine prevented women from becoming persistently infected with a [type of human papilloma virus called HPV-16] that is associated with half of all cervical cancers, researchers reported.... The study involved 2,392 women from 16 to 23 years in age. Participants were randomly assigned to receive three shots of either an HPV-16 vaccine or a placebo (a dummy substance). The study was double-blinded—that is, neither the investigators nor the study participants knew who got the vaccine and who got the placebo. Participants were followed for an average of 17 months after getting the third shot.... [Forty-one] women developed HPV-16 infection—all of these women were in the placebo group.... By comparison, no one who got all three vaccine shots developed an HPV-16 infection.' (National Cancer Institute)

4. The endorsement of the Canadian Auto Workers' union is essential to getting elected in Oshawa. No one has ever been elected to represent Oshawa in Parliament without the support of the CAW.

5. For most of the school year the number of disciplinary actions taken weekly because of student misconduct at North High School has remained about the same—roughly 10 a week. But for the last month the number of actions per week has gone down considerably—to about six per week. There can be only one reason: last month a new Code of Student Conduct was posted in the hallway outside the principal's office.

6. In Instance 1, when factors X, Y, and Z were present, E happened. In Instance 2, when factors X, Y, and P were present, E happened. In Instance 3, when factors

X and Z were present, E did not happen. In Instance 4, when Z and P were present, E did not happen. And in Instance 5, when X, Z, and P were present, E did not happen. Therefore, Y caused E.

* 7. Educators have frequently noted the connection between education level and salary. The higher a person's education level is, the higher his or her annual salary is likely to be. Education increases people's earning power.

8. 'On 20 May 1747, I took twelve patients [with] scurvy on board the *Salisbury* at sea. Their cases were as similar as I could have them. They all in general had putrid gums, the spots and lassitude, with weakness of their knees. They lay together in one place, being a proper apartment for the sick in the fore-hold; and had one diet in common to all. . . . Two of these were ordered each a quart of cider a day. Two others took [twenty-five drops of] vitriol three times a day. . . . Two others took two spoonfuls of vinegar three times a day. . . . Two of the worst patients [were given a half pint of sea water daily]. . . . Two others had each two oranges and one lemon given them everyday. . . . The two remaining patients took [small doses of nutmeg, garlic, mustard seed, and a few other ingredients]. The consequence was that the most sudden and visible good effects were perceived from the use of the oranges and lemons; one of those who had taken them being at the end of six days fit for duty. . . . The other was the best recovered of any in his condition, and being now deemed pretty well was appointed nurse to the rest of the sick. As I shall have occasion elsewhere to take notice of the effects of other medicines in this disease, I shall here only observe that the result of all my experiments was that oranges and lemons were the most effectual remedies for this distemper at sea.' (James Lind, *Of the Prevention of the Scurvy*, 1753)

9. On Tuesday 52 people ate ham sandwiches at Johnny's Deli, and half of these came down with hepatitis. The board of health discovered that the people who became ill had eaten ham sandwiches made by Johnny's brother, who had hepatitis at the time. This was the only relevant common element among those who got sick. Seems Johnny's brother was the cause of this outbreak.

10. Scientists wanted to see whether giving pre-puberty children dietary supplements of calcium could significantly increase the density of the children's bones. (Bone density is a key part of bone strength.) So they selected 71 pairs of identical twins and gave one twin of each pair a daily supplement of extra calcium and the other twin a sugar pill (placebo). All the twins had diets that contained adequate amounts of all nutrients. The investigators monitored the twins and their diets for three years. The only relevant difference between the twins was the extra calcium that half of them received. At the end of the three years, the scientists found that the twins who had received the extra calcium had significantly greater bone density. They concluded that the extra calcium caused the increased density.

11. For years vehicular accidents at the intersection of Fifth and Main Streets have consistently averaged two to four per month. After a traffic light was installed there, the rate has been one or two accidents every three months. That new traffic light has made quite a difference.

12. The risk of atherosclerosis (hardening of the arteries) is linked to the amount of cholesterol in the bloodstream (called serum cholesterol). The higher the serum cholesterol levels, the greater the risk of atherosclerosis. There's a causal connection between serum cholesterol levels and risk of atherosclerosis.

* 13. Investigators tested the performance of four gasoline-powered lawnmowers before and after a tune-up. The machines differed in age, manufacturer, engine type, and controls. The performance of every mower was better after the tune-up, leading the testers to conclude that tune-ups can improve the performance of lawnmowers.

14. The reason there have been so many terrorist attacks in Western countries in the past 10 years is that the rights of Palestinians have been violated by Westerners. Every time large numbers of innocent Palestinians have been jailed, persecuted, or killed in Western countries, there has been a terrorist attack in the West.

15. Charlie was pretty happy all week, but then he started moping around as if he'd lost his dog or something. I think he's upset because he got word that his grades weren't good enough to get into medical school.

* 16. The price of a barrel of oil on the world market has hit $40 only 12 times in the last 30 years. Sometimes major world economies were in recession, and sometimes they weren't. Sometimes there was an increase in the average fuel-consumption of cars; sometimes not. War has been the only constant.

17. Sometimes my television reception is excellent, and sometimes it's terrible. There's only one important factor that seems to make a difference. When the reception is excellent, no other major appliances are running in the house. When it's terrible, at least one major appliance—like the dishwasher—is running. For some reason, running a major appliance interferes with my TV reception.

18. In our test, after people washed their hands with Lather-Up Germicidal Soap, no germs whatsoever could be detected on their hands. But under exactly the same conditions, after they washed their hands with Brand X germicidal soap, plenty of germs were found on their hands. Lather-Up is better.

* 19. Just five people got As on the mid-term exam. The only common factor in their success is that they all studied the night before and reviewed their notes just before walking into class to take the test.

20. The cause of Jackie M's criminal behaviour—his involvement in petty theft and assaults—is no mystery. Jackie commits most of his criminal acts when the outdoor temperatures are highest. When outdoor temperatures are lowest,

he behaves himself. In fact, the incidence of his criminal behaviour rises as the temperature rises. Jackie's problem is that he has a heat-sensitive personality.

Exercise 8.11

For each argument in Exercise 8.10, identify errors in causal reasoning that are most likely to occur in the circumstances indicated. The possibilities include (a) misidentifying or overlooking relevant factors, (b) being misled by coincidence, (c) falling for the post hoc fallacy, and (d) confusing cause and effect. Answers are provided for 2, 7, 13, 16, and 19.

Exercise 8.12

For each of the following causal statements, say whether the specified cause is (a) a necessary condition, (b) a sufficient condition, (c) a necessary and sufficient condition, or (d) neither a necessary nor a sufficient condition.

* 1.   Sylvia's exposure to the influenza virus caused her to get the flu.
  2.   Sergio's eagerness to get to the airport caused him to get a speeding ticket.
  3.   Giving the roses water and nourishing soil caused them to flourish.
* 4.   Chopping off the head of the king put an end to him.
  5.   The mighty Casey hit the ball out of the park, winning the game by one run.
  6.   The straw broke the camel's back.
  7.   The proper combining of sodium and chlorine produced salt, sodium chloride.
  8.   Johann got a good grade on the exam because he studied the night before.
* 9.   A single spark started the internal combustion engine.
  10. Simone lost weight by exercising regularly.

Mixed Arguments

We noted in Chapter 3 the distinction between deductive and inductive arguments. We said that a deductive argument is intended to provide logically *conclusive* support for its conclusion, and that an inductive argument is intended to provide *probable*—not conclusive—support for its conclusion. In Chapters 6 and 7 we discussed deductive reasoning in more detail and ways of evaluating deductive arguments. And here in Chapter 8 we've discussed several forms of inductive reasoning and ways of evaluating them. Since the processes for evaluating deductive and inductive arguments are so different, it makes sense to learn about them separately. But in real life, arguers will very often combine inductive and deductive elements within a single, compound argument. Let's look briefly at the notion of *mixed arguments*, and how to evaluate them.

There are no limits to the ways in which arguers may try to combine deductive and inductive elements within a single, mixed argument. One of the simplest ways in which deductive and inductive elements may be combined is seen when one of the *premises* of a categorical syllogism is actually the *conclusion* of an inductive argument—say, an argument that uses enumerative induction.

Here's an example:

> 'In our study, we gave 100 average Canadian consumers a simple quiz about basic science. None of them passed it. It seems average Canadian consumers just don't have an understanding of basic science. Only people who understand science should get to have a say on scientific issues like the safety of genetically modified wheat. So, average Canadians consumers should not have a say on genetically modified wheat.'

The first part of that argument is an example of enumerative induction: it's a kind of survey, one that reaches a dramatic conclusion based on a rather small sample.

- *target population:* Canadian consumer
- *sample:* 100 Canadian consumers
- *relevant property:* understand basic science.
- *conclusion:* 0 per cent of Canadian consumers understand basic science.

The second part of the argument is a categorical syllogism.

Premise 1: No Canadian consumers understand basic science.

Premise 2: All people who should get a say on the safety of genetically modified wheat are people who understand basic science.

Conclusion: No Canadian consumers are people who should get a say on the safety of genetically modified wheat.

Let's look at those two components of the argument, beginning with the inductive part. How strong is the argument that 'no Canadian consumers understand basic science?' The first thing to note, of course, is that the sample is very small: a sample of just 100 people leaves a very large margin of error. We also need more information about whether the sample was random or representative. We would also, ideally, want to ask questions about just what kind of quiz was administered and what the quiz givers count as 'basic' science. But even with the minimal information available here, and especially given the small sample, it looks as if this inductive part of the argument is pretty weak. But let's accept it for now, for the sake of argument, and move on to assess the deductive component of the argument.

Since the conclusion is about Canadian consumers and whether they're the sort who should have a say, we'll assign S & P (Subject and Predicate) this way:

S = Canadian consumers
P = people who should get a say on the safety of genetically modified wheat

We'll assign M (for 'Middle Term') to the term that's left, namely the bit about understanding basic science.

M = people who understand basic science

Next, let's take the categorical syllogism expressed above and put it into standard form, using the letters we just assigned:

No S are M.

All P are M.

Therefore, no S are P.

Now we can ask, is this a valid argument? Let's do a Venn diagram to figure it out. Diagramming the two premises produces a diagram like this:

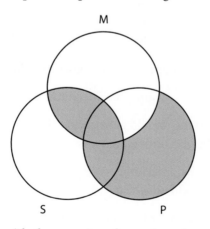

Does this diagram—with the premises drawn in—show the thing that is stated in the conclusion, namely that 'No S are P'? Yes, you can clearly see that the area of overlap between the S circle and the P circle is entirely shaded out. It's empty, just as it should be to show that 'no S are P.' The deductive part of our overall argument, then, is valid.

So, what about our mixed argument as a whole? Well, the deductive part is fine. But since the inductive argument offered in support of one of the premises for the deductive part is quite weak, we should consider mixed argument, as a whole, to be weak.

Summary

An inductive argument is intended to provide only probable support for its conclusion, being considered strong if it succeeds in providing such support and weak if it does not.

Inductive arguments come in several forms, including enumerative, analogical, and causal. In enumerative induction, we argue from premises about some members of a group to a generalization about the entire group. The entire group is called the target group; the observed members of the group, the sample; and the group characteristics we're interested in, the relevant property. An enumerative induction can fail to be strong by having a sample that's too small or not representative. When we draw a conclusion about a target group on the basis of too small a sample, we are said to commit the error of hasty generalization. Opinion polls are enumerative inductive arguments, or the basis of enumerative inductive arguments, and must be judged by the same general criteria used to judge any other enumerative induction.

In analogical induction, or argument by analogy, we reason that since two or more things are similar in several respects, they must be similar in some further respect. We evaluate arguments by analogy according to several criteria: (1) the number of relevant similarities between things being compared, (2) the number of relevant dissimilarities, (3) the number of instances (or cases) of similarities or dissimilarities, and (4) the diversity among the cases.

A causal argument is an inductive argument whose conclusion contains a causal claim. There are several inductive patterns of reasoning used to assess causal connections. These include the Method of Agreement, the Method of Difference, the Method of Agreement and Difference, and the Method of Concomitant Variation. Errors in cause-and-effect reasoning are common. They include misidentifying relevant factors in a causal process, overlooking relevant factors, confusing cause with coincidence, confusing cause with temporal order, and mixing up cause and effect.

Crucial to an understanding of cause-and-effect relationships are the notions of necessary and sufficient conditions. A necessary condition for the occurrence of an event is one without which the event cannot occur. A sufficient condition for the occurrence of an event is one that guarantees that the event occurs.

Key Terms

Analogy: A comparison of two or more things alike in specific respects.

Argument by analogy (analogical induction): An argument making use of analogy, reasoning that because two or more things are similar in several respects, they must be similar in some further respect.

Biased sample: A sample that does not properly represent the target group.

Causal argument: An inductive argument whose conclusion contains a causal claim.

Causal claim: A statement about the causes of things.

Confidence level: In statistical theory, the probability that the sample will accurately represent the target group within the margin of error.

Enumerative induction: An inductive-argument pattern in which we reason from premises about individual members of a group to conclusions about the group as a whole.

Hasty generalization: The fallacy of drawing a conclusion about a target group on the basis of too small a sample.

Inference to the best explanation: A form of inductive reasoning in which we reason from premises about a state of affairs to an explanation for that state of affairs:

    Phenomenon Q.

    E provides the best explanation for Q.

    Therefore, it is probable that E is true.

Margin of error: The variation between the values derived from a sample and the true values of the whole target group.

Mixed argument: An argument that includes both inductive and deductive elements.

Necessary condition: A condition for the occurrence of an event without which the event cannot occur.

Random sample: A sample that is selected randomly from a target group in such a way as to ensure that the sample is representative. In a simple random selection, every member of the target group has an equal chance of being selected for the sample.

Relevant property (property in question): In enumerative induction, a property, or characteristic, that is of interest in the target group.

Representative sample: In enumerative induction, a sample that resembles the target group in all relevant ways.

Sample (sample member): In enumerative induction, the observed members of the target group.

Sufficient condition: A condition for the occurrence of an event that guarantees that the event occurs.

Target group (target population): In enumerative induction, the whole collection of individuals under study.

Field Problems

1. Design an opinion poll to determine the percentage of people on campus who believe that 'young offenders' should get the same penalty (for the same crime) as adult offenders.

   Specify all the following parameters: (1) the target group, (2) the makeup and size of the sample, (3) the methods for ensuring a random sample, (4) the methods for ensuring a representative sample, (5) the exact phrasing of the polling question(s), (6) the method for gathering the responses (telephone survey, 'man on the street' poll, email questionnaire, etc.), and (7) the acceptable margin of error. Explain the reasons for your choices.

2. Devise an extended argument by analogy (200–300 words) to support the proposition that the Earth is not a mere planet of rock and soil but is a living organism, a notion that has come to be known as the Gaia theory. You'll need to research this term on the Internet. (The original idea that inspired this view was not that the planet was an organism, but that it *could be usefully viewed* as an organism that is self-regulating.) People who take the idea literally might say, for example, that just as billions of cells in the human body perform the functions that sustain the body, so billions of organisms on the Earth perform the functions that sustain the life of the Earth. Use several relevant similarities in your argument. Then write a critique of your argument, focusing especially on relevant dissimilarities and the number of relevant similarities.

3. Select a causal argument on a political issue from recent op-ed pages (in newspapers or on websites). Then critique it, explaining why it's strong or weak, specifically noting whether it misidentifies or overlooks relevant factors, confuses cause with coincidence, commits the post hoc fallacy, confuses cause and effect, or mishandles or misunderstands necessary and sufficient conditions.

Self-Assessment Quiz

1. What is the logical form of enumerative induction, indicated schematically?
2. In enumerative induction, what are the target group, the sample, and the relevant property?
3. What are the two major ways in which an enumerative induction can fail to be strong?
4. What is the logical form of analogical induction, indicated schematically?

For each of the following enumerative inductions, say whether the argument is strong or weak. If it's weak, say whether the problem is a sample that's too small, not representative, or both.

5. All the women in my yoga class are in favour of a national child-care program. Ninety per cent of the members of a national women's group (3,000 members) are in favour of a national child-care program. And all my women friends are in favour of a national child-care program. The fact is, almost all Canadian women are in favour of a national child-care program.

6. David Milgaard was wrongly convicted of murder in Saskatchewan in 1970. Donald Marshall Jr was wrongfully convicted of murder in Nova Scotia in 1971. And Guy Paul Morin was wrongfully convicted of murder in Ontario in 1984. People whose last names begin with an 'M' get a raw deal from the Canadian justice system!

7. Most professors at this university are not grading as strictly as they used to. They now give Bs for work that once would have earned Cs. The grading standards at Canadian universities are dropping.

8. The first time Ariana encountered trigonometry, she couldn't understand it. And the first time she read Shakespeare, she didn't get it. She will never understand anything.

9. Canadians are quite satisfied with Canada's current laws regarding polygamy. An online poll conducted by *The Globe and Mail* got over twenty thousand responses—and 79 per cent of them said that polygamy should *not* be legalized.

10. Judging from what I've seen, anti-globalization protestors are just a bunch of hooligans, tree huggers, and Luddites.

Evaluate each of the following arguments by analogy, indicating (1) the two things being compared, (2) the conclusion, and (3) whether the argument is strong or weak.

11. 'Suppose that someone tells me that he has had a tooth extracted without an anaesthetic, and I express my sympathy, and suppose that I am then asked, How do you know that it hurt him? I might reasonably reply, 'Well, I know that it would hurt me. I have been to the dentist and know how painful it is to have a tooth stopped without an anaesthetic, let alone taken out. And he has the same sort of nervous system as I have. I infer, therefore, that in these conditions he felt considerable pain, just as I should myself.' (Alfred J. Ayer)

12. 'As for one who is choosy about what he learns . . . we shall not call him a lover of learning or a philosopher, just as we shall not say that a man who is difficult about his food is hungry or has an appetite for food. We shall not call him a lover of food but a poor eater. . . . But we shall call a philosopher the man who is easily willing to learn every kind of knowledge, gladly turns to learning things, and is insatiable in this respect.' (Socrates)

13. 'Let us begin with a parable [showing that statements about God have no mean-ing]. . . . Once upon a time two explorers came upon a clearing in the jungle. In the clearing were growing many flowers and many weeds. One explorer says, 'Some gardener must tend this plot.' The other disagrees, 'There is no gardener.' So they pitch their tents and set a watch. No gardener is ever seen. 'But perhaps he is an invisible gardener.' So they set up a barbed-wire fence. They electrify it. . . . But no shrieks ever suggest that some intruder has received a shock. No movements of the wire ever betray an invisible climber. . . . Yet still the Believer is not convinced. 'But there is a gardener, invisible, intangible, insensible.' . . . At last the Skeptic despairs, 'But what remains of your original assertion? Just how does what you call an invisible, intangible, eternally elusive gardener differ from an imaginary gardener or even from no gardener at all?' (Antony Flew)

Analyze each of the following causal arguments. Identify the conclusion and whether the argument is weak or strong. If it's weak, explain why with reference to the material in this chapter.

14. School violence is caused mainly by teens playing violent video games. Inci-dents of violence in schools have increased as more and more teens are playing violent video games, as the video games themselves have become more graphi-cally and realistically violent, and as the number and variety of video games have expanded dramatically.

15. Smoking and exposure to second-hand smoke among pregnant women pose a significant risk to both infants and the unborn. According to numerous studies, each year the use of tobacco causes thousands of spontaneous births, infant deaths, and deaths from SIDS. Death rates for fetuses are 35 per cent higher among pregnant women who smoke than among pregnant women who don't smoke.

16. Why are crime rates so high, the economy so bad, and our children so prone to violence, promiscuity, and vulgarity? These social ills have arisen—as they always have—from the 'moral vacuum' created when Canadians turn away from religion. Our current slide into chaos started when kids stopped saying 'The Lord's Prayer' before class, and families stopped saying grace before dinner. And as God has slowly faded from public life, we have got deeper in the hole.

17. The 12 of us went on a hike through the mountains. We all drank bottled water except Lisa, who drank from a stream. Later she got really sick. Some intestinal thing. But the rest of us were fine. We've repeated this adventure many times on other hikes, with all but one of us drinking bottled water and one drinking from a stream. Everything else was the same. Each time, the person who drank from the stream got really ill. Drinking from streams on these hikes causes intestinal illness. Don't do it.

18. Ever since I started drinking herbal tea in the morning, my energy level has improved and I'm a lot calmer during the day. That stuff works.

19. Yesterday my astrological chart—prepared by a top astrologer—said that I would meet an attractive person today, and I did. Last week, it said I'd come

into some money, and I did. (Jack paid me that $100 he owed me.) Now I'm a believer. The stars really do rule.

20. Most of the terminal-cancer patients in this ward who had positive attitudes about their disease lived longer than expected. Most of the negative-attitude patients didn't live as long as expected. A positive attitude can increase the life expectancy of people with terminal cancer.

Integrative Exercises

These exercises pertain to material in Chapters 3 and 6–8.

For each of the following arguments, specify the conclusion and premises and say whether it is deductive or inductive. If it's deductive, use Venn diagrams or truth tables to determine its validity. If it's inductive, say whether it's an enumerative, analogical, or causal induction and whether it's strong or weak. If necessary, add implicit premises and conclusions.

1. It's clear that if the allies accidentally damage any holy sites when they attack enemy forces, the local people will never give the allies any respect or co-operation. The allies, though, will not damage any holy sites. Therefore, the locals will respect the allies and co-operate with them.

2. By routing suburban buses through downtown, the Transit Authority has created serious traffic congestion. The buses get in each other's way and in the way of drivers of cars. I've lived here for 20 years and have never seen a serious traffic jam downtown. Now it's a daily occurrence.

3. If people have free will, they can be held morally responsible for what they do. But—as our judicial system demonstrates—people cannot really be held morally responsible for their actions. Thus, people do not have free will.

4. 'If we take in hand any volume; of divinity or school metaphysics, for instance; let us ask, *Does it contain any abstract reasoning concerning quantity or number?* No. *Does it contain any experimental reasoning concerning matter of fact and existence?* No. Commit it then to the flames; for it can contain nothing but sophistry and illusion.' (David Hume)

5. No philosophy majors are persons without a brain. All students without a brain are persons who spend most of their time partying. So no philosophy majors are persons who spend most of their time partying.

6. The new rules for student loans say that anyone who has missed two or more payments on any of their debts can be denied a loan. But anyone can miss a payment or two; in some cases, it happens because people just can't afford the payments. These new rules are punishing people for being poor.

7. All politicians are corrupt manipulators, so some corrupt manipulators are effective leaders, since some effective leaders are politicians.

8. If we increase security in the country because of terrorist attacks, our personal freedoms will be curtailed. If we do not increase security in the country, terrorist attacks will increase. So either our personal freedoms will be curtailed or terrorist attacks will increase.

9. Because the core values of the Canada Health Act are universality and accessibility, we believe it is crucial that health care in Canada remain a public good, and that we reject two-tier health care of any kind.

10. As former Prime Minister Pierre Elliott Trudeau argued when he was Justice Minister, 'The state has no place in the bedrooms of the nation.' This implies that governments should take no notice of people's gender or sexual orientation. When it comes to issuing marriage licences, then, all people must be equal under the law.

11. [Be careful: This one has an unstated conclusion.] The standard of living in Canada ranks among the very highest in the world. Yet that fact glosses over the terrible living conditions endured by many of Canada's Aboriginal peoples. Despite its promises and obligations, the Canadian government has done little to improve the lot of its Aboriginal citizens, many of whom continue to struggle with poverty, poor health care, substandard educational opportunities. And many Aboriginal communities continue to be plagued by crime and addiction.

12. Almost all of the owners of restaurants, bars, and clubs in Halifax are opposed to the city's total ban on smoking in indoor public places. The vast majority of Haligonians simply do not like this law.

13. Every student Maria knows who wears glasses also has a high grade-point average. So most students who wear glasses probably have high grade-point averages.

14. 'The evils of the world are due to moral defects quite as much as to lack of intelligence. But the human race has not hitherto discovered any method of eradicating moral defects. . . . Intelligence, on the contrary, is easily improved by methods known to every competent educator. Therefore, until some method of teaching virtue has been discovered, progress will have to be sought by improvement of intelligence rather than of morals.' (Bertrand Russell)

15. Television is destroying morality in this country. As TV violence, sex, and vulgarity have increased, so have violent crimes, sexual assaults, and violations of obscenity laws.

16. In the past 20 years, several planes and a number of ships have disappeared in the Bermuda Triangle. These odd vanishings cannot be mere coincidence. The Bermuda Triangle is the centre of mysterious forces unknown to science.

17. 'Some people would have us believe that the Supreme Court of Canada, emboldened by the Charter of Rights and Freedoms, has adopted an increasingly 'activist' stance and is now usurping powers that should legitimately be exercised by the legislature. . . . [But] it is highly misleading to speak as though the Supreme Court is taking power away from the legislature when it rules on

charter cases. The role of the Supreme Court is to decide whether the legislature has satisfied the conditions required for the creation of legitimate law. Thus the only power that the Supreme Court takes away, when it rules against the legislature is the power to engage in an illegitimate use of force. And this is not a power that anyone should want the legislature to have.' (Joseph Heath, 'Why Have a Constitution at All?' *Policy Options*, October 2003)

18. Eighty-three per cent of the letters to the editor received by this newspaper are adamantly in favour of a national day-care plan. And since the *Daily Planet* is the only major newspaper in the city and it provides the primary forum for discussion of local issues, we must conclude that this town is also overwhelmingly in favour of a national day-care plan.

19. The big grandfather clock in the hallway struck midnight—and then the old man died. This doesn't prove that the striking of the clock killed him, but it does show that the two events—the clock's striking and the death of the old man—were somehow causally linked.

20. If the recession continues, people will lose billions of dollars in failed investments. People will indeed lose billions of dollars in failed investments, so the recession will continue.

Writing Assignments

1. In a 250-word essay use an enumerative inductive argument to argue that your campus is (or is not) relatively free of crime.

2. Using either enumerative induction or argument by analogy, write a 500-word rebuttal to Essay 6 ('Misleading the Patient for Fun and Profit') in Appendix A.

3. In a 400-word essay argue for or against one of these claims:
   - Men are better at science than women are.
   - Everyone does what is in his or her own best interests.
   - Deadbeat dads (fathers who don't or won't pay child support that they are legally obligated to pay) should be put in jail.
   - Sexual harassment is not a problem on this campus.
   - Competition is always a good thing.
   - Pornography should never be banned on a university campus.

Part Four
Explanations

Chapter
9

Inference to the Best Explanation

Chapter Objectives

Explanations and Inference

You will be able to

○ define inference to the best explanation and understand how it differs from other kinds of induction.

○ clarify what an explanation (including theoretical explanation) is and how it differs from an argument.

○ appreciate how inference to the best explanation is used in all disciplines and in everyday life.

○ demonstrate how to use inference to the best explanation in many different situations.

Theories and Consistency

You will be able to

○ check an explanation for internal and external consistency.

Theories and Criteria

You will be able to

○ understand the importance of using criteria to judge the adequacy of theories.

○ list and explain the five criteria of adequacy.

○ apply the criteria of adequacy to simple causal theories.

○ define and explain an ad hoc hypothesis.

You will be able to

○ memorize and explain the four steps in the TEST formula.

○ recognize the importance of considering alternative explanations.

○ use the TEST formula to evaluate theories.

Let's take stock of the inductive terrain travelled thus far. In Chapter 8 we closely examined the nature and uses of inductive reasoning. We were reminded that a deductive argument, unlike an inductive one, is intended to provide logically conclusive support for its conclusion. If it succeeds in providing such support, it is said to be valid; if it does not, invalid. If a valid argument has true premises, it is said to be sound. But an inductive argument is intended to supply only probable support for its conclusion. If it manages to provide such support, it is said to be strong; if it does not, weak. The conclusion of an inductively strong argument is simply more likely to be true than not. If a strong argument has true premises, it's said to be cogent.

We also saw that inductive arguments come in several forms. One of them is enumerative induction, in which we reason from premises about *some* members of a group to a conclusion, or generalization, about the group *as a whole*. All the swans you have ever seen are white, so *all* swans must be white. Forty per cent of the students at your university have a driver's licence, so 40 per cent of all students everywhere must have a driver's licence. (Whether these enumerative inductive arguments are strong or cogent is another matter.)

Another kind of inductive argument is argument by analogy (or analogical induction), in which we reason that since two or more things are similar in several respects, they must be similar in some additional respect. In an analogical induction you might argue that (1) since humans can move about, solve mathematical equations, win chess games, and feel pain, *and* (2) since computers (or robots) are like humans in that they can move about, solve mathematical equations, and win chess games, it is therefore probable that computers can also feel pain. Analogical induction, like all inductive reasoning, can establish conclusions only with a degree of probability.

Review Notes

A Look Back at the Basics

- *Statement (claim)*: An assertion that something is or is not the case.
- *Premise*: A statement given in support of another statement.
- *Conclusion*: A statement that premises are intended to support.
- *Argument*: A group of statements in which some of them (the premises) are intended to support another of them (the conclusion).
- *Indicator words*: Words that frequently accompany arguments and signal that a premise or conclusion is present.
- *Deductive argument*: An argument intended to provide conclusive support for its conclusion.
- *Inductive argument*: An argument intended to provide probable support for its conclusion.

Finally, we saw that causal arguments—inductive arguments whose conclusions contain causal claims—can be enumerative inductions, analogical inductions, or arguments that rely on Mill's methods and similar kinds of inferences. Reasoning well about causal connections means avoiding numerous common errors, including misidentifying or overlooking relevant factors, confusing coincidence with cause, and committing the post hoc fallacy.

We noted only in passing that there is another kind of inductive reasoning that is so important that all of Part 4 of this book is devoted to it: **inference to the best explanation**. Well, here we are in Part 4, and it's time to delve deep into this kind of inductive reasoning, perhaps the most commonly used form of inference and arguably the most empowering in daily life.

Explanations and Inference

Recall from Chapter 1 that an explanation is a statement (or statements) asserting why or how something is the case. For example: The bucket leaks because there's a hole in it. He was sad because his dog had died. She broke the pipe by hitting it with a wrench. These explanations and all others are intended to clarify and elucidate, and thus to increase our understanding. Remember too our discussion of the important distinction between an explanation and an argument. Whereas an explanation tells us *why or how something is the case*, an argument gives us reasons for believing *that something is the case*.

As you've probably already guessed, there are also different kinds of explanations (see the box 'The Lore of Explanations'). For instance, some explanations are what we might call procedural—they try to explain how something is done or how an action is carried out. ('She opened up the engine, then examined the valves, and then checked the cylinders.') Some are interpretive—they try to explain the meaning of terms or states of affairs. ('This word means "fancy" or "showy".') And some are functional—they try to explain how something functions. ('The heart circulates and oxygenates the blood.')

But the kind of explanation we're concerned with here—and the kind we bump into most often—is what we'll call, for lack of something snappier, a **theoretical explanation**. Such explanations are theories, or hypotheses, that try to explain why something is the way it is, why something is the case, or why something happened. In this category we must include all explanations intended to explain the cause of events—the causal explanations that are so important to both science and daily life. Theoretical explanations, of course, are claims. They assert that something is or is not the case.

Now, even though an explanation is not an argument, an explanation can be *part* of an argument. It can be the heart of the kind of inductive argument known as 'inference to the best explanation'. And in this kind of inference, the explanations we use are theoretical explanations.

In inference to the best explanation, *we reason from premises about a state of affairs to an explanation for that state of affairs*. The premises are statements about observations or other evidence to be explained. The explanation is a claim about why the state of affairs is the way it is. The key question that this type of inference tries to answer is 'What is the best explanation for the existence or nature of this state of affairs?' The best explanation is the one most likely to be true, even though there is no guarantee of its truth as there is in deductive inference.

Recall that enumerative induction has this pattern:

X per cent of the observed members of group A have property P.
Therefore, X per cent of all members of group A probably have property P.

And that analogical induction has this pattern:

Thing A has properties P_1, P_2, and P_3, plus the property P_4.
Thing B has properties P_1, P_2, and P_3.
Therefore, thing B probably has property P_4.

Inference to the best explanation, however, has this pattern:

Phenomenon Q.
E provides the best explanation for Q.
Therefore, it is probable that E is true.

'There is nothing more practical than a good theory.'
—Leonid Ilich Brezhnev

For example:

The new quarterback dropped the ball again. The best explanation for that screw-up is that he's nervous. So he's definitely nervous.

The best explanation for Maria's absence today is that she's angry at the boss. Yep, she's mad at the boss.

The defendant's fingerprints were all over the crime scene, the police found the victim's blood on his shirt, and he was in possession of the murder weapon. The only explanation for all this that makes any sense is that the defendant actually committed the crime. He's guilty.

If the explanations in these arguments really are the best, then the arguments are inductively strong. And if the premises are also true, then the arguments are cogent. If they are cogent, we are justified in believing that the explanations for the phenomena are in fact correct.

Notice that an inference to the best explanation always goes 'beyond the evidence'—it tries to explain facts but does so by positing a theory that is not derived entirely from those facts. It tries to understand the known by putting forth—through inference and imagination—a theoretical pattern that encompasses both the known and unknown. It proposes a plausible pattern that expands our understanding.

The fact that there are *best* explanations, of course, implies that not all explanations for a state of affairs are created equal; some are better than others. Just because you've devised an explanation for something doesn't mean that you're justified in believing that the explanation is the right one. If other explanations are just as good, your explanation is in doubt. If other explanations are better than yours, you are not justified in believing it. But much of the time, after further study or thought, you can reasonably conclude that a particular explanation really is the best explanation. (More on how to evaluate the relative worth of explanations later.) In this way you can come to understand the state of affairs more than you did before.

Inference to the best explanation probably seems very familiar to you. That's because you use it all the time—and need it all the time. Often when we try to understand something in the world, we construct explanations for why this something is the way it is, and we try to determine which of these is the best. Devising explanations helps increase our

"WELL WHICH DO YOU THINK IS MORE LIKELY, YOUR PILLOW IS GROWING HAIR OR YOU'RE LOSING YOURS?"

Review Notes

The Lore of Explanations

An explanation is a statement (or statements) asserting why or how something is the case. In traditional terminology, that which is to be explained in an explanation is called the *explanandum*, and that which does the explaining is called the *explanans*. Take this explanation: 'The dog barked because a prowler was nearby.' The explanandum is 'the dog barked,' and the explanans is 'a prowler was nearby.'

You can categorize explanations in many ways, depending on the kind of explanandum you're interested in. Here are a few of the more common categories:

- Teleological explanations try to explain the purpose of something, how it functions, or how it fits into a plan. (*Telos* is a Greek word meaning 'end' or 'purpose'.)

  Example: The wall switch is there so you can turn off the lamp from across the room.
  Example: These wildflowers are here as a blessing from God.

- Interpretive explanations concern the meaning of terms or states of affairs. These explanations seek to understand, not the purpose or cause of something, but rather its sense or semantic meaning.

  Example: When Mary smiled, she was signalling her agreement.
  Example: 'Effect' means to accomplish, but 'affect' means to influence.

- Procedural explanations try to explain how something is done or how an action is carried out.

  Example: To stop the chemical reaction, Ariana added sulphur.
  Example: He paid his taxes online by downloading the forms and then using his credit card number.

understanding by fitting our experiences and background knowledge into a coherent pattern. At every turn we are confronted with phenomena that we can only fully understand by explaining them.

Sometimes we're barely aware that we're using inference to the best explanation. If we awaken and see that the streets outside are wet, we may immediately posit this explanation: it's been raining. Without thinking much about it, we may also quickly consider whether a better explanation is that a street-sweeper machine has wet the street. Just as quickly we may dismiss this explanation because we see that the houses and cars are also wet. After reasoning in this fashion, we may decide to carry an umbrella that day.

Let's consider a more elaborate example. Say that you discover that your car won't start in the morning (the phenomenon to be explained). You would like to know why it won't start (the explanation for the failure) because you can't repair the car unless you know what the problem is. You know that there are several possible explanations or theories.

1. The battery is dead.
2. The fuel tank is empty.
3. The starter has malfunctioned.
4. A vandal has sabotaged the car.
5. All or several of the above.

So you try to figure out which theory is the most plausible, that is, most likely to be true. You see right away that there is snow around the car from yesterday's snowstorm—but there are no tracks (except yours) and no signs of tampering anywhere. So you dismiss theory 4. You remember that you filled up the gas tank yesterday, the fuel gauge says that the tank is full, and you don't see any signs of leakage. So you can safely ignore theory 2. You notice that the lights, heater, and radio work fine, and the battery gauge indicates a fully charged battery. So you discard theory 1. When you try to start the car, you hear a clicking sound like the one you heard when the starter had failed previously. Among the theories you started with, then,

> 'A superstition is a premature explanation that overstays its time.'
> —George Iles

Food For Thought

Darwin and the Best Explanation

Charles Darwin (1809–82) offered the theory of evolution by natural selection as the best explanation for a wide variety of natural phenomena. He catalogued an extensive list of facts about nature and showed that his theory explained them well. He argued, however, that the alternative theory of the day—the view that God independently created species—did not explain them. Darwin declared:

> It can hardly be supposed that a false theory would explain, in so satisfactory a manner as does the theory of natural selection, the several large classes of facts above specified. It has recently been objected that this is an unsafe method of arguing; but it is a method used in judging of the common events of life, and has often been used by the greatest natural philosophers.[1]

Charles Darwin (1809–1882). Photo: © Stapleton Collection/Corbis theory 3 now seems the most plausible. This means that theory 5 cannot be correct since it entails two or more of the theories.

If you wanted to, you could state your argument like this:

(1) Your car won't start in the morning.
(2) The theory that the starter has malfunctioned is the best explanation for the car's not starting in the morning.
(3) Therefore, it's probable that the malfunctioning starter caused the car not to start in the morning.

Food For Thought

Sherlock Holmes and Inference to the Best Explanation

The fictional character, Sherlock Holmes, owed his great success as a detective primarily to inference to the best explanation. He was so good at this kind of inference that people (especially Watson) were frequently astonished at his skill. Holmes, however, was guilty of spreading some confusion about his ability. He called his method deduction, though it was clearly inductive. Holmes in action:

Photo: Getty Images

I knew you came from Afghanistan. From long habit the train of thoughts ran so swiftly through my mind that I arrived at the conclusion without being conscious of intermediate steps. There were such steps, however. The train of reasoning ran, 'Here is a gentleman of medical type, but with the air of a military man. Clearly an army doctor, then. He has just come from the tropics, for his face is dark, and that is not the natural tint of his skin, for his wrists are fair. He has undergone hardship and sickness, as his haggard face says clearly. His left arm has been injured. He holds it in a stiff and unnatural manner. Where in the tropics would an English army doctor have seen much hardship and got his arm wounded? Clearly in Afghanistan.'[2]

Here Holmes explains how he knew that a man had 'gone about in fear of some personal attack within the last twelve-month':

'You have a very handsome stick,' I answered. 'By the inscription I observed that you had not had it more than a year. But you have taken some pains to bore the head of it and pour melted lead into the hole so as to make it a formidable weapon. I argued that you would not take such precautions unless you had some danger to fear.'[3]

In science, where inference to the best explanation is an essential tool, usually the theories of interest are causal theories, in which events are the things to be explained and the proposed causes of the events are the explanations. Just as we do in everyday life, scientists often consider several competing theories for the same event or phenomenon. Then—through scientific testing and careful thinking—they systematically eliminate inadequate theories and eventually arrive at the one that's rightly regarded as the best of the bunch. Using this form of inference, scientists discover planets, viruses, cures, subatomic particles, black holes—and many things that can't even be directly observed.

And then there are all those other professionals who rely on inference to the best explanation. Physicians use it to pinpoint the cause of multiple symptoms in patients. Police detectives use it to track down lawbreakers. Judges and juries use it to determine the guilt or innocence of accused persons. And philosophers use it to assess the worth of conceptual theories.

With so many people in so many areas of inquiry using inference to the best explanation, you would expect the world to be filled with countless theories proposed by innumerable people looking to explain all sorts of things. And so there are. Here's a very brief table of notable or interesting proposed theories and the phenomena they are meant to explain:

Theory	To Explain...
Atomic	Behaviour of subatomic particles
Germ	Spread of disease
HIV	Cause of AIDS
Oedipus complex	Behaviour of men and boys
Placebo effect	Apparent cure of disease
Bleak winters	Why Canadians are funny
Violent video games	Violence in children
El Niño	Bad weather
El Niño	Good weather
Incumbent politicians	A bad economy
Political sex scandals	Immoral behaviour of young people

Of course, it's often easy to make up theories to explain things we don't understand. The harder job is sorting out good theories from bad, and that's the topic of the next few pages.

Exercise 9.1

1. What is an explanation?
2. What is inference to the best explanation?
3. Is inference to the best explanation inductive or deductive?
* 4. What is a theoretical explanation?
5. What is the basic logical pattern of inference to the best explanation? For enumerative induction? For analogical induction?
6. Under what circumstances can an inference to the best explanation be deemed strong? Cogent?
7. What is a teleological explanation? Interpretive explanation? Procedural explanation
* 8. What is a causal explanation? Are causal explanations used in inference to the best explanation?
9. How does the kind of explanation used in inference to the best explanation differ from a teleological explanation or an interpretive explanation?
10. Have you used inference to the best explanation today? If so, how did you use it? (Supply an example from the events of your day.)

Exercise 9.2

For each of the following explanations, say what state of affairs is being explained and what the explanation is.

1. Most students love Professor Walton's class because she takes dull material and makes it interesting.
* 2. We all know that the spotted owl is endangered, and the only explanation for that is the political clout of the logging industry.
3. Why is Georgia wearing orange goggles? Because she's a bit eccentric, and she likes how they look.
4. Crimes committed by high-school students are increasing because school boards refuse to mandate harsh punishments for criminal acts.
* 5. I'll tell you why we're seeing so many hurricanes: gas-guzzling SUVs are causing global warming!
6. Binge drinking is on the rise at Canadian universities. This can best be explained by the permissive attitudes of the university presidents.
7. Americans are fond of the death penalty, but Europeans and Canadians are not. Americans just never got over the old Wild West eye-for-an-eye mentality. Europeans never had a Wild West.
* 8. I believe that psychics really can predict the future because many things that psychics have told me have come true.

9. Rock stars make more money than teachers because they are smarter than teachers.
10. Global terrorism is caused by worldwide injustice and deprivation.

Exercise 9.3

For each of the following, determine whether the type of explanation offered is theoretical (the kind used in inference to the best explanation) or non-theoretical (e.g., teleological, interpretive, procedural). Be careful to note any borderline cases (explanations that could be either theoretical or non-theoretical).

1. There is no peace in the Middle East—and there never will be—because of the stubbornness of both sides in the conflict.
2. 'Creation science' is controversial because mainstream scientists hate it.
* 3. Ethics is the critical study of morality.
4. John built himself a solar house so he could thumb his nose at the power company.
5. Jack is soaking wet because he stood in the rain.
6. When Jill raises her hand that means she's going to ask a question that no one can answer.
* 7. When you experience memory loss that can only mean one thing: Alzheimer's disease.
8. I wear this medallion for good luck.
9. He got that song by downloading it from a website onto his hard drive and then loading it from his hard drive onto his iPod.
10. Evil exists in the world because God allows it.
11. You are always sick because you don't take care of yourself.
* 12. That painting is without vibrancy or cohesion. Just look at the dull colours and mishmash of forms.
13. Jill bombed her courses because she liked to party too much.
14. Sam has been weight training, so he's pretty buff.
15. Jane is studying hard so she can get a better job.
16. No one noticed the comet before because of cloud cover.
17. He broke the lock and pushed open the door—that's how he got in.

Exercise 9.4

In each of the following examples, a state of affairs is described. Devise two theories to explain each one. Include one theory that you consider plausible and one theory that you think is not plausible.

1. Mutilated cows have been found in several pastures in Western Canada. In each case organs are missing from the carcasses. There are never any signs of vehicle tracks or footprints. The cause of death is unknown. The method used to remove the organs is also unknown, although the wounds show indications of precision surgical tools.

* 2. When Jack came home, he noticed the window in the kitchen was broken, there were muddy footprints on the kitchen on the floor, and some valuable silverware was missing.

3. Carl has vivid memories of his being in a past life. Sometimes he remembers himself being a stable boy; other times he recalls that he was a Roman soldier. All of these memories come to light only when Carl is under hypnosis.

4. In many Islamic countries women have fewer rights than men do.

5. During the 1980s, the demand for food assistance rose dramatically and a massive charitable food-assistance system emerged.

* 6. Alice has been taking vitamin C every day for a year, and during that time she has not had a cold or a sore throat.

7. Teenagers are now having sex at earlier ages.

8. Scientists have discovered that there is a direct correlation between fat in people's diets and heart disease. The more fat, the greater the risk of heart disease.

9. The incidence of violent crimes in Canada has decreased in recent years.

Exercise 9.5

Read each of the following passages and answer these questions:
1. What is the phenomenon being explained?
2. What theory is suggested as a possible explanation for the phenomenon?
3. Is the theory plausible? If not, why not?
4. Is there a plausible theory that the writer has overlooked? If so, what is it?

Passage 1

Many people believe that drinking a warm glass of milk at bedtime helps them fall asleep. The reason must be the tryptophan in the milk. Tryptophan is an essential amino acid that is converted into serotonin. Serotonin affects sleep patterns and the perception of pain.

Passage 2

'Shark attacks around the world declined in 2003 for a third straight year, partly because swimmers and surfers grew more accustomed to thinking of the ocean as a wild and dangerous place. . . .

'The University of Florida, which houses the International Shark Attack File, said there were 55 unprovoked attacks worldwide, down from 63 reported in 2002 and lower than the previous year's 68 attacks.

'Four people were killed, compared to three in 2002, four in 2001 and 11 in the year 2000.

'Normally, scientists do not put much stock in year-to-year fluctuations in the number of attacks because they can be affected by such things as the weather and oceanographic conditions that drive bait fish closer to shore.

'But the third consecutive year of decline could indicate a longer term trend, the university said.

'"I think people are beginning to get a little more intelligent about when and where they enter the water," George Burgess, director of the International Shark Attack File, said in a statement.

'"There seems to be more of an understanding that when we enter the sea, it's a wilderness experience and we're intruders in that environment."'[4]

Passage 3

'Women who have been coloring their hair for 24 years or more have a higher risk of developing a cancer called non-Hodgkin lymphoma, researchers reported.

'They said their study of 1,300 women could help explain a mysterious rise in the number of cases of the cancer that affects the lymphatic system.

'Writing in the *American Journal of Epidemiology*, they said women who dyed their hair starting before 1980 were one-third more likely to develop non-Hodgkin lymphoma, or NHL, and those who used the darkest dyes for more than 25 years were twice as likely to develop the cancer.

'"Women who used darker permanent hair coloring products for more than 25 years showed the highest increased risk," Tongzhang Zheng, associate professor of epidemiology and environmental health at Yale School of Medicine, said in a statement.

'Cancer experts note that a person's absolute risk of developing lymphoma is very low, so doubling that risk still means a woman who dyes her hair is very unlikely to develop lymphoma.'[5]

Passage 4

Spontaneous human combustion (SHC) is the theory that under certain rare circumstances, a human body mysteriously ignites, burns, and is almost entirely consumed. Investigators have encountered a few cases in which the burnt remains of a human body (usually only a limb or two) are found in an enclosed room, with nearby flammable objects completely unaffected by fire. The other parts of the body, including the torso, are entirely incinerated. There is usually, or always, a source of flame in the room—a lit pipe or candle, for example. And the victim is often elderly, alcoholic, or in some way incapacitated. SHC is the only reasonable explanation for these strange facts.

Theories and Consistency

Very often we may propose a theory as an explanation for a phenomenon, or we may have a theory thrust upon us for consideration. In either case, we will likely be dealing with an argument in the form of inference to the best explanation. The conclusion of the argument will always say, in effect, *this* theory is the best explanation of the facts. And we will be on the hot seat trying to decide if it really is. How do we do that?

The work is not always easy, but there are special criteria we can use to get the job done. Before we apply these criteria, though, we have to make sure that the theory in question meets the minimum requirement of *consistency*. A theory that does not meet this minimum requirement is worthless, so there is no need to use the special criteria to evaluate the theory. A theory that meets the requirement is eligible for further consideration. Here we are concerned with both *internal* and *external* consistency. A theory that is internally consistent is consistent with itself—it's free of contradictions. A theory that is externally consistent is consistent with the data it's supposed to explain—it fully accounts for the observable data.

If we show that a theory contains a contradiction, we have refuted it. A theory that implies that something both is and is not the case cannot possibly be true. By exposing an internal contradiction, Galileo once refuted Aristotle's famous theory of motion, a venerable hypothesis that had stood tall for centuries. He showed that the theory implied that one falling object falls both faster and slower than another one.

If a theory is externally inconsistent, we have reason to believe that it's false. Suppose you leave your car parked on the street overnight and the next morning discover that (1) the windshield has a large round hole in it, (2) there's blood on the steering wheel, and (3) there's a brick on the front seat. And let's say that your friend Charlie offers this theory to explain these facts: someone threw a brick through your windshield. What would you think about this theory?

You would probably think that Charlie had not been paying attention. His theory is consistent with the fact that the windshield is broken, and it would explain why there's a brick on the seat. And it's not inconsistent with the observation of

> 'In making theories, keep a window open so that you can throw one out if necessary.'
> —Bela Schick

Review Notes

Minimum Requirement: Consistency
- *Internal consistency:* A theory that is internally consistent is free of contradictions.
- *External consistency:* A theory that is externally consistent is consistent with the data it's supposed to explain.

blood, though it doesn't explain it, either. But most important, Charlie's theory (that someone threw a brick—a sharp-edged, rectangular object—through your windshield) is inconsistent with the fact that the hole in the windshield is round. Charlie's theory is a good try, but it doesn't work. It's externally inconsistent. Keep looking for a better answer!

Theories and Criteria

For a moment let's return to our example of the car that won't start. Recall that we examined five possible explanations for the non-start phenomenon:

1. The battery is dead.
2. The fuel tank is empty.
3. The starter has malfunctioned.
4. A vandal has sabotaged the car.
5. All or several of the above.

But what if someone suggested that our analysis of this problem was incomplete because we failed to consider several other possible theories that are at least as plausible as these five? Consider these, for example:

6. Each night, you are sabotaging your own car while you sleepwalk.
7. Your 90-year-old uncle, who lives a 1,000 kilometres away from you, has secretly been going for joyrides in your car, thus damaging the engine.
8. A poltergeist (a noisy, mischievous ghost) has damaged the car's carburetor.
9. Yesterday, you scrambled the electrical system by accidentally driving the car through an alternative space-time dimension.

What do you think of these theories? More specifically, are the last four theories *really* at least as plausible as the first five? If you think so, *why*? If you think not, *why not*? Remember that the strangeness of a theory is no good reason to discount it. It will not do to say that theories 6 to 9 are too weird to be true. In the history of science plenty of bizarre theories have turned out to be correct. (Quantum theory in physics, for example, is about as weird as you can get.) Earlier we concluded that theory 3 was better (more likely to be true) than 1, 2, 4, and 5. But what criteria did we use to arrive at this judgment? And on the basis of what criteria can we say that theory 3 is any better than theories 6 to 9? There must be *some* criteria because it is implausible that every theory is equally correct. Surely there is a difference in quality between a theory that explains rainfall by positing some natural meteorological forces and one that alleges that Donald Duck causes weather phenomena.

A simplified answer to the problem of theory choice is this. Just weigh the evidence for each theory, and the theory with the most evidence wins. As we will soon see, the amount or degree of evidence that a theory has is indeed a crucial factor—but it cannot be the sole criterion by which we assess explanations.

Throughout the history of science, major theories—from the heliocentric theory of the solar system to Einstein's General Theory of Relativity—have never been established by empirical evidence alone.

The task of determining the best explanation has another complication. If we accept such extraordinary theories as 6 to 9 as legitimate possibilities, there must be no end to the number of theories that we could devise to explain the data at hand. In fact, we could come up with an infinite number of possible theories for any phenomenon simply by repeatedly adding one more element. For example, we could propose the one-poltergeist theory (a single entity causing the trouble), a two-poltergeist theory, a three-poltergeist theory, and so on.

Fortunately, despite these complications, there are reasonable criteria and reliable procedures for judging the merits of eligible theories and for arriving at a defensible judgment of which theory is best. The **criteria of adequacy** are the essential tools of science and have been used by scientists throughout history to uncover the best explanations for all sorts of events and states of affairs. Science, though, doesn't own these criteria. They are as useful—and as used—among non-scientists as they are among men and women of science.

An alternative explanation of all our perceptions is that everything we experience is simply computer-generated inputs, as depicted in the film *The Matrix*. Photo: Warner Bros / The Kobal Collection

Applying the criteria of adequacy to a set of theories constitutes the ultimate test of a theory's value, for *the best theory is the eligible theory that meets the criteria of adequacy better than any of its competitors*. Here, 'eligible' means that the theory has already met the minimum requirement for consistency.

All of this implies that the evaluation of a particular theory is not complete until alternative, or competing, theories are considered. As we've seen, there is an indefinite number of theories that could be offered to explain a given set of data. The main challenge is to give a fair assessment of the relevant theories in relation to each other. To fail to somehow address the alternatives is to overlook or deny relevant evidence, to risk biased conclusions, and to court error. Such failure is probably the most common error in the appraisal of theories.

A theory judged by these criteria to be the best explanation for certain facts is worthy of our belief, and we may legitimately claim to know that such a theory is true. But the theory is not then necessarily or certainly true in the way that the conclusion of a sound deductive argument is necessarily or certainly true. Inference to the best explanation, like other forms of induction, cannot guarantee the truth of the best explanation. That is, it is not truth-preserving. The best theory we have may actually be false. Nevertheless we would have excellent reasons for supposing our best theory to be a true theory.

The criteria of adequacy are *testability, fruitfulness, scope, simplicity,* and *conservatism*. Let's examine each one in detail.

Food For Thought

Inference to the Best Explanation and the External World

In Chapters 10 and 11 we will explore in detail how inference to the best explanation can be used to tackle some big issues. Here we just want to mention one of the 'big questions' to which philosophers and other thinkers have applied inference to the best explanation.

A problem that has historically occupied thinkers in the history of philosophy is whether we have any good reasons to believe that there is a world outside our own thoughts. That is, is there an *external world* independent of the way we represent it to ourselves? Some people, called skeptics, have denied that we have any such good reasons because we can never get 'outside our skins' to objectively compare our subjective experiences with reality. All we know is the nature of our perceptions—which may or may not be linked to the 'real world' in any way.

To this puzzle many philosophers have applied inference to the best explanation. They argue that we can indeed know that there is an external reality because that belief is the best explanation of the peculiar pattern of our perceptions. In other words, the best explanation of why we seem to see a tree in front of us is that there *really is a real tree in front of us*.

Testability

Most of the theories that we encounter every day and all the theories that scientists take seriously are **testable**—*there is some way to determine whether the theories are true or false*. If a theory is untestable—if there is no possible procedure for checking its truth—then it is worthless as an explanatory theory. Suppose someone says that an invisible, undetectable spirit is causing your headaches. What possible test could we perform to tell if the spirit actually exists? None. So the spirit theory is entirely empty. We can assign no weight to such a claim.

Here's another way to look at it. Theories are explanations, and explanations are designed to increase our understanding of the world. But an untestable theory does not—and cannot—explain anything. It is equivalent to saying that an unknown thing with unknown properties acts in an unknown way to cause a phenomenon—which is the same thing as offering no explanation at all.

We often run into untestable theories in daily life, just as scientists sometimes encounter them in their work. Many practitioners of alternative medicine claim that health problems are caused by an imbalance in people's *chi*, an unmeasurable form of mystical energy that is said to flow through everyone. Some people say that their misfortunes are caused by God or the Devil. Others believe that certain

Review Notes

Criteria of Adequacy
- *Testability:* Whether there is some way to determine if a theory is true.
- *Fruitfulness:* The number of novel predictions made.
- *Scope:* The amount of diverse phenomena explained.
- *Simplicity:* The number of assumptions made.
- *Conservatism:* How well a theory fits with existing knowledge.

events in their lives happen (and are inevitable) because of fate. And parents may hear their young daughter say that she did not break the lamp, but her invisible friend did.

Many theories throughout history have been untestable. Some of the more influential untestable theories are the theory of witches (some people called witches are controlled by the Devil), the moral fault theory of disease (immoral behaviour causes illness), and the divine-placement theory of fossils (God created geological fossils to give the false impression of an ancient Earth).

But what does it mean that a theory is testable or untestable? A theory is testable *if it predicts something other than what it was introduced to explain.* Suppose your electric clock stops each time you touch it. One theory to explain this event is that there is an electrical short in the clock's wiring. Another theory is that an invisible, undetectable demon causes the clock to stop. The wiring theory predicts that if the wiring is repaired, the clock will no longer shut off when touched. So it is testable—there is something that the theory predicts other than the obvious fact that the clock will stop when you touch it. But the demon theory makes no predictions about anything, *except* the obvious, the very fact that the theory was introduced to explain. It predicts that the clock will stop if you touch it, but we already know this. So our understanding is not increased, and the demon theory is untestable.

Now, if the demon theory says that the demon can be detected with x-rays, then there is something the theory predicts other than the clock's stopping when touched. You can x-ray the clock and examine the film for demon silhouettes. If the theory says the demon can't be seen but can be heard with sensitive sound equipment, then you have a prediction, something to look for other than clock stoppage.

So other things being equal, testable theories are superior to untestable ones; they may be able to increase our understanding of a phenomenon. But an untestable theory is just an oddity.

'The weakness of the man who, when his theory works out into a flagrant contradiction of the facts, concludes "So much the worse for the facts: let them be altered," instead of "So much the worse for my theory."'
—George Bernard Shaw

Fruitfulness

Imagine that we have two testable theories, theory 1 and theory 2, that attempt to explain the same phenomenon. Theory 1 and theory 2 seem comparable in most respects when measured against the criteria of adequacy. Theory 1, however, successfully predicts the existence of a previously unknown entity, say, a star in an uncharted part of the sky. What would you conclude about the relative worth of these two theories?

If you thought carefully about the issue, you would probably conclude that theory 1 is the better theory—and you would be right. Other things being equal, theories that perform this way—that successfully predict previously unknown phenomena—are more credible than those that don't. They are said to be **fruitful**, to yield new insights that can open up whole new areas of research and discovery. This fruitfulness suggests that the theories are more likely to be true.

Food For Thought

The Importance (and Fun) of Crazy Theories

Many theories proposed throughout the history of science have been, well, crazy. That is, they have been unorthodox or heretical, with a shockingly different take on the world. The heliocentric theory of our solar system is a prime example. Some of these crazy theories have turned out to be good theories—they measured up to the criteria of adequacy very well. So a crazy theory is not necessarily a bad theory. Science as a whole has always been open to offbeat explanations, but they had to be judged to have merit. Most crazy theories in science or on the fringes of science, though, usually fail the criteria of adequacy miserably. The challenge for scientists and other critical thinkers is to remain open to unorthodox theories but not be afraid to test them through critical reasoning. Besides, offbeat theories are fun. These following theories were gleaned from the Web.

Trepanation: formerly for the release of evil spirits and later for the achievement of enlightenment. Erich Lessing/Art Resource, NY

- 'It is my belief that Mars was once a beautiful, fertile planet capable of sustaining life, much like our own, until some cataclysmic, global event changed everything. I believe that the survivors went searching for another planet, on which to live, and that they chose the Earth. We are their descendants. They were an advanced civilization who brought their technology with them. Upon reaching Earth, they proceeded to build the same type of structures that were familiar to them on Mars. That way, if there were more survivors they'd recognize the structures and know where the others were.'

- 'Trepanation is the practice of making a hole in the skull. It is sometimes spelled trephination. . . . Trepanation was practised on every continent through every time period and by every race of mankind until the advent of brain surgery in this century. Doctors today have been taught that trepanation was done in past centuries for superstitious, magical, or religious reasons. They generally look on trepanation as a practice akin to blood letting. They scoff at it. . . . The risk-to-benefit ratio would have to have been very favourable for the practice to have been so widely practised, but official investigators haven't been able to see that there is both a rationale and a benefit to this procedure.'
- 'Have you ever dreamed of travelling in time? Now you can experience what you have only dreamed of. With the Hyper Dimensional Resonator you can travel into the past or explore the future. The world will be at your beck and call and you will have all the time in the world to explore it. . . . I sell an instrument which can be used for both out of the body time travel and can also be used to help heal the sick.'

If a friend of yours is walking through a forest where she has never been before, yet she seems to be able to predict exactly what's up ahead, you would probably conclude that she possessed some kind of accurate information about the forest, such as a map. Likewise, if a theory successfully predicts some surprising state of affairs, you are likely to think that the predictions are not just lucky guesses.

All empirical theories are testable (they predict something beyond the thing to be explained). But fruitful theories are testable and then some. They not only predict something, but they also predict something that no one expected. The element of surprise is hard to ignore.

Decades ago Einstein's theory of relativity gained a great deal of credibility by successfully predicting a phenomenon that was extraordinary and entirely novel. The theory predicts that light travelling close to massive objects (such as stars) will appear to be bent because the space around such objects is curved. The curve in space causes a curve in nearby light rays. At the time, however, the prevailing opinion was that light always travels in straight lines—no bends, no curves, no breaks. In 1919 the physicist Sir Arthur Eddington devised a way to test this prediction. He managed to take two sets of photographs of exactly the same portion of the sky—when the sun was overhead (in daylight) and when it was not (at night). He was able to get a good photo of the sky during daylight because there was a total eclipse of the sun at the time. If light rays really were bent when they passed near massive objects, then stars whose light passes near the sun should appear to be shifted slightly from their true position (as seen at night). Eddington discovered that stars near the sun did appear to have moved and that the amount of their apparent movement was just what the theory predicted. This novel prediction then demonstrated the fruitfulness of Einstein's theory, provided a degree of confirmation for the theory, and opened up new areas of research.

So the moral is that other things being equal, fruitful theories are superior to those that aren't fruitful. Certainly many good theories make no novel predictions but are accepted nonetheless. The reason is usually that they excel in other criteria of adequacy.

Scope

Suppose theory 1 and theory 2 are two equally plausible theories to explain phenomenon X. Theory 1 can explain X well, and so can theory 2. But theory 1 can explain or predict *only* X, whereas theory 2 can explain or predict X—as well as phenomena Y and Z. Which is the better theory?

We must conclude that theory 2 is better because it explains more diverse phenomena. That is, it has more **scope** than the other theory. The more a theory explains or predicts, the more it extends our understanding. And the more a theory explains or predicts, the less likely it is to be false because it has more evidence in its favour.

A major strength of Newton's theory of gravity and motion, for example, was that it explained more than any previous theory. Then came Einstein's theory of relativity. It could explain everything that Newton's theory could explain plus many phenomena that Newton's theory could not explain. This increased scope of Einstein's theory helped convince scientists that it was the better theory.

Here's a more down-to-earth example. For decades psychologists have known about a phenomenon called *constructive perception* (discussed in Chapter 4). In constructive perception, what we perceive (see, hear, feel, etc.) is determined in part by what we expect, know, or believe. Studies have shown that when people expect to perceive a certain stimulus (say, a flashing light, a certain colour or shape, or a shadow), they often *do* perceive it, even if there is no stimulus present. The phenomenon of constructive perception then can be used to explain many instances in which people seem to perceive something when it is not really there or when it is actually very different from the way people think it is.

One kind of case that investigators sometimes explain as an instance of constructive perception is the UFO sighting. Many times people report seeing lights in the night sky that look to them like alien spacecraft, and they explain their perception by saying that the lights were caused by alien spacecraft. So we have two theories to explain the experience: constructive perception and UFOs from space. If these two theories differ only in the degree of scope provided by each one, however, we must conclude that the constructive-perception theory is better. (In reality, theories about incredible events usually differ on several criteria.) The constructive-perception theory can explain not only UFO sightings but also all kinds of ordinary and extraordinary experiences—hallucinations, feelings of an unknown 'presence', mis-identification of crime suspects, contradictory reports in car accidents, and more. The UFO theory, however, is (usually) designed to explain just one thing: an experience of seeing strange lights in the sky.

Scope is often a crucial factor in a jury's evaluation of theories put forth by both the prosecution and the defence. The prosecution will have a very powerful case against the defendant if the prosecutor's theory (that the defendant did it) explains all the evidence and many other things while the defence theory (innocence) does not. The defendant will be in big trouble if the prosecutor's theory explains the blood on the defendant's shirt, the eyewitness accounts, the defendant's fingerprints on the wall, and the sudden change in his usual routine—*and* if the innocence theory renders these facts downright mysterious.

Other things being equal, then, the best theory is the one with the greatest scope. And if other things aren't equal, a theory with superior scope doesn't necessarily win the day because it may do poorly on the other criteria or another theory might do better.

Simplicity

Let's return one last time to the scenario about the non-starting car. Recall that the last four theories are:

6. Each night, you are sabotaging your own car while you sleepwalk.
7. Your 90-year-old uncle, who lives a 1,000 kilometres away from you, has been damaging the engine by secretly been going for joyrides in your car.
8. A poltergeist (a noisy, mischievous ghost) has damaged the car's carburetor.
9. Yesterday, you accidentally drove the car through an alternative space-time dimension, scrambling the electrical system.

By now you probably suspect that these explanations are somehow unacceptable, and so they are. One important characteristic that they each lack is **simplicity**. Other things being equal, the best theory is the one that is the simplest—that is, the one that makes the fewest assumptions. The theory making the fewest assumptions is less likely to be false because there are fewer ways for it to go wrong. Another way to look at it is that since a simpler theory is based on fewer assumptions, less evidence is required to support it.

'I cannot help fearing that men may reach a point where they look on every new theory as a danger, every innovation as a toilsome trouble, every social advance as a first step toward revolution, and that they may absolutely refuse to move at all for fear of being carried off their feet.'
—Alexis de Tocqueville

Food For Thought

There's No Theory Like a Conspiracy Theory

Conspiracy theories try to explain events by positing the secret participation of numerous conspirators. The assassination of President John F. Kennedy, the terrorist attacks of 9/11, the Watergate scandal, the AIDS crisis—all these and more have been the subject of countless conspiracy theories, both elaborate and provocative. Some conspiracy theories, of course, have been found to be true after all. But most of them are implausible. The main problem with them is that they usually fail to meet the criterion of simplicity. They would have us make numerous assumptions that raise more questions than they answer. How do the conspirators manage to keep their activities secret? How do they control all the players? Where is the evidence that all the parts of the conspiracy have come together just so?

Nonetheless, many conspiracy theories remain quite popular, perhaps because they engage our imaginations. Here's a short list of things that, we are told, are the centre of a massive conspiracy:

- The death of Elvis Presley
- The assassination of Martin Luther King Jr
- The Oklahoma City bombing
- The death of Princess Diana
- The terrorist attacks of 9/11
- The death of former Enron CEO, Ken Lay

And here are a few of the alleged cabals that are doing all the dirty deeds:

- The US government
- The Vatican
- The CIA
- The Illuminati, a secret society controlling the government
- Doctors
- The Freemasons
- The pharmaceutical industry

Explanations 8 and 9 lack simplicity because they each must assume the existence of an unknown entity (poltergeists and another dimension that scrambles electrical circuits). Such assumptions about the existence of unknown objects, forces, and dimensions are common in occult or paranormal theories. Explanations 6 and 7 assume no new entities, but they do assume complex chains of events. This alone makes them less plausible than the simple explanation of 3, the starter malfunction.

The criterion of simplicity has often been a major factor in the acceptance or rejection of important theories. For example, simplicity is an important advantage that the theory of evolution has over creationism, the theory that the world was created at once by a divine being (see Chapter 10). Creationism must assume the existence of a creator and the existence of unknown forces (supernatural forces used by the creator). But evolution does not make either of these assumptions.

Scientists eventually accepted Copernicus's theory of planetary motion (helio-centric orbits) over Ptolemy's (Earth-centred orbits) because the former was simpler (see Chapter 10). In order to account for apparent irregularities in the movement of certain planets, Ptolemy's theory had to assume that planets have extremely complex orbits (orbits within orbits). Copernicus's theory, however, had no need for so much extra baggage. His theory could account for the observational data without so many orbits within orbits.

Sometimes a theory's lack of simplicity is the result of constructing ad hoc hypotheses. An **ad hoc hypothesis** is one that cannot be verified independently of the phenomenon it's supposed to explain. If a theory is in trouble because it is not matching up with the observational data of the phenomenon, you might be able to rescue it by altering it—by positing additional entities or properties that can account for the data. Such tinkering is legitimate (scientists do it all the time) if there is an independent way of confirming the existence of these proposed entities and properties. But if there is no way to verify their existence, the modifications are ad hoc hypotheses. Ad hoc hypotheses always make a theory less simple—and therefore less credible.

Conservatism

What if a trusted friend told you that—believe it or not—some dogs lay eggs just as chickens do? Let's assume that your friend is being perfectly serious and believes what she is saying. Would you accept this claim about egg-laying dogs? Not likely. But why not?

Probably your main reason for rejecting such an extraordinary claim would be that it fails the criterion of **conservatism**, though you probably wouldn't state it that way. (Note: This sense of 'conservatism' has nothing to do with politics!) This criterion says that other things being equal, *the best theory is the one that fits best with our established beliefs*. We would reject the canine-egg theory because, among other things, it conflicts with our well-founded beliefs about mammals, evolution, canine anatomy, and much more. Humans have an enormous amount of experience with dogs (scientific and otherwise), and none of it suggests that dogs can lay eggs. In fact, a great deal of what we know about dogs suggests that they *cannot* lay eggs. To accept the canine-egg theory despite its conflict with a mountain of solid evidence would be irrational—and destructive of whatever understanding we had on the subject.

Perhaps one day we may be shocked to learn that, contrary to all expectations,—dogs do lay eggs. But given that this belief is contrary to a massive amount of credible experience, we must assign a very low probability to it.

We are naturally reluctant to accept explanations that conflict with what we already know, and we should be. Accepting beliefs that fly in the face of our knowledge has several risks:

1. The chances of the new belief being true are not good (because it has no evidence in its favour, while our well-established beliefs have plenty of evidence on their side).
2. The conflict of beliefs undermines our knowledge (because we cannot know something that is in doubt, and the conflict would be cause for doubt).
3. The conflict of beliefs lessens our understanding (because the new beliefs cannot be plausibly integrated into our other beliefs).

So everything considered, the more conservative a theory is, the more plausible it is.[6]

Here's another example. Let's say that someone claims to have built a perpetual motion machine. A perpetual motion machine is supposed to function without ever stopping and without requiring any energy input from outside the machine; it is designed to continuously supply its own energy.

Now, this is an intriguing idea—which we shouldn't take too seriously. The problem is that the notion of a perpetual motion machine is not conservative at all. It conflicts with a very well-established belief, namely, one of the scientific laws of thermodynamics. The law of conservation of mass-energy says that mass-energy cannot be created or destroyed. A perpetual motion machine, though, would have to create energy out of nothing. Like any law of nature, however, the law of conservation of mass-energy is supported by a vast amount of empirical evidence. We must conclude, then, that it is extremely unlikely that anyone could escape the law of conservation of mass-energy through the use of any machine. (This fact, however, has not stopped countless optimistic inventers from claiming that they've invented such devices. When the devices are put to the test, they invariably fail to perform as advertised.)

It's possible, of course, that a new theory that conflicts with what we know could turn out to be right and a more conservative theory wrong. But we would need good reasons to show that the new theory was correct before we would be justified in tossing out the old theory and bringing in the new.

Science looks for conservative theories, but it still sometimes embraces theories that are departures (sometimes *radical* departures) from the well-worn, accepted explanations. When this dramatic change happens, it's frequently because other criteria of adequacy outweigh conservatism. We'll explore the creation and evaluation of scientific theories in the next chapter.

Food For Thought

Was the Moon Landing a Hoax?

A stunning conspiracy theory says yes. NASA faked the whole thing, you see. Here's NASA's side of the story:

Photo: NASA

> All the buzz about the Moon began on February 15th when Fox television aired a program called Conspiracy Theory: Did We Land on the Moon? Guests on the show argued that NASA technology in the 1960s wasn't up to the task of a real Moon landing. Instead, anxious to win the Space Race any way it could, NASA acted out the Apollo program in movie studios. Neil Armstrong's historic first steps on another world, the rollicking Moon Buggy rides, even Al Shepard's arcing golf shot over Fra Mauro—it was all a fake! ...

According to the show NASA was a blundering movie producer thirty years ago. For example, Conspiracy Theory pundits pointed out a seeming discrepancy in Apollo imagery: Pictures of astronauts transmitted from the Moon don't include stars in the dark lunar sky—an obvious production error! What happened? Did NASA film-makers forget to turn on the constellations?

Most photographers already know the answer: It's difficult to capture something very bright and something else very dim on the same piece of film—typical emulsions don't have enough 'dynamic range'. Astronauts striding across the bright lunar soil in their sun-lit spacesuits were literally dazzling. Setting a camera with the proper exposure for a glaring spacesuit would naturally render background stars too faint to see.

Here's another one: Pictures of Apollo astronauts erecting a US flag on the Moon show the flag bending and rippling. How can that be? After all, there's no breeze on the Moon....

Not every waving flag needs a breeze—at least not in space. When astronauts were planting the flagpole they rotated it back and forth to better penetrate the lunar soil (anyone who's set a blunt tent-post will know how this works). So of course the flag waved! Unfurling a piece of rolled-up cloth with stored angular momentum will naturally result in waves and ripples—no breeze required! ...

The best rebuttal to allegations of a 'Moon Hoax', however, is common sense. Evidence that the Apollo program really happened is compelling: A dozen astronauts (laden with cameras) walked on the Moon between 1969 and 1972. Nine of them are still alive and can testify to their experience. They didn't return from the Moon empty-handed, either. Just as Columbus carried a few hundred natives back to Spain as evidence of his trip to the New World, Apollo astronauts brought 841 pounds of Moon rock home to Earth.

'Moon rocks are absolutely unique,' says Dr David McKay, Chief Scientist for Planetary Science and Exploration at NASA's Johnson Space Center (JSC). McKay is a member of the group that oversees the Lunar Sample Laboratory Facility at JSC where most of the Moon rocks are stored. 'They differ from Earth rocks in many respects,' he added.

'For example,' explains Dr Marc Norman, a lunar geologist at the University of Tasmania, 'lunar samples have almost no water trapped in their crystal structure, and common substances such as clay minerals that are ubiquitous on Earth are totally absent in Moon rocks.'

'We've found particles of fresh glass in Moon rocks that were produced by explosive volcanic activity and by meteorite impacts over 3 billion years ago,' added Norman. 'The presence of water on Earth rapidly breaks down such volcanic glass in only a few million years. These rocks must have come from the Moon!'[7]

Occult or paranormal theories often run afoul of the criterion of conservatism. Take *dowsing*, for instance. Dowsing is the practice of detecting underground water by using a Y-shaped stick (known as a divining rod or dowsing rod), a pendulum, or another device. It's a folk tradition that's hundreds of years old. Dowsers claim to be able to detect the presence of underground water by walking over a given terrain and holding the two branches of the dowsing rod (one in each hand) with its point facing skyward away from the body. (This claim, as it turns out, is unsupported.) When the point of the rod dips toward the ground, that's supposed to indicate that water is beneath the dowser. It seems to the dowser (and sometimes to observers) that the rod moves on its own, as though under the influence of some hidden force.

One theory to account for the rod's movements is that an unknown form of radiation emanating from the underground water pulls on the diving rod, causing it to move. (A well-supported alternative theory is that the movement of the divining rod in the dowser's hands is caused by suggestion and unconscious muscular activity in the dowser.) As it stands, the radiation theory is not testable, fruitful, or simple. But its major failing is its lack of conservatism. The claim about the strange, occult radiation conflicts with what scientists know about energy, radiation, and human sensory systems. It is possible that the dowser's radiation exists, but there is no reason to believe that it does and good reason to doubt it.

We will look at many more examples shortly, but before we go any further, you need to fully understand two crucial points about the nature of theory appraisal.

First, there is no strict formula or protocol for applying the criteria of adequacy. In deductive arguments there are rules of inference that are precise and invariable. But inference to the best explanation is a different animal. There are no precise rules for applying the criteria, no way to quantify how a theory measures up according to each criterion, and no way to rank each criterion according to its importance. Sometimes we may assign more weight to the criterion of scope if the theory in question seems similar to other theories on the basis of all the remaining criteria. Other times we may weight simplicity more when considering theories that seem equally conservative or fruitful. The process of theory evaluation is not like solving a math problem—but more like diagnosing an illness or making a judicial decision. It is rational but not formulaic, and it depends on the dynamics of human judgment. The best we can do is follow some guidelines for evaluating theories generally and for applying the criteria of adequacy. Fortunately, this kind of help is usually all we need. (You'll get this kind of guidance in the following pages.)

Second, despite the lack of formula in theory assessment, the process is far from subjective or arbitrary. There are many judgments that we successfully make every day that are not quantifiable or formulaic—but they are still objective. We can agree, for example, on many key features that go into making a car a good one: various safety features, fuel-efficiency, cargo space, and so on. We cannot say exactly how to rank those features, but that doesn't stop us from arriving at sound judgments; leaving aside questions of price, a BMW 520i is a better car than a Ford Fiesta. Of course, there are cases that are not so clear-cut that give rise to reasonable disagreement among reasonable people—various luxury sedans may be very similar in quality, with only minor differences. But there are also many instances that are manifestly unambiguous. Pretending that these questions of quality are unclear would be irrational. It would simply be incorrect to believe that a Toyota Yaris is 'just as good' a car as an S-Class Mercedes. The same goes for evaluating theories. The criteria that apply are well understood. The fact that there's no formula for applying those criteria does nothing to prevent us from applying them in a sensible manner to tell good theories from bad ones.

Exercise 9.6

1. When you are trying to decide between two theories, can you just rely on evidence alone to determine which theory is better?
* 2. In theory evaluation, what is the minimum requirement of consistency?
3. According to the text, what is a 'best theory'?
4. According to the text, what are the criteria of adequacy?

5. What does it mean for a theory to be testable? Fruitful? Conservative?
* 6. What does it mean to say that a theory does not have much scope?
7. According to the text, are theories that posit paranormal entities simple? If not, why not?
8. What are the risks involved in accepting a non-conservative theory?

Exercise 9.7

Following are several pairs of theories used to explain various phenomena. For each pair, determine (1) which theory is simpler and (2) which one is more conservative.

1. Phenomenon: A sudden remission of cancer in a patient. Theories: Part of the natural cycle of the disease; the result of taking an elixir with 'healing properties' unknown to science.
* 2. Phenomenon: The survival of a group of sailors whose ship sank at sea. Theories: Quick action by a group of magic dolphins; quick action by the Coast Guard rescue team.
3. Phenomenon: The winning of an election by a relatively unknown candidate. Theories: A last-minute blitz of TV ads; the candidate's endorsement by a famous convicted murderer.
* 4. Phenomenon: A 'precognitive' dream (having one's dream come true).Theories: Coincidence; psychic energy emanating from the dreamer.
5. Phenomenon: The sudden friendliness of the Canadian government towards the conservative American government. Theories: The election of a Conservative government in Canada; change in attitude among Canadians regarding their neighbours to the south.
6. Phenomenon: The bizarre and dangerous behaviour of your best friend. Theories: An allergy attack; the result of taking LSD; possession by demons.
* 7. Phenomenon: A hurricane hitting Nova Scotia. Theories: El Niño; radiation from outer space.
8. Phenomenon: A huge drop in the incidence of childhood disease over the last 50 years. Theories: Mandatory immunization; lower levels of air pollution.

Telling Good Theories from Bad

Many (perhaps most) explanatory theories that you run into every day are easy to assess. They are clearly the best (or not the best) explanations for the facts at hand. The dog barked because someone was approaching the house. Your friend blushed because he was embarrassed. The cabinet minister resigned because of a scandal. In such cases, you may make inferences to the best explanation (using some or all of the criteria of adequacy) without any deep reflection. But at other times, you may need and want to be more deliberate, to think more carefully about which explanation is really best. In either case, it helps to have a set of guidelines that tells you how your inquiry *should* proceed if you're to make cogent inferences. Here, then, is the **TEST formula**, four steps to finding the best explanation:

Step 1. State the **T**heory and check for consistency.
Step 2. Assess the **E**vidence for the theory.
Step 3. **S**crutinize alternative theories.
Step 4. **T**est the theories with the criteria of adequacy.

(In the next chapter, you will see that this formula is also one way of describing the general approach used in science to evaluate sets of theories.)

Step 1. State the theory and check for consistency. Before you can evaluate an explanatory theory, you must express it in a statement that's as clear and specific as possible. Once you do this, you can check to see if the theory meets the minimum requirement for consistency. If it fails the consistency test, you can have no good grounds for believing that it's correct. And, obviously, if the theory fails step 1, there's no reason to go to step 2.

Step 2. Assess the evidence for the theory. To evaluate any theory critically, you must understand any reasons in its favour—the empirical evidence or logical arguments that may support or undermine it. Essentially, this step involves an honest assessment of the empirical evidence relevant to the truth (or falsity) of the theory. To make this assessment, you must put to use what you already know about the credibility of sources, causal reasoning, and evidence from personal and scientific observations (topics covered in Chapters 4 and 8).

In this step, you may discover that the evidence in favour of a theory is strong, weak, or non-existent. You may find that there is good evidence that seems to count against the theory. Or you may learn that the phenomenon under investigation did not occur at all. Whatever the case, you must have the courage to face up to reality. You must be ready to admit that your favourite theory has little to recommend it.

Step 3. Scrutinize alternative theories. Inference to the best explanation will not help us very much if we aren't willing to consider alternative explanations. Simply examining the evidence relevant to an eligible theory is not enough.

Theories can often appear stronger than they really are if we don't bother to compare them with others. To take an outrageous example, consider this theory designed to explain the popularity and seeming omnipresence of an American icon. Mickey Mouse is not an animated character but a living, breathing creature that lives in Hollywood. The evidence for this explanation is the following: (1) Millions of people (mostly children) worldwide believe that Mickey is real; (2) Walt Disney (Mickey's alleged creator) always talked about Mickey as if the mouse were real; (3) millions of ads, books, movies, and TV shows portray Mickey as real; (4)

it's possible that through millions of years of Earth history a biological creature with Mickey's physical characteristics could have evolved; and (5) some say that if enough people believe that Mickey is real, then—through psychic wish fulfillment or some other paranormal process—he will become real.

Now, you don't believe that Mickey is real (do you?), even in the face of reasons 1–5. But you might admit that the Mickey theory is starting to sound more plausible. And if you never hear any alternative explanations, you might eventually become a true believer. (Anthropologists can plausibly argue that various cultures have come to believe in many very unlikely phenomena and exotic deities in large part because of *a lack of alternative explanations.*)

When you do consider an alternative explanation—for example, that Mickey is an imaginary character of brilliant animation marketed relentlessly to the world—the Mickey-is-real theory looks a little silly. And once you consider the evidence for this alternative theory (for example, documentation that Walt Disney created Mickey with pen and ink and that countless marketing campaigns have been launched to promote his creation), the other explanation looks even sillier.

Step 3 requires us to have an open mind, to think outside the box, to ask if there are other ways to explain the phenomenon in question and to consider the evidence for those theories. Specifically, in this step we must conscientiously look for competing theories, *then apply both step 1 and step 2 to each one of them.* This process may leave us with many or few eligible theories to examine. In any case, it's sure to tell us something important about the strength or weakness of competing theories.

Many times the criteria of adequacy can help us do a preliminary assessment of a theory's plausibility without our surveying alternative theories. For example, a theory may do so poorly regarding a particular criterion that we can conclude that, whatever the merits of alternative explanations, the theory at hand is not very credible. Such a clear lack of credibility is often apparent when a theory is obviously neither simple nor conservative.

Skipping step 3 is an extremely common error in the evaluation of explanations of all kinds. It is a supreme example of many types of errors discussed in earlier chapters—overlooking evidence, preferring available evidence, looking only for confirming evidence, and denying the evidence.

Step 3 goes against our grain. The human tendency is to grab hold of a favourite theory—and to halt any further critical thinking right there. Our built-in bias is to seize on a theory immediately—because we find it comforting or because we just 'know' it's the right one—then ignore or resist all other possibilities. The result is a greatly increased likelihood of error and delusion and a significantly decreased opportunity to achieve true understanding.

Failure to consider alternative theories is the archetypal mistake in inquiries into the paranormal or supernatural (a topic we discuss in Chapter 10). The usual pattern is this: (1) you come across an extraordinary or impressive phenomenon, (2) you can't think of a natural explanation of the facts, and (3) you conclude that the phenomenon must not be natural but paranormal or supernatural. This conclusion, however, would be unwarranted. Just because you can't think of a natural explanation doesn't mean that there isn't one. You may simply be unaware of the correct natural explanation. In the past, scientists have often been confronted with extraordinary phenomena that they couldn't explain—phenomena that were later found to have a natural explanation.

Step 4. Test the theories with the criteria of adequacy. As we've seen, simply toting up the evidence for each of the competing theories and checking to see which one gets the highest score will not do. We need to measure the plausibility of the theories by using the criteria of adequacy. The criteria can help us put any applicable evidence in perspective and allow us to make a judgment about theory plausibility even when there's little or no evidence to consider.

By applying the criteria to all the competing theories, we can often accomplish several important feats. We may be able to eliminate some theories immediately, assign more weight to some than others, and distinguish between theories that at first glance seem equally strong.

The best way to learn how to do step 4, as well as steps 1–3, is by example. Watch what happens when we assess the plausibility of theories for the following two phenomena.

Review Notes

Evaluating Theories: The TEST Formula
Step 1: State the **T**heory and check for consistency.
Step 2: Assess the **E**vidence for the theory.
Step 3: **S**crutinize alternative theories
Step 4: **T**est the theories with the criteria of adequacy.

A Doomed Flight

On 2 September 1998, Swissair Flight 111 crashed into the Atlantic Ocean not far from Peggy's Cove, Nova Scotia, killing all 229 people on board. The incident, like most airline disasters, prompted a search for explanations for the crash. The ensuing investigation was led by the Canadian Transportation Safety Board (TSB), with the co-operation of the US Federal Aviation Administration (FAA) and the aircraft manufacturers Pratt & Whitney. The investigation relied heavily on criteria of adequacy to sort through competing theories. After an investigation lasting five years, the TSB concluded that faulty wiring in the aircraft's entertainment system had started a fire that eventually brought the plane down.

Using this incident as inspiration and guide, let's devise another story of a mysterious jetliner crash and examine the main theories to explain it. We will assume that all the facts in the case are known, that all relevant reports are honest (no intent to deceive), and that no other information is forthcoming. In other words, this is a very contrived case. But it suits our purposes here just fine. Here goes.

The (made-up) facts of the case are these: at 8:30 pm, Flight 222, a McDonnell Douglas MD-11, left JFK airport in New York on its way to Oslo, Norway. At 9:38 pm the crew issued a 'Mayday' call, and at 9:42 the plane crashed into the ocean 50 km off the coast of Newfoundland. The crash happened during a time of heightened awareness of possible terrorist attacks on aircraft.

Now let's try steps 1–4 on a supposedly popular theory and some of its leading alternatives. Here's the pop theory in question. Theory 1: *A missile fired by a terrorist brought down the plane.* This one meets the requirement for consistency, so our first concern is to assess the evidence for the theory. Those who favour this theory point to several pieces of evidence. Eyewitnesses said that they had seen a bright streak of light or flame speeding toward the plane. A few people said that they thought they were watching a missile intercept the plane. And a journalist reported on the Internet that the plane had been shot down by a missile fired from a boat.

There are, however, some problems with this evidence. Eyewitness reports of the movements of bright lights in a dark sky are notoriously unreliable, even when the eyewitnesses are experts. Under such viewing conditions, the actual size of a bright object, its distance from the observer, its speed, and even whether it's moving are extremely difficult to determine accurately by sight. Also another phenomenon could have easily been mistaken for a speeding missile. It's known that an explosion rupturing a fuel tank on an aircraft's wing can ignite long streams of fuel, which from the ground may look like a missile heading toward the plane. In addition, the Canadian Coast Guard monitors boats and ships in the area in which Flight 222 crashed, and it says that there were none in the immediate area when the crash occurred. Because of the distances involved and other factors, firing a missile from the ground at Flight 222 and hitting it was virtually impossible. Finally, an unsupported allegation—whether from a journalist or anyone else—is not good evidence for anything.

Then we have this explanation. Theory 2: *An alien spacecraft shot the plane down.* For the sake of illustration, we will assume that this explanation meets the consistency requirement. The evidence is this. Several people say that they saw a UFO fly near the plane just before the plane exploded. And tapes of radar images show an unknown object flying close to the MD-11.

These eyewitness accounts suffer from the same weakness as those mentioned in theory 1. Observations under the conditions described are not reliable. Thus many alleged alien craft have turned out to be airplanes, helicopters, blimps, meteors, and even the planet Venus, an extremely bright object in the sky. Radar tapes may show many objects that are 'unknown' to untrained observers but are identified precisely by experts. The radar evidence would be more impressive if the flight controllers had not been able to account for an object flying close to Flight 222.

Theory 3: *A bomb on board the plane exploded, bringing the aircraft down.* This explanation is internally and externally consistent. The main evidence for it is the existence of trace amounts of explosive residue on a few of the recovered aircraft parts. Also, the story of the crash of Flight 222 resembles the media account of the crash of another jetliner that's known to have been brought down by an onboard bomb.

This resemblance, though, is only that—it's not evidence that counts in favour of the bomb theory. And the explosive residue is not so tell-tale after all. Investigators determined that the residues are most likely left over from a security training exercise conducted on the plane a week earlier. Moreover, examination of the wreckage and patterns of damage to it suggests that a bomb was not detonated inside the aircraft.

Theory 4: *A mechanical failure involving the fuel tanks caused the explosion that brought the plane down.* This is an eligible theory. It's backed by evidence showing that an explosion occurred in one of the plane's fuel tanks. Experts know that a short circuit in wiring outside a fuel tank can cause excess voltage in wiring that's inside the tank and thus ignite the fuel. Investigators found that there was indeed a short circuit in some of the fuel-tank wiring. In addition, explosions in several other large jets, some smaller planes, and various machine engines have been linked to faulty wiring in fuel tanks.

Theory 5: *A solar flare disrupted electrical circuits in the plane, releasing a spark that made the fuel tanks explode.* This too is an eligible theory. Solar flares are massive electromagnetic explosions on the surface of the sun. They can sometimes disrupt radio communications and even cause radio blackouts. Theory 5 says that a solar flare so dramatically affected electrical circuits in the plane that a spark was emitted that ignited the fuel. The rationale behind this theory is that flying planes, being closer to the sun, are more susceptible to the powerful effects of solar flares.

The evidence for this theory, however, is nil. There is no good reason to believe that a solar flare could ever cause a spark in an electrical circuit.

Now let's apply the criteria of adequacy to these explanations. We can see right away that all the theories do equally well in terms of testability and fruitfulness. They're all testable, and none has yielded any surprising predictions. Except for theory 4, they also have equal scope because they explain only the phenomenon they were introduced to explain, the crash of Flight 222 (and perhaps similar airline crashes). Theory 4, however, has a slight edge because it can explain certain airline crashes as well as explosions in other systems that have wired fuel tanks. So if we are to distinguish between the theories, we must rely on the other criteria.

This is bad news for theories 2 and 5 because they fail the criteria of simplicity and conservatism. The evidence in favour of the alien spacecraft theory is extremely weak. Even worse, it conflicts with a great deal of human experience regarding visitors from outer space. We simply have no good evidence that anyone has ever detected any beings or technology from outer space. Moreover, the probability of the Earth being visited by beings from outer space must be considered low (but not zero) in light of what we know about the size of the universe and the physical requirements of space travel. Likewise, the solar flare theory has no evidence to support it, and it too conflicts with what we know. There are no documented cases of solar flares causing sparks in electrical wiring. And neither theory is simple. Theory 2 assumes an unknown entity (aliens), and theory 5 assumes unknown processes (solar flares causing sparks in wiring). These are excellent grounds for eliminating theories 2 and 5 from the running.

That leaves theories 1, 3, and 4, which we must also sort out by using the criteria of simplicity and conservatism. They fare equally well in terms of simplicity because none assumes any unknown or mysterious entities or processes. Conservatism, though, is a different story. Neither theory 1 nor 3 accords with the evidence. In each case, existing evidence counts *against* the theory. Theory 4, though, accords well with the evidence. It not only doesn't conflict with what we know, but the evidence also supports the theory in important ways. Theory 4, then, is the best explanation for the crash of Flight 222 and the theory most likely to be true. And the explanation we started with, theory 1, is implausible.

Without a detailed formula, without a weighting system, and without quantifying any criteria, we have arrived at a verdict regarding competing theories. Deciding among theories is not always so straightforward, of course. But this lack of clear-cut answers is what gives rise to more research and more critical thinking.

> 'Science is organized common sense where many a beautiful theory was killed by an ugly fact.'
> —Thomas H. Huxley

Exercise 9.8

On the basis of what you already know and the criteria of adequacy, determine which theory in each group is most plausible.

1. Phenomenon: a deadly illness striking everyone in a small town.
   Theories: (1) resurgence of smallpox, (2) poison in the drinking water, (3) a failure to think positively.
2. Phenomenon: a sudden and dramatic drop in the price of most corporate stocks.
   Theories: (1) rumours of a recession, (2) manipulation of the stock market by one powerful shareholder, (3) particularly nasty weather on the East Coast.
* 3. Phenomenon: extraordinarily large humanlike footprints in the snow on a mountainside.
   Theories: (1) the legendary man-beast known as the Yeti, (2) falling rocks from the sky, (3) a very big human mountain climber.

4. Phenomenon: the construction of the Egyptian pyramids.

   Theories: (1) the work of clever Egyptian engineers and many slaves, (2) the work of Egyptians with the help of extraterrestrial beings, (3) the work, not of the Egyptians, but the ancient Romans.

5. Phenomenon: a large increase in the incidence of heart disease among middle-aged women.

   Theories: (1) the result of an increase in violence against women, (2) an increase in the amount of fat consumed by women over age 45, (3) an increase in the number of women who marry late in life.

Exercise 9.9

Evaluate the following theories by using the TEST formula. As part of your evaluation:

   a. State the claim to be evaluated.
   b. Indicate what phenomenon is being explained.
   c. Specify at least one alternative theory.
   d. Use the criteria of adequacy to assess the two theories and determine which one is more plausible.
   e. Write a paragraph detailing your reasons for your choice. Use your background knowledge to fill in any information about the theories and how well they do regarding each criteria.

1. A religious sect based in Montreal predicts that the end of the world will occur on 1 January 2001. The world, of course, did not end then. The leader of sect explains that the prophecy failed to come true because members of the sect did not have enough faith in it.

2. A small, secret society of corporate CEOs and international bankers runs the economies of Canada, the United States, and Europe. For its own benefit and for its own reasons, the society decides when these nations go into and come out of recession, what levels of production will be achieved by the oil industry, and what each country's gross national product will be. Members of the society are so rich and powerful that they are able to hide the society's activities from public view and operate without the knowledge of governments and ordinary citizen.

3. What is the greatest influence on the course of human history, its social and cultural development? Some say it's powerful ideas like socialism, democracy, human dignity, and scientific method. Some say it's the social movements that embody and promote these ideas. But the greatest influences are wrought by great leaders, who are not necessarily great thinkers. Throughout history, every time a great leader appeared—Moses, Alexander, Caesar, Napoleon, and the like—the world was irrevocably changed regardless of what ideas or social movements were in existence.

4.   The primary cause of all wars is fear. When people are afraid of others—because of ignorance or perceived threats—they naturally respond with belligerence and acts of violence. If they have no fear of others, they tend to react rationally and calmly and to seek some sort of fair accommodation.

5.   Scientists studied 20 terminal-cancer patients, taking note of the overall mental attitudes of the patients. Some of them were characterized as having negative attitudes; they were often angry at their situation and experienced feelings of hopelessness and regret. But other patients were thought to have positive attitudes; they were generally upbeat, optimistic about their treatment, and hopeful. Most of those with positive attitudes lived longer than most of those with negative attitudes. A positive attitude can lengthen cancer patients' lives.

6.   Anaïs said farewell to her favourite uncle as he boarded a plane for Paris. That night she dreamed that he was flying in a jetliner that suddenly ran into a powerful thunderstorm and extreme turbulence. The plane rocked from side to side, then descended rapidly into the night. The jetliner crashed into a mountain, killing all onboard. When she awoke the next day, she learned that her uncle's plane had encountered violent turbulence on the way to Paris and that several passengers, including her uncle, had been injured during the flight. She had just had one of those rare experiences known as a prophetic dream.

Exercise 9.10

Read the following passages and answer these questions for each one:

1.   What is the phenomenon being explained?
2.   What theories are given to explain the phenomenon? (Some theories may be unstated.)
3.   Which theory seems the most plausible and why? (Use the criteria of adequacy.)
4.   Which theory is the least plausible and why?
5.   Regarding the most credible theory, what factors would convince you to regard it as even more plausible?
6.   What factors would persuade you to regard the least credible theory as much more plausible?

Passage 1

'Since Venus rotates so slowly, we might be tempted to conclude that Venus, like Mercury, keeps one face always toward the Sun. If this hypothesis were correct we should expect that the dark side would be exceedingly cold. Pettit and Nicholson have measured the temperature of the dark side of Venus. They find that the temperature is not low, its value being only –9F [–22.8°C] degrees, much warmer than our stratosphere in broad daylight. It is unlikely that atmospheric currents from the bright side of Venus could perpetually heat the dark side. The planet must rotate fairly often to keep the dark side from cooling excessively.'[8]

Passage 2

'Parapsychologists claim man's ability to know when he is being stared at has existed since the time of primitive man and served, in those days, to warn him of impending danger and attack from savage beasts. They also believe this ability still exists in modern men and women today. Skeptics deny this claim and believe it is nothing more than superstition and/or a response to subtle signals from the environment that are not strong enough to let us know exactly what caused them. For example, if we are in a very dark room and we suddenly sense the presence of another person—even though we do not see or hear him—we may know he is there because of the person's shaving lotion, movement of air currents in the room, body heat, etc. In other words if we are warned of another's presence, it is likely due to subtle physical cues in the environment that we normally do not attend to—not to any so-called "psychic" or paranormal ability!

'To determine if people can tell when they are being stared at, two demonstrations were completed. In the first, forty individuals were stared at for an average time of 8.6 minutes while they were eating, reading, or watching a computer screen or television. When they finished they were asked if they were aware they were being stared at. Of the forty a total of thirty-five reported they were "totally unaware that anyone was looking at them". For the other five there is good reason to believe they also were not aware they were being viewed. In the second demonstration fifty students sat at a table in front of a one-way mirror and were observed by two experimenters, one minute at a time, five times during a twenty-minute observation period. The students' task was to try to guess when they were being stared at and report their degree of certainty. None of the fifty were able to correctly guess when they were being stared at. The mean accuracy score for the group was 1.24; the chance score for guessing was 1.25 out of a total of five guesses.'[9]

Summary

Even though an explanation is not an argument, an explanation can be part of an argument—a powerful inductive argument known as inference to the best explanation. In inference to the best explanation, we reason from premises about a state of affairs to an explanation for that state of affairs. Such explanations are called theoretical explanations, or theories.

To be worthy of consideration, a theory must meet the minimum requirement for consistency. We use the criteria of adequacy to judge the plausibility of a theory in relation to competing theories. The best theory is the one that meets the criteria of adequacy better than any of its competitors. The criteria of adequacy are testability (whether there is some way to determine if a theory is true), fruitfulness (the number of novel predictions made), scope (the amount of diverse phenomena explained), simplicity (the number of assumptions made), and conservatism (how well a theory fits with existing knowledge).

Judging the worth of a theory is a four-step process called the TEST formula: (1) Stating the theory and checking for consistency, (2) assessing the evidence for the theory, (3) scrutinizing alternative theories, and (4) testing the theories with the criteria of adequacy.

Key Terms

Ad hoc hypothesis: A hypothesis, or theory, that cannot be verified independently of the phenomenon it is supposed to explain. Ad hoc hypotheses always make a theory less simple—and therefore less credible.

Conservatism: A criterion of adequacy for judging the worth of theories. A conservative theory is one that fits with our established beliefs.

Criteria of adequacy: The standards used to judge the worth of explanatory theories. They include *testability*, *fruitfulness*, *scope*, *simplicity*, and *conservatism*.

Fruitfulness: A criterion of adequacy for judging the worth of theories. A fruitful theory is one that makes novel predictions.

Inference to the best explanation: A form of inductive reasoning in which we reason from premises about a state of affairs to an explanation for that state of affairs:

    Phenomenon Q.

    E provides the best explanation for Q.

    Therefore, it is probable that E is true.

Scope: A criterion of adequacy for judging the worth of theories. A theory with scope is one that explains or predicts phenomena other than that which it was introduced to explain.

Simplicity: A criterion of adequacy for judging how simple a theory is. A simple theory is one that makes as few assumptions as possible.

TEST formula: A four-step procedure for evaluating the worth of a theory:

    Step 1. State the Theory and check for consistency.

    Step 2. Assess the Evidence for the theory.

    Step 3. Scrutinize alternative theories.

    Step 4. Test the theories with the criteria of adequacy.

Testability: A criterion of adequacy for judging the worth of theories. A testable theory is one in which there is some way to determine whether the theory is true or false—that is, it predicts something other than what it was introduced to explain.

Theoretical explanation: A theory, or hypothesis, that tries to explain why something is the way it is, why something is the case, or why something happened.

Field Problems

1. Many companies have recently marketed products that are supposed to relieve various ills (arthritis, low back pain, migraine headaches, tennis elbow, etc.) through the use of simple magnets. This 'magnetic therapy' is said to work because magnetic fields generated by the magnets act on the body's processes or structures. Look at ads in magazines, on TV, or on the Internet to find a health claim made for one of these products. Then in a 150-word paragraph evaluate the claim in light of the criteria of simplicity and conservatism. Check for any relevant scientific research and information at www.quackwatch.com or www.sram.org/(*The Scientific Review of Alternative Medicine*).

2. Using the TEST formula, evaluate the theory that people are more likely to behave strangely or violently during a full moon than at other times. Do some research to uncover any evidence pertaining to this theory. Write a 200-word essay summarizing your findings.

Self-Assessment Quiz

1. What is the basic pattern of inference to the best explanation? How does this pattern differ from that of enumerative induction? Analogical induction?
2. What is the minimum requirement for consistency?
3. What are the criteria of adequacy?
4. According to the text, what does it mean for a theory to be testable or untestable?
5. What is the TEST formula?
6. According to the text, in theory evaluation, when is a theory properly considered the best?

Each of the following theories is offered to explain John's apparently prophetic dream that a distant cousin would die in a plane crash. Indicate which theory (a) lacks simplicity, (b) is not conservative, (c) is untestable, and (d) has the most scope. (Some theories may merit more than one of these designations.)

7. The fact that John's dream happened to be about a plane crash involving his cousin was coincidence. We have many dreams, and some are likely to match real events from time to time.
8. In his dream, John was able to see into the future and 'view' the plane crash.
9. The incident was an example of 'synchronicity', in which events are paired in unusual but predetermined ways by cosmic forces.
10. John had calculated the odds of the crash even before he dreamed about it, so the dream was not a prophecy, but a memory of his calculation.

Indicate which theory in each of the following groups is most plausible.

11. Phenomenon: The rise in popularity of a newly elected prime minister.
    Theories: (1) The so-called 'honeymoon effect' in which a new prime minister enjoys popularity until he or she is involved in serious or controversial decisions, (2) the systematic manipulation of all polling organizations by the prime minister's staff, (3) the influence of a powerful secret society controlling the media.

12. Phenomenon: your friend has been skipping class, and you haven't seen her in days.
    Theories: (1) she's in bed with the flu, (2) she has been kidnapped, (3) she has inherited millions of dollars and has decided to hang out with a better class of friends.

13. Phenomenon: ships, boats, and planes have been disappearing off the coast of Prince Edward Island for years.
    Theories: (1) considering the meteorological and atmospheric conditions of the area, it's normal for some craft to be lost from time to time; (2) the craft have been hijacked; (3) the ships, boats, and planes are simply off course.

14. Phenomenon: the rapid spread of an unknown, dangerous, viral disease throughout North America.
    Theories: (1) the lack of awareness and defences against a new mutated virus, (2) bureaucratic bungling at the Public Health Agency of Canada, (3) a massive conspiracy of doctors who want higher fees for treating seriously ill patients.

Evaluate the following theories using the TEST formula. As part of your evaluation, (1) state the claim to be evaluated, (2) indicate what phenomenon is being explained, (3) specify at least one alternative theory, and (4) use the criteria of adequacy to assess the two theories and determine which one is more plausible.

15. People buy high-ticket merchandise because of subliminal advertising—their minds are being influenced by imperceptible stimuli designed by ad execs.

16. Skeptical scientists have never been able to find evidence for cold fusion, try as they may. That's because their skepticism skews their observations.

17. Eleanor won the lottery twice in nine months. She must have a system that enables her to pick winning numbers.

18. He embezzled that money because his parents were divorced when he was very young.

19. School children who do poorly in school are not dumb or handicapped. They perform poorly for one reason only: low or negative expectations of their teachers.

20. The woman has been displaying bizarre behaviour for years, but recently she seems worse than ever. Sometimes she suddenly begins screaming, saying that there are snakes crawling on the walls. She shakes uncontrollably at the slightest noise. And she has started to bleed from her palms. The priest says that she's possessed by demons, and he's right.

Integrative Exercises

These exercises refer to lessons in Chapters 3 and 6–9.

1. What is a deductive argument?
2. What is a valid argument?
3. What is an inductive argument?
4. What is the logical pattern of *modus ponens*?

For each of the following arguments, specify the conclusion and premises and say whether it is deductive or inductive. If it's deductive, use Venn diagrams or truth tables to determine its validity. If it's inductive, say whether it's an enumerative, analogical, or causal induction and whether it's strong or weak. If necessary, add implicit premises and conclusions.

5. The problem is that if people realize that they can do their own buying and selling of stocks, they won't use brokers any more. But people don't realize that yet. So people will continue to use brokers.
6. I've read a lot about relations between Canadian soldiers and the people of Afghanistan. Almost everything I've read has been positive. The Afghanis realize that our soldiers are there to help and have welcomed them with open arms. I even read about one woman whose house was damaged in a firefight between Canadian soldiers and Taliban fighters, and she said she was glad the Canadians were there.
7. Every man I know has some kind of hang-up about sex. What is it with men? They're all a bunch of sexual neurotics.
8. Either the Prime Minister visited Quebec City to shore up support for his party among Quebecers, or he went there for the poutine. He didn't go there for the poutine, so he must have gone to shore up support for his party.
9. 'Hence a young man is not a proper hearer of lectures on political science; for he is inexperienced in the actions that occur in life, but its discussions start from these and are about these; and, further, since he tends to follow his passions, his study will be vain and unprofitable, because the end aimed at is not knowledge but action.' (Aristotle, *Nichomachean Ethics*)
10. Why should Canada be sending aid to foreign countries when there are people right here in Canada who need help? Every dollar spent on foreign aid could be better spent on problems right here at home!
11. No kings are persons without power. All people without power are persons who spend their days being victims. Therefore, no kings are victims.
12. Vulgarity is rampant across the land, and Hollywood is to blame. As vulgar, sexually explicit, tasteless movies have proliferated, so has the amount of vulgarity increased.
13. He's afraid of her. He avoids her all the time, and he won't look her in the eye.
14. Most teens arrested for committing some act of violence also play a lot of violent video games. These games are causing violent behaviour among our youth.

Evaluate each of the following theories and indicate whether it is plausible or implausible.

15. The positions and movements of the stars and planets at the time of your birth can have a powerful effect on your life.

16. David Milgaard was sent to prison for raping and murdering a nursing assistant, Gail Miller, and he spent 21 years behind bars. Three of Milgaard's friends testified against him in court. Milgaard was released in 1997 after DNA evidence supposedly proved he didn't commit the crime. But I'll trust the word of three witnesses over some fancy scientific test any day!

17. In Area 51, the famous portion of a military base near Groom Dry Lake in Nevada, the government is concealing real alien visitors or an actual space vehicle used by the visitors to reach Earth.

18. If people are homeless, it's because they chose to be homeless. In Canada, there are a hundred ways to get out of poverty—if you want to.

19. The large network news organizations have ignored most of the anti-war protests staged since 9/11. Coverage of any anti-war sentiment seems to be against media policy. This can only mean that top network execs have decided together that such coverage is not in their best interests.

20. When the streetlights lit up the side of the building, a vague image appeared on the wall, a mixture of shadows and light. Most people say that the image shows the face of Jesus. This image is a holy sign from God.

 ## Writing Assignments

1. In a one-page essay evaluate the theory that all major decisions made by the Canadian prime minister or the premier of your province are politically motivated and have very little to do with the merits of ideas or programs. Use the TEST formula.

2. Think of the last time you caught a cold or the flu. Write a 250-word paper evaluating at least two theories that explain how you first came into contact with the virus. Use the TEST formula.

3. Write a 500-word paper in which you use the TEST formula to assess two theories for UFO abductions. One theory is the alien theory (Hypothesis 1) as discussed in Essay 9 ('UFO Abductions') in Appendix A; the other one is the hypnosis theory, the view that no one is actually abducted but instead the idea of being abducted by aliens is inadvertently implanted in people's minds when they undergo hypnosis.

Chapter 10

Judging Scientific Theories

Chapter Objectives

Science and Not Science

You will be able to

○ understand why science is not the same thing as technology, ideology, or scientism.

The Scientific Method

You will be able to

○ list the five steps of the scientific method.
○ understand the logic of scientific testing.
○ understand why no scientific hypothesis can be conclusively confirmed or conclusively confuted.

Testing Scientific Theories

You will be able to

○ use the steps of the scientific method, and be able to explain how a scientist would go about testing a simple hypothesis in medical science.
○ understand why scientists use control groups, make studies double-blind, include placebos in testing, and seek replication of their work.

Judging Scientific Theories

You will be able to

○ list the five criteria of adequacy and explain what they mean.
○ understand how to apply the criteria of adequacy to the theories of evolution and creationism and why the text says that evolution is the better theory.

Science and Weird Theories

You will be able to

○ explain why evaluating weird claims might be worthwhile.

Making Weird Mistakes

You will be able to

○ understand why it can be so easy to err when trying to evaluate weird theories.

○ explain three major errors that people often make when they are trying to assess extraordinary experiences and theories.

○ explain the distinction between logical and physical possibility.

Judging Weird Theories

You will be able to

○ use the TEST formula to evaluate extraordinary theories.

○ understand why eyewitness testimony is often unreliable.

So the world is chockablock with claims in the form of explanations—*theoretical explanations*, to be more precise, about why something is the case or why something happens. An overwhelming number of such theories are offered to explain the cause of events, such as why the window broke, why the moon looks so pale, why Ralph stole the bike, why the stock market tanked. As critical thinkers, we do the best we can in evaluating these theories that come our way, testing them if possible, looking for alternative theories, and applying the criteria of adequacy. As it turns out, science is in the same line of work.

Science seeks to acquire knowledge and an understanding of reality, and it does so through the formulation, testing, and evaluation of theories. When this kind of search for answers is both systematic and careful, science is being done. And when we ourselves search for answers by scrutinizing possible theories—and we do so systematically and carefully—we are searching scientifically.

Let's examine the scientific process more closely.

Science and Not Science

First, let's explore what science is *not*.

Science is not technology. Science is a way of searching for truth—a way that uses what is often referred to as *the scientific method*. Technology, on the other hand, is not a search for truth; technology is the use of knowledge to do things in the world, and it is often embodied in products—DVDs, cell phones, laptop computers, robots that vacuum the carpet, better mousetraps. Technology applies knowledge acquired through science to practical problems that science generally doesn't care about, such as the creation of electronic gadgets. Technology seeks facts to use in producing stuff. Science tries to understand how the world works, not by merely cataloguing specific facts, but by discovering general principles that both explain and predict phenomena.

This nice distinction sometimes gets blurry when technologists do scientific research in order to build a better product or scientists create gadgets in order to do better scientific research. But, in general, science pursues knowledge; technology makes things.

Science is not ideology. Some people say that science is not a way of finding out how the world works, but a world view affirming how the world is, just as Catholicism or socialism affirms a view of things. To some, science is not only an ideology, but a most objectionable one—one that posits a universe that is entirely material, mechanistic, and deterministic. On this 'scientific view', the world—including us—is nothing more than bits of matter forming a big machine that turns and whirs in predetermined ways. This mechanistic notion is thought to demean humans and human endeavours by reducing us to the role of cogs and sprockets.

But we can't identify science with a specific world view. At any given time, a particular world view may predominate in the scientific community, but this fact doesn't mean that the world view is what science is all about. Predominant world views among scientists have changed over the centuries, but the general nature of science as a way of searching for truth has not. For example, the mechanistic view of the universe, so common among scientists in the seventeenth century, has now given way to other views. Discoveries in quantum mechanics (the study of sub-atomic particles) have shown that the old mechanistic perspective is incorrect.

Science is not scientism. One definition of *scientism* is the view that science is the only reliable way to acquire knowledge. Put another way, science is the only reliable road to truth. But in light of the reliability of our sense experience under standard, unhindered conditions (see Chapter 4), this claim is dubious. We obviously do know many things without the aid of scientific methodology.

But there is a related point that is not so dubious. Science may not be the only road to truth, but it is an extremely reliable way of acquiring knowledge about the empirical world. (Many philosophers of science would go a step further and say that science is our *most reliable* source of knowledge about the world.) Why is science so reliable? Science embodies to a high degree what is essential to a reliable knowledge of empirical facts: systematic consideration of alternative solutions or theories, rigorous testing of them, and careful checking and rechecking of the conclusions.

Some would say that science is reliable because it is self-correcting. Science does not grab hold of an explanation and never let go. Instead, it looks at alternative ways to explain a phenomenon, tests these alternatives, and opens up the conclusions to

> 'Science is not gadgetry. The desirable adjuncts of modern living, although in many instances made possible by science, certainly do not constitute science.'
> —Warren Weaver

criticism from scientists everywhere. Eventually, the conclusions may turn out to be false and scientists will have to abandon the answers they thought were solid. But usually, after much testing and thinking, scientists hit upon a theory that does hold up under scrutiny. They are then justified in believing that the theory is true, even though there is some chance that it is flawed.

The Scientific Method

The scientific method cannot be identified with any particular set of experimental or observational procedures because there are many different methods for evaluating the worth of a hypothesis. In some sciences, such as physics and biology, hypotheses can be assessed through controlled experimental tests. In other sciences, such as astronomy and geology, hypotheses must usually be tested through observations. For example, an astronomical hypothesis may predict the existence of certain gases in a part of the Milky Way, and astronomers can use their telescopes to check whether those gases exist as predicted.

The scientific method, however, does involve several steps, regardless of the specific procedures involved:

1. Identify the problem or pose a question.
2. Devise a hypothesis to explain the event or phenomenon.
3. Derive a test implication or prediction.
4. Perform the test.
5. Accept or reject the hypothesis.

Scientific inquiry begins with a problem to solve or a question to answer. So in step 1 scientists may ask: What causes X? Why did Y happen? Does hormone therapy cause breast cancer? Does Aspirin lower the risk of stroke? How is it possible for whales to navigate over long distances? How did early hominids communicate with one another? Was the Big Bang an uncaused event?

In step 2 scientists formulate a hypothesis that will constitute an answer to their question. In every case there are facts to explain, and the hypothesis is an explanation for them. The hypothesis guides the research, suggesting what kinds of observations or data would be relevant to the problem at hand. Without a hypothesis, scientists couldn't tell which data are important and which are worthless.

Where do hypotheses come from? One notion is that hypotheses are generated through induction—by collecting the data and drawing a generalization from them to get a hypothesis. But this can't be the way that most hypotheses are formulated because they often contain concepts that aren't in the data. (Remember, theories generally reach beyond the known data to posit the existence of things unknown.) The construction of hypotheses is not usually based on any such mechanical procedure. In many ways, they are created just as works of art are created. Scientists dream them up. They, however, are guided in hypothesis creation by certain criteria—namely, the criteria of adequacy we examined in the last chapter. With testability, fruitfulness, scope, simplicity, and conservatism as their guide, they devise hypotheses from the raw material of the imagination.

Remember, though, that scientists must consider not just their favourite hypothesis, but alternative hypotheses as well. The scientific method calls for consideration of competing explanations and for their examination or testing at some point in the process. Sometimes applying the criteria of adequacy can immediately eliminate some theories from the running, and sometimes theories must be tested along with the original hypothesis.

In step 3 scientists derive implications, or consequences, of the hypothesis to test. As we've seen, sometimes we can test a theory directly, as when we simply check the gas tank of the lawnmower to confirm the theory that it won't run because it's out of gas. But often theories cannot be tested directly. How would we directly test, for example, the hypothesis that chemical X is causing leukemia in menopausal women? We can't.

> 'The whole of science is nothing more than a refinement of everyday thinking.'
> —Albert Einstein

Food For Thought

Are You Scientifically Literate?

According to poll results reported in a July 2006 issue of *MacLean's*, 57 per cent of Canadians believe in ESP (Extra-Sensory Perception). This is despite the fact that:

- No credible scientific evidence of ESP has *ever* been produced.
- The existence of ESP would contradict much of what is known about physics and human neurophysiology.

A little scientific literacy can help you avoid unreasonable beliefs!

Test *Your* Scientific Literacy!

True or False?

1. Lasers work by focusing sound waves.
2. Electrons are smaller than atoms.
3. The universe began with a huge explosion, the 'Big Bang'.
4. The earliest humans lived at the same time as the dinosaurs.
5. The hole in the ozone layer is responsible for global warming.
6. Artificial cloning usually involves transplanting the nucleus from one cell into another cell.

Answers: 1. False, 2. True, 3. True, 4. False, 5. False, 6. True.

So scientists test indirectly by first deriving a test implication from a hypothesis and then putting that implication to the test. Deriving such an observational consequence involves figuring out what a hypothesis implies or predicts. Scientists ask, 'If this hypothesis were true, what consequences would follow? What phenomena or events would have to obtain?'

Recall that we derived test implications in the problem of the car that wouldn't start in Chapter 9. One hypothesis was that the car wouldn't start because a vandal had sabotaged it. We reasoned that if a vandal had indeed sabotaged the car, there would be tracks in the snow around it. But there were no tracks, disconfirming the sabotage hypothesis.

The logic of hypothesis testing, then, works like this. When we derive a test implication, we know that if the hypothesis to be tested (H) is true, then there is a specific predicted consequence (C). If the consequence turns out to be false (that is, if it does not obtain as predicted), then the hypothesis is probably false, and we can reject it. The hypothesis, in other words, is disconfirmed. We can represent this outcome in a conditional, or hypothetical, argument:

If H, then C.
not-C.
Therefore, not-H.

This is, remember, an instance of *modus tollens*, a valid argument form. In this case, H would be false even if only one of several of its consequences (test implications) turned out to be false.

On the other hand, we would get a very different situation if C turned out to be true:

If H, then C.
C.
Therefore, H.

Notice that this is an instance of affirming the consequent, an invalid argument form. So just because C is true, that doesn't necessarily mean that H is true. If a consequence turns out to be true, that doesn't *prove* that the hypothesis is correct. In such a result, the hypothesis is confirmed, and the test provides at least some evidence that the hypothesis is true. But the hypothesis isn't then established. If other consequences for the hypothesis are tested, and all the results are again positive, then there is more evidence that the hypothesis is correct. As more and more consequences are tested, and they are shown to be true, we can have increasing confidence that the hypothesis is in fact true. As this evidence accumulates, the likelihood that the hypothesis is actually false decreases—and the probability that it's true increases.

In step 4 scientists carry out the testing. Usually this experimentation is not as simple as testing one implication and calling it quits. Scientists may test many consequences of several competing hypotheses. As the testing proceeds, some hypotheses are found wanting, and they're dropped. If all goes well, eventually one hypothesis remains, with considerable evidence in its favour. Then step 5 can happen, as the hypothesis or hypotheses are accepted or rejected.

Because scientists want to quickly eliminate unworthy hypotheses and zero in on the best one, they try to devise the most telling tests. This means that they are on the lookout for situations in which competing hypotheses have different test consequences. If hypothesis 1 says that *C* is true, and hypothesis 2 says that *C* is false, a test of *C* can then help eliminate one of the hypotheses from further consideration.

As we've seen, implicit in all this is the fact that no hypothesis can ever be *conclusively* confirmed. It's always possible that we will someday find evidence that undermines or conflicts with the evidence we have now.

Likewise, no hypothesis can ever be *conclusively* confuted. When scientists test hypotheses, they never really test a single hypothesis—they test a hypothesis together with a variety of background assumptions and theories. So a hypothesis can always be saved from refutation by making changes in the background claims. (As we detailed in the previous chapter, sometimes these changes are made by constructing ad hoc hypotheses—by postulating unverifiable entities or properties.) In such situations, no amount of evidence logically compels us to conclusively reject a hypothesis.

But our inability to confirm or confute a hypothesis conclusively does not mean that all hypotheses are equally acceptable. Maintaining a hypothesis in the face of mounting negative evidence is unreasonable, and so is refusing to accept a hypothesis despite accumulating confirming evidence. Through the use of carefully controlled experiments, scientists can often affirm or deny a hypothesis with a high degree of confidence.

Review Notes

Steps in the Scientific Method
1. Identify the problem or pose a question.
2. Devise a hypothesis to explain the event or phenomenon.
3. Derive a test implication or prediction.
4. Perform the test.
5. Accept or reject the hypothesis.

Testing Scientific Theories

Let's see how we might use the five-step procedure to test a fairly simple hypothesis. Suppose you hear reports that some terminal cancer patients have lived longer than expected because they received high doses of vitamin C. And say that the favoured hypothesis among many observers is that the best explanation for the patients' surviving longer is that vitamin C is an effective treatment against cancer. So you decide to test the hypothesis that high doses of vitamin C can increase the survival time of people with terminal cancer. (Years ago, this hypothesis was actually proposed and tested in three well-controlled clinical trials.[1]) An obvious alternative hypothesis is that vitamin C actually has no effect on the survival of terminal-cancer patients and that any apparent benefits are due mainly to the placebo effect (the tendency for people to feel better temporarily after they're treated, even if the treatment is a fake). The placebo effect could be leading observers to believe that people taking vitamin C are being cured of cancer and are thus living longer. Or the placebo effect could be making patients feel better, thereby enabling them to take better care of themselves (by eating right or complying with standard medical treatment, for example) and increasing survival time.

Now, if your hypothesis is true, what would you expect to happen? That is, what test implication could you derive? If your hypothesis is true, you would expect that terminal cancer patients given high doses of vitamin C would live longer than terminal cancer patients who didn't receive the vitamin (or anything else).

How would you conduct such a test? To begin with, you could prescribe vitamin C to a group of terminal cancer patients (called the experimental group) but not to another group of similar cancer patients (called the control group) and keep track of their survival times. Then you could compare the survival rates of the two groups. But many people who knowingly receive a treatment will report feeling better—even if the treatment is an inactive placebo. So any positive results you see in the treated group might be due not to vitamin C but to the placebo effect.

To get around this problem, you would need to treat both groups, one with vitamin C and the other with a placebo. That way, if most of the people getting the vitamin C live longer than expected and fewer of those in the placebo group do, you can have slightly better reason for believing that vitamin C works as advertised.

But even this study design is not good enough. It's possible for the people conducting the experiment, the experimenters, to bias the results unknowingly. Through subtle behavioural cues, they can unconsciously inform the test subjects which treatments are real and which ones are placebos—and this, of course, would allow the placebo effect to have full reign. Also, if the experimenters know which treatment is the real one, they can unintentionally misinterpret or skew the study results in line with their own expectations.

This problem can be solved by making the study *double-blind*. In double-blind experiments, neither the subjects nor the experimenters know who receives the real treatment and who the inactive one. A double-blind protocol for your vitamin study would ensure that none of the subjects would know who's getting vitamin C, and neither would the experimenters.

What if you have a double-blind set-up but most of the subjects in the vitamin C group were sicker to begin with than those in the placebo control group? Obviously, this would bias the results, making the vitamin C treatment look less effective—even if it *is* effective. To avoid this skewing, you would need to ensure that both groups are as much alike as possible to start—with all subjects being around the same age, having the same physical condition, being at the same stage of cancer, and so on.

Finally, you would need to run some statistical tests to ensure that your results are not a fluke. Even in the most tightly controlled studies, it's possible that the outcome is the result of random factors that cannot be controlled. Statisticians have standard methods for determining when experiment results are likely, or not likely, to be due to chance.

Suppose you design your study well and you conduct it. The results are that the patients receiving the high doses of vitamin C did not live longer than the placebo group. In fact, all the subjects lived about the same length of time. Therefore, your hypothesis is disconfirmed. On the other hand, the alternative hypothesis—that vitamin C has no measurable effect on the survival of terminal cancer patients—is confirmed.

Should you now reject the vitamin C theory? Not yet. Even apparently well-conducted studies can have hidden mistakes in them, or there can be factors that the experimenters failed to take into account. This is why scientists insist on study *replication*—the repeating of an experiment by different groups of scientists. If other scientists replicate the study and the study results hold up, then you can be more confident that the results are solid. In such a case, you could safely reject the vitamin C hypothesis. (This is, in fact, what scientists did in the real-life studies of vitamin C and cancer survival.)

At this point, when evidence has been gathered that can bear on the truth of the hypothesis in question, good scientific judgment is crucial. It's here that consideration of other competing hypotheses and the criteria of adequacy again come into play. At this stage, scientists need to decide whether to reject or accept a hypothesis—or modify it to improve it.

Judging Scientific Theories

As you can see, theory testing is part of the broader effort to assess the merits of one theory against a field of alternatives. And as you know by now, this broader effort will always involve, explicitly or implicitly, the application of the criteria of adequacy to the theories in question:

- Testability: Whether there's some way to determine if a theory is true.
- Fruitfulness: The number of novel predictions made.

- Scope: The amount of diverse phenomena explained.
- Simplicity: The number of assumptions made.
- Conservatism: How well a theory fits with existing knowledge.

Let's study two important examples to see how scientists manage this task. The first is a classic case from the history of science; the second, a contemporary tale of what many perceive as a battle between science and religion. Notice that the steps itemized by the TEST formula are implicit in the evaluation process.

Copernicus Versus Ptolemy

Consider the historic clash between the geocentric (Earth-centred) and the heliocentric (sun-centred) theories of planetary motion. It's difficult to imagine two rival theories that have more profoundly influenced how humanity views itself and its place in the universe.

In the beginning was the geocentric view. Aristotle got things going by putting forth the theory that a spherical Earth was at the centre of a spherical universe consisting of a series of concentric, transparent spheres. On one celestial sphere we see the sun, the moon, and the known planets. On the outermost sphere we behold the stars. All the heavenly bodies rotate in perfect circles around the stationary Earth. The heavenly bodies are pure, incorruptible, and unchanging; the Earth, impure, corruptible, and transient.

Food For Thought

Copernicus on Ptolemy's System

Copernicus was shocked at how complex and seemingly arbitrary Ptolemy's revered system was. He thought that Ptolemy, through countless revisions and additions, had created not a beautiful model—but a kind of monster. As Copernicus put it,

> It is as though an artist were to gather the hands, feet, head and other members for his images from diverse models, each part excellently drawn, but not related to a single body, and since they in no way match each other, the result would be a monster rather than a man.

Nicolaus Copernicus (1473–1543). Erich Lessing/Art Resource, NY

Then came the great astronomer and mathematician Ptolemy, who flourished in Alexandria between 127 and 148 CE. He discovered inconsistencies in the traditional geocentric system between the predicted and observed motions of the planets. He found, in other words, that Aristotle's theory was not conservative, a crucial failing. So he fine-tuned the old view, adding little circular motions (called epicycles) along the planet orbits and many other minor adjustments. He also allowed for an odd asymmetry in which the centre of planet orbits was not exactly the centre of Earth—all this so the theory would match up to astronomical observations. By the time Ptolemy finished tinkering he had posited 80 circles and epicycles—80 different planetary motions—to explain the movements of the sun, moon, and five known planets.

"IT'S BLACK, AND IT LOOKS LIKE A HOLE. I'D SAY IT'S A BLACK HOLE."

© 2002 by Sidney Harris. www.ScienceCartoonsPlus.com

The result was a system far more complex than Aristotle's. But the revised theory worked well enough for the times, and it agreed better than the earlier theory did with observational data. Despite the complications, learned people could use Ptolemy's system to calculate the positions of the planets with enough accuracy to manage calendars and astrological charts. So for 15 centuries astronomers used Ptolemy's unwieldy, complex theory to predict celestial events and locations. In the West, at least, Earth stood still in the centre of everything as the rest of the universe circled around it.

The chief virtue of the Ptolemaic system, then, was conservatism. It fitted, mostly, with what astronomers knew about celestial goings-on. It was also testable, as any scientific theory should be. Its biggest failing was simplicity—or the lack thereof. The theory was propped up by numerous assumptions for the purpose of making the theory fit the data.

Enter Nicolaus Copernicus (1473–1543). He was disturbed by the complexity of Ptolemy's system. It was a far cry from the simple theory that Aristotle had bequeathed to the West. Copernicus proposed a heliocentric theory in which Earth and the other planets orbit the sun, which is the true centre of the universe. In doing so, he greatly simplified both the picture of the heavens and the calculations required to predict the positions of planets.

Copernicus's theory was simpler than Ptolemy's on many counts, but one of the most impressive was retrograde motion, a phenomenon that had stumped astronomers for centuries. From time to time, certain planets seem to reverse their customary direction of travel across the skies—to move backward! Ptolemy had explained this retrograde motion by positing yet more epicycles, asserting that planets orbiting Earth will often orbit around a point on the larger orbital path. Seeing these orbits within orbits from Earth, an observer would naturally see the planets sometimes backing up.

But the Copernican theory could easily explain retrograde motion without all those complicated epicycles. As the outer planets (Mars, Jupiter, and Saturn) orbit the sun, so does Earth, one of the inner planets. The outer planets, though, move much more slowly than Earth does. On its own orbital track, Earth sometimes passes the outer planets as they lumber along on their orbital track, just as a train passes a slower train on a parallel track. When this happens, the planets appear to move backward, just as the slower train seems to reverse course when the faster train overtakes it.

Copernicus's theory, however, was not superior on every count. It explained a great many astronomical observations, but Ptolemy's theory did too, so they were about even in scope. It had no big advantage in fruitfulness over the Ptolemaic system. It made no impressive predictions of unknown phenomena. Much more troubling, it seemed to conflict with some observational data.

One test implication of the Copernican theory is the phenomenon known as *parallax*. Critics of the heliocentric view claimed that if the theory were true, then as Earth moved through its orbit, stars closest to it should seem to shift their position relative to stars farther away. There should, in other words, be parallax. But no one had observed parallax.

Copernicus and his followers responded to this criticism by saying that stars were too far away for parallax to occur. As it turned out, they were right about this, but confirmation didn't come until 1832, when parallax was observed with more powerful telescopes.

Another test implication seemed to conflict with the heliocentric model. Copernicus reasoned that if the planets rotate around the sun, then they should show phases just as the moon shows phases because of the light of the sun falling on it at different times. But in Copernicus's day, no one could see any such planetary phases. Fifty years later, though, Galileo used his new telescope to confirm that Venus had phases.

Ultimately, scientists accepted the Copernican model over Ptolemy's because of its simplicity—despite what seemed at the time like evidence against the theory. As Copernicus said, 'I think it is easier to believe this [sun-centred view] than to confuse the issue by assuming a vast number of Spheres, which those who keep the Earth at the center must do.'[2]

Evolution versus Creationism

Few scientific theories have been more hotly debated among non-scientists than evolution and its rival, creationism (or creation science). Both theories purport to explain the origin and existence of biological life on Earth, and each claims to be a better explanation than the other. Can science decide this contest? Yes. Despite the complexity of the issues involved and the mixing of religious themes with the non-religious, good science can figure out which theory is best. Remember that the best theory is the one that explains the phenomenon and measures up to the criteria of adequacy better than any of its competitors. There is no reason that the scientific approach cannot provide an answer here—even in this thorniest of thorny issues.

Neither the term 'evolution' nor the concept began with Charles Darwin (1809–82), the father of evolutionary theory. The word showed up in English as early as 1647. The ancient Greek philosopher Anaximander (c. 611–547 BCE) was actually the first evolutionary theorist, who inferred from some simple observations that humans must have evolved from an animal and that this evolution must have

> 'It is a good morning exercise for a research scientist to discard a pet hypothesis every day before breakfast. It keeps him young.'
> —Konrad Lorenz

Food For Thought

Can You See Evolution?
Critics of the theory of evolution often ask, 'If evolution occurs, why can't we see it?' Here's how the US's National Academy of Sciences responds to this objection (http://books.nap.edu/html/creationism/evidence.html):

> Special creationists argue that 'no one has ever seen evolution occur.' This misses the point about how science tests hypotheses. We don't see Earth going around the sun or the atoms that make up matter. We 'see' their consequences. Scientists infer that atoms exist and Earth revolves because they have tested predictions derived from these concepts by extensive observation and experimentation.

> Furthermore, on a minor scale, we 'experience' evolution occurring every day. The annual changes in influenza viruses and the emergence of antibiotic-resistant bacteria are both products of evolutionary forces....On a larger scale, the evolution of mosquitoes resistant to insecticides is another example of the tenacity and adaptability of organisms under environmental stress. Similarly, malaria parasites have become resistant to the drugs that were used extensively to combat them for many years. As a consequence, malaria is on the increase, with more than 300 million clinical cases of malaria occurring every year.

begun in the sea. But in his famous book *The Origin of Species* (1859), Darwin distilled the theory of evolution into its most influential statement.

Scientists have been fine-tuning the theory ever since as new evidence and new insights pour in from many different fields, such as biochemistry and genetics. But the basic idea has not changed: living organisms adapt to their environments through inherited characteristics, which results in changes in to successive generations. Specifically, the offspring of organisms differ physically from their parents in various ways, and these differences can be passed on genetically to their offspring. If an offspring has an inherited trait (such as sharper vision or a larger brain) that increases its chances of surviving long enough to reproduce, that individual is more likely to survive and pass the trait on to the next generation. After several generations, this useful trait, or adaptation, spreads throughout a whole population of individuals and differentiates the population from its ancestors. The name that Darwin gave to this process is *natural selection.*

Creation science, on the other hand, maintains that (1) the universe and all life was created suddenly, out of nothing, only a few thousand years ago (6,000–10,000 is the usual range); (2) natural selection could not have produced living things from a single organism; (3) species change very little over time; (4) man and apes have a separate ancestry; and (5) the earth's geology can be explained by catastrophism, including a worldwide flood.[3]

The first thing we should ask about these two theories is whether they're testable. The answer is yes. Recall that a theory is testable if it predicts or explains something other than what it was introduced to explain. On this criterion, evolution is surely testable. It explains, among other things, why bacteria develop resistance to antibiotics, why there are so many similarities between humans and other primates, why new infectious diseases emerge, why the chromosomes of closely related species are so similar, why the fossil record shows the peculiar progression of fossils that it does, and why the embryos of related species have such similar structure and appearance.

Creationism is also testable. It too explains something other than what it was introduced to explain. It claims that Earth's geology was changed in a worldwide flood, that the universe is only a few thousand years old, that all species were created at the same time, and that species change very little over time.

Innumerable test implications have been derived from evolutionary theory, and innumerable experiments have been conducted, confirming the theory. For example, if evolution is true, then we would expect to see a systematic change in the fossil record from simple creatures at the earlier levels to more complex individuals at the more recent levels. We would expect not to see a reversal of this configuration. And this sequence is exactly what scientists see time and time again.

Creationism, however, has not fared as well. Its claims have not been borne out by evidence. In fact, they have consistently conflicted with well-established scientific findings.

This latter point means that creationism fails the criterion of conservatism—it conflicts with what we already know. For example, the scientific evidence shows that Earth is not 6,000–10,000 years old—but billions of years old. According to the US National Academy of Sciences,

> There are no valid scientific data or calculations to substantiate the belief that Earth was created just a few thousand years ago. [There is a] vast amount of evidence for the great age of the universe, our galaxy, the Solar system, and Earth from astronomy, astrophysics, nuclear physics, geology, geochemistry, and geophysics. Independent scientific methods consistently give an age for Earth and the Solar system of about 5 billion years, and an age for our galaxy and the universe that is two to three times greater.[4]

Creationism also fails the criterion of conservatism on the issue of a geology-transforming universal flood. Again, the National Academy of Sciences:

> Nor is there any evidence that the entire geological record, with its orderly succession of fossils, is the product of a single universal flood that occurred a few thousand years ago, lasted a little longer than a year, and covered the highest mountains to a depth of several meters. On the contrary, intertidal and terrestrial deposits demonstrate that at no recorded time in the past has the entire planet been under water. . . . The belief that Earth's sediments, with their fossils, were deposited in an orderly sequence in a year's time defies all geological observations and physical principles concerning sedimentation rates and possible quantities of suspended solid matter.[5]

Has either theory yielded any novel predictions? Evolution has. It has predicted, for example, that new species should still be evolving today; that the fossil record should show a movement from older, simpler organisms to younger, more complex ones; that proteins and chromosomes of related species should be similar; and that organisms should adapt to changing environments. These and many other novel predictions have been confirmed. Creationism has made some novel claims, as we saw earlier, but none of these have been supported by good evidence. Creationism is not a fruitful theory.

The criterion of simplicity also draws a sharp contrast between the two theories. Simplicity is a measure of the number of assumptions that a theory makes. Both theories make assumptions, but creationism assumes much more. Creationism assumes the existence of a creator and unknown forces. Proponents of creationism readily admit that we do not know how the creator created nor what creative processes were used.

In this contest of theories, the criterion of scope—the number of diverse phenomena explained—is probably more telling than any of the others. Biological evolution explains a vast array of phenomena in many fields of science. In fact, a great deal of the content of numerous scientific fields—genetics, physiology,

'If we are going to teach creation science as an alternative to evolution, then we should also teach the stork theory as an alternative to biological reproduction.'
—Judith Hayes

biochemistry, neurobiology, and more—would be deeply perplexing without the theory of evolution. As the eminent geneticist Theodosius Dobzhansky put it, 'Nothing in biology makes sense except in the light of evolution.'[6]

Virtually all scientists would agree—and go much further:

> It [evolution] helps to explain the emergence of new infectious diseases, the development of antibiotic resistance in bacteria, the agricultural relationships among wild and domestic plants and animals, the composition of Earth's atmosphere, the molecular machinery of the cell, the similarities between human beings and other primates, and countless other features of the biological and physical world.[7]

Food For Thought

Gaps in the Fossil Record?

Creationists hold that if evolution were true, then there should be fossil remains of transitional organisms. But, they insist, there are gaps where transitional fossils should be, so evolution didn't happen. But this claim is incorrect. There are transitional fossils:

> Gaps in the fossil record are not even a critical test of evolution vs. progressive creation, as evolution also predicts gaps. There are some 2 million described species of living animals, but only 200,000 described fossil species. Thus, it is impossible to provide a minutely detailed history for every living species. This is because, first, the fossil record has not been completely explored. It is pretty hard to overlook a dinosaur bone! Yet, though dinosaurs have been

In 2006 scientists discovered this 375-million-year-old fossil of a species that spans the gap between fish and land animals.
Photo: © Ted Daeschler/Academy of Natural Sciences/VIREO

> excavated for over 150 years, 40 per cent of the known species were found in the last 20 years or so (*Discover*, March 1987, p. 46). It is likely many more dinosaur species remain to be found. Second, sedimentary rocks were formed locally in lakes, oceans, and river deltas, so many upland species were never fossilized. Third, many deposits that were formed have been lost to erosion. Thus, a complete record is impossible.

> However, there is a critical test. Evolution predicts that some complete series should be found, while [creationists predict] that none should ever be found. In fact, many excellent

series exist. The evolution of the horse is known in exquisite detail from Hyracotherium (Eohippus) to the modern horse (G.G. Simpson, *Horses*, 2nd ed. Oxford, 1961). Scientific creationists have been forced to claim that the series is but allowed variation within a created 'kind'. If so, then rhinoceroses, tapirs, and horses are all the same 'kind', as they can be traced to ancestors nearly identical to Hyracotherium! All of these fossils lie in the correct order by both stratigraphic and radioisotope dating.

Another critical test is Darwin's prediction that '... our early ancestors lived on the African continent....' (The *Descent of Man*, p. 158). An excellent, detailed series of skulls and some nearly complete skeletons now connect modern man to African australopithecines. Some of the extinct australopithecines had brains about the size and shape of those of chimpanzees.[8]

Creationism, however, can explain none of this. And it provokes, not solves, innumerable mysteries. What caused the worldwide flood? Where did all that water come from? Where did it all go? Why does Earth seem so ancient (when it's said to be so young)? How did the creator create the entire universe suddenly—out of nothing? Why does the fossil record seem to suggest evolution and not creation? So many questions are an indication of diminished scope and decreased understanding.

'My theory of evolution is that Darwin was adopted.'
—Steven Wright

Note that creationism tries to explain biological facts by appealing to something that's incomprehensible—a creator and his means of creating. The creationist view is that something incomprehensible using incomprehensible means created the universe. But appealing to the incomprehensible does not increase our understanding. Creationism, then, explains nothing. Creationism has zero scope.

Good scientists must be prepared to admit this much: If creationism meets the criteria of adequacy as well as evolution does, then creationism must be as good a theory as evolution. But creationism fails to measure up to the criteria of adequacy. On every count it shows itself to be inferior. Scientists then are justified in rejecting creationism in favour of evolution. And this is exactly what they do.

Exercise 10.1

Review Questions

1. How does science differ from technology?
2. What is the scientific method?
3. Can science be identified with a particular world view?

4. According to the text, what is scientism?
5. According to the text, why is science such a reliable way of knowing?
* 6. What are the five steps of the scientific method?
7. Can hypotheses be generated through induction? Why or why not?
8. What does it mean to derive a test implication from a theory?
* 9. What is the conditional argument reflecting the fact that a theory is disconfirmed?
10. What is the conditional argument reflecting the fact that a theory is confirmed?
11. Can theories be conclusively confirmed? Why or why not?
* 12. Can theories be conclusively disconfirmed? Why or why not?
13. According to the text, is creationism as good a scientific theory as evolution? Why or why not?

Exercise 10.2

For each of the following phenomena, devise a hypothesis to explain it and derive a test implication to test the hypothesis.

1. In a recent study of scientific literacy, women performed better than men in understanding the scientific process and in answering questions about basic scientific facts and concepts.
* 2. Jamal found giant footprints in his backyard and mysterious tufts of brown fur clinging to bushes in the area. Rumours persist that Bigfoot, the giant primate unknown to science, is frequenting the area. Two guys living nearby also claim to be perpetrating a hoax about the existence of the creature.
3. The rates of automobile crashes are higher among teenage boys than any other age group.
4. For months after the tragedy of September 11, there were no major terrorist attacks in the United States or Canada.
5. Students who tend to 'skim' when they read also tend to commit plagiarism more often.
* 6. Weight trainers swear that the supplement creatine dramatically improves their performance.
7. Many people who take B vitamins for their headaches report a lower incidence of headaches.
8. Recent research confirms a link between diets high in saturated fat and a higher risk of coronary-artery disease.
9. When John got home, he found that the lock on his door had been broken and his colour TV was missing.
10. The economic gap between the very rich and the very poor widened considerably in 2009.

Exercise 10.3

Using your background knowledge and any other information you may have about the subject, devise a competing theory for each of the following and then apply the criteria of adequacy to both of them—that is, ascertain how well each theory does in relation to its competitor on the criteria of testability, fruitfulness, scope, simplicity, and conservatism.

1. Phenomenon: People report feeling less pain after trying acupuncture.
     Theory: Treatment with acupuncture needles can alleviate pain.

2. Phenomenon: Your mild-mannered friend suddenly going into a violent rage.
     Theory: Schizophrenia.

* 3. Phenomenon: The unexpected melting of massive chunks of the world's glaciers.
     Theory: Local climate changes.

4. Phenomenon: A rare species of fungus grows in only one place in the world—the wing tips of a beetle that inhabits caves in France.
     Theory: Evolution.

5. Phenomenon: As the job market worsens, blacks lose jobs faster than whites.
     Theory: Racial prejudice.

6. Phenomenon: The psychic was able to recount a number of personal details about a recently deceased person he never met.
     Theory: Psychic ability.

* 7. Phenomenon: Almost all of the terrorist attacks in the world in the past five years have been perpetrated by religious fanatics.
     Theory: Religion fosters terrorism.

8. Phenomenon: Twenty patients with severe arthritis pain were prayed for by 50 people, and 14 out of those 20 reported a significant lessening of pain.
     Theory: Prayer heals.

9. Phenomenon: Over the past year, two terminally ill cancer patients in Broderick Hospital were found to be cancer-free.
     Theory: Treatment with a new type of chemotherapy.

10. Phenomenon: Entrance marks required to get into most Canadian universities are at their highest level in years.
     Theory: Increased immigration is resulting in greater competition from new Canadians, which drives up the entrance requirements.

Exercise 10.4

For each of the following theories, derive a test implication and indicate whether you believe that such a test would likely confirm or disconfirm the theory.

1. Elise has the power to move physical objects with her mind alone.
* 2. Ever since the city installed brighter streetlights, the crime rate has been declining steadily.
3. The Ultra-Sonic 2000 pest-control device can rid a house of roaches by emitting a particular sound frequency that humans can't hear.
4. The Dodge Intrepid is a more fuel-efficient car than any other on the road.
5. Practitioners of transcendental meditation (TM) can levitate—actually ascend unaided off the ground without physical means of propulsion.
* 6. Eating foods high in fat contributes more to being overweight than eating foods high in carbohydrates.
7. Lemmings often commit mass suicide.
8. The English sparrow will build nests only in trees.

Exercise 10.5

Read the following passages and answer the following questions for each one:

1. What is the phenomenon being explained?
2. What theories are advanced to explain the phenomenon? (Some theories may be unstated.)
3. Which theory seems the most plausible and why? (Use the criteria of adequacy.)
4. Regarding the most credible theory, is there a test implication mentioned? If so, what is it? If not, what would be a good test implication for the theory?
5. What test results would persuade you to change your mind about your preferred theory?

Passage 1

'In the past several years, a researcher named David Oates has been advocating his discovery of a most interesting phenomenon. Oates claims that backward messages are hidden unintentionally in all human speech. The messages can be understood by recording normal speech and playing it in reverse.... [According to Oates] "Any thought, any emotion, any motive that any person has can appear backwards in human speech. The implications are mind boggling because reverse speech opens up the Truth.". . . To our knowledge there is not one empirical investigation of reverse speech in any peer-reviewed journal. If reverse speech did exist it would be, at the very least, a noteworthy scientific discovery. However, there are no data to support the existence of reverse speech or Oates's theories about its implications.'[9]

Passage 2

'Michael Behe, a Lehigh University biochemist, claims that a light-sensitive cell, for example, couldn't have arisen through evolution because it is "irreducibly complex". Unlike the scientific creationists, however, he doesn't deny that the universe is billions of years old. Nor does he deny that evolution has occurred. He only denies that every biological system arose through natural selection.

'Behe's favorite example of an irreducibly complex mechanism is a mouse trap. A mouse trap consists of five parts: (1) a wooden platform, (2) a metal hammer, (3) a spring, (4) a catch, and (5) a metal bar that holds the hammer down when the trap is set. What makes this mechanism irreducibly complex is that if any one of the parts were removed, it would no longer work. Behe claims that many biological systems, such as cilium, vision, and blood clotting, are also irreducibly complex because each of these systems would cease to function if any of their parts were removed.

'Irreducibly complex biochemical systems pose a problem for evolutionary theory because it seems that they could not have arisen through natural selection. A trait such as vision can improve an organism's ability to survive only if it works. And it works only if all the parts of the visual system are present. So, Behe concludes, vision couldn't have arisen through slight modifications of a previous system. It must have been created all at once by some intelligent designer. . . .

'Most biologists do not believe that Behe's argument is sound, however, because they reject the notion that the parts of an irreducibly complex systems could not have evolved independently of that system. As Nobel Prize-winning biologist H. J. Muller noted in 1939, a genetic sequence that is, at first, inessential to a system may later become essential to it. Biologist H. Allen Orr describes the processes as follows: "Some part (A) initially does some job (and not very well, perhaps). Another part (B) later gets added because it helps A. This new part isn't essential, it merely improves things. But later on A (or something else) may change in such a way that B now becomes indispensable." For example, air bladders—primitive lungs—made it possible for certain fish to acquire new sources of food. But the air bladders were not necessary to the survival of the fish. As the fish acquired additional features, however, such as legs and arms, lungs became essential. So, contrary to what Behe would have us believe, the parts of an irreducibly complex system need not have come into existence all at once.'[10]

Exercise 10.6

Read the following passage about a study conducted on the use of vitamin C to treat cancer. Identify the hypothesis being tested, the consequences (test implication) used to test it, and whether the hypothesis was confirmed or disconfirmed.

Passage 1

'In 1978, the Mayo Clinic embarked on a prospective, controlled, double-blind study designed to test Pauling and Cameron's claims [for the effectiveness of vitamin C]. Each patient in this study had biopsy-proven cancer that was considered incurable and unsuitable for further chemotherapy, surgery, or radiation. The patients were randomized to receive 10 grams of vitamin C per day or a comparably flavored lactose placebo. All patients took a glycerin-coated capsule four times a day.

'The patients were carefully selected so that those [in the] vitamin C [and] placebo groups were equally matched. There were 60 patients in the vitamin C group and 63 in the placebo group. The age distributions were similar. There was a slight predominance of males, but the ratio of males to females was virtually identical. Performance status was measured using the Eastern Cooperative Oncology Group Scale, a clinical scale well recognized by cancer researchers. Most study patients had some disability from their disease, but only a small proportion were bedridden. Most patients had advanced gastrointestinal or lung cancer. Almost all had received chemotherapy, and a smaller proportion had undergone radiation therapy.

'The results were noteworthy. About 25 per cent of patients in both groups showed some improvement in appetite. Forty-two per cent of the patients on placebo alone experienced enhancement of their level of activity. About 40 per cent of the patients experienced mild nausea and vomiting, but the two groups had no statistically significant differences in the number of episodes. There were no survival differences between patients receiving vitamin C and those receiving the placebo. The median survival time was approximately seven weeks from the onset of therapy. The longest surviving patient in this trial had received the placebo. Overall, the study showed no benefit from vitamin C.'[11]

Science and Weird Theories

What good are science and inference to the best explanation in the realm that seems to lie *beyond* common sense and scientific inquiry—the zone of the extraordinary, the paranormal, and the supernatural? In this land of the wonderfully weird—the interesting and mysterious domain of UFOs, ESP, ghosts, psychic predictions, tarot card readings, and the like—exactly what work can science do?

From reading Chapter 9, you probably have already guessed that science and critical reasoning can be as useful in assessing weird claims as they are in sizing up mundane ones. Inference to the best explanation—whether wielded in science or everyday life—can be successfully applied to extraordinary theories of all kinds. Fortunately for critical thinkers, the TEST formula outlined in Chapter 9 for finding the best theoretical explanation is not afraid of ghosts, monsters, or space aliens. In the next few pages, we will get a good demonstration of these points by examining some extraordinary theories in much greater detail than we have previously.

'I maintain there is much more wonder in science than in pseudoscience. And in addition, to whatever measure this term has any meaning, science has the additional virtue, and it is not an inconsiderable one, of being true.'
—Carl Sagan

Science has always been interested in the mysterious, and from time to time it has also ventured into the weird. In the past 150 years, scientists have tested spiritualism, clairvoyance, telepathy, telekinesis (moving physical objects with the mind alone), astrology, dowsing, the Loch Ness monster, faith healing, firewalking, and more. Among these we should also count some bizarre phenomena that scientists never tire of studying—black holes, alternative dimensions of space, and the microworld of subatomic particles (the weirdest of the weird), where the laws of physics are crazy enough to make Alice in Wonderland scream.

But why should anyone bother to learn how to evaluate weird claims in the first place? Well, for one thing, they are widely believed and often difficult to ignore. They are, after all, heavily promoted in countless television programs, movies, books, magazines, and tabloids. And—like claims in politics, medicine, and many other fields—they can dramatically affect people's lives, for better or worse. It's important then for anyone confronted with such popular and influential claims to be able to assess them carefully.

Captain Pointy was beginning to review his skeptical opinions on the existence of aliens.

www.CartoonStock.com

Food For Thought

How Many People Believe in Weird Things?

According to a survey completed by Ipsos-Reid for *Reader's Digest* in mid-2003:

- 61 per cent of adult Canadians believe in angels;
- 37 per cent believe in ghosts;
- 29 per cent believe in astrology and horoscopes;
- 43 per cent believe in out-of-body experiences.

According to poll results reported in *Maclean's*, in July 2006:

- 57 per cent of Canadians believe in ESP (extra-sensory perception)
- Two-thirds believe in life after death;
- 31 per cent believe we can *communicate* with the dead.

In addition, if you really care whether an extraordinary claim is true or false, there is no substitute for the kind of critical evaluation discussed here. Accepting (or rejecting) a weird claim solely because it's weird will not do. A horse laugh is not an argument, and neither is a sneer. Weird claims often turn out to be false, and as the history of science shows, they sometimes surprise everyone by being true.

Making Weird Mistakes

So in science and in our own lives, the critical assessment of weird theories is possible, but that doesn't mean the process is without risks. It's easy for a scientist or anyone else to err when thinking about extraordinary claims. Weird claims and experiences have a way of provoking strong emotions, preconceived attitudes, and long-held biases. In the world of the weird, people (including scientists and other experts) are often prone to the kinds of errors in reasoning we discussed in Chapter 4, including resisting contrary evidence, looking for confirming evidence, and preferring available evidence. Those who contemplate extraordinary things also seem to be especially susceptible to the following errors.

Leaping to the Weirdest Theory

When people have an extraordinary experience, they usually try to make sense of it. They may have a seemingly prophetic dream, see a ghostly shape in the dark, watch their astrologer's prediction come true, think they've witnessed a miracle, or feel they have somehow lived another life centuries ago. Then they cast about for an explanation for such experiences. And when they cannot think of a natural explanation, they often conclude that the explanation must be paranormal or supernatural. This line of reasoning is common but fallacious. *Just because you can't think of a natural explanation doesn't mean that there isn't one.* You may just be ignorant of the correct explanation. Throughout history, scientists have often been confronted with astonishing phenomena that they could not explain in natural terms at the time. But they didn't assume that the phenomena must be paranormal or supernatural.

"TELL THEM ABOUT YOUR PSORIASIS, BETTY. MAYBE THEY CAN CURE IT."

Harley Schwadron.

They simply kept investigating—and they eventually found natural explanations. Comets, solar eclipses, meteors, mental illness, infectious diseases, and epilepsy were all once thought to be supernatural or paranormal but were later found through scientific investigation to have natural explanations. When confronted then with a phenomenon that you don't understand, the most reasonable response is to search for a natural explanation.

The fallacious leap to a non-natural explanation is an example of the appeal to ignorance discussed in Chapter 5. People think that since a paranormal or supernatural explanation has not been shown to be false, it must be true. This line, though logically fallacious, can be very persuasive.

The failure to consider alternative explanations is probably the most common error in assessing paranormal claims. As we've seen, this failure can be willful. People can refuse to consider seriously a viable alternative. But honest and intelligent people can also simply be unaware of possible natural explanations. Looking for alternative explanations requires imagination and a deliberate attempt to 'think outside the box'.

Mixing What Seems with What Is

Sometimes people leap prematurely to an extraordinary theory by ignoring this elementary principle: *Just because something seems real doesn't mean that it is.* Because of the nature of our perceptual equipment and processes, we humans are bound to have many experiences in which something appears to be real but is not. The corrective for mistaking the unreal for the real is to apply another important principle that we discussed in Chapter 4. That is, it's reasonable to accept the evidence provided by personal experience only if there's no good reason to doubt it. We have reason to doubt if our perceptual abilities are impaired (we are under stress, drugged, afraid, excited, etc.), we have strong expectations about a particular

Review Notes

Common Errors in Evaluating Extraordinary Theories

1. Believing that just because you can't think of a natural explanation, a phenomenon must be paranormal.
2. Thinking that just because something seems real, it is real. (A better principle is that it's reasonable to accept the evidence provided by personal experience only if there's no good reason to doubt it.)
3. Misunderstanding logical possibility and physical possibility. Also, believing that if something is logically possible, it must be actual.

experience (we strongly expect to see a UFO or hear spooky noises, for example), and observations are made under poor conditions (the stimuli are vague and ambiguous or the environment is too dark, too noisy, too hazy, etc.). Since scientists can falter here just as anyone else can, they try to use research methods that minimize reasons for doubt.

Misunderstanding the Possibilities

Debates about weird theories often turn on the ideas of possibility and impossibility. Skeptics may dismiss a weird theory by saying, 'That's impossible!' Believers may insist that a state of affairs is indeed possible, or they may proclaim, '*Anything is possible!*' Such protestations, however, are often based on misunderstandings.

The experts on the subject of possibility (namely, philosophers) often talk about *logical possibility* and *logical impossibility*. Something is logically impossible if it violates a principle of logic (that is, if it involves a logical contradiction). Something is logically possible if it does not violate a principle of logic (does not involve a logical contradiction). Anything that is logically impossible can't exist. We know, for example, that there are no married bachelors because these things involve logical contradictions (male humans who are both married and not married). Likewise we know that there are no square circles because they involve logical contradictions (things that are both circles and not circles). We must conclude from all this that, despite what some people sincerely believe, it is not the case that anything is possible. If a weird phenomenon is logically impossible, we needn't investigate it further because it can't exist. Most alleged paranormal phenomenon, however, are not logically impossible. ESP, UFOs, reincarnation, dowsing, spontaneous human combustion, out-of-body experiences, for example, do not generally involve any logical contradiction.

Philosophers also refer to *physical possibility* and *physical impossibility*. Something is physically impossible if it violates a law of science. Whatever violates a law of science cannot occur. We know that travelling faster than the speed of light is physically impossible because such an occurrence violates a law of science. Perpetual motion machines are physically impossible because they violate the law of science known as

A faked UFO photo. UFOs are logically and physically possible—but not necessarily actual. Photo: Dale O'Dell/Alamy

the conservation of mass-energy. Thus, if an extraordinary phenomenon violates a law of science, we know that it cannot be.

Some things that are logically possible, however, are physically impossible. It's logically possible for Vaughn's dog to fly to another galaxy in 60 seconds. This astounding performance does not violate a principle of logic. But it does violate laws of science pertaining to speed-of-light travel and gravitation. It is therefore physically impossible. The upshot of all this is that, contrary to what some people would have us believe, if something is logically possible, that doesn't mean it's physically possible. That is, if something is logically possible, that doesn't mean it's actual. Many logically possible things may not be real.

Judging Weird Theories

Now let's do a detailed evaluation of two extraordinary theories using the TEST formula from Chapter 9. Recall the four steps of the procedure:

Step 1. State the theory and check for consistency.
Step 2. Assess the evidence for the theory.
Step 3. Scrutinize alternative theories.
Step 4. Test the theories with the criteria of adequacy.

Science uses such a procedure to assess all manner of extraordinary explanations, and—by proceeding carefully and systematically—so can you.

Crop Circles

Crop circles are large-scale geometric designs pressed or stamped into fields of grain. They are often circular but can be almost any shape, ranging from simple patterns to complex pictograms or symbols. They can measure a few feet in diameter or span the length of several football fields. The current wave of popular interest in crop circles began in the 1970s, when they started mysteriously appearing overnight in the grain fields of southern England. The crops would be neatly flattened with the stalks pressed together and sometimes impressively interlaced. In the 1980s and 1990s, interest in the phenomenon grew as crop circles proliferated

Photo: Robert Harding Picture Library Ltd./Alamy

throughout the world, showing up in Canada, Europe, Africa, Australia, the United States, and elsewhere. In 2002 Hollywood got into the act with the movie *Signs*, starring Mel Gibson as a Pennsylvania farmer who discovers massive crop circles in his fields and is soon drawn into encounters with extraterrestrial beings.

From the beginning, crop circles have been both intriguing and controversial. The controversy has centred mostly on one question: what theory best explains the existence of crop circles? Many explanations for the cause of the phenomenon have been offered and debated, with plenty of people making the case for their favourite theory in books and magazine articles and, of course, on the Internet. Let's examine some of these theories and see if we can separate the good from the bad.

Food For Thought

Alternative Explanations and Ghosts

Suppose you awake in the middle of the night to see an apparition at your bedside. Later you arrive at the only explanation you can think of: you saw a ghost. But, as paranormal investigator Joe Nickell explains, there are other theories to consider.

One of William Mumler's fake ghost photos produced by simple double exposures. He was a nineteenth-century spiritualist who made a good living producing what he called 'spirit photographs' for clients. Photo: Wm. B. Becker Collection/American Museum of Photography

The experience [of seeing an apparition] is a common type of hallucination, known popularly as a 'waking dream', which takes place between being fully asleep and fully awake. Such experiences typically include bizarre imagery (bright lights or apparitions of demons, ghosts, aliens, etc.) and/or auditory hallucinations. 'Sleep paralysis' may also occur, whereby there is an inability to move because the body is still in the sleep mode.

A good example of an obvious waking dream is reported by 'A. C'. She was asleep on board the Queen Mary, the former ocean liner that, since 1971, has been permanently docked at Long Beach, California. As the woman relates:

I awoke from a deep sleep around midnight. I saw a figure walking near my daughter's sleeping bag toward the door. Thinking it was my sister, I called out. There was no answer. It was then that I noticed my sister was lying next to me. I sat up in bed and watched the person in white walk through the door!

Step 1. We begin with a theory that has received a great deal of attention from skeptics and believers alike.

Theory 1: Crop circles are created by small whirlwinds of electrified air (also called wind vortices). The idea here is that crop circles are made by columns of whirling, charged air—similar to dust devils or miniature tornadoes. These vortices form above grain fields and then plunge to the ground, discharging the electricity and flattening the grain in swirled patterns. But unlike tornadoes, wind vortices leave the stalks of grain undamaged.

Step 2. What is the evidence for this theory? The evidence is indirect. Natural crop-circle vortices are unknown to science, but similar vortices are reported to have been produced artificially in laboratories. A few people claim to have seen the

…. To be sure, not all sightings of ghostly figures are of the waking-dream variety, many in fact occurring during normal activity. Some are like the report of 'J. M.' who was at the Queen Mary's Purser's Desk when, he stated, 'I caught a brief glimpse out of the corner of my eye, of someone or something moving,' or like that of 'P. T.' who said, 'I saw something move out of the corner of my eye … a brief glimpse of someone or something.' Actually, the illusion that something is moving in the peripheral vision is quite common. The typical cause may be a 'floater', a bit of drifting material in the eye's vitreous humour, although a twitching eyelid, or other occurrence is also possible.

Such an illusion or a different stimulus—a noise, a subjective feeling, etc.—might trigger, as in one experiencer aboard the Queen Mary, a 'mental image'. In that case it was of a man 'wearing a blue mechanic's uniform'—a 'feeling' which left after a few moments. In certain especially imaginative individuals the mental image might be superimposed upon the visual scene, thus creating a seemingly apparitional event.…

Indeed, personal experience as well as research data demonstrate that ghostly perceptions often derive from daydreams or other altered states of consciousness. Haraldsson for instance specifically determined that apparitional sightings were linked to periods of reverie. As well, Andrew MacKenzie demonstrated that a third of the hallucinatory cases he studied occurred either just before or after sleep, or while the percipient was in a relaxed state or concentrating on some activity like reading, or was performing routine work. The association of apparitional experiences with a dream-like state was also reported by G.N.M. Terrell. He observed that apparitions of people invariably appear fully clothed and are frequently accompanied by objects, just as they are in dreams, because the clothing and other objects are required by the apparitional drama.…That the apparitions vanish when the observer's gaze is shifted could be explained by the hypothesis that the reverie is merely broken.[12]

vortices in open fields. An electrified vortex might produce light during discharge, and sure enough eyewitnesses have reported seeing 'balls of light' and other light phenomena in or near crop circles. Many crop-circle enthusiasts (known as 'cereologists' or 'croppies') have photographed what they claim are mysterious lights near crop circles, and the photographs show impressive balls of light and strange glowing arcs. Some croppies also report hearing strange sounds near crop circles (humming noises, for example). Finally, some cereologists have reported that the plants in crop circles differ anatomically from those outside the circles. The joints in stalks, for example, may be bigger in crop-circle plants than in plants growing elsewhere.

This evidence, however, is weak. Producing a vortex in a laboratory does not prove that it exists 'in the wild'. In fact, there is no good evidence that crop-circle vortices exist in nature. As with most unfamiliar and provocative phenomena, eyewitness accounts of vortices are generally unreliable, especially since people generally don't know what a true crop-circle vortex looks like. Sightings of various light phenomena are not direct evidence for the existence of vortices because they can be explained in other ways. The lights could come from many other sources, including ball lightning (a documented phenomenon), commercial aircraft, military aircraft, the parachute flares of pranksters, and the flashlights of people making crop circles (there are plenty of people who make crop circles as hoaxes or works of art). The photographs of light phenomena also have other explanations. The arcs and balls of light in these photos can be easily produced when the flash reflects off of the camera strap, insects, droplets of water, and the like. Photos of weird lights are also easily faked. Reports of strange sounds, like the reports of weird lights, are not good evidence of vortices at work because the sounds could have several other causes (farm machinery, wind, etc.). And even if there are anatomical differences between crop-circle plants and non-circle plants, this would not show that crop circles are made by vortices. At most, it would suggest only that crop-circle plants are different, however the circles are made. (This same point applies to claims about other kinds of differences between crop-circle areas and non-circle locations, including alleged magnetic or soil anomalies. The anomalies, if they exist, do not confirm that crop circles are made in any particular way.)

The biggest problem for the crop-circle vortex theory is that it doesn't explain the evidence. The theory seems adequate to explain circular crop-circle designs (a whirlwind would seem to be just the thing to make a circle on the ground), but not all crop circles are circular. Many are incredibly complex amalgams of squares, triangles, straight lines, and shapes that have no names.

Step 3. Now let's examine a popular alternative theory.

"Bloody hell! Crap circles."

Theory 2: Crop circles are made by extraterrestrial beings (space aliens). This explanation asserts only that crop circles are the work of aliens; it does not specify how the aliens do it. The circles could be created by alien spacecraft, energy beams

Food For Thought

I Confess: I'm a Crop-Circle Prankster

Other than to make great art, why would anyone want to go skulking around in the night to make crop circles in someone's wheat field? Maybe this confession from an unrepentant circle-maker will clear things up:

> I made my first crop circle in 1991. My motive was to prove how easy they were to create, because I was convinced that all crop circles were man-made. It was the only explanation nobody seemed interested in testing. Late one August night, with one accomplice—my brother-in-law from Texas—I stepped into a field of nearly ripe wheat in northern England, anchored a rope into the ground with a spike and began walking in a circle with the rope held near the ground. It did not work very well: the rope rode up over the plants. But with a bit of help from our feet to hold down the rope, we soon had a respectable circle of flattened wheat.

> Two days later there was an excited call to the authorities from the local farmer: I had fooled my first victim. I subsequently made two more crop circles using far superior techniques. A light garden roller, designed to be filled with water, proved helpful. Next, I hit on the 'plank walking' technique that was used by the original circle makers, Doug Bower and the late Dave Chorley, who started it all in 1978. It's done by pushing down the crop with a plank suspended from two ropes. To render the depression circular is a simple matter of keeping an anchored rope taut. I soon found that I could make a sophisticated pattern with very neat edges in less than an hour.

> Getting into the field without leaving traces is a lot easier than is usually claimed. In dry weather, and if you step carefully, you can leave no footprints or tracks at all. There are other, even stealthier ways of getting into the crop. One group of circle makers uses two tall bar stools, jumping from one to another.

> But to my astonishment, throughout the early 1990s the media continued to report that it was impossible that all crop circles could be man-made. They cited 'cerealogists'— those who study crop circles—and never checked for themselves. There were said to be too many circles to be the work of a few 'hoaxers' (but this assumed that each circle took many hours to make), or that circles appeared in well-watched crops (simply not true), or that circle creation was accompanied by unearthly noises (when these sounds were played back, even I recognized the nocturnal song of the grasshopper warbler).[13]

from space, or 'thought energy' from places unknown. This theory has seemed plausible to some people in light of the intricacy and beauty of crop-circle pictograms, with a few croppies insisting that aliens must be communicating in geometrical language. To some, the circles have seemed much too complicated and elegant to be the result of human ingenuity.

The evidence for this alien explanation? The elegant complexity of crop circles has been thought to be pretty good support for the theory. Who else but aliens would create such brilliant masterpieces on such a large scale—masterpieces that are best viewed from the air or space itself? A few people have announced that they found very intricate mathematics in the more elaborate crop-circle designs. Some have also reported seeing odd lights in the vicinity of crop circles, and others have claimed that they saw actual alien craft in the night sky not far from the crop-circle fields. A few cereologists have even claimed that they caught sight of UFOs in the process of making crop circles.

This evidence, however, is problematic and has some of the same weaknesses as the wind vortex evidence. The complexity and beauty of crop circles do not lend support to the alien theory, because the artistry of the crop formations has an obvious alternative explanation: that the circles were made by people. In fact, there are numerous documented cases of people—either hoaxers or artists—having created stunningly exquisite and elaborate crop circles, some with plenty of mathematics built in. Because the human-artist explanation is at least as plausible as the alien artist one, the artistic or intellectual impressiveness of crop circles can give no weight to the alien theory. As mentioned earlier, light phenomena near crop circles also have other explanations. Nighttime UFO sightings might seem to be good evidence that aliens are up to something. But such sightings are susceptible to many of the doubt-producing factors that we discussed in Chapter 4, namely, darkness, ambiguous stimuli, lack of cues to the true position and size of moving objects, perceptual construction, stress, strong emotions, expectancy, and more. Eyewitness reports of aliens actually constructing crop circles constitute very weak evidence for theory 2. Such extraordinary reports require reliable corroborating evidence, but no alien activity of any kind has ever been scientifically documented, despite allegations to the contrary.

Many people favour a more down-to-earth theory.

Theory 3: Crop circles are made by people using ordinary means. This explanation encompasses the creation of crop circles by hoaxers, artists, or any other humans. The relevant evidence suggests that people have indeed produced many crop circles. In 1991 two English artists with a sense of humor, Doug Bower and Dave Chorley, declared that they had been making crop circles for years to fool gullible people who believed in UFOs. They demonstrated their circle-making skills for reporters and television audiences, easily producing very elaborate crop circles in a short time. To create their designs, they used only ropes and planks. They showed that crop circles thought to be way beyond human ability were in fact made by people using incredibly simple techniques. Their formations fooled many people,

> 'It is easier to attribute UFO sightings to the known irrationalities of terrestrials than to the unknown efforts of extraterrestrials.'
> —Richard Feynman

including at least one prominent cereologist. Many circle watchers conceded that human hoaxers were making crop circles and that it was no cinch to distinguish 'true' circles from fake ones. A leading cereologist admitted that 80 per cent of crop circles in Britain were made by humans.

It is clear, however, that Bower and Chorley could not have created all the known crop circles. From southern England, crop-circle creation spread all over the globe, appearing in increasing numbers. This spread of the phenomenon, though, seemed to correlate with increased international media coverage of crop circles, suggesting that other people may have been inspired to copy English circle-making. In addition, many artists have been fascinated by the aesthetics of crop circles and have generated their own masterpieces in grain.

Croppies have argued that humans can't be responsible for some crop circles because there are often no signs of human activity at formation sites (no footprints, paths through the grain, etc.). But as the circle building of hoaxers suggests, people can produce crop circles without leaving evidence of human activity behind. Hoaxers, for example, can often avoid leaving footprints in a grain field by walking along the narrow footpaths created by farm machinery.

Also, as suggested earlier, physical anomalies in crop-circle plants or soil do not prove that crop circles are made in any particular way. It's possible that anomalies are produced by the techniques used in human circle making. Some have suggested, for example, that enlarged joints in grain stalks are the result of the bent stalks baking in the hot sun.

Step 4. Now let's see what happens when we apply the criteria of adequacy to these three theories. Theories 1 and 3 seem equal in terms of testability. Both predict something other than what they were introduced to explain. Theory 1, for example, predicts that in the creation of a crop circle, an electrified vortex forms above the formation area—something that should be detectable by the right kind of scientific instruments. Theory 3 is certainly testable because human activity is detectable and measurable. Theory 2 (aliens) may or may not be testable, depending on how alien activity is construed. We will give the theory the benefit of the doubt and say that it too is testable.

Theories 1 and 2 are not fruitful, for they have yielded no surprising predictions. We could argue, though, that theory 3 is fruitful because the creation of specific crop circles at designated times and places has been successfully predicted by hoaxers (the ones who created the circles).

In terms of scope, neither theory 1 nor 2 gets any points. The vortex theory does not explain anything other than the creation of crop circles. Theory 2 could be construed as explaining many things in which aliens are involved (UFO sightings, abductions, UFO crashes, etc.). But positing the existence of mysterious beings that act in mysterious ways for mysterious reasons does not seem to explain much of anything. Theory 3, on the other hand, can be used to explain many strange phenomena because humans, after all, are responsible for many hoaxes and bizarre happenings.

Food For Thought

Eyewitness Testimony and Extraordinary Things

A great deal of the evidence for paranormal phenomena is eyewitness testimony. Unfortunately, research suggests that eyewitness testimony generally can't be trusted—especially when the testimony concerns the paranormal. For example, in some studies people who had participated in seances later gave wildly inaccurate descriptions of what had taken place. Researchers have found that people's beliefs and expectations seem to play a big role in the unreliability of testimony about the paranormal.

Different people clearly have different beliefs and expectations prior to observing a supposed psychic—skeptics might expect to see some kind of trickery; believers may expect a display of genuine psi [parapsychological phenomena]. Some 70 years ago Eric Dingwall in Britain speculated that such expectations may distort eyewitness testimony: The frame of mind in which a person goes to see magic and to a medium cannot be compared. In one case he goes either purely for amusement or possibly with the idea of discovering 'how it was done', whilst in the other he usually goes with the thought that it is possible that he will come into direct contact with the other world.

Recent experimental evidence suggests that Dingwall's speculations are correct.

Wiseman and Morris in Britain carried out two studies investigating the effect that belief in the paranormal has on the observation of conjuring tricks. Individuals taking part in the experiment were first asked several questions concerning their belief in the paranormal. On the basis of their answers they were classified as either believers (labelled 'sheep') or skeptics (labelled 'goats').

In both experiments individuals were first shown a film containing fake psychic demonstrations. In the first demonstration the 'psychic' apparently bent a key by concentrating on it; in the second demonstration he supposedly bent a spoon simply by rubbing it.

After they watched the film, witnesses were asked to rate the 'paranormal' content of the demonstrations and complete a set of recall questions. Wiseman and Morris wanted to discover if, as Hodgson and Dingwall had suggested, sheep really did tend to misremember those parts of the demonstrations that were central to solving the tricks. For this reason, half of the questions concerned the methods used to fake the phenomena. For example, the psychic faked the key-bending demonstration by secretly switching the straight key for a pre-bent duplicate by passing the straight key from one hand to the other. During the switch the straight key could not be seen. This was clearly central to the trick's method; and one of the 'important' questions asked was whether the straight key had always remained in sight. A second set of 'unimportant' questions asked about parts of the demonstration that were not related to the tricks' methods. Overall, the results suggested that sheep rated the demonstrations as more 'paranormal' than goats did, and that goats did indeed recall significantly more 'important' information than sheep. There was no such difference for the recall of the 'unimportant' information.[14]

As far as simplicity is concerned, theories 1 and 2 are in deep trouble. Like most paranormal explanations, they both posit the existence of unknown entities (charged, naturally occurring vortices and space aliens). Theory 3 sticks with known entities and processes.

On the criterion of conservatism, theories 1 and 2 are again in trouble. There is no good evidence that the hypothesized vortex has ever occurred anywhere. And we have no good reason to believe that either space aliens or alien technology have ever visited Earth, let alone created some nice designs in a wheat field.

We can summarize these judgments as in the following table:

Criterion	Vortices	Aliens	Humans
Testable	Yes	Yes	Yes
Fruitful	No	No	Yes
Scope	No	No	Yes
Simple	No	No	Yes
Conservative	No	No	Yes

We can see immediately that the three theories are equal in testability, but theory 3 wins on all other counts. It is clearly the superior theory. Both the vortex theory and the alien theory fail the tests of fruitfulness, scope, simplicity, and conservatism. Of these four criteria, simplicity and conservatism carry the most weight here. In general, the plausibility of a theory is weakened considerably when it posits unknown entities and processes. Likewise, a theory that doesn't fit with what we already know takes a hit in credibility. An unconservative theory, of course, can acquire some credibility if it excels in the other criteria of adequacy. But theories 1 and 2 fall short in all the criteria except testability. We can see then that theories 1 and 2 are not good explanations for crop circles. They are most likely false. Theory 3—human creation of crop circles—is a much better theory.

There are other crop-circle theories that we haven't examined. None of them seem to measure up to the criteria of adequacy as well as theory 3 does. If this is the case, then we can give an even stronger endorsement of theory 3: Crop circles are probably human-made.

Talking with the Dead

Some people claim that they can communicate with the dead, providing impressive and seemingly accurate information about a person's dead loved ones. They are called psychics (a century ago they were called mediums), and they have gained the respect of many who have come to them in search of messages from the deceased. They appear on television programs, publish books, and offer seminars to thousands. The most famous among these modern-day mediums are psychics James Van Praagh, Sylvia Browne, and John Edward. Their performances assure many people that their loved ones who 'have passed over' are fine and that any unsettled issues of guilt and forgiveness can be resolved.

'We [psychics] are here to heal people and to help people grow ... skeptics ... they're just here to destroy people. They're not here to encourage people, to enlighten people. They're just here to destroy people.'
—James Van Praagh

What is the best explanation for these otherworldly performances in which the psychics appear to be in contact with the dead? Several theories have been proposed. One is that the psychics are getting information about the dead and their loved ones ahead of time (before the performances begin). Another is that the psychics are using telepathy to read the minds of the living to discover facts about the dead. But for simplicity's sake let's narrow the list of theories down to the two leading ones.

Step 1. Here's the psychics' theory.

Theory 1: The psychics are communicating information or messages to and from the disembodied spirits of people who have died. In other words, the psychics are doing exactly what they claim to be doing. They are somehow identifying the appropriate deceased spirit, receiving and decoding transmissions from that spirit, conveying the information to the living, and sending messages back to the dead.

Step 2. The main evidence in support of this theory is the psychics' performance. They usually perform before an audience and talk to audience members who have lost loved ones. The psychics appear to know facts about the dead that they could only know if they were actually communicating with the dead. They also seem to inexplicably know things about members of the audience. Often they also provide incorrect information (such as saying that a member of the audience has lost her mother when in fact the mother is very much alive). But their 'hits' (times when they produce correct information) occur often enough and seem to be specific enough to impress.

> 'Death is a part of life, and pretending that the dead are gathering in a television studio in New York to talk twaddle with a former ballroom-dance instructor is an insult to the intelligence and humanity of the living.'
> —Michael Shermer

Food For Thought

Why People Believe Psychic Readings

Ray Hyman is professor emeritus of psychology at the University of Oregon and an expert on the scientific investigation of paranormal claims, including psychic readings. Years of research have led him to be skeptical of the validity of psychic readings, but he used to be a true believer. He explains why he went from believer to skeptic:

> Now it so happens that I have devoted more than half a century to the study of psychic and cold readings. I have been especially concerned with why such readings can seem so concrete and compelling, even to skeptics. As a way to earn extra income, I began reading palms when I was in my teens. At first, I was skeptical. I thought that people believed in palmistry and other divination procedures because they could easily fit very general statements to their particular situation. To establish credibility with my clients, I read books on palmistry and gave readings according to the accepted interpretations for the

lines, shape of the fingers, mounds, and other indicators. I was astonished by the reactions of my clients. My clients consistently praised me for my accuracy even when I told them very specific things about problems with their health and other personal matters. I even would get phone calls from clients telling me that a prediction that I had made for them had come true. Within months of my entry into palm reading, I became a staunch believer in its validity. My conviction was so strong that I convinced my skeptical high school English teacher by giving him readings and arguing with him. I later also convinced the head of the psychology department where I was an undergraduate.

When I was a sophomore, majoring in journalism, a well-known mentalist and trusted friend persuaded me to try an experiment in which I would deliberately read a client's hand opposite to what the signs in her hand indicated. I was shocked to discover that this client insisted that this was the most accurate reading she had ever experienced. As a result, I carried out more experiments with the same outcome. It dawned on me that something important was going on. Whatever it was, it had nothing to do with the lines in the hand. I changed my major from journalism to psychology so that I could learn why not only other people, but also I, could be so badly led astray. My subsequent career has focused on the reasons why cold readings can appear to be so compelling and seemingly specific.

HEART

HEAD

LIFE

What is this palm saying? Psychologists think they know. Photo: iStock / © Emrah Turudu

Psychologists have uncovered a number of factors that can make an ambiguous reading seem highly specific, unique, and uncannily accurate. And once the observer or client has been struck with the apparent accuracy of the reading, it becomes virtually impossible to dislodge the belief in the uniqueness and specificity of the reading. Research from many areas demonstrates this finding. The principles go under such names as the fallacy of personal validation, subjective validation, confirmation bias, belief perseverance, the illusion of invulnerability, compliance, demand characteristics, false uniqueness effect, foot-in-the-door phenomenon, illusory correlation, integrative agreements, self-reference effect, the principle of individuation, and many, many others. Much of this is facilitated by the illusion of specificity that surrounds language. All language is inherently ambiguous and depends much more than we realize upon the context and non-linguistic cues to fix its meaning in a given situation.[15]

"Ahh.. I see your future. Get up, go to work go to bed. Get up, go to work, go to bed. Get..."

www.CartoonStock.com

Psychics have rarely been tested scientifically. The few experiments conducted to date have been severely criticized for sloppy methodology. So there is no good scientific evidence to support theory 1. Investigators who have seen the psychics' live performances (not just the edited versions of the TV programs) report that the hit rates (the percentage of hits out of the total number of statements or questions) are actually much lower than most people realize. They have found hit rates as low as 5 per cent with the highest being well under 50 per cent. The low hit rate, though, may not be apparent on TV shows because misses are often edited out. Psychics tend to explain their misses with ad hoc hypotheses (explanations that cannot be verified).

Step 3. Here's the main alternative to the psychics' theory.

Theory 2: The psychics are doing 'cold reading'. Cold reading is a very old skill practised by fortune tellers, tarot-card readers, and mentalists (performers who pretend to read minds). When done well, cold reading can astonish and appear to be paranormal. In cold reading, the psychic reader surreptitiously acquires information from people (the subjects) by asking them questions, making statements, observing how people behave, and listening to what they say. Good cold readers always give the impression that the information actually comes from some mysterious source, such as the spirits of the departed. Anyone can learn to do cold reading. It doesn't require any exotic skills or special powers. All that's needed is the practised ability to deftly manipulate a conversation to elicit information from the subject.

Note that theory 2 does not say that the cold reading is necessarily done to deliberately deceive an audience. Cold reading can be done either consciously or unconsciously. It's possible for people to do cold reading while believing that they are getting information via their psychic powers.

To get the relevant information (or appear to have it), a psychic reader can use several cold-reading techniques. These include the following.

1. The reader encourages the subject to fill in the blanks.

    READER: I'm sensing something about the face or head or brow.
    SUBJECT: You're right, my father used to have terrible headaches.
    READER: I'm feeling something about money or finances.
    SUBJECT: Yes, my mother always struggled to pay the bills.

2. The reader makes statements with multiple variables so that a hit is very likely.

> READER: I'm feeling that your father was dealing with a lot of frustration, anguish, or anger.
> SUBJECT: Yes, he was always arguing with my brother.

3. The reader makes accurate and obvious inferences from information given by the subject.

> READER: Why was your father in the hospital?
> SUBJECT: He had had a heart attack.
> READER: Yes, he struggled with heart disease for years and had to take heart medication for a long time. You were really worried that he would have another heart attack.

4. The reader asks many questions and treats answers as though they confirmed the reader's insight.

> READER: Who was the person who got a divorce?
> SUBJECT: That was my daughter. She divorced her husband in 1992.
> READER: Because I feel that the divorce was very painful for her, that she was sad and depressed for a while.

5. The reader makes statements that could apply to almost anyone.

> READER: I'm sensing something about a cat or a small animal.
> SUBJECT: Yes, my mother owned a poodle.

With such cold-reading techniques a reader can appear to read minds. Theory 2 is bolstered by the fact that the psychics' amazing performances can be duplicated by anyone skilled in the use of cold reading. In fact, magicians, mentalists, and other non-psychic entertainers have used cold-reading techniques to give performances that rival those of the top psychics. Regardless of their authenticity, the performances of Van Praagh, Edward, and other psychics seem to be indistinguishable from those based on cold reading. The psychics may indeed be communicating with the dead, but they look as if they're using cold-reading techniques.

Step 4. Now we can apply the criteria of adequacy to these two competing explanations. Both theories are testable, and neither has yielded any novel predictions. So we must judge the theories in terms of scope, simplicity, and conservatism. And on each of these criteria, theory 2 is clearly superior. Theory 1 explains only the psychics' performances as described earlier, but theory 2 explains these performances plus other kinds of seemingly psychic readings, including tarot-card reading, fortune-telling, mentalist acts, and old-fashioned spiritualist seances. Theory 1, of course, fails the criterion of simplicity because it assumes the existence of unknown entities (disembodied spirits with certain abilities) and unknown processes (communication to and from the dead). Theory 2 makes no such assumptions. Finally, theory 1 is not conservative. It conflicts with everything we know about death, the mind, and communication. Theory 2, though, fits with existing knowledge just fine.

Here are these judgments in table form:

Criterion	Theory 1	Theory 2
Testable	Yes	Yes
Fruitful	No	No
Scope	No	Yes
Simple	No	Yes
Conservative	No	Yes

We must conclude that theory 1 is a seriously defective theory. It is unlikely to be true. Theory 2, however, is strong. It is not only superior to theory 1, but it is also a better explanation than other competing theories we haven't discussed in that it can explain most or all of the psychics' hits. If the cold-reading theory really is better than all these others, then we have good reasons to believe that Van Praagh, Edward, and other psychics perform their amazing feats through simple cold reading.

Exercise 10.7

1. Is it reasonable to accept or reject an extraordinary claim solely because of its weirdness?
2. According to a 2003 Ipsos-Reid poll, what percentage of Canadians believes in ghosts?
3. Is it reasonable to conclude that a phenomenon is paranormal just because you cannot think of a natural explanation?
* 4. Of what logical fallacy is the fallacious leap to a non-natural explanation an example?
5. What is the critical thinking principle that can help you avoid mistaking how something seems for how something is?
* 6. What is logical possibility? What is logical impossibility?
7. What is physical possibility? What is physical impossibility?
8. Are dogs that lay eggs logically possible?
9. Is it true that anything possible? If not, why not?
10. What is the four-step method for evaluating a theory?

Exercise 10.8

In each of the following examples, a state of affairs is described. Devise three theories to explain each one. Include two plausible theories that are natural explanations and one competing theory that is paranormal.

1. Jack spent the night in a hotel that had a reputation for being haunted. He slept in the very room (number 666) in which a horrible murder had been committed in the 1930s. He fell asleep thinking about the crime. At 3:00 AM he awoke to see the apparition of a man sitting at the foot of his bed.

* 2. Jacques lived in a house built back in the 1940s and that was now in disrepair. As he sat reading in the living room, he heard creaking sounds coming from upstairs.

3. Selena found herself thinking about the camping trip that she had gone on in British Columbia. She was remembering the morning she woke up to find her tent crawling with ladybugs. As she was pondering the ladybugs, she suddenly noticed a ladybug on the windowsill near her chair.

4. Some people report that in the past when they needed help in a risky situation (for example, when they were in a car accident or when they were lost in a crime-ridden neighbourhood), they were aided by a stranger who never gave his or her name and who left the scene quickly after rendering assistance. They claim that the stranger must have been their guardian angel.

5. According to a recent survey, 37 per cent of Canadians believe in ghosts or spirits of the dead.

6. Lil's horoscope said that she would meet someone interesting. Three days after reading it, she did.

* 7. Wayne dreamed that his uncle was killed by a bear in Algonquin Provincial Park. When Wayne woke up, he got a call from his mother saying that his uncle had been injured in a car accident near the park.

8. Eleanor has a reputation for acting strangely. Recently when her priest visited her in her home, she fell to the floor writhing with convulsions.

9. Nelly made a fresh batch of tortillas. On one of them she noticed that the scorch marks were unusual. She was sure that she could see the face of Jesus in the design made by the scorch marks.

10. Ali was not feeling well. He heard that a crazy woman in his village had put a curse on him because he had called her a witch. The next day Ali broke his arm when he slipped and fell against some rocks.

Exercise 10.9

Using your background knowledge and any other information you may have about the subject, devise a competing, naturalistic theory for each paranormal theory that follows, and then apply the criteria of adequacy to both of them—that is, ascertain how well each theory does in relation to its competitor on the criteria of testability, fruitfulness, scope, simplicity, and conservatism.

1. Phenomenon: George and Jan have been married for 20 years. Many times George seems to know exactly what Jan is thinking, as though he can read her mind.

    Theory: George is telepathic.

2. Phenomenon: Yolanda awoke one morning and remembered having a strange dream. She dreamed that space aliens came into her bedroom while she was sleeping and abducted her. The dream seemed extremely vivid. Later in the day, she noticed some scratches on her ankle. She didn't know how they got there.

    Theory: Yolanda was abducted by aliens.

* 3. Phenomenon: In 1917 in Cottingley, England, three little girls claimed to have taken photos of fairies who played with them in the garden. The photos showed the girls in the garden with what appeared to be tiny fairies dancing around them. (The 1997 movie *Fairy Tale* was about the girls and their story.)

    Theory: Fairies really do exist, and the girls photographed them.

4. Phenomenon: Ogopogo is alleged to be a large water serpent inhabiting Okanagan Lake in British Columbia. The creature is unknown to science. The serpent was known as N'ha-a-itk by the Interior Salish First Nations tribe, and there have been many reported sightings over the years. There is no hard evidence proving that the monster exists.

    Theory: Ogopogo actually exists.

5. Phenomenon: The famous Israeli psychic Uri Geller seems to be able to bend spoons and keys with his mind. He has been performing this feat for audiences for years. Magicians claim that Geller is a fraud and that they can also bend spoons and keys with simple sleight-of-hand magic tricks.

    Theory: Geller's psychic powers enable him to bend metal with his mind.

6. Phenomenon: When there's a full moon people seem to act in weird ways. All you have to do to confirm this is to go downtown and observe people when there's a full moon.

    Theory: Through some unknown force, the moon exerts influence on people's behaviour.

7. Phenomenon: Some people claim to be psychic detectives, that is, psychics who help the police solve crimes. The psychics sometimes mention the police departments that they have assisted. This psychic detective work is hard to

verify, and skeptics claim that either the psychics lie about their successes or they hit upon a solution to a crime by chance.

Theory: The psychic abilities of psychic detectives enable them to solve crimes.

Exercise 10.10

Read the following passages and answer these questions for each one.

1. What is the phenomenon being explained?
2. What theories—stated or implied—are used to explain the phenomenon?
3. Which theory seems the most plausible and why? (Base your judgment on the evidence cited in the passage as well as any other information you might have on the subject, and use the criteria of adequacy.)
4. What kind of evidence would persuade you to change your mind about your preferred theory?

Passage 1

'A Ouija board is used in divination and spiritualism. The board usually has the letters of the alphabet inscribed on it, along with words such as "yes", "no", "good-bye" and "maybe". A planchette (a slidable 3-legged device) or pointer of some sort is manipulated by those using the board. The users ask the board a question and together, or one of them singly, moves the pointer or the board until a letter is "selected" by the pointer. The selections "spell" out an answer to the question asked.

'Some users believe that paranormal or supernatural forces are at work in spelling out Ouija board answers. Skeptics believe that those using the board either consciously or unconsciously select what is read. To prove this, simply try it blindfolded for some time, having an innocent bystander take notes on what letters are selected. Usually, the result will be unintelligible nonsense.

'The movement of the planchette is not due to paranormal forces but to unnoticeable movements by those controlling the pointer, known as the *ideomotor effect*. The same kind of unnoticeable movement is at work in dowsing.

'The Ouija board was first introduced . . . in 1890 as a parlor game sold in novelty shops.'[16]

Passage 2

'Most scientists discount the existence of Bigfoot because the evidence supporting belief in the survival of a prehistoric bipedal apelike creature of such dimensions is scant. The only notable exception is Grover S. Krantz (1931–2002), an anthropologist at Washington State University. For nearly 40 years, Krantz argued for the probable existence of Bigfoot, but was unable to convince the majority of scientists. The evidence for Bigfoot's existence consists mainly of testimony from Bigfoot enthusiasts, footprints of questionable origin, and pictures that could easily have been of apes or humans in ape suits. There are no bones, no scat, no artifacts, no dead bodies, no mothers with babies, no adolescents, no fur, no nothing. There is no evidence that any individual or community of such creatures dwells anywhere near any of the "sightings". In short, the evidence points more towards hoaxing and delusion than real discovery. Some believers dismiss all such criticism and claim that Bigfoot exists in another dimension and travels by astral projection. Such claims reinforce the skeptic's view that the Bigfoot legend is a function of passionate fans of the paranormal, aided greatly by the mass media's eagerness to cater to such enthusiasm.'[17]

Passage 3

'Trickery aside, what about reports of apparent animal ESP? Anecdotal evidence suggests some animals may have precognitive awareness of various types of natural catastrophes, becoming agitated before earthquakes, volcanic eruptions, cyclones, and other events. However, the creatures may actually be responding to subtle sensory factors—like variations in air pressure and tremors in the ground—that are beyond the range of human perception.

'Something of the sort may explain some instances of apparent animal prescience. For example, a Kentucky friend of mine insists that his dogs seem to know when he has decided to go hunting, exhibiting a marked excitement even though they are lodged some distance away from the house. However, it seems possible that they are either responding to some unintended signal (such as recognizing certain noises associated with his getting ready for a hunting trip) or that he is selectively remembering those occasions when the dogs' excitement happens to coincide with his intentions. Another friend says he once had dogs who seemed to know when he was going to take them for a walk, but he decided he must have unconsciously signaled them (such as by glancing in the direction of their hanging leashes).'[18]

Passage 4

'Ever since humans gained the ability to look down at the Earth from airplanes, space shuttles, and satellites, we've discovered a number of unusual markings. We know very little about them. [There are some] mysterious lines that are found on the Nazca Desert of Peru. They stretch for several miles, crossing over cliffs and hills. A Swiss author named Erich von Daniken claims in his book, *Chariots of the Gods*, that these lines were made by aliens who visited the Earth long ago. A German scientist, Maria Reicher, says that von Daniken's idea is ridiculous, and she has her own theory. . . .

'Von Daniken claims that aliens landed in the Nazca Desert back when humans were still evolving from primitive beings. When the alien vehicles touched down, they gouged tracks into the desert plain. According to his theory, the ancient Nazcan natives would have believed that these lines were made by the "fiery chariots of the sky gods". They carefully preserved the tracks the "gods' chariots" had made and even extended them in all directions.

'Maria Reicher believes that the Nazca lines were created by ancient Peruvians to form a kind of calendar. She found that the lines aren't formed by marks in the earth, but by dark, purplish rocks that form borders and rows. The Nazcan people separated these rocks, which litter the desert, from the yellowish sand. Ancient Peruvians depended on the annual spring rains for their very existence. Since they needed time to prepare their fields before rainy season began, they made a point of learning when the seasons changed. Reicher noticed that the lines of rocks point to a place on the horizon where the sun rose and set during the winter and summer solstice—the times when the seasons change. Her theory is that the Nazcans used these lines as a sort of grand astronomical calendar, to help them get ready for the all-important change of seasons.'[19]

Passage 5

The renowned prophet Michel Nostradamus (1503–66) composed a thousand verses that foretold historical events. Here's proof. Verse XXVII reads like this:

> Underneath the cord, Guien struck from the sky,
> Near where is hid a great treasure,
> Which has been many years a gathering,
> Being found, he shall die, the eye put out by a spring.[20]

This is a clear reference to the Second World War. It means 'paratroopers alight near the Nazi's plunder hoard and, captured, they are executed.' Some people think that the verses are so vague that anyone can read anything they want into them. But they're not ambiguous at all.

Summary

Science seeks knowledge and understanding of reality, and it does so through the formulation, testing, and evaluation of theories. Science is a way of searching for truth. Technology, though, is the production of products. Science is not a world view, and we can't identify it with a particular ideology. A particular world view may predominate in the scientific community, but this doesn't mean that the world view is what science is all about. Science is not scientism—it is not the only way to acquire knowledge. It is, however, a highly reliable way of acquiring knowledge of empirical facts.

The scientific method cannot be identified with any particular set of experimental or observational procedures. But it does involve several general steps: (1) identifying the problem, (2) devising a hypothesis, (3) deriving a test implication, (4) performing the test, and (5) accepting or rejecting the hypothesis.

This kind of theory testing is part of a broader effort to evaluate a theory against its competitors. This kind of evaluation always involves, implicitly or explicitly, the criteria of adequacy.

Inference to the best explanation can be used to assess weird theories as well as more commonplace explanations in science and everyday life. However, when people try to evaluate extraordinary theories, they often make certain typical mistakes. They may believe that because they can't think of a natural explanation, a paranormal explanation must be correct. They may mistake what seems for what is, forgetting that we shouldn't accept the evidence provided by personal experience if we have good reason to doubt it. And they may not fully understand the concepts of logical and physical possibility. In both science and everyday life, the TEST formula enables us to appraise fairly the worth of all sorts of weird theories, including those about crop circles and communication with the dead, the two cases we examined in this chapter.

Field Problems

1. Find a controversial health or medical theory on the Internet and design a study to test it. Indicate the makeup and characteristics of any group in the study, whether a placebo group is used, whether the study is double-blind, and what study results would confirm and disconfirm the theory.

2. Find a controversial theory in the social sciences (e.g., anthropology, economics, psychology, political science) on the Internet and design a study to test it. Indicate the makeup and characteristics of any group in the study, whether a placebo group is used, whether the study is double-blind, and what study results would confirm and disconfirm the theory. If the theory is one that you strongly believe, indicate the kind and level of evidence that could convince you to change your mind about it.

3. Do research on the Internet to find information on spontaneous human combustion, the theory that a human body can catch on fire because of an unknown internal chemical or biological process. Apply the TEST formula to evaluate the theory. Consider at least one plausible alternative theory. Look for background information at *The Skeptic's Dictionary* (http://skepdic.com), the Committee for Skeptical Inquiry (CSI) (http://www.csicop.org), or *Skeptic Magazine* (http://www.skeptic.com).

Self-Assessment Quiz

1. What is a test implication?
2. Are hypotheses generated purely through induction? Why or why not?
3. When a test implication is disconfirmed, what conditional argument is exemplified?

4. When a test implication is confirmed, what conditional argument is exemplified?
5. Why can't scientific hypotheses be conclusively confirmed?
6. Why can't scientific hypotheses be conclusively disconfirmed?

For each of the following phenomena, devise a hypothesis to explain it and derive a test implication to test the hypothesis.

7. Car accidents on Blind Man's Curve have increased lately, especially since the streetlight was broken and not replaced.
8. Juan was found two hours after the fatal stabbing sitting in Stanley Park with blood on his shirt.
9. Mysterious lights appeared in the night sky. They looked like alien spacecraft.

For each of the following phenomena, suggest (1) a possible hypothesis to explain it, (2) a possible competing hypothesis, (3) a test implication for each hypothesis, and (4) what testing results would confirm and disconfirm the hypothesis.

10. While camping in the provincial park, Maria came down with a gastrointestinal illness.
11. The students who were put in a class with two teachers instead of one showed an improvement in their grades.
12. Public health officials report a significant increase in levels of stress in people who live or work in Toronto.
13. Since the Vaughn family started using Super Cold-Stopper With Beta-Carotene they have had 50 per cent fewer colds.

For each of the following hypotheses, specify a test implication and say what evidence would convince you to accept the hypothesis.

14. Esther stole the book from the library.
15. Most people—regardless of ethnicity—are economically better off now than their parents were 30 years ago.
16. Canada is closer to a two-tier health-care system today than it was 10 years ago.

Each of the theories that follow is offered to explain why an astrological reading by a famous astrologer turned out to be wildly inaccurate. On the basis of a person's horoscope, he had predicted that the person was a nice man who could work with other people very well. The person turned out to be Josef Mengele, the Nazi mass murderer. Say which theory (a) lacks simplicity, (b) is not conservative, (c) is untestable, and (d) has the most scope. (Some theories may merit more than one of these designations.)

17. Theory: Astrology—the notion that the position of the stars and planets at your birth controls your destiny—has no basis in fact.

18. Theory: Astrology works, but the astrologer read the horoscope wrong.
19. Theory: An unknown planetary force interfered with the astrological factors that normally determine a person's destiny.

Evaluate the following theory by using the TEST formula. Say what phenomenon is being explained. Use your background knowledge to assess the evidence. Specify one alternative theory, use the criteria of adequacy to assess the two theories, and determine which one is more plausible.

20. Joseph has acted strangely for years—always wearing black clothes and sometimes having seizures in public. He's possessed.

Integrative Exercises

These exercises pertain to material in Chapters 3–5 and 8–10.
1. What is an enumerative induction?
2. What is an analogical induction?
3. What is a necessary condition? What is a sufficient condition?
4. What is the appeal to ignorance?

For each of the following arguments, specify the conclusion and premises. If necessary, add implicit premises and conclusions.

5. 'The proper thing for the state to do, faced with disagreement about the nature of marriage that goes to the very core of what marriage is, is to get out of marriage as the relevant factor for the determination of state benefits. There should be no marriages (civil or religious) that the state should care about. Leave "marriage" to those who have some kind of theory about it. The non-religious marriages will be tiny in number in comparison with traditional marriages in any case.' (Iain T. Benson, http://centreblog.blogspot.com)

6. 'Privatization is neither an efficient nor an effective response to the shortage of long-term care facilities. Some Regional Health Authorities see [privatization] as an obstacle to the provision of well-coordinated and fiscally-responsible care. Centralized administration of public health care provides both lower administrative costs and economies of scale. Indeed, the fact that health care costs so much more in the US than in Canada—13.5 per cent of GDP in the US compared with 9.2 per cent in Canada—is largely the result of higher administrative costs in a system comprised of numerous competitive insurance firms, hospitals, clinics, and so on.' (Editorial, *Canadian Centre for Policy Alternatives*, http://www.policyalternatives.ca)

7. (This argument refers to protests in Ottawa and Toronto over the American invasion of Iraq). 'This kind of infantile posturing would be funny were it not so terrifying. That folks who may have smoked a little too much dope or gone to one

too many love-ins might still like to fight the establishment is cute. Except that in this case it does not simply represent an opinion. It represents, I think, a frightening set of values—and by that I don't mean the belief that tie-dyed shirts or the Grateful Dead are fashionable. I mean values that have convinced these people that peace is preferable to freedom, and that the protector of our freedom, the United States, deserves only to be loathed.' (Rondi Adamson, 'Peaceniks should grow up instead of just pretending to', *Ottawa Citizen*, 23 February 2003)

8. Our forests are Canada's greatest national treasure. They must be protected at all cost. Without our forests, Canada would be a land of lakes and tundra: our forests give our landscape depth and vibrancy. And don't forget that trees soak up carbon dioxide and give off oxygen. So we should also value our forests for their contribution to the very air we breathe. Finally, consider the economic value of our great forests. Every year the forestry industry exports tens of billions of dollars worth of products, contributing significantly to the standard of living enjoyed by all Canadians.

For each of the following phenomena, suggest (1) a possible hypothesis to explain it, (2) a possible competing hypothesis, and (3) a test implication for each hypothesis.

9. The accident rate on Highway 401 was very high but was reduced considerably after the speed limit was lowered to 90 km/h and billboards urged drivers to obey the law.
10. In stressful situations, women appear to adapt better and more quickly to the emotional demands of the situation than men do.
11. The percentage of high school seniors engaging in sexual intercourse has risen dramatically in the past six years.
12. The mosquito population in the township has decreased drastically in the past year even though county workers have curtailed the use of insecticides and have stopped urging residents to get rid of standing water on their property, which is a breeding ground for the insects.

Evaluate each of the following theories and say whether it is plausible or implausible.

13. Treatment for HIV/AIDS is much more effective than it used to be because of global warming.
14. Six thousand years ago a worldwide flood devastated the Earth, killing all but a handful of human beings who survived by building an ark.
15. The universe is so vast, with billions of stars that could have planets that will sustain life, that it is probable that intelligent life exists in other places besides Earth.
16. Transcendental meditation shows us that if enough people meditate together on the prevention of crime, the crime rate in an area will decrease.

Evaluate each of the following theories by using the TEST formula. Use your background knowledge to assess the evidence. Specify one alternative theory, use the criteria of adequacy to assess the two theories, and determine which one is more plausible.

17. Canada's prominent role as an international peacekeeper has resulted from the respect our military has earned through aggressive use of its awesome firepower over the last 30 years.

18. Because of accounting errors, the population of Canada has falsely been said to be over 30 million. It's actually much closer to 20 million.

19. The NDP has never formed a federal government in Canada because influential Americans have worked hard to prevent Canada from becoming 'too left-wing'.

20. Everyone who has ever beaten cancer—that is, been cured—has done so because of a wholesome diet.

Writing Assignments

1. In a one-page essay use the TEST formula to evaluate the following theories:
   a. Phenomenon: People report feeling less arthritis pain after taking fish oil capsules.

   > Theory 1: Fish oil relieves joint pain.
   > Theory 2: The placebo effect.

   b. Phenomenon: A temporary drop in the crime rate in Regina just after a transcendental meditation (TM) group meditated for three days on a lower crime rate.

   > Theory 1: TM meditation lowers crime rates.
   > Theory 2: Normal fluctuations in Regina's crime rate.

   c. Phenomenon: Fifty patients with severe arthritis pain were prayed for by 100 people, and 25 out of those 50 patients reported a significant lessening of pain.

   > Theory 1: Prayer heals.
   > Theory 2: Normal pain remission that is characteristic of arthritis.

2. Read Essay 9 ('UFO Abductions') in Appendix A and write a 500-word essay evaluating one of the more plausible theories mentioned in the reading, comparing it to this theory: reports of UFO abductions are the result of US government doctors implanting 'memories' of abductions in people to secretly test the reliability of their implantation techniques. Use the TEST formula.

3. Devise two theories to explain the low test scores of most of the students in your calculus course, and then write a 500-word paper evaluating the worth of the two theories.

4. Rewrite Essay 10 ('Amityville: The Horror of It All') in Appendix A so that it makes more explicit use of the TEST formula, identifying the phenomenon to be explained and the theories offered to explain it.

Chapter 11

Judging Moral Arguments and Theories

Chapter Objectives

Moral Arguments

You will be able to

- understand the distinction between moral statements, arguments, and theories.
- explain the difference between moral and non-moral statements.
- outline the structure of moral arguments.
- know the reason why a moral argument requires at least one moral premise.
- supply the missing moral premise in a moral argument.
- use the counter-example method to evaluate moral premises.

Moral Theories

You will be able to

- recognize the differences among moral judgments, principles, and theories.
- recognize that everyone has a moral theory and that it's important to ensure that your moral theory is coherent.
- understand the similarities between moral theories and scientific theories.
- list the three moral criteria of adequacy and apply the criteria moral theories.

A Coherent World View

You will be able to

- understand what a world view is and why having a coherent world view is so important.
- understand how a world view can fail to be coherent.
- explain how and why the criterion of internal consistency is applied to world views.

We have come a long way. We have seen that we can apply critical thinking productively to everyday claims, arguments, and problems; to explanations in a wide range of subject areas; to scientific theories of all sorts; and to offbeat theories of the paranormal and supernatural kind. Now we can go even further. We can now venture into a vast and complex sphere that is often thought to be off limits to critical reasoning: *morality*. Morality concerns beliefs about right and wrong, good and bad, and just and unjust. It's an aspect of life that we deal with every day because we have little choice. In countless situations we must decide what we ought to do or not do, what is moral or immoral, and what is good or bad. To do these things, we are forced to accept or reject moral statements, make and criticize moral arguments, and wrestle with moral theories.

In this process of contending with moral issues, we inevitably formulate our own moral theory—our own beliefs about what morality is or is not, what actions are right or wrong, and what things are good or bad. To an astonishing degree, our moral theory charts the course of our lives. If the course matters, then we must try to fashion the best moral theory we can.

If we are to be intellectually mature, we must also try to integrate the results of these moral analyses and deliberations into a comprehensive picture of reality, what is known as a world view. A **world view** is a philosophy of life, a set of beliefs and theories that helps us make sense of a wide range of issues in life. It defines for us what exists, what should be, and what we can know. We all have a world view, and our notions about morality are an important part of it. A good critical thinker tries to ensure that his or her world view contains no internal contradictions and that it offers reliable guidance in dealing with the world.

So in this chapter we set out to apply critical thinking to some big ideas and broad questions. We explore procedures for evaluating moral discourse—specifically, moral judgments, arguments, and theories—and look at ways that we can incorporate our understanding into a coherent world view.

Moral Arguments

A moral argument, like any other kind of argument, has premises and a conclusion. The premises (and sometimes the conclusion) may be implied, not stated, and they may be simple or complex—just as in other arguments. Moral arguments, however, differ from non-moral ones in that their conclusions are moral statements. In general, a **moral statement** is a statement asserting that an action is right or wrong (moral or immoral) or that something (such as a person or motive) is good or bad. Here are some moral statements:

- Serena should keep her promise to you.
- It is wrong to treat James so harshly.
- Abortion is immoral.

'A system of morality which is based on relative emotional values is a mere illusion, a thoroughly vulgar conception which has nothing sound in it and nothing true.'
—Socrates

- We ought to protect Liu from the angry mob.
- My father is a good man.

Moral statements are plainly different from non-moral, or descriptive, statements. Non-moral statements do not assert that something is right or wrong, good or bad—they simply describe a state of affairs without giving it a value one way or the other. Compare these non-moral statements with the moral statements just given:

- Serena did not keep her promise to you.
- James was treated harshly.
- Some people think abortion is immoral.
- Liu was protected from the angry mob.
- My father tried to be a good man.

Food For Thought

Is Moral Reasoning Possible?

Some people claim that reasoning about morality is not possible because moral statements are not statements at all. This view is a moral theory known as *emotivism*. Emotivism says that moral statements are just not the kinds of things that can be true or false. They are more like exclamations, such as 'Hooray!' or 'Bah!' They are expressions of emotion, not statements of fact. So according to emotivism, the sentence 'Racial discrimination is wrong' means something like 'Racial discrimination—boo!'

But this theory has been severely criticized by moral philosophers. They contend, for example, that in several ways the theory conflicts with our experience of the moral life. Our everyday moral experience seems to suggest that we sometimes have moral disagreements with others. The notion that we do have disagreements seems to most people like a simple matter of common sense. But according to emotivism, moral disagreements are impossible. Since moral utterances are not statements, they cannot contradict one another. If you say 'sushi—yum!' and someone else says 'sushi—yuk!' the two of you are not disagreeing; you're just each telling us how *you* feel about sushi. But our moral experience seems to show that in moral disagreements we are doing much more than expressing emotion. In addition, emotivism says that nothing is good or bad, right or wrong, because these terms don't refer to anything. But our moral experience appears to suggest that some things really are good or bad, right or wrong. Many moral philosophers believe that these considerations show that emotivism must be mistaken.

Critics who take this line of argument against emotivism admit that our common-sense moral experience may be misleading. It's possible that emotivism is correct after all. Common-sense views of the world have been wrong in the past. But, these critics assert, we are justified in believing what common sense tells us unless we have good reason to doubt it.

The standard moral argument is a mixture of moral and non-moral statements. At least one premise is a moral statement that asserts a general moral principle or moral standard. At least one premise makes a non-moral claim. And the conclusion is a moral statement, or judgment, about a particular case (usually a particular kind of action). For example:

Argument 1
(1) It is wrong to inflict unnecessary pain on a child.
(2) Spanking inflicts unnecessary pain on a child.
(3) Therefore, spanking is wrong.

In this simple argument, premise 1 is a moral statement, affirming a general moral principle. Premise 2 is a non-moral statement describing the nature of a specific kind of action. And the conclusion is the moral statement that the argument is intended to establish. It is about a specific kind of action.

A standard moral argument has this form for good reason. In a moral argument, we simply cannot establish the conclusion (a moral statement) without a moral premise. A moral argument with only non-moral premises does not work. To put it another way, we cannot infer what *should be or ought to be* (in the conclusion) from statements about *what is*. Suppose the previous argument reads like this (and there are no missing premises):

Spanking inflicts unnecessary pain on a child.
Therefore, spanking is wrong.

The premise doesn't say anything about right or wrong; it just makes a descriptive claim. The conclusion, though, does assert something about right or wrong. So the conclusion is not supported by the premise; it does not follow from the descriptive statement.

Food For Thought

Moral and Non-moral Statements

Is this a moral statement: 'I am opposed to abortion'? How about this one: 'I feel very strongly that abortion is wrong'? Actually in many contexts, statements like these are not meant to be moral statements at all; they are not meant to assert that an action is right or wrong or that a person is good or bad. They are used instead to report on someone's state of mind. Saying that you feel a certain way toward an action is not the same thing as stating that the action is wrong. But be careful. Sometimes statements like these really are meant as moral statements. Context will usually tell you which kind of statement is intended.

Here's another example:

Dumping oil in a lake does unnecessary damage to the environment.
You shouldn't dump oil in a lake.

This argument, as it is, fails because the moral premise is missing. We need a moral premise to connect the non-moral premise to the conclusion, like this:

Argument 2
You should avoid unnecessary damage to the environment.
Dumping oil in a lake does unnecessary damage to the environment.
You shouldn't dump oil in a lake.

Food For Thought

Can't We All Just Get Along?

Despite the prevalence of moral disagreements on countless issues, there is a surprising amount of agreement on basic moral principles. Often, the bone of contention in moral arguments is not the moral premises (which may be widely accepted), but the non-moral ones. In debates about 'pulling the plug' on severely comatose patients, for example, all parties may agree that murder is wrong but disagree about the nature of comatose patients. Some may insist that comatose patients are entities that can be murdered (because they are fully human, true persons, etc.); others, that comatose patients are not the kind of entities that can be murdered (because they are not persons, for example). So there may not be as much moral disagreement in the world as you might think. Here's a list of moral principles that both parties in moral debates often accept:

- Personal benefit: Acknowledge the extent to which an action produces beneficial consequences for the individual in question.
- Principle of benevolence: Help those in need.
- Principle of harm: Do not harm others.
- Principle of honesty: Do not deceive others.
- Principle of lawfulness: Do not violate the law.
- Principle of autonomy: Acknowledge a person's freedom over his or her actions or physical body.
- Principle of justice: Acknowledge a person's right to due process, fair compensation for harm done, and fair distribution of benefits.
- Rights: Acknowledge a person's rights to life, information, privacy, free expression, and safety.[1]

In the standard moral argument, we also need a non-moral premise. Remember that the conclusion is a moral statement (judgment) about a particular kind of action. The moral premise, however, is a statement expressing a general moral principle about a much broader class of actions. In order to infer the narrower conclusion from a much broader premise, we need a non-moral statement to bridge the gap. For example, from the general moral principle that 'you should avoid unnecessary damage to the environment,' we cannot conclude that 'you shouldn't dump oil into a lake' unless there is a non-moral premise stating that dumping oil in a lake does unnecessary damage to the environment. Likewise from the general moral principle that 'plagiarism is wrong', we cannot conclude that 'copying ideas from the Internet without proper citation is wrong' unless there's a factual premise telling us that copying ideas from the Internet without proper citation is a kind of plagiarism.

Now, very often when you encounter moral arguments, they are abbreviated and missing the moral premise (the general moral principle), like the arguments discussed earlier:

Spanking inflicts unnecessary pain on a child.
Therefore, spanking is wrong.

Dumping oil in a lake does unnecessary damage to the environment.
You shouldn't dump oil in a lake.

Usually, the moral premise is missing because it's implicit. In such cases, to make sense of the argument, you must supply the implicit premise. Sometimes you may automatically add the implicit premise in your head without bothering to properly fill out the argument. But if you want to evaluate moral arguments carefully, it's best to spell out any missing premises. Implicit moral premises are often dubious and need to be studied closely. General moral principles that are taken for granted may turn out to be unfounded or incomplete. Also, laying everything out on the table like this is essential if you wish to improve the argument—an important exercise if you want your positions on moral issues to be well supported.

The best approach to identifying implicit premises is to treat moral arguments as deductive. (Notice that arguments 1 and 2 are valid deductive arguments.) Your task, then, is to supply plausible premises that will make the argument valid. (We used this same procedure in Chapter 3 for finding implicit premises.) Consider this argument:

Cloning humans is unnatural.
Therefore, cloning humans is morally wrong.

As it stands, this argument is not valid, and we can see right away that the missing premise is a general moral principle. A plausible premise to make this argument valid, then, is 'Anything unnatural is morally wrong,' a general moral principle. The revised version is:

Argument 3
Anything unnatural is morally wrong.
Cloning humans is unnatural.
Therefore, cloning humans is morally wrong.

Here's another incomplete argument:

Meg lied to her sister for no good reason.
Therefore, Meg should not have lied to her sister.

To make this argument valid and to supply a general moral principle, we can add this premise:

"Do everything ethically ... within reason, of course."

www.CartoonStock.com

Argument 4
One should not lie without good reason.
Meg lied to her sister for no good reason.
Therefore, Meg should not have lied to her sister.

Another advantage to treating moral arguments as deductive (and to supplying explicit premises that will make the arguments valid) is ease of analysis. Generally, moral arguments are easier to evaluate and modify when they are deductive. And if they are deductively valid, you know that any flaws in the arguments will likely be the result of false premises. For example, if you have a deductively valid argument, and the conclusion is false, you know that at least one of the premises is false.

Often the problematic premise in a moral argument is the moral premise that states a general moral principle. How do we evaluate such a premise? Actually, we can often assess the premise the same way we might assess any other kind of universal generalization—by trying to think of counterexamples to it. Consider this deductively valid argument, a modified version of argument 3:

> 'So, if we can support our [moral] judgments with good reasons, and provide explanations of why these reasons matter, and show that the case on the other side is weak, what more in the way of "proof" could anyone possibly want?'
> —James Rachels

Argument 5
(1) The medical cloning of humans is unnatural because it is something that would not occur without human intervention.
(2) All actions that are unnatural and that are not done for religious reasons should not be done.
(3) The medical cloning of humans is never done for religious reasons.
(4) Therefore, cloning humans should not be done.

Premise 2 is the general moral principle here. Is it true? At the very least it is questionable. We know that it's questionable because we can think of counter-examples to it. That is, we can think of instances in which the principle would not hold. For example, what about the use of antibiotics to treat infections? The use of antibiotics is unnatural as defined in the argument (they are a good example of human intervention in the natural course of illness), and few would claim that antibiotics

"BUT ISN'T IT MORE IMPORTANT to LEARN How to BE A DECENT HUMAN BEING?"

are employed for religious reasons. (The term 'for religious reasons' is vague, but we will assume for the sake of this example that it means something like 'as an integral part of established religious practice'.) But despite its unnaturalness, the use of antibiotics seems to be morally acceptable. So premise 2 appears to be false. We could probably refute premise 2 by using many other counter-examples, such as wearing clothes, drinking bottled water, and riding a bicycle.

Of course, the non-moral premises in a moral argument can also be questionable. As noted in previous chapters, accurately assessing the truth of these premises depends on your knowledge of the subject matter, including the results of relevant scientific research and your background information. Sometimes, however, all parties to a moral dispute accept the non-moral premises but debate the moral ones.

Remember that most of what you learned about arguments in previous chapters applies here. Assessing arguments of any kind is a matter of studying a passage until you understand it, finding the conclusion, identifying the premises, and checking the quality of the reasoning.

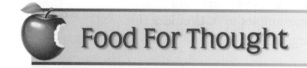

Food For Thought

Morality and Ethics

The activity of critically examining moral arguments is also sometimes known as *ethics*. In fact, that's the word attached to that activity when it is taught in university courses dedicated to the topic. Morality (as noted above) concerns our beliefs about right and wrong; ethics is the process of reflecting critically on those beliefs and asking which of our moral beliefs are well-founded. So, university courses on health-care ethics (or bioethics) will ask you to *think critically* about personal beliefs and social policies related to health care. Courses in business ethics ask students to *think critically* about claims regarding the moral standards to which corporations should be held. And courses in environmental ethics are an opportunity to *think critically* about the moral status of the natural environment and about various claims regarding our obligation to safeguard it.

Moral Theories

When we assess moral arguments and in other ways think critically about morality, we are ultimately trying to evaluate or develop three immeasurably valuable things: moral judgments, moral principles, and moral theories. Moral judgments are decisions about the morality of specific classes of actions or of the goodness of people and their motives. They are the final, prized product of our moral deliberation. They are also, as we've seen, the conclusions of moral arguments. Moral judgments are usually justified by appeals to general moral principles—moral standards that apply to broad areas of conduct. As the previous section shows, moral principles are crucial premises in moral arguments. But where do moral principles come from? Moral philosophers (those who study the nature of morality) and other critical thinkers try to devise a comprehensive moral theory from which moral principles can be derived. Theories of morality are attempts to explain what makes an action right or what makes a person good. They try to specify what all right actions and all good things have in common. As such, they give ultimate support, guidance, and validation to our moral decision making.

Interestingly enough, we all have a moral theory. Whether we articulate it or not, we all have some kind of view of what makes actions right or persons good. Even the notion that there is no such thing as right or wrong is a moral theory. Even the idea that all moral theories are worthless or that all moral judgments are subjective, objective, relative, or meaningless is a moral theory. The critical question then is not whether you have a moral theory but whether the theory you have is a good one.

Many people embrace the moral theory given to them by their parents. Others adopt moral theories that have been developed by great thinkers of the past. One theory that many people find attractive, for example, is the divine-command theory. This is the view that what makes an action right is that God commands it or wills it. Some who accept this theory believe that God's commandments are embodied in rules laid out in the Bible or the Torah or the Koran, and that an action is therefore right if it conforms to those rules. Another interesting—and very influential—moral theory is act-utilitarianism, the view that what makes an action right is that it maximizes overall happiness, everyone considered. If, out of all possible actions in a situation, a particular action produces the greatest amount of happiness, then the action is right. What counts here is not commandments or abstract concepts such as rights and justice, but the consequences of actions. There is a multiplicity of moral theories with conflicting takes on morality, each varying in its worth as a plausible guide to conduct.

This brings us round to a more focused version of the question asked earlier: Which moral theory is best, and how can we judge that it's the best? Recall that we asked this type of question in Chapters 9 and 10 when we discussed inference to the best explanation and several types of theories (everyday, scientific, and weird). The answer in this chapter is the same as the answer in those chapters. To identify

> 'In my view moral theorizing is something that real people do in everyday life. It is not just the domain of professors, expounding in their lecture halls. Moral theorizing can be found on the highways and byways, practiced by everyone from bartenders to politicians.'
> —Dale Jamieson

Food For Thought

Critiquing Moral Theories

Most moral philosophers don't buy the idea that one moral theory is as good as any other. They spend a good deal of time evaluating moral theories to gauge their worth, and some theories don't fare very well under this scrutiny. Here, for example, are some typical criticisms of three controversial moral theories.

Subjective Relativism

This view states that what makes an action right for someone is that that person approves it. Moral judgments are relative to what each person believes. If you say that stealing is wrong, then it's wrong (for you). If someone else says that stealing is right, then it's right (for her). Moral philosophers, though, think that the theory has several problematic implications. For example, the theory implies that each person is morally infallible. If you truly approve of an action, then it's right, and you cannot be wrong. Subjective relativism also makes moral disagreement nearly impossible. You disagree with others when you think they are mistaken. But according to subjective relativism, no one could be mistaken. These and other implications, critics say, render the theory implausible.

Cultural Relativism

This view claims that what makes an action right is that it's approved by one's culture. If your culture deems something to be right, it's right. Moral truth is relative to cultures. As you might expect, this view is criticized for many of the same problems that plague subjective relativism. It implies that cultures are infallible. This means that if most people living in Nazi Germany during the Second World War had approved of the extermination of the Jews, then the Holocaust was morally right. It seems, though, that societies are no more infallible than individuals. What's more, cultural relativism implies that it would be impossible to disagree with one's culture and be right. Social reformers such as Martin Luther King Jr or Gandhi could not claim that an action approved of by society is wrong, for if society approves of it, the action is right. For these and other reasons, most moral philosophers view cultural relativism as a questionable moral theory.

Ethical Egoism

In this view, what makes an action right is that it promotes one's own best interest. It doesn't imply that you should do anything you want because, in the long run, that may not be in your own best interest. Ethical egoism could even condone generosity to others, on the grounds that being nice to other people is in your best interest. Critics, however, say that the theory is implausible because it sanctions all sorts of abominable acts. For example, if it's in your best interest to kill your boss, and if you could do it without suffering any negative consequences (such as getting caught), then ethical egoism says that your moral duty is to kill him.

the best theory, we must compare competing theories and use the criteria of adequacy to appraise their worth. The criteria of adequacy that we use in judging moral theories are a little different from those we use to assess other types of theories, though the two sets of criteria have much in common. In addition, in some significant ways, moral theories are much like scientific theories, and the process of theory evaluation is similar in both cases.

How are moral theories like scientific theories? Recall that scientific theories try to explain the causes of events, everything from the growth of tumours to exploding stars. A plausible scientific theory is one that's consistent with all the relevant data. A theory explaining the cause of a fatal illness, for example, must take into account facts about the patient's symptoms, the results of medical tests, medical histories, environmental factors, and more. Moral theories, on the other hand, try to explain what makes an action right or what makes a person good. A plausible moral theory must also be consistent with the relevant data. The data that moral theories try to explain are our considered moral judgments—those moral judgments that we accept after we reason about them carefully. Any plausible moral theory must be consistent with those considered moral judgments. If it isn't consistent with them—if, for example, it approves of obviously immoral acts (such as inflicting pain on innocent children for no good reason or treating equals unequally)—the theory must be rejected. So the first criterion of adequacy for moral theories is *consistency with considered moral judgments.*

In science (and many other fields of inquiry) there is an interesting relationship between theory and data. The data have an impact on the theory because the theory explains the data. A good theory, on the other hand, can lead scientists to reject certain data. Scientists want the data and theory to match up as closely as possible. They want the match to be so close that significant changes in either the data or theory aren't necessary. Moral theories work this way too. Our moral data (our considered moral judgments) influence our moral theory. And our moral theory can lead us to accept or reject certain data. Ideally, we want the fit between data and theory to be as close as possible. In other words, we want to achieve what moral philosophers refer to as a 'reflective equilibrium' between facts and theory. We want the fit to be so close that significant adjustments in either data or theory are not necessary.

In addition to being consistent with the data, a plausible scientific theory must also be conservative. It must be consistent with background information—that is, with well-founded beliefs, such as reliable scientific findings and well-established theories. Plausible moral theories must also be consistent with the relevant background information—that is, with our experience of the moral life. Whatever else our moral experience involves, it certainly includes (1) making moral judgments (we do this constantly), (2) having moral disagreements (we occasionally do this), and (3) sometimes acting immorally (we recognize that we are not morally perfect). If a moral theory suggests that we do not have these experiences, we must view the theory with suspicion. Another criterion of adequacy for moral theories, then, is *consistency with our experience of the moral life.*

Now, it's possible that our experience of the moral life is an illusion and that it only seems to involve making moral judgments, having moral disagreements, and acting morally. But unless we have good reason to believe that our moral experience is an illusion, we are justified in accepting it at face value.

A scientific theory gains in credibility if it helps to solve problems (has fruitfulness and scope). A plausible moral theory must also help to solve problems. That is, it must help us make moral decisions, especially those that involve moral dilemmas—instances where moral principles or moral judgments are in conflict. After all, the reason we want a moral theory is that it helps guide our actions and reconcile clashing moral beliefs. A moral theory that offers no help with such moral problems is said to be *unworkable.* Unworkable moral theories are inferior. So a final criterion of adequacy for moral theories is *workability in real-life situations.*

Now let's see how we can use these criteria to judge the merits of a moral theory. For the sake of illustration, we will focus on just one theory without doing a comprehensive comparison with others. And we will zero in on a theory that's relatively simple—act-utilitarianism.

This moral theory was conceived by Jeremy Bentham (1748–1832) and later refined by John Stuart Mill (1806–73). Bentham's idea was that right actions are those that achieve the greatest happiness for the greatest number. He declared that by this simple standard all actions could be judged. Many people embraced the theory because it seemed so much more rational than moral theories of the time, which often rested on dubious assumptions. In the nineteenth century, act-utilitarianism inspired reformers who worked to abolish slavery, eliminate child labour, and promote equal rights for women.

To be more precise, act-utilitarianism says that what makes an action right is that it maximizes overall happiness, everyone considered. Acting morally in any given situation, then, involves calculating how much happiness each of several possible actions can produce, identifying the persons who will be affected by those actions, and opting for the one action that produces the greatest amount of happiness in the world. Notice that what matters in act-utilitarianism is the *consequences*

Review Notes

Moral Criteria of Adequacy
1. Consistency with our considered moral judgments.
2. Consistency with our experience of the moral life.
3. Workability in real-life situations.

![apple logo]

Food For Thought

Jeremy Bentham, Father of Utilitarianism

Jeremy Bentham (1748–1832) was a philosopher who devoted his considerable intellectual talent to ethics and political-legal theory. Early on, he was dismayed by the injustice in law and morals that seemed rampant in British society. So he developed his own moral theory (utilitarianism) and tried to put his ideas into practice. At the time Bentham proposed it, utilitarianism was considered a radical departure in moral philosophy. But it seemed to be the antidote to conventional moral theories that he thought condemned actions that did no harm and encouraged actions that did great harm. Utilitarianism cut through all that with just one simple principle about maximizing happiness. Inspired by his theory, Bentham advocated many ideas that are now taken for granted but seemed shock-

Jeremy Bentham (1748–1832). National portrait gallery, London

ing at the time: the reform of prisons, equal rights for women, the liberalization of laws concerning sexual activity, and the use of civil service exams for government employees.

To some people, the most interesting fact about Bentham is that he is still hanging around the old school that he helped found, University College in London. Well, actually his embalmed body is still hanging around, on display, topped by a wax model of his head.

of an action—not whether the action breaks a rule or violates some moral principle. If happiness is maximized by a particular action, then the action is morally right, regardless of any other considerations. By the lights of act-utilitarianism, the end justifies the means.

How does act-utilitarianism fare when judged by the moral criteria of adequacy? For starters, the theory does seem to be consistent with key aspects of our experience of the moral life. The theory assumes that we can and do make moral judgments, have moral disagreements, and act morally.

Some critics, however, have questioned whether act-utilitarianism is a workable theory because calculating amounts of happiness seems to be extremely difficult or impossible. For example, each action we perform has consequences indefinitely into the future. At what point, then, should we make our calculation of the happiness produced? Should we figure into our calculations the happiness that will accrue by next Tuesday? Next year? Next decade? Some actions may produce very little happiness in the short run but a great deal of happiness over the long haul. Some actions work the other way round—they have big short-term benefits, no long-term payback. Act-utilitarianism offers no help in resolving this problem, and so critics have accused the theory of being unworkable.

Many moral philosophers think that act-utilitarianism faces a much bigger problem than unworkability in that it seems to conflict with many of our considered moral judgments. For instance, the theory seems to conflict with our considered moral judgments involving rights. We tend to think that certain things should not be done to people even if doing them would produce the greatest amount of happiness in the world. We would not think it right to falsely accuse and punish an innocent person just because doing so would make a whole town of people happy. We would not think it right to torture one person just because the action would make a dozen other people extremely happy. Our considered moral judgments say that such actions are wrong, but act-utilitarian says they're right.

Suppose that two possible actions will produce exactly the same amount of overall happiness. But one of the actions involves the violation of someone's rights or causes a serious injustice. According to act-utilitarianism, the two actions are equally right. But to many, this evaluation of the situation seems to conflict with our considered moral judgments.

The same kind of conflict arises in regard to moral duties. Most of us believe that we have certain duties to other people that often seem more weighty than considerations of happiness. For example, we believe that, in general, we have a duty to keep our promises to people. But act-utilitarianism does not recognize any such duties. It says that our only goal should be to maximize happiness—regardless of whether we have to break a promise to do it.

So for these reasons (and a few others), many critics have accused act-utilitarianism of being acutely inconsistent with relevant moral data. They believe that any theory that runs afoul of the criterion of consistency in this way cannot be correct.

But take note. Even the fiercest critics of act-utilitarianism have admitted that the theory does seem to capture something essential to moral theories—the notion that the consequences of actions are indeed relevant to moral judgments. Probably very few people would want to say that in moral decision making the consequences of their actions never matter.

For the record, the sketch of act-utilitarianism given here has been oversimplified so we can focus on the process of theory assessment. Over the years, utilitarians have modified the original theory to make it more plausible. Critics, however, still claim that the theory is flawed . . . but that's another story.

A Coherent World View

Making a coherent and powerful world view for yourself is the work of a lifetime, requiring reflection, critical thinking, and (often) personal anguish. So there is no way that this chapter—or *any* chapter, book, or person—can provide you with ready-made content for your world view. But we can trace out some characteristics that any good world view should possess.

A world view is a massive intellectual construct with many elements. We can get a handle on it, though, by thinking of it as primarily a composite of theories—theories about morality, God, science, mind, personhood, society, knowledge, and much more. We all have our own beliefs about these things, and our most general beliefs often congeal into theories. Since world views are framed out of theories, good world views will, as a minimum requirement, consist of good theories. So much of the job of devising a good world view consists of ensuring that our theories are the best theoretical explanations available. We do that, of course, by putting our theories to the test as we did in previous chapters.

But there's more to crafting a plausible world view than that. Recall our discussion of theories and inference to the best explanation in Chapter 9. We saw that a theory helps increase our understanding by fitting our beliefs into a coherent pattern. When some of our most fundamental beliefs conflict with one another, the relevant theory is in trouble and our understanding is decreased. After all, if two of

© 2002 by Sidney Harris. www.ScienceCartoonsPlus.com

our beliefs are inconsistent with one another, we know that at least one of them must be false. To achieve true understanding, we must somehow resolve the inconsistency. Likewise, if the theories that make up our world view are inconsistent with one another, there is obviously something wrong with our world view. At least one of our theories must be flawed, and some of our beliefs must be wrong. Our understanding of the world is decreased, and our prospects for success (however we define it) are dimmed. A crucial criterion, then, for judging a world view is *internal consistency*—the requirement that the theories composing our world view not conflict.

How can our best theories conflict? Here are some ways:

- *Our moral theory can conflict with our view of human freedom.* Most people believe that persons can be held morally responsible for their actions—as long as they act freely. That is, persons can be praised or blamed only for those actions over which they have control. But many people also think that humans *cannot* act freely, that they do not have free will. They believe in causal determinism, the view that every event in the universe has a cause (is determined). This means that everything that happens (including human actions) has a preceding cause, so that the chain of causes stretches back into the indefinite past—out of our control. Many would see this situation as an unacceptable conflict between their moral theory and their view of the way the world is.
- *Our theory about the existence of God can conflict with our scientific theory about*

the nature of the universe. Some people argue that God must exist because everything, including the universe, has a cause and the only thing that could have caused the universe is God. Modern physics, however, shows that some things in the universe (namely, certain subatomic particles) often occur uncaused, so it's not true that everything has a cause. Thus, in this instance science seems to be at odds with a certain brand of theology.

- *Our theory about the mind can be in conflict with theories of personal survival after death.* Some believe that people can live on in some ethereal form, as souls or disembodied minds, for example, after death. This notion accords well with the idea that the mind (our true essence) is the kind of thing that can exist independently of the body. But this kind of survival after death would not be possible if the mind is identical to the body, as some people believe.

The work of building plausible world views will always involve eliminating inconsistencies. If you really want to understand the world and your place in it, you must wrestle with these inconsistencies. Reconciling conflicting beliefs (by eliminating them or modifying them) is a necessary condition for creating theories and a world view that can successfully guide your thinking, your choices, and your deeds.

Summary

A moral argument is an argument in which the conclusion is a moral statement. A moral statement is a statement asserting that an action is right or wrong (moral or immoral) or that a person or motive is good or bad. In a moral argument, we cannot establish the conclusion without a moral premise. A standard moral argument has at least one premise that asserts a general moral principle, at least one premise that is a non-moral claim, and a conclusion that is a moral statement. Often a moral premise in a moral argument is implicit. In evaluating any moral argument, it's best to specify any implicit premises. The best approach to identifying the implicit premises is to treat moral arguments as deductive. Your job then is to supply plausible premises that will make the argument valid. You can test a premise that is a general moral principle by trying to think of counterexamples to it.

Theories of morality are attempts to explain what makes an action right or what makes a person good. We test moral theories the same way we test any other theory—by applying criteria of adequacy to a theory and its competitors. The criteria of adequacy for moral theories are (1) consistency with considered moral judgments, (2) consistency with our experience of the moral life, and (3) workability in real-life situations.

Making a coherent world view is the work of a lifetime. World views are composites of theories, including theories of morality. A good world view must consist of good theories. But it also must be have internal consistency—the theories composing our world view must not conflict.

Key Terms

Moral statement: A statement asserting that an action is right or wrong (moral or immoral) or that something (such as a person or motive) is good or bad.

World view: A philosophy of life; a set of fundamental ideas that helps us make sense of a wide range of important issues in life. A world view defines for us what exists, what should be, and what we can know.

Exercises

Exercise 11.1

Review Questions

1. What is a moral theory?
2. According to the text, what is a world view?
3. What is a moral statement?
4. What is the basic structure of a standard moral argument?
* 5. Why can't we infer a moral statement from non-moral statements alone?
6. Why is it important to spell out implicit premises in a moral argument?
7. What technique can we use to determine whether a general moral principle is true?
8. What is a moral judgment?
* 9. According to the text, what precisely does a moral theory try to explain?
10. What are the criteria of adequacy for appraising moral theories?
11. According to the text, how are moral theories like scientific theories?
12. Who founded the moral theory known as act-utilitarianism?
* 13. According to the text, what is a crucial criterion for judging a world view?

Exercise 11.2

Specify whether the following statements are moral or non-moral.

* 1. Joan worries whether she's doing the right thing.
2. When the government restricts freedom of the press, it harms every citizen.
3. The government should not restrict freedom of the press.
4. Paul was sure that he saw Gregory steal the book from the library.
5. Because of the terrible results of the bombing, it's clear that the entire war effort was immoral.

* 6. The Church should never have allowed pedophile priests to stay in the priesthood.
  7. The officer was justified in using deadly force because his life was threatened.
  8. The officer used deadly force because his life was threatened.
* 9. Lying is wrong unless the lie involves trivial matters.
  10. The officials should never have allowed the abuse to continue.

Exercise 11.3

In each of the following passages, add a moral premise to turn it into a valid moral argument.

1. Noah promised to drive Thelma to Vancouver, so he should stop bellyaching and do it.
2. The conflict between loggers and activists got violent, and the government did nothing to stop it. The government should have intervened.
3. There was never any imminent threat from the Iraqi government, so the United States should not have invaded Iraq.
* 4. The Indian government posed an imminent threat to Pakistan and the world, so the Pakistanis were justified in attacking Indian troops.
5. Marc took office supplies from work to use at home. Therefore he should be fired.
6. Ellen knew that a murder was going to take place. It was her duty to try to stop it.
7. Ahmed should never have allowed his daughter to receive *in vitro* fertilization. Such a procedure is unnatural.
8. The doctors performed the experiment on 20 patients without their consent. Obviously, that was wrong.
* 9. What you did was immoral. You hacked into a database containing personal information on thousands of people and invaded their privacy.
10. Ling spent all day weeding Mrs Black's garden for no pay. The least Mrs Black should do is let Ling borrow some gardening tools.

Exercise 11.4

Use counter-examples to test each of the following general moral principles.

1. Anything that is unnatural is immoral.
2. It is always and everywhere wrong to tell a lie.
* 3. In all circumstances the killing of a human being is wrong.
4. In all situations in which our actions can contribute to the welfare, safety, or happiness of others, we should treat all persons equally.
5. Any action that serves one's own best interests is morally permissible.
6. Any action that is approved of by one's society is moral.

* 7. Assisted suicide is never morally justified.

8. Whatever actions a person approves of are morally right.

9. Making a promise to someone incurs a moral obligation to keep the promise in all circumstances.

10. Any action done for religious reasons is morally acceptable because religious reasons carry more weight than secular ones.

Exercise 11.5

Identify the moral argument in each of the following passages. Specify the premises and the conclusion, adding implicit premises where needed.

1. The movie *Lorenzo's Oil* is about a family's struggle to find a cure for their young son's fatal genetic disease, an illness that usually kills boys before they reach their 11th birthday. The script is based on the true story of a family's attempt to save Lorenzo, their son, from this fatal genetic disease through the use of a medicinal oil. The movie is a tear-jerker, but it ends on a hopeful note that suggests that the oil will eventually cure Lorenzo and that the oil is an effective treatment for the genetic disease. The problem is, there is no cure for the disease and no good scientific evidence showing that the oil works. But the movie touts the oil anyway—and gives false hope to every family whose son suffers from this terrible illness. Worse, the movie overplays the worth of the oil, seriously misleading people about the medical facts. The movie, therefore, is immoral. It violates the ageless moral dictum to, above all else, 'do no harm'. *Lorenzo's Oil* may be just a movie, but it has done harm nonetheless.

2. 'I, like many of my fellow Muslims, was appalled by the latest bombings in Saudi Arabia ("Among the Saudis, Attack Has Soured Qaeda Supporters", front page, 11 Nov). Yet I was disturbed to get the sense that Saudis were angered by this latest act of barbarity because the targets were mainly Arab and Muslim.

    'You quote one person as saying of the bombing in Riyadh in May, "At that time it was seen as justifiable because there was an invasion of a foreign country, there was frustration." Another says, "Jihad is not against your own people."

    'Regardless of whether the victims are Muslim or not, the vicious murder of innocent human beings is reprehensible and repugnant, an affront to everything Islam stands for. Any sympathy for Al Qaeda among the minority of Saudis should have evaporated after the May bombings in Riyadh, and it should have surprised no one in Saudi Arabia that Al Qaeda would attack a housing complex full of Arabs and Muslims.

    'That is what Al Qaeda is: a band of bloodthirsty murderers.' (Letter to the editor, *New York Times*, 11 November 2003.)

3. John and Nancy Jones had a two-year-old son who suffered from a serious but very curable bowel obstruction. For religious reasons, the Joneses decided to

treat their son with prayer instead of modern medicine. They refused medical treatment even though several doctors told them that the child would die unless he was treated medically As it turned out, the boy did die. The Joneses were arrested and charged with involuntary manslaughter. Were the Joneses wrong to refuse treatment for their son? The answer is yes. Regardless of what faith or religious dogma would have the Joneses do, they allowed their child to die. According to just about any moral outlook, the care of a child by the parents is a fundamental obligation. Above all other concerns, parents have a duty to ensure the health and safety of their children and to use whatever means are most likely to secure those benefits. The Joneses ignored this basic moral principle. They were wrong—and deserve whatever punishment the state deems appropriate.

Exercise 11.6

Read the following description of a moral theory and answer the questions that follow.

> **The Ethics of Love Theory**
> According to the Ethics of Love Theory, what makes an action right is that it is based on love toward others. Love is the only universal moral good. In any situation where a moral choice must be made, this theory says that we must ask ourselves, 'Which action would demonstrate the greatest degree of love for others, everyone considered?' So in this theory, actions that demonstrate love (such as respecting others, telling the truth, treating people equally, caring for them, protecting them from harm) would always be preferred over actions that do not demonstrate love (discriminating against persons, lying to them, harming them, stealing from them, ignoring them if they ask for help). Furthermore, actions that demonstrate great love (such as risking your life to save theirs) would be preferred over those that exhibit only small degrees of love (such as being courteous).

1. Is this theory consistent with our considered moral judgments? Is it consistent with our judgments regarding the punishment of criminals? Acts of war? Providing for one's family as opposed to providing for all persons equally? If the theory conflicts with our considered moral judgments, give an example demonstrating the conflict.
2. Is this theory consistent with our experience of the moral life? According to this theory, are moral judgments possible? Can we have moral disagreements? Can we ever act immorally?
3. Is this theory workable? Does it help you make moral decisions in these situations?
    a. Your beloved mother has a terminal illness that causes her unimaginable pain, and she begs you to kill her.

b. You promise to buy your beloved spouse a car, but a half dozen homeless people beg you to give them the money that you had set aside for the car.

c. You are a doctor who must decide which of 100 patients should receive a life-saving organ transplant. You can choose only one, though you love all of them. Some are elderly and some are in great pain; some are very young and some are Nobel laureates.

d. What is your final assessment of the ethics of love theory? Is it a good theory? Is it a better theory than act-utilitarianism?

Field Problems

1. Check the Internet to find out about rule-utilitarianism, a moral theory meant to be an improvement over act-utilitarianism. A good place to start is *The Internet Encyclopedia of Philosophy* (http://www.utm.edu/research/iep); see the entry 'Moral Philosophy'. Write a 300-word assessment of the theory, using the moral criteria of adequacy.

2. From the opinion and editorial page (including letters to the editor) of a newspaper, select a passage containing a moral argument. Write a brief assessment of the argument, identifying the premises and conclusion, adding implicit premises (to make the argument valid), and stating whether the revised argument is sound or unsound.

Self-Assessment Quiz

1. What is a moral statement?
2. What are the elements of a standard moral argument?
3. According to the text, what are the moral criteria of adequacy?
4. According to the text, how can you test whether a general moral principle is true?
5. Is it possible to derive a moral statement from a non-moral statement?

In each of the following passages, add a moral premise to turn it into a valid moral argument.

6. Of course we should have offered protection to the Kurds. They were in grave danger and they asked for our help.
7. The supplement manufacturers knew that the herb ephedra was dangerous, so they should have removed it from the market.
8. The Liberals insulted the prime minister. They should never have been allowed to do that.
9. The Smiths were consenting adults who were having sex in the privacy of their own homes. These actions by the Smiths are morally permissible.

10. Randi killed his neighbour, and the killing was not in self-defence. He should not have committed such an act.

Use counter-examples to test each of the following general moral principles.

11. Lying is wrong under all circumstances.
12. People who commit crimes should not be punished—they should be retrained to act legally.
13. All humans, whatever their circumstances, have full moral rights.
14. All creatures that are alive and sensitive to stimulation are equally valuable and should be accorded equal respect.
15. The morally right action is the one that produces the most happiness, everyone considered.
16. Right actions are those that are in one's own self-interest.

Defend the following actions from a utilitarian standpoint.

17. Medical experimentation on a patient without her consent.
18. Taking food, shelter, and other resources from rich people and distributing them equally among poor people.

Evaluate each of the following arguments.

19. Any form of expression or speech that offends people of faith should not be tolerated. Penthouse.com definitely offends people of faith. Ban it!
20. Anyone who disagrees with the basic moral dictums of the prevailing culture should be censored. Dr Tilden's graduation speech clearly was inconsistent with the prevailing moral opinions on campus. She should be reprimanded.

 Integrative Exercises

These exercises pertain to material in Chapters 3, 5, and 8–11.

For each of the following arguments, specify the conclusion and premises and indicate where possible whether it is cogent or sound. Decide whether any fallacies are used and, if so, name them.

1. Ninety per cent of famous scientists do not believe in God, so 90 per cent of all scientists probably do not believe in God.
2. If Vaughn buys that flat-screen TV, he will spend all of his time watching television. And if he spends all of his time watching television, he will get fat. Well, Vaughn did buy that flat-screen TV. Therefore, he will get fat.
3. Anyone who runs away from a car accident should be arrested. Janet ran away from a car accident. She should be arrested.
4. I found five jelly beans in the yard this morning, and I found 30 more in the kitchen this afternoon. So I've found 35 jelly beans today.

5. Ann is taller than Jacob, and Jacob is taller than Jane. Therefore, Ann is taller than Jane.

6. 'I write in response to the 4 Nov. news article, "Plans for group home, storage facility opposed." As the sister and guardian of a profoundly retarded woman who lives in a group home, I can assure the gentlemen quoted that their fears are very much unfounded. The home in which my sister resides is large, lovely, brand new, well staffed and well maintained. It does nothing but enhance the community, bring neighbors together and create a wonderfully diverse neighborhood.' (Letter to the editor, *Buffalo News*)

7. '...freedom of the press is not absolute and I disagree with the notion that the press has absolute control over everything at press. There is also a responsibility to balance it with justice, to portray things properly. So there is a level as a liberal democracy in Canada of having freedom to express what we want to but there is also a level of control and in terms of the ethical side, . . . if you are balancing the publication of a cartoon versus people who had real concerns about their safety and really about offending the entire Muslim community which I thinks is 1.1 to 1.3 billion people around the world. . . the frivolous publication of a cartoon that has little or no value is definitely not enough to outweigh those other consequences.' (From a CBC interview with Ryan Gallant, President of the UPEI Student Union, criticizing the publication of cartoons of the Muslim prophet Mohammed by UPEI's student newspaper, www.upei.ca/president/the_cartoon_controversy_and_th.)

8. We have interviewed 100 NHL players, and 70 of them admit to extramarital affairs. So most NHL players are adulterers.

9. You think you're going to drive cross-country in that 1978 Chevy disaster-on-wheels? Forget it. It's old, has 250,000 kilometres on it, and it has worn belts and bad cylinders.

10. Take it easy. Deborah will arrive soon to give you a lift into town, just as she promised. She has never broken a promise, and her car is in excellent shape.

11. Melissa took the money from petty cash even though she had plenty of money in her pocket. People shouldn't steal unless they are destitute. She shouldn't have taken that money.

12. There is one principle we can never avoid: we should never do anything that shows disrespect for human life. The artificial use of human cells—as scientists are now doing in stem cell research—shows a complete disregard for human life. Stem cell research is immoral.

13. Krista is always on her Blackberry. Therefore, she's probably got lots of important business stuff going on.

14. This new BMW will give you a sense of style, assurance, and class. See your BMW dealer today!

15. The depiction of Hollywood stars in movies puffing away on cigarettes is teaching our kids to smoke. Recent research reveals a cause-and-effect relationship between exposing children to movie smoking and their subsequent decision to take up the habit.

For each of the following phenomena, (1) devise two theories to explain it, and (2) apply the criteria of adequacy to them to determine which theory is best.

16. The number of delayed and cancelled flights in the airline industry has tripled in the last year.
17. After taking a new food supplement known as Max10, hundreds of people have reported having more energy, feeling more alert, and having an enhanced sense of well-being.
18. Ever since the average classroom size at Earl of March Secondary School dropped from 42 to 25, grades have improved dramatically and discipline problems are at an all-time low.
19. Over the past 10 years there has been a surprising rise in the incidence of leukemia in children who live in the Kingston area.
20. Multiracial neighbourhoods seem much friendlier than neighbourhoods that are segregated or are dominated by one ethnic or cultural group.

Writing Assignments

1. Complete Exercise 11.6 and then write a 500-word essay assessing the worth of the ethics of love theory. Use the moral criteria of adequacy.
2. Write a one-paragraph summary of the moral argument put forth in Essay 6 ('Misleading the Patient for Fun and Profit') in Appendix A. Be sure to identify clearly the argument's premises and conclusion.
3. Write 500-word assessment of the moral theory known as ethical egoism (discussed in the box 'Critiquing Moral Theories'). Use the moral criteria of adequacy.

Appendix A

Essays for Evaluation

Essay 1 *

Deterrence
by David M. Paciocco

The theory of deterrence has two components. The first, known as 'specific' or 'individual' deterrence, is that punishment will discourage the offender from committing further offences in the future. The second, known as 'general deterrence', is that punishing offenders will discourage other like-minded people from committing offences.

Based on its 1987 study, *Sentencing Reform*, the Canadian Sentencing Commission gave up on specific deterrence. It acknowledged that the claim that punishment is effective in reducing the tendency to reoffend is undermined by rates of recidivism (or repeat offending), the apparent 'undeterrability' of certain groups of offenders, and the 'acknowledged fact' that most prison inmates have been convicted on prior occasions.[1] Anyone who has the time should sit in provincial court and watch offenders being sentenced. As a prosecutor, I became so accustomed to finding a copy of the criminal record in the file that if there wasn't one, I would look around the floor to see if I had dropped it.

In spite of our failure to intimidate offenders from reoffending by punishing them, we continue to rely on specific deterrence as a justification for punishment. If we are going to send a first offender to jail, our preference is to give a 'short, sharp' sentence that will 'send a message' to him or her. This practice shares a philosophical kinship with giving a child a sharp smack to the back of the head, and is probably about as effective. It is, however, a lot more expensive.

General deterrence, the theory that punishing offenders will intimidate others into being law-abiding, is even more central to our theories of punishment. For the most hated crimes, those involving sexual assault, violence causing bodily harm, robbery, and drugs, the primary sentencing principle is general deterrence. Trial judges are overruled by appeal courts when they fail to give general deterrence sufficient weight in sentencing offenders. Yet, paradoxically, most of the crimes for which we emphasize this sentencing principle are the kinds of offences that are most resistant to general deterrence.

The official position appears to be that we must accept the general deterrence theory as a matter of faith, but that we cannot put too much faith in it. The Canadian Sentencing Commission asked Professor Cousineau of Simon Fraser University to review the latest literature. He concluded that 'there is little or no evidence to sustain an empirically justified belief in the deterrent effect of legal sanctions.'[2] In spite of this report, the commission could not bring itself to reject the intuitively appealing notion that if people know there is a heavy cost associated with their conduct, they may, as rational people, opt not to engage in that behaviour.[3] But even the Sentencing Commission was guarded in its assessment. It cautioned that there is no reason to believe that legal sanctions can be used to deter specific crimes, or to believe that making an example out of a particular offender will have any effect on other potential offenders. It therefore concluded its discussion of general deterrence by saying that 'deterrence is a general and limited consequence of sentencing.'[4]

A moment's reflection will demonstrate why general deterrence is so ineffective. Deterrence is based on theories of rational decision making. It presupposes that actors weigh to a nicety the pros and cons of their acts before action. The most dangerous criminals do not fit that model. They are not people renowned for their good judgment and considered action. At the same time, the most horrendous crimes do not lend themselves to this kind of judgment. Sexual offenders give in to vile urges. Assailants strike out in anger. Homicide, in particular, is primarily a crime of passion. It is only rarely a contract hit or a neatly planned exercise. It is more often the worst result of the free reign of jealousy, rage, vindictiveness, hatred, and anger, the most powerful of human emotions. Even when not spontaneous, it is still most commonly done in the throes of extreme emotion. In 1995, by no means an exceptional year, 9 per cent of killers committed suicide, almost invariably immediately after they had killed.[5] If these people are not afraid to inflict mortal violence on themselves as the price for their crime, what makes us think we can deter them by threatening a cell with a television?

Some Canadians believe that the television in the cell is part of the reason that general deterrence does not work; we are not hard enough on criminals. If we ratcheted up the sentences, they believe, and began to treat criminals as criminals, we might just reduce crime. In fact, there is 'a great deal of empirical research in the United States and elsewhere [that] has shown that crime rates are not greatly affected by changes to the severity of penalties imposed.'[6] The Canadian Sentencing Commission came to the same conclusion.[7] This result has been effectively demonstrated in Canada with respect to the offence of murder. Murder rates did not rise with the abolition of capital punishment in 1976. They went down and stayed down. One of the great American ironies is that those states with the highest murder rates are the same ones that invoke the death penalty most frequently.

The Ontario Court of Appeal was recently asked to increase the typical sentencing range for men who attempt to murder their female partners. Sentences for that offence range around ten years. The court was right to reject the submission that imposing higher sentences would discourage men from trying.[8] By definition, these men are attempting to succeed in killing their spouses. If they succeeded, they would get life imprisonment, subject to lengthy parole ineligibility. How can anyone think that a man who knows he might get life if he succeeds is going to sit down and say, 'OK. If I fail they are going to give me 12 years instead of ten, so I had better not do it.' This is simply silly. Even at 20 or 30 or 40 years, there would be no difference. The violent among us are destructive actors, not constructive thinkers.

Cesare Beccaria, sometimes called the father of criminology, was a proponent of general deterrence. He nonetheless sensed that employing brutal punishments would do nothing to reduce crime rates: 'The countries and times most notorious for severity of penalties have always been those in which the bloodiest and most inhumane deeds were committed, for the same spirit of ferocity that guided the hand of the legislators also ruled that of the parricide and assassin.'[9] Savage punishments reinforce savage attitudes in some people. For the just, savage punishments defeat themselves. They can cause a humane public to rebel against the values demonstrated by the administration of justice, thereby undermining the educational effect of criminal prosecutions. Experience has shown that they can even cause courts to rebel by finding technical ways to prevent imposing the punishment.[10] When felons were executed for minor felonies in England, judges became creative in finding ways not to convict.

Even if the theory of general deterrence is sound, its promise is easily defeated in practice. It is universally accepted that to be effective systematically, general deterrence depends more than anything else on the certainty of punishment. That is why high-profile RIDE programs and high police presence in crime areas can help produce a reduction in crime rates, but an abstract fear of being caught is tremendously less effective. Some commentators have added that the punishment must also be swift for general deterrence to work. For reasons we can do nothing about, punishment in our system is neither certain nor swift. In terms of the certainty of punishment, with the exception of homicide, where detection and conviction rates are high, only a very small percentage of offenders are even sentenced. This is partially because of the chronic underreporting of most offences, and partially because some crimes are simply not solved by the police. There are also incredibly high attrition rates for most offences. Complaints tend not to get to trial, either because there is insufficient evidence, the complainants recant, witnesses disappear, the accused disappears, the matter is judged not serious enough to proceed, or the case otherwise falls through the cracks. Some cases end up in acquittals. A leading English academic, Andrew Ashworth, estimates that, in Britain, only 3 per cent of actual offences end up at the sentencing stage.[11] The John Howard Society of Alberta estimated that the clearance rate by conviction in Canada in 1987 was unlikely to exceed 20 per cent.[12] Even if both these figures are gross under estimates, they demonstrate poignantly that we will never attain certainty of punishment, no matter how much money we throw at the system or how much we tinker with its rules.

All indications are that general deterrence, in the form of creating conditions through the punishment of offenders that will make others decide not to offend, is woefully ineffective for most crimes. It is particularly so for crimes of violence. If the marginal return of general deterrence was the only gain to be made by incarcerating violent offenders, it would not make economic sense to do so. Our continued reliance on it as a reason for the punitive sentencing of such people is therefore misleading and distorting. It creates a public expectation that cannot be satisfied.

Notes

1. Canadian Sentencing Commission, *Sentencing Reform: A Canadian Approach* (Ottawa: Ministry of Supply and Services, 1987) at 135. Between 1975 and 1985, 60 per cent of those released on mandatory supervision were readmitted to federal penitentiary, while 49 per cent of those who had been released on parole were readmitted.
2. *Ibid* at 136.
3. *Ibid* at 136–7.
4. *Ibid* at 138.
5. Statistics Canada, Canadian Centre for Justices Statistics, *Homicide in Canada—1995*, vol. 16, no. 11 (1996) at 5.
6. Julian V. Roberts, 'New Data on Sentencing Trends in Provincial Courts' (1994), 34 CR (4th) 181 at 194.
7. Canadian Sentencing Commission, *Sentencing Reform* at 137.
8. *R. v. Edwards* (1996), 28 OR (3d) 54 (CA).
9. Daniel J. Curran and Claire M. Renzetti, *Theories of Crime* (Boston: Allyn and Bacon, 1994) at 13.
10. H.R.S. Ryan, *The Theory of Punishment* (1970), Study Note, reproduced in Don Stuart and R.J. Delisle, *Learning Canadian Criminal Law*, 5th ed. (Carswell: Toronto, 1995) at 139.
11. Andrew Ashworth, *Sentencing and Criminal Justice* (London: Weidenfeld & Nicoloson, 1992) at 23.
12. Canadian Sentencing Commission, *Sentencing Reform* at 148.

Essay 2 *

Hurray! No One's Watching: The Olympics'
Decline Signals Their Success, But Now What?
by Andrew Potter

Has the Olympic movement run its course? Television ratings in both Canada and the United States were way down for these Games, with both the CBC and NBC prime-time broadcasts losing out to new programming from their competitors. Over in Turin, many supposedly marquee events, notably figure skating, took place in half-empty arenas. Is this the beginning of the end for the largest sporting event in the world?

---

*Source: 'Hurray! No One's Watching. The Olympics' Decline Signals Their Success. But Now What?', by Andrew Potter. From *Maclean's* 1 March 2006.

The *Wall Street Journal* thinks so. In an editorial published just days into the Turin Games, the paper argued that the chief appeal of the Olympics in the past was that, of all the proxy wars fought between the forces of freedom and the forces of totalitarianism, ice dancing and the luge were probably the most benignly entertaining. With the end of the Cold War and the rise of globalization, international events such as the Olympics are obsolete. But, if the *Journal* is right, then perhaps we shouldn't actually think of the declining interest in the Olympics as a sign of the movement's failure, but as its success.

The relationship between Olympism and nationalism has always been pretty confused. On the one hand, the fundamental principles of the Olympic movement sound like the lyrics to John Lennon's *Imagine* remixed in bureaucratese. The Olympic Charter explicitly states that the Games 'are competitions between athletes in individual or team events and not between countries'. The Olympic Truce, first declared in 1992, holds that athletic competition has the power to promote unity and peace by abolishing boundaries.

You could have fooled me. The charter may endorse sport as 'a way of life based on the joy found in effort', but it promotes that way of life through flag-waving, anthem playing, and a rank ordering of nations by medal count. The fact is, for all its hippyish ideology, the Olympic movement has always found raw nationalism convenient. It is all well and fine for everyone to routinely denounce Hitler for using the 1936 Berlin Games as a showpiece for Nazism, or to express horror at the 1972 Munich murder of 11 members of the Israeli team by Palestinian terrorists, but that's what happens when you allow sport to become the pursuit of politics by other means.

As countries stop mattering at the Games, we shouldn't be surprised to find that fewer people are tuning in to watch. Many of the traditional events don't really pull their weight as spectator sports, as evidenced by the absence of a serious luge league or Nordic combined circuit. More often than not, the athletes' skill or training or art is invisible to the untrained viewer, revealed through microsecond differences in split times or hinted at in the inscrutable decisions of an anonymous politburo of judges. What makes the Olympics worth watching is not what the athletes are doing, but the uniforms they are wearing. Those of us who cheered on Pierre Lueders in the bobsleigh event did so because he's Canadian, not because we have the foggiest appreciation for why the sport even exists.

There was always something rather ridiculous about the International Olympic Committee founder Pierre de Coubertin's idea that a quadrennial gathering of leisured aristocrats would lead the way to a borderless world of peace and harmony. Unsurprisingly, commercialization and professionalization appeared at the modern Games almost immediately, along with other complications such as drug use and the participation of women. In his excellent book *Olympics in Athens 1896*, the British diplomat Michael Llewellyn Smith suggests that, instead of lamenting the tawdry affair that the Olympics has become, we should embrace it 'as a triumph of modernity, capitalism, commerce, sporting prowess and celebrity culture'.

To really embrace the modern world, the IOC just needs to go an extra step and become truly cosmopolitan by doing away with countries at the Olympics altogether: get rid of the flags and make the Games a genuine competition between individuals under the Olympic banner. Or, if we must have teams, here's an idea. Many athletes already get the bulk of their funding from corporate sponsorships, so why not let corporations sponsor entire teams? I'd just as soon see Wal-Mart or Starbucks at the top of the medal standings as I would China or Sweden.

One likely consequence of all of this would be a serious overhaul of the schedule of events: out with the old and aristocratic, in with the extreme and populist. This is in fact what the IOC is already doing, to a certain extent. The sports that got most of the attention (and fans) at Turin were the ones with all of the fancy branding and the hyper marketing. Events such as snowboarding and freestyle skiing ruled the Winter Games, just as beach volleyball is far and away the most popular sport at the Summer Games. Not only might such a move help revive the Games' sagging fortunes, but it would be more faithful to the transnationalist spirit of the Olympic movement.

Meanwhile, nothing would prevent countries from continuing to invest in amateur sport. Indeed, if we truly value one of the fundamental principles of the Olympic movement—that 'sport is at the service of the harmonious development of man, with a view to encouraging the establishment of a peaceful society'— then national pride is irrelevant, is it not? Governments should invest in amateur sport simply because it makes better citizens, and if it doesn't, then it isn't clear why governments should be involved. If the Games can't survive a move to true commercialized cosmopolitanism, then Olympism is a more obsolete ideal than it already seems.

Essay 3 *

Marine Parks
by Bill Daly

The issue of whether we should allow marine parks to stay open has been widely debated in our community recently. It is an important issue because it concerns fundamental moral and economic questions about the way we use our native wildlife. A variety of different arguments have been put forward about this issue. This essay will consider arguments for having marine parks and point to some of the problems with these views. It will then put forward reasons for the introduction of laws that prohibit these unnecessary and cruel institutions.

It has been argued that dolphin parks provide the only opportunity for much of the public to see marine mammals (Smith, 1992). Most Australians, so this argument goes, live in cities and never get to see these animals. It is claimed that marine parks allow the average Australian to appreciate our marine wildlife. However, as Smith states, dolphins, whales, and seals can be viewed in the wild at a number of places on the Australian coast. In fact, there are more places where they can be seen in the wild than places where they can be seen in captivity. Moreover, most Australians would have to travel less to get to these locations than they would to get to the marine parks on the Gold Coast. In addition, places where there are wild marine mammals do not charge an exorbitant entry fee—they are free.

Dr Alison Lane, the director of the Cairns Marine Science Institute, contends that we need marine parks for scientific research (*The Age*, 19 Feb., 1993). She argues that much of our knowledge of marine mammals comes from studies that were undertaken at marine parks. The knowledge obtained at marine parks, so this argument goes, can be useful for planning for the conservation of marine mammal species. However, as Jones (1991) explains, park research is only useful for understanding captive animals and is not useful for learning about animals in the wild. Dolphin and whale biology changes in marine park conditions. Their diets are different, they have significantly lower life spans and they are more prone to disease. In addition, marine mammals in dolphin parks are trained and this means that their patterns of social behaviour are changed. Therefore research undertaken at marine parks is generally not reliable.

It is the contention of the Marine Park Owners Association that marine parks attract a lot of foreign tourists (*The Sun-Herald*, 12 April 1993). This position goes on to assert that these tourists spend a lot of money, increasing our foreign exchange earnings and assisting our national balance of payments. However, foreign tourists would still come to Australia if the parks were closed down. Indeed, surveys of overseas tourists show that they come here for a variety of other reasons and not to visit places like Seaworld (*The Age, Good Weekend*, 16 Aug. 1993). Tourists come here to see our native wildlife in its natural environment and not to see it in cages and cement pools. They can see animals in those conditions in their own countries. Furthermore, we should be promoting our beautiful natural environment to tourists and not the ugly concrete marine park venues.

Dolphin parks are unnecessary and cruel. The dolphins and whales in these parks are kept in very small, cramped ponds, whereas in the wild they are used to roaming long distances across the seas. Furthermore, the concrete walls of the pools interfere with the animals' sonar systems of communication. In addition, keeping them in pools is a terrible restriction of the freedom of fellow creatures who may have very high levels of intelligence and a sophisticated language ability. Moreover, there are many documented cases of marine mammals helping humans who are in danger at sea or helping fisherman with their work.

In conclusion, these parks should be closed, or at the very least, no new animals should be captured for marine parks in the future. Our society is no longer prepared to tolerate unnecessary cruelty to animals for science and entertainment. If we continue with our past crimes against these creatures we will be remembered as cruel and inhuman by the generations of the future.

References

Jones, G. 1991. 'The Myths About Animal Research in Marine Parks', *Scientific Australian* 12, 3.

Smith, H. 1992. 'Marine Parks: Good for Business, Good for Australia', *Leisure Business Review* 24, 4.

The Age. 19 February 1993.

The Age, Good Weekend. 16 August 1993.

The Sun-Herald. 12 April 1993.

Essay 4 *

The Kalam Cosmological Argument
by Theodore Schick

Although it may be possible for the universe to be infinitely old, many believe that the universe was created less than fifteen billion years ago in a cataclysmic explosion known as the 'big bang'. The existence of such a creation event explains a number of phenomena including the expansion of the universe, the existence of the cosmic background radiation, and the relative proportions of various sorts of matter. As the theory has been refined, more specific predictions have been derived from it. A number of these predictions have recently been confirmed. Although this is a major scientific achievement, many believe that it has theological implications as well. Specifically, they believe that it provides scientific evidence for the existence of God. Astronomer George Smoot suggested as much when he exclaimed at a press conference reporting the findings of the Cosmic Background Explorer (COBE) satellite, 'If you're religious it's like looking at the face of God.' Why? Because something must have caused the big bang, and who else but God could have done such a thing? Astronomer Hugh Ross, in his book *The Creator and the Cosmos*, puts the argument this way: 'If the universe arose out of a big bang, it must have had a beginning. If it had a beginning, it must have a beginner' (Ross, 1995: 14). And that beginner, Ross believes, is God.

The Kalam cosmological argument follows along these lines. It goes like this:

1. Whatever begins to exist has a cause.
2. The universe began to exist.
3. Therefore, the universe had a cause, namely God.

This argument gets its name from the Arabic work *Kalam*, which means 'to argue or discuss'. It originated with Islamic theologians who sought to challenge the Greek view of the eternity of matter.

The Kalam cosmological argument doesn't require that everything have a cause, only those things that begin to exist. Since God is eternal, he doesn't require a cause. The universe, however, is not eternal. So it does require a cause.

As with the traditional cosmological argument, however, the Kalam cosmological argument gives us no reason for believing that the first cause is God. The universe that came from the big bang is finite, and it doesn't take a being of infinite power to create a finite universe. The same goes for the properties of intelligence and goodness. So even if the Kalam cosmological argument did prove the existence of a first cause, it doesn't prove the existence of God.

There's reason to believe it doesn't even prove the existence of a first cause, however, for modern physics explicitly repudiates premise 1 and provides good reason for rejecting premise 2.

Remarkably enough, modern physics rejects the claim that whatever begins to exist has a cause. On the contrary, it maintains that things like subatomic particles can come into existence without a cause. As physicist Edward Tryon tells us:

> . . . quantum electrodynamics reveals that an electron, positron, and photon occasionally emerge spontaneously in a perfect vacuum. When this happens, the three particles exist for a brief time, and then annihilate each other, leaving no trace behind. . . . The spontaneous, temporary emergence of particles from a vacuum is called a vacuum fluctuation, and is utterly commonplace in quantum field theory (Tryon, 1973: 396–7).

Vacuum fluctuations are random events, and random events have no cause. So anything produced by a vacuum fluctuation is uncaused.

What's even more remarkable is that according to modern physics, the universe itself could be the result of a vacuum fluctuation! Tryon explains:

> If it is true that our Universe has a zero net value for all conserved quantities, then it may simply be a fluctuation of a vacuum, the vacuum of some larger space in which our universe is imbedded. In answer to the question of why it happened, I offer the modest proposal that our Universe is simply one of those things which happen from time to time (Tyron, 1973: 397).

According to Tryon, universes happen; they come into existence spontaneously without being caused to exist.

Wouldn't a universe produced by a vacuum fluctuation violate the Law of Conservation of Mass-Energy? Not if the total amount of mass-energy of the universe is zero. How is that possible? Physicist Paul Davies explains:

> There is a . . . remarkable possibility, which is the creation of matter from a state of zero energy. This possibility arises because energy can be both positive and negative. The energy of motion or the energy of mass is always positive, but the energy of attraction, such as that due to certain types of gravitational or electromagnetic field is negative. Circumstances can arise in which the positive energy that goes to make up the mass of newly created particles of matter is exactly offset by the negative energy of gravity or electromagnetism. . . . Some have suggested that there is a deep cosmic principle at work which requires the universe to have exactly zero energy. If that is so, the cosmos can follow the path of least resistance, coming into existence without requiring any input of matter or energy at all (Davies, 1983: 31–2).

If our universe has zero total energy, as measurements seem to indicate, it could be the result of a vacuum fluctuation. But if it was the result of a vacuum fluctuation, it was not caused to exist by anyone or anything.

The second premise of the Kalam cosmological argument says that the universe began to exist. Evidence for the big bang is usually presented as evidence for this claim. But the fact that the big bang occurred doesn't prove that the universe began to exist, for the big bang may itself have been the result of a prior big crunch!

It has long been known that if the amount of matter in the universe is great enough, then the universe will someday stop expanding and start contracting. Eventually, all the matter in the universe will be drawn back to a single point in what has come to be known as 'the big crunch'. Because matter supposedly cannot be crushed out of existence, the contraction cannot go on indefinitely. At some point the compressed matter may bounce back in another big bang. If so, the big bang would have been caused by a prior big crunch rather than by some supernatural being.

The view that the universe oscillates between periods of expansion and contraction in an endless—and beginningless—cycle of creation and destruction is a very Eastern one. Hindus, for example, believe that everything in the universe—as well as the universe itself—undergoes a continuous process of death and rebirth. For them, time is circular; the beginning and end are one and the same. Thus the notion of a first cause makes no sense. Only for those who have a linear view of time is the question of the origin of the universe a problem.

Recent estimates indicate that there is not enough mass in the universe to stop its expansion. So the big bang may not have been the result of a prior big crunch. But even if the universe as a whole never contracts, we know that certain parts of it do. When a star has used up its fuel, the force of gravity causes it to contract. If the star is massive enough, this contraction results in a black hole. The matter in a black hole is compressed toward a point of infinite density known as a 'singularity'. Before it reaches the singularity, however, some physicists, most notably Lee Smolin, believe that the matter in the black hole may start expanding again and give rise to another universe. In a sense, then, according to Smolin, our universe may reproduce itself by budding off. He writes:

> A collapsing star forms a black hole, within which it is compressed to a very dense state. The universe began in a similarly very dense state from which it expands. Is it possible that these are one and the same dense state? That is, is it possible that what is beyond the horizon of a black hole is the beginning of another universe?

> This could happen if the collapsing star exploded once it reached a very dense state, but after the black hole horizon had formed around it. . . .

> What we are doing is applying this bounce hypothesis, not to the universe as a whole, but to every black hole in it. If this is true, then we live not in a single universe, which is eternally passing through the same recurring cycle of collapse and rebirth. We live instead in a continually growing community of 'universes', each of which is born from an explosion following the collapse of a star to a black hole (Smolin, 1997: 87–8).

Smolin's vision of a self-reproducing universe is an appealing one. It suggests that the universe is more like a living thing than an artifact and thus that its coming into being doesn't require an external agent.

Smolin's theory is simpler than the God hypothesis because it does not postulate the existence of any supernatural entities. It is also more conservative because it doesn't contradict any laws of science. In addition, it is potentially more fruitful because it is possible to draw testable predictions from it. Other things being equal, the simpler, the more conservative, and the more fruitful a theory, the better. So even if the big bang occurred fifteen billion years ago, we don't have to assume that it was caused by God.

References
Davies, P. 1983. *God and the New Physics*. New York: Simon and Schuster.
Ross, H. 1995. *The Creator and the Cosmos*. Colorado Springs, NV: Navpress.
Smolin, L. 1997. *the Life of the Cosmos*. New York: Oxford University Press.
Tyron, E. 1973. 'Is the Universe a Vacuum Fluctuation?', *Nature* 246.

Essay 5 *

The Naturalist and the Supernaturalist
by C.S. Lewis

I use the word *Miracle* to mean an interference with Nature by supernatural power.[1] Unless there exists, in addition to Nature, something else which we may call the supernatural, there can be no miracles. Some people believe that nothing exists except Nature; I call these people *Naturalists*. Others think that, besides Nature, there exists something else: I call them *Supernaturalists*. Our first question, therefore, is whether the Naturalists or the Supernaturalists are right. And here comes our first difficulty.

Before the Naturalist and the Supernaturalist can begin to discuss their difference of opinion, they must surely have an agreed definition both of Nature and of Supernature. But unfortunately it is almost impossible to get such a definition. Just because the Naturalist thinks that nothing but Nature exists, the word *Nature* means to him merely 'everything' or 'the whole show' or 'whatever there is'. And if that is what we mean by Nature, then of course nothing else exists. The real question between him and the Supernaturalist has evaded us. Some philosophers have defined Nature as 'What we perceive with our five senses.' But this also is unsatisfactory; for we do not perceive our own emotions in that way, and yet they are presumably 'natural' events. In order to avoid this deadlock and to discover what the Naturalist and the Supernaturalist are really differing about, we must approach our problem in a more roundabout way.

I begin by considering the following sentences: (1) Are those his natural teeth or a set? (2) The dog in his natural state is covered with fleas. (3) I love to get away from tilled lands and metalled roads and be alone with Nature. (4) Do be natural. Why are you so affected? (5) It may have been wrong to kiss her but it was very natural.

A common thread of meaning in all these usages can easily be discovered. The natural teeth are those which grow in the mouth; we do not have to design them, make them, or fit them. The dog's natural state is the one he will be in if no one takes soap and water and prevents it. The countryside where Nature reigns supreme is the one where soil, weather and vegetation produce their results unhelped and unimpeded by man. Natural behaviour is the behaviour which people would exhibit if they were not at the pains to alter it. The natural kiss is the kiss which will be given if moral or prudential considerations do not intervene. In all the examples Nature means what happens 'of itself' or 'of its own accord': what you do not need to labour for; what you will get if you take no measures to stop it. The Greek word

---

*Source: 'The Naturalist and the Supernaturalist', by C.S. Lewis. From *Miracles*. Copyright © C.S. Lewis Pte. Ltd. 1947, 1960.

for Nature (Physis) is connected with the Greek verb for 'to grow'; Latin *Natura*, with the verb 'to be born'. The Natural is what springs up, or comes forth, or arrives, or goes on, *of its own accord*: the given, what is there already: the spontaneous, the unintended, the unsolicited.

What the Naturalist believes is that the ultimate Fact, the thing you can't go behind, is a vast process in space and time which is *going on of its own accord*. Inside that total system every particular event (such as your sitting reading this book) happens because some other event has happened; in the long run, because the Total Event is happening. Each particular thing (such as this page) is what it is because other things are what they are; and so, eventually, because the whole system is what it is. All the things and events are so completely interlocked that no one of them can claim the slightest independence from 'the whole show'. None of them exists 'on its own' or 'goes on of its own accord' except in the sense that it exhibits, at some particular place and time, that general 'existence on its own' or 'behaviour of its own accord' which belongs to 'Nature' (the great total interlocked event) as a whole. Thus no thoroughgoing Naturalist believes in free will: for free will would mean that human beings have the power of independent action, the power of doing something more or other than what was involved by the total series of events. And any such separate power of originating events is what the Naturalist denies. Spontaneity, originality, action 'on its own', is a privilege reserved for 'the whole show', which he calls *Nature*.

The Supernaturalist agrees with the Naturalist that there must be something which exists in its own right; some basic Fact whose existence it would be nonsensical to try to explain because this Fact is itself the ground or starting-point of all explanations. But he does not identify this Fact with 'the whole show'. He thinks that things fall into two classes. In the first class we find either things or (more probably) One Thing which is basic and original, which exists on its own. In the second we find things which are merely derivative from that One Thing. The one basic Thing has caused all the other things to be. It exists on its own; they exist because it exists. They will cease to exist if it ever ceases to maintain them in existence; they will be altered if it ever alters them.

The difference between the two views might be expressed by saying that Naturalism gives us a democratic, Supernaturalism a monarchical, picture of reality. The Naturalist thinks that the privilege of 'being on its own' resides in the total mass of things, just as in a democracy sovereignty resides in the whole mass of the people. The Supernaturalist thinks that this privilege belongs to some things or (more probably) One Thing and not to others—just as, in a real monarchy, the king has sovereignty and the people have not. And just as, in a democracy, all citizens are equal, so for the Naturalist one thing or event is as good as another, in the sense that they are all equally dependent on the total system of things. Indeed each of them is only the way in which the character of that total system exhibits itself at a particular point in space and time. The Supernaturalist, on the other hand, believes that the one original or self-existent thing is on a different level from, and more important than, all other things.

At this point a suspicion may occur that Supernaturalism first arose from reading into the universe the structure of monarchical societies. But then of course it may with equal reason be suspected that Naturalism has arisen from reading into it the structure of modern democracies. The two suspicions thus cancel out and give us no help in deciding which theory is more likely to be true. They do indeed remind us that Supernaturalism is the characteristic philosophy of a monarchical age and Naturalism of a democratic, in the sense that Supernaturalism, even if false, would have been believed by the great mass of unthinking people four hundred years ago, just as Naturalism, even if false, will be believed by the great mass of unthinking people today.

Everyone will have seen that the One Self-existent Thing—or the small class of self-existent things—in which Supernaturalists believe, is what we call God or the gods. I propose for the rest of this book to treat only that form of Supernaturalism which believes in one God; partly because polytheism is not likely to be a live issue for most of my readers, and partly because those who believed in many gods very seldom, in fact, regarded their gods as creators of the universe and as self-existent. The gods of Greece were not really supernatural in the strict sense which I am giving to the word. They were products of the total system of things and included within it. This introduces an important distinction.

The difference between Naturalism and Supernaturalism is not exactly the same as the difference between belief in a God and disbelief. Naturalism, without ceasing to be itself, could admit a certain kind of God. The great interlocking event called Nature might be such as to produce at some state a great cosmic consciousness, an indwelling 'God' arising from the whole process as human mind arises (according to the Naturalists) from human organisms. A Naturalist would not object to that sort of God. The reason is this. Such a God would not stand outside Nature or the total system, would not be existing 'on his own'. It would still be 'the whole show' which was the basic Fact, and such a God would merely be one of the things (even if he were the most interesting) which the basic Fact contained. What Naturalism cannot accept is the idea of a God who stands outside Nature and made it.

We are now in a position to state the difference between the Naturalist and the Supernaturalist despite the fact that they do not mean the same by the word Nature. The Naturalist believes that a great process, or 'becoming', exists 'on its own' in space and time, and that nothing else exists—what we call particular things and events being only the parts into which we analyze the great process or the shapes which that process takes at given moments and given points in space. This single, total reality he calls Nature. The Supernaturalist believes that one Thing exists on its own and has produced the framework of space and time and the procession of systematically connected events which fill them. This framework, and this filling, he calls Nature. It may, or may not, be the only reality which the one Primary Thing has produced. There might be other systems in addition to the one we call Nature.

In that sense there might be several 'Natures'. This conception must be kept quite distinct from what is commonly called 'plurality of worlds'—i.e. different solar systems or different galaxies, 'island universes' existing in widely separated parts of a single space and time. These, however remote, would be parts of the same Nature as our own sun: it and they would be interlocked by being in relations to one another, spatial and temporal relations and causal relations as well. And it is just this reciprocal interlocking within a system which makes it what we call a Nature. Other Natures might not be spatio-temporal at all: or, if any of them were, their space and time would have no spatial or temporal relation to ours. It is just this discontinuity, this failure of interlocking, which would justify us in calling them different Natures. This does not mean that there would be absolutely no relation between them; they would be related by their common derivation from a single Supernatural source. They would, in this respect, be like different novels by a single author; the events in one story have no relation to the events in another *except* that they are invented by the same author. To find the relation between them you must go right back to the author's mind: there is no cutting across from anything Mr Pickwick says in *Pickwick Papers* to anything Mrs Gamp hears in *Martin Chuzzlewit*. Similarly there would be no normal cutting across from an event in one Nature to an event in any other. By a 'normal' relation I mean one which occurs in virtue of the character of the two systems. We have to put in the qualification 'normal' because we do not know in advance that God might not bring two Natures into partial contact at some particular point: that is, He might allow *selected* events in the one to produce results in the other. There would thus be, at certain points, a partial interlocking; but this would not turn the two Natures into one, for the total reciprocity which makes a Nature would still be lacking, and the anomalous interlockings would arise not from what either system was in itself but from the Divine act which was bringing them together. If this occurred each of the two Natures would be 'supernatural' in relation to the other: but the fact of their contact would be supernatural in a more absolute sense—not as being beyond this or that Nature but beyond any and every Nature. It would be one kind of Miracle. The other kind would be Divine 'interference' not by the bringing together of two Natures, but simply.

All this is, at present, purely speculative. It by no means follows from Supernaturalism that Miracles of any sort do in fact occur. God (the primary thing) may never in fact interfere with the natural system He has created. If He has created more natural systems than one, He may never cause them to impinge on one another.

But that is a question for further consideration. If we decide that Nature is not the only thing there is, then we cannot say in advance whether she is safe from miracles or not. There are things outside her: we do not yet know whether they can get in. The gates may be barred, or they may not. But if Naturalism is true, then we do know in advance that miracles are impossible: nothing can come into Nature from the outside because there is nothing outside to come in, Nature being everything. No doubt, events which we in our ignorance should mistake for miracles might occur: but they would in reality be (just like the commonest events) an inevitable result of the character of the whole system.

Our first choice, therefore, must be between Naturalism and Supernaturalism.

Note
1.   This definition is not that which would be given by many theologians. I am adopting it not because I think it an improvement upon theirs but precisely because, being crude and 'popular', it enables me most easily to treat those questions which 'the common reader' probably has in mind when he takes up a book on Miracles.

Essay 6 *

Misleading the Patient for Fun and Profit
by Lewis Vaughn

Romance is in the air. The media, the public, the gurus, and the hucksters have gazed upon acupuncture, homeopathy, chelation therapy, herbal concoctions, magnetic therapy, and any other treatments called 'alternative medicine' . . . and *have fallen in love*. So, as in any romance, current talk about a beloved 'alternative' therapy is usually marked by uncritical acceptance, blind commitment, feverish thinking, and occasional cooing.

In this atmosphere, there are two politically incorrect questions that you must never utter: (1) *Is this true?* (Are there good grounds for believing this claim?) and (2) *Is this right?* (Is it morally permissible to use or promote this treatment?) We are told that to ask question 1 (and the relevant accompanying questions about evidence and reasons for believing) is to reveal an annoying and pernicious bias in favor of Western science and rational ways of knowing. It is to show a callous disregard for the kind of validation that can come from people's subjective experiences. It is—worst of all—to give offense to those who have strong beliefs about the effectiveness of a treatment.

Fortunately, scientists—being the pigheaded realists that they are—have persisted in asking question 1 and have thus discovered, among other things, that acupuncture is no better than placebo, homeopathy doesn't work, and chelation therapy can kill you.

*Source: 'Misleading the Patient for Fun and Profit' by Lewis Vaughn. Copyright © 1998 by the Council for Secular Humanism (CSH). This article originally appeared in *Free Inquiry* magazine, volume 18, number 3 (Summer), published by the CSH in Amherst, New York. Reprinted with permission.

Question 2, however, is almost never asked. One version of it is particularly rare: Is it ethical to recommend or promote an unproven treatment—one that has little or no scientific evidence supporting its efficacy?

The issue is important because companies, advertisers, special interest groups, magazines, newspapers, television talk-shows, health practitioners, and others often do promote remedies and health practices that are unproven. This practice—for better or worse—can have enormous consequences for all of us.

Most medical scientists and health officials oppose the practice, sometimes warning that there isn't yet enough evidence to recommend a certain treatment to the public. Promoters of unproven treatments strongly disagree and sometimes ridicule officials for being 'overly cautious' or 'too conservative'. Their most plausible arguments usually involve an appeal to the relative costs and benefits of a treatment. 'What's the harm?' they may ask. 'If the treatment itself is harmless, why shouldn't suffering people be given a chance to try it? There may be no strong evidence that it works, but if it does, the benefits to many people would be substantial. The costs to people—in terms of potential physical harm—are low. So on balance, it's best to urge people to try it; the possible benefits outweigh the possible costs.' Promoters may believe that this argument is especially strong if the treatment has some preliminary evidence in its favor or if the monetary outlay for the treatment is low.

But is this really a good argument? Many on both sides in the debate would probably agree that weighing costs and benefits is a valid way to judge the issue. (This approach is based on the fundamental ethical insight that we ought to do what's likely to benefit people and avoid doing what's likely to harm them.) So the question reduces to whether promoting unproven treatments is likely to result in a net benefit to people. Does the promoter's argument show that his promoting leads to such benefit?

Actually, his argument fails. It fails because it's too simplistic, neglecting to take into account important factors in the cost-benefit equation.

One such factor is *probability*. Few people would judge a treatment solely on the magnitude of its proposed benefit or harm. Most would want to take into account the probability that the proposed effects would happen. Someone may claim that rubbing a stone on your belly will cure cancer. The alleged benefit is enormous—but the likelihood of receiving this benefit is almost nil. If someone wanted to sell you such a 'cancer-curing' stone for ten dollars, would you buy it? Probably not. The proposed benefit is great but not likely to happen. The cost, though, is a sure thing: if you want the stone, you'll have to pay the price. So on balance, the likely cost, though small, outweighs the unlikely benefits, though great.

But what's the probability that any unproven remedy will be effective? The evidence relating to the remedy can't tell us; by definition, it's too weak to help us figure probabilities. We can, however, make a reasonable assumption. Scientists know that the chances of new hypotheses being correct are very low simply because it's far easier to be wrong than to be right. For the same reason, the likelihood of new health claims turning out to be true is also low. Historically, most health hypotheses, when adequately tested, have been found to be false. In drug testing, for example, scientists may begin with thousands of substances proposed as medicines, some with preliminary evidence in their favor. In the end, after assessing them all, only a meager handful are proven effective in humans. Some promoters misjudge the cost-benefit of recommending a treatment because they either overestimate the probability of its effectiveness or don't consider the factor at all. They seem to assume that the odds of any proposed remedy being effective are close to 50–50, especially if there's some preliminary evidence in its favor. This assumption is false.

When we plug realistic probabilities into our moral equation, the wisdom of promoting unproven treatments becomes suspect. Even if an unproven treatment has considerable possible benefits, is harmless, and costs little, it may be no bargain. In general, given the realistic probabilities, the most likely prospect is that the treatment will be ineffective. So, in fact, the odds are excellent that people who buy the treatment will waste their time and money. The likely cost outweighs the unlikely benefits. Promoting the treatment is not likely to result in a net benefit for people, but net harm. The possible benefit of a ten-dollar 'cancer-fighting' rock may be great, but the low probability of its working makes buying it a bad deal. Promoting it would be unethical.

Clearly, the higher the cost of an unproven treatment, the less likely that promoting it will result in a net benefit. But there's more to the cost of an unproven treatment than many promoters realize. The monetary cost can vary tremendously and may not be low at all. (Many unconventional treatments cost hundreds or even thousands of dollars.) Other costs include the direct physical harm that a treatment can cause (nearly all treatments—drugs, surgery, herbs, vitamins, and others—cause some side effects). There's also an indirect cost: A few people (maybe many people) may take the promoter seriously and stop, postpone, or refuse a proven therapy to try the unproven one—a gamble that sometimes has tragic consequences. Then there's the very real emotional pain that false hope can often bring. In these ways, even a harmless therapy can cause harm. All these costs must be factored into the cost-benefit equation. Usually, they just make the promoter's argument weaker.

But, some will say, what about the placebo effect, the well-documented phenomenon of people tending to feel better after being given a bogus or inactive treatment? If someone who tries an unproven treatment experiences the placebo effect and therefore feels better, doesn't this mean that there is benefit to trying an unproven treatment after all? Doesn't the placebo effect thus change our moral equation?

The placebo effect (which happens in 30 per cent or more of cases) would change the equation if it were unequivocally beneficial. But it is not. First, the placebo effect does not happen in every case. In fact, it is probable that in *most* cases it does not happen. Even when it does, it is often of short duration. So there is no guarantee that anyone will benefit from a placebo in any particular case. Second, placebos can cause adverse side effects (when they do, they're called nocebos). So they're not uniformly helpful. Third, placebo effects can encourage people to continue to use an ineffective treatment when more effective treatments are available. Placebo effects, after all, are not cures, but temporary feel-good phenomena. Fourth, placebo effects often inspire people to promote a remedy to friends and relatives—even though the remedy may be ineffective or harmful. This simply multiplies the problems that accrue to use of placebos. So in the promotion of unproven treatments, the placebo effect is usually not a point in the promoter's favor. Our moral equation still stands—generally *against* the promotion of meritless remedies.

Now, it's possible that a person could apply the cost-benefit approach in her own life and rightly conclude that she *should* try an unproven remedy. She could calculate that any possible benefit, though very unlikely, is well worth the cost because no other treatment is possible or because she considers the cost inconsequential. Promoters, however, aren't privy to such personal information about those who try unproven remedies. Promoters can only weigh the probable impact of their actions on other people. If they do so honestly, they'll have to conclude that, generally, promoting unproven treatments does more harm than good.

Essay 7 *

Yes, Human Cloning Should Be Permitted
by Chris MacDonald

Patricia Baird's discussion of human cloning (*Annals RCPSC*, June 2000) challenges the prospect of nuclear-transfer cloning for the purposes of human reproduction. Baird reviews a long list of familiar worries about human cloning, but the most striking feature of her discussion is its frankness in placing the onus of justification on the shoulders of those who would permit human cloning. The reasons for permitting cloning, she argues, are 'insufficiently compelling', so cloning should be prohibited. The implication is that any new technology should be forbidden unless and until enough justification can be found for allowing its use.

Baird is to be commended for her frankness. But the onus is misplaced, or at least too severe. One need not be a single-minded defender of liberty to think that, contrary to Baird's implication, we need good reasons to limit the actions of others, particularly when those actions do no clear and specific harm. The fact that a portion of society—even a majority—finds an activity distasteful is insufficient grounds for passing a law forbidding it. For example, it is presumably true that at one point, roughly 90 per cent of the public (the same proportion that Baird says

*Source: 'Yes, Human Cloning Should Be Permitted', by Chris MacDonald. From *Annals of the Royal College of Physicians and Surgeons of Canada*. Reprinted by permission of the author.

is against human cloning) was opposed to homosexuality. Does (or did) this justify action on the part of government to ban homosexual lifestyles? Surely not.

There may be a flaw in my analogy. Human cloning, according to critics, has harmful effects (or at least risks). Indeed, Baird suggests that the arguments regarding potential physical and psychological harm to clones have been 'well delineated'. In fact, a convincing case has yet to be made for the claim that the physical and psychological risks to clones are more severe than, or different in kind from, those faced by children produced in more traditional ways. Identical twins live with the psychological 'burden' of not being genetically unique. Children born to women over 35 are at an increased risk of genetic illness. Children resulting from in-vitro fertilization or other reproductive technologies live with the knowledge that their origins were unusual. They may even live with the knowledge that their genetic profile has been manipulated (for example, through pre-implantation selection of embryos). Human cloning for reproductive purposes is another novel—and as yet untested—medical technology. As such, it should be approached with caution. Thorough animal trials should be completed before attempts on humans are contemplated. But this is true of any new medical technology.

Baird worries about the shift that human cloning might provoke in the way that we view children. This in turn would change the type of community that we are. The central worry is that human cloning 'commodifies' children (i.e. that cloning may make us think of children as a commodity or product to be bought and sold). Why would cloning have this effect? Is it simply because it is likely to be expensive, so that it costs money to have children? Surely this is insufficient to worry us. Raising children already costs money—the statistics show us how many hundreds of thousands of dollars it costs to raise a child through to adulthood. Yet no one has suggested that we see our children as products, or love them any less. (In the mid 1940s—before publicly funded health care—my grandparents sold their car to pay the hospital bill related to my father's birth, so 'purchasing' the birth of a child is nothing new!)

Baird argues that an 'important part of human identity is the sense of arising from a maternal and a paternal line while at the same time being a unique individual.' Yet without supporting evidence, this sounds like pop psychology. And we can reply in kind: most people I know do not identify with both their maternal and paternal lineages. One of my friends, who was raised by a single mother, identifies with her maternal eastern European heritage, and not with the French paternal heritage implied by her surname. Another friend identifies with his father's black heritage, rather than with his maternal Chinese lineage, despite his Asian physical features. Such patterns are not unusual. Dual heritage may be normal, but it hardly seems central to our conception of ourselves as humans. And identical twins seem none the worse for the knowledge that they are not genetically unique individuals.

Claims about challenges to what makes us 'human' may be powerful rhetorical devices, but they must be substantiated if they are to be convincing.

Baird is correct to exhort us to look beyond harms to identifiable individuals, to the social implications that human cloning might have. As a comparison, think of fetal sex selection. Most of us think that sex selection is a bad thing not because of any purported harm to the child, but because we worry about the social implications of valuing children of one sex over those of another. So Baird rightly reminds us that focusing on potential harms to individuals constitutes a 'dangerously incomplete framing' of the problem. Furthermore, cloning (and genetic technology in general) is sufficiently new—and its implications sufficiently poorly understood—to warrant a healthy respect, and even the allowance of a margin of safety. But this does not suggest the need for the ban that Baird (with others) proposes. What these worries suggest is a need for caution, for discussion, and for regulation. For instance, laws limiting the number of clones that might be created from one individual, restricting the combination of cloning with genetic modification, and defining lines of parental obligation, would alleviate many of the concerns associated with human cloning. (Françoise Baylis argues that cloning is so likely to be used in combination with gene transfer that we should think of cloning as an enhancement technology rather than as a reproductive technology, in her article 'Human Cloning: Three Mistakes and A Solution', which has been accepted for publication in the *Journal of Medicine and Philosophy*.)

What I have said here should not be taken as an absolute defence of human cloning in all circumstances. (Indeed, there may be only a few circumstances in which cloning is appropriate.) Nor have I suggested that public monies should be spent on cloning research. All I have suggested is that a ban on research leading toward human cloning is unwarranted by the arguments raised thus far. Caution and discretion are warranted; a ban is not.

Finally, I worry that Baird's point of view exemplifies the way in which human reproductive cloning is being singled out, among cloning-related techniques, as a bogeyman. Almost in chorus, scientists are pleading with regulators not to place restrictions on cloning experimentation per se. At the same time, most scientists seem to be more than willing to swear off reproductive cloning, and indeed to wring their hands over the moral implications of its use. Yet this has the air of a too-hasty concession. The scientific community seems to be too willing to condemn one unpopular application of cloning technology, on the basis of too little convincing argumentation, to appease those who oppose cloning technology in general. But human cloning for reproductive purposes has legitimate, morally acceptable applications—for example, for infertile couples, and for gay couples. And none of the criticisms have been convincingly made. We should not let reproductive human cloning be abandoned as the moral sacrificial lamb of the cloning debate.

Essay 8*

RIM is Dead

by Henry Blodget (CEO/EIC, Business Insider)

By creating the BlackBerry, Research In Motion revolutionized mobile productivity. For nearly a decade, the company easily fended off the competition by providing the best personal-information gadget on the market. It silenced its critics. It reduced Palm, a previous leader in mobile gadgets, to a pile of rubble. And it made its shareholders rich.

But now, Research In Motion's amazing run appears to be over. The company has lost its lead in the smartphone market, and its market share is falling rapidly. And many long-time addicts like me have switched to iPhones or Android phones.

There are three main reasons RIM's fortunes have turned south.

First and foremost, RIM's products are no longer the best on the market. Although some diehard business users still cling to their BlackBerrys—and insist that the devices are better for e-mail and calendar management than anything else out there—these folks are increasingly a minority. The rest of smartphone users prefer the broader capabilities of iPhones and Android phones, especially apps and web browsing.

Second, the smartphone market has become a 'platform' game. As Microsoft's Windows demonstrated in the PC era, technology markets in which third-party companies build programs or applications to run on top of a particular operating system or other product—'platform markets'—tend to standardize around one or two market leaders. Thanks to the explosion of 'apps' available for iPhones and Android phones, the smartphone market is increasingly becoming a platform market. Research In Motion has fewer developers building apps for BlackBerry than Apple and Google do for their platforms, and this lack of apps makes the products less useful for consumers. RIM has tried to encourage developers in recent years, but it still lags badly as an app-development platform.

Third, one of the biggest selling points for BlackBerrys has always been their security and integration with corporate computing systems, most notably Microsoft's Exchange. Increasingly, however, companies are allowing employees to use whichever devices they prefer. And many employees are choosing iPhones and Android phones. In addition, many companies are officially equipping employees with iPhones and iPads, something that was nearly unheard of only a few years ago.

Is there anything that could turn RIM's fortunes around?

Yes. If RIM actually could deliver a product that was a 'quantum leap' over the latest iPhone or Android phone, consumers would respond accordingly. The one

---

*Source: 'RIM is Dead' by Henry Blodget and 'Long Live RIM' by Nick Waddell. Both from Canadian Business, 19 May 2011.

benefit about competing in the smartphone market is that consumers tend to upgrade their phones every year or two, and they tend to be seduced by the latest, greatest phone on the market.

The most likely scenario for RIM is that it becomes Nokia, a company that once dominated the cellphone market but lost several steps and is now scrambling to stay relevant. A worse scenario would be that RIM becomes the next Palm, a one-time leader that falls on its face and is eventually sold for scrap to a larger technology player.

Long Live RIM
by Nick Waddell (Founding Editor, Cantech Letter)

To a certain class of pundit, Research In Motion is already a dinosaur. The Waterloo tech giant, which made its name by practically inventing the smartphone category, sells products that to some seemed antiquated compared to slicker iPhones, iPads, and Android devices. But all is not lost for RIM. Its obsession with making its devices secure now shows extended vision, given recent high-profile security gaffes from industry leaders Amazon, Apple, and Sony. And RIM is hardly floundering financially; the global mobile player is in outstanding fiscal shape. Marked for extinction by many, RIM itself is preparing for evolution instead.

It's hard to ignore that RIM's transformation into an also-ran occurred alongside Apple's stunning and sustained resurgence. Comparisons between RIM and Apple are commonplace. Nervy analysts these days are just as likely to set RIM against beleaguered mobile pioneer Palm.

Palm's Palm Pilot popularized the personal digital assistant, or PDA. Released in 1996, the device effectively launched an industry that ultimately morphed into the devices we see today. But for numerous reasons, many related to a seemingly endless string of spinoffs and corporate restructurings, Palm lost its way and failed to jump on the lucrative opportunity of combining an electronic organizer with a cellular phone. Palm was ultimately acquired by HP for a fraction of the value it once commanded.

In a recent interview with Forbes, Rob Enderle of the Enderle Group said RIM 'started out as a much-loved enterprise product, but that market has changed to one that is more consumer-driven in that the business line managers are more inclined to make IT decisions.' His conclusion about RIM? 'They are trending to be the next Palm.' Others, however, say the RIM-Palm comparison doesn't really stand up to examination.

Casual observers might be surprised to learn of the company's astonishing growth over the past three years. Between fiscal 2008 and 2011, RIM's top-line revenue more than tripled, from just over $6 billion to nearly $20 billion. Of course, this number is less than a third of the $65 billion that Apple posted in fiscal 2010. But dig a little deeper into the books of both companies and a curious stat stands out. In the most recent fiscal year, Apple spent $1.78 billion on research and development, a number equal to 2.73 per cent of its top line. In contrast, RIM has been much more R&D intensive; the $1.35 billion it spent on R&D in the last fiscal year was 6.78 per cent of its total revenue.

So what is RIM up to with all this spending? Paradigm Capital analyst Barry Richards sees evidence of a sea change at RIM that is punctuated by 14 recent acquisitions, including last year's snagging of highly regarded QNX Software, which makes operating systems used in 'mission critical' environments such as high-speed trains and nuclear power plants. QNX is now expected to become nothing less than the default operating system for all BlackBerry devices.

The acquisition of QNX was another in a series of RIM moves that had tech geeks buzzing. Navneet Alang, a writer for the Techi website, agrees, saying, 'Blackberry have suddenly got a lot of talent for creating a successor to their clunky and old-fashioned—if eminently practical—Blackberry OS.' Richards believes RIM's new PlayBook tablet, which also operates on the QNX architecture, 'takes RIM back to its roots in secure data for enterprises.'

Indeed, a growing amount of evidence suggests that mobile security could be the issue that slowly levels the playing field between RIM and the more tony Android and Apple devices. In April, security researchers discovered that the location-based services in Apple's iOS 4+ devices, including the iPhone, had been collecting comprehensive and detailed information on their users' location in an unencrypted file. Apple is now facing at least one class-action lawsuit....

With a strong balance sheet, a robust and powerful new operating system, and a global smartphone market that is growing at a frenetic pace, rumours of RIM's demise may […] be greatly exaggerated. In the meantime, tech investors looking to identify the next killer app might be surprised to find that apps in general are fast being overshadowed by more menacing security concerns. To the great favour of Research In Motion, 2011 will almost certainly be more about encryption, and less about Angry Birds.

Essay 9*

UFO Abductions
by Theodore Schick and Lewis Vaughn

In recent years, books, magazines, movies, and television talk shows have circulated an amazing hypothesis: Alien beings are abducting ordinary people, manipulating them in strange ways (performing experiments on them, having sex with them, or otherwise terrifying them), and then releasing their victims and vanishing. In the best-selling book *Communion*, author Whitley Strieber suggested that he was abducted by aliens with large heads and strange eyes and that they forced him to

---

*Source: 'UFO Abductions', by Theodore Schick and Lewis Vaughn. From *How to Think About Weird Things*.

endure horrific treatment, including having a needle inserted into his head and an instrument put into his anus (Strieber, 1987). Later the book was made into a movie with the same name. The book *Intruders* by Budd Hopkins presents dramatic case histories of people who claim to have endured UFO abductions (Hopkins, 1987). Hopkins suggests that aliens have abducted hundreds of people and used them in disturbing genetic experiments, then released them.

In many cases, before any abduction story surfaces, the victims first experience a vivid dream or nightmare (sometimes in childhood) involving eerie, otherworldly creatures. Or they experience 'missing time', the realization that they don't remember what happened to them during a certain period. Or they see an odd light in the night sky that they identify as a UFO. Later, when the victims are hypnotized to try to learn more about these strange occurrences, an abduction experience is fully revealed. While under hypnosis, the abductees report in stunning detail what they believe they saw or felt during abduction, what the aliens looked like, and, in some cases, what the aliens said. The technique called *regressive hypnosis* has been the favored method for uncovering details of an abduction and for authenticating it. Some people, however, have recounted a UFO-abduction experience or produced details about it without undergoing hypnosis.

Now let's apply the SEARCH formula to the abduction hypothesis and to some of the leading alternatives and see what happens.

Hypothesis 1: *Alien beings have abducted several people, interacted with them in various ways, and then released them.* Proponents of this hypothesis point to several pieces of evidence. First and foremost, there's the striking testimony elicited during hypnosis, which is thought to be a kind of truth serum, a way to retrieve accurate details about a person's experience of past events. There's also testimony that arises without the aid of hypnosis. There's the fact that the alleged abductees' stories seem to be so similar, that many abductees report the experience of missing time, and that a few of them (including Whitley Strieber) have passed lie detector tests. There's also physical evidence, like mysterious scars on abductees' bodies and areas of dead grass on the ground suggesting a UFO landing.

As for hypnosis, it's not the revealer of truth that many believe it to be. Research has shown that even deeply hypnotized people can willfully lie and that a person can fake hypnosis and fool even very experienced hypnotists. More to the point, research also shows that when hypnotized subjects are asked to recall a past event, they will fantasize freely, creating memories of things that never happened. Martin T. Orne, one of the world's leading experts on the use of hypnosis to obtain information about past events, sums up the situation like this:

> The hypnotic suggestion to relive a past event, particularly when accompanied by questions about specific details, puts pressure on the subject to provide information. . . . This situation may jog the subject's memory and produce some increased recall, but it will also cause him to fill in details that are plausible but consist of memories or fantasies from other times. It is extremely difficult

to know which aspects of hypnotically aided recall are historically accurate and which aspects have been confabulated [made up and confused with real events]. . . . There is no way, however, by which anyone—even a psychologist or psychiatrist with extensive training in the field of hypnosis—can for any particular piece of information determine whether it is actual memory versus a confabulation unless there is independent verification (Orne, 1979).

Orne and other experts have also emphasized how extremely suggestible hypnotic subjects are and how easy it is for a hypnotist to unintentionally induce pseudomemories in the subject:

If a witness is hypnotized and has factual information casually gleaned from newspapers or inadvertent comments made during prior interrogation or in discussion with others who might have knowledge about the facts, many of these bits of knowledge will become incorporated and form the basis of any pseudo-memories that develop. . . . If the hypnotist has beliefs about what actually occurred, it is exceedingly difficult for him to prevent himself from inadvertently guiding the subject's recall so that [the subject] will eventually 'remember' what he, the hypnotist, believes actually happened (Orne, 1979).

Orne describes a simple experiment he has repeatedly conducted that shows the limits of hypnotism. First he verifies that a subject went to bed at a certain time at night and slept straight through until morning. Then he hypnotizes the subject and asks her to relive that night. Orne asks the subject if she heard two loud noises during the night (noises that didn't, in fact, happen). Typically, the subject says that she was awakened by the noises and then describes how she arose from bed to investigate. If Orne asks her to look at the clock, the subject identifies a specific time—at which point the subject was actually asleep and in bed. After hypnosis, the subject remembers the nonevent as though it actually happened. A pseudomemory was thus created by a leading question that may seem perfectly neutral.

A study has even been conducted to see if people who had never seen a UFO nor were well informed about UFOs could, under hypnosis, tell 'realistic' stories about being abducted by aliens. The conclusion was that they can. The imaginary abductees easily and eagerly invented many specific details of abductions. The researchers found 'no substantive differences' between these descriptions and those given by people who have claimed to be abducted (Lawson and McCall, 1977).

Research also suggests that hypnosis not only induces pseudomemories, but also increases the likelihood that they'll become firmly established. As psychologist Terence Hines says:

What hypnosis does do—and this is especially relevant to the UFO cases— is to greatly increase hypnotized subjects' confidence that their hypnotically induced memories are true. This increase in confidence occurs for both correct and incorrect memories. Thus, hypnosis can create false memories, but the individual will be especially convinced that those memories are true. People repeating such false memories will seem credible because they really believe their false memories are true. Their belief, or course, does not indicate whether the memory is actually true or false (Hines, 1988: 195).

Proponents of the abduction hypothesis, however, point out that a few people have told of being abducted by a UFO before they were hypnotized. This testimony is relevant to the issue—but it's also subject to all the questions of reliability that we must ask of any human testimony. Given what we know about the witnesses and the circumstances of their experience (to be discussed shortly), we must rate this testimonial evidence as weak.

The similarity of abductee stories also gives little support to hypothesis 1. Critics point out that there's little wonder that the stories have so much in common since UFO abduction has become a universally familiar theme, thanks to books, movies, and television. Psychologist Robert A. Baker says:

Any one of us, if asked to pretend that we had been kidnapped by aliens from outer space or another dimension, would make up a story that would vary little, either in details or in the supposed motives of the abductors, from the stories told by any and all of the kidnap victims reported by [Budd] Hopkins. Our imaginative tales would be remarkably similar in plot, dialogue, description, and characterization to the close encounters of the third kind and conversations with little gray aliens described in *Communion* or *Intruders*. The means of transportation would be saucer-shaped, the aliens would be small, humanoid, two-eyed, and gray or white or green, and the purpose of their visits would be to: (1) save our planet; (2) find a better home for themselves; (3) end nuclear war and the threat we pose to the peaceful life in the rest of the galaxy; (4) bring us knowledge and enlightenment; and (5) increase the aliens' knowledge and understanding of other forms of life (Baker, 1990: 247).

The similarities in many abduction stories can also be created by a hypnotist who has unwittingly cued the same pseudomemories in all his or her subjects. This cuing is most likely to happen when the hypnotist lacks proper training in hypnotism and has strong beliefs about what actually happened to the subject—a state of affairs that may be the norm.

On closer inspection, the phenomenon of missing time seems to provide little support for the abduction hypothesis either. One reason is that the phenomenon is actually a common, ordinary experience—especially when people are anxious or under stress:

Typically, motorists will report after a long drive that at some point in the journey they woke up to realize they had no awareness of a preceding period of time. With some justification, people will describe this as a 'gap in time', a 'lost half-hour', or a 'piece out of my life' (Baker, 1990: 252).

In addition, many cases of missing time in abduction stories have been investigated and found to have fairly prosaic explanations (Klass, 1989).

Passing a lie detector test doesn't lend credence to an abduction story either. Polygraph tests are still used in criminal investigations, employment screenings, and elsewhere. Nevertheless, recent research has established that polygraph testing is an extremely unreliable guide to someone's truthfulness (Lykken, 1981; US Office of Technology Assessment, 1993).

The physical evidence is equivocal. Scars or cuts on abductees could have been caused by aliens—or they could have happened accidentally without the subject's knowing how, just as we all occasionally discover scratches or cuts on our bodies without remembering how they got there. They also could have been intentionally self-inflicted. There's no corroborating evidence to show that they are, in fact, alien-inflicted. The story is much the same with dead-grass areas. There's no direct evidence linking them to UFO landings. Some of them, however, have been shown to be the work of a type of fungus that dehydrates the grass (sometimes in a circular pattern called a fairy ring) and makes it appear burnt. Let us consider some alternative explanations.

Hypothesis 2: *People who report being abducted by aliens are suffering from serious mental illness.* In other words, nobody has been abducted; people who make abduction claims are just plain crazy. Actually, it wouldn't be surprising to find that a few of these people were psychotic. But the idea that a large proportion of them are crazy isn't supported by the evidence.

Not every alleged abductee has undergone psychological testing, but a few have. The Fund for UFO Research asked Elizabeth Slater, a professional psychologist, to study nine people who claimed to have been abducted by aliens. During the study, Slater wasn't aware of the subjects' abduction claims. After extensive testing of these nine, she concluded that none of them were psychotic or crazy (Slater, 1985). Other research has come up with similar findings.

Of course, psychologists and psychiatrists know that a person needn't be insane to exhibit extremely strange behavior or to have very weird experiences. It is also worth noting that Slater commented that the subjects, though sane, couldn't be considered completely normal. She said that they 'did not represent any ordinary cross-section of the population', that several of them could be characterized as 'odd or eccentric', and that under stressful conditions six of the nine showed a 'potential for more or less transient psychotic experiences involving a loss of reality testing along with confused and disordered thinking that can be bizarre' (Slater, 1985).

Hypothesis 3: *People who report being abducted by aliens are perpetrating a hoax.* A few tales of UFO abduction are suspicious or have been found to be hoaxes. Philip Klass, for example, has shown that the Travis Walton abduction story (eventually made into the movie *Fire in the Sky*) was a probable hoax (Klass, 1989). But there's no evidence that the majority of abduction tales are put-ons. Most observers agree that those who make abduction claims are apparently sincere.

Hypothesis 4: *Reports of alien abductions are fantasies arising from people with 'fantasy-prone personalities', and these fantasies may be further elaborated and strengthened through hypnosis.* Scientists have discovered that some people, though they appear normal and well-adjusted, frequently have very realistic wide-awake hallucinations and fantasies and often have experiences that resemble those induced by hypnosis. The researchers who uncovered this phenomenon describe it this way:

> [This research] has shown that there exists a small group of individuals (possibly 4 per cent of the population) who fantasize a large part of the time, who typically 'see', 'hear', 'smell', and 'touch' and fully experience what they fantasize; and who can be labeled fantasy-prone personalities. Their extensive and deep involvement in fantasy seems to be their basic characteristic and their other major talents—their ability to hallucinate voluntarily, their superb hypnotic performances, their vivid memories of their life experiences, and their talents as psychics or sensitives—seem to derive from or grow out of their profound fantasy life (Wilson and Barber, 1983).

When these people are deep in fantasy, they have a decreased awareness of time and place, just as many abductees say they do (the experience of missing time). Also, not only are they easily hypnotized, but they show hypnotic behavior all the time, even when not hypnotized:

> When we give them 'hypnotic suggestions' such as suggestions for visual and auditory hallucinations, negative hallucinations, age regression, limb rigidity, anesthesia, and sensory hallucinations, we are asking them to do for us the kind of thing they can do independently of us in their daily lives (Wilson and Barber, 1983).

Interestingly enough, some research suggests that people who claim to have been abducted by aliens are in fact fantasy-prone personalities. In one study, a biographical analysis was done on 154 people who said they had been abducted or had several contacts with aliens. It was found that 132 of these subjects seemed normal and healthy but had many fantasy-prone personality characteristics (Basterfield and Bartholomew, 1988). Baker has suggested that Whitley Strieber, author of *Communion*, fits the fantasy-prone personality mold:

> Anyone familiar with the fantasy-prone personality who reads Strieber's *Communion* will suffer an immediate shock of recognition! Strieber is a classic example of the fantasy-prone type: easily hypnotized, amnesiac, from a very religious background, with vivid memories of his early years and a very active fantasy life—a writer of occult and highly imaginative novels featuring unusually strong sensory experiences, particularly smells and sounds and vivid dreams.

Strieber's wife was questioned under hypnosis by Hopkins. With regard to some of Strieber's visions, she says, 'Whitley saw a lot of things that I didn't see at that time.' 'Did you look for [a bright crystal in the sky]?' 'Oh, no. Because I knew it wasn't real.' 'How did you know it wasn't real? Whitley's a fairly down-to-earth guy—' 'No, he isn't. . . .' 'It didn't surprise you hearing Whitley, that he sees things like that?' 'No' (Baker, 1990: 247).

There's also evidence that sleep-related hallucinations (called, you may remember, hypnogogic and hypnopompic hallucinations) happen more frequently to fantasy-prone people. And there's reason to believe that these phenomena play a role in UFO-abduction stories. We know that many UFO abductions allegedly happen after the victim has gone to bed and involve the feeling of being paralyzed or seeming to float outside the body. Such hallucinations seem absolutely real and thus are referred to as waking dreams. They're not an indication of mental illness; they happen to normal, sane, and rational people. Baker explains their telltale signs:

> There are a number of characteristic clues that tell you whether a perception is or is not a hypnogogic or hypnopompic hallucination. First, it always occurs before or after falling asleep; second, one is paralyzed or has difficulty in moving, or on the other hand, one may float out of one's body and have an out-of-body experience; third, the hallucination is unusually bizarre, i.e., one sees ghosts, aliens, monsters, etc.; fourth, after the hallucination is over, the hallucinatory typically goes back to sleep; and, fifth, the hallucinator is unalterably convinced of the reality of the entire experience (Baker, 1990: 250).

Strieber himself, says Baker, had such a hallucination:

> Strieber's *Communion* contains a classic, textbook description of a hypnopompic hallucination, complete with the wakening from a sound sleep, the strong sense of reality and of being awake, the paralysis (due to the fact that the body's neural circuits keep our muscles relaxed to help preserve our sleep), and the encounter with strange beings. Following the encounter, instead of jumping out of bed and going in search of the strangers, Strieber, typically, goes back to sleep. He even reports that the burglar alarm had not gone off—proof again that the intruders were mental rather than physical. On another occasion Strieber reports awakening and believing that the roof of his house is on fire and that aliens are threatening his family. Yet his only response to this is to go peacefully back to sleep—again, clear evidence of a hypnopompic dream.
>
> Strieber, of course, is convinced of the reality of these experiences. This, too, is expected. If he were not convinced of their reality, the experience would not be hypnopompic nor hallucinatory (Baker, 1990: 251).

Finally, it's clear that if a fantasy-prone person experiences a fantasy about being abducted by aliens and then is hypnotized by a hypnotist who asks leading questions and believes in UFO abductions, the fantasy is likely to be confirmed or elaborated, to be very convincing to others, and to be believed as absolutely true by the abductee.

Hypothesis 5: *Reports of alien abductions arise from dreams and are then elaborated or strengthened through hypnosis.* We know that the adventures of many people claiming to be abductees actually began with compelling dreams. First they said that they dreamed that they had had contact with a UFO or were abducted; then—while under hypnosis—they told in detail of an actual alien abduction. Many of the abductees featured in Hopkins's *Intruders*, for example, described such a pattern of events. As Hines says:

> It is thus easy to understand how, for example, a frightening dream about being abducted by a UFO can come to seem real to an individual who is repeatedly hypnotized to recall further details of the experience and is explicitly told by the hypnotist that the experience is real. If the individual already has difficulty telling reality from fantasy, the process of becoming convinced that the dream or fantasy was real will occur more rapidly. It is no rare event for someone to have a dream that, at least briefly, may seem to have really happened. In fact, almost everyone has had dreams that, upon awakening, were so vivid that it was not possible, for a while at least, to decide whether they really happened or not (Hines, 1988: 203).

Hypothesis 6: *People who report being abducted are suffering from excessive bursts of electrical activity in their temporal lobes.* Neuroscientist Michael Persinger claims that mystical experiences, out-of-body experiences, and even abduction-like experiences are associated with some unusual activity going on inside the brain—specifically, surges of electrical activity in the temporal lobes. Some people have what is called high 'temporal lobe lability'. Their temporal lobes are 'unstable' and frequently surge with electrical activity. Persinger discovered that compared with people who have 'normal' lability, those with high temporal lobe lability more often report mystical or psychic experiences and feelings of flying or leaving the body. In experiments, Persinger has actually induced such experiences—including abduction-like experiences—in people by applying magnetic fields across the brain, thereby instigating bursts of electrical activity in the temporal lobes (Blackmore, 1994).

Persinger says that people with high lability are likely to have abduction-type experiences occasionally. The surges are likely to occur during sleep, thus inducing a nighttime abduction experience (which is exactly what many people have reported).

Earthquakes, which produce strong magnetic effects, could trigger temporal lobe surges. So Persinger predicted that reports of UFO abductions and sightings would correspond to the dates of seismic activity. When he tested his prediction, he found that he was right; there was a strong correlation between seismic events and the weird experiences.

Now let's apply the criteria of adequacy to these alternative hypotheses. All are testable, so we must rely on the other four criteria to help us choose among the possibilities. Using these four criteria, let's first see if we can eliminate some of the hypotheses.

Hypotheses 4 (fantasy-prone personalities), 5 (dream material), and 6 (electrical activity) can probably be given similar weight in terms of fruitfulness, scope, and simplicity (except that 6 has an edge in fruitfulness). Hypotheses 2 (mental illness) and 3 (hoaxes) are clearly inferior to 4, 5, and 6 in conservatism. They conflict with existing evidence; hypotheses 4, 5, and 6, on the other hand, are consistent with a great deal of evidence.

Now the contest is between hypotheses 1 (authentic abductions), 4, 5, and 6. We can now see that hypothesis 1 comes out the loser to the other three on every count. Hypothesis 1 has yielded no novel predictions. Hypotheses 4, 5, and 6 have greater scope, for they offer explanations that can be applied to several phenomena, not just claims of alien abductions. In terms of simplicity, hypothesis 1 must be given less credence than the other hypotheses because it postulates new entities—aliens.

In light of the criterion of conservatism, we see that the evidence in favor of hypothesis 1 is extremely weak; the evidence for the other three alternatives is much stronger. In addition, hypothesis 1 conflicts with a great deal of human experience regarding visitors from outer space; so far, we have no good evidence that anyone has ever detected any aliens. Moreover, the probability of the Earth being visited by aliens from outer space must be considered very low (but not zero) in light of what we know about the size of the universe, the estimated likelihood of extraterrestrial life, and the physical requirements of space travel.

For all these reasons, the abduction hypothesis must be considered improbable. Hypotheses 4, 5, and 6 appear much more likely. If there is a winner among these three, it would have to be hypothesis 6. It excels in fruitfulness, for it has yielded a surprising prediction—the odd correlation between abduction reports and seismic activity. It is still possible, however, that each of our remaining three hypotheses is a correct explanation for a portion of alien abduction claims. Also, these hypotheses may not be the only ones. Our list of alternative hypotheses isn't intended to be exhaustive. Further research could narrow—or widen—the field. In the meantime, our analysis has given us a conclusion supported by good reasons: The abduction hypothesis is untenable, and there are indeed reasonable alternatives.

References
Baker, R.A. 1990. *They Call It Hypnosis*. Buffalo: Prometheus Books.
Basterfield, K., and R. Bartholomew. 1988. 'Abductions: The Fantasy-Prone Personality Hypothesis', *International UFO Review* 10, 3 (May/June): 9–11.
Blackmore, S. 1994. 'Alien Abduction', *New Scientist* 19 November: 29–31.
Hines, T. 1988. *Pseudoscience and the Paranormal*. Buffalo: Prometheus Books.
Hopkins, B. 1987. *Intruders*. New York: Random House.
Klass, P.J. 1989. *UFO Abductions: A Dangerous Game*. Buffalo: Promethus Books.
Lawson, A.H., and W.C. McCall. 1977. 'What Can We Learn from the Hypnosis of Imaginary Attackers?', *MUFON UFO Symposium Proceedings*. Seguin, TX: Mutual UFO Network.
Lykken, D. 1981. *A Tremor in the Blood*. New York: McGraw-Hill.

Orne, M.T. 1979. 'The Use and Misuse of Hypnosis in Court', *International Journal of Clinical and Experimental Hypnosis* (October): 311–41.

Slater, E. 1985. 'Conclusions on Nine Psychologies', in *Final Report on the Psychological Testing of UFO "Abductee"*, ed. R. Westrum. Mt. Rainier, DS: Fund for UFO Research, pp. 17–31.

Strieber, W. 1987. *Communion*. New York: William Morrow.

US Office of Technology Assessment. 1993. *Scientific Validity of Polygraph Testing: A Research Review and Evaluation*. Washington, DC: Office of Technology Assessement, OTA-TMH-15.

Wilson, S.C., and T.X. Barber. 1983. 'The Fantasy-Prone Personality: Implications for Understanding Imagery, Hypnosis, and Parapsychological Phenomena', in *Imagery, Current Theory, Research, and Application*, ed. A.A. Sheikh. New York: John Wiley.

Essay 10*

Amityville: The Horror of It All
by Joe Nickell

The bestselling book *The Amityville Horror: A True Story* was followed by a movie of the same title and a sequel, *Amityville II: The Possession*. Although the original event proved to be a hoax, that fact does not seem well known to the general public. . . . Now a new book sheds new light on the sordid affair and reviews the multiple-murder case that preceded it. Written by Ric Osuna, it is titled *The Night the DeFeos Died: Reinvestigating the Amityville Murders*.

The saga began on 13 November 1974, with the murders of Ronald DeFeo Sr, his wife Louise, and their two sons and two daughters. The six were shot while they slept in their home in Amityville, New York, a community on Long Island. Subsequently the sole remaining family member—Ronald Jr, nicknamed 'Butch'—confessed to the slaughter and was sentenced to 25 years to life. Just two weeks after his sentencing late the following year, George and Kathy Lutz and their three children moved into the tragic home where—allegedly—a new round of horrors began.

The six-bedroom Dutch Colonial house was to be the Lutzes' residence for only 28 days. They claimed they were driven out by sinister forces that ripped open a heavy door, leaving it hanging from one hinge; threw open windows, bending their locks; caused green slime to ooze from a ceiling; peered into the house at night with red eyes and left cloven-hooved tracks in the snow outside; infested a room in mid-winter with hundreds of houseflies; and produced myriad other supposedly paranormal phenomena, including inflicting a priest with inexplicable, painful blisters on his hands.

Local New York television's Channel 5 'investigated' the alleged haunting by bringing in alleged psychics together with 'demonologist' Ed Warren and his wife Lorraine, a professed 'clairvoyant'. The group held a series of séances in the house. One psychic claimed to be ill and to 'feel personally threatened' by shadowy forces. Lorraine Warren pronounced that there was a negative entity 'right from the bowels of the earth'. A further séance was unproductive but psychics agreed a 'demonic spirit' possessed the house and recommended exorcism (Nickell, 1995).

In September 1977 *The Amityville Horror: A True Story* appeared. Written by Jay Anson, a professional writer commissioned by Prentice-Hall to tell the Lutzes' story, it became a runaway best seller. Anson asserted: 'There is simply too much independent corroboration of their narrative to support the speculation that they either imagined or fabricated these events,' although he conceded that the strange occurrences had ceased after the Lutzes moved out.

Indeed, a man who later lived there for eight months said he had experienced nothing more horrible than a stream of gawkers who tramped onto the property. Similarly the couple who purchased the house after it was given up by the Lutzes, James and Barbara Cromarty, poured ice water on the hellish tale. They confirmed the suspicions of various investigators that it was a bogus admixture of phenomena: part traditional haunting, part poltergeist disturbance, and part demonic possession, including elements that seemed to have been lifted from the movie *The Exorcist*.

Researchers Rick Moran and Peter Jordan (1978) discovered that the police had not been called to the house and that there had been no snowfall when the Lutzes claimed to have discovered cloven hoofprints in the snow. Other claims were similarly disproved (Kaplan and Kaplan, 1995).

I talked with Barbara Cromarty on three occasions, including when I visited Amityville as a consultant to the *In Search Of* television series. She told me not only that her family had experienced no supernatural occurrences in the house, but that she had evidence the whole affair was a hoax. Subsequently I recommended to a producer of the then-forthcoming TV series *That's Incredible*, who had called for my advice about filming inside the house, that they have Mrs Cromarty point out various discrepancies for close-up viewing. For example, recalling the extensive damage to doors and windows detailed by the Lutzes, she noted that the old hardware—hinges, locks, doorknob, etc.—were still in place. Upon close inspection, one could see that there were no disturbances in the paint and varnish (Nickell, 1995).

In time, Ronald DeFeo's attorney, William Weber, told how the Lutzes had come to him after leaving the house, and he had told them their 'experiences' could be useful to him in preparing a book. 'We created this horror story over many bottles of wine that George Lutz was drinking,' Weber told the Associated Press. 'We were creating something the public wanted to hear about.' Weber later filed a two-million-dollar lawsuit against the couple, charging them with reneging on their book deal. The Cromartys also sued the Lutzes, Anson, and the publishers, maintaining that the fraudulent haunting claims had resulted in sightseers destroying any privacy they might have had. During the trials the Lutzes admitted that virtually everything in *The Amityville Horror* was pure fiction (Kaplan and Kaplan, 1995; Nickell, 1995).

Now Ric Osuna's *The Night the DeFeos Died* adds to the evidence. Ronald DeFeo's wife Geraldine allegedly confirms much of Weber's account. To her, it was clear that the hoax had been planned for some time. Weber had intended to use the haunting claims to help obtain a new trial for his client (Osuna, 2002: 282–6).

As to George Lutz—now divorced from his wife and criticized by his former stepsons—Osuna states that 'George informed me that setting the record straight was not as important as making money off fictional sequels.' Osuna details numerous contradictions in the story that Lutz continues to offer versions of (286–9).

For his part, Osuna has his own story to tell. He buys Ronald 'Butch' DeFeo's current story about the murders, assuring his readers that it 'is true and has never been made public' (18, 22). DeFeo now alleges that his sister Dawn urged him to kill the entire family and that she and two of Butch's friends had participated in the crimes.

In fact, Butch maintains that Dawn began the carnage by shooting their domineering father with the .35-caliber Marlin rifle. Butch then shot his mother, whom he felt would have turned him in for the crime, but claims he never intended to kill his siblings. He left the house to look for one of his friends who had left the scene and, when he returned to find that Dawn had murdered her sister and other two brothers, he was enraged. He fought with her for the gun and sent her flying into a bedpost where she was knocked out. He then shot her.

Osuna tries to make this admittedly 'incredible' tale believable by explaining away contradictory evidence. He accepts DeFeo's claim that he altered the crime scene and asserts that the authorities engaged in abuses and distortions of evidence to support their theory of the crimes. Even so, Osuna concedes that 'Butch had offered several different, if ludicrous, versions of what had occurred' (33), and that he might again change his story. But he asserts that 'Too much independent corroboration exists to believe it was just another one of his lies' (370).

I remain unconvinced. Butch DeFeo has forfeited his right to be believed, and his current tale is full of implausibilities and contradictions. Osuna appears to me to simply have become yet another of his victims.

References
Anson, J. 1977. *The Amityville Horror: A True Story*. New York: Bantam Books.
Kaplan, S., and R.S. Kaplan. 1995. *The Amityville Horror Conspiracy*. Lacyville, PA: Belfrey Books.
Moran, R., and P. Jordan. 1978. 'The Amityville Horror Hoax', *Fate* May: 44–6.
Nickell, J. 1995. *Entities: Angels, Spirits, Demons, and Other Alien Beings*. Amherst, NY: Prometheus Books, 122–9. (Background for the present article has been abridged from this source.)
Osuna, R. 2002. *The Night the DeFeos Died: Reinvestigating the Amityville Murders*. np: Xlibris Corporation.

Appendix B

Answers to Exercises

Chapter 1

Exercise 1.1

1. Critical thinking is the systematic evaluation or formulation of beliefs, or statements, by rational standards.
4. Critical thinking operates according to rational standards in that beliefs are judged by how well they are supported by reasons.
6. The *critical* in critical thinking refers to the exercising of careful judgment and judicious evaluation.
8. A statement is an assertion that something is or is not the case.
11. An argument is a group of statements in which some of them (the premises) are intended to support another of them (the conclusion).
14. In an argument, a conclusion is a statement that premises are intended to support.
17. No.
19. Indicator words are words that frequently accompany arguments and signal that a premise or conclusion is present.
23. Look for the conclusion first.

Exercise 1.2

1. No statement.
4. No statement.
7. Statement.
10. No statement.

Exercise 1.3

1. Argument.
   Conclusion: He should avoid her.

4. No argument.
7. No argument.
11. Argument.
    Conclusion: Don't outlaw guns.
15. Argument.
    Conclusion: Noisy car alarms should be banned.

Exercise 1.4

1. Argument.
    Conclusion: Faster-than-light travel is not possible.
    Premise: Faster-than-light travel would violate a law of nature.
4. Argument.
    Conclusion: The flu epidemic on the East Coast is real.
    Premise: Government health officials say so.
    Premise: I personally have read at least a dozen news stories that characterize the situation as a 'flu epidemic'.
7. No argument.
10. No argument.

Exercise 1.5

3. Premise: Freedom to seek out food to sustain oneself and one's family is a basic moral right.
    Premise: The right to hunt and fish was guaranteed to Aboriginal Canadians by treaties signed by the Canadian government.
6. Premise: MacDonald has admitted that he knows nothing about animals.
    Premise: The Society for the Prevention of Cruelty to Animals has declared MacDonald a dummy when it comes to animals.
9. Premise: The Internet has led to the capture of more terrorists than anything else.
    Premise: The Attorney General of Canada has asserted that the Internet is the best friend that anti-terrorist teams have.
12. Premise: All the top TV critics agree that *The Sopranos* is the greatest series in TV history.
    Premise: I have compared *The Sopranos* to all other TV series and found that the show outshines them all.

Exercise 1.6

2. Conclusion: Several Canadian cities can expect to see an overall decline in smoking.
4. Conclusion: As a married person, you are happier than people who aren't married.
8. Conclusion: The government does not do anything about pornography on the Internet even though kids have access to all kinds of porn.

Exercise 1.7

1. Argument.
   Conclusion: Advertising isn't manipulative.
   Premise: The main thing advertising does is provide information about products.
   Premise: Ads that don't seem to feature much information are really just trying to entertain us, not manipulate us.
3. Argument.
   Conclusion: There is no archaeological evidence for the [biblical] Flood.
   Premise: If a universal Flood occurred between five and six thousand years ago, killing all humans except the eight on board the Ark, it would be abundantly clear in the archaeological record.
   Premise: The destruction of all but eight of the world's people left no mark on the archaeology of human cultural evolution.

Chapter 2

Exercise 2.1

1. For critical thinking to be realized, the process must be systematic, it must be a true evaluation or formulation of claims, and it must be based on rational standards.
5. We take things too far when we accept claims for no reason.
7. You are most likely to let your self-interest get in the way of clear thinking when you have a significant personal stake in the conclusions you reach.
11. Group pressure can affect your attempts to think critically by allowing your need to be part of a group or your identification with a group to undermine critical thinking.

14. A world view is a set of fundamental ideas that helps us make sense of a wide range of issues in life.
17. Critical thinking is concerned with objective truth claims.
21. Reasonable doubt, not certainty, is central to the acquisition of knowledge.

Exercise 2.2

1. Self-interest.
4. Group pressure (in this case, the we-are-better-than-them type).
7. Group pressure.
10. Self-interest.

Exercise 2.3

1. a. The charges are false.
   c. Important evidence that would exonerate Father Miller was not mentioned in the newspaper account.
3. a. A study from McGill shows that women are less violent and less emotional than men.
6. No good reasons listed.

Exercise 2.4

1. Better-than-others group pressure. Possible negative consequence: Failure to consider other points of view; discrimination against people who disagree with Marie-Eve.
3. It's not entirely clear what the group's motivations are. This passage could easily be an example of better-than-others group pressure.
7. Appeal to popularity. Possible negative consequence: Overlooking other factors that might be a lot more important than popularity.

Exercise 2.5

1. Face-saving. Possible negative consequences: Poor academic performance due to overconfidence; embarrassment at failure after being so cocky; alienation of friends.
2. Self-interest; Possible negative consequences: Wasting the taxpayer's money; being thrown out of office for misconduct.

Chapter 3

Exercise 3.1

4. Deductive.
8. Sound.
12. No.

Exercise 3.2

1. Step 1: Conclusion: She has a superior intellect.
    Premises: Ethel graduated from Queen's University. If she graduated from Queen's, she probably has a superior intellect.
    Step 2: Not deductively valid.
    Step 3: Inductively strong.
    Step 4: Does not apply.
6. Step 1: Conclusion: Thus, every musician has a university degree.
    Premises: Every musician has had special training, and everyone with special training has a university degree.
    Step 2: Deductively valid.
    Step 3: Does not apply.
    Step 4: Does not apply.
9. Step 1: Conclusion: So some actors who sing also play a musical instrument.
    Premises: Some actors sing, and some play a musical instrument.
    Step 2: Not deductively valid.
    Step 3: Not inductively strong.
    Step 4: Intended to be deductive.
15. Step 1: Conclusion: So it's impossible for androids to have minds.
    Premises: If minds are identical to brains—that is, if one's mind is nothing but a brain—androids could never have minds because they wouldn't have brains. Clearly, a mind is nothing but a brain.
    Step 2: Deductively valid.
    Step 3: Does not apply.
    Step 4: Does not apply.

Exercise 3.3

3. Valid.
8. Valid.
14. Valid.
18. Valid.
23. Invalid.

Exercise 3.4

I.
1. The Honourable Member from Algoma-Manitoulin-Kapuskasing was caught misusing campaign funds.
5. She's not incompetent.
9. The engine started right away.

II.
3. Sixty per cent of the teenagers in several scientific surveys love rap music.
6. Assad's fingerprints are on the vase.
9. The murder rates in almost all cities in the central Canada are very low.

Exercise 3.5

1. Valid; *modus tollens*.
6. Valid; *modus tollens*.
9. Valid; *modus ponens*.

Exercise 3.6

2. If Lino is telling the truth, he will admit to all charges.
   Lino is telling the truth.
   So he will admit to all charges.
   If Lino is telling the truth, he will admit to all charges.
   He will not admit to all charges.
   So he is not telling the truth.
5. If religious conflict in Nigeria continues, thousands more will die.
   The religious conflict in Nigeria will continue.
   Therefore, thousands more will die.
   If religious conflict in Nigeria continues, thousands more will die.
   Thousands more will not die.
   Therefore, religious conflict in Nigeria will not continue.
9. If solar power can supply six megawatts of power in Vancouver (which is certainly not the sunniest place in the world), then solar power can transform the energy systems in sunnier places like Edmonton and Calgary.
   Solar power can supply six megawatts of power in Vancouver.
   So solar power can transform the energy systems in sunnier places like Edmonton and Calgary.
   If solar power can supply six megawatts of power in Vancouver (which is certainly not the sunniest place in the world), then solar power can transform the energy systems in sunnier places like Edmonton and Calgary.

But solar power cannot transform the energy systems in sunnier places like Edmonton and Calgary.

So solar power cannot supply six megawatts of power in Vancouver.

Exercise 3.7

4. If the Queen of England were a man, she would be mortal.
    She is mortal.
    Therefore, the Queen of England is a man.
    If a, then b.
    b.
    Therefore, a.

5. If Bill Clinton was the president of the US in 1970, then he would be an American.
    Bill Clinton was not president of the US in 1970. Therefore, he is not an American.
    If a, then b.
    Not a.
    Therefore, not b.

7. If Vaughn is a dog, he is a mammal.
    He is a mammal.
    Therefore, he is a dog.
    If a, then b.
    b.
    Therefore, a.

8. If ducks are sea turtles, then they are at home in the water.
    Ducks are not sea turtles.
    Therefore, ducks are not at home in the water.
    If a, then b.
    Not a.
    Therefore, not b.

11. If Chicago is the capital of Illinois, then Chicago is in Illinois.
    Chicago is in Illinois.
    Therefore, Chicago is the capital of Illinois.
    If a, then b.
    b.
    Therefore, a.

Exercise 3.8

1. Any argument that provides 3 separate, stand-alone reasons supporting a single conclusion will do. For example:

    (1) The stores are closed. (2) We have no money. (3) And we have no way of travelling to any place of business. (4) Therefore, we are just not going to be able to go shopping right now.

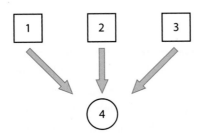

4. (1) If the pipes have burst, there will be no running water. (2) The pipes have burst. (3) And if all the water is rusty, we won't be able to use it anyway, (4) and all the water is rusty. (5) So we have no usable water at this point.

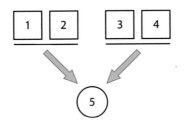

Exercise 3.9

6. (1) If Marla buys the house in the suburbs, she will be happier and healthier. (2) She is buying the house in the suburbs. (3) So she will be happier and healthier.

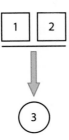

10. (1) The existence of planets outside our solar system is a myth. (2) There is no reliable empirical evidence at all showing that planets exist outside our solar system.

17. (1) ~~There are at least two main views regarding the morality of war.~~ (2) ~~Pacifism is the view that no war is ever justified because it involves the taking of human life.~~ (3) ~~Just-war theory is the view that *some* wars are justified for various reasons—mostly because they help prevent great evils (such as massacres, 'ethnic cleansing', or world domination by a madman like Hitler) or because they are a means of self-defence.~~ (4) I think that our own moral sense tells us that sometimes (in the case of the Second World War, for example) violence is occasionally morally justified. (5) ~~It would be hard for anyone to deny that a war to prevent something like the Holocaust is morally right.~~ [Implied conclusion] (6) Just-war theory is correct.

20. (1) The picnic will probably be spoiled because (2) there is a 90 per cent probability of rain.

Exercise 3.10

1. Conclusion: (3) The idea that God is required to be the enforcer of the moral law is not plausible.

   Premises: (4) In the first place, as an empirical hypothesis about the psychology of human beings, it is questionable. (5) There is no unambiguous evidence that theists are more moral than non-theists. (6) Not only have psychological studies failed to find a significant correlation between frequency of religious worship and moral conduct, but convicted criminals are much more likely to be theists than atheists. (7) Second, the threat of divine punishment cannot impose a moral obligation. (8) Might does not make right.

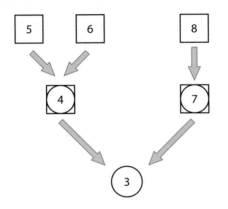

Chapter 4

Exercise 4.1

4. We should proportion our belief to the evidence.
10. Two additional indicators are reputation among peers and professional accomplishments.
17. By making a conscious effort to consider not only information that supports what we believe, but also the information that conflicts with it.

Exercise 4.2

4. Proportion belief to the evidence; the claim is not dubious enough to dismiss out of hand, and not worthy of complete acceptance. Low plausibility.
6. Reject it; it conflicts with a great deal of background information.

10. Proportion belief to the evidence; the claim is not dubious enough to dismiss out of hand, and not worthy of complete acceptance. Moderate plausibility.
14. Reject it; it conflicts with a great deal of background information.
17. Reject it; it conflicts with a great deal of background information.

Exercise 4.3

3. Do not agree. Persuasive evidence would include the body of an alien or the alien craft itself, both scientifically documented as being of extraterrestrial origin.
8. Do not agree. Persuasive evidence would include several double-blind, controlled trials demonstrating that meditation and controlled breathing shrink tumours.

Chapter 5

Exercise 5.1

4. The fallacy of composition is arguing that what is true of the parts must be true of the whole.
10. They are fallacious because they assume that a proposition is true merely because a great number of people believe it, but as far as the truth of a claim is concerned, what many people believe is irrelevant.
15. Yes.
19. People are often taken in by false dilemmas because they don't think beyond the alternatives laid before them.

Exercise 5.2

1. Composition.
5. Genetic fallacy.
10. Genetic fallacy.
14. Equivocation.
20. Genetic fallacy.

Exercise 5.3

4. False dilemma.
6. Hasty generalization.
10. False dilemma.

Exercise 5.4

3. Jones says that Mrs Anan deserves the Nobel Prize. But he's a real jerk. Clearly then Mrs Anan does not deserve the Nobel Prize.
6. In light of ethical considerations, Scouts Canada should allow gay kids to be members. The reason is that banning gay kids from the organization would be in conflict with basic moral principles.
11. Newfoundland's fisheries are a mess because the Department of Fisheries and Oceans—a federal department—has too much power over them. Nobody likes intrusive governments!

Chapter 6

Exercise 6.1

1. Conjunction. Components: The Liberals raised taxes, The Conservatives cut programs; &
5. Conditional. Components: Taslima can read your mind, You're in trouble; →
7. Conditional; Components: God is all-powerful, He can prevent evil in the world; →

Exercise 6.2

1. $p \vee q$
4. $e \& f$
8. $\sim g \& \sim h$
14. $\sim\sim p$

Exercise 6.3

2. False.
6. True.
8. False.

Exercise 6.4

2. True.
5. True.
10. True.

Exercise 6.5

2. Either John is home or Mary is home.
5. If the sun is not shining, then we will not go outside.
10. If the day goes well, then we will not regret our efforts.

Exercise 6.6

2. $p \lor q$
5. $\sim a \rightarrow \sim b$
9. $p \rightarrow q$

Exercise 6.7

2. Alligators are reptiles and dogs are reptiles.

a	d	a & d
T	T	T
T	F	F
F	T	F
F	F	F

6. Either dogs are not mammals, or snakes are reptiles. [Hint: To avoid confusion, you can *add* columns after the guide columns, such as the one for ~d in this truth table. This extra column reminds you that the truth values for ~d are the flip side of those for d.]

d	s	~d	~d v s
T	T	F	T
T	F	F	F
F	T	T	T
F	F	T	T

8. Alligators can bark, and dogs are not reptiles.

a	d	~d	a & ~d
T	T	F	F
T	F	T	T
F	T	F	F
F	F	T	F

Exercise 6.8

2. Valid.

$$p \to q$$
$$p$$
$$\therefore q$$

p	q	$p \to q$	p	q
T	T	T	T	T
T	F	F	T	F
F	T	T	F	T
F	F	T	F	F

7. Valid.

$$p \to q$$
$$\sim q \,\&\, r$$
$$\therefore r$$

	p	q	r	$\sim q$	$p \to q$	$\sim q \,\&\, r$	r
1	T	T	T	F	T	F	T
2	T	T	F	F	T	F	F
3	T	F	T	T	F	T	T
4	T	F	F	T	F	F	F
5	F	T	T	F	T	F	T
6	F	T	F	F	T	F	F
7	F	F	T	T	T	T	T
8	F	F	F	T	T	F	F

14. Valid.

$$p \to q$$
$$\sim(q \lor r)$$
$$\therefore \sim p$$

	p	q	r	$\sim p$	$p \to q$	$\sim(q \lor r)$	$\sim p$
1	T	T	T	F	T	F	F
2	T	T	F	F	T	F	F
3	T	F	T	F	F	F	F
4	T	F	F	F	F	T	F
5	F	T	T	T	T	F	T
6	F	T	F	T	T	F	T
7	F	F	T	T	T	F	T
8	F	F	F	T	T	T	T

Exercise 6.9

3. Jake is the plumber or Jake is the carpenter. Jake is not the carpenter. Therefore, Jake is the plumber.

    $p \lor c$

    $\sim c$

    $\therefore p$

p	c	p ∨ c	~ c	p
T	T	T	F	T
T	F	T	T	T
F	T	T	F	F
F	F	F	T	F

Valid.

11. Unless both Mary goes and Henry goes, the party will be a disaster. The party will be a disaster. Therefore, both Mary and Henry will not go.

    $\sim(m \,\&\, h) \to p$

    p

    $\therefore \sim(m \,\&\, h)$

	m	h	p	~(m & h)	~(m & h) → p	p	~(m & h)
1	T	T	T	F	T	T	F
2	T	T	F	F	T	F	F
3	T	F	T	T	T	T	T
4	T	F	F	T	F	F	T
5	F	T	T	T	T	T	T
6	F	T	F	T	F	F	T
7	F	F	T	T	T	T	T
8	F	F	F	T	F	F	T

Invalid.

Exercise 6.10

3. $p \lor q$

    p

    $\therefore \sim q$

    T   T   F

    $p \;\lor\; q \qquad p \quad \sim q$

    T   T   T   T

    Invalid.

10. $p \rightarrow q$

    $\therefore p \rightarrow (p \,\&\, q)$

<table>
<tr><td></td><td>F</td><td></td><td></td><td>F</td><td></td></tr>
<tr><td colspan="2">$p \rightarrow q$</td><td></td><td colspan="3">$p \rightarrow (p \,\&\, q)$</td></tr>
<tr><td>T</td><td>F</td><td></td><td>T</td><td>T</td><td>F</td></tr>
</table>

    Valid.

15. $(d \vee e) \rightarrow (d \,\&\, e)$

    $\sim(d \vee e)$

    $\therefore \sim(d \,\&\, e)$

<table>
<tr><td></td><td></td><td>T</td><td></td><td></td><td></td><td>F</td><td></td><td></td><td>F</td><td></td></tr>
<tr><td colspan="4">$(d \vee e) \rightarrow (d \,\&\, e)$</td><td></td><td colspan="3">$\sim(d \vee e)$</td><td colspan="3">$\sim(d \,\&\, e)$</td></tr>
<tr><td>T</td><td>T</td><td>T</td><td>T</td><td></td><td></td><td>T</td><td>T</td><td></td><td>T</td><td>T</td></tr>
</table>

    Valid.

Chapter 7

Exercise 7.1

1. S = scientists, P = Baptists; universal negative; E.
5. S = theologians who have studied arguments for the existence of God, P = scholars with serious misgivings about the traditional notion of omnipotence; universal affirmative; A.
8. S = people who play the stock market, P = millionaires; particular negative; O.
12. S = terrorists, P = Saudi citizens; particular affirmative; I.
16. S = new Canadians, P = immigration reform supporters; universal negative; E.

Exercise 7.2

1.   All Habs fans are fanatics [or, are people who are fanatical]. A.
5.   All good investments are cell phone companies that keep up with the latest technology. A.
9.   All intelligent thoughts are thoughts that have already happened. A.
13. Some things are things meant to be forgotten. I.

Exercise 7.3

1.   All guardians of the soul are poets. A.
4.   All androids like Commander Data are nonhumans. A.
5.   No things that satisfy the heart are material things. E.

8. Some treatments said to be part of 'alternative medicine' are treatments that are unproven. I.

12. All days that give her any joy are Fridays. A.

15. All pictures identical with the one hanging on the wall are things that are crooked. A.

20. All nations without a conscience are nations without souls. A.

Exercise 7.4

1. No persons are persons exempt from federal income tax.
   S = persons; P = persons exempt federal income tax.

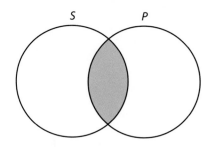

5. No things are things more pitiable than the reasons of an unreasonable man.
   S = things; P = things more pitiable than the reasons of an unreasonable man.

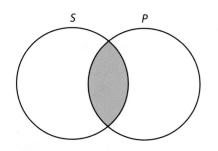

8. Some good talkers are good listeners.
   S = good talkers; P = good listeners.

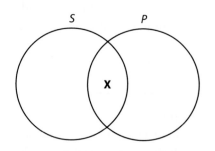

12. All corporations are corporations with social obligations.
    S = corporations; P = corporations with social obligations.

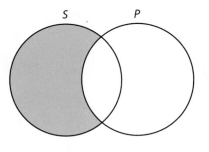

Exercise 7.5

1. No P are S; No S are P.

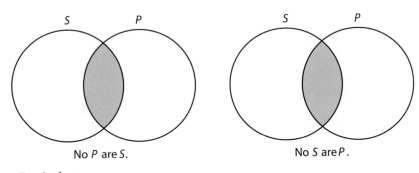

No P are S.   No S are P.

Equivalent.

3. All S are P; All P are S.

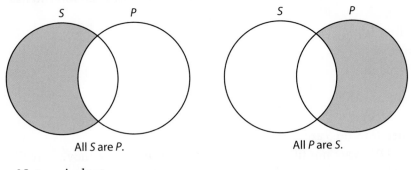

All S are P.   All P are S.

Not equivalent.

6. All *P* are non-*S*; All *S* are non-*P*.

All *P* are non-*S*.   All *S* are non-*P*.

Equivalent.

9. Some *S* are not *P*; Some *P* are not *S*.

Some *S* are not *P*.   Some *P* are not *S*.

Not equivalent.

Exercise 7.6

2. All horses are mammals, and no mammals are lizards. Therefore, no lizards are horses.
   S = lizards
   P = horses
   M = mammals

   All *P* are *M*.
   No *M* are *S*.
   Therefore, no *S* are *P*.

6. Some DVDs are not film classics, but all black and white movies are film classics. Therefore, some black and white movies are not DVDs.

   S = black and white movies
   P = DVDs
   M = film classics

   Some *P* are not *M*.
   All *S* are *M*.
   Therefore, some *S* are not *P*.

9. No elm trees are cacti. Some tall plants are elm trees. So some tall plants are not cacti.

    S = tall plants

    P = cacti

    M = elm trees

    No *M* are *P*.
    Some *S* are *M*.
    Therefore, some *S* are not *P*.

Exercise 7.7

2. All *P* are *M*.
    No *M* are *S*.
    Therefore, no *S* are *P*.

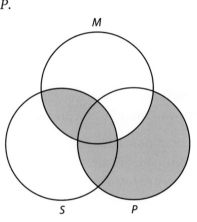

    Valid.

6. Some *P* are not *M*.
    All *S* are *M*.
    Therefore, some *S* are not *P*.

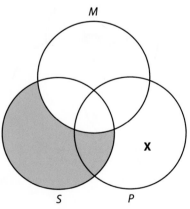

    Invalid.

9. No *M* are *P*.
    Some *S* are *M*.
    Therefore, some *S* are not *P*.

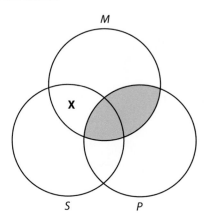

Valid.

Exercise 7.8

1. Some architectural structures are non-traditional designs, for all houses are
    architectural structures, and some houses are non-traditional designs.

    Some houses are nontraditional designs.
    All houses are architectural structures.
    Therefore, some architectural structures are non-traditional designs.

    Some *M* are *P*.
    All *M* are *S*.
    Therefore, some *S* are *P*.

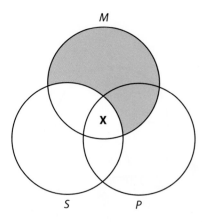

Valid.

3. All SUVs are evil vehicles because all SUVs are gas guzzlers, and all gas guzzlers are evil vehicles.

All gas guzzlers are evil.
All SUVs are gas-guzzlers.
Therefore, all SUVs are evil vehicles.

All *M* are *P*.
All *S* are *M*.
Therefore, all *S* are *P*.

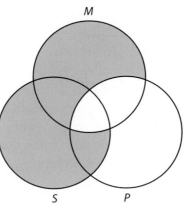

Valid.

8. No wimps are social activists because no wimps are people of honest and strong conviction. And all social activists are people of honest and strong conviction.

All social activists are people of honest and strong conviction.
No wimps are people of honest and strong conviction.
Therefore, no wimps are social activists.

All *P* are *M*.
No *S* are *M*.
Therefore, no *S* are *P*.

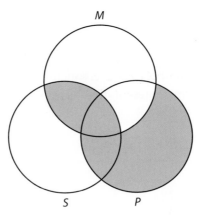

Valid.

Chapter 8

Exercise 8.1

1. Target group: people in the country; sample: adults in Montreal and Toronto; relevant property: being in favour of gay marriage. The argument is weak because the sample is not representative.
4. Target group: students at this university; sample: first-year students at this university; relevant property: being against the US war in Iraq. The argument is weak because the sample is both too small and not representative.
8. Target group: dentists; sample: dentists who suggest that their patients chew gum; relevant property: recommending Brand X gum. The argument is weak because the sample is not representative.
12. Target group: Canadians; sample: adults with an annual income of $48,000–$60,000; relevant property: being happy and satisfied with one's job. The argument is weak because the sample is not representative. (Middle-income workers are likely to have attitudes toward job satisfaction that are different from those of workers in other income brackets, especially lower ones.)

Exercise 8.2

1. Weak. To ensure a strong argument, draw the sample randomly from the entire Canadian population, not just from the two biggest cities in the country.
4. Weak. To ensure a strong argument, randomly draw a sample of several hundred students from the whole university population, not just the first-year students.
8. Weak. To ensure a strong argument, draw the sample randomly from the set of all dentists, not just the dentists who recommend gum.
12. Weak. To ensure a strong argument, draw the sample randomly from the set of all Canadian workers, including respondents representative of all income groups.

Exercise 8.3

1. Does not offer strong support for the conclusion. The problem is non-random—and therefore non-representative—sampling.

Exercise 8.4

1. a, c.

Exercise 8.5

1. Not more likely to be true.

Exercise 8.6

1. Individual: June; group: geeks; characteristic: play computer games; proportion: 67%.
4. Individual: next meal eaten at the Poolhouse Café; group: meals eaten at the Poolhouse Café; characteristic: being wonderful; proportion: almost every.
5. Individual: your car; group: Fords; characteristic: work poorly; proportion: most.

Exercise 8.7

1. unacceptable premise (90% of women are not left-handed)
2. non-typical individual (being a professor makes Professor Norman unusual; professors are more likely than most people to have read Plato.)
4. statistically weak (53% might be technically 'most', but just barely.)

Exercise 8.8

2. Literary analogy.
6. Argument by analogy. Two things being compared; relevant similarity: working with numbers; conclusion: 'he'll be a whiz at algebra'; weak argument.
8. Argument by analogy; four things being compared; relevant similarity: being beef; conclusion: 'I will like tripe'; weak argument.
12. Argument by analogy; two things being compared; relevant similarity: being foundations; conclusions: 'no lasting reputation worthy of respect can be built on a weak character'; strong argument.

Exercise 8.9

1. Instances being compared: the personality traits of Pierre Elliott Trudeau and Michael Ignatieff; relevant similarities: fearsome intellectual, charismatic speaker, passionate defender of social justice; diversity among cases not a significant factor; conclusion: 'Ignatieff, too, will likely eventually be one of Canada's great Prime Ministers'; weak argument (because of several unmentioned dissimilarities—including very different opponents, a different political environment, and so on.)

5. Instances being compared: having terminal cancer and being threatened by an assailant; relevant similarities: being threatened with death or great pain; diversity among cases not a significant factor. Conclusion: 'suicide must sometimes be morally justified when it is an act of self-defence against a terminal disease that threatens death or great pain.' This is a strong argument—*if* all the relevant similarities and dissimilarities have indeed been taken into account. A critic could argue, though, that killing oneself in self-defence is just not relevantly similar to killing another human in self-defence. The critic, then, would have to specify what the significant difference is.

Exercise 8.10

2. Conclusion: 'Research suggests that eating lots of fruits and vegetables may provide some protection against several types of cancer.' Correlation. The argument is strong. The conclusion is a limited claim ('*may* provide some protection . . .'), which the stated correlation could easily support.
7. Conclusion: 'Education increases people's earning power.' Correlation. The argument is strong.
13. Conclusion: 'Tune-ups can improve the performance of lawnmowers.' Method of difference. The argument is strong.
16. Conclusion: [Implied] 'Having a major war somewhere in the world causes the price of oil to hit $40 a barrel.' Method of Agreement. The argument is strong if all relevant factors have been taken into account, which may not be the case.
19. Conclusion: [Implied] 'Only five students got A's on the mid-term exam because they studied the night before the exam and reviewed their notes just before walking into class to take the test.' Method of Agreement. The argument is strong.

Exercise 8.11

2. a, d.
7. a.
13. a.
16. a, b, d.
19. a, b.

Exercise 8.12

1. a.
4. b.
9. a.

Chapter 9

Exercise 9.1

4. A theoretical explanation is an explanation that serves as a theory, or hypothesis, used to explain why something is the way it is, why something is the case, or why something happened.
8. A causal explanation is a kind of theoretical explanation. Like all theoretical explanations, causal explanations are used in inference to the best explanation.

Exercise 9.2

2. The state of affairs being explained is the endangered status of the spotted owl. The explanation is the powerful influence of the logging industry.
5. The state of affairs being explained is an increase in the number of hurricanes. The explanation is that SUVs are causing global warming.
8. The state of affairs being explained is the many times that psychics have seemed to predict the future. The explanation is that that psychics really can predict the future.

Exercise 9.3

3. Interpretive.
7. Theoretical.
12. Interpretive.

Exercise 9.4

2. Theory 1: Jack's house was burglarized.
   Theory 2: Jack's dog went on a rampage.
6. Theory 1: Alice was not exposed to any germs.
   Theory 2: Vitamin C supercharged Alice's immune system.

Exercise 9.6

2. The minimum requirement of consistency is the criterion that any theory worth considering must have both internal and external consistency—that is, be free of contradictions and be consistent with the data the theory is supposed to explain.
6. A theory that does not have much scope is one that explains very little—perhaps only the phenomenon it was introduced to explain and not much else.

Exercise 9.7

2. The second theory is both simpler and more conservative.
4. The first theory is both simpler and more conservative.
7. The first theory is both simpler and more conservative.

Exercise 9.8

3. Theory 3.

Chapter 10

Exercise 10.1

6. (1) Identify the problem or pose a question, (2) devise a hypothesis to explain the event or phenomenon, (3) derive a test implication or prediction, (4) perform the test, (5) accept or reject the hypothesis.
9. If H, then C. Not-C. Therefore, not-H.
12. No. Hypotheses are tested together with other hypotheses. A hypothesis can always be saved from refutation by making changes in one of the accompanying hypotheses.

Exercise 10.2

2. Hypothesis: Two guys are perpetrating a Bigfoot hoax. Test implication: If the two guys are perpetrating a hoax, then monitoring their behaviour day and night should yield evidence of hoaxing activity.
6. Hypothesis: Creatine dramatically increases the performance of weight trainers. Test implication: If creatine increases performance, then giving creatine to weight trainers in a controlled way (in a double-blind controlled trial) should increase various measures of performance in the trainers compared to weight trainers who get a placebo (inactive substance).

Exercise 10.3

3. Theory: Local climate changes.
   Competing theory: Heat from volcanic activity around the planet is melting the glaciers.
   Both theories are about equal in terms of testability, fruitfulness, and scope. The volcanic theory, however, is neither simple nor conservative. It's not simple

because it assumes an unknown process. It's not conservative because it is not consistent with what is known about the effects of heat from volcanoes.

7. Theory: Religion fosters terrorism.
Competing theory: Terrorists commit terrorist acts because they are insane.
Both theories are about equal in terms of testability, fruitfulness, scope, and simplicity. The insanity theory, though, is not conservative. It conflicts with what we know about those who commit terrorist acts. In general, terrorists may be fanatical, but they do not seem to be clinically insane.

Exercise 10.4

2. Test implication: If brighter street lights decrease the crime rate, then reducing the brightness of the lights (while keeping constant all other factors, such as police patrols) should increase the crime rate. The test would likely confirm the theory.

6. Test implication: If eating foods high in fat contributes more to being overweight than eating foods high in carbohydrates, then over time people should gain more weight when they are eating X number of grams of fat per day than when they are eating the same number of grams of carbohydrates per day.

Exercise 10.7

4. The appeal to ignorance.
6. Something is logically impossible if it violates a principle of logic; something is logically possible if it does not violate a principle of logic.

Exercise 10.8

2. Theory 1: The aging of the building materials in the house caused creaking.
Theory 2: The wind blowing against the house caused the creaking.
Theory 3: A ghost caused the creaking.

7. Theory 1: A coincidental matching between the dream and real events made the dream seem prophetic.
Theory 2: Wayne had the same dream every night because he was concerned about his uncle, so there was a good chance that the dream would match something in reality.
Theory 3: The dream was a genuine prophetic dream.

Exercise 10.9

3. Alternative theory: As a prank, the little girls cut drawings of fairies out of a book, posed them in the garden, and took photos of themselves with the

cutouts. Then they claimed that the photos showed actual fairies. Both theories seem to be about equal in testability and fruitfulness. The prank theory has more scope because faked photos can explain many other phenomena, including many different kinds of paranormal hoaxes. The fairy theory is neither simple nor conservative. Fairies are unknown to science, and claims about their existence conflict with many things that we know.

Chapter 11

Exercise 11.1

5. We cannot infer what should be or ought to be from what is.
9. Moral theories try to explain what makes an action right or what makes a person good.
13. Internal consistency—the requirement that the theories composing our world view do not conflict.

Exercise 11.2

1. Non-moral.
6. Moral.
9. Moral.

Exercise 11.3

4. The Indian government posed an imminent threat to Pakistan and the world. When a foreign government poses an imminent threat to Pakistan and the world, Pakistanis are justified in attacking that government. So the Pakistanis were justified in attacking Indian troops.
9. Hacking into a database containing personal information on thousands of people and invading their privacy is immoral. You hacked into a database containing personal information on thousands of people and invaded their privacy. Therefore, what you did was immoral.

Exercise 11.4

3. Killing another human being in self-defence is morally permissible. So it is not the case that in all circumstances the killing of a human being is wrong.
7. If helping someone to commit suicide would somehow save the lives of millions of people, the act would seem to be morally permissible. So it is not the case that assisted suicide is never morally justified.

Glossary

ad hoc **hypothesis**: A hypothesis, or theory, that cannot be verified independently of the phenomenon it is supposed to explain. *Ad hoc* hypotheses always make a theory less simple—and therefore less credible.

ad hominem **(appeal to the person)**: The fallacy of rejecting a claim by criticizing the person who makes it rather than the claim itself. *Ad hominem* means 'to the man'.

affirming the antecedent: *See* **modus ponens**.

affirming the consequent: An invalid argument form:
> If *p*, then *q*.
>
> *q*.
> Therefore, *p*.

analogical induction: *See* **argument by analogy**.

analogy: A comparison of two or more things alike in specific respects.

antecedent: The first part of a conditional statement (If *p*, then *q*), the component that begins with the word *if*. *See* **conditional statement**.

appeal to authority: The fallacy of relying on the opinion of someone deemed to be an expert who in fact is *not* an expert.

appeal to common practice: The fallacy of accepting or rejecting a claim solely on the basis of what groups of people generally do or how they behave (when the action or behaviour is irrelevant to the truth of the claim).

appeal to emotion: The fallacy of using emotions in place of relevant reasons as premises in an argument.

appeal to ignorance: The fallacy of arguing that a lack of evidence proves something. In one type of this fallacy, the problem arises by thinking that a claim must be true because it hasn't been shown to be false. In another type, the breakdown in logic comes when you argue that a claim must be false because it hasn't been proved to be true.

appeal to popularity (or **to the masses**): The fallacy of arguing that a claim must be true merely because a substantial number of people believe it.

appeal to the person: *See **ad hominem**.*

appeal to tradition: The fallacy of arguing that a claim must be true just because it's part of a tradition.

argument: A group of statements in which some of them (the premises) are intended to support another of them (the conclusion).

argument by analogy (analogical induction): An argument that makes use of analogy by reasoning that because two or more things are similar in several respects, they must be similar in some further respect.

background information: The large collection of very well-supported beliefs that we all rely on to inform our actions and choices. It consists of basic facts about everyday things, beliefs based on very good evidence (including our own personal observations and excellent authority), and justified claims that we would regard as 'common sense' or 'common knowledge'.

begging the question: The fallacy of attempting to establish the conclusion of an argument by using that conclusion as a premise. Also called arguing in a circle.

biased sample: A sample that does not properly represent the target group. *See* **representative sample**.

burden of proof: The weight of evidence or argument required by one side in a debate or disagreement.

categorical logic: A form of logic whose focus is categorical statements, which make assertions about categories, or classes, of things.

categorical statement: A statement, or claim, that makes a simple assertion about categories, or classes, of things.

causal argument: An inductive argument whose conclusion contains a causal claim.

causal claim: A statement about the causes of things.

claim: A statement; an assertion that something is or is not the case.

cogent argument: A strong inductive argument with all true premises.

composition: The fallacy of arguing that what is true of the parts must be true of the whole. The error is to think that the characteristics of the parts are somehow transferred to the whole, something that is not always the case.

compound statement: A statement composed of at least two constituent, or simple, statements.

conclusion: In an argument, the statement that the premises are intended to support.

conditional statement: An 'if-then' statement; it consists of the antecedent (the part introduced by the word *if*) and the consequent (the part introduced by the word *then*).

confidence level: In statistical theory, the probability that the sample will accurately represent the target group within the margin of error.

conjunct: One of two simple statements joined by a connective to form a compound statement.

conjunction: Two simple statements joined by a connective to form a compound statement.

consequent: The part of a conditional statement (If *p*, then *q*) introduced by the word *then*.

conservatism: A criterion of adequacy for judging the worth of theories. A conservative theory is one that fits with our established beliefs.

copula: One of four components of a standard-form categorical statement; a linking verb—either 'are' or 'are not'—that joins the subject term and the predicate term.

criteria of adequacy: The standards used to judge the worth of explanatory theories. They include *testability, fruitfulness, scope, simplicity,* and *conservatism.*

critical thinking: The systematic evaluation or formulation of beliefs, or statements, by rational standards.

deductive argument: An argument intended to provide logically conclusive support for its conclusion.

denying the antecedent: An invalid argument form:
> If *p*, then *q*.
> Not *p*.
> Therefore, not *q*.

denying the consequent: *See **modus tollens**.*

dependent premise: A premise that depends on at least one other premise to provide joint support to a conclusion. If a dependent premise is removed, the support that its linked dependent premises supply to the conclusion is undermined or completely cancelled out.

disjunct: A simple statement that is a component of a disjunction.

disjunction: A compound statement of the form 'Either *p* or *q*.' A disjunction is true even if only one disjunct is true, and false only if both disjuncts are false.

disjunctive syllogism: A valid argument form:
>   Either p or q.
>   Not p.
>   Therefore, q.

In the second premise of a syllogism, either disjunct can be denied.

division: The fallacy of arguing that what is true of the whole must be true of the parts. The error is thinking that characteristics of the whole must transfer to the parts or that traits of the group must be the same as traits of individuals in the group.

enumerative induction: An inductive argument pattern in which we reason from premises about individual members of a group to conclusions about the group as a whole.

equivocation: The fallacy of using a word in two different senses in an argument.

expert: Someone who is more knowledgeable in a particular subject area or field than most others are.

explanation: A statement or statements intended to tell why or how something is the case.

fallacy: An argument form that is both common and defective; a recurring mistake in reasoning.

false dilemma: The fallacy of asserting that there are only two alternatives to consider when there are actually more than two.

faulty analogy: A defective argument by analogy.

fruitfulness: A criterion of adequacy for judging the worth of theories. A fruitful theory is one that makes novel predictions.

gambler's fallacy: The error of thinking that previous events can affect the probabilities in the random event at hand.

genetic fallacy: The fallacy of arguing that a claim is true or false solely because of its origin.

hasty generalization: The fallacy of drawing a conclusion about a target group on the basis of too small a sample.

hypothetical syllogism: A valid argument made up of three hypothetical, or conditional, statements:
>   If p, then q.
>   If q, then r.
>   Therefore, if p, then r.

independent premise: A premise that does not depend on other premises to provide support to a conclusion. If an independent premise is removed, the support that other premises supply to the conclusion is not affected.

indicator words: Words that frequently accompany arguments and signal that a premise or conclusion is present.

inductive argument: An argument in which the premises are intended to provide probable, not conclusive, support for its conclusion.

inference: The process of reasoning from a premise or premises to a conclusion based on those premises.

inference to the best explanation: A form of inductive reasoning in which we reason from premises about a state of affairs to an explanation for that state of affairs:
   Phenomenon Q.
   E provides the best explanation for Q.
   Therefore, it is probable that E is true.

invalid argument: A deductive argument that fails to provide conclusive support for its conclusion.

logic: The study of good reasoning, or inference, and the rules that govern it.

margin of error: The variation between the values derived from a sample and the true values of the whole target group.

mixed argument: An argument that includes both inductive and deductive elements.

***modus ponens* (affirming the antecedent):** A valid argument form:
   If p, then q.
   p.
   Therefore, q.

***modus tollens* (denying the consequent):** A valid argument form:
   If p, then q.
   Not q.
   Therefore, not p.

moral statement: A statement asserting that an action is right or wrong (moral or immoral) or that something (such as a person or motive) is good or bad.

necessary condition: A condition for the occurrence of an event without which the event cannot occur.

peer pressure: Group pressure to accept or reject a claim solely on the basis of what one's peers think or do.

philosophical skepticism: The view that we know much less than we think we do or that we know nothing at all.

philosophical skeptics: Those who embrace philosophical skepticism.

***post hoc, ergo propter hoc* ('after that, therefore because of that'):** The fallacy of reasoning that just because B followed A, A must have caused B.

predicate term: The second class, or group, named in a standard-form categorical statement.

premise: In an argument, a statement, or reason, given in support of the conclusion.

property in question: *See* **relevant property**.

propositional logic: The branch of deductive reasoning that deals with the logical relationships among statements.

quality: A characteristic of a categorical statement, based on whether the statement affirms or denies that a class is entirely or partly included in another class. A categorical statement that affirms is said to be affirmative in quality; one that denies is said to be negative in quality.

quantifier: In categorical statements, a word used to indicate the number of things with specified characteristics. The acceptable quantifiers are 'all', 'no', or 'some'. The quantifiers 'all' and 'no' in front of a categorical statement tell us that it's *universal*—that is, that it applies to every member of a class. The quantifier 'some' at the beginning of a categorical statement says that the statement is *particular*—it applies to some but not all members of a class.

quantity: In categorical statements, the attribute of number, specified by the words 'all', 'no', or 'some'.

random sample: A sample that is selected randomly from a target group in such a way as to ensure that the sample is representative. In a simple random selection, every member of the target group has an equal chance of being selected for the sample.

red herring: The fallacy of deliberately raising an irrelevant issue during an argument. The basic pattern is to put forth a claim and then couple it with additional claims that may seem to support it but that, in fact, are mere distractions.

relevant property (property in question): In enumerative induction, a property, or characteristic, that is of interest in the target group.

representative sample: In enumerative induction, a sample that resembles the target group in all relevant ways. *See* **biased sample**.

sample (sample member): In enumerative induction, the observed members of the target group.

scope: A criterion of adequacy for judging the worth of theories. A theory with scope is one that explains or predicts phenomena other than that which it was introduced to explain.

simple statement: A statement that doesn't contain any other statements as constituents. *See* **compound statement**.

simplicity: A criterion of adequacy for judging the worth of theories. A simple theory is one that makes minimal assumptions.

singular statements: In categorical logic, statements that assert something about a single person or thing, including objects, places, and times.

slippery slope: The fallacy of arguing, without good reasons, that taking a particular step will inevitably lead to further, undesirable steps.

social relativism: The view that truth is relative to societies.

sound argument: A deductively valid argument that has true premises.

standard-form categorical statement: In categorical logic, a categorical statement that takes one of these four forms:
1. All S are P. (All cats are carnivores.)
2. No S are P. (No cats are carnivores.)
3. Some S are P. (Some cats are carnivores.)
4. Some S are not P. (Some cats are not carnivores.)

statement (claim): An assertion that something is or is not the case.

stereotyping: Drawing conclusions about people without sufficient reasons.

straw man: The fallacy of distorting, weakening, or oversimplifying someone's position so it can be more easily attacked or refuted.

strong argument: An inductive argument that succeeds in providing probable—but not conclusive—support for its conclusion.

subjective relativism: The idea that truth depends on what someone believes.

subjectivist fallacy: Accepting the notion of subjective relativism or using it to try to support a claim.

subject term: The first class, or group, named in a standard-form categorical statement.

sufficient condition: A condition for the occurrence of an event that guarantees that the event occurs.

syllogism: A deductive argument made up of three statements—two premises and a conclusion. *See* ***modus ponens*** and ***modus tollens***.

symbolic logic: Modern deductive logic that uses symbolic language to do its work.

target group (target population): In enumerative induction, the whole collection of individuals under study.

testability: A criterion of adequacy for judging the worth of theories. A testable theory is one in which there is some way to determine whether the theory is true or false—that is, it predicts something other than what it was introduced to explain.

TEST formula: A four-step procedure for evaluating the worth of a theory:

Step 1. State the Theory and check for consistency.

Step 2. Assess the Evidence for the theory.

Step 3. Scrutinize alternative theories.

Step 4. Test the theories with the criteria of adequacy.

theoretical explanation: A theory, or hypothesis, that tries to explain why something is the way it is, why something is the case, or why something happened.

truth-preserving: A characteristic of a valid deductive argument in which the logical structure guarantees the truth of the conclusion if the premises are true.

truth table: A table that specifies the truth values for claim variables and combinations of claim variables in symbolized statements or arguments.

***tu quoque* ('you're another'):** A type of *ad hominem* fallacy that argues that a claim must be true (or false) just because the claimant is hypocritical.

valid argument: A deductive argument that succeeds in providing conclusive support for its conclusion.

variables: In modern logic, the symbols, or letters, used to express a statement.

Venn diagrams: Diagrams consisting of overlapping circles that graphically represent the relationships between subject and predicate terms in categorical statements.

weak argument: An inductive argument that fails to provide strong support for its conclusion.

world view: A philosophy of life; a set of fundamental ideas that helps us make sense of a wide range of important issues in life. A world view defines for us what exists, what should be, and what we can know.

Notes

Chapter 2

1. Francis Bacon, 'Idols of the Mind', in *Novum Organum, The Works*, 3 vols., ed. and trans. Basil Montague (Philadelphia: Parry & MacMillan, 1854).
2. *Ibid.*
3. Bertrand Russell, *Let the People Think* (London: William Clowes, 1941), 2.
4. W.K. Clifford, 'The Ethics of Belief', in *The Rationality of Belief in God*, ed. George I. Mavrodes (Englewood Cliffs, NJ: Prentice-Hall, 1970), 159–60.
5. Shirley MacLaine, *It's All in the Playing* (New York: Bantam Books, 1987), 171–2.
6. For a thorough review of various forms of relativism, see Theodore Schick and Lewis Vaughn, *How to Think about Weird Things*, 3d ed. (Mountain View, CA: Mayfield, 1999), 68–92.

Chapter 3

1. This step-by-step procedure is inspired, in part, by Greg Bassham et al., *Critical Thinking: A Student's Introduction* (San Francisco: McGraw-Hill, 2002), 56–62.
2. Dave Barry, 'How to Win Arguments, As It Were', *The Miami Herald*.
3. This procedure is inspired, in part, by Brooke Noel Moore and Richard Parker, *Critical Thinking*, 6th ed. (Mountain View, CA: Mayfield, 2001), 274–5.

Chapter 4

1. Bertrand Russell, *Let the People Think* (London: William Clowes, 1941), 1.
2. Adapted from Duke University Libraries, 'Guide to Library Research', http://library.duke.edu/services/instruction/libraryguide/evalwebpages.html (accessed 8 September 2009).
3. Elizabeth Loftus and Hunter G. Hoffman, 'Misinformation and Memory: The Creation of New Memories', *Journal of Experimental Psychology: General* 118(1) (March 1989): 100–4.
4. Terence Hines, *Pseudoscience and the Paranormal* (Buffalo, NY: Prometheus Books, 1988), 170.
5. This example was inspired by L.W. Alvarez, letter to the editors, *Science* (18 June 1965): 1541.

6. Hines, *Pseudoscience and the Paranormal*, 4–5.

7. Thomas Gilovich, *How We Know What Isn't So* (New York: Free Press, 1991), 54.

8. J. Cocker, 'Biased Questions in Judgment of Covariation Studies', *Personality and Social Psychology Bulletin* 8 (June 1982): 214–20.

9. Michael Sivak and Michael Flannagan, 'Flying and Driving after the September 11 Attacks', *American Scientist*, January-February 2003, 6-8.

10. John Ruscio, 'Risky Business', *Skeptical Inquirer* (March 2000).

11. Peter Kan, Sara E. Simonsen, Joseph L. Lyon, and John R. W. Kestle, 'Cellular Phone Use and Brain Tumor: A Meta-analysis', *Journal of Neurooncology* (2008) 86: 71–78; Institute of Medicine, *Immunization Safety Review: Vaccines and Autism*, National Academies Press, 2004.

12. Leonard Downie Jr. and Robert G. Kaiser, *The News About the News* (New York: Vintage Books, 2003), 9–10.

13. 'Work Farce', *New York Post*, 26 June 2003.

14. 'Soldiers Sweep Up Saddam's Hit Goons', *New York Post*, 1 July 2003.

Chapter 5

1. The inspiration for this unconventional categorization comes primarily from Ludwig F. Schlecht, 'Classifying Fallacies Logically', *Teaching Philosophy* 14(1) (1991): 53–64 and Greg Bassham et al., *Critical Thinking: A Student's Introduction* (San Francisco: McGraw-Hill, 2002).

2. W. Ross Winterowd and Geoffrey R. Winterowd, *The Critical Reader, Thinker, and Writer* (Mountain View, CA: Mayfield, 1992), 447–8.

3. Reported in Richard Whately, *Elements of Logic* (London: Longmans, Green, and Co., 1826).

4. Theodore Schick and Lewis Vaughn, *How to Think About Weird Things*, 3d ed. (Mountain View, CA: Mayfield, 1999), 192.

5. Student paper reproduced by permission of Mitchell S. McKinney, University of Missouri, http://www.missouri.edu/_commpjb/comm104/Sample_Papers/Free_Speech/free_speech.html.

Chapter 6

1. *Annals of Improbable Research*, www.improbable.com.

Chapter 8

1. Susan Blackmore, 'Psychic Experiences: Psychic Illusions', *Skeptical Inquirer* 16: 367–76.

2. David G. Myers, 'The Power of Coincidence', *Skeptic Magazine* 9(4) (September 2002).

Chapter 9

1. Charles Darwin, *The Origin of Species* (New York: Collier, 1962), 476.

2. Arthur Conan Doyle, *A Study in Scarlet* (New York: P.F. Collier and Son, 1906), 29–30.

3. Arthur Conan Doyle, 'The "Gloria Scott"', *Memoirs of Sherlock Holmes* (London: George Newnes, 1894).

4. 'Shark Attacks Are Down for Third Year in a Row', CNN.com (29 January 2004).

5. 'Study Examines Cancer Risk from Hair Dye', CNN.com (28 January 2004).

6. W.V. Quine and J.S. Ullman, *The Web of Belief* (New York: Random House, 1970), 43–4.

7. NASA, 'The Great Moon Hoax', Science@NASA website, http://science.nasa.gov.

8. Fred L. Whipple, *Earth, Moon and Planets* (Boston: Harvard University Press, 1968).

9. Robert A. Baker, 'Can We Tell When Someone Is Staring at Us?', *Skeptical Inquirer*, March/April 2000.

Chapter 10

1. See Stephen Barrett et al., *Consumer Health*, 6th ed. (New York: WCB/McGraw-Hill, 1993), 239–40.

2. Thomas S. Kuhn, *The Copernican Revolution: Planetary Astronomy in the Development of Western Thought* (Cambridge, MA: Harvard University Press, 1957), 179.

3. Section 4a of Act 590 of the Acts of Arkansas of 1981, 'Balanced Treatment for Creation-Science and Evolution-Science Act'.

4. National Academy of Sciences, *Science and Creationism* (Washington, DC: National Academy Press, 1998).

5. *Ibid.*

6. Theodosius Dobzhansky, quoted in National Academy of Sciences, *Science and Creationism*, http://books.nap.edu.

7. National Academy of Sciences, 'Preface', in *Science and Creationism*.

8. George S. Bakken, 'Creation or Evolution?' National Center for Science Education website, www.ncseweb.org.

9. Tom Byrne and Matthew Normand, 'The Demon-Haunted Sentence', *Skeptical Inquirer*, March/April 2000.

10. Theodore Schick and Lewis Vaughn, *How to Think about Weird Things*, 3d ed. (San Francisco: McGraw-Hill, 2002), 190–1.

11. Stephen Barrett, 'High Doses of Vitamin C Are Not Effective as a Cancer Treatment', Quackwatch.com (6 July 2003).

12. Joe Nickell, 'Haunted Inns: Tales of Spectral Guests', *Skeptical Inquirer*, September/October 2000.

13. Matt Ridley, 'Crop Circle Confession', *Scientific American*, August 2002.

14. Richard Wiseman, Matthew Smith, and Jeff Wiseman, 'Eyewitness Testimony and the Paranormal', *Skeptical Inquirer*, November/December 1995.

15. Ray Hyman, 'How *Not* to Test Mediums', *Skeptical Inquirer*, January/February 2003.

16. Robert T. Carroll, 'Ouija Board', *The Skeptic's Dictionary*, http://Skepdic.com (27 October 2003).

17. Robert T. Carroll, 'Bigfoot', *The Skeptic's Dictionary*, http://Skepdic.com (27 October 2003).

18. Joe Nickell, 'Psychic Pets and Pet Psychics', *Skeptical Inquirer*, November/December 2002.

19. NOVA Online, 'Hot Science, Alien Evidence?' www.pbs.org/wgbh/alienactivity (27 October 2003).

20. Henry Roberts, *The Complete Prophecies of Nostradamus (Great Neck, NY: Nostradamus, 1969), 18, as cited in Andrew Neher, The Psychology of Transcendence* (Englewood Cliffs, NJ: Prentice Hall, 1980), 188.

Chapter 11

1. 'Ethics', *Internet Encyclopedia of Philosophy*, www.utm.edu/research/iep.

Index